COEVOLUTION

Genes, Culture, and Human Diversity

WILLIAM H. DURHAM

COEVOLUTION

GENES, CULTURE, AND HUMAN DIVERSITY

STANFORD UNIVERSITY PRESS 1991

STANFORD, CALIFORNIA

Stanford University Press, Stanford, California
© 1991 by the Board of Trustees of the Leland Stanford Junior University
Printed in the United States of America

CIP data appear at the end of the book

TO KATHY, JOEY, AND ANDY

PREFACE

This book proposes an evolutionary theory of cultural change and uses that theory to examine the range of relationships between genes and culture in human populations. I have called the theory "coevolution" not only to emphasize the fact that genes and culture are copartners in shaping human diversity, but also to acknowledge from the start that human cultural systems are all related by historical derivation or "descent," in much the way that human gene pools are all related by descent. The challenge, I believe, is not to show that cultures have, in fact, evolved from common ancestry (although skeptics may want to consult Ruhlen 1987, Cavalli-Sforza et al. 1988, and Durham 1990 for evidence to that effect); rather, the challenge is to show just *how* this has happened. The book before you is a step in that direction.

Like all cultural phenomena, the ideas and concepts described in this book have themselves "descended with modification" from earlier forms. To begin with, their conceptual phylogeny winds back through earlier efforts at building an evolutionary theory of culture and at relating it to the older theoretical framework of organic evolution. In recognition of this phylogeny and of my debt to the ancestors, I devote a good portion of Chapters 4 and 8 to discussing earlier efforts along the same lines. In both places, I attempt to clarify the main similarities and differences between the theory offered here and its predecessors. Although every author must surely find some advantage in his or her own perspective, I would also be the first to admit that the work before you remains provisional and incomplete in many respects. There is much still to be done.

Coevolution has also evolved as a manuscript through quite a number of revisions—sometimes small and gradual, sometimes extensive and episodic—that go back almost a decade. Consider, for example, the evolution of the case studies assembled here to illustrate the value of the book's theoretical propositions. Although partly chosen on the basis of previous scholarly attention, each case required at least a year's additional research, often with the help of a team of assistants (acknowledged below). Even then, some cases proved problematic. For instance, my original outline of the book called for Chapter 1 to begin with a close look at *kuru*, a lethal nerve-degeneration disease among certain populations of Highland New Guinea. Although the lessons of kuru remain positively central to the goals of the book, the case soon proved to be too complex and controversial for the starting point; it has since been moved to a more appropriate home in Chapter 7.

In the place of kuru, I then developed a second opening example—an analysis of West Africa's New Yam Festivals—that met with yet another fate. My interest in these local "first fruits" ceremonies traced to a report by Jere Haas and Gail Harrison (1977: 78) that African yams were among the "significant sources" of a chemical compound called thiocyanate, said to be a metabolic precursor to cyanate (CNO). Cyanate, in turn, was known from experimental clinical work to inhibit the harmful sickling of red blood cells in individuals with sickle-cell anemia, itself a genetic evolutionary response to locally endemic malaria. If all of this were true, then one would expect to find, in a group of otherwise similar populations, that those with yams as a dietary staple would show a more benign form of sickle-cell anemia and thus (for reasons explained in Chapter 3) a higher frequency of the responsible gene—but only if yams have actually been shunned for the main malaria season, thereby allowing sickling to have its usual antimalarial effect. Having stated aloud this rather bold hypothesis in my introductory anthropology course, I was naturally quite pleased when two of the students tracked down an article, by the yam experts D. G. Coursey and Cecilia Coursey (1972), showing that the consumption of new yams (which would be physiologically most potent, I figured) is widely and strictly prohibited in West Africa until the New Yam Festivals are celebrated. The trap was fully set when I then found a reasonably strong correlation between the timing of the local festivals— and thus the end of the prohibition—and a midsummer dry spell that marks the end of the main malaria season.

At this point in its history, the case appeared to be a marvelous example of the evolutionary influence of genes and culture on each other, and I promptly began to build it into the first two chapters of the book. A few months later, in response to some last minute double-checking, I received a series of letters from D. G. Coursey and his fellow yam authority R. D. Cooke of the Tropical Products Institute in London (personal communications, 1982) with convincing laboratory evidence that the pertinent species of yams are altogether lacking in metabolic precursors to cyanate. They suggested that earlier papers on the subject may simply have confused yams with a different root crop, manioc, which *does* contain cyanate precursors, but which has only recently been introduced to West Africa (on which see Jackson 1981, 1986). To make a long story short, *Coevolution* had to be thoroughly revised, and an associated conference paper withdrawn from publication (see Gruter and Bohannan 1983:

129). Today, all that remains of this example is the analysis of sickle-cell gene frequencies in Chapter 3.

But the most important events in *Coevolution*'s evolution were still to come. In autumn 1983, I submitted the first complete draft to Stanford Press, and to less impartial friends, for critical feedback. Abundant helpful remarks from these reviewers (acknowledged below) prompted the second draft, completed in July 1985, featuring the same basic structure and organization as the present version. At their prodding, for example, I greatly expanded the review in Chapter 4 of other recent models of gene-culture relations. Yet the most consequential evolutionary changes were to come in the period 1985 to present, while I was working with the benefit of editorial guidance from J. M. B. Edwards of Berkeley, California. Although cultural phenomena, in my view, always have editors, they are rarely as thoughtful or as thorough as is Edwards, who brought to the task his own training in analytic philosophy at Oxford University. So helpful were his critical comments that I have ended up recasting major portions of the text for yet a third time, bringing clearer definition to theoretical points, better balance to the case studies, and a whole new concluding chapter to tie loose ends together. My debts to him, and to William Carver of Stanford Press for arranging his services, which also included the copy-editing, are immeasurable.

Finally, let me turn to the question of origins, for surely all evolving entities, including this one, can be traced to some starting point. The idea of writing this book first occurred to me years ago as a graduate student in a tropical ecology course in Costa Rica given by the Organization for Tropical Studies (OTS). One of the organizers of the course, the ecologist John Vandermeer, proposed a field project in which a group of us were to assess the extent of individual variation within the "traditional" agricultural practices of Costa Rican *campesinos* (small farmers). Vandermeer's description of the project began with a provocative comparison:

It is well known in tropical situations that local farmers have a reasonably complicated set of understandings and beliefs which they utilize in running their farms. It is frequently assumed that these beliefs are in some sense adaptive in that they have been handed down from generation to generation and the ones that work for one reason or another are the ones that survive. . . . If in fact there is a natural selective process operating, such that poor techniques are slowly weeded out and the good ones remain, we can expect at any given time that a relatively large number of poor techniques will be commonly employed. [Vandermeer 1972: 279]

The suggestion of an analogous, if sketchy, "natural selective process" operating on campesino beliefs stirred considerable interest among OTS participants, and groups of us went out to interview local agriculturalists at two different field sites.

In retrospect, I would not say that our findings were all that enlightening (a report accompanies Vandermeer 1972). We easily confirmed the existence of variability both in space (between neighboring families) and in time (the same family in successive years, based on recall). However, there seemed to be much greater potential in the idea that a process like natural selection may be an important force in cultural evolution. In subsequent years, I came to realize both that similar arguments had previously been expressed by a number of scholars (see, for example, the works cited in Chapter 4, note 5), and that the constraints upon this "selective process" were often far more important than the process itself. Moreover, I came to realize that the *real* analogy had been in Darwin's use of the term "natural selection" in the first place (on which see Young 1985). Nevertheless, it was initially this OTS experience that prompted me to begin to assemble the files and thoughts that have led, years later, to the study before you.

Throughout this eventful evolutionary history, I have tried to keep two principal audiences in mind. First, I have tried to write a book of interest to academic anthropologists, particularly cultural anthropologists, whose stock-in-trade is the analysis of contemporary cultural systems, and biological anthropologists, who have traditionally focused on the causes and consequences of genetic evolutionary change in human populations. My reason is simple: I am firmly convinced that anthropology as a whole (and particularly these two subfields) has much to gain from an evolutionary dimension of cultural analysis. I believe it is a dimension that has the potential to complement and supplement other kinds of cultural analysis, to amplify the intellectual "common ground" (and language) that lies between cultural and biological anthropology and, similarly, to help build new and better conceptual bridges between the social and biological sciences. At the same time, I realize that the very term "evolution" is today a dirty word to many cultural anthropologists—and understandably so, given the long history of its incorrect application in the social sciences (see Chapter 1). Nevertheless, I believe the time has come to move beyond that history, and any hang-up it has left us with, in order to reconsider the merits of developing an evolutionary dimension to culture theory.

The second main audience I have had in mind is the population of interested university-level students. Every year as I gear up for teaching courses in anthropology and human biology, I have a difficult time finding adequate, accessible readings on evolutionary theory and gene-culture relationships for undergraduate and graduate students. To begin with, many of the pertinent works have a heavy disciplinary bias toward either genes (biology) or culture (anthropology), and so toward corresponding orthodox theory. For example, some of the biological literature speaks of a program to "biologicize" the social sciences, while some texts in cultural anthropology are self-consciously antibiological. In addition, some sources are simply too quantitative and technical for a student audience, and often the examples employed for illustration are simplistic or obscure at that. I therefore felt I might help to fill the gap by addressing a student audience as well. Although this decision has added to the quantity of background material in the chapters below, it has also made my treatment more thorough and balanced.

In the attempt to take both audiences into account and yet avoid lengthy sections of data, methods, and background, I have included two appendixes at the back of the book. The first of these, "Methods and Supporting Analysis," gives a chapter-by-chapter summary of the more detailed material behind the case studies described in the text. In the interest of keeping down publication costs, however, this appendix does not include tables of all the raw data used in the case studies; those missing are available on request. The second appendix, "First Principles of Genetics," includes a brief introduction to the molecular biology of genes and proteins, and an explanation of some basic concepts in population genetics. My hope is that this material will increase the pedagogical value of the book, both for readers who are new to these subjects and also for instructors who may wish to use this as background material for their students. My misgivings about concluding this project without even an appendix on human paleontology have been allayed by the fortuitous publication of two recent books (Richards 1987; Foley 1987) that can be read to great advantage alongside this one (the Foley work is the more technical of the two).

Many people have given generously of their time, effort, and expertise to this project in the course of its evolution. First, I would like to express my appreciation to colleagues, students, and staff of the Department of Anthropology and the Program in Human Biology at Stanford University for providing such a stimulating environment in which to carry out this investigation. In particular, I owe special gratitude to the more than 35 students who have helped at one time or another as research assistants in the tasks of data collection and analysis. Their dedication and energy made it possible, indeed enjoyable, for me to combine to an unusual degree the dual professorial challenges of research and teaching. I thank each of them (specific assistance is acknowledged by initials at corresponding points in the text): Karin Asimus, Judy Brandel, Brad Brockbank, Anna Carey, Cindy Carlson, Mike Charlson, Brad Chen, Macall Dunahee, John Farr, Jeff Gerard, Heather Gordon, Debbie Guatelli, Frances Hayashida, James Henley, Hans Henriquez, Michelle Henry, Frank Hicks, Pam Ison, Greg Jouriles, Susan Keefe, Jon Kraft, Eliza Lim, Joy MacIver, Julie Martinez, Nina Miller, David Posner, Maria Quintana, Rob Randall, William Ring, Jose Rivera, Laurel Roberts, Toshiyuki Sano, Peter Schein, Toby Shih, Carol Smithson, Quynh Tran, Marilyn Tseng, Tim Warren, Robert Wendland, and Maria Zebouni. Without the help of these hardworking people, this undertaking would simply not have been possible. Additional thanks are due to Stewart Patrick for the helpful critical feedback in his 1987 Stanford Humanities Honors Essay, "Toward a Systematic Evolutionary View of Human Culture."

I would also like to offer my appreciation to the following colleagues who offered suggestions on particular topics discussed in the manuscript: Peter Abrams, Harumi Befu, Merton Bernfield, Luca Cavalli-Sforza, George Collier, Jane Collier, R. D. Cooke, D. G. Coursey, Larry Epstein, Nina Etkin, Marcus Feldman, James Fox, Milton J. Friedman, James Gibbs, David Groff, Craig Heller, Nancy Howell, Allen Johnson, Ronald Johnson, Solomon Katz, Olga Linares, Henry McHenry, William Mentzer, Jim Moore, Robert Netting, Donald H. Perkel, Charles Rick, John Rick, D. F. Roberts, George E. Simpson, G. William Skinner, Elliot Sperling, Robert Williams, H. Clyde Wilson, Terrence Wylie, Sylvia Yanagisako, and Steven Zegura. Criticisms of my earlier arguments by Martin Daly (1982), Mark Flinn and Richard Alexander (1982), Sandra Mitchell (1987), and members of the "Ecology and Evolution Seminar" in the Anthropology Department at Stanford have helped to improve the theoretical propositions advanced here.

For their extra time and effort in commenting on earlier drafts of specific chapters, I thank: John Crook, Melvyn Goldstein, Nancy E. Levine, Ken Wachter, and Ron Weigel (Chapter 2); Anthony Allison, Peter J. Brown, Joseph Greenberg, and Frank Livingstone (Chapter 3); Richard N. Adams, Brent Berlin, and Charles Hale (Chapter 4); Cynthia Ferré, Gebhard Flatz, John D. Johnson, Ellen Messer, Moses Moon, and Frederick Simoons (Chapter 5); Patrick Bateson, Melvin Ember, Joseph Shepher, and Arthur Wolf (Chapter 6); Charles Hale and Marie-Dominique Irvine (Chapter 7); and John Dupré, Davydd Greenwood, Donald Kennedy, Melvin Konner, Sandra Mitchell, Barbara Herrnstein Smith, and Bruce Winterhalder (Chapter 8).

Special acknowledgment is due the following colleagues for their thoughtful critiques of the full text in an earlier draft: Clifford Barnett, Robert Dorit, Davydd Greenwood, Ralph Holloway, Sam Karlin, Carolyn Kline, Peter Richerson, David S. Wilson, Bruce Winterhalder, Arthur Wolf, and two anonymous reviewers. I offer special thanks to Eric A. Smith for his chapter-by-chapter comments on the 1985 draft. Although the book is vastly improved for their efforts, responsibility for all remaining errors and ambiguities is entirely my own. Additional thanks are due Robert Boyd and Peter J. Richerson, John H. Crook, Davydd Greenwood, Nancy E. Levine, and Ronald Weigel for their willingness to exchange unpublished manuscripts and to allow me to cite and quote from theirs.

As editor of Stanford University Press, William Carver heroically supported, encouraged, and prodded me throughout the history of this project, as did Karen Brown Davison in her capacity as associate editor. I am deeply grateful for both of their efforts. For invaluable help with organization and bibliography, sometimes at long distance, I thank Marie-Dominique Irvine, Anna Carey, Laurel Roberts, and Quynh Tran. For hours and hours of help with artwork, I thank Catherine Vafis, Macall Dunahee, Priscilla Murray, Joan Takenaka, and Linda Toda. It was my good fortune to complete this project during a Fellowship at the Center for Advanced Study in the Behavioral Sciences. For able assistance with proofs and permissions, I thank Center staff members Kathleen Much and Virginia Heaton, respectively.

An earlier draft of the manuscript was completed in the peace and quiet of a cabin near Baton Rouge, generously made available when I needed it most by Karen Foote and Mike Olinde. Finally, this book is dedicated to my wife and sons as a hopelessly inadequate acknowledgment of their forbearance and support throughout the project, which at times seemed interminable to us all.

Portions of the text have been modified from previous publications, including the analysis of sickle-cell gene frequencies in Chapter 3 (Durham 1983), the conceptual framework for relating genetic and cultural change in Chapter 4 (Durham 1982), and the analysis of Mundurucú headhunting in Chapter 7 (Durham 1976a). I have presented portions of Chapters 2, 5, 6, and 7 earlier, at conferences, but have held back their publication until my information and analysis were more complete.

I am grateful for the financial assistance, early in this project, of a National Science Foundation Postdoctoral Fellowship and two NIH Biomedical Research Grants. More recently, *Coevolution* and I have been supported by a MacArthur Prize Fellowship; without this timely aid and encouragement, I doubt that I could ever have completed this project.

W.H.D.

CONTENTS

TABLES

FIGURES

COEVOLUTION

Genes, Culture, and Human Diversity

1 / INTRODUCTION: Genes and Culture in Evolutionary Perspective

One of the major intellectual challenges facing the behavioral sciences today concerns the relationship between genes, culture, and human diversity. The objective is both to develop a body of theory relating genetic and cultural processes to the evolution of human differences, and to test and retest such theory against the accumulated data of the behavioral and social sciences. Although the challenge is similar for all aspects of human variation, whether morphological, physiological, or behavioral, it is particularly great with respect to human behavior, where genes and culture may each have direct and simultaneous influence. There is pressing need for a body of theory that explains differences in human behavior patterns and does so without prejudging whether the appropriate principles are those of genetics, cultural analysis, or some combination of the two.

This challenge, of course, is hardly a new one. Many of the underlying issues have been recognized and studied for years as part of the age-old debate about "nature versus nurture" and "instinct versus learning." In addition, many of the lessons learned have already been incorporated into the research and teaching of the disciplines most affected, including anthropology, biology, psychology, and sociology. It is therefore appropriate to ask two questions at the start of this endeavor: (1) Why study genes, culture, and human diversity still further? and (2) Why presume that new insights can be gained today? Although one could offer many reasons, particularly if one were to survey the range of current opinion on the matter, my view is that two stand out in each case.

Why Study Genes, Culture, and Human Diversity Still Further?

The first and most important reason concerns the accelerating reduction of human differences in the world today. Scholars continue to debate the causes of this "homogenization," which is especially acute in the social and cultural realm (see, for example, Bodley 1982; Burger 1987), but its consequences are clear: the last few hundred years have successfully reversed the general trend of prior millennia toward increasing human diversity. Worse still, the process appears to be self-reinforcing. The remaining variation seems subject to ever greater depreciation and intolerance. In my opinion, it is important not only to enhance our understanding of the causes of diversity before the very variance to be explained has more seriously diminished, but also to restore a sense of respect and tolerance for human differences before they are lost forever. One hope I had in starting this project was that I might help in some small way to make human diversity more understandable, less threatening, and more highly valued than it is at present. This seems to me to be a timely and exigent task.

A second problem that gives urgency to this topic is the growing hostility in some quarters between the biological sciences on the one hand and the social sciences on the other. For years the subject of human social behavior has been contested territory between them, reminiscent of the uneasy border that sometimes separates hostile tribes. Sociobiology, calling itself "the new synthesis," came rushing into that territory in the mid-1970's advocating the "biologicization" of the social sciences and precipitating new and sometimes severe border incidents. The debate over sociobiology that ensued (it is discussed in more detail below) made clear both that important issues remained unresolved in the study of genes and culture in human populations, and that sociobiology, at least in its early form, was not likely to resolve them. It appeared to me not so much that sociobiology was wrong (although I have read a number of arguments to which that claim did apply) as that sociobiology was intrinsically incomplete as a theory for explaining human behavioral diversity. I came away from the early days of the debate thinking that a more encompassing, systematic study of gene-culture relations was needed lest both sides retreat and dig themselves into the trenches of the status quo ante bellum. This, too, seemed an urgent task. The question was not *whether* genes and culture are related in their influences on human diversity, but *how*. Here, then, were two important reasons for pushing onward.

Why Presume That New Insights Can Be Gained Today?

But can one realistically hope that new solutions will be found today for the age-old issues of nature versus nurture? Will this not be just another indecisive round in an endless debate? My response to these questions is optimistic, thanks to recent developments in both anthropology and evolutionary biology. In my opinion, a hard new look at this subject is not only possible today in light of these advances, it is also logically required. The time has come to re-examine the influences of genes and culture on the evolution of human diversity.

The Emergence of Ideational Theories of Culture

In anthropology, one of the more significant of these recent developments is the emergence of what Roger M. Keesing (1974) has called "ideational theories" of culture. These new approaches offer a more explicit and more analytic conceptualization of culture than has been possible since Edward B. Tylor introduced the term to anthropology, calling it "that complex whole which includes knowledge, belief, art, morals, custom and any other capabilities and habits acquired by man as a member of society." (1871, 1: 1.) For years, anthropologists have debated about the range of phenomena to be included within that "complex whole" (for reviews see Kroeber and Kluckhohn 1952; M. Harris 1968; J. Moore 1974). The trend in recent years has been to move away from the ambiguous and overgeneralized expressions of Tylor and other early writers and to "narrow the concept of 'culture,'" as Keesing put it, "so that it includes less and reveals more." (1974: 73.)

Although there is certainly no complete agreement on the best way to achieve that goal, ideational theory has encouraged a new consensus about a number of key properties of culture. In my view, five of these properties are especially important to the study of human diversity and gene-culture relations (specific examples of these properties are given in Chapters 2 and 6; see LeVine 1984 for a similar list).

Conceptual reality. The first and most basic property of culture in the new consensus is its conceptual reality: culture consists of shared ideational phenomena (values, ideas, beliefs, and the like) in the minds of human beings.[1] It refers to a body or "pool" of information that is both public (socially shared) and prescriptive (in the sense of actually or potentially guiding behavior). As the anthropologist Ward Goodenough (1981: 56) puts it, the culture of a human population is "a system of standards for behavior."

This property of culture has been described in many ways by recent authors, but two examples may be cited to emphasize the basic point. Morris Freilich has offered this formal conceptualization.

Culture belongs to the family "guidance system". A guide is a bit of information . . . which makes one type of behavior more probable than [another]. . . .

[1] The conceptual reality of culture has been argued persuasively by Sir Karl Popper, the noted philosopher of science, who differentiates the reality of ideational phenomena as "World 3": the world of knowledge, principles, and statements in and of themselves. This world, consisting of "the products of the human mind" is distinguished by Popper from the world of physical objects or things ("World 1") and from the world of subjective experiences like emotional responses or thought processes ("World 2"). But, argues Popper, World 3 is in no way "less real" than Worlds 1 and 2; the influence of culture on human behavior proves its reality (Popper 1972: ch. 4, 1976: 180 ff.; see also Eccles 1973).

People who share space—members of the same geographic community—share a number of . . . guides. Among such shared guides I will distinguish *natural guides* ([physiological] drives, climate, etc.) from *standards* (guides which are man-made and developed as a by-product of social interaction). Culture as a member of the family guidance system belongs to the subfamily *standards*. . . . [1977: 90–91]

The same basic message is expressed in different terms in the writings of Clifford Geertz, a leader of one ideational approach, the so-called symbols-and-meanings view of culture.

One of the more useful ways—but far from the only one—of distinguishing between culture and social system is to see the former as an ordered system of meaning and of symbols, in terms of which social interaction takes place; and to see the latter as the pattern of social interaction itself. On the one hand there is the framework of beliefs, expressive symbols, and values in terms of which individuals define their world, express their feelings, and make their judgments; on the other level there is the ongoing process of interactive behavior, whose persistent form we call social structure. Culture is the fabric of meaning in terms of which human beings interpret their experience and guide their action; social structure is the form that action takes, the actually existing network of social relations. [1973: 144–45]

An important corollary of this first property can be seen in both passages, namely that a distinction must be drawn between culture and human behavior. According to current theory, culture is properly regarded neither as a subset of behavior (that is, as the special "habits of action" or "way of life" of a people) nor as a superset of behavior (as part of a people's total "artifacts, mentifacts, and sociofacts," as in Huxley 1955). One reason for making this distinction is that the conceptual phenomena of culture are only one guiding force of several that may influence the nature and form of behavior. Genes, of course, constitute another guiding force, as do features of the natural and social environment (see Chapters 3 and 4). Given that two or more of these forces may be confounded in a given action or set of actions, it is misleading to say, for instance, that culture is behavior transmitted from one individual to another by learning and teaching. Behaviors may certainly be *culturally variable* in the sense that if the guiding ideas, values, or beliefs of a population change, then associated behaviors will also change. But to include the behaviors *as culture* imposes a futile nature/nurture categorization upon attributes that may be influenced by genes *and* culture *and* environment.[2] In short, culture should be thought of not as behavior but as part of the information that specifies its form.

Social transmission. A second important property of culture in the new consensus, although recognized for years, is its distinctive mecha-

[2] The anthropologist Eric A. Smith first pointed this out to me in 1977 (pers. comm.) in response to my paper, "The Adaptive Significance of Cultural Behavior" (1976b), which made this mistake in its very title. For additional discussion of this distinction and its consequences see Durham 1982.

nism of transmission: culture is conveyed socially within or between populations. To qualify as cultural, a given unit of information must be learned from other individuals ("socially learned"), not transmitted genetically (see Chapter 3) or acquired from isolated individual experience, as in trial-and-error learning. In other words, as the anthropologist Roy D'Andrade has well said in his article "The Cultural Part of Cognition": "A good part of what any person knows is learned from other people. The teaching by others can be formal or informal, intended or unintended, and the learning can occur through observation or by being taught rules. However accomplished, the result is a body of learnings, called culture, transmitted from one generation to the next." (1981: 179.) In a similar vein, the "social learning theory" of the psychologist Albert Bandura emphasizes social conveyance, particularly modeling and "observational learning," as fundamental to the acquisition and dissemination of culture. According to Bandura, "it is difficult to imagine a social transmission process in which the language, lifestyles, and institutional practices of a culture are taught to each new member by selective reinforcement of fortuitous behaviors, without the benefit of models who exemplify the cultural patterns." (1977: 12.) The point is not simply that culture is learned information but that it is learned in a distinctive *social* way, through modeling.[3]

In recent years, this property has been emphasized as one of the key differences between genetic and cultural inheritance. In his book *The Evolution of Culture in Animals*, for example, the biologist John Bonner goes so far as to define culture as "the transfer of information by behavioral means, most particularly by the process of teaching and learning"; he contrasts it directly with "the transmission of genetic information passed by the direct inheritance of genes from one generation to the next." (1980: 10; for similar definitions, see Bajema 1978; Mainardi 1980; Cavalli-Sforza and Feldman 1981; Plotkin and Odling-Smee 1981; Boyd and Richerson 1985.) This definition of culture duly emphasizes its informational content and the fact of its social transmission through learning. Moreover Bonner, Danilo Mainardi (1980), and others have been able to document a fair number of examples of the social transmission of behavioral "traditions" among nonhuman animals (see also Galef 1976; McGrew and Tutin 1978; Mundinger 1980). On the other hand, as Mainardi (1980: 227) is first to admit, "this is a simplified definition of culture"; it is also one that explicitly focuses on "direct phenotypic copying unmediated by arbitrarily meaningful codes." (Boyd and Richerson 1985:

---

[3] As a by-product of such social conveyance, cultural information is always shared in a population. Some authors (for instance; Parsons 1951: 15; LeVine 1984: 68) have made this a separate defining property of culture, arguing that a "community of thought" is necessary in order for culture to promote regularities and patterns among individual behaviors. Although I agree that this *is* a property of culture, it seems to me to follow from, or be derivative of, the more basic property of social transmission.

37.) It is therefore a definition that fails to include a third property of culture, crucial in the emerging consensus, a property having to do with the nature of the socially transmitted information itself.

Symbolic encoding. In the view of most anthropologists today, culture is heavily dependent upon "symboling," or symbolic encoding, which is the bestowing of conventional, nonsensory meaning upon things or acts (as defined, for example, by White 1959b). Through symboling, particularly the form of symboling we call language, the information content, accuracy, and efficiency of social transmission are all enormously increased over nonsymbolic modeling and behavioral imitation. In addition, information conveyed symbolically has, by definition, socially bestowed significance. It does not merely guide or instruct behavior; it also makes sense, holds value, and has some "point" to those who take part.

Although recognition of this property of culture is not particularly new (Kroeber and Kluckhohn 1952, for instance, traces it to the early 1940's), it is especially prominent in recent anthropological conceptualizations of culture. Clifford Geertz, to take a leading example, describes culture as "an historically transmitted pattern of meanings embodied in symbols, a system of inherited conceptions expressed in symbolic forms by means of which men communicate, perpetuate, and develop their knowledge about and attitudes toward life." (1973: 89; see also 1983.) Similarly, David Schneider (1976b: 202–3) refers to culture as "a system of symbols and meanings . . . a body of . . . postulates, presumptions, propositions, and perceptions about the universe and man's place in it." Roy D'Andrade (1984: 116), for a third example, views culture as "consisting of learned systems of meaning, communicated by means of natural language and other symbols."

In the emerging consensus this property of culture has special significance, for two reasons. First, many anthropologists agree with Marshall Sahlins that the relative "arbitrariness of the symbol is the indicative condition of human culture." (1976b: 62.) This arbitrariness, of course, greatly enhances the information density of social transmission, in that simple symbols can stand for complex concepts. For the same reason, social transmission is also much more creative than any system dependent upon things or acts with inherent sensory meaning (icons), or upon fixed vocal or behavioral signals. The consensus also seems to be that "the creation of meaning is the distinguishing and constituting quality of men." (Sahlins 1976b: 62, 102; see also White 1949.) The argument is both that cultural information has a *constitutive* function—it "creates realities" (D'Andrade 1984: 93) and "organizes relations" (Sahlins 1976b: 102)—and that this meaningfulness makes culture "ours alone," an exclusively *"human* domain." (Holloway 1969: 407, 395.) Although the last word is surely not yet in on the symbols-and-meanings capabilities of the great apes and other primates (see reviews in Bright 1984; Lieberman

1984), our human meaning systems do exhibit, at the very least, an impressive difference of scale from theirs.[4]

Systemic organization. The fourth basic property of culture concerns its structure and organization: culture takes the form of a "system of knowledge" within a population (Keesing 1974: 89). It is an assemblage that "tends to form an integrated whole" marked by a "strain toward consistency." (Murdock 1971: 331–32.) The logical structure is both hierarchical (that is, some of the information is more basic and of higher order than the rest) and coherent (component beliefs are often linked together and embedded within the whole). Similarly (although it will be noted that he included patterns of action in his formulation as well as of belief), Clyde Kluckhohn emphasized that "every culture is a structure—not just a haphazard collection of all the different physically possible and functionally effective patterns of belief and action, but an interdependent *system* with its forms segregated and arranged in a manner which is *felt* as appropriate." (1951: 100.)

Although this fourth property of culture is widely accepted by anthropologists today, there remains fairly strenuous debate about how best to characterize the system under study. Here Keesing (1974: 77 ff.) has reviewed three of the most recent views: that cultures are "cognitive systems" (that is, "systems of inferred ideational codes lying behind the realm of observable events"); that they are "structural systems" (in which "universal processes of mind [create] substantially diverse but formally similar patterns" of thought and expression); and that they are "symbolic systems" (that is, systems of "shared symbols and meanings"). These three approaches lead to quite different views of the content and functions of culture, as D'Andrade (1984: 116) has pointed out, but they all agree that culture is organized as a more or less integrated system.[5]

Social history. The fifth important property of culture in the new consensus is its social history: the shared ideas, values, and beliefs of a culture have all been handed down from prior forms. They simply do not emerge full-blown as if put into place by a single, immutable act of spe-

---

[4] Charles Darwin was one of the first authors to make this argument, noting that humans differ from other animals "in [their] almost infinitely larger power of associating together the most diversified sounds and ideas." (1922 [1871]: 131.) For Darwin, this "power of associating together" was one good example of the fact that "the difference in mind between man and the higher animals, great as it is, certainly is one of degree and not of kind." (1922 [1871]: 193.) More recently, the biologist Alfred Emerson has offered a similar view: "[Human] symbolic communication produces almost a qualitative difference from animals. I am sure that it was quantitative as it [evolved] in time; as it is now manifested, it is practically qualitative." (1956: 151.)

[5] Clifford Geertz (1966: 66) compares the systemic organization of culture to an octopus, integrated but "neurally quite poorly connected." There is also widespread agreement concerning the hierarchical nature of the information in culture. Nevertheless, leading theoreticians conceptualize the levels and basic elements of the hierarchy quite differently: thus Victor Turner (1977) speaks of "root paradigms" and Roy Rappaport (1979) of "ultimate sacred postulates."

cial creation. In a very real sense, the conceptual phenomena characterizing a given population at any one time are the surviving variants of all the conceptual phenomena ever introduced and socially transmitted. According to Freilich, for example, "while culture is indeed a set of standards, all standards are not culture. Cultural standards have a history (they are 'historically created designs for living') and it is this aging process which gives to culture its unique quality." (1977: 91.)

His argument has two implications of special importance for our purposes.[6] First, it suggests that a history of social conveyance is one key property distinguishing cultural rules and regulations from "natural guides," that is, "our basic drives [like] hunger, thirst, sex, etc. . . . [and natural environmental] phenomena such as temperature, humidity, rainfall, and altitude." (p. 90.) Second, it emphasizes that history has shaped and molded the standards of a population that we observe today. If we seek an understanding of culture, and of culture's influence on behavior, we can scarcely afford to ignore this social history.

Despite the validity of arguments like Freilich's, this fifth property of culture has not often been given its due in ethnography or cultural analysis. Of course, pertinent social history may not be remembered or recorded adequately within a population. But it has also often been ignored or discredited by ethnographers working in the thin time-slice of synchronic research. Lacking that history, anthropological data have too often consisted of only the current versions of values, ideas, and beliefs. This has contributed to a false impression of timelessness in culture, and so has impeded our understanding of pattern and process in cultural change. This unfortunate trend has shown some signs of reversing itself in what Sherry Ortner (1984: 159) calls "anthropology's rapprochement with history." However, it remains to be seen if, in the future, social history will be treated less as (in Ortner's words) "a chain of external events to which people react," and more as a creative, molding influence on the information content of cultural systems. We will return to this point in Chapter 2.

Culture as "Social Heredity"

To summarize, then, the new consensus in anthropology regards cultures as systems of symbolically encoded conceptual phenomena that are

---

[6]Although I heartily concur with Freilich's observation that cultural standards have a history, I disagree with his subsequent argument in the same essay that "time works on standards the way it works on most other phenomena; it erodes function and highlights form. Cultural standards have no obvious function (they may be irrational or nonrational) hence their essential meaning lies in their form: the manner in which one standard interrelates with other standards. We can no more easily demonstrate the functionality of matrilateral cross-cousin marriage than we can show the utility of Mona Lisa's smile. Both examples belong to the same realm, aesthetics. Cultural standards are then *conventions* or *logical standards*: phenomena given meaning within a logical system." (1977: 91.) Aesthetic standards certainly do play a role in cultural change (see Chapter 7), but I disagree

socially and historically transmitted within and between populations. As Keesing (1974) has pointed out, this view contrasts markedly with earlier conceptualizations of culture as adaptive behavioral systems, for instance, or as the means by which human populations maintain themselves in local environments. The conceptual elements of culture—ideas, values, beliefs, and the like—certainly help to organize and shape human behavior, but they are logically and empirically distinct from the actions themselves. As Geertz argued some years ago, "culture is best seen not as complexes of concrete behavior patterns—customs, usages, traditions, habit clusters—as has, by and large, been the case up to now, but as a set of control mechanisms—plans, recipes, rules, instructions (what computer engineers call 'programs')—for the governing of behavior." (1973: 44.)

This view of culture has profound implications for the social sciences and their relationship to the natural sciences. In the first place, it leads us back to the heart of the problem of relating genes and culture—not away from it, as has sometimes been claimed. The development of ideational theory in anthropology re-emphasizes that human beings are possessed of *two* major information systems, one genetic, and one cultural. It forcefully reminds us that *both* of these systems have the potential for transmission or "inheritance" across space and time, that *both* have profound effects on the behavior of the organism, and that *both* are simultaneously co-resident in each and every living human being. The question, then, of the relationship between these two systems of information cannot be escaped. It is raised by the very opening premises of the new ideational approaches to culture.

Second, the emergence of an ideational conception of culture makes possible new advances in the study of cultural evolution. For example, ideational theory points the way to operationalizing the unit or units of cultural transmission. We can now appreciate that culture is handed down through time and space in units that are conceptual, socially conveyed, symbolically coded, parts of a system, and so on (a subject we return to in Chapter 4). In addition, as we shall see, ideational theory points the way to a clearer understanding of the mechanisms of cultural change—the set of forces that shape the social history, successful or unsuccessful, of such conceptual units. I believe it is no exaggeration to suggest that ideational theory clears the way, for the first time in the history of anthropology, for a unified general model of cultural evolution.

In my view, these developments virtually compel us to re-examine the subject of relations between genes and culture. First, the time has come to reconsider the old but superficial argument that "cultural heredity is analogous to genetic heredity." (Emerson 1965: 56.) It seems to me that

---

with the general assertion that "cultural standards have no obvious function," particularly if he means *all* cultural standards. Chapter 2 presents a striking counterexample to this part of Freilich's argument.

advances in culture theory, together with the advances in genetic theory described in the next section, have put us in a position *either* to give that analogy substantial meaning for the first time—and therefore to flesh out what Alfred Emerson calls the "similar but not identical events, functions, and processes of change"—*or* to drop it once and for all. For reasons explained in subsequent chapters, I am beginning to think that there can now be real analytic value in the metaphor of culture as social heredity and in the reanalysis of the "relationship" described by Geertz:

As the order of bases in a strand of DNA forms a coded program, a set of instructions, or a recipe, for the synthesis of the structurally complex proteins which shape organic functioning [see App. B], so culture patterns provide such programs for the institution of the social and psychological processes which shape public behavior. Though the sort of information and the mode of transmission are vastly different in the two cases, this comparison of gene and symbol is more than a strained analogy. . . . It is actually a substantial relationship. [1973: 92; see also Emerson 1956, 1965; Swanson 1983]

Second, it is also time to reconsider the general subject of relationships between the dynamics of genetic and cultural change. For example, we need to look closely again at the matter of *interaction* between these two information systems. The anthropologist Frank B. Livingstone, in a now-classic study (1958), elucidated culture's role in the genetic evolution of sickle-cell anemia. This study, reviewed in Chapter 3, suggested a conceptual framework, which might be called "interactionism," to scholars interested in human evolution (see Montagu 1962, 1968a for pertinent examples). In the words of the geneticist Theodosius Dobzhansky (1962: 18): "Human evolution cannot be understood as a purely biological process, nor can it be adequately described as a history of culture. It is the interaction of biology and culture. There exists a feedback between biological and cultural processes."

Although interest in these "biocultural" interactions remains high (a point we will return to in Chapters 4 and 5), subsequent decades of research have also made it clear that reciprocally causal feedback is both difficult to document (although there are exceptions, as we shall see) and apparently quite rare. It is therefore useful to re-examine the whole question today of when—that is, under what conditions—and how the changes in one information system induce or impede changes in the other. Alternatively, when interaction is not implied—as, for example, when culture changes independently of genetic change—we need to look again at the *comparative* rates and directions of change in the two systems. The point is then to ask when and why does cultural change complement, oppose, or vary indifferently with respect to genetic change. In both cases, I maintain, the emergence of ideational theories of culture helps both to formulate the questions and to find out how they may be answered.

The Emergence of Genetic Theories of Social Behavior

In biology, meanwhile, recent developments have certainly been no less important to the general goal of understanding human diversity. Among the more significant of these has been the emergence—indeed the cultural evolution—of sociobiology itself. Although, like many others, I am critical of sociobiological attempts to explain human behavioral diversity as the product of natural selection acting on genes, I am equally impressed by the valuable extensions of Darwinian theory made in this new field. For all practical purposes, these extensions can be traced back to twin papers by W. D. Hamilton (1964) on "the genetical evolution of social behavior." Hamilton proposed that the evolutionary process of natural selection (defined below and described in some detail in Chapter 3) does not treat all individual organisms as independent entities in the contest described as "survival of the fittest," but permits certain advantages to arise from kinship and social relations.

Hamilton's insight, generally referred to as the "principle of inclusive fitness" because it redefines evolutionary fitness to include the reproduction of relatives, led to a rapid resurgence of interest among biologists in the analysis of animal social behavior. Within a few years, theoretical advances followed on a number of related topics: individual versus group selection, the costs and benefits of sociality, reciprocal altruism, sexual selection, and parent-offspring conflict. Each contributed new insights to the evolutionary biology of social behavior (see, for example, Alexander and Tinkle 1981; Daly and Wilson 1983; Brandon and Burian 1984). Newly focused empirical studies (reviewed in Gray 1984, 1985) appeared shortly thereafter; they largely confirmed the utility of the approach while suggesting further modifications. This area of study evolved so rapidly itself that, by 1975, it was recognized as a whole new subfield of biology, commonly known as "sociobiology" (E. Wilson 1975). Although a full review is beyond the scope of the present study, it will be useful to introduce briefly a few of the terms and principles central to sociobiology, many of which it shares with the more general subfield of evolutionary biology (for more thorough discussion, with examples, see Wittenberger 1981; Barash 1982; Trivers 1985).

Genotype and phenotype. One of the most basic of all principles in genetic evolutionary theory is the distinction between "genotype," the specific genetic constitution of an organism, and "phenotype," its observable properties or attributes whether they be morphological, physiological, or behavioral.[7] To take a simple example, human eye color is a phe-

---

[7] As discussed in Mayr (1982: 782), the terms "genotype" and "phenotype" were coined in 1909, along with the word "gene" itself, by the Danish geneticist Wilhelm Johannsen. From the start, Johannsen realized that "a given phenotype may be an expression for a biological unity [that is, a specific genotype], but by no means does it need to be." (1909: 123,

notypic property whose "character states" (brown, blue, green, hazel, etc.) vary from individual to individual. An important part of that variation, but by no means all of it, comes from variation in the genotypes of individuals, that is to say, from differences in the genes responsible for directing or "instructing" the biochemical synthesis of the pigments in the iris (the instructional role of genes is described in more detail in Chapter 3 and App. B).

The distinction between genotype and phenotype is particularly important in the study of human diversity because of common confusion in vernacular usage: we are used to speaking of "inherited traits" as if phenotypic properties could themselves be transmitted from parents to children. But as the geneticist Richard Lewontin, among others, has emphasized, "the *genotype* comprises what is inherited, through the sperm and egg, at the moment of conception: a set of DNA molecules, the genes, which are contained in the nucleus of the fertilized egg. The *phenotype*, on the other hand, is made up of all aspects of the organism. . . . We do not inherit our phenotypes. They develop throughout our lifetimes partly as a consequence of our genotypes—but only partly." (Lewontin 1982: 18, emphasis added.) In Chapter 3 we will return to this distinction, and to the important if evasive relationship between genotypes and phenotypes. For now it should be noted that sociobiology regards social behavior as simply another aspect of an organism's phenotype, on a par with its morphology and physiology, and therefore subject to some degree of change under the influence of genetic evolution.

Genetic selection. The process that Darwin called natural selection, "the preservation of favourable variations and the rejection of injurious variations" (1964 [1859]: 81), has been redefined over the years to its current meaning in sociobiology: the differential reproduction of genotypes. Among evolutionists in other subfields, however, natural selection is beginning to take on a larger and more variable meaning that reflects the arguments of the paleontologist Stephen Jay Gould (1980a, 1982a) and others concerning "higher forms" of differential reproduction, such as species selection.[8] To reduce confusion, let me simply refer to the sociobiological concept as "genetic selection." As we will see in Chapter 3, where the topic is explored in more detail, genetic selection amounts to a gene and genotype sorting process: genotypes whose net effect on pheno-

---

quoted from Mayr.) The observable characteristics of an individual result from a complex interplay of genetic and extragenetic influences, including the biophysical environment and, as we shall see in later chapters, culture. As noted by Stuart-Fox (1986), the anthropologist Julian Steward (1960: 170) was one of the first authors to point out that the culturally influenced behavior of human beings is "phenotypical."

[8] Vrba and Eldredge (1984) have extended the concept of natural selection to cover the "sorting by differential birth and death" at any given "focal level" in the organizational hierarchy of nature, such as organisms, populations, species, or monophyletic taxa. To make matters still more confusing, not only I but other authors (for example, Cavalli-Sforza and Feldman 1981: ch. 1; Boyd and Richerson 1985: ch. 4) now speak of "the natural selection of cultural variation."

types results in a better-than-average design for survival and/or reproduction in a given environment will tend to increase in frequency in a population. Such genotypes, and the specific genes within them, are said to be "favored" or "selected for" by the environment. In this way, genetic selection acts as one major force of organic evolutionary change.

Reproductive fitness. In sociobiology, as in evolutionary biology more generally, an individual or a genotype is considered "fit" if its phenotypic characteristics are "such as to make it likely to contribute a more than average number of genes to future generations. Fitness may [thus] be defined as 'effective design for reproductive survival.'" (Williams 1966: 158.) This kind of fitness, which can be called "reproductive fitness" to distinguish it from physical fitness or fitness of other kinds, is a probabilistic concept; it refers to the number of offspring that an organism may be expected to produce—"expected" because of its specific architecture—in a given environment, where the expected number is simply "a probabilistically weighted average of the possible values." (Kitcher 1985: 51; see also Sober 1984b: 43.) In contrast, an organism's actual reproductive performance—that is, the total number of surviving offspring it happens to produce—is conventionally called its "lifetime reproductive success" or simply "reproductive success" (designated S). Evolutionary theorists have found it useful to distinguish two kinds of reproductive fitness: the "Darwinian fitness" of individuals or of specific genotypes, defined as their expected personal contribution of offspring to the next generation; and the "inclusive fitness" of individuals or specific genotypes (the concept Hamilton introduced in 1964), defined as their total expected contribution of genetic "offspring equivalents" to the next generation. By a special formula,[9] inclusive fitness takes into account not only their personal Darwinian fitness but also the effects of an individual or genotype on the Darwinian fitnesses of his or her kin (see West Eberhard 1975; Brandon and Burian 1984: 183). Both of these measures are often standardized on a 0.0 to 1.0 scale, where 1.0 means the greatest relative success in passing on genes under existing conditions and therefore being most "fit." Before standardization, the units for both kinds of fitness are adult offspring or their genetic equivalents.

Because it adjusts the calculation of fitness to include the influence of interactions among individuals with shared genes, inclusive fitness is generally regarded as a better indicator of "effective design" for passing on

[9] Following its formal quantitative derivation, Hamilton summarized this formula as follows: "Inclusive fitness may be imagined as the personal fitness which an individual actually expresses in its production of adult offspring as it becomes after it has been first stripped and then augmented in a certain way. It is stripped of all components which can be considered as due to the individual's social environment. . . . This quantity is then augmented by certain fractions of the quantities of harm and benefit which the individual himself causes to the fitnesses of his neighbours. The fractions in question are simply the coefficients of relationship [a measure of the proportion of genes identical by descent in two individuals] appropriate to the neighbours whom he affects." (1964: 8.)

genes. But it is also somewhat more difficult to estimate. In principle, an "ego's" effects on the Darwinian fitnesses of associates are added to, or subtracted from, ego's own "nonsocial" (or noninteractive) fitness, each weighted by the appropriate coefficient of relationship (for sample calculations see West Eberhard 1975: 6). According to the folklore of evolutionary biology, this procedure was first utilized years ago by the British geneticist J. B. S. Haldane during a conversation in an English pub. "Asked if he would be prepared, on evolutionary grounds, ever to sacrifice his life for another, Haldane is supposed to have grabbed a beer mat and a pencil and, after a few quick calculations, to have declared that he would willingly lay down his life if he could save more than two brothers, four half brothers, or eight first cousins." (Kitcher 1985: 79.) Haldane's calculations, anticipating the concept of inclusive fitness, follow from the coefficient of relationship, which equals 0.5 for brothers (that is, on average, half of their genes are identical by descent), 0.25 for half brothers, and 0.125 for first cousins.

Adaptation. Another important concept in sociobiology, one whose generality and significance are hotly debated today, is that of "adaptation," the appropriateness or "fit" of an organism's form and function to prevailing environmental conditions. In sociobiology, "an adaptation can be considered as any characteristic of an organism that increases its fitness." (Barash 1982: 24; for additional definition and discussion see Pittendrigh 1958; Williams 1966; Stern 1970; Holland 1975; Brandon 1978; Lewontin 1979b, 1984).[10]

The subject has been controversial, in part because of terminological confusion. To take one example, Stephen Gould and Elisabeth Vrba have argued in an influential paper that a feature should be considered an adaptation if and only if it both "promotes fitness" and "was built *by [genetic] selection* for the function it now performs." (1982: 5, emphasis added; see also Brandon 1985.) They suggest the term "exaptation" for those "useful structures . . . that are fit for their current role [but] were not designed for it [by genetic selection]." This argument, however, contrasts strikingly with one made just three years earlier by Gould and Lewontin, who noted that adaptations can be shaped by a number of different processes, not simply by genetic selection.

First, we have what physiologists call "adaptation": the phenotypic plasticity that permits organisms to mold their form to prevailing circumstances during ontogeny. . . . Physiological adaptations are not heritable, though the capacity to develop them presumably is. Secondly, we have a "heritable" form of non-

[10] The concept of adaptation is also central to a large portion of anthropological theory, particularly the subfield of ecological anthropology. For reviews of its meaning and uses in this context, see Alland and McCay 1973; Alland 1975; Bennett 1976; Burnham 1973; Kirsch 1980; Little 1983; Borgerhoff Mulder 1987a; and Caro and Borgerhoff Mulder 1987. On maladaptation in human social systems, see Rappaport 1977; Weiss 1980. For a critical assessment, see Bargatzky 1984.

Darwinian adaptation in humans (and, in rudimentary ways, in a few other advanced social species): cultural adaptation (with heritability imposed by learning). . . . Finally, we have adaptation arising from the conventional Darwinian mechanism of selection upon genetic variation. *The mere existence of a good fit between organism and environment is insufficient evidence for inferring the action of [genetic] selection.* [1979: 592–93, emphasis added]

To their list one could add a level corresponding to behavioral adaptation (the moment-to-moment behavioral adjustments of organisms); one might also distinguish the class of reversible physiological changes (like an increase in red–blood cell density) from irreversible developmental adaptations (see discussion in Maynard Smith 1966: ch. 1). Thus organisms in general, and the human organism in particular, have a full inventory of adaptive response mechanisms, each with different properties and time constants (see Slobodkin 1968; Slobodkin and Rapoport 1974; Bonner 1980: 62–64).

This discrepancy in the definition of adaptation can be resolved readily enough if one uses the term "organic adaptation" (after Williams 1966: 96) for features that promote fitness and were built by genetic selection for their current role; the terms "physiological" and "developmental" adaptation for features of phenotypic plasticity that are not socially transmitted; and "cultural adaptation" for features that are similarly functional in terms of fitness but were shaped by sociocultural processes for correlated benefits.[11] These distinctions also help to reduce what Gould and Lewontin (1979: 593) call the "confused thinking" in human sociobiology that arises from a failure to differentiate genetic from cultural modes of adaptation. Even so, the debate over adaptation is certain to continue for some time.

Genotypic selfishness. Where genetic selection has been the major force in the evolution of the behavior of a species, individuals are expected to behave in ways that maximize the propagation of their specific genes. In other words, they are expected to behave in "a genotypically selfish fashion," engaging in acts of apparent self-sacrifice only when, in fact, the acts enhance their individual inclusive fitness (see R. Alexander 1974). It should be emphasized that the concept of genotypic selfishness applies only where the evolution of phenotypes has been guided by the differential reproduction of genotypes, as opposed to other evolutionary forces like migration or drift (as discussed in Chapter 3), or to differential reproduction at other levels (see Wilson 1983).

Phenotypic altruism. Given the baseline prediction of genotypic selfishness, one of the central problems of sociobiology is to explain the evolution of the sharing, caring, and sacrifice that are found in various forms

---

[11] These distinctions are useful for theoretical and conceptual clarity. As I have argued earlier (Durham 1976a, 1976b), actual instances of human adaptation may sometimes confound two or more mechanisms and categories.

among social animals. There are now quite a number of sociobiological theories for the evolution of such "phenotypic altruism," that is, for the evolution of behaviors that appear altruistic but that, from a genetic perspective, are actually selfish. Let me simply mention three of the more important ones. First, there is Hamilton's argument (1964) that genetic selection can favor the evolution of altruistic behaviors by individuals for the benefit of close kin. The requirements are two. First, there must be genetic differences between the altruists-toward-kin and nonaltruists. Second, this behavior must yield the highest net inclusive fitness or, in other words, the fitness value of ego's effect on relatives must do more than compensate for any attendant decrease in ego's own Darwinian fitness. Where these conditions are met, phenotypic altruism is said to evolve by the special form of genetic selection called "kin selection" (for discussion and elaboration, see West Eberhard 1975).

A second important argument is that of Robert Trivers, who has showed that genetic selection *can* favor the evolution of temporary reproductive sacrifice by an organism toward nonrelatives, so long as there is an eventual net "return benefit."

One human being saving another, who is not closely related and is about to drown, is an instance of altruism. Assume that the chance of the drowning man dying is one-half if no one leaps in to save him, but that the chance that his potential rescuer will drown if he leaps in to save him is much smaller, say, one in twenty. Assume that the drowning man always drowns when his rescuer does and that he is always saved when the rescuer survives the rescue attempt. . . . Were this an isolated event, it is clear [in terms of fitness] that the rescuer should not bother to save the drowning man. But if the drowning man reciprocates at some future time, and if the survival chances are then exactly reversed, it will have been to the benefit of each participant to have risked his life for the other. . . . If we assume that the entire population is sooner or later exposed to the same risk of drowning, the two individuals who risk their lives to save each other *will be selected over* those who face drowning on their own. [1971: 36, emphasis added]

The implication is that lifesaving behavior, an example of what sociobiologists call "reciprocal altruism," would evolve by the differential reproduction of genotypes.

By itself, the logic of the argument seems solid and generalizable, and there is now supporting evidence from field studies of animal behavior for reciprocal altruism of other kinds (reviewed in Trivers 1985: ch. 15). Moreover, the logic has proved useful for identifying key variables and for making certain predictions. For example, Trivers (1971) notes that the advantage under genetic selection of such reciprocity depends upon the fitness benefit of the altruistic act to the recipient being greater than its fitness cost to the performer, and upon the probability that the benefit will one day be reciprocated. Opportunity for the evolution by genetic selection of reciprocal altruism is thus expected to vary positively with species' longevity and inversely with their dispersal rates. Where the preceding illustration is on shaky grounds, however, is with its assumption that reciprocated lifesaving in human populations evolves by genetic selection. We will return to this and related problems in the next section.

Finally, a number of sociobiologists have pointed out that the mechanism Darwin called "sexual selection" (1964 [1859]: 87 ff.) can also cause the genetic evolution of seemingly altruistic phenotypes. "What I call Sexual Selection," Darwin wrote, "depends, not on a struggle for existence, but on a struggle between males for [access to] the females; the result is [usually] not death to the unsuccessful competitor, but few or no offspring." (p. 88.) Through this mechanism, the mating preferences of adult females can cause the differential reproduction of genotypes to favor a greater degree of self-sacrifice on the part of males than would otherwise be the case. In addition, as Darwin was first to point out, sexual selection can cause size dimorphism and other sex-specific behavior patterns, as when the males of a species are larger, more ornate, or better equipped for fighting than are the females (see, for example, Dawkins 1976: 153 ff.).

The Sociobiology Debate

An interest in the human applications of sociobiological principles and concepts had been evident all along, but their successful employment elsewhere in the animal kingdom added momentum to the development of an explicit human sociobiology (see, for example, R. Alexander 1974; E. Wilson 1975: ch. 27; Chagnon and Irons 1979). This, in turn, touched off the debate mentioned above, with many and far-reaching consequences for the study of human behavioral diversity (see Caplan 1978; Barlow and Silverberg 1980; Kitcher 1985).

At the heart of the matter were two related conceptual issues. Issue 1 stemmed from an emergent ambiguity in the definition and conceptualization of sociobiology itself. On the one hand, sociobiology was given broad definition at its formal inception, when the biologist Edward O. Wilson described it as "the systematic study of the biological basis of all social behavior." (1975: 4.) The breadth of this definition came from the words "biological basis": although Wilson himself sometimes equated this expression with "reference to evolutionary explanations in the true genetic sense" (as when, in the same context, he contrasted sociobiology and sociology), that was not a necessary connotation. As Wilson later emphasized, sociobiology was intended to be "a scientific discipline, not a particular theory concerning the genetic basis of human [or nonhuman] social behavior." (1982: xii.) On the other hand, sociobiology was quickly given a narrow definition both by its proponents, eager to use genetics and Darwinian theory in examples of a "biological basis" to social behavior (see, for example, Lockard 1980; Barash 1977), and by its critics (see, for example, Lewontin et al. 1984; Montagu 1980).[12] In this conception, so-

[12] This narrower definition emerged via three pathways: (1) through formal declarations by proponents, such as David Barash's statement that "sociobiology is the *application of*

ciobiology meant a genetic explanation of social behavior. Observed differences in behavior were attributed to differences in genetic composition, to the action of genetic selection, or to some other process of genetic differentiation.[13] Trivers's example of lifesaving is a case in point.

Issue 2 concerned the conceptualization of culture in the sociobiological analysis of human behavior. Although many of the field's proponents have regarded culture as important to the study of human behavior, few have treated it as an ideational system capable of evolutionary change in its own right. Instead, as we will examine in more detail in Chapter 4, culture has been viewed as the set of specific behaviors or "traits" of a population (an approach that inevitably confounds the effects of genes and ideational phenomena) or as some sort of reflective "self-expression" of the genes. It has thus been treated as an aspect of phenotype, much as physiology and morphology are. Culture has generally not been treated as a coparticipant in evolutionary change in human populations; for the most part, evolution has been defined as a genetic process.

The implications of Issue 2 have been profound. First, in the absence of an ideational conceptualization of culture, and without a theory of cultural evolutionary change, sociobiological explanations of human social behavior have reinforced the narrow definition of sociobiology (see Durham 1979b), despite the efforts of Wilson, Roger Masters (1982), and a few other scholars to reinforce the broad one.[14] Indeed, the sociobiology literature of the 1970's and early 1980's is peppered with fairly sophomoric behavioral analyses suggesting causation by genetic selection where the data imply, at best, simple correlation. Consider, for example, the following passage from David Barash's influential 1977 textbook, *Sociobiology and Behavior.*

---

evolutionary biology to the social behavior of animals" (1977: 2, emphasis added); (2) through attempts by proponents to operationalize sociobiology in specific hypotheses and research reports (see Lockard et al. 1976 for a classic early example; for other examples, see Lewontin, Rose, and Kamin 1984: ch. 9); and (3) through the arguments of critics who emphasized that natural selection is, in sociobiological theory, a genetic mechanism (see, for example, Durham 1976b, 1978, 1979b; Gould 1978, 1980b, 1983a; Gould and Lewontin 1979; Lewontin 1979b).

[13] Sociobiology's proponents and critics all agree that the process of genetic selection can cause the evolution of a phenotypic property if and only if there is "some correlation between the genotype and the phenotype in question." (Barash 1982: 29.) As further evidence of ambiguity in the definition of sociobiology, Barash calls this the "central principle of sociobiology" within 47 pages of Wilson's (1982) statement, quoted above, that sociobiology is "not a particular theory concerning the genetic basis of human behavior."

[14] Personally, I was initially sympathetic to the term "sociobiology" because of its formal broad definition by Wilson. That definition seemed to me to invite the expansion of models of evolutionary change "to accommodate the retention of traits whether based on chemical instructions genetically inherited at conception, or on accumulated 'wisdom' passed along sometimes continuously and from many 'parents'" (Durham 1976a: 386), and so I used the term in its broad sense in my first paper on the relationship of genes and culture. Within a matter of months, however, it became clear that most readers and writers associated "sociobiology" with the narrow definition, in part because there was no complementary cultural theory of the type that I was arguing for.

Given the peculiar biology of *Homo sapiens*, males probably maximize their fitness by a degree of reproductive, parental commitment to their mate(s). However, optimal male strategy would include remaining susceptible to additional copulations, so long as they did not require further investment. Women *may also have been selected* for an interest in copulations outside the pair-bond but, because of their greater involvement in the consequences of such activity [i.e., pregnancy], women should be more fussy than men. Men are predicted to feel more threatened by the activities of their women than women should feel as a result of sexual dalliance by their men. . . . *In effect, I am suggesting a potential biological basis for the double standard.*[15] [1977: 293, emphasis added]

The argument views both behavioral tendencies and the "double standard" as products of the differential reproduction of genotypes. But note that the double standard is a fitting—if morally objectionable—illustration of the ideational phenomena of culture, one that exhibits all five of the basic properties discussed earlier, including social history. In the absence of any semblance of ideational theory, arguments like Barash's imply that the double standard and other cultural phenomena are the direct expressions of genetic "whisperings within" (Barash 1979). In essence, they offer a presumptive genetic history in reply to the call for an actual social history.

In my opinion, it is arguments of this type that explain why the narrow conception of sociobiology has become the generally accepted one in both the public and the academic view today, particularly in the social sciences. Sociobiology is now widely regarded as "the genetic viewpoint" and is inextricably associated with the idea of "genetically transmitted social strategies" by both its proponents (as by Wenegrat 1984 and Wind 1984, to take recent examples) and its critics (as by Lewontin, Rose, and Kamin 1984). In an effort to reduce confusion and semantic controversy, I feel compelled to use the narrow, consensual definition of sociobiology in these pages.[16]

[15] Of course Barash is not alone in this argument; for review and discussion see Hrdy and Williams 1983. For other examples of the urge to equate correlation with causation, see Barash on "a possible evolutionary basis for human racial prejudice" (1977: 311), on the causes of human male-male competition (p. 301), and on "why it is usually the mother's parents who help out most when [a] new baby arrives." (p. 302.)

[16] To be sure, there continues an "evolution and refinement of sociobiological theory" (see Caplan 1983; for applications see Dickemann 1985; Borgerhoff Mulder 1987b), and there are exceptions to the consensual view. Boyd and Richerson, for instance, provide an instructive exception, defining human sociobiology as the view that the processes of cultural evolution "will usually enhance genetic fitness." (Boyd and Richerson 1985: 13.) Two problems inhere in this definition. First, processes of cultural change that "enhance genetic fitness" promote, by definition, the adaptation of human populations to their environments. By implication, the label "sociobiology" would then apply to any subfield of inquiry that views culture as promoting adaptation, including the much older "ecological" subfield of cultural anthropology (see, for example, Orlove 1980). Second, if we use the dictionary meaning of "usually" ("on the average"), Boyd and Richerson's own work becomes fully sociobiological by their own definition, since they admit that the various mechanisms of cultural change in their theory that sometimes permit maladaptation (see Chapter 4 of this book) are probably "adaptive when averaged over many characters and many societies." (Boyd and Richerson 1985: 268.)

Second, in the absence of an adequate conceptualization of culture, the implications of sociobiology have clearly been anathema to the social sciences. This has certainly been the case in anthropology where, for years, culture has been treated as a supplementary system of evolutionary change (see Peters 1982). While that treatment has often been vague or (as I shall try to show) erroneously stage-like, and while no specific theory of cultural evolution has ever gained general acceptance, the point remains that many social scientists have long taken for granted that cultural systems do evolve and that their evolution has had profound effects on human behavior. The focus of their attention, unlike the sociobiologists', has been on the *social* processes that guide the "descent with modification" of cultures as they are handed down from ancestral populations. To social scientists, there has been no reason to presume that cultural differences have a genetic history.

Not surprisingly, reactions on both sides of the issue were often hostile. Anthropologists and others were quick to criticize sociobiologists for "dragging genes into the analysis" of human social behaviors and for offering a genetic justification for certain social ills. Sociobiologists, in turn, criticized anthropologists for ignoring Darwinian theory and for assuming that genes play little or no role in behavioral diversity (on these issues see Caplan 1978; Ruse 1979; Fetzer 1985). There was, once again, precious little middle ground. Clearly, sociobiology in its narrow form was not the "new synthesis" that had been promised, at least with respect to human behavior. But, at the same time, it was also making impressive gains in the explanation of the social behavior of other species, particularly through the use of the inclusive fitness concept. The question remained, Could the idea of inclusive fitness be gainfully employed outside the narrow purview of sociobiology, and could it be teamed up in some meaningful way with an ideational approach to culture? It seemed to me that it could.

Toward an Evolutionary Anthropology

The concerns of this book can therefore be seen as a direct outgrowth of two parallel sets of advances, each an example of cultural evolution in its own right: the emergence of ideational theories of culture in anthropology, and the emergence of theories for the genetic evolution of social behavior in biology. Both advances make possible new forms of rapprochement between biology and the social sciences; each of them, although in different ways, invites new efforts toward bridging the historical gap between these fields. In addition, each points directly to the need for further theoretical and empirical research on two key subjects: the patterns and processes of cultural evolution, and the nature of relationships between cultural dynamics and genetic evolution.

Happily, such efforts are now beginning to appear in the literature. Luigi Cavalli-Sforza and Marcus Feldman's *Cultural Transmission and Evolution* (1981), Charles Lumsden and Edward O. Wilson's *Genes, Mind, and Culture* (1981), and Robert Boyd and Peter Richerson's *Culture and the Evolutionary Process* (1985), all reviewed in Chapter 4, particularly deserve note. This growing field of inquiry has been called by many names, including "biocultural anthropology" (Bennett, Osborne, and Miller 1975; Katz 1982; Ortner 1983), "cultural Darwinism" (Richerson and Boyd 1984), and the "new sociobiology" (Caplan 1983), each of which I find vague, inaccurate, or pejorative. For the sake of clarity, and to suggest a parallel with the position of evolutionary biology within the biological sciences and the newer evolutionary psychology within that discipline (see, for example, Cosmides and Tooby 1987; Tooby and Cosmides 1989), let me simply call this subfield "evolutionary anthropology." Although the term has been used before (for example, in Bliebtreu 1969), there is today, for the first time, a substantial theoretical literature with this focus, and a growing amount of new case study material. The book before you represents an attempt to summarize and extend our understanding of this subject area.

The Concept of Evolution

Because the concept of evolution, for reasons we will turn to shortly, has had a less than illustrious career in the social sciences, it will be useful to begin with a brief discussion of just what it means and implies today (for an insightful history of the concept, see Bowler 1989; on the word "evolution" itself, see Carneiro 1972 and Gould 1977: ch. 3). From the start it will be useful to bear in mind three things that evolution, popular usage to the contrary, is *not*: progress or improvement (it is simply cumulative and transmissible change); genetic selection or "Darwin's theory" (these are instead ideas about the mechanisms of evolution in a specific context, namely, organic evolution); or an exclusive property of genetic systems (many things can and do evolve).

The best concise definition of evolution remains Charles Darwin's famous one-liner from *On the Origin of Species* (1964 [1859]): "descent with modification." The success of this definition through the years—itself an impressive cultural evolutionary phenomenon—can be attributed to three of its implications. First, the phrase has general applicability: it implies that many things can evolve, not just the species of Darwin's original concern. Second, the phrase implies derivation with change or "modification" but does not presuppose any particular form or process of change. It therefore encompasses a theoretically unlimited set of possible processes, not simply Darwin's own emphasis upon natural selection. Third, the phrase seems to suggest nearly the full set of conceptual elements that we now recognize as "system requirements" for evolution in

TABLE I.I

The System Requirements for Evolution

1. Units of Transmission
2. Sources of Variation
3. Mechanisms of Transmission
4. Processes of Transformation
5. Sources of Isolation

any given system (see Table 1.1).[17] It implies some class of things that descend and are modified (Requirement 1); some mechanism of continuity by which these things "descend" and persist (Requirement 3); and some process of modification (Requirement 4), which, in turn, assumes some source of novelty or variation (Requirement 2) within the class of objects. Requirement 5, sources of isolation or discontinuity, permits the accumulation of differences in incipient subsystems and thus eventual diversification. Arguably, it is the only requirement not represented in the phrase (although Darwin was clearly aware of its evolutionary significance; see, for example, 1964 [1859]: 104–5).

To improve upon Darwin's definition today, or at least to be more explicit, one has to be considerably more technical and long-winded. Lewontin, for instance, has argued that an "evolutionary perspective" or an interest in "evolutionary dynamics" is equivalent to being interested "in the change of state of some universe in time"; whether that universe consists of societies, languages, species, geological features, or stars, there is a "formal representation" of the evolutionary process that is common to all (1974: 6). The formal representation in question depicts evolution as the sequential transformation of a given system. If we let S_t denote the state of the system at time t, and let T represent the processes of transformation, then

$$\ldots S_1 \xrightarrow{\quad T \quad} S_2 \xrightarrow{\quad T \quad} S_3 \xrightarrow{\quad T \quad} S_4 \ldots$$

In this way, sequential transformation gives rise to both continuity and cumulative change. Of course, the process or processes behind that transformation may themselves vary through time, and thus all the T's in the schema need not be identical or even consistently weighted. Nevertheless, the result will always be a process of "descent with modification"; in the schema above, S_4 has descended with modification from S_3, which in turn has descended from S_2, and so on.

According to Lewontin, two basic challenges confront any evolutionary theory: how to represent S, in order to specify the changes (if any) be-

[17] Table 1.1 is an elaboration on Campbell's (1965: 27) "three basic requirements" for a Darwinian model of evolution, namely, "the occurrence of variations," "consistent selection criteria," and "a mechanism for the preservation, duplication, or propagation of positively selected variants." Citing Campbell, Naroll and Wirsing (1976: 189–90) give four similar requirements, adding as number one "a population of entities competing for survival."

tween times 1 and 2; and how to characterize *T*. This conceptual rendering, he believes, can be generalized to a wide range of systems, including geological features, stars, and the others referred to above. But "organic" or "genetic" evolution remains the prototype example. Again we may take Darwin's "descent with modification" as a useful description of this kind of evolution.

Implicit in Darwin's theory, however, is one property of evolution in living systems that is ignored or at least downplayed in Lewontin's schema: the transmission of units through space and time is, in such systems, accomplished by serial *replication*, that is to say, by the actual re-creation of units rather than by their simple endurance (the former is arguably what Darwin meant by "descent" in the first place). This mechanism of transmission, in turn, creates the possibility of a special process of transformation within systems of replicating entities: evolution can occur as a consequence of the relative success or failure of units at replication. This property of evolution in living systems has been duly emphasized by the biologist Richard Dawkins (1976, 1982a), who has argued that genes are, in fact, the world's original replicators.

As many authors, including Dawkins, have pointed out, evolution as sequential transformation in a system of replicating entities is not limited to genetic systems. Cultures, too, fit this definition. Indeed, as we shall see in later chapters, the systems of shared ideational phenomena in human populations are, in many ways, *model systems* for this particular kind of evolutionary transformation. According to this definition of terms, then, cultures surely do evolve.

Key Questions in the Study of Evolution

Given the "system requirements" listed in Table 1.1, it is no surprise that the most important (and often the most hotly debated) questions asked about the evolution of a system are also five in number. These questions have particular prominence in evolutionary biology today (as can be seen, for example, in Sober 1984a), but they will also be key questions in the emergence of an evolutionary anthropology.

What are the best units for describing the system? The study of evolution in any system requires identifying the units whose changes provide the best description of sequential transformation in the system. In the case of living systems, one can be more specific: we need to know what are the fundamental units of replication, or what are the things that replicate differentially through space and time. More specifically, in the case of organic evolution, the challenge is to identify the objects—for example, genotypes, individuals, or species—that vary in fitness (Brandon and Burian 1984). In the case of cultural evolution (to be taken up in later chapters), the "units question" will be parallel: In what units are the ideational phenomena of culture differentially transmitted?

What are the sources of variation? Given a successful answer to the first question, it becomes important to ask about the origins and variation of units. By what process or processes is variation introduced into the system of units undergoing sequential change? In the case of organic evolution, two different kinds of processes have been identified as "primary," or initial, sources of variation: mutation, or the spontaneous introduction of variation at the level of genotypes and individuals; and speciation, the formation of variable, noninterbreeding descendant populations. Secondary sources of variation would include migration and the reshuffling of variants known as recombination. From the arguments of Gould (1982a, 1982b) and others, it would seem that both primary processes may be required for a full answer to the "origins question" in organic evolution. With respect to cultural evolution, approximate equivalents would be innovation, or the introduction of new concepts into a population (see Barnett 1953), and diversification or "cultural speciation," (as in Diener 1980: 427), the formation of new and distinct cultural systems from old ones.

What are the mechanisms of transmission? Given variation, what then governs the transmission of units through space and time and either maintains or erodes variability? In the case of organic evolution, the answer to this "transmission question" has long been supplied through reference to Gregor Mendel's laws of inheritance (see, for example, Stern and Sherwood 1966; Olby 1985), that is, through reference to the regularities of gene transmission caused by actual biological reproduction. Today, however, there is increasing evidence for irregularities or "violations" of Mendel's laws (see Crow 1979), and for non-Mendelian processes of gene duplication and transmission within and between species (see Temin and Engels 1984; Syvanen 1984). Ironically, these findings now force us to reconsider what were earlier points of difference between genetic and cultural transmission, such as the assertion of the anthropologist Alfred Kroeber that whereas organic evolution "really does nothing but diverge," culture "diverges, but it syncretizes and anastomoses, too," as a consequence of interpopulational diffusion and borrowing (1963: 68). Now there would seem to be possibilities for coalescence and assimilation in the transmission processes of both systems.

What are the main causes of transformation? It was in response to this question that Darwin so clearly set his views apart from those of other early theorists, including Lamarck and Wallace, and left his greatest mark on modern biology. In addition to defining and describing the process he called natural selection, Darwin identified and qualified it as "the main but not exclusive means of modification." (1964 [1859]: 6.) Although he recognized the process of preservation by reproductive advantage as "by far the predominant Power" in the evolution of organic forms (p. 43), Darwin avoided "Wallace's fatal flaw" of hyperselectionism (Gould 1985), that is, of attributing each and every phenotypic attribute of a given organism (or, indeed, of *all* organisms) to an evolutionary derivation by natural selection.[18]

Darwin also recognized that natural selection commonly acts through individual-level differences. Whatever the reasons for parent-child differences, he argued, it was "the steady accumulation, through natural selection, of such differences, *when beneficial to the individual*, that [gave] rise to all the more important modifications of structure." (1964 [1859]: 170, emphasis added.) But if natural selection generally favored "slight variations, each good for the individual possessor" (p. 459), there were direct implications for the pattern of change in organic evolution, or what are now called the *tempo* and *mode* of transformation. Here, too, Darwin was explicit: "That natural selection will always act with extreme slowness I fully admit." (p. 108.) "As natural selection acts solely by accumulating slight, successive, favorable variations, it can produce no great or sudden modification; it can act only by very short and slow steps. Hence the canon of 'Natura non facit saltum' [nature does not make leaps]." (p. 471.)

In short, Darwin was the first to admit that his predominant Power "must be slow and gradual" in operation (p. 317), a view that is today called "phyletic gradualism," and he was the first to defend this position with reference to the geological record.[19] His proposal was aptly summarized in a schematic rendition of the "great Tree of Life," a portion of which is redrawn in Fig. 1.1, panel A. The figure shows clearly that, to Darwin, organic evolution proceeds through the gradual accumulation of slight variations. Speciation occurs (the branching points of the tree), but species formation does not itself cause significant directional trends.

In recent years, this view of life has been contrasted with one introduced by Niles Eldredge and Stephen Gould in 1972. Called the theory of "punctuated equilibria," it maintains "speaking of mode, that significant evolutionary change arises in coincidence with events of branching speciation, and not primarily through the *in toto* transformation of lineages [classical Darwinism]. It [also] maintains, speaking of tempo, that the proper geological scaling of speciation renders branching events as geo-

---

[18] A number of recent authors, many of them writing in the name of sociobiology, have fallen into the same trap as Wallace, provoking Gould and Lewontin (1979; also Lewontin 1979b) into writing "a critique of the adaptationist programme." It has proven all too easy for modern evolutionists to forget or ignore Darwin's argument about the "main but not exclusive means" of organic evolution. Thus one finds such statements in the literature as Daly and Wilson's (from their textbook): "Natural selection is *the* mechanism that causes evolution." (1983: 5, emphasis added.)

[19] In his theory, Darwin likened the "very slow, intermittent action of natural selection" to "what geology tells us of the rate and manner at which the inhabitants of this world have changed." However slow the process of selection, he could see "no limit to the amount of change, to the beauty and infinite complexity of the coadaptations between all organic beings, one with another and with their physical conditions of life, which may be effected in the long course of time by nature's power of selection." (1964 [1859]: 109.) Even if "Darwin was not entirely a gradualist," as authors such as Arthur (1984: 118–19) have claimed, it is clear that he felt compelled to justify a gradual view of change.

Panel A

Panel B

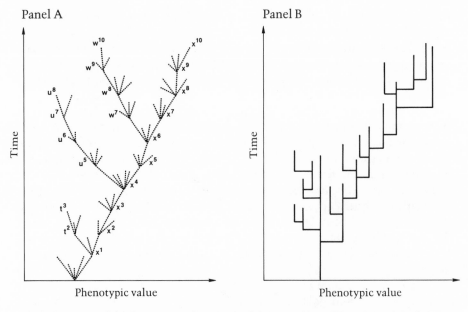

Fig. 1.1. Two models of organic evolution. Panel A is a portion of Darwin's original "Tree of Life" diagram showing the evolutionary emergence of new species (x^1, x^2, x^3, etc.) from a common ancestor. The X axis (unlabeled in Darwin's original figure) measures the mean value of a given phenotypic character in the evolving populations. In this model, organic evolution results from the gradual accumulation of incremental changes, a view now called "phyletic gradualism." Speciation occurs (at the branching points) but is not responsible for the trends shown. Panel B shows the contrasting pattern of "punctuated equilibria," in which evolutionary trends result from sudden shifts caused by the origin and extinction of species. Each hypothetical shift is followed by a period of stasis (idealized here as complete) in the mean phenotypic value of each species. In this model, organic evolution occurs through rapid speciation events. The two models shown represent polar extremes; actual evolutionary histories could conceivably follow an intermediate pattern or even some mixture of the two. Panel A redrawn from Darwin 1964 [1859]: facing p. 117; panel B redrawn from Gould 1982b: 91.

logically instantaneous and that, following this rapid origin, most species fluctuate only mildly in morphology during a period of stasis that usually lasts for several million years." (Gould 1982b: 83.) Accordingly, evolution by punctuated equilibria is predicted to generate a pattern of organic evolution resembling Fig. 1.1, panel B. In this relatively pure, hypothetical case—"pure" in the sense that lineages show no gradualistic change—the directional trend of evolution is fueled entirely by branching. The overall pattern is more that of a bush than a tree (Gould 1977: ch. 6).

Needless to say, the conflicting claims of these theories have generated considerable debate in recent years (see, for example, Gould 1980a; Stebbins and Ayala 1981; Gould 1982a; Stebbins and Ayala 1985). Argument has been intense, partly because both sides claim causal priority. On the one hand is Darwin's argument for the predominant Power of natural selection; on the other is Gould's assertion that while "gradual phyletic transformation can and does occur . . . its relative frequency is low and punctuated equilibrium is the predominant mode and tempo of evolutionary change."[20] (1982b: 84.) The issue remains far from resolved for a number of reasons, of which two may be mentioned here. First, recent theoretical work suggests that what Darwin called "slight, successive, favorable variations" and natural selection can, at least in principle, create punctuated equilibria (see, for instance, Newman, Cohen, and Kipnis 1985). This implies that Darwin could be both right about the "major means of modification" and, simultaneously, wrong about its "extreme slowness."

Second, gaps or temporal discontinuities in the fossil record often preclude decisive tests of the rival proposals even in specific, relatively well-documented cases. Nowhere is this better seen than in the fossil evidence for the rapid evolutionary expansion of the human brain, itself a worthy, if unusual, example of organic evolution. On axes like those in the previous figure, Fig. 1.2 summarizes the available data on the "endocranial volume" (ECV), or the internal size of the braincase, for all fossil species of hominids between 3 million and 30 thousand years B.P. (before present). (For details on data and methods, see App. A.8.1.) The figure includes data both from species believed to be directly ancestral to ourselves (such as the gracile Australopithecines, *Homo habilis*, and *Homo erectus*), and from species believed to have died out without descendants (such as the robust Australopithecines and perhaps the Neanderthals). The figure reveals no obvious pattern of gradual or punctuational change, nor even a discernible mixture of the two. Interpretation of trends is clearly difficult because of small sample sizes for most time periods, and because of substantial gaps in the fossil record at key junctures (as, for example, in the vicinity of 2 million years B.P.). Of the small but increasing number of quantitative analyses of these data, some have led to completely opposite conclusions. For example, a 1981 study of endocranial volumes and other fossil hominid data by J. E. Cronin and others reported "no well-documented examples of either stasis or punctuation" (p. 113), while one by G. Philip Rightmire in the same year found that *"Homo erectus* was apparently a stable taxon, exhibiting little morphological change throughout most of its long history." (p. 246; but see Wolpoff 1984.) In Chapter 8 we will return to these data and to some of their other implications for evolutionary anthropology. But for now we must conclude that Fig. 1.2 leaves open the question of what processes have been the main causes of transformation in this important example, the rapid evolution of the human brain.

[20] Gould (1982a: 84) admits that "it is hard to put a number on 'low' and 'predominant'" as used in this passage. He adds: "Would an off-the-cuff claim for 90 percent be sufficient to rescue me from a charge of winning my own argument by defining it for easy victory?"

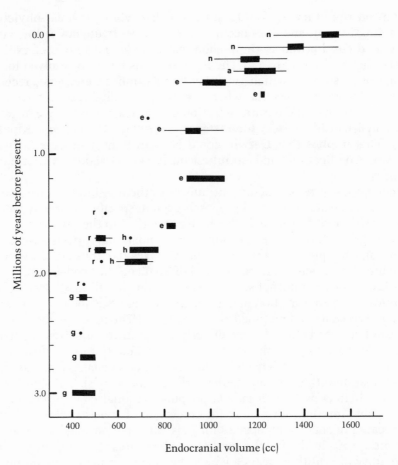

Fig. 1.2. Organic evolution as illustrated by the increase in cranial capacity among our hominid ancestors. The figure illustrates the expansion of endocranial (internal braincase) volume among pooled samples of fossil hominid skulls, where each sample contains specimens of a single species dated to within fifty thousand years of the time shown (e.g., the bar at 0.8 million years B.P. represents data for 8 skulls, each dated between 0.751 and 0.850 million years B.P.). For each sample, the light bar represents the range of endocranial volumes and the heavy bar, the standard error of their mean (the latter is roughly equivalent to a standard deviation that controls for sample size); dots represent single specimens. Letters to the left of the bars designate different ancestral species or groups of species. From the bottom: **g** = gracile Australopithecines (*A. afarensis* and *A. africanus*); **r** = robust Australopithecines (*A. robustus* and *A. boisei*); **h** = *Homo habilis*; **e** = *Homo erectus*; **a** = archaic *Homo sapiens*; and **n** = Neanderthals (who may or may not have been our direct ancestors). Only a small fraction of the total increase in endocranial volume shown here can be attributed to concomitant increase in body size; consequently, these data document the extraordinary evolutionary increase in the size of the organ most crucial to our "capacity for culture." At the same time, however, the data remain too sparse to say with certainty whether the trends fit the gradualism model, the punctuational model, or some combination of the two. See App. A.8.1 for sources and additional discussion of data and methods.

What are the sources of isolation and discontinuity among incipient subsystems? In other words, what permits descendant subunits to diverge? In organic evolution, this is equivalent to asking about the causes of reproductive isolation as required for species formation, or what Gould (1982c: xxvi) has termed "the central problem of [organic] evolution." The question calls for the identification of the most important modes of speciation (as reviewed, for example, in Bush 1975; Barton and Charlesworth 1984), itself a controversial subject, and for the identification of major reproductive isolating mechanisms that allow genetic differences to accumulate between subpopulations. The importance of the "isolation question" to organic evolution has been emphasized by many authors, including the biologist Richard Alexander who notes that "without isolation there would be but a single species." (1979: 14.) The role of isolation in the divergence of cultures, as discussed for example by J. Hill (1971) and P. Diener (1980), has generally not received the attention that is its due, except perhaps in the study of linguistic change (see, for example, Samuels 1972: ch. 6).

Cultural Evolution: An "Untried Theory"?

If cultures do evolve, then the concept of evolution and the questions it raises would seem to offer a valuable perspective for the study of human cultural systems.[21] Ironically, although anthropology actually began during the last century as an evolutionary science, on the very coattails of the Darwinian revolution in biology (see, for example, Kroeber 1960; Carneiro 1973a, 1973b), mainstream concerns in the discipline have focused elsewhere for most of this century, sometimes with a deliberate bias against evolution (White 1960).[22] One reason is that "theories of cultural evolution did not originate with Darwin nor were they borrowed from biology. They are as old as the ancient Greeks," and they are decidedly non-Darwinian in orientation and mechanism (White 1959c: 107). In contrast

[21] As evidence of this value, in the late 1780's (that is to say, well before Darwin) Sir William Jones "recognized the common origin and diverging descent of the Indo-European languages—an insight which grouped species of idioms into genera and genera into a family, resulting in a genuine phylogeny, perhaps the first in any field of knowledge." (Kroeber 1960: 8; see also Greenberg 1959: 65.) A number of linguists, including a contemporary of Darwin's named Max Mueller (quoted by Greenberg), were therefore able to say, "In language, I was a Darwinian before Darwin."

[22] Antievolutionary sentiments have usually been directed at specific models and formalizations, especially unilinear ones, rather than at the concept of cultural evolution itself. Consider, for example, the antievolutionism associated with the anthropologist Franz Boas and his followers earlier this century. On the one hand (as expressed by B. Laufer, quoted in White 1960: v), this group regarded the theory of cultural evolution developed by that time as "the most inane, sterile, and pernicious theory in the whole theory of science." On the other hand, as Mead (1964: 6) observed, "at no point did Boas challenge the general propositions of evolution or question the theory that human cultures had evolved from initially simpler forms." A recent example of antievolutionary bias is given in Stocking (1986: 505) who quotes the words of an unnamed sociocultural anthropologist, "I am not interested in the evolution of anything."

to the branching-tree pattern of diversification engendered in Darwinian theory (not to mention the bush pattern of the recent punctuationalists), the works of Henry Maine, Lewis Henry Morgan, Edward Tylor, John McLennan, and others in the 1860's to 1890's were unilinear "stage theories of history." (See Blute 1979.) As such they heavily emphasized a notion of social progress through a sequence of uniform stages leading from "savagery," "barbarism," and the like among nonstate societies through to the "civilization," of course, of Western Europe.[23]

Subsequent generations of social scientists overwhelmingly rejected these theories, and sometimes the whole idea of cultural evolution along with them, even while embracing more appropriate—and often more Darwinian—notions of "culture change." As a result, the study of cultural evolution remained thoroughly "contaminated," as Donald Campbell (1965: 23) once put it, by the "reactionary political viewpoints of the privileged classes and racial supremacist apologists for colonialism, exclusionist immigration laws, etc."

In retrospect, it seems that a part of the problem stemmed from the failure of these early theorists to differentiate between "culture" and "social system" and thus, to borrow again from Geertz (1973: 144–45), to distinguish between change in the "ordered system of meaning and of symbols" and change in "the actually existing network of social relations." Surely changes in these systems can be, and often *are*, interrelated, as when new symbols and meanings are introduced to justify or, indeed, to mystify some change in a social system. And surely it would have been foolhardy, then as now (see Hull 1982), to propose theories of cultural evolution that ignore social context and thus disregard, for example, the cultural implications of power relations in a society. But it was also a mistake to confound these two phenomena, particularly if, as more recent authors insist (see, e.g., Hallpike 1986; Johnson and Earle 1987), there can be similar trajectories of "social evolution" in societies with very different cultural systems. Of course, there may also be different outcomes to social evolution in societies that began with the same cultural heritage (see especially Kirch 1984; Kirch and Green 1987). There may thus be two distinctive patterns of change, one for each system: stage-wise pathways of development in social relations, and divergent, branching trees of differentiation in culture. Whatever the case, attempts by the so-called classical evolutionists of the nineteenth century to subsume all social and cultural change within unilinear schemes were surely destined to fail.

Eventually, in the mid-1940's, there began something of a rebirth of interest in formal evolutionary theories of culture (reviewed in Phillips 1971, for example), but scholars were still notably uneasy about the con-

[23] For fuller discussion of these theories and their impact on anthropology, see works by Burrow (1966), Harris (1968), and Stocking (1987). The writings of Edward B. Tylor, particularly as reviewed by Burrow (1966: ch. 7), Opler (1964, 1965), and Stocking (1968: ch. 5), offer an instructive case example of the unilinear approach.

cept of evolution and even about the use of the word. Thus Julian Steward was to write in his 1955 monograph, *Theory of Culture Change*: "Since 'evolution' still strongly connotes the nineteenth-century view, I hesitate to use it but find no better term." (p. 5.) Consequently, cultural evolution has remained at the fringes of respectable, mainstream anthropology and is today, as Marion Blute (1979) has argued, "an untried theory." Not surprisingly, culture is therefore analyzed "much as it would have been at any time in Western history before Darwin." (Greenwood 1984: 20.)

I would like to offer three reasons why it is important today for contemporary anthropology to try again to develop a genuine theory of cultural evolution. The first is simply to avoid any impression of an analogous "cultural creationism," that is, any (presumably unintended) impression that cultural systems have persisted in fixed, unmodified form from the moment of their creation. This reason rests upon the inference, wholly justified by available evidence,[24] that human cultures are all related by "descent"—that is to say, by derivation or extraction—and that the differences we observe today are the cumulative results of some set of historical diversifying processes. In short, anthropology needs a sequential transformation theory of cultural evolution to support its own assumptions about human cultures and to avoid false and misleading impressions.

The second reason is that our understanding of cultural systems will be substantially improved by greater attention to the diachronic or evolutionary dimension to culture. Here let me frame the argument with an instructive metaphor. It seems to me that the emerging anthropological consensus, described above, treats cultures very much like cryptographers' codes—that is, like the systems of symbols with certain more or less arbitrary meanings that people use to transmit messages through time and space (on this similarity, see also Douglas 1971). Accordingly, one can reasonably imagine three complementary approaches to the study of the "codes," two of which, in anthropology, are already quite sophisticated. First, cultures can be, and are, "deciphered," that is to say their meaning, in what is often referred to as symbolic or semiotic anthropol-

[24] Anthropological evidence has long suggested that human cultural systems are all related by descent, forming what Kroeber (1963: 68) called the "tree of human culture." In a book specifically challenging unilinear views of "social evolution," for example, V. Gordon Childe (1951: 166) wrote, "It is not in the least surprising that the development of societies observed in different parts of the Old World, to say nothing of the New, should exhibit divergence rather than parallelism" in a pattern analogous to organic evolution. Similarly, in his posthumously published *Roster of Civilizations and Culture* (1962), Kroeber concluded that "the many past and present cultures grade into one another in space and time in a vast continuum," such that "the classification of history and culture seems bound to be somewhat like the classification of the forms of life." (pp. 10, 12.) Among the many attempts to provide detailed case studies of "descent with modification" in a specific subsample of cultures, one may cite the works of Greenberg on the languages of Africa (J. Greenberg 1966a; see also Fivaz and Scott 1977; Chapter 3 of this book) and the Americas (J. Greenberg 1987); those of Lincoln (1981, 1986; Chapter 5 of this book) on Indo-European mythology; and those of Epling et al. (1973) and Marshall (1984) on the "genetic relations" of Polynesian sibling terminologies and of Austronesian languages more generally.

ogy, is interpreted or translated. This can be thought of as the interpretive or "horizontal" dimension of cultural analysis (horizontal in the sense of being within or between codes). To quote from Geertz (1973: 14), "the whole point of a semiotic approach to culture is to aid us in gaining access to the conceptual world in which our subjects live." Second, cultures can be, and are, studied in order to predict or explain human behavior. This can be thought of as the explanatory or "vertical" dimension of cultural analysis (vertical in the sense of studying links between codes on one level and behaviors on another). Much in the way that the interception and translation of cryptographers' codes can lead to the prediction or understanding of secretive actions, so too can the analysis of cultures help to explain the diversity of human behavioral customs.

But consider now the third dimension here: one can also study the evolutionary emergence of the code. That is to say, one can legitimately seek to comprehend the historical processes through which people have composed, edited, and revised the codes that give meaning and direction to their lives. It should be noted that this "temporal" or evolutionary dimension is, at least in principle, fully complementary to the other two: it can be used to establish the history of how codes have come to have their present configuration and meaning, and how they have historically affected social behavior and been affected themselves in return. But, as noted earlier, this dimension has received the least attention of the three by mainstream anthropology. Indeed, as Frank Livingstone and others have noted, "an adequate model of cultural evolution . . . is still the major theoretical problem facing anthropology today." (1981: 645.) It takes little imagination, therefore, to predict that the development of such a model and, with it, a fully three-dimensional approach to culture will add valuable perspective to cultural analysis.

The third reason why anthropology will benefit from cultural evolutionary theory concerns the concept of culture itself: that concept cannot help but be strengthened, and our understanding of it enhanced, if we can one day account for trends in the historical emergence and divergence of ideational systems. As one example of this benefit, it seems to me that the significance of culture for understanding human behavior stands to be greatly clarified and reinforced by renewed attempts to resolve some key issues about genes and culture left hanging by the sociobiology debate. With this goal in mind, let me briefly outline some of the more important of these issues in order to have them clearly before us from the start.

Some Key Issues in Evolutionary Anthropology

Most of the conceptual issues remaining today in the study of genes, culture, and human diversity relate to two problems: how best to describe the evolutionary dynamics of culture; and how to characterize the relationships between those dynamics and the processes of genetic change. In my assessment, there remain five issues of paramount importance; each is described below.

The Issue of Distinction

The most basic of all issues facing evolutionary anthropology concerns the question, Does culture provide human populations with a second system of information inheritance that is truly distinct from the genes? Is it genuinely appropriate and/or necessary for us to distinguish between genes and culture as two different kinds of influence on human diversity? What, after all, is to be gained by this distinction?

That there remains some disagreement on this subject may come as a surprise to many readers, particularly to specialists in cultural anthropology on the one hand and in human genetics on the other. Historically, it would seem that these fields of inquiry were founded on the assumption that genes and culture do provide the human organism with two distinct modes of inheritance, each with specialized features that justify and reinforce the specialized study of them. Recently, however, a number of authors have challenged that assumption, arguing that it leads to a false and misleading dichotomy.

The clearest and strongest of these pronouncements was raised in a paper by the anthropologist Mark Flinn and the biologist Richard Alexander (1982). Their critical review of culture theory (including a number of my own arguments) explicitly challenged the assumptions, first, that the units of inheritance are distinct between genetic and cultural systems; and second, that the mechanisms for the transmission of these units can also be differentiated. In their argument, Flinn and Alexander take the answer to the "units question" of cultural evolution to be "traits," that is, specific phenotypic properties of the organism. They then point out that, without exception, the transmission of traits through time in a population also depends upon environmental influence, the underlying genetic integrity of the organism, and the organism's entire history of evolution by genetic selection. In short, they say, a trait is never really "cultural" as opposed to, or differentiated from, "genetic"; it is, at best, both of these confounded. A dichotomy between genetic transmission and cultural transmission is therefore, in their words (p. 390), "unacceptable." This criticism leads them to challenge the argument that human diversity is a product of two inheritance systems, one genetic and one cultural, and of two corresponding sets of units (called "instructions" in the specific passage they cite).

This is a common theme (Cloak 1975; Boyd and Richerson [1976]; Lumsden and Wilson 1981; others). However, two sets of instructions occur in the development of all traits of all organisms: genetic and environmental. No rationale has ever been advanced for regarding the influence of culture on the development and expression of behavior as other than a special subset of the environment. The remarkable persistence of such unsupportable dichotomies seems to attest primarily to the human reluctance to see ourselves as natural objects in the universe, subject, even if in a special way, to the same rules that govern all life. [p. 391]

In the chapters that follow, we will look closely at this issue, particularly at two aspects of it raised by Flinn and Alexander. First, we will investigate the question of proper units for the study of cultural transmission, in part because so much of the debate follows from the assumption of a "trait" unit. On this subject there has arisen considerable diversity of opinion among students of cultural evolution (as reviewed, for example, in Stuart-Fox 1986), if only because of the difficulty of finding an explicit analog in culture for the role of the gene in organic evolution. The problem, as Martin Daly (1982: 402) has succinctly noted, is that "there are no segregating particles underlying culture," or at least no one has satisfactorily identified them. Second, we will also take a closer look at the properties of culture that purportedly qualify it as a "special subset" of the environment. How well does culture fit into the conventional genes/environment dichotomy on which this argument is based? Are there properties of culture that warrant its distinction from both genes and environment? It is my contention that in order to resolve this "distinction issue" we should integrate more fully into our conception of culture a number of lessons from the new ideational theories in anthropology.

The Issue of Independence

If we assume for the moment that culture is a distinct inheritance system, the question naturally follows, Is cultural evolution also an autonomous force in the shaping of human diversity? The question is all the more necessary because we know that the structures and functions of our "capacity for culture" (as described, for example, in Spuhler 1959; Holloway 1975b; Graubard 1985), particularly those of the brain and vocal tract, are themselves products of organic evolution. How much freedom from the genes can one expect in such a "derived" information system, that is to say, one whose existence depends so directly upon the products of organic evolution? In what ways does culture remain influenced by its supporting structures, and thus by the genes, and in what ways has the cultural system evolved a measure of its own independence?

This issue has been raised in many different contexts and by many different authors but never so pointedly as by the biologist Edward O. Wilson. In his book *On Human Nature*, Wilson discusses the development of moral systems and asks: "Can the cultural evolution of higher ethical values gain a direction and momentum of its own and completely replace genetic evolution? I think not. The genes hold culture on a leash. The leash is very long, but inevitably values will be constrained in accordance with their effects on the human gene pool." (1978: 167.) The metaphor is clear and concise yet deceptively simple. Contained within the image of genes holding culture on a leash are a number of important questions or groups of questions like: (1) Is the leash the same length at all times and all places? Why or why not? (2) Are there ever instances when the chain of command is reversed, and culture "drags along" the leash bearers? When does this occur, if ever? (3) Is the leash ever so long as to be ineffective, allowing the "domesticated pet" to run free, in effect? When does this happen? And so on. On close examination, we can see that the value of Wilson's metaphor lies not so much in the initial image it presents as in the array of unanswered questions it raises. These are key questions in the study of evolutionary anthropology—questions to which we must return in this investigation.

The Issue of Transformation

If it is true that all human cultures are related by descent, the question immediately arises, What have been the mechanisms of change responsible for transforming earlier, ancestral systems (including the original, universal culture) into the vast, if dwindling, array of contemporary cultures? Using Lewontin's schema presented above, we may actually distinguish two key questions in this regard. First, what is the full range of processes responsible for transformation? What are the various mechanisms through which the state of a given cultural system at some given time t can be modified into a new state at time $t + 1$? What are the properties of these mechanisms? Do they follow general patterns and regular rules? Second, of that range, which mechanism or mechanisms have been most important in the sense of having the greatest and most enduring effects? In other words, is there a cultural equivalent to Darwin's predominant Power?

As before, there exists less than complete agreement on these topics in the recent literature, but in the chapters that follow we will explore some of the progress that has been made. As we will see, there are already some impressive results to report with respect to the range of forces. A number of authors, most notably Cavalli-Sforza and Feldman (1981) and Boyd and Richerson (1985), have compiled substantial inventories of the various mechanisms that may, in principle, act in transforming cultural systems. In my view, however, the single most important failure of these attempts is that none of them has forwarded a convincing argument, as did Darwin, for the "main but not exclusive means." Hence one goal of the book before you is to attempt such an argument. It is no longer enough to say, as Margaret Mead (1964) and others have in the past, that cultural evolution consists of "directional cultural change." We need to understand why and in what sense it is directional and just how it is transformed. We need, in short, a systematic theory of cultural kinetics.

This, however, leads immediately to a fourth concern.

The Issue of Difference

If, for the sake of argument, we now assume some resolution of the preceding issues, such that cultural systems are indeed (1) distinct from genetic systems, (2) in some ways independent of genetic systems, and (3) fully capable of transformation, then a whole new issue presents itself: Is cultural evolution then fundamentally different from organic evolution in either its operation or its effects? In other words, does cultural evolution entail processes or principles that are either unprecedented in the evolution of life or at least substantially different in their logic or function from those in the organic realm? Is there then a basic, qualitative difference between the evolutionary dynamics of genes and of culture?

On this issue the emerging literature of evolutionary anthropology seems to be divided according to each author's view of the distinction between "ultimate" and "proximate" forms of causation, and how it applies to culture. This longstanding distinction, formally introduced to modern biology by Ernst Mayr (1961: 1503; see review in Losco 1981), requires that causal influences on behavior be distributed between these discrete, polar categories so that "proximate causes govern the responses of [an] individual to immediate factors of the environment, while ultimate causes are responsible for the evolution of the particular DNA program of information [i.e., the genes] with which every individual of every species is endowed."[25] Following this convention, a number of recent authors have seen fit to treat culture as a system of proximate causation and therefore as completely consistent with the logic and function of the ultimate causes. By this view, culture is the metaphorical "handmaiden" of the genes (Alexander 1979: 142–43). In contrast, other authors have argued that culture provides the human organism with essentially a second source of ultimate causation. Asserting that there are "novel forces" in the cultural system, unparalleled in organic evolution, these authors suggest that "the existence of culture causes human evolution to be fundamentally different from that of noncultural organisms." (Boyd and Richerson 1985: 99.)

In the chapters that follow, we will return to this issue of difference and the associated problem of causation. As we will see, the confusion and disagreement here arises from the fact that cultural causes are neither as

[25] In his book, *The Evolution of Human Sexuality*, Donald Symons (1979: 7–8) offered this useful elaboration of Mayr's argument. "Proximate, or immediate, causal analyses consider *how* the behavior came to exist. . . . In other words, questions about the proximate causes of behavior deal with development, physiology, and immediate stimulus: they consider the individual animal's history and present circumstances. . . . Ultimate, or evolutionary, causal analyses consider *why* the behavior exists. The answers to questions about ultimate causation will be that the behavior functions in specific ways to maximize the animal's inclusive fitness [as already defined]. Functions result from the operation of natural selection in the populations from which the animal is descended. . . . Questions about the ultimate causes of behavior thus consider primarily the species's history."

"ultimate" as genetic causes (for the simple reason, again, that genetic selection molded the human capacity for culture in the first place) nor are they as "proximate" as developmental and physiological causes. In a very real sense, cultural evolution is *intermediate* between the poles of this conventional dichotomy, and I will argue that this special status has important implications for the issue of difference.

The Issue of Coexistence

Assuming, then, that we are able to make some headway on Issues 1 through 4 of this series, the key problem remains: How do the processes of genetic and cultural evolution relate? What is the range of possible relationships between genetic and cultural change, and which of these relationships are most important to understanding the evolution of human diversity? Although, as noted earlier, such questions are not entirely new, they have recently returned to prominence as a result of the sociobiology debate. Researchers have asked: (1) When does genetic evolution cause cultural change? (2) When, conversely, does cultural evolution cause genetic change? and (3) When do genes and culture evolve independently, so that change in one is not accompanied by change in the other? The answers to these questions have not come easily, and even the most earnest of attempts have sometimes engendered great controversy and polemics. In retrospect, however, my impression is that the debate on this issue has been compounded with differences of opinion arising from all of the previous four issues. If we are able to provide some resolution on those more basic concerns, Issue 5 may prove less problematic than it has thus far appeared.

About This Book

The book before you represents a first effort toward the resolution of these and related issues. It is an attempt to formulate a general theory of cultural evolution, to use that theory to predict basic modes of relationship between genetic and cultural dynamics, and to test those predictions against a sample of demanding case studies. In a general sense its goal is to demonstrate that an evolutionary dimension to the study of culture has much to contribute both to our understanding of human diversity, particularly behavioral diversity, and to the resolution of age-old questions about nature and nurture, genes and culture. The book is another example of evolutionary anthropology as previously defined; it attempts the dual task of summarizing, with critical evaluation, other major works in this subject area and of extending the body of evolving theory in what I believe to be crucial new directions. Building (not uncritically) on my own earlier arguments, I present three main hypotheses that, together, form the heart of the theory of *coevolution*. Like a boat builder launching a new ship, naturally I wish the theory well. In the long run, however, it matters not how well or long this boat will sail; what matters is whether or not better boats can now be built.

The chapters that follow build sequentially from basic principles of cultural and genetic analysis toward the proposal of a cultural evolutionary theory that is parallel in many respects to Darwin's theory of organic evolution. I use the proposal, which I call a "theory of evolution by *cultural* selection," to formulate a general conceptual framework for the study of gene-culture relationships. Through comparison of rates and directions of change in the two evolving systems, the framework predicts the existence of five major patterns or "modes" of relationship between genes and culture, two that are fully interactive in the sense described above, and three that are instead comparative. In later chapters, each of these modes is discussed in some detail and its existence confirmed through one or more case studies chosen for their heuristic value and broader implications. But coevolution predicts not simply the existence of these five modes of gene-culture relations; it also predicts their relative importance in the ongoing dynamics of cultural change. We are thus led, by the end of the book, to a general prediction about the cooperative evolution of genes and culture in the genesis of human diversity.

In addition to differences between the theory and predictions of this book and others in evolutionary anthropology, there are also differences in content and organization. The first difference concerns strategies of model building and model testing. Nearly every other recent scholarly work on the relations of genes and culture is heavily abstract and quantitative, requiring readers to have at least a working knowledge of calculus. Important assumptions and arguments have sometimes been hidden behind overly technical jargon, or locked up inside partial derivatives and double integrals, almost completely inaccessible to nonmathematicians. Moreover, these attempts have all run headlong into what has been termed the "modeler's dilemma": in most instances one cannot be precise, general, and realistic all at once (Levins 1966). In contrast, my goal has been to strive for generality and realism at the expense of precision. I have therefore put more emphasis on basic concepts, principles, and definitions than I have on formulas (most of which, in fact, have been relegated to the appendixes). For example, I devote considerable attention in later chapters to the "units question" of cultural evolution, because earlier quantitative studies have relied upon easily modeled units that are also misleading and unfaithful to the recognized basic properties of culture. In addition, the framework and models of gene-culture relationships that I propose make use of some simple graphic schemas that deliberately sacrifice precision in the pursuit of what, I hope, are gains in the other dimensions. In this way, I have tried to make accessible both the issues that have surfaced in this area of inquiry and my ideas for their resolution.

The second difference concerns my use of case studies. Early in this project, I became convinced that more insight was to be gained from an in-depth treatment of a few such studies than by any attempt to survey many subjects. Also, it seemed to me that the lack of detailed empirical analysis was another of the serious shortcomings common to other recent investigations in this area. I therefore selected a small number of promising cases to investigate in as much depth as time and resources would allow. Generally speaking, these cases focus on human behavioral diversity, not because interesting questions and good examples are lacking in the physiological and morphological aspects of human diversity, but because I needed a more circumscribed universe and because behavior is an especially good place in which to study the effects of both genes and culture. I do take up a number of physiological and morphological topics along the way, but in each instance the inquiry is related to or motivated by specific differences in human behavior. Let me also emphasize that I make no claim about the greater "representativeness" of the cases presented below, particularly since some of them were chosen deliberately for their unusual or exaggerated qualities. Instead, the cases are meant to illustrate theoretical arguments. They also illustrate an approach to empirical inquiry that I believe for other reasons to have more general applicability.

In concluding this chapter, let me sketch a brief outline of the subsequent chapters, with their mixture of theoretical material and case studies. I begin in Chapter 2 with a case study of human behavioral diversity that illustrates both the explanatory dimension of cultural analysis and the need for a complementary evolutionary dimension. The case concerns the diversity of marriage patterns in Tibetan populations, an example that stands out in all of social science for the variety (and fluidity) of marriage forms observed in a single population. My analysis will demonstrate the power of culture's ideational code for explaining even these very complex patterns of behavior, but it will also raise important questions about how that code, after all, evolved to have its current information content. The attempt to answer this second question will lead us to some provocative hypotheses regarding the persistence of ideational phenomena and on to a more general framework for understanding cultural change.

That framework, in turn, shares a number of features with the conceptual structure of organic microevolutionary theory, which is a subject we turn to in Chapter 3. The focus here is on a second case study, namely, an attempt to explain the gene-frequency differentials that are responsible for the variable rates of sickle-cell anemia among the native populations of tropical West Africa. This is another classic case of diversity in the annals of anthropology, one that provides the opportunity to review some basic concepts and principles of population genetics, and one that brings us back, through no coincidence, to culture. The analysis will show, first, that genetic selection can explain most of the difference between West African populations in the occurrence of sickling disease, but second, that genetic selection differentials themselves can be traced, in part, to cultural differences among the human inhabitants of the region.

After a brief critical review of previous models for relating genes and culture, Chapter 4 integrates principles from Chapters 2 and 3 into a general theory of cultural evolution. In essence, the theory proposes that two intergraded forces, one called "selection by choice" and the other "selection by imposition," are the main but not exclusive means of modification in cultural evolution. Primarily through these forces, I argue, the ideational phenomena of culture are differentially socially transmitted through space and time. Chapter 4 then assembles these and other forms of cultural selection into a conceptual framework for interrelating the dynamics of genetic and cultural change. Central to that framework is the special capacity of culture for what I call self-selection, that is, the capacity for previously evolved ideational phenomena to govern the rates of social transmission and hence direct cultural selection. That capacity, in turn, leads me to propose models of five distinct modes of gene-culture relations. Called "genetic mediation," "cultural mediation," "enhancement," "neutrality," and "opposition," these modes constitute the theoretical backbone for the remainder of the book. Together, they suggest a new, more integrated theory of evolutionary change in human populations. I call this theory "coevolution," both because it portrays genes and culture as distinct but interacting "tracks" of evolutionary change, and also because it hypothesizes that genes and culture often, though not always, cooperate in the evolution of adaptively advantageous human attributes. In the balance of Chapter 4, as a case examination of the mode called genetic mediation, we shall investigate the hypothesized influence of genes on the cultural evolution of basic color terms.

Chapter 5 takes up the logically symmetrical case of cultural mediation, in which culture is hypothesized to play a guiding role in the course of genetic evolution. This mode of relationship is exemplified by the influence that dairying and associated cultural phenomena appear to have had in the genetic evolution of adult lactose absorption. In a similar vein, Chapter 6 explores the relationship called enhancement, in which culture evolves in the direction of improved human adaptation but does so independently of genetic change. This mode is illustrated by a comparative analysis of incest taboos compiled from a world sample of human populations. From there, Chapter 7 goes on to look at neutral and opposing relations between genes and culture. The chapter includes discussion of two suspected examples of opposition: the headhunting tradition of the Mundurucú Indians of Amazonia, a tradition sustained by choice for generations despite its presumed dysfunctionality; and the case of *kuru*, a lethal nerve-degeneration disease that reached epidemic proportions among the Fore people of New Guinea as a consequence of beliefs maintained by choice. We will see that opposition can and does exist within human populations, but also that its relatively stable manifestation generally results from imposition rather than choice.

We return from this odyssey through theory and examples to a review, in the final chapter, of the major assumptions, hypotheses, and implications of coevolution. Special emphasis is placed on the relative importance of the different modes of gene-culture relations. We also return to the "key issues" of evolutionary anthropology, which are used to draw distinctions between coevolutionary theory and other leading proposals. I conclude with three predictions: that comparative modes of gene-culture relations are more common than interactive modes; that selection by choice usually produces enhancement grading into neutrality; and that most cases of sustained opposition reflect the action of imposition.

2 / CULTURE AND HUMAN DIVERSITY: A Case Study of Marriage in Tibet

Among the inhabitants of the arid and austere Tibetan plateau, so-called rooftop of the world, one finds the greatest diversity of socially sanctioned marriage customs known to anthropology. On the one hand, Tibetan tradition embraces the entire range of recognized marital forms, including monogamy (one spouse per individual), polygyny (two or more wives simultaneously per husband), polyandry (two or more husbands simultaneously per wife), and polygynandry or "group marriage" (two or more husbands simultaneously married to two or more wives). On the other hand, the tradition also includes patterned variation in the location of postmarital residences of married couples. Some of them live in the husband's natal household (a practice called "virilocality") or the wife's natal household ("uxorilocality"); others construct and occupy a new residence of their own ("neolocality").[1] In addition, there is further variation among plural marriages in the kinship relations and generational standing of co-husbands and co-wives. The husbands in polyandrous marriages, for example, range from unrelated males to full brothers and on to father and son under certain conditions. The resulting Tibetan "marriage system," as it is called, represents an unparalleled example of human behavioral diversity.

In this chapter, I would like to explore the Tibetan marriage system with three specific goals in mind. First, drawing on a number of recent ethnographic descriptions, I would like to examine the full pattern of variation within the system. Second, I would like to assess the validity and utility of a cultural explanation of this pattern of variation, thereby demonstrating the role of "vertical" cultural analysis introduced in Chapter 1 (regrettably, space precludes an exploration of its "horizontal" equivalent). Finally, I would like also to examine the social history of the ideational phenomena that lie behind and guide the observed patterns of behavior, thereby attempting to add an evolutionary dimension.

---

[1] The terms "virilocality" and "uxorilocality" (with prefixes derived from the Latin words *vir*, "man," and *uxor*, "wife," respectively) are used today in preference to the older but misleading "patrilocality" and "matrilocality" (see Barnard and Good 1984: ch. 5).

Because marriage in Tibet is not an altogether obvious choice of topic, let me mention a few of the reasons why it offers an especially good starting point for our inquiry. As we shall see, the example nicely illustrates both the five basic properties of culture introduced in Chapter 1 and the strength of culture's influence on human behavior. In so doing, the Tibetan material serves to clarify the causal, instructional role of culture in the genesis of human behavioral diversity. In addition, the study of marriage and family also relates directly to the genes and culture controversy. These institutions are clearly central to human reproduction: it is largely through marriage and family that human genes are, or are not, propagated through space and time. Yet marriage and family arrangements are also directly related to human cultural systems. In all known societies, these arrangements are shaped and regulated by specific rules and/or beliefs governing the relations between adults of both sexes and the relations between parents and their children. As the sociologist Pierre van den Berghe (1979: 113) half-jokingly put it, "man mates much like other mammals do, but he makes much more fuss about it." Last but not least, marriage and the family have been topics of central concern within cultural anthropology for over a century. One of the main reasons for this is their key role in the organization and structure of human societies, particularly the small and relatively simple nonstate societies traditionally studied by anthropologists. If one can determine the validity and utility of a coevolutionary perspective in such an area, albeit only in selected cases at the outset, a small but significant step will have been made toward evaluating this perspective's more general potential. Let me begin, then, with this illustrative—even dramatic—case study of human behavioral diversity.

Marriage in Tibetan Populations

In 1965 the anthropologist Melvyn Goldstein began a study of Tibetan immigrants living in a refugee settlement at Mysore, India. Goldstein chose Mysore as his location because China had closed Tibet to Western social scientists after the takeover of 1959. But his choice of subject was prompted by a discrepancy among the reports concerning marriage practices in traditional Tibetan society. Observers seemed to concur about the range of marriage forms observed among Tibetans, including monogamy, polygyny, *and* polyandry, but there was considerable disagreement concerning their relative prevalence. Was polyandry the predominant form of marriage as claimed, for example, by Prince Peter (1965: 193), or were the majority of Tibetan unions actually monogamous as asserted by Robert Ekvall (1968: 26)? Hoping to resolve the issue, Goldstein set about interviewing immigrants in India, many of whom were from the same cluster of villages in the Gyantse district of central Tibet (see Fig. 2.1; see Dargyay 1982 for a second study based on the reports of immigrants from this district).

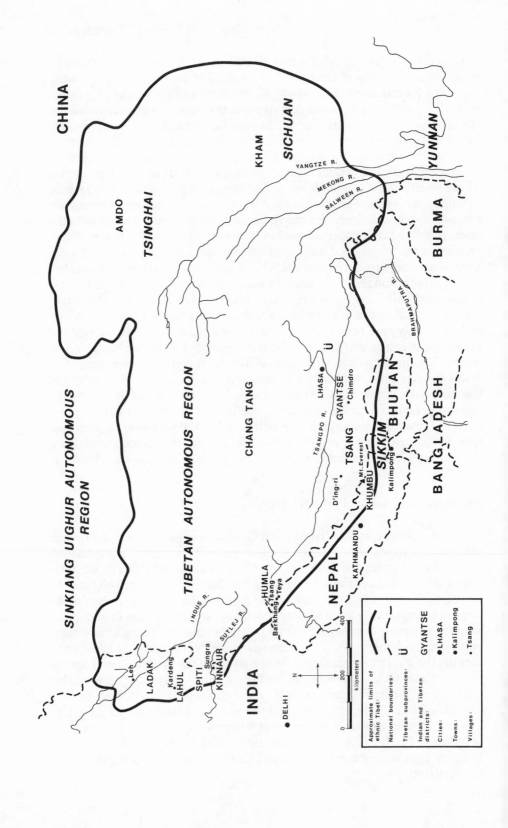

Marriage Patterns in Central Tibet

Goldstein did not take long to discover that both the diversity in marriage forms and the disagreement over their frequencies were direct consequences of social structure in Tibetan society. Most of his data applied to immigrant serfs from central Tibet, that is, to people who had made their living farming small plots on the estates of powerful overlords—a living supplemented by sheep and yak herding as resources allowed. But the data included a couple of different categories of serfs that corresponded to distinct socioeconomic strata in Tibetan society. Goldstein found that the predominant form of marriage varied widely across these strata and across associated differences in family ecology and economy. The discrepant reports of earlier observers had thus resulted from ignoring social structure and pooling observations from disparate strata.

Consider, first, the category of serfs called *dü-jung* (see Table 2.1), the small householders (literally, "small smoke") who were the vast majority of all inhabitants of the Gyantse District.[2] Some serfs in this category were bound to the large estates by an arrangement with the lord that provided them with individual use rights to small plots in return for a tax of periodic unpaid labor (a form of corvée). Other dü-jung, a majority in the areas described to Goldstein, were free, "human lease" serfs: they leased their own freedom from the overlord in return for cash payments, and then leased land from wealthier landholding serfs on a labor-rent basis. The farms of this second group were also small (up to two acres) and their tenure even more temporary than in the case of their bound counterparts. Consequently, both kinds of dü-jung gained access to land as individuals, and their resources in both cases were not heritable.

According to Goldstein's informants, dü-jung of both kinds "character-

[2] In referring to the traditional culture and social system of Tibet, I use the past tense to avoid the impression that conditions have remained unaltered since the Chinese takeover of 1959. There are, however, a good number of Tibetan-speaking populations who continue to live outside Tibet proper (for instance in Nepal, for which see Fig. 2.1) and thus outside the sphere of direct Chinese influence. Although subject to other outside influences (on which see Goldstein 1981b), many of these populations have retained key elements of the traditional Tibetan marriage system.

Fig. 2.1 (opposite). A map of ethnic Tibet, including the locations of places described in the text. Tibetan-speaking peoples, numbering some four million today, have traditionally occupied an area of about one and a half million square miles (enclosed by solid line), most of it at 11,000 feet or more above sea level. As shown, this area is substantially larger than the Tibetan Autonomous Region of the People's Republic of China, or what was called "Tibet proper" before the Chinese takeover of 1959. The northern three-sevenths of ethnic Tibet is a cold, dry desert almost completely lacking in permanent settlements. To the south of the desert, occupying roughly two-sevenths of the total area, is a semicircular band of rolling plateaux and sparse grasslands supporting a low-density population of nomadic herders. The remaining two-sevenths is a semicircular band of river valleys, centering on the Tsangpo, with sufficient water to support irrigated agriculture and sedentary populations. The agricultural communities described in the text inhabit this southernmost region. Adapted from Ekvall 1968.

TABLE 2.1

Socioeconomic Characteristics and Marriage Patterns
of the Dü-jung and Thongpa Serfs of South-Central Tibet

	Category of serf	
Feature	Dü-jung	Thongpa
Socioeconomic characteristics		
Bondage	Free or bound (majority free)	Always bound
Land holdings	0–2 acres	20–300 acres
Land tenure	Individual use rights (non-heritable)	Corporate family rights (heritable)
Tax obligations (taxable unit)	Corvée labor (individual)	Corvée labor Animal services Money and crops (family)
Marriage patterns		
Initiative for marriage	Individual	Parental arrangement
Form of marriage	Monogamy	Monogamy Polyandry Polygyny Polygynandry[a]
Postmarital residence	Neolocal	Commonly virilocal (sometimes uxorilocal)

SOURCE: Data from Goldstein 1971a.

[a]Not reported in Goldstein 1971a but documented subsequently in Goldstein 1976 and Levine 1977.

istically married out of love and almost always married monogamously."
(1971a: 72.) Young men and women were relatively free to marry whom-
ever they pleased—parents were not deeply involved in the arrangements—and the newly wedded couple generally established their own
independent, neolocal postmarital residence. The reasons Goldstein gave
for this pattern were largely economic. As laborers and cultivators of very
small parcels, the dü-jung did not have the resources to support an extended family, nor were they able to attract and maintain more than one
spouse at a time. Moreover, since resources, rents, and tax obligations all
devolved upon individuals, not families, there existed little economic incentive for a large and complex family structure. Goldstein concluded
(p. 71) that "since the dü-jung gained access to land as individuals rather
than as parceners in family corporations, the importance of the family
unit was greatly diminished. Normally, there was a continual process of
splitting off as the children [of a given generation] married and established
their own households."

The circumstances of the *thongpa* (literally "people of the house") contrasted sharply (Table 2.1).[3] In this stratum, serfs lived within corporate

[3]The Tibetan term *thongpa* is transcribed many different ways in the literature, including *dr'ong-pa* (as in Aziz 1978), and *trongba* (as in Levine 1977, 1988; Schuler 1987). In addition, different areas of ethnic Tibet apparently had different terms for this stratum of serfs,
including the term *tre-ba* in Central Tibet (see Goldstein 1971a, 1978a). To minimize confu-

family units that were given both much larger parcels of land (on the order of 20 to 300 acres according to Goldstein's informants) and permanent hereditary rights to them. As part of the arrangement, however, the thongpa were also bound to their parcels "unilaterally and permanently," and were subject to heavy annual taxes of money, crops, labor, and loaned animal services. Unlike a dü-jung family, a thongpa family had the same tax obligations regardless of family size.

Under these contrasting conditions, traditional marriage practices of the thongpa varied from those of the dü-jung in three important ways. First, thongpa marriages were nearly always arranged by the parents.[4] "Marriage was a serious matter which entailed subtle strategies" (p. 72) and deliberate parental manipulation. Second, the form of marriage was highly variable, ranging from monogamy (as among the dü-jung) to sororal polygyny (that is, co-wives were sisters), to fraternal polyandry (co-husbands were brothers), and on to polygynandry (see Table 2.1, note *a*). Indeed, Goldstein was told of thongpa marriages involving as many as five or six adults at once. Third, the custom of postmarital residence was both different from the dü-jung's and variable. Monogamous marriages were carefully arranged to be either virilocal (again, in the husband's natal household) or uxorilocal (in the wife's). Neolocality was consciously and consistently avoided. Polygynous marriages, in turn, were usually uxorilocal, whereas polyandrous marriages were usually virilocal. Thus, as Table 2.1 shows, marriage among the thongpa was an institution considerably more variable and complex than it was among the dü-jung.

A clearer idea of this variation and complexity is provided by Goldstein's data on thongpa marriages in the village of Chimdro, Gyantse district. Table 2.2 summarizes his findings with respect to the 62 "primary" marriages in the village—that is, those marriages perpetuating the named, corporate households. As the table shows, just over half of the primary marriages were fraternally polyandrous. In addition, Goldstein noted, their composition closely paralleled the nature of the sibling group in which the marriage took place. Thus, for example, each of the twenty families with two sons arranged a bi-fraternal polyandrous marriage between the brothers and a single wife who then came to live with them virilocally. In a similar fashion, single virilocal marriages proved to be the rule even where families had more than two sons. As Goldstein concluded, "in no instance with multiple sons was a joint family [of separate monogamous marriages] established." (p. 70.)

There were, however, variations on the theme. Several families with three or more sons sent one or more of them to a local Buddhist monas-

---

sion, I therefore use the one term *thongpa* (following the transcription of Goldstein 1978b) throughout this chapter.

[4] Among Tibetan-speakers in Bhutan, the right of thongpa parents to arrange the marriages of their children was even guaranteed by law. The traditional legal code stipulated that "marriages must not be contracted in defiance of the wishes of parents." (See Bell 1928: 175.)

TABLE 2.2

Marriage Forms and Postmarital Residences of the Thongpa Serfs of Chimdro Village, Gyantse, South-Central Tibet, by Number of Sons in Family

Number of sons[a]	Families		Primary marriages[b]			Postmarital residences	
	Number	Percent	Number	Percent	Form	Primary marriages[b]	Secondary marriages[c]
0	6[d]	9.7%	6	9.7%	Monogamy	Uxorilocal	(None)
1	24	38.7	24	38.7	Monogamy	Virilocal	(None)
2	20	32.3	20	32.3	Bi-fraternal polyandry	Virilocal	(None)
3	8	12.9	6	9.7	Tri-fraternal polyandry	Virilocal	(None)
			2	3.2	Bi-fraternal polyandry	Virilocal	Uxorilocal
4	4	6.5	1	1.6	Quatri-fraternal polyandry	Virilocal	Uxorilocal (?)
			1	1.6	Tri-fraternal polyandry	Virilocal	Uxorilocal (?)
			2	3.2	Bi-fraternal polyandry	Virilocal	
TOTAL	62	100.1%[e]	30	48.4%	Monogamy	6 (9.7%) Uxorilocal	
			32	51.6%	Polyandry	56 (90.3%) Virilocal	
			24	38.7	Bi-fraternal polyandry		
			7	11.3	Tri-fraternal polyandry		
			1	1.6	Quatri-fraternal polyandry		

SOURCE: Data from Goldstein 1971a: 70.

[a] Number of daughters was not reported except for families with o sons (see Note d).
[b] Marriages maintaining the corporate family unit are called "primary."
[c] Marriages outside and away from the corporate family are called "secondary."
[d] Five of these families had only one daughter, for whom a bridegroom was brought in through uxorilocal, monogamous marriage. One of the families had two daughters; the option of sororal polygyny was avoided by sending the younger daughter to a nunnery while still a child.
[e] Total exceeds 100 percent because of rounding error.

tery,[5] to a "secondary" marriage (that is, to a marriage in which the young man was required to move out of his natal household and into uxorilocal residence in the house of a sonless thongpa family), or to both. The end result was that, of the 62 primary thongpa marriages, 24 were bi-fraternal polyandry, 7 were tri-fraternal polyandry, and 1 was quatri-fraternal polyandry. The remaining 30 were monogamous; as shown in Table 2.2, these were all described to Goldstein as cases in which there had been no more than one son in the family. On the basis of these data, Goldstein inferred that traditional patterns of marriage in the central region of Tibet were both highly variable, as earlier observers had noted, but also highly organized with respect to economic strata and the demographic features of the family. It seems likely, then, that if marriage were similarly organized in other regions of Tibet, the relative frequencies of monogamy, polygyny, and polyandry would vary in space and time as a function of (1) the relative sizes of local dü-jung and thongpa populations, and (2) the specific demographic features of resident thongpa households. It is little wonder that the earlier literature was so ambiguous and confusing on this subject.

Goldstein's study was essentially the first to demonstrate that Tibetan marriage customs were internally organized and systematic, not at all random or capricious as had sometimes been implied.[6] The research of other scholars not only confirms the basic pattern described by Goldstein, but extends it both to other regions of ethnic Tibet and to still other forms of socially sanctioned marriage.

Marriage Patterns in D'ing-ri

A second study of Tibetan refugees, conducted in the Khumbu region of Nepal from 1969 through 1971 by the anthropologist Barbara Aziz (1978), documented similar patterns of marital diversity among former inhabitants of the D'ing-ri Valley of southwestern Tibet. Like Chimdro, the villages of D'ing-ri Valley are located in the southern portion of the Tibetan plateau (elevation 4,000 to 4,600 meters) along streams that provide seasonal irrigation for fields of barley, turnips, peas, and mustard. And, as in Chimdro before the Chinese takeover, the largest rural subpopulations in D'ing-ri were thongpa and dü-jung serfs with socioeconomic positions and tax requirements closely parallel to those described for central Tibet.

---

[5] In this region of Tibet and others, local monasteries had the right to levy a "monk tax" on thongpa families. When a monastery could not maintain its size by voluntary entrance, it could require thongpa families with three or more sons to make one a monk for life (usually the second born: see Goldstein 1971c: 21; Aziz 1978: 269). This tax was partly responsible for the fact that "in precommunist Tibet . . . as many as 20 percent of the males were celibate monks throughout their lives." (Goldstein 1981a: 733.)

[6] The Western image of Tibet as a land of promiscuity traces back at least to the thirteenth century and the travels of Marco Polo. Although his tales do not mention polygamous marriages per se, they do claim that, by local custom, passing male travelers would find "perhaps 20 or 30 girls at their disposal" (Yule 1903: 44) in any given village or hamlet. Polo, however, claimed that this behavior was characteristic of mature females only before marriage.

Unlike Chimdro, however, D'ing-ri has long been a "frontier" community, bordering on the monogamous Hindu populations to the south, and subject for many years to their proselytizing influences.

Nevertheless, Aziz's description of marriage in D'ing-ri nicely corroborates the major findings of Goldstein's earlier study. First, her information clearly confirms the correlation between marriage form and family position in the social structure of rural Tibet. For example, she found that according to a 1959 census of the area the vast majority of all dü-jung marriages were monogamous and, by implication, neolocal. The census, conducted in the same year as the Chinese takeover, attributed a full 96.8 percent of all polygamous households to the landholding thongpa and once again established that marital diversity originated in the thongpa stratum (Aziz 1978: 140).

Second, Aziz was able to document the form and frequency of marriages in a large sample ($N = 430$) from all strata of the D'ing-ri population, including thongpa and dü-jung serfs as well as a small number of nobles and hereditary priests. These data, summarized in Table 2.3, yielded a pattern with several familiar features. First, fraternal polyandry was both the most prevalent and the most variable form of plural marriage, and was exclusively virilocal.[7] Second, the sample also included cases of sororal polygyny, a form of marriage that usually occurs when a *magpa* (literally "son-in-law," but reserved in conventional usage for those in uxorilocal residence) is brought into a house without male issue. Although most polygyny in the sample was therefore uxorilocal, it sometimes developed from virilocal monogamy and polyandry, particularly when a first wife proved infertile. Third, the sample included eight instances of *bi-generational* polyandry, a form of marriage previously described to Goldstein (1971a: 69) but not present in his Chimdro sample. In D'ing-ri these unions typically formed when a widower remarried virilocally and included one or more of his sons in the union. Although these were regarded as unusual or "irregular" marriages according to Aziz, they were not considered improper so long as incest avoidance rules were obeyed.[8]

The D'ing-ri sample also extended Goldstein's list to include three more forms of marriage. One of these was bi-generational polygyny, a union that formed in much the same way as bi-generational polyandry (as when a widow would invite one or more of her daughters to join a new matrilocal marriage). Less frequent, but still in evidence, were polygyny

[7] As mentioned in Table 2.3 (note *a*), 15 percent of all cases of "fraternal polyandry" in Aziz's sample are actually marriages between more distant kinsmen and one wife. Because a more specific breakdown of these marriages is not available, I will also treat them as "fraternal" polyandry, but it should be noted that they actually add still further diversity to the pattern of Tibetan marriage.

[8] On the subject of bigenerational polyandry, Aziz was told that "if there is any kinship tie between the second and the first wife, it precludes *any possibility* of sexual association with the boy" (1978: 153, emphasis added), that is, with the son of the first wife.

TABLE 2.3

*Forms and Frequencies of Marriage in a Cross-Sectional Sample
of the Population of D'ing-ri Valley, Southwestern Tibet*

Form of marriage	Number	Percent of total
1. Monogamy	308	71.6%
2. Fraternal polyandry (2 to 6 brothers)[a]	80	18.6
3. Sororal polygyny (2 or 3 sisters)	14	3.3
4. Bi-generational polygyny (mother/daughter)	10	2.3
5. Bi-generational polyandry (father/son)	8	1.9
6. Other polygyny (unrelated females)	8	1.9
7. Other polyandry (unrelated males)	2	0.5
TOTAL	430	100.1%[b]

SOURCE: Data from Aziz 1978: 139.

NOTE: This multigenerational sample is based on the family histories of immigrants from all strata of D'ing-ri society (thongpa and dü-jung serfs, nobles, and hereditary priests). The representativeness of the sample is suggested by the similarity between the frequencies of polygamy in the sample (28.4 percent) and in a 1959 regional census (27 percent).

[a] Aziz (1978: 148) states that 15 percent of the marriages listed here as fraternal polyandry are actually "unions of more distant kinsmen with one wife: unions of parallel cousins [that is, children of siblings of the same sex], of cross cousins [children of siblings of opposite sex], and of step brothers." In each instance, however, the co-husbands were raised from infancy in the same residence and were said to "feel as close as full brothers."

[b] Total exceeds 100 percent because of rounding error.

involving unrelated females (Form 6 in Table 2.3) and polyandry involving unrelated males (Form 7). Aziz noted that all cases of Form 6 developed from virilocal marriages where the first wife had proven infertile, and that one of the polyandrous cases similarly involved an additional "partner" for a childless couple. She regarded these cases as a testimonial to the importance of family heirs among the Tibetans of D'ing-ri.

In short, Aziz provides confirming evidence that "Tibet probably exhibits a greater diversity of marriage types than any other society." (1978: 134.) As in Chimdro, most of the diversity in D'ing-ri arises from the thongpa stratum of landholding serfs. By implication, then, this opening case study contains within it a contrast between (1) a social stratum with one of the most variable systems of marriage in the world and (2) other strata, of the same society, whose marital diversity is certainly not above the median. Nevertheless, as impressive as these data may seem, the account is not yet complete. Still other forms of socially sanctioned thongpa marriage will be presented in the third and final ethnographic case, which is in many ways the most detailed and systematic one.

Marriage Patterns Among the Nyinba

Working among the Nyinba in the Humla District of northwestern Nepal, the anthropologist Nancy E. Levine (1977, 1988) has documented a pattern of marital diversity that closely parallels the pattern for the thongpa of Chimdro and D'ing-ri. The similarity is all the more striking in light of the contrasts between these communities. For several hundred years the Nyinba have been tax-paying subjects of Hindu lords (who themselves practiced partible inheritance of land and rights over serfs); they have utilized actual slave labor, not dü-jung, to assist in their fields; and they have cultivated plots that are both much lower (at 3,000 meters) and much smaller (less than two acres apiece on average) than those in Chimdro and D'ing-ri.

In the village of Barkhang, for example, Levine's survey of 60 thongpa households (89 marriages in all) produced the marriage pattern shown in Table 2.4. As in Chimdro, virilocal fraternal polyandry proved to be the most common form of matrimony, characterizing nearly 52 percent of the marriages and, again, the form varied with the number of sons in the sibling set (to a noteworthy maximum of seven!). However, in addition to the instances of "simple polyandry," Levine found two forms of polyandrous matrimony not seen in Chimdro and D'ing-ri. Her survey turned up two cases of bona fide polygynandry and three more she called "conjoint marriages"—polygynandrous unions that developed internal behavioral subdivisions over time, almost like marriages within a marriage. Monogamy, as also in Chimdro, was the second most prevalent form of marriage, accounting for about 43 percent of the total. Given that Nyinba norms seem actually to favor polyandry, Levine was initially surprised by this finding. But she soon found that "the relatively high number of monogamous unions may be explained simply as due to developmental and demographic factors: the presence of only one heir in a particular generation or the loss of participants [from polygamous unions] over time." (Levine 1977: 222.) Only four monogamous marriages were formed where fraternal polyandry had been a real option. The overall pattern was thus quite similar to Chimdro's.

Finally, Levine documented five cases of polygyny in Barkhang and heard of still other cases in neighboring Nyinba villages. Two forms of polygyny were apparent, aside from polygynandry: a virilocal form instigated by a male (normally a single son) whose first wife proved infertile or bore exclusively female offspring (males are the preferred heirs); and a uxorilocal form created "when a woman who has brought a magpa invites her sister to join in the marriage." (p. 206.) In short, Levine's findings corroborated the reports of Goldstein and Aziz and extended them to include still other forms of marriage among Tibetans. In addition, Levine's analysis demonstrated that Nyinba unions truly did constitute marriage rather than simple "polykoity" (plural mating), a debate that has lingered in the literature on polyandry since Edmund R. Leach's (1955) review of the problem (see also Gough 1959). Levine found that each of the surveyed forms of union could do both of two things: confer social legitimation upon the children born to such unions; and bestow rights and duties of affinity (in-law relations) between the kin of one married partner and his or her spouse (see discussion in Levine and Sangree 1980).

TABLE 2.4

Forms and Frequencies of Marriage Among Thongpa Serfs in Chimdro, Central Tibet, and in Barkhang, Northwestern Nepal

	Chimdro[a]		Barkhang[b]	
Form of marriage	Number	Percent	Number	Percent
All Marriages				
Monogamy	30	48.4%	38	42.7%
Polygyny	—[c]	—[c]	5	5.6
Polyandry	32	51.6	46[d]	51.7[d]
TOTAL	62	100.0%	89	100.0%
Polyandrous Marriages[e]				
Bi-fraternal	24	38.7%	11	12.6%
Tri-fraternal	7	11.3	16	18.4
Quatri-fraternal	1	1.6	11	12.6
Penta-fraternal	—	—	4	4.6
Hexa-fraternal	—	—	1	1.1
Septi-fraternal	—	—	1	1.1
TOTAL	32	51.6%	44	50.4[f]%

SOURCE: Data from Goldstein 1971a: 70 (for Chimdro); Levine 1977: 213, 221 (for Barkhang).
  [a]Data are based on the memory recall of Tibetan refugees surveyed in Mysore, India, three to five years after their departure from Tibet.
  [b]Data pertain to marriages at the time of Levine's household survey.
  [c]Although there were no instances of polygyny in Goldstein's sample, informants insisted that such marriages did sometimes occur.
  [d]These figures include 41 cases of what Levine terms "simple polyandry," 2 of polygynandry, and 3 of conjoint marriage.
  [e]Includes polygynandry in Barkhang.
  [f]Levine does not explain the discrepancy between this total and the one above; the sample sizes also differ slightly.

Looking back over the cases reviewed here and still others in the literature,[9] we may reasonably conclude that marital diversity was a regular, systematic feature of social life in Tibetan populations. The variations of marital form originally documented for Chimdro were by no means local or idiosyncratic, but were instead part of a much larger pan-Tibetan ideology of marriage before the Chinese takeover. Because of that ideology, there were striking consistencies in the patterns of matrimony within populations separated by hundreds of miles, by different subsistence strategies, and by distinct political organizations. Of course there were also "variations on the theme" at the local level, reflecting outside influ-

  [9]For other ethnographic accounts, see Prince Peter 1963, Mann 1978, Crook 1980b, Sander 1983, Crook and Osmaston 1989, and Crook and Crook 1988 on Ladak; Nag 1960 and Prince Peter 1963 on Lahul; Chandra 1973, Raha 1978, and Bajpai 1981 on Kinnaur; Goldstein 1976, 1977, and 1987 on the Limis of Humla District, Nepal; Ross 1981 on the Dhingaba of Humla District, Nepal; Schuler 1987 on the Chumikwa of Mustang District, Nepal; Fürer-Haimendorf 1964 on the Sherpas of Solukhumbu District, Nepal; Gorer 1967 and Nakane 1966 on the Lepchas of Sikkim; and Ekvall 1968 on Tibetan nomads. Although some authors, notably Cassinelli and Ekvall (1969: 224–29), describe thongpa-like marriage customs among Tibetan nobles, for simplicity this chapter must focus on the subpopulation of serfs (and their freeholding descendants living in Nepal).

ences in some cases and possible adjustments of the ideology to local conditions in other cases. But there remained an underlying unity of logic and form—a unity indicative of an earlier common origin. Indeed, that unity extended even beyond agriculturalists to Tibet's renowned nomadic yak herders (see Ekvall 1968).[10] The evidence confirms that the ideology of marriage was, until very recently, a bona fide cultural tradition in Tibet.

Analytic Challenges of This Case

We now have before us an appropriately complex case of human diversity, an example that embraces variations in the form and frequency of marriage and in the postmarital residence of the participants. The dimensions of the case are summarized in Table 2.5. If we focus for the moment on thongpa marriages alone, we can see that out of eighteen possible combinations (nine documented forms of marriage times two traditional choices of postmarital residence), a full thirteen have been reported: eight varieties of virilocal marriage and five varieties of uxorilocal. This variability must surely stand as a benchmark in the study of human behavioral diversity.[11] Of equal importance for our purposes, however, are the forms of marriage in Table 2.5 that do *not* occur among the thongpa, such as virilocal bigenerational polygyny. A full explanation of Tibetan marital diversity must account for the blanks as well as the *T*'s in this tabulation.

When the marriage practices of the dü-jung are added to the picture, we arrive at a total of fifteen socially acceptable ways of being married in rural Tibet. The analytic challenges of the case, then, include these questions:

1. Why is there such a great diversity of marriage forms within the thongpa stratum of Tibetan serfs?

2. Why are there such contrasting marriage patterns between the thongpa and dü-jung populations? and

3. Why, after all, is it in Tibet that we find the most diverse marital system in the world?

[10] There was some confusion in the early literature on Tibet as to whether or not nomadic pastoralists were participants in the plural marriage system. On the one hand, Baber (1886: 97) refered to polyandrous nomadic families in the east, calling them "husbandmen . . . a word not devoid of appropriateness in this connection." On the other hand, Rockhill (1891: 212) claimed to find polyandry "unknown among them." Although, as we shall see, there may well have been some regional variation in prevalence, more recent authors all confirm the existence of the plural marriage system among the nomads (see, for example, Harrer 1982 [1953]: 105; Ekvall 1968; and App. A.2.3).

[11] Even by itself, socially sanctioned polyandry is unusual, as can be seen from the worldwide sample of the *Ethnographic Atlas* and its successor (Murdock 1967, 1981). Categorizing a total of 862 societies on the basis of the "prevailing form of domestic or familial organization," the *Atlas* lists 712 societies with prevalent polygyny, 137 with prevalent monogamy, and only 4 (2 of them actually different samples of Tibetans) with prevalent polyandry. At the same time, considering the impressive variability we have just seen in the forms and

TABLE 2.5

Documented Marriage Forms Among Tibetan Serf Populations

	Postmarital residence		
Form of marriage[a]	Virilocal	Uxorilocal	Neolocal
Monogamy			
1. Monogamy	T	T	D
Polygyny			
2. Sororal polygyny	T	T	
3. Bigenerational polygyny		T	(D)[b]
4. Other polygyny[c]	T	T	
Polyandry			
5. Fraternal polyandry	T		
6. Bigenerational polyandry	T		
7. Other polyandry[c]	T	T	
Polygynandry			
8. Fraternal polygynandry	T		
9. Conjoint marriage[d]	T		

SOURCE: Data from Goldstein, especially 1971a, 1976, 1978b; Levine 1977, 1988; Aziz 1978.

[a]Includes all forms of socially sanctioned matrimony. T's indicate forms of marriage documented among thongpa landholders; D's indicate forms of marriage among the dü-jung.

[b]Documented by Aziz (1978: 156) as a relatively infrequent form of marriage among the dü-jung.

[c]"Other" refers to polygyny including unrelated females and to polyandry including unrelated males. Although most instances of "other polygyny" are virilocal and, likewise, most instances of "other polyandry" are uxorilocal, Levine reports that uxorilocal "other polygyny" (1988: 147) and virilocal "other polyandry" (1988: 161) occur under certain special conditions.

[d]Term used by Levine (1977: 215ff.) to refer to polygynandrous unions that develop discernible internal subgroups ("marriages within a marriage").

Taken as a group, these questions comprise the first of three analytic problems that we will consider in the course of this chapter, namely, the problem of explaining the diversity of marriage patterns among Tibetans. But let us also not forget the more general questions concerning genes and culture that were raised by our discussion in Chapter 1. For example, we might ask in this context whether Questions 1 through 3 above can be answered fully by the information contained within either inheritance system—genes or culture—by itself, or whether these questions instead require information from both systems. If the questions can be answered satisfactorily by reference to only one system, then what does this imply more generally about the relationships between genes and culture? Alternatively, if they can be answered only by reference to both systems, then what would be implied about the nature of causal analysis in the case of an organism with two channels of information inheritance? In my view these questions, too, should be borne in mind as we turn to the challenge of explaining the special behavioral diversity of this, our opening case. Let

frequencies of Tibetan marriage, one can see just how much is lost in coding Tibetan society as one with "prevalent polyandry." There is obviously much more involved.

us begin, then, with a brief review of the published arguments for the diversity of marriages in Tibet.

Candidate Explanations

In his book *A Study of Polyandry* (1963), Prince Peter of Greece and Denmark presented the most complete review to date of contending explanations for the marriage customs of Tibetans. Unfortunately, Prince Peter sought only to explain the occurrence of polyandry, "something really at variance with our [Western] way of conducting family affairs" (p. 14), rather than to analyze the full pattern of diversity. But because this was a common preoccupation, his review included the full set of existing explanations organized into five categories (see his section III):

1. *Historical explanations,* suggesting that Tibetan polyandry is either the product of a historical diffusion from other regions or that it constitutes a relic from an earlier "polyandrous stage" in some unilinear scheme of human social evolution

2. *Demographic explanations,* suggesting that polyandry derives from recurrent competition for wives in areas with predominantly male adult sex ratios

3. *Sociological explanations,* including the arguments that (a) polyandry is a strategy to increase wealth, prestige, or social position and (b) polyandry emerges where social conditions permit the expression of male "sibling solidarity"

4. *Economic explanations,* proposing that polyandry forms (a) as a last resort in situations where males cannot each afford a wife, (b) to reduce divisive conflicts of interest that would occur if brother/heirs took separate wives with separate inheritances, (c) to prevent the erosive partitioning of heritable property, or (d) to concentrate adult labor power in the family

5. *Personal explanations,* in which polyandry purportedly serves more idiosyncratic needs such as ensuring the sexual satisfaction or fertility of a wife, or reducing the quarrels among brothers in a family or among sisters-in-law.

To these one could add a sixth category to accommodate Prince Peter's own explanation and a seventh to include an older, "political-economic" hypothesis that he overlooked:

6. *Psychological explanations,* among which is the argument that polyandry forms when austere environments permit the expression of "latent tendencies" both for incest and for male homosexuality (see Prince Peter 1965: 206–7)

7. *Political-economic explanations,* namely the argument that polyandry reflects "the interest of the state [or other landlords] . . . to keep a

fixed tax roll" by preventing multiple marriages and the subdivision of estates (Carrasco 1959: 45, 61).

Finally, one could add an eighth category in order to include the most recent arguments, namely, sociobiological ones:

8. *Sociobiological explanations*, such as the suggestion that polyandry arises from "some specific genetic base for fraternal sexual sharing," perhaps from the expression of "genes for fraternal tolerance" (see discussion in Hiatt 1980: 598).

At the outset, it should be clear that most of these arguments are necessarily weak in the Tibetan context because of their nearly exclusive focus on polyandry. They simply ignore many of the empirical properties of the Tibetan system that require explanation, such as the coexistence of polygyny and polygynandry in the very same populations. In this respect, nearly all of the arguments qualify as examples of what the anthropologist Gerald Berreman calls his "law of polyandry": "The occurrence of polyandry drives all other forms of marriage from the minds of anthropological observers."[12] (1978: 340.) Ironically, a truly valid explanation of Tibetan marital diversity must therefore violate Berreman's law.

In addition to this major shortcoming, there are other, more specific problems inherent in each of the arguments on this list (see App. A.2.1). To take an example—one with special relevance to the concerns of this book—let us consider briefly the specific problem confronting sociobiological explanations.

The Problem with Sociobiological Explanations

In their 1977 paper on the implications of sociobiology for the study of human family structures, Pierre van den Berghe and David Barash offered the following explanation for the occurrence of fraternal polyandry in societies like Tibet: "In the few cases of polyandrous mating in humans, *kin selection theory would lead one to expect* that if several men shared a wife and contributed to the fitness of her offspring, they would want to maximize the probability of her children sharing genes with them. This probability would be maximized in the case of fraternal polyandry." (1977: 812, emphasis added.) The mode of argument here is properly "sociobiological" by the definition of Chapter 1 (compare with Emlen and Oring 1977; Wittenberger 1979; Vehrencamp and Bradbury 1984 on polyandrous mating in nonhuman species). It is another good example of what

---

[12]Berreman (1978: 340) also gives a corollary to his law: "The term 'polyandry' obscures recognition of variation among and within the systems to which it is applied." These criticisms are based on the important observation that polyandry is not everywhere the same simple phenomenon. Instead, argues Berreman, polyandrous unions are commonly but part of greater systems of marriage that have highly contrasting cultural and structural features (see, for example, the studies in Levine and Sangree 1980).

Richard Dawkins (1982a: 27), reacting to a parallel suggestion about human polyandry, called "dragging genes in," for the simple reason that kin selection is a genetic theory. As discussed in Chapter 1, kin selection is actually a form of genetic selection and can only explain (or "lead one to expect") behavior when behavioral variation is correlated with genetic variation—a point Barash himself, in other writings, calls the "central principle of sociobiology." (1982: 42.) Thus the van den Berghe and Barash argument assumes that there are genetic differences between people who marry in the fraternal polyandrous fashion and those who do not.[13] One may then fairly ask, Is there evidence from polyandry in Tibet or elsewhere to support this assumption?

Consider, first, L. R. Hiatt's (1980) review of socially sanctioned polyandry among the Kandyan Sinhalese of Sri Lanka. On the one hand, Hiatt argued that Sinhalese polyandry appears to "conform to" and "be compatible with" sociobiological theory, at least as concerns the stated objectives of the participants themselves; for example, males mentioned defense against cuckoldry as a motivating concern. On the other hand, Hiatt reviewed specific evidence casting doubt on the idea of "genes for fraternal tolerance," including Stanley J. Tambiah's observation (1966) that the children of polyandrous Sinhalese unions rarely adopt polyandry themselves. He concluded that the "behavioral strategies involved in polyandry . . . do not correspond to particular genes or gene-combinations." Instead, he argued that the match of theory and behavior resulted from individual-level "constitutional factors . . . such as intelligence, cortical control [over impulses], and certain affective states." But these, Hiatt pointed out, are actually "general properties of the species" even if, in the Sinhalese environment, they have led to rather special consequences (1980: 583).

In the Tibetan case, the evidence against a genetic explanation is still stronger. Not only do the children of polyandry readily adopt other marriage forms on the list, but polyandry is frequently only a transient marital status within any given thongpa household. Indeed, as Levine notes (1977: 217 ff.), polyandry is but one of many passing phases in a "domestic cycle" that may take any multiple-son household from polyandry to polygynandry to polygyny and on to monogamy simply as a function of inter-

[13] Compare the passage by van den Berghe and Barash to this statement by Alexander on polyandrous Tibetan families: "that the 'hired hand' is generally a brother (or brothers) and that limited access to the wife of the older male (even, sometimes, the father when a wife dies early) has become part of the inducement to cooperativeness in parental behavior, *is obviously commensurate with* predictions from kin selection and parental manipulation." (1974: 371–72, emphasis added.) By the definition discussed in Chapter 1, this statement is not sociobiological, comments by Beall and Goldstein (1981) notwithstanding, although it requires close reading to appreciate the distinction. It says only that the behavior "is commensurate with" the predictions of organic evolutionary theory. Strictly speaking, the passage does not imply that kin selection provides causal explanation; instead, it leaves open the possibility that the behavior came to have the described form through some other process. By the same token, however, it must also be noted that Alexander does not discuss what such a process might be.

nal demographic events (births, deaths, and migrations). Thus there can hardly be systematic genetic differences between groups of people who, at any given moment of sampling, may be monogamous, polygynous, or polyandrous. But even more revealing in my opinion are the results of Goldstein's study of Tibetan refugees living in Mysore, India. Although there were surely few changes in thongpa gene frequencies during the six or seven years the immigrants lived in India before Goldstein's arrival, settlement records indicated that *not one* polyandrous marriage had been contracted in the new location (Goldstein 1971a: 73). Instead, thongpa marriages quickly converged on the dü-jung pattern, monogamy, and remain in that pattern today. The record from ethnic Tibet is thus fully consistent with the null hypothesis that there are, in fact, no genetic differences underlying the behavioral differences between thongpa and dü-jung or, for that matter, between Tibetans as a whole and other peoples.

On the basis of these observations and others discussed in Apps. A.2.1–A.2.3, all but two of the preceding hypotheses can be ruled out as explanations of the Tibetan marital system. These two hypotheses, 4c and 4d above, form the basis of what I will call the "domestic economy theory" of Tibetan marital diversity. Not only, as I will show below, do they produce the best fit to the empirical properties of polyandry in Chimdro, D'ing-ri, and Barkhang, but they also go far beyond polyandry toward explaining the greater variation in the Tibetan marriage system. In addition, they have what I view as the distinct advantage of close correspondence with the reasons Tibetans themselves give for their marital customs. In the sections that follow, let us consider each of them in turn.

Explaining Diversity: The Domestic Economy Theory

Hypothesis 1: The Conservation of Family Property

A domestic economy argument for polyandry can be traced back as far as the early eighteenth century, to an Italian traveler named Desideri who visited Tibet between 1715 and 1721. Accounts of Desideri's journey reveal that he morally objected to the polyandry he encountered, calling it "infamy and abomination." But he also argued that "the fundamental reason for such an abominable custom is the sterility of the land, and the scarcity of the land able to support cultivation, due to the lack of water. As all the brothers make up one single family, the crops they harvest can suffice to maintain them comfortably; but if they divided themselves into several families, each one would be extremely poor and reduced to begging."[14] (Quoted in Puini 1904: 131; also translated in De Filippi 1971 [1932]: 194.)

[14] After Desideri, the same basic idea was repeated by a dozen or more authors cited in Westermarck (1921), but by none more concisely than W. Rockhill (1891: 211 ff.; see also Nag 1960: 193–94).

However, the first author to make the argument comprehensive, and to show its power to explain the larger pattern of marriage diversity in Tibet, was Goldstein (1971a). His analysis was derived from a number of cultural beliefs held by the thongpa and described to him by refugee informants. These beliefs were of two main kinds: "principles," that is, beliefs about what is appropriate and acceptable conduct; and "rules" or "legal norms," that is, in this context, principles supported by actual or potential legal sanction. In both cases, these beliefs were consciously articulated statements about proper procedure for the thongpa in matters of family continuity and inheritance. They were therefore a small but crucial part of the larger web of values, beliefs, and meanings that guided traditional Tibetan social life. Consider, first, two very basic beliefs—one a rule, the other a principle—central to thongpa marriage and inheritance.

Partible patrilineal inheritance. Goldstein's argument began with "the basic inheritance rule" of the thongpa. The rule provided that "all males in a family were coparceners with demand rights to a share of the family corporation's land [and domesticated animals]." (p. 68; see also 1978a.) Inheritance was thus patrilineal (through the father's line) and partible: any male in a family had a litigable right to split off from the corporate unit and demand his own portion of the estate. Daughters were excluded from property inheritance by this rule except in the case of thongpa families with no sons of their own. In that event, the daughters were said to have "residual rights" to the land of their natal family corporation. A magpa marriage would be arranged and the new son-in-law would take charge of family agricultural production. If sons were then born to the magpa generation, land and animal rights would eventually revert to them under the patrilineal rule.[15]

The monomarital principle. Given this basic inheritance rule, Goldstein argued, the thongpa considered it "unstable" for there to be two or more conjugal families per generation, owing to the potential for conflict between the families and to their right to withdraw, with inheritance, from the corporate household.[16] To prevent this instability, thongpa par-

[15] Theoretically this inheritance rule would entitle each male of a thongpa household to demand an equal share of land and animals. But in actual practice the rule favored (sometimes grossly) elder sons and stay-at-homes because of a "covert assumption" that property division need not be equitable (see Goldstein 1978b: 328–29). In most places the result was only a "generalized preference" for particular heirs; in Ladak, however, it was apparently formalized into something more like primogeniture (Mann 1978; Goldstein, pers. comm.). But either way, the consequences meant disproportional hardship for the departing heirs.

[16] In Goldstein's account, the partible patrilineal inheritance rule is accepted without question by the thongpa even as they follow the monomarital principle to circumvent its consequences. One wonders why the thongpa did not simply abolish the partibility aspect of the rule even if, as Arthur Wolf (pers. comm.) suggests, that aspect is part of an older East Asian tradition that the original immigrants to the Tibetan plateau brought with them. One possibility is that a rule for primogeniture or other single-heir transmission may simply have been unacceptable to the aristocratic overlords who owned most of the arable land of Tibet. Because the thongpa were hereditarily bound from birth to a particular estate and to a share of their family's tax obligation (see Goldstein 1971d), these lords had long had a direct, vested interest in thongpa inheritance practices. A second possibility was suggested to me by Eric A. Smith (pers. comm.): partibility may have been retained in the face of the mono-

ents therefore followed a "monomarital principle" in arranging the marriages of their children. This principle held that "in each generation of a thongpa family one and only one [primary] marriage can be contracted, the children of which are considered full family members with full jural rights," including land inheritance (Goldstein 1971a: 68). Thus all legal heirs were either included in the one primary marriage (thereby creating polyandry or polygyny, as the case might be), or else they were effectively disinherited and sent off to Lamaistic institutions or to secondary marriages outside and away from the corporate household, as in the uxorilocal case.[17]

By Goldstein's account, the application of this monomarital principle was motivated by a strong, conscious desire to prevent partition of the family's estate and its predictable economic consequences, including the difficulty of meeting family tax obligations (1971a, 1971c). The preservation of the family corporation's land appears, therefore, to be "the foremost value" behind the establishment of a single, monomarital family each generation (1971a: 69). From this I infer that other pertinent values and motivations among the thongpa can be expected to exert much less influence on the family structures created by marriage. Diversity should follow largely from the observance of the one-marriage principle in varying demographic situations.

The resulting hypothesis is both simple and elegant: Marriage patterns among the thongpa are expected to vary with the composition of the sibling group so that in each generation (1) one and only one primary marriage is formed and (2) family property remains intact. This can be called "the hypothesis of family property conservation." It predicts that both the forms of marriage and the frequencies of those forms will vary in space and time as functions of the demographic attributes of thongpa families, particularly the number of surviving sons. More specifically, it can be used to predict that thongpa parents with one son will arrange virilocal monogamy for his marriage; parents with two sons will arrange virilocal bifraternal polyandry; parents with three sons virilocal tri-fraternal polyandry—and so on. Similarly, thongpa parents with no sons are predicted to arrange marriages consistent with the number of their daughters and their daughters' desires for plural spouses. In these cases, however, the hypothesis predicts uxorilocality as a way of keeping land tied to the original thongpa house and family name.

---

marital principle because of its perceived advantages under special conditions, such as the founding of a new community or the inheritance of an extinct estate. In these circumstances, the subdivision of family property once, twice, or a few times may actually be beneficial in terms of family demography and economics (leading, as we shall see, to an increased number of surviving descendants), but only if held in check by the monomarital principle thereafter. The coexistence of the two, despite their apparent contradiction, may thus have permitted greater situational flexibility than would either alone.

[17] The monomarital principle has sometimes been described as a "prescriptive ideal" (as in Levine 1980: 285) and sometimes as a "rule" (Briffault 1927: 651–52, citing two earlier reports). But in all cases the net effect seems to be the same: one primary marriage per generation.

TABLE 2.6

Explanation of Marital Diversity in Chimdro by the Domestic Economy Theory

Composition of sibling group	Predicted form of marriage	Hypothesis 1: The conservation of family property			Exceptions		Accounted for by "family harmony"?
		Number expected[a]	Number observed[b]	Percent accounted for	Number	Nature	
Families with no sons							
1 daughter	Uxorilocal monogamy	5	5	100.0%	0	—	—
2 daughters	Uxorilocal polygyny	1	0	0.0	1	Monogamy plus 1 nun	?
Families with one or more sons							
1 son	Virilocal monogamy	24	24	100.0	0	—	—
2 sons	Virilocal bi-fraternal polyandry	20	20	100.0	0	—	—
3 sons	Virilocal tri-fraternal polyandry	8	6	75.0	2	Bi-fraternal polyandry plus 1 *magpa*	Yes
4 sons	Virilocal quatri-fraternal polyandry	4	1	25.0	1	Tri-fraternal polyandry[c]	Yes
					2	Bi-fraternal polyandry[c]	Yes
TOTAL		62	56	90.3%	6		

SOURCE: Table 2.2.
[a] Refers to the number of thongpa families in Chimdro with the predicted form of marriage.
[b] Refers to the number of thongpa families in Chimdro with a given sibling group composition.
[c] Information is lacking on the fate of the son or sons not included in the primary marriage.

Testing Hypothesis 1 in Chimdro. Let us compare these predictions with the observed marriage patterns of the thongpa of Chimdro as shown in Table 2.6. The 24 families with 1 male heir gave rise to 24 marriages of virilocal monogamy; the 20 families with 2 male heirs gave rise to 20 marriages of virilocal bi-fraternal polyandry; the 8 families with 3 male heirs gave rise to 6 marriages of virilocal tri-fraternal polyandry; and the 4 families with 4 heirs gave rise to 1 case of virilocal quatri-fraternal polyandry. Likewise, of 6 families with no male heirs all 6 arranged uxorilocal marriages as predicted, 5 were monogamous as predicted, and the sixth also arranged for monogamy, having earlier committed a daughter to a nunnery.

In sum, the hypothesis of family property conservation accounts, by itself, for the nature of thongpa marriages in 56 of 62 actual cases, an impressive 90.3 percent of the total. In other words, these two basic beliefs of the thongpa, partible patrilineal inheritance and the monomarital principle, successfully account for nine-tenths of the total variation in the marriages of thongpa serfs in Chimdro. Moreover, this result is also consistent with the complete lack of diversity among dü-jung marriages. Lacking heritable rights to their plots, one would not expect the dü-jung to adhere to a monomarital principle and indeed they did not.[18] Still more revealing are the marriages of *chi-mi* serfs (literally, "common man," a term referring to their status as serfs of a thongpa village as a collective entity), those malcontents from thongpa families who opted not for litigation and partition of their family estate but for the relatively simple option of relinquishing thongpa status and setting out on their own. Lacking heritable land, the chi-mi almost always married monogamously, by choice rather than arrangement, and neolocally, in the manner of the dü-jung (Goldstein 1971b: 532).

Hypothesis 2: The Optimization of Family Labor

To the argument about family property Goldstein added a second: "Maintenance of an optimum adult labor force is a secondary, although significant, motivating factor with respect to polyandry [and other forms of plural marriage in Tibet]." (1976: 231.) The suggestion, which I reformulate and test later, is that the thongpa attempted to manipulate the human resources of their families through marriage so as to produce "eco-

[18] The same phenomenon was reported by Nag (1960: 191–92) in a smaller but structurally parallel sample in the village of Kardeng, Lahul. Nag found no exceptions to monogamous marriage in a sample of 6 "landless menials" known as Lohars, in contrast to only 18 monogamous marriages in a sample of 35 landholding Kanets. Much as in Chimdro, about half the Kanet marriages were polyandrous (presumably fraternal). Indeed, most instances of Kanet monogamy were "circumstantial," there being only one son in the family at the time of Nag's survey. Similarly, Chandra (1973) reported a high frequency of plural marriages (including two cases of polygyny and two of polygynandry) among the Kanets of Sungra, a village in Kinnaur District (although the marriage classification schemes in that study are problematic in other regards).

nomic units well adapted to complex economic patterns." (Goldstein 1971a: 73.) Like the preceding hypothesis, this argument, too, was derived from a number of explicit thongpa beliefs.

Diversified family economy. According to the first of these beliefs, diversified economic activity is essential to thongpa household prosperity. Ideally, say the thongpa, a given family should include enough adult members for there to be concurrent income from intensive agriculture, the thongpa's economic mainstay; from the herding of yak, *dzo* (hybrids of yak and common cattle), sheep, goats, and other animals; and from salt trading or other forms of regional commerce. When Aziz asked informants about the motivations behind fraternal polyandry, she found that "whatever else this form of marriage may mean, it is seen by Tibetans themselves as primarily an economic arrangement. All persons believe that polyandry functions to increase the labor force available to the household—the taxable and productive unit. When a number of sons remain together the family is able to diversify its economic interests, and it is that diversification, more than intensive cultivation, that brings wealth to a household." (1978: 106.) Her informants also gave this reason for resenting the loss of sons to local D'ing-ri monasteries. So important was the household's economic production that parents commonly searched for someone to substitute for a son when the monk tax was levied against them (see note 5).

Two features of this belief are especially worth noting here. First, the claim was evidently accurate. Data collected by Goldstein (1971a: 73), Aziz (1978: 108), and Levine (1988: ch. 9) all indicated a strong positive correlation between the number of adult family members, the diversity of income sources, and the economic success of thongpa families. Second, the belief made particularly good sense given the natural and social environment of the thongpa. Situated in the Himalayan rain shadow at an average elevation of over 4,000 meters, the thongpa have long lived in a habitat that combines all the ecological challenges of aridity—particularly the problem of low and unpredictable primary productivity (a measure of the rate of photosynthesis by plants)—with the special stresses of high altitude (see, for example, Baker 1978). In such circumstances, a diverse resource procurement strategy helps not only to increase the harvest of free energy but also to reduce the risks of specialization, if only at the cost of high labor inputs. Although applicable to all Tibetans to some extent, these advantages were especially pronounced for the thongpa, whose tillable land was notoriously scarce and inelastic. Even the early Western visitors to the region had noted that (as summarized by Linton 1936: 183 from the reports of Desideri [in Puini 1904], Rockhill 1891, and others) "in Tibet all arable land has long since passed into family holdings." In addition, recent historical studies confirm that land scarcity, while "pervasive and intense," led only to the "circulation of estates" and not to the opening of new fields (Goldstein 1973; see also Carrasco 1959).

On the one hand, this inelasticity is inherent in the natural ecological conditions of the Tibetan plateau, including impoverished, boulder-strewn soils and acute shortages of irrigation water, which serve to make agricultural areas into "encapsulated environments." (Goldstein 1981b.) On the other hand, resource constraints were also imposed by the social and political organization of traditional Tibetan society, and particularly by the system of land tenure and taxation. That system ensured, first, that many thongpa had to pay dearly through taxation for their access to primary productivity; and second, that there was little turnover in land rights, especially in multiple-male households (Carrasco 1959: 30; Levine 1977: 238). On the death of any given household head, there was generally no shortage of younger males ready to carry on with the agricultural activities of the estate. Herding and salt trading were viewed as about the only practical avenues to increase a family's livelihood, since they alone entailed no additional need for land or imposition of taxes. The result of these natural and social conditions, then, was a strong positive incentive for a diversified family economy.[19]

The sexual division of labor. Levine reports that, as a consequence of these incentives, an especially acute demand for labor existed within thongpa households. Tibetan rules for the division of labor by sex translated this demand for labor into an explicit preference for multiple adult males in each household. These principles specified, for example, that salt trading and herding were exclusively "men's work," as were the agricultural activities of ploughing, planting, and terrace construction (Levine 1988: ch. 9; for other examples, see Raha 1978; R. Chandra 1981). Having a diversified family economy, therefore, meant having a deliberately high household sex ratio—a goal that was, one might say, openly espoused. The benefits of such an economy provided some of the strongest continuing support for polyandry. Indeed, they are the reason behind the rare instances of virilocal polyandry among unrelated men (given as "other polyandry" in Table 2.5); according to Levine, this type of marital arrangement exists only where a "lone man, incapable of managing his estate, [seeks] the approval of his wife and then [adds] a friend to their marriage . . . mostly for [his] labor." (1988: 161.)

Family harmony. At the same time, limits to the plurality of adult males were also recognized. Once more than two or three co-husbands were involved, the perceived economic advantages of polyandry tended to be outweighed by domestic strife, sexual jealousy, and frequent quarrel-

---

[19] Although traditional Tibetan social structure certainly contributed to the constraints on thongpa resources, the experience of Tibetan-speakers living outside the reach of that structure (such as the Nyinba and Sherpa of Nepal) emphasizes that scarcity and inelasticity are inherent in the natural ecological conditions of the habitat. Thus, although Goldstein (1981b: 6) and others are correct in suggesting that the traditional marriage system was "as much an adaptation to serfdom as it was to the climatic and geomorphological limitations of the high-altitude environment," limitations of the latter kind have been sufficient by themselves to sustain the tradition.

ing. According to Goldstein, "Tibetans believed that marriages involving tri-fraternal polyandry . . . and especially quatri-fraternal polyandry were much more difficult than bi-fraternal polyandrous marriages to maintain harmoniously, and various mechanisms were employed to decrease [in effect] the number of siblings, such as making one son a celibate monk or sending one as an adoptive bridegroom to a family with no male children." (1971a: 68–69.) The basic notion—the fifth and last belief to be extracted from Goldstein's account—was that marriages should therefore be formed of a size and composition that could function harmoniously in day-to-day life, benefiting from a diversified multi-male economy on the one hand, but also avoiding the risk of estate subdivision on the other. If more than the optimal number of sons existed in a given family, parents simply acted in the interest of family harmony and dispatched "surplus" males to other options.

As in the case of the inheritance rule and monomarital principle, a noteworthy feature of these last three principles—diversified income, division of labor, and family harmony—was their conscious articulation by the thongpa. Nyinba women told Levine, for example, that they preferred polyandry, and ideally two husbands, because of the benefits of economic diversity.[20] In their view, "three husbands are also acceptable, four less so, because of the threat of partition. . . . The same logic concerning household welfare is expressed regarding numbers of sons: two or three are desirable, because they can attract a good wife and maintain an estimable living standard." (Levine 1981–82: 8–9.) On the basis of these explicit beliefs, therefore, the labor optimization hypothesis predicts that thongpa parents should have arranged the plural marriages of their offspring in an attempt to achieve the simultaneous goals of economic diversity and domestic tranquility.

Testing Hypothesis 2 in Chimdro. In Goldstein's argument, the thongpa's concern with optimizing the use of family labor is described as "secondary" to their goal of conserving family property.[21] Hypothetically, this means that this concern should modify the monomarital principle, increasing the range of marriage options utilized by thongpa families while at the same time preserving the goal of a single primary marriage per generation. If the hypothesis is true, then the desire for family harmony should account for most or all of the "exceptional" marriages we encountered above. And indeed it can be used to explain at least five of them.

Consider, first, the exceptions shown in Table 2.6 for sibling groups of 3 sons. Given that tri-fraternal polyandry was believed to be "much more

[20] Nyinba men, on the other hand, tended to view *tri*-fraternal polyandry as the ideal because it allowed simultaneous specialization in agriculture, herding, and trade (Levine, pers. comm.). This ideal is also reflected in Nyinba clan legends, which commonly feature village founders, as well as their descendants in later generations, as three brothers (see Levine 1976).

[21] This motivation was also described as "secondary" during Prince Peter's visit to Ladak in 1938 (1963: 378).

difficult" than bi-fraternal polyandry to maintain harmoniously, one can understand why thongpa parents sometimes opted for the bi-fraternal form, marrying one son outside the household in the uxorilocal magpa tradition. In the Chimdro data, this arrangement was found established in 2 of 8 possible cases (although we lack sufficient detail to explain why these 2 and not the others). Similarly, in thongpa families with 4 sons, we should expect an even greater proportion of exceptions given that family harmony was described as "especially difficult" in the quatri-fraternal context. Although the subsample is very small, this, too, is confirmed in the Chimdro data: 3 of the 4 marriages in 4-son families were less-than-quatri-fraternal polyandry (but again we lack details concerning the fate of the brothers outside the primary marriage). In all, then, 61 of 62 total cases can be accounted for by the combination of arguments presented above. The one exception in Chimdro is the monogamous uxorilocal marriage formed from a sibling group of 2 sisters. Family harmony may have been a concern in such potentially polygynous contexts, too, but such a motive is not mentioned by Goldstein.

Table 2.6 therefore confirms the domestic economy theory as a good explanation for the diversity of thongpa marriages in Chimdro. The evidence convincingly supports Goldstein's claim that "the varying forms of marriage as well as the other alternatives, such as the monastic and nun orders, were all derived from the basic desire (or the perceived need) to maintain the family corporation intact across generations through the implementation of a monomarital principle." (Goldstein 1971a: 70.) In addition, the evidence suggests that a concern for optimizing the use of family labor modified this basic desire, adding still more diversity to the marriage customs.

The explanatory power of Goldstein's argument is noteworthy as we have seen. But equally noteworthy, it seems to me, is the fact that the argument rests on explicit and consciously recognized beliefs. This last feature renders Goldstein's argument testable by what is sometimes called a "natural experiment," that is, by study of the behavioral changes (if any) that result when people voluntarily live under conditions that vary from the usual in a way that resembles—but is not—experimental manipulation. If, for example, a group of thongpa came to live under conditions that pre-empted the normal inheritance process, so that it became impossible to transmit estate property via the monomarital route, one would expect thongpa marriage patterns to change rather drastically. Specifically, one would expect a rapid decline in the frequency of plural marriages and especially polyandry, given informants' statements that the latter is regarded as, at best, the lesser of evils.

As noted earlier, such a natural experiment occurred at the Mysore refugee settlement, providing striking confirmation of this prediction. Under the terms of the settlement agreement, one-acre plots were allocated to individual refugees as permanent but not heritable possessions, a pattern that "fits precisely the tied dü-jung land-tenure pattern in Tibet." This brought a sudden end to the thongpa tradition: among all migrants, regardless of their former status in Tibet, "the marriage and family pattern was clearly of the [monogamous] dü-jung type."[22] (Goldstein 1971a: 73.)

An important inference can be drawn from this finding: the behavioral diversity manifest in the traditional thongpa marriage system was a direct consequence of cultural beliefs in the minds of the actors. In this instance, five beliefs—one rule and four principles—acted as conventional guides to behavior, creating through their observance a complex but comprehensible pattern of marital diversity. When one or more of the beliefs were changed or blocked, as in the refugee settlement project, behavior patterns also changed.[23] I conclude, then, that if one is to understand this pattern of behavior, one cannot ignore the beliefs that create and shape it. The beliefs themselves are necessary to the explanation.

Hypothesis 3: The Reproduction of the Household

Although the domestic economy theory seems convincing to this point, it does have one major shortcoming. The data we have from D'ing-ri, the Nyinba, and other communities contain four forms of matrimony that are not easily explained in terms of the principles we have examined: virilocal sororal polygyny (no. 2 in Table 2.5), virilocal and uxorilocal "other" polygyny (no. 4), fraternal polygynandry (no. 8), and conjoint marriage (no. 9). As noted earlier, each of these is an accepted and recurrent form of marriage within the population where it occurs, and at least three of the four are Tibetan institutions of considerable geographic distribution. Polygynandry, to take one example, has been reported in at least five locations: in Ladak and Lahul (Prince Peter 1963); in the Nyinba villages of the Humla District of Nepal (Levine 1977, 1988); in Tsang, another village of Tibetan-speakers in Humla, Nepal (Goldstein 1976); and in the Sherpa villages of Khumbu, Nepal (Fürer-Haimendorf 1964). Only the conjoint marriage of the Nyinba seems a bit unusual in that it has been described and documented in that one locale. But even if we set that

---

[22] A reverse "natural experiment," described by Nancy Levine (1977, 1988), seems also to be producing the results one would expect. Former slaves of the Nyinba, the landless descendants of an earlier, ethnically distinct population in Humla, traditionally married in a monogamous, uxorilocal manner before emancipation in 1926. In recent years, they have begun to convert, house by house, to the thongpa marriage system—and particularly to fraternal polyandry with virilocal residence—just as soon as they are able obtain the important heritable resources: land and grazing animals. The results of yet another "experiment"— one involving D'ing-ri immigrants in Nepal—are more ambiguous (see Aziz 1978: 159, note 8), but so are the immigrants' new living conditions.

[23] An example of a blocked monomarital principle has been reported by Sherry Ortner among the Tibetan-speaking Sherpas of Nepal, where "the Nepalese government has outlawed polyandry (although there are still a few cases), and the problem [of shrinking land resources through partition] is now handled in a variety of ways. A father may enlarge his holding by buying land from someone who, for whatever reason, wants to sell. Alternatively—this is the most common practice today—a son may sell his small share to one of his brothers and go off to seek his fortune elsewhere." (1978: 16.)

form aside for now (to come back to it later), there are still three common Tibetan marriage forms remaining to be accounted for. Each of these unexplained forms was also described to Levine by her informants in the Nyinba community. She contends that these marriages were regular, understandable by-products of at least one additional belief about marriage and the family, a belief about household reproduction. As she describes it, this belief both reinforced the validity of the domestic economy theory and extended its explanatory power.

The reproductive interest of the household. Levine's hypothesis, like Goldstein's, is derived from the articulated concerns of thongpa household members. Informants expressed the belief not only that each household was entitled to one or more legitimate heirs, but also that the set of corporate heirs might restructure a given primary marriage in order to achieve that end. According to her information, this general principle acted as a guide to the formation of plural virilocal matrimonies in the following manner. In the course of each generation, there were always a few marriages in which the "primary" or original wife proved to be infertile. For the thongpa this was a serious problem: infertile wives posed "a real threat of heirlessness and subsequent extinction." (Levine 1977: 202.) At the same time, however, "sterility of the wife [was] not sufficient grounds for divorce or even for mistreatment of the unfortunate woman. *The only acceptable solution* [was] to incorporate a second wife into the existing marital union." (p. 203, emphasis added.) The result was therefore polygyny or polygynandry: a "junior wife" was invited into a pre-existing monogamous union of either the virilocal or uxorilocal kind, or into a preexisting, virilocal polyandrous union.[24] As informants explained, thongpa households simply must have an heir, someone to carry forward with the household, the family property, and the family name (see also Prince Peter 1963: 420).

Testing Hypothesis 3 in Barkhang and D'ing-ri. Although it is not possible to test Hypothesis 3 with the same detailed tabulation as before, it does derive considerable support from the ethnographic data provided by Levine (1977) and Aziz (1978). Consider, for example, two key circumstances in which the reproductive interests of the household were invoked by the Nyinba.

1. A primary wife proved infertile, jeopardizing the continuity of the household. In this situation, tradition specified that the infertile wife was not entitled to oppose the addition of a second spouse. However, her coop-

[24] In D'ing-ri, as in Barkhang, an explicit concern for family harmony also influenced the nature of the resulting union. Sororal polygyny therefore arose when a primary wife was "barren or unagreeable to stay in her husband's house. Her family, reluctant to withdraw her or allow a stranger to eclipse her, therefore provide[d] another daughter, usually the younger sister of the [primary wife]. . . . It [was] also believed that when a junior wife [was] the kinswoman of the other, there [would] be no jealousy or tension between the women." (Aziz 1978: 151.) In these cases, noted Aziz, a primary wife generally accepted her sister's children as her own and developed a "matronly attitude" toward her sister.

eration was desired because dissension among co-wives was seen as a major problem inherent in polygyny and polygynandry. Guided also by their interest in family harmony, then, and by the folk wisdom that "sisters are said to be, and do seem to be, more compatible," brothers would often try to recruit a sister of the first wife (Levine 1977: 203). The result was that out of 24 multi-female marriages known to Levine in the greater Nyinba region, many of them polygynandrous, a full third were sororal.

2. A primary wife was not infertile but had given birth to female children only. Since Nyinba men preferred male heirs, this too could prompt them to bring in one or more junior wives, but in this instance the primary wife was entitled to oppose the addition (p. 208). In an attempt to keep an inheritance and the right to magpa marriage for her daughters, she might even try to initiate a partition.

The very same principles appeared to guide the formation of multi-wife marriages among the thongpa of D'ing-ri, although cases of polygynandry were not reported in that community. Normally in D'ing-ri the strict rule was that there must be one and only one primary wife per household; the aim was to produce a single, relatively noncontentious set of heirs (Aziz 1978: 105, 144). However, the concern for heirs was paramount: "Where a couple is childless, *a second wife should be brought in* and if a family has still no heir, it often feels obliged to adopt a child." (p. 103, emphasis added.) So important is this concern that infertility is considered "the only condition" under which unrelated women will share one husband, and "a barren *na-ma* ['primary wife'] may even accept her husband's illegitimate child (born to a mistress or servant girl)." (p. 151.)

Curiously, the infertility of husbands was considered much less of a problem. Among the Nyinba, this seemed to be both because polyandry was frequent (presumably two or more males are less likely to be infertile than one female), and because "otherwise childless men tend to be willing to accept children whose legitimacy they suspect." (Levine 1977: 202.) Prince Peter, however, did report cases of concern over male infertility among other Tibetans, and he described an institutionalized mechanism for resolving the problem. An informant from Lahul told him that "when a family had no issue, a man from the outside was called in in an attempt to sire a child for them. Such a man was called a *p'horjag* (*P'hor-Jag*) as in other parts of the Himalayas and in Tibet where the custom was also followed. It was not particularly well looked upon in Lahul, and was only rarely resorted to. Monogamous families seemed to favor it more than polyandrous ones, he added." (1963: 326.) Unfortunately, Prince Peter's discussion does not make clear whether a *p'horjag* ("extra man") union was bona fide marriage (adding a sixteenth form of matrimony to the list for Tibet) or simply a form of polykoity. However it does make clear that any child so born was named as if it had been fathered by the barren son or sons of the estate family.

Levine (1977: 218) is quite correct, then, in adding a household reproductive interest to Goldstein's list of principles governing thongpa marriage decisions.[25] It helps to account for virilocal sororal polygyny, nonsororal polygyny of both virilocal and uxorilocal residence, polygynandry, and the unusual custom of the p'horjag. It must be admitted, however, that the principle can also be seen at work in the formation of magpa marriages, in which case it is also certainly implied by Goldstein's analysis. Once again, it is Prince Peter (1963: 316) who makes the point most explicitly:

The heiress' children take her name [not the *magpa's*] and the bridegroom is really nothing more than the man she has chosen to enable her to have the children she needs to hand down the property she has inherited undivided. . . . Even if there are children of the union, the *mag-pa* or *mag-pas* can be dismissed, it being considered that he or they have fulfilled their mission [i.e., to provide heirs] and are no longer of any use. Offspring remain with the house, namely in this case, with the mother.

A Cultural Explanation of Diversity

With the addition of the hypothesis of household reproduction, the domestic economy theory arrives at a fairly comprehensive set of answers to our three main analytic questions about the Tibetan marital system. First, with respect to the thongpa stratum, the theory proposes that marital diversity resulted from adherence to a set of beliefs that acted as guides or instructions to the formation of new unions. So influential were these beliefs among the thongpa that they are able to explain, as we have seen, a full twelve of the thirteen marriage forms shown in Table 2.5 (we will return in a later section to examine the remaining "conjoint marriage"). Second, the theory accounts for the contrasting marriage patterns of thongpa and dü-jung serfs. Unlike the thongpa, the dü-jung had no heritable land rights and this left them with little desire to conserve land resources through the careful arrangement of plural marriages. Third, we can also now understand why Tibet, after all, was the home of this benchmark example of behavioral diversity. The "social ecology" of the thongpa is characterized by a highly unusual constellation of features: scarce and inelastic arable lands, low and highly seasonal primary productivity, and a system of land tenure and taxation that effectively made arable land still scarcer and less productive for the thongpa. These special challenges were

[25] Paradoxically, thongpa concerns over household reproduction (plus property conservation and labor optimization) also played a central role in the maintenance of traditional monastic celibacy in Tibet. In their efforts to produce a set of (relatively noncontentious) heirs for the household, and to fulfill the local monk tax (see note 5), thongpa parents commonly dispatched their second sons, while still quite young, to a lamasery. Although these sons were sometimes later able to rejoin their brother(s) in a polyandrous marriage, the decisions imposed by thongpa parents remained a major—if not *the* major—source of recruitment for traditional Tibetan celibacy (see also note 27; Goldstein 1971a; Grimshaw 1983).

surmounted, at least in part, by an equally unusual system of marriage which acted both to conserve inelastic agricultural potential and to concentrate adult labor—and thus productivity—in the household. Alternative strategies of marriage and inheritance, as for example with multiple primary marriages per generation or with a single heir and therefore less labor, would have led only to poverty under these circumstances.[26]

The domestic economy theory has a number of other features that warrant emphasis. First, the argument implies that behavioral diversity of an almost bewildering magnitude may nevertheless result from a relatively small set of beliefs in the minds of the actors. Moreover, there appear to be few, if any, forms of thongpa marriage that are routinely exempt from these beliefs. As a result, once the beliefs are made clear, it becomes quite easy to understand how thongpa families acquire their particular forms and frequencies. Second, it should be emphasized that these beliefs are part of the "common knowledge" of the populations and subpopulations where they exist. They constitute, in essence, a shared pool of instructions that guide the process of marital decision making. Among other features, they are part of the everyday understandings that organize and shape Tibetan social life. They are consciously identified and articulated by the natives themselves, and they have explanatory force for them as well as for outside analysts. They are, in short, elements of thongpa culture and quite influential ones at that. Indeed, the strength of their influence over the behavior of Tibetans is strikingly confirmed by the success of the preceding analysis. When the beliefs we have discussed are in place and functioning (as we may infer was once the case throughout much of ethnic Tibet), similar patterns of marriage and family structure are observed in communities that are quite distinct in other ways. When the same beliefs are pre-empted or blocked, as in the case of the refugees in India, marital diversity collapses into a common monogamous pattern.

Third, as elements of thongpa culture, the component beliefs of the domestic economy theory exemplify each of the five basic properties of culture introduced in Chapter 1. Consider, to begin with, the matter of conceptual reality. The phenomena properly regarded as part of culture in this case study are not the behaviors themselves, that is, the various marital arrangements of the thongpa and dü-jung families. Rather, the phenomena of culture are the conceptual entities—the beliefs, whether rules or principles—behind such behavior. By extension, "Tibetan culture" re-

---

[26] The thongpa are thus an exceptionally good case in point of Goody's argument about "production and reproduction" in Eurasian societies. As befits a population with scarce and intensively used productive resources, the thongpa illustrate "the tendency towards the retention of these resources within the basic productive and reproductive unit." (Goody 1976: 20.) They do so through the positive control of marriage arrangements, as we have seen, and through a "strategy of heirship" that both "adds wives," specifically to produce heirs, and (through celibacy and secondary marriages) "subtracts children," specifically to control their numbers.

fers to the full set of such "knowledge and values, signs and/or symbols" in the minds of Tibetans (Boehm 1978: 278); it is the total pool of shared conceptual phenomena that creates the special features of the Tibetan way of life. In short, Tibetan culture is manifest in the marital arrangements of the serfs. Although it can be known from and studied in that behavior, Tibetan culture has a reality distinct from the forms and frequencies of thongpa and dü-jung matrimonies. The point, I think, is crucial.

Consider next the properties of social transmission and symbolic encoding. As we have seen, evidence from the Mysore refugee settlement indicates quite clearly that the information organizing the forms and frequencies of thongpa marriage was not transmitted genetically. But neither was this information individually rediscovered by Tibetans on the basis of their own experience each generation. Instead, there is ample evidence that their behavior was guided by beliefs conveyed both socially and symbolically—in this case, through language. Among the Nyinba, for example, adults describe at least a couple of relatively recent cases of partitioning that resulted in "devastation" for one or more of the heirs. Such cases not only indicate recurrent experimentation with the rule at the local level; they also reflect a specific social memory of the consequences. In addition, the Nyinba cite the customary partitioning of their Nepalese neighbors of Teya—and their subsequent poverty—as examples of a fate that simply must be avoided. "The situation of neighboring Nepalese communities is seen as a prime example of the evils of household divisions. Nepalese men establish separate residences when they marry and receive equal portions of the divided patrimony. The Nyinba assert that the end result of this is very small land shares per son and a low standard of living for each household. This explanation is widely propounded and stands as a salutary warning against the effects of dividing up patrimonies." (Levine 1977: 238–39; see Ross 1981: 175 for an equivalent example from another community of Tibetan-speakers.) Thus the monomarital principle is clearly passed along through a form of social learning. It is perpetuated with a reinforcement that stems not simply from social experience, but also from a whole different society's social experience.

A number of the systemic properties of culture can also be seen in the set of beliefs that underlie the marriage practices. For example, some member elements of the set (particularly the inheritance rule and the monomarital principle) are clearly more basic than others, since they have greater explanatory power in the analysis and are referred to by informants as more important. "Embeddedness," too, is manifest in this set of beliefs, none of which can stand alone in explaining marital diversity and all of which are related to still other aspects of Tibetan culture—religion, ritual, aesthetics, and so on.[27] In short, the systemic nature and organiza-

---

[27] An interpretive anthropological study of the relationship between Tibetan Buddhism and other aspects of Sherpa society makes the point about embeddedness quite nicely. The

tion of Tibetan culture shows through clearly despite my deliberate, specific focus on marriage and the family.

Finally, this analysis also implies that the beliefs behind Tibetan marriage have a long and persistent social history. Goldstein and others imply that at least some of today's beliefs have characterized Tibetan populations "since antiquity" (see, for example, Beall and Goldstein 1981: 6) and that they "must be indefinitely old" (Wilson 1886: 190). Indeed, there is direct evidence to confirm these inferences: by 600 A.D. Chinese analysts of the Sui dynasty reported that among the Fu Guo people along their borders (ancestors to contemporary Tibetans) "a man can marry his father's wives and his elder brother's wives." (Wei Zheng et al. 1973: 1858; for a related report from the Tang Dynasty see Bushnell 1880: 528.)[28] This report, together with the historical reconstruction of early Tibetan culture by Wolfram Eberhard (1937: 518; 1982: 69; see also 1942) and other evidence summarized in App. A.2.2, implies that the beliefs behind plural marriages were already part of a fully established tradition by that time.

Explaining Beliefs: The Cultural Evolution of the Monomarital Principle

To this point, our analysis of marriage in Tibet exemplifies the vertical or explanatory dimension of cultural analysis introduced in Chapter 1. In essence, the idea is that much of the patterned variation in human behavior can be explained by variation in the ideas and beliefs in people's minds, that is, from component elements of their culture. In such arguments, culture is viewed as a source of information that gives specific form to human action and renders it both meaningful to the actors and intelligible to outside observers.[29]

---

anthropologist Sherry Ortner (1978) shows that the organized rituals of the Sherpa and the institution of the Sherpa family are dynamically interdependent. In her account, Tibetan Buddhism functioned as a "lightning rod" for the ills of society (including the excessive individualism of corporate families) and was in turn reinforced by the domestic cycle of the family, which created, as we have seen, consecrated celibates in each generation.

[28] It is possible that the passage refers to levirate marriage, that is, to the right (or obligation) of a male to marry the wive(s) of a deceased brother (the subsequent line in Wei Zheng et al. 1973 is: "On the death of a son or a younger brother, the father or the elder brother also takes their wives"). On the other hand, the Chinese annalists may not have appreciated the distinction between polyandrous and levirate marriage, and they may therefore have described either or both practices in this way. This would have been particularly confusing to the Chinese had polyandry developed historically out of levirate marriage as some authors have proposed. (The passage quoted in the text and other early Chinese descriptions of Tibetan marriage were found and translated for me by Toby Shih, a Stanford graduate student from the People's Republic of China.)

[29] For a complementary interpretive analysis of Tibetan culture, see Ortner's (1978) study of religious ritual among the Sherpas of the Khumbu area of Nepal. Particularly germane is her analysis of the antisocial bias of Sherpa Buddhism: "A relatively orthodox, individualistic Buddhism . . . is sustained by the Sherpas not only for historical reasons [following their immigration to Nepal from eastern Tibet some 400 years ago], *but because*

Although the Tibetan example nicely illustrates the power and value of this kind of explanation, it also raises a number of unanswered questions concerning the cultural evolution of the beliefs themselves, that is to say, questions concerning their "descent with modification" from earlier beliefs (as discussed in Chapter 1). One could well ask, in this context, all five "key questions" pertinent to the evolution of a given system. However, let us simply focus here on two of them. Consider, first, the "origins question" introduced in Chapter 1: How did this set of beliefs—the partible patrilineal inheritance rule, the monomarital principle, and the several principles of household economy and reproduction—first become part of thongpa culture? Were they, for example, carried in by the first settlers of the Tibetan plateau, and thus the product of earlier cultural evolution elsewhere? Or were they later introductions and thus a specific innovation of the thongpa or else the product of some subsequent diffusion from outside? To date, at least two sets of authors have attempted answers to this question, both postulating an indigenous origin among the thongpa and suggesting that "the people must have been made to think of reshaping the [marriage] system in the context of resource limitation." (Mann 1978: 23; see also Crook and Crook 1987.) Unfortunately, the dearth of information on early Tibetan culture history (for which see Stein 1972; Snellgrove and Richardson 1968) means that the origins question cannot be answered today with any degree of certainty.

Consider, then, the "transformation question": What process or processes have had the greatest impact upon the descent with modification of the relevant thongpa beliefs? For present purposes, let us further differentiate questions about change per se from questions about the stability and persistence of favored forms. Thus, we might first ask, What were the guiding forces of change during the cultural evolution of thongpa marriage beliefs and what were their tempo and mode? Did the thongpa come to settle on the monomarital principle in, for example, a gradual fashion, that is, through small and continuous decrements from an original "multiple marriage" principle or even from no principle at all? Or did new and substantially different variants spread rapidly and in nearly final form through the population, as in the punctuational model? Such differences in the patterns of change can indicate important differences in mechanism (see Fig. 1.1). Sadly, as in the case of the origins question, current information appears insufficient to trace the historical record of change in thongpa beliefs—even to match, for this cultural example, the incomplete fossil record of Fig. 1.2.

On the other hand, information is somewhat better on the subject of persistence. Judging from the historical material described above, we can

---

it remains experientially apt for them in relation to the contemporary structures of their world"—structures that include the inelastic land base and diversified, family-centered economy (1978: 160, emphasis added). This argument parallels the cultural evolutionary analysis offered below. On the Tibetan "symbolic world" more generally, see also Paul 1982.

infer that the main ideational guides to thongpa marriage date back in recognizable form at least thirteen hundred years. We may fairly ask, therefore, Why did the thongpa perpetuate, generation after generation, this rather special set of guidelines for behavior? Why did they adhere to these particular beliefs and not to any number of the countless alternatives one can imagine, such as beliefs in impartible inheritance, multiple marriage, or even infanticide? And why were these favored guidelines so remarkably persistent and stable through space and time (at least until the political events of recent years)? In short, what kept these ideas alive for so many years in Tibetan society?[30]

In answer to these questions the literature contains what I view as two related categories of hypotheses. The first category explains persistence as a product of *choice*: the inheritance rule, the monomarital principle, and the other beliefs are viewed as consciously and deliberately maintained by the thongpa for the thongpa. In one such argument, for example, based on a study of marriage in Ladak, R. S. Mann (1978: 25) claims that "finding polyandry [to be] an adequate means of adjustment to particular situations, the Ladakhis could think of its sustaining devices" and implement them. His suggestion is that polyandry and, I hasten to add, other forms of marriage have been sustained through thongpa choices to "devise and adopt" appropriate land inheritance practices, religious celibacy, and values supportive of the men's and women's roles in plural marriages.

In contrast, the second category of hypotheses explains persistence as a product of *imposition*: the thongpa adhere to this set of beliefs because they are required to do so by the state, by the church, or by other powerful, self-interested landlords. Thus one finds an argument by J. H. Crook and S. J. Crook (1987) that the institution of hereditary estates in Tibet "forced the [thongpa] into adopting [and perpetuating] modes of production and a labor organization of family members most suited to the maximization of their productive role" for the landlords.[31] Although this suggestion, like the related "political explanation" discussed earlier, derives some support from the legal codes of Tibet and Bhutan (see the discussion in Crook and Crook 1987), it faces two serious challenges. First (as will be shown in App. A.2.2) the thongpa marital system appears to predate, by a wide margin, not only the first of the recorded historical de-

[30] I use the metaphor of "living beliefs" deliberately but guardedly. As I will argue more fully below, there is a sense in which beliefs can be kept "alive" by virtue of their sequential replication and transmission within populations. But this is a special, dependent "life" whose continuity is always at the mercy of those who believe and transmit.

[31] Anna Grimshaw (1983: 132) offers a second imposition argument, suggesting that "polyandrous marriage [and presumably the ideational basis for the full marriage system] is a response to the demands of a society founded upon celibate domination [and needing] to support a large monastic population." As a general explanation for persistence, however, this hypothesis is challenged both by the historical record, which indicates that plural marriages existed before the introduction of Buddhism to Tibet (see App. A.2.2), and by the persistence of thongpa marriage customs in communities of Tibetan-speakers that lack monastic institutions. The Sherpas, for example, had no monastery for over 300 years after their exodus from Tibet (Ortner 1978: 160).

crees to formalize it in law, but even the emergence, sometime in the sixth to seventh centuries A.D., of a centralized polity with the legal authority to issue such decrees. Second, thongpa marriage beliefs have persisted for many generations among groups like the Nyinba and Sherpa of Nepal who live outside the jurisdiction of the Tibetan state and have not been forced to carry on this tradition by powerful overlords.[32] As Goldstein (1987: 41) concludes, "the widespread practice of polyandry [for example] is not the outcome of a law requiring brothers to marry jointly. There is choice."

It therefore seemed reasonable to suggest that some process of local decision making was probably the most important single force behind the persistence of the thongpa marriage beliefs, particularly among Tibetan-speakers living outside Tibet proper. The problem remained to elucidate, if possible, that process and to test its ability to explain the persistence of thongpa ideational phenomena. In the remaining sections of this chapter, then, I shall attempt both of these goals, focusing specifically on the monomarital principle. The subject is intrinsically difficult because ideational phenomena generally leave behind even fewer "fossil imprints" than do their genetic counterparts in the course of organic evolution. Still, we must try.

The analysis that follows is based on one final attribute of the Tibetan belief system. Running throughout the marital beliefs of the thongpa is a common underlying theme of concern over reproduction, particularly over the procreation of heirs. On the one hand, this interest is manifest as an apparent concern for the reproduction of the household as a corporate unit. The emphasis is on family continuity and on the production of one or more heirs to carry on the family name and to manage the estate. The concern is collective, an interest in the long-term viability of the family and its direct descendants. In Tsang, a village of Limi Valley, Nepal, for example, Goldstein (1977: 53) found that "since land is scarce, most families having less than 1 acre of arable land, the people of Limi consider the maintenance of this land intact, i.e., without being split into smaller and smaller parcels, a critical factor in sustaining a satisfactory standard of living, though not necessarily essential for sheer survival." We will return below to the question of standard of living versus sheer survival, but for now it is important to note the explicit concern for the maintenance of family resources through time. This concern, formalized into the monomarital principle, assures the perpetuation of the named, estate households of close kin.

On the other hand, it must also be noted that an individual reproduc-

---

[32] Aware of this difficulty, Crook and Crook (1987) suggest that the marriage system may well have had an earlier, "very ancient origin" among the thongpa themselves or their ancestors, only to become codified at a later point, during the emergence of the landed aristocracy. "It seems entirely plausible that early tribal settlements on the same patchy resources may have evolved [this cultural tradition] as a way of solving their ecological problems."

tive interest sometimes shows through this collective concern, for instance in the case of the women who marry in the virilocal fashion and
find their own reproductive concerns (such as arranging a magpa husband
for one or more daughters) at odds with the desires of their husband(s) for
male progeny. It is also manifest in the "only condition"—infertility—
under which unrelated women will share a husband and an estate. To
these examples must be added the observation of Prince Peter that males,
too, have an individual interest in reproduction. Interviewing Tibetan
men about their motivations for polyandry, he was told "that someone
had to stay at home and care for the wife and children when one of the
brothers went off on commercial travels. . . . [Polyandry is regarded as]
the ideal solution to the problem, for if the wife were tempted in the absence of her husband to have sexual relations with someone else, at least
by having them with his brother, her offspring will always be of the same
family blood."[33] (1963: 453; see also 558.) On close scrutiny, therefore,
one comes away with the impression that two underlying, organizing
concerns of Tibetan marriage are (1) the overlapping reproductive interests of the family as a unit, and (2) the distinctive, sometimes conflicting,
reproductive interests of its individual members.

Looking back over our analysis to this point, one might reasonably
wonder whether the last two implications—the biological reproduction
of the thongpa and the historical persistence of their marital beliefs—are
somehow related. My suspicion, arising from earlier research on other
topics in cultural evolution, such as the headhunting ideology of certain
Amazonian peoples (Durham 1976a; see also Chapter 7 of this book) and
the milk-drinking preferences of European populations (Durham 1982;
see also Chapter 5), was not that the reproductive success of the thongpa
was itself the main determinant of the persistence of their marital beliefs,
although it may well have made some contribution. Instead, my hunch
was that both of these things were mainly products of a third parameter:
the perceived and valued *consequences* of the marital beliefs. In other
words, it seemed to me that the locally recognized benefits of the marital
system—including property conservation and labor optimization—promoted both the reproductive success of thongpa parents and what we
might call the "replicative success" of the marital beliefs themselves. My
hypotheses were thus two: first, that the marital ideology had, by virtue
of its consequences under local conditions, net reproductive benefit for
thongpa parents; and second, that the marriage beliefs themselves had
been preserved within the cultural system primarily as a result of a
thongpa preference for them because of their consequences.

The former idea was not particularly new. It has always seemed implicit

---

[33] Prince Peter also found concern over "the same family blood" to motivate fraternal
polyandry among the Kandyan Sinhalese of Sri Lanka. "When I asked whether the associated husbands [in a polyandrous union] were ever anything else than brothers, I was told
they were not. I heard that the men who share a woman must be of the same blood, so that
the issue will also be of that blood." (1963: 132.)

in the domestic economy theory.[34] But the second idea was new, or so it seemed to me. It proposed that thongpa marriage beliefs had been preserved in the course of cultural evolution mainly by a preference for their consequences—in this case economic consequences that seemed, in turn, to have reproductive advantage. I began, therefore, to look more closely at the cultural evolutionary history of thongpa beliefs, particularly one of them. The obvious choice was the monomarital principle. Why do the thongpa adhere to the belief in one primary marriage per generation, a belief I will abbreviate as $M = 1.0$, as opposed to other variants like $M = 2.0$, $M = 3.0$, or some mixture? And why has $M = 1.0$ enjoyed such endurance and tenacity through the ages in the minds of this stratum of Tibetans?

Hypothesis 4: Preservation by Preference

Drawing on the observations above, I suggest a two-part answer to these questions. The first part concerns the adherence of the thongpa to the monomarital principle even when other options are clearly available. My hypothesis here is that this principle has been favored over its alternatives by the value-guided choices of the effective decision makers. More specifically, I propose that $M = 1.0$ has been *preserved by the preference* of thongpa parents for its perceived and valued consequences. Because of this preference, the monomarital principle enjoys a substantial social transmission advantage among the thongpa; it is taught and learned with far greater frequency than are its alternatives.

In the absence of pertinent historical data, I attempted a two-stage test of this hypothesis drawing on the contemporary ethnographic record. First, I combed the literature on the thongpa in an effort to substantiate, if only for selected locations, the assumptions behind the hypothesis. I found the accounts of Levine (1977, 1988) and of James Ross (1981) to be especially convincing in their demonstration that alternatives to the monomarital principle are a persistent and recognized feature of thongpa culture. Indeed, the existence of variation appears to be guaranteed by the marriage system itself: because of the strains of plural marriages to family harmony in each generation, departures from $M = 1$ are regularly produced by partition (examples are discussed later in this chapter). Not surprisingly, people are fully aware of this option and articulate the view, at least in the villages within Nepal, that their adherence to the norm is a matter of their own free choice.

The second stage entailed a comparative "emic analysis" (that is, an

---

[34] More than that, it was made explicit by the biologist Richard Alexander. In his words, the polyandry of the thongpa "is easily related to the low *and* reliable productivity of farms, with the result that additional labor without additional children (thus, more than a single male per family) has come to be the best route to long-term maximization of reproduction because of the necessity of retaining the minimal acceptable plot of land. . . . In effect a parent may dramatically increase the parental care available to its grandchildren [and thus their survival] by adding parents in the form of nonbreeding offspring [or at least ones that bred less]." (1974: 371–72.)

analysis from the native viewpoint; see Harris 1968: ch. 20) of the reasons Tibetans give for adhering to the monomarital principle. My goal was basically to test Goldstein's original findings in Chimdro for their generalizability. Did the thongpa of other communities observe the monomarital principle for the same set of reasons? Did they always cite the same economic advantages? Although the universe of detailed community studies remains quite small, the available evidence is uniformly affirmative, as can be seen from the following summary (for additional discussion, see App. A.2.3).

Consider, first, Goldstein's later study of the Tibetan-speakers of Tsang, a village in Humla District, Nepal. Informants explained that they explicitly choose fraternal polyandry in cases of multi-male sibling sets in order to "preserve the productive resources of their family units (primarily land and secondarily animals) across generations. *Polyandry is perceived and consciously selected* as a means of precluding the division of a family's resources among its male heirs." (1976: 231, emphasis added.) Thus the value placed on land and specifically on an adequate family-sized land base consciously motivates adherence to the monomarital principle and the choice of polyandrous marriage—otherwise seen as a less-than-desirable matrimonial arrangement.

In D'ing-ri, the local explanation is much the same. Informants told Aziz that "a strong ideal is the indivisibility of the plot of land attached to the household." (1978: 105.) In a deliberate, calculated response to the overlord's tax requirements of these families, and to the general scarcity of labor reported by Aziz, the thongpa here concentrate both land and labor by means of the monomarital principle, and strive to maintain the greatest possible family resource revenue. They told Aziz that partitioning is strenuously avoided; a familiar saying with them is *ch'ug-po dr'ong chig, mon döi dr'ong nyi, zer* (prosperity in one house, poverty in two). (p. 140.) Equivalent motives were also described to Levine in her study of the Nyinba. First, it is patently clear that the monomarital principle does have perceived consequences in this community. "Economic considerations are said to be the primary reason behind the low rate of partitioning. Partition is thought to dissipate household wealth and to be injurious to the interests of the estate household as a corporation. Brothers can only weaken their own economic position and that of their offspring by dividing up an estate." (1977: 237–38.) Second, it is also clear that these consequences are given great weight by the Nyinba. They have two main reasons. First, land and other productive resources are highly emphasized in their cultural value system.[35] Second, they view marriage decisions as central to a household's general strategy for consolidating wealth and social prestige.

---

[35] Pertinent Nyinba values show through clearly in their discussions of wealth, particularly in the context of arranging marriages. According to Levine (1988: 233), "Nyinba evaluate a household's wealth primarily by the extent of its landholdings. As they put it, land

Finally, Prince Peter's travels in Ladak and Lahul also produced abundant evidence in support of Hypothesis 4. His questions about polyandry were repeatedly answered in terms of family property conservation and family labor supply, but nowhere more pointedly than by a key informant, one Lobsang Tok-Tok, of Leh, Ladak.

[Lobsang] asked me how it was that we were so wealthy in Europe without being polyandrous. It seemed to him incomprehensible that one could stay rich while dividing up the family property with each monogamous marriage, as we do in our countries. It would be impossible to do this in Ladak, he said, because there would never be enough to go round, and everybody would quickly be reduced to famine.
. . . When we married, I said, each of us goes off with his wife and tries to fend for himself and build up a family life based on his own earnings. . . .
Lobsang agreed that it would not be possible to do otherwise if one did not live in polyandry on the same piece of land, in the same household, generation after generation, without dividing it up. . . . [After some thought, Lobsang said] he could now grasp why Europeans had colonies throughout the world, why they came to India and even to Ladak. It was obviously because, with the family system that they had, they did not have enough to live on at home, and the fact that they did not practice polyandry led them to go overseas to seek a livelihood. [1963: 361–64]

As Prince Peter concluded, the conversation revealed "better than anything else" the way in which polyandry—and the other forms of plural marriage—were related to "the economic necessities of the environment." (p. 64.)

From these accounts and many others, it is clear that the thongpa perceive and value a certain "payoff" from the monomarital principle at each generation. That payoff—which I will call, for the sake of convenience, the "ecological consequences" of the belief—is described in various ways, sometimes as land area, sometimes as agricultural production, sometimes as general "wealth," and sometimes as social prestige.[36] But the local perception is that thongpa who sustain the principle are rewarded for their efforts. Family members are better off as a result.

These findings all lend direct support to Hypothesis 4: the thongpa themselves see the monomarital principle as preserved by their own preferences. The available evidence leaves little doubt that the consequences of the principle are both perceived by the thongpa and highly

---

gives a household a 'name.' In arranging a marriage, the girl's parents look first to landholdings and second to levels of engagement in the salt trade. This is because landholdings presage a household's economic future, while salt trading involvements stand mostly as an index of present income and standard of living. After these considerations comes ownership of valuables: money, gold, jewelry, brass utensils, carpets, silk, and special clothing. The number of cattle matters, but is less important, since animals die so often and the area is not well suited to livestock raising."

[36] For present purposes, the "ecological consequences" of a belief may be defined as its specific reinforcing effects for carriers—that is, its "rewards" and "punishments" (Campbell 1965: 33; Murdock 1971: 330). It is important to note that not all consequences of a belief will have reinforcing effects. Some may not be perceived; others may be perceived but not culturally valued; still others may be perceived and valued but not linked or associated with their ideational source. We will return to these topics in Chapter 4.

valued by traditional standards. The result is strong cultural deterrence to partitioning.

Hypothesis 5: Valued Consequences Enhance Reproductive Success

The second part of my answer concerns the longer-term effects of the monomarital principle. My hypothesis here is that the perceived and valued ecological consequences of $M = 1$ have themselves enhanced thongpa survival and reproduction in the special social and natural environment of the Tibetan plateau. The implication is that the value system of the thongpa has favored the social transmission of beliefs that enhance the "reproductive success" of thongpa parents, which is to say, their personal contributions of descendants to future generations.[37]

I had two particular goals in mind as I began to formulate a test for this hypothesis. First, although I had no reason to doubt the thongpa rationale for the monomarital rule, I felt it appropriate to attempt an independent check of what the anthropologist Roy Rappaport (1979: ch. 4) would call their "cognized model" of its consequences. I was interested to know whether or not the rule-based marital decisions of the thongpa were actually the best of the available options in terms of human survival and reproduction.

Second, I wanted to explore an apparent difference between what some thongpa describe as the "devastating hardship" produced by partitioning of corporate estates, and what Goldstein has described as more of a loss in the general "quality of life." "Polyandry," Goldstein has asserted, "is primarily selected not for bread-and-butter motives—fear of starvation in a difficult environment—but rather primarily for the Tibetan equivalent of oysters, champagne, and social esteem." (1978b: 329.) His description contrasts markedly with some thongpa accounts, but it occurred to me that both perceptions might be justified depending on the time scale of the argument. In the thongpa context, estate partitioning might quickly convert the "oysters, champagne, and social esteem" concerns of one generation into serious "bread-and-butter" issues for their descendants.

A paper by Cynthia Beall and Goldstein (1981) highlights both of these sets of issues. Appropriately, the paper focuses on the persistence question, asking why the thongpa marriage system—particularly its fraternal polyandry—has existed "since antiquity" (p. 6), and answering, as before, that polyandry has long been "perceived and consciously selected" (p. 10) as a means to consolidate the household's economic resources within and between generations. However, they also attempt to show that this form of marriage entails a relative reproductive sacrifice for thongpa males.

[37] Formally, the reproductive success, S_{ij} of an individual, i, is defined as the number of his or her surviving descendants in the population j generations later (for discussion, see Durham 1976a). It is thus a measure of a person's success as an ancestor. For $j = 1$, reproductive success is an approximate index of an individual's Darwinian fitness as defined in Chapter 1.

Using detailed demographic statistics for Tsang, they show that the reproductive success of males who marry (and reproduce) polyandrously is, after one generation, substantially *less* than it is for those who marry monogamously.[38] Counter to my hypothesis, they conclude that the Tibetan example "strongly suggests that sociocultural, economic, and political factors can perpetuate mating systems that entail significant reproductive sacrifice." (p. 11.) In addition, the paper reaffirms Goldstein's earlier argument that "the motivation underlying the selection of fraternal polyandry is economic in nature but is concerned with wealth and social status, not subsistence survival." (p. 10.)

My concern was simply this: although these conclusions seemed reasonable at first glance, both were argued from the perspective of a single thongpa generation. Would the arguments still hold two, three, or four generations hence? Remembering, for example, that thongpa monogamy requires partition in multi-male sibling sets, and also that departing sons tend to get shortchanged (see note 15), one wonders how a monogamous man's own sons would fare in their attempts to attract spouses and raise families—especially if they, too, chose monogamy and partition. It seemed possible, indeed likely, that both of Beall and Goldstein's conclusions would be reversed in a longer time frame. At any rate, the issues seemed to warrant further study.

A Simulation Study

The challenge was to design a test of Hypothesis 5 with a greater time depth than that used by Beall and Goldstein.[39] Finding that little social history was available on the monomarital principle, I decided to use a computer model to "simulate history," that is, to study *what would have been* the consequences for thongpa families had they experimented with the monomarital principle.[40] More specifically, my goals were two: first, I

[38] More specifically, Beall and Goldstein used fertility statistics from Tsang to calculate a first-generation comparison of the individual inclusive fitnesses of males marrying in various combinations of monogamy and fraternal polyandry. They found that the average "inclusive fitness for a male with three brothers is nearly five times greater if all brothers marry monogamously . . . than if they all marry polyandrously." (1981: 9.) As discussed in Chapter 1, inclusive fitness is a more accurate, if also more complex, measure than reproductive success for assessing a person's net contribution of genes to the next generation. For critical reviews of their analysis, see Abernethy 1981; Fernandez 1981; Fleising 1982; Weigel and Taylor 1982; and Goldstein and Beall 1982 (a reply).

[39] My original hope was to attempt a modest Tibetan analog of Robert Netting's thorough historical analysis of the cultural rules of Törbel, a community in the Swiss Alps. In that study, Netting linked the origin and persistence of a group of social rules to their specific benefits for peasant cultivators in an environment of "restricted but renewable natural resources." (1981: 58.) Unfortunately, I soon learned that detailed historical information like Netting's is not currently available for Tibetan communities, at least not in the English language (T. Wylie and N. Levine, pers. comms.). Reluctantly, I chose the alternative strategy described below.

[40] Independently, Weigel and Weigel (1987) also came to the conclusion that computer simulation could help to understand the social and ecological conditions favoring polyandry. Theirs is a stochastic model, focused on the demographic conditions (births, deaths, marriages, etc.), that would make polyandry an "adaptive alternative" to monogamy within any

wanted to predict the economic and demographic effects of modifying the principle from $M = 1.0$ (one primary marriage per generation) to such alternative principles as $M = 2.0$ (two primary marriages with equal inheritance per generation), or $M = 3.0$, or even $M = 1.3$ or 1.5 (as an average number of primary marriages per generation in a hypothetical sample of thongpa households). Here, my hypothesis—I will call it Hypothesis 5a— was that the simulation would confirm a survival and reproduction advantage to the thongpa's monomarital principle, the arguments of Beall and Goldstein notwithstanding. Second, I wanted to ask when, if ever, and under what circumstances would a given set of thongpa parents achieve higher reproductive success by ignoring the monomarital principle for one generation and allowing (indeed encouraging) the partition of the corporate estate.[41] Here, I proposed to test Hypothesis 5b: Limited, one-time-only partition *would* be reproductively advantageous for the thongpa above certain well-defined thresholds of estate size. Moreover, I expected to find a general correspondence between these theoretical thresholds and the actual circumstances under which the monomarital principle is relaxed as, for example, it sometimes is among the Nyinba (Levine 1977: ch. 6).

As a first attempt to test these hypotheses, and with the able assistance of B.C. and H.H., I designed and built a minicomputer simulation program that modeled the demographic consequences of alternative thongpa marriage strategies (for discussion of the simulation's assumptions and equations see App. A.2.4). The program was designed to represent as accurately as possible the conditions of thongpa living in the high valleys of Nepal. There, as noted earlier, clear indications exist that the monomarital principle has long been maintained through choice. I then simulated the demographic histories of several thousand hypothetical thongpa households. In so doing, I varied both the parameter values assumed by the simulation and the initial conditions of the households—land base and labor supply, for example—within reasonable ranges of values for the thongpa in those communities. The simulations were of two kinds, one for each of the two hypotheses. "Type 1" simulations modeled the fate of specific thongpa households through the generations, calculating S, the number of surviving descendants, through time as a function of land base allocations and the marriage principle.[42] "Type 2" simulations modeled

given generation. Under the assumption of equal fertility for monogamous and polyandrous marriages, for example, they find that chance effects, about one-third of the time, cause males in polyandrous unions to have inclusive fitnesses equal to or greater than those of their monogamous counterparts. Were Weigel and Weigel to add the effects of land inheritance and partitioning to the model, and then to simulate survival and reproduction through multiple generations, it seems likely that their results would converge with my own.

[41] I thank both Eric A. Smith and David S. Wilson for independently suggesting to me the second simulation.

[42] The simulations calculate the number of surviving descendants of each thongpa family as a unit, but, under the assumptions of the simulation (see App. A.2.4), that number is the same as the individual reproductive success of the fertile wife of the first generation. It is

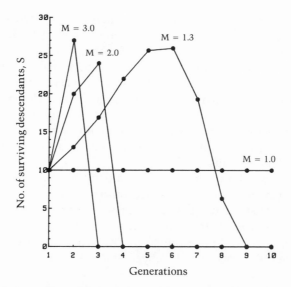

Fig. 2.2. The simulated reproductive success of thongpa families as a function of time and marriage principle. By assumption, family reproductive success equals the number of surviving descendants, *S*, of a given fertile wife in the first generation. The graph shows the results of four simulations, each predicting the average number of surviving descendants among thongpa families who adhere to one of the marriage principles *M* = 1.0, 1.3, 2.0, or 3.0, as shown. Initially, all families were assumed to have a generous (for conditions in Nepal) but inelastic land base of five acres. Fertility, mortality, and land per heir were calculated as shown in App. A.2.4. The results show that partitioning families would generate an initial surge in the average number of their surviving descendants. But they also show that the surge would be followed by rapid extinction in every case—as rapid as two generations later for the marriage principle *M* = 3.0. In this simulation, adherence to the monomarital principle optimizes the long-term reproductive success of the thongpa.

the impact of one-time-only partitions, calculating *S* as a function of the initial size of the corporate estate.

Type 1 simulations. Sample results of the Type 1 simulations, characteristic of a broad range of parameter values and initial conditions, are shown in Fig. 2.2. Two implications are immediately clear. First and foremost, all values of *M* greater than 1.0 cause a relatively rapid extinction of the named corporate household and all its heirs. On the one hand, this result is not particularly surprising: it stands to reason that repeated partitions will eventually distribute a resource base into pieces too small to sustain their inheritors. On the other hand, the time course *is* surprising. The extinctions are remarkably quick, ranging from the two short generations for marriage rule *M* = 3, to a more protracted "average extinction" at nine generations for a sample mean of *M* = 1.3. In other words, disas-

─────────────

also the sum of the individual reproductive successes of the various co-husbands in generation one. I lacked the data on which to base a simulation of how reproductive success was distributed among the males, but for this particular analysis those data were not crucial.

trous life-and-death consequences of experimenting with the monomarital principle are but a few short generations away.[43] The simulation
unequivocally supports Hypothesis 5a. Second, however, Fig. 2.2 shows
that the short-term effects of the partitions are actually to *increase* the
number of surviving descendants. For one or two generations ($M = 3$ and
$M = 2$, respectively), partition and monogamy actually do confer the
greater reproductive success, just as Beall and Goldstein (1981) suggested
they would. However, the simulation also makes clear that such a strategy quickly backfires. In all cases of M greater than 1.0, extinction is the
inevitable and precipitous result.

In short, the results of the Type 1 simulation appear to reconcile the
conflict between the view that partitioning causes "devastating hardship" for the thongpa and the view that partitioning causes a loss of "the
Tibetan equivalent of oysters, champagne, and social esteem." In a very
real sense, both are right: sustained partitioning can reduce "quality of
life" concerns to a matter of "sheer survival" in just two or three
generations.

Type 2 simulations. The simulations of "one-time-only" partitions
produced the results summarized in Fig. 2.3. There it can be seen that
strict adherence to the monomarital principle produces the highest reproductive success at all initial estate sizes below about 2.2 acres. Then,
from 2.2 acres to about 3.7 acres, the number of surviving descendants is
predicted to be highest following a one-time $M_o = 2$ partition (the subscript o designates once only).[44] Finally, at initial estate sizes over 3.7
acres, the $M_o = 3$ procedure is the one to optimize the number of surviving descendants ($M_o = 4$ and above were not simulated because such cases
have not been documented in the literature).

The real test of Hypothesis 5b, of course, would come from comparing
the predictions of Fig. 2.3 with actual cases of partitioning by the
thongpa. Unfortunately, the available data are not as detailed as one
would like. Still, they suggest that we may be on the right track. For example, one prediction implied by Fig. 2.3 is that households with fewer
than 2.2 acres of arable land should do all they can to avoid partition *unless and until* they inherit a second estate from an extinction. But once
they do receive such an inheritance, we would predict an eventual one-

[43] Ken Wachter (pers. comm.) correctly notes that the long-term stability of the monomarital strategy depends on variables and institutions not included in my simulation. For
example, in every generation, the monomarital principle guarantees substantial numbers of
nonreproducing adult females (nearly one per household under the demographic assumptions of the model). The simulation assumes that these women remain completely out of
thongpa household reproduction, becoming either religious celibates or *morang* (unmarried
women with independent households; see Goldstein 1976), or else migrating (see Levine
1977: 312) or otherwise marrying out of the community altogether (see Prince Peter 1963:
349 ff. on the "Argons" of Ladak). In future simulations, it would be useful to keep track of
the number of these females.

[44] Lacking error terms on the estimates of fertility, mortality, and agricultural production,
I was unable to calculate confidence limits for these curves or their intersections. As a
guess, I would imagine a ± 0.5 acres for each of the intersection points. The threshold values
of 2.2 and 3.7 acres should therefore be regarded as approximations only.

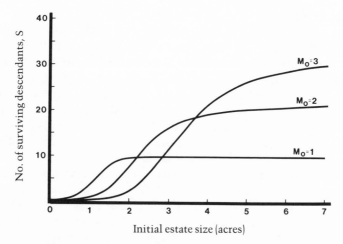

Fig. 2.3. The simulated reproductive success of thongpa families who conduct a one-time-only partition at a given initial estate size. As in Fig. 2.2, it is assumed that family reproductive success equals the number of surviving descendants, S, of a given fertile wife in the first generation. Three curves are shown, each based on the same demographic assumptions as before, and each representing the number of surviving descendants three or more generations after a *single* partition by the marriage principles $M_o = 1$, $M_o = 2$, and $M_o = 3$ (the subscript o designates once only). The plot indicates that the reproductive success of thongpa parents can be enhanced by (1) a single two-way partition at initial estate sizes of 2.2 to 3.7 acres, and (2) a single three-way partition at initial estate sizes of over 3.7 acres. If the thongpa do tend to make partitioning decisions in a reproductively advantageous manner, then actual case histories should show a general correspondence with these predictions. For example, below 2.2 acres, estate holders should vigorously oppose all forms of partition, especially $M_o = 3$. In addition, three-way partition should be extremely rare on estates below 2.8 acres because both $M_o = 1$ and $M_o = 2$ are better options, reproductively speaking.

time-only partition into two new estates if the aggregate land base were in the range of 2.2 to 3.7 acres, and directly into three new estates if it were over 3.7. In addition, the figure predicts that thongpa families with less than about 2.8 acres (the intersection of the curves $M_o = 1$ and $M_o = 3$) would virtually never try the $M_o = 3$ procedure because in this range there are *two* reproductively more advantageous options. Given the additional likelihood that the thongpa estates to become extinct most often will be smaller than average in size, we would expect to find that (1) there is a general relaxation of the monomarital principle in virtually any household that has inherited the estate of another, and that (2) by far the most common partition is of the one-time $M_o = 2$ variety. Partition in households with less than 2.2 acres should be relatively rare and, in accordance with Hypothesis 1, such cases should be viewed locally as a grave tragedy, to be avoided. Moreover, three-way partitions should be relatively unusual and reserved for truly large inheritances.

Probably the best of the empirical data are again from Levine's study of the Nyinba (see especially 1977: ch. 6). The sample is small (only 7 households out of 53, or 13.2 percent, have partitioned in the last 25 years), but the cases are nonetheless revealing. They form three distinct categories.

1. *Partition of relatively large estates*. Levine found 3 cases, all two-way partitions. Without exception, households with "abundant wealth in land" were divided into two new households, each "more than adequately provided for." Significantly, all three of the initial estates had inherited additional lands from extinct households (pp. 244, 271).

2. *Partition of middle-sized estates*. Again there were 3 cases, all of them complicated asymmetrical partitions in which one of the new households received only "a small fraction" of the original estate. In one, the partition was "maneuvered" by the remaining brothers; in the other two, partition was initiated by Buddhist lamas with supplemental income from ritual services. But even the lamas could "never hope to be well-off by Nyinba standards." (p. 245.)

3. *Partition of small estates*. In the remaining case, a small estate (almost certainly less than 2.2 acres) was divided between two households that, according to Levine, are now "so poor they cannot provide an adequate standard of living for their members." (p. 244.)

Levine concluded that (1) "partition creates two, or rarely, three, households out of one" (p. 238); (2) "each [such] household is considered poorer in the eyes of the community" (ibid.), sometimes much poorer and "barely viable"; and (3) "the possession of abundant wealth in land appears to be a primary factor in weakening the restraints on partition." (p. 270.) In the last case, the economic consequences of partition do not impoverish the new domestic units. Not surprisingly, Levine also found a general, temporal association of extinctions and partitions within Nyinba villages (Barkhang had had three extinctions and three partitions in the last four decades). In short, her examples make clear that partitions are relatively rare—and dreaded—among the smallest estate holders; that they are especially complicated and contested in the case of middle-sized estates; but that they occur with weakened restraints and little negative sanction in the case of larger estates, particularly if they have recently inherited additional lands.[45] Comparing these conclusions to the simulation results above, one would guess that the smallest estate category involved less than 2.2 acres, say 0.8 to 1.8, the medium one 1.8 to about 2.5 acres, and the largest one from 2.5 to 3.7 or so acres. But in any event, Levine's findings suggest a reasonable qualitative match to our predictions.

In summary, I would offer the following tentative conclusions. First, the simulation results suggest that the monomarital principle does in-

---

[45] The Nyinba also say that the monomarital principle was relaxed by their ancestors during the founding of Barkhang and other villages. According to Levine, "legends always portray the first settlers and their sons as marrying separately and partitioning. How the first settlers—who are supposed to have come from polyandrous Tibet—actually married is a moot point. What is significant is the notion that they would have married monogamously. People say that polyandry prevents the dispersion of household wealth and the fragmentation of land and that it avoids the proliferation of households, thus restricting village growth. They also suggest that household partition was less problematic in the past, when much land stood unclaimed and when it was necessary to expand village numbers and enhance village political strength." (Levine 1988: 32; see also 1976.)

deed have the long-term effect of optimizing human survival and reproduction in the special environment of the thongpa. Among alternative marriage principles, $M = 1.0$ is the only sustainable variant given the social and ecological circumstances of the thongpa and their other cultural beliefs. In addition, the principle includes, in effect, a waiver clause that maintains a degree of flexibility and promotes additional reproductive success whenever a household resource base can be expanded. The principle may thus be seen as a strategic rule of thumb, guiding the thongpa to make the most, reproductively speaking, of a difficult situation. It is both invoked and relaxed in a manner that enhances the reproductive success of thongpa parents.

Second, we have also found evidence from an emic analysis that the monomarital principle persists through time because of its perceived and valued consequences. The principle is clearly valued both as a way to conserve estate property through the generations, and as a way to optimize adult labor power. It is clearly *not* valued in reproductive terms per se, and this is, perhaps, quite fortunate. Unless Tibetans were to act on the basis of a sophisticated and far-reaching concern for great- or great-great grandchildren, they could easily be misled by short-term reproductive efficiency into a belief in fatal multiple-marriage principles (as implied by Fig. 2.2). Nevertheless, the principle's valued consequences seem to have had a beneficial reproductive effect over several generations. The implication is that the value system of the thongpa, while ostensibly weighting other phenomena, has had the effect of favoring beliefs that enhance reproductive success. The key link seems to reside in the thongpa equivalent of endowment. Parents strive not simply for children, on the one hand, nor simply for land, social standing, or economic income on the other. Instead, they seem to strive for well-endowed heirs, so much so that the endowment includes labor and even the organization of marriage, as well as land and wealth.[46] The concern is for a sizable, smoothly running *estate* for their heirs, or even better (when circumstances permit), two or more such estates. It is this concern, I maintain, and the beliefs that shape it, that are adaptive for the thongpa given the constraints and opportunities of their particular environment. Moreover, they are "adaptive" by both of the criteria discussed in Chapter 1: they are both reproductively advantageous and the product of a selective historical process, namely, "preservation by preference."

Explaining a Special Case: Conjoint Marriage

In an earlier section we found that Levine's principle of household reproductive interest helped to explain the occurrence of polygynandry

[46] The thongpa offer a good example of what Irons (1979) has called "a positive association of cultural and biological success." The computer simulations above support Irons's suggestion "that striving for wealth equates with striving for reproductive success." (p. 272.)

among Tibetan speakers, but we set aside conjoint marriage as something of a special case. Let us now return to that case, and to the folk explanations for it and for some cases of polygynandry, too, as it turns out.

Hypothesis 6: The Reproductive Interests of Individuals

In her analysis of Nyinba marriages, Levine (1981–82: 12) emphasizes the paramount importance of the reproductive interest of the household. At the same time, however, she points out that "the Nyinba recognize the very real problems that barrenness or sonlessness can pose for individual women, and the disappointment of not having children of their own for individual men." (p. 12.) While these individual-level concerns may well "pale in comparison with the threat posed to everyone else in the household in the present and future," they are nevertheless a real and significant force in the shaping of Nyinba marriages. Indeed, we have already seen some evidence for this in the concern of traveling males, for example, that their wives have children by a brother rather than by an unrelated male (presumably if this were only a household interest, it would not matter who the father was). However, in the Nyinba case, the individual-level concerns are even more pronounced and highly refined.

One important reason for this concern is a permutation in the basic Tibetan inheritance rule. In contrast to most Tibetan-speakers, the Nyinba follow a rule of land acquisition that is *per stirpes* (Latin for "through [the root and] offshoots"). Rather than supporting the ideal that land is equipartible among the male progeny of a household, the Nyinba subscribe to the view that land rights are instead determined by the *paternity* of the heirs. At best, sons can claim an equal share of their father's land rights.[47] Although it is unclear exactly where this additional rule came from and how far it has spread among Tibetan speakers, there is evidence to suggest it is of Indian (Hindu) origin (Levine 1988: 169, 179).

Paternity therefore plays a crucial role in the size (and quality) of Nyinba inheritances and, not surprisingly, there is heightened interest in the subject of paternity and heirship in this community. Because land inheritance is so highly valued (and so crucial to the long-term viability of

---

[47] The way per stirpes inheritance works can best be seen in a hypothetical example, a case described by Levine and based upon an actual thongpa partition in Barkhang. According to her account, four half brothers named Tragpa (the eldest), Gangri, Sonam, and Yangjur had lived together in quatri-fraternal polyandry for some years when one of the younger brothers married again and brought a junior wife into the household. At that time, "partition proceedings began almost immediately. Tragpa separated with the primary wife, while his younger brothers stayed together with the junior wife." (Levine 1977: 242.) By the per stirpes inheritance rule, the estate was then partitioned according to the paternity of the brothers. Since the four brothers had among them three fathers, Angdu, Tharba, and Tashi (from tri-fraternal polyandry in the preceding generation), the estate was said to consist of three one-third shares. Yangjur, as the only son of Angdu, was entitled to a full one-third share from his father, as was Gangri from his father Tashi. But because Tragpa and Sonam were both sons of Tharba, Tragpa was entitled to only a one-sixth share. The consequence was one of those described as "devastating": Tragpa's portion was "hardly adequate to support himself, his wife, and their small child."

descendants), males take a special interest in the procreation of heirs and in the issue of their biological paternity. Levine discovered that this is still another factor motivating the formation of polygynandry among the Nyinba.

The reproductive interests of co-husbands. Among many Tibetan populations described in the literature, it is said that brothers in a polyandrous marriage share a joint and equal "social fatherhood" of the children born to the union (see, for instance, Prince Peter 1963: 325–26; Fürer-Haimendorf 1964: 73–74; see also Levine 1987). Children are spoken of as the undifferentiated, collective property of the household, "like the fields." This is most definitely *not* the case among the Nyinba, asserts Levine, and one reason is the per stirpes inheritance procedure. In Barkhang she found that each co-husband in a polyandrous union takes a separate, special interest in procreation, with particular "hopes for the birth of children recognized as his own." (1977: 191.) Differential paternity is therefore clearly recognized within the household (as well as between households, in cases of suspected infidelity); indeed, this recognition is the basis for establishing the child's full set of rights and duties in the house and in the greater Nyinba community.[48] With consequences like this, paternity is not treated lightly by the Nyinba, but is instead carefully ascribed within the sibling set on a "first-refusal" basis: one of the brothers must accept the child as his own or else the marriage ends in divorce.[49]

This explicit reproductive interest of co-husbands provides another socially condoned route to polygynandry. Moreover, it is often invoked even if a first wife has proven repeatedly fertile. "A brother who is part of an already fertile [polyandrous] marriage may elect to marry a junior wife if he has no recognized offspring or heirs"—and if he is not likely to gain any under the existing arrangement (p. 218). The inference is that each brother is entitled to the paternity of at least one child and that, in fact, he must essentially be convinced of that role. If he does not accept pater-

[48] Under certain circumstances, it must be noted, Tibetan-speakers without per stirpes inheritance also recognize differential paternity. For example, Gorer (1967: 171; see also Fürer-Haimendorf 1964: 73) wrote of the Lepchas of Sikkim that "the co-husbands sleep with their common wife on alternate nights but all children are presumed to be begotten by the first husband, and he alone has to observe the prenatal precautions; an exception is only made to this rule if the first husband's prolonged absence makes his paternity a physiological impossibility."

[49] According to Levine (1977: 192), "Nyinba ideas about the timing of conception are not unlike our own." Women are said to be most fertile during the second week of the menstrual cycle and pregnant women "are thought to be able to pinpoint a short stretch of time during which conception occurred." Because it is "uncommon" for all of a woman's husbands to be present in the household simultaneously (due to trading and herding activities), paternity attribution is often straightforward. But "if paternity is attributable to more than one husband, the parents will wait for the child's birth to compare its appearance with that of possible genitors. Here again the wife will make the attribution of paternity and it is up to her husbands to accept or reject her decision. If husbands refuse to acknowledge their role in a child's conception, the child is considered illegitimate. . . . Drawing public attention to the conception of an illegitimate child is tantamount to instigating a divorce." (p. 193.)

nity for any of the children born to the primary wife, he is entitled to bring in a second, junior spouse. Whether or not he actually does so, however, depends upon still another principle.

The principle of sibling solidarity. Among the co-husbands of a polyandrous union, Levine also found "a great sense of trust . . . which is expressed in continual cooperation in the household and in the sharings of wives." (1977: 210; see also 1988: ch. 11.) She argues that such "sibling solidarity" is, particularly in the case of brothers, another important cultural principle behind the formation of plural marriages among the Nyinba. The principle, although not a strong enough belief to promote fraternal polyandry or polygynandry during times of relative economic abundance (as when one household inherits the estate of another, for example), clearly does play a role in men's decisions to convert polyandrous unions to polygynandry. Thus Levine found that if two or more "brothers" were in fact descended from different mothers (and were therefore actually double first cousins or "three-quarter brothers" at best), then this seemed to weaken support for the ideal of fraternal solidarity. In particular, the sons of co-wives were "less likely to remain in a simple polyandrous arrangement and more apt to take more than one wife for themselves." (1977: 210.) Once again, this tendency was fully recognized by the natives. "The Nyinba assert that there is a relationship between filiation and the willingness to make do with a single fertile woman. A principal informant once told me that men with different genitors often took additional wives and that men with different genetrices were very likely to do so." (Ibid.)

This pattern showed through clearly in data obtained by Levine from genealogies and family surveys. Omitting cases of polygynandrous unions motivated by infertility, she found that "brothers" from different fathers had married plural fertile women in 7 of 26 matrimonies, but that for "brothers" from different mothers the corresponding figures were 6 out of 6 (p. 211). In addition, Levine found that the incidence of polygynandry was also partly a function of the number of males in the sibling groups. Specifically, the tendency to acquire an additional wife or wives increased with the number of brothers born to the same mother, but was uniformly high among "brothers" born to different mothers. Data from Levine (1977), assembled in Table 2.7, indicate that brothers of identical maternity arranged polygynandrous marriages in 40 percent or fewer of all cases in which the sibling set numbered two to five males. Polygynandry reached 100 percent only when the marriage included six or seven brothers, each presumably wanting one or more children recognized as his own. On the other hand, brothers of differential maternity arranged polygynandrous marriages in all cases, regardless of the size of the sibling groups; there was even one such marriage of just two "brothers" (probably, in fact, cousins). Although the sample size is admittedly quite small, the difference between the distributions is statistically significant accord-

TABLE 2.7

Differential Maternity Among Brothers and Frequency of
Polygynandry in a Sample of Nyinba Households

| No. of brothers | Marriages among brothers of identical maternity | | | Marriages among "brothers" of differential maternity | | |
| | Polyandry[a] | Polygynandry | | Polyandry[a] | Polygynandry | |
	Number	Number	Percent	Number	Number	Percent
Two	10	0	0.0%	1	1	100.0%
Three	15	6	40.0	1	1	100.0
Four	8	3	37.5	3	3	100.0
Five	3	1	33.3	1	1	100.0
Six	1	1	100.0	—	—	—
Seven	1	1	100.0	—	—	—
TOTAL[b]	38[c]	12	31.6%	6	6	100.0%

SOURCE: Data from Levine 1977: 213.
[a]Includes all cases of polygynandry.
[b]Based upon genealogical and census data collected by Levine. Omitted from this sample were marriages includ-ing one or more infertile women or males aged thirty or less. The sample is not directly comparable to that of Table 2.4.
[c]Includes 26 marriages among brothers of differential *paternity*, 7 of which (18.4 percent) were polygynandrous.

ing to a chi-square test of independence ($\chi^2 = 10.0$ with $p < 0.005$). The data confirm what the Nyinba have said all along: the binding power of fraternal solidarity is noticeably reduced if "brothers" have different mothers.[50] Levine traces this reduction, in turn, to the "brothers'" having grown up amid the competitive, even hostile relations between their mothers as co-wives (1988: 153).

To summarize up to this point, then, Levine succeeds in explaining the occurrence of polygynandrous marriages among the Nyinba by using three principles that she adds to the domestic economy model: the spe-cial local rule of per stirpes inheritance; the reproductive interests of co-husbands; and the principle of sibling solidarity. Adult males, however, are not the only ones with recognized reproductive interests in Nyinba society, and this brings us to Levine's final principle.

The reproductive interests of co-wives. The one remaining challenge from Table 2.5 concerns the appearance of "conjoint marriage," a form of polygynandrous marriage with enduring behavioral subgroups. Levine notes that such "marriage within a marriage" is found only among poly-gynandrous households with fertile co-wives and is conspicuously lack-ing among polygynandrous marriages with but one fertile woman. The reason she gives is as follows.

In the latter, only one of the women is capable of producing heirs or successors for the household. Therefore the procreative identities of the two women become merged. However, in the former case, the women retain separate identities in pro-

[50]Hiatt (1980: 587) concludes similarly from Tambiah's (1966) study of nonpolygynous fraternal polyandry among Kandyan Sinhalese ($N = 17$) that "the closer the genetic relation-ship between the co-husbands, the greater the likelihood of enduring cooperation between

creative concerns and pursue conflicting goals. These women feel bound by few, if any, ties. Even full sisters are motivated in this respect more by individual self-interest than by any feelings of sibling solidarity, let alone concern for the welfare of the group. [Levine 1977: 214]

This reproductive self-interest among fertile co-wives is recognized and respected by others, so that "fertile women are not expected to work together in rearing one another's children. . . . In this way, two mothers in a single household become the focus of separate uterine familial units. Men in this situation have alternative means of realizing their aims of fatherhood and thus can direct their attention to one woman or another." (pp. 214–15.) Moreover, the co-husbands in such a union encourage and are said to be "pleased by increased chances of becoming fathers and more satisfactory conjugal arrangements." (p. 215.) As we have seen, it is often the reproductive self-interest of the males that creates polygynandry in the first place and engenders this conflict of interest between fertile females. From the start, "most fertile women vociferously oppose the addition of more wives to their marriage." (p. 209.) But once polygynandry is imposed upon a primary wife, the conjoint form of marriage, Levine argues, follows from the recognized right of women's reproductive self-interest.

Finally, Levine notes there is evidence that fertile co-wives in a conjoint marriage deliberately manipulate the size of the corporate household and heirship. Given that polygynandry "tends to be condemned as selfishness," Levine says that she

had often wondered why the rate of conjoint marriages was so high . . . 15.1% of women initially entered into such unions. But in fact, as I found out, such marriages did not necessarily entail a large number of children for the next generation. . . . Women who lived their lives in such unions had [significantly] fewer children than their polyandrously and monogamously married sisters. . . . Thus such a form of marriage doesn't necessarily pose an immediate danger to household solidarity. [1981–82: 12–13]

Levine suggests that Nyinba women in conjoint marriages, apparently out of fear of partition and the chances of reduced wealth and status, intentionally reduce their fertility through voluntary abstinence. Paradoxically, she implies, their individual reproductive interest is here served by less procreation. Conjoint marriage is thus the monomarital principle stretched to its limit: there may well be only one family, legally speaking, in a conjoint household, but there are effectively two or more reproductive units.

With the addition of this last principle, the reproductive interests of co-wives, we arrive at a tentatively complete explanation of the diversity of marriage forms among Tibetan populations. While I may seem to have exhausted the documented marriage patterns, I wish to emphasize that fur-

---

them; and the more distant the genetic relationship, the greater the likelihood of strain, conflict, and dissolution."

ther study may always reveal additional, unexplained variation in the forms and frequencies of Tibetan marriage—not to mention additional principles to explain that variation.[51]

The evidence reviewed in this section provides solid support for Hypothesis 6, that conjoint marriage among the Nyinba forms as a consequence of individual reproductive interests. Far from being subordinated to the greater household's reproductive concerns, individuals express some rather finely tuned reproductive interests of their own, particularly in the case of "brothers" of the same household. As Levine (1977, 1988) explains, these individual interests reflect both the per stirpes inheritance rule that is characteristic of this population and also the differential development of sibling solidarity in various contexts. At the same time, however, they also point to limitations inherent in the unrefined measures of reproductive success—the household's reproductive success, for instance—that I have used for analytical purposes in most of this chapter. An important implication is that the measure called individual inclusive fitness, defined in Chapter 1, should prove to be a useful tool in this kind of cultural analysis. We will return to this suggestion in Chapter 4.

Cultural Analysis: Explanation and Evolution

To conclude this opening case study of human diversity, let me summarize the three main problems addressed in this chapter and the implications of our proposed solutions.

Explaining Behavior

The first problem we confronted in this chapter was the problem of explaining behavioral differences: how to account for the almost bewildering diversity of the Tibetan marriage system. In particular, the goal was to account for the existence of no fewer than fifteen distinct kinds of marriage, including virtually all the major types known to anthropology, among thongpa and dü-jung serfs. After a brief critical review of eight different categories of previous hypotheses, we looked in some detail at the most plausible one to date, the domestic economy theory. According to that theory, as developed by Melvyn Goldstein, Tibetan marital diversity resulted from the adherence of the rural population, particularly the thongpa serfs, to a set of beliefs that organized their behavior to meet a number of complementary goals.

[51] This section makes tentatively complete the explanation of marital diversity, but it has not attempted to complete the explanation of the social history of all component principles and beliefs. That is a larger project that I leave for another time. It should be noted, however, that a social history of the per stirpes inheritance rule of the Nyinba warrants special priority in this regard. Not only is the rule relatively unusual among Tibetan-speakers, it also seems responsible for the refinement of articulated individual interests in the subject of reproduction.

The first goal we considered was also described as the most important: the thongpa articulated a conscious concern for conserving family property intact through the generations. To achieve this goal, as we have seen, the thongpa purposefully adhered to a monomarital principle, a belief that effectively contravened the Tibetan legal provision for partible patrilineal inheritance. The second goal, that of adult labor optimization, was similarly promoted through adherence to traditional beliefs, including the principle of family harmony. The third and final goal we considered, the desire of each household to reproduce itself through time, was also supported by a belief, namely, that the heirs had a right to manipulate their marriage(s) in order to achieve smooth succession. In a series of empirical tests, predictions generated from these goals were matched against the evidence for marital diversity in three well-studied Tibetan communities, Chimdro, D'ing-ri, and Barkhang. Our analyses confirmed that their highly complex pattern of matrimonial arrangements can be explained in terms of a relatively small set of beliefs in the minds of the actors.

To this point, our analysis illustrated the explanatory or "vertical" dimension to cultural analysis that was described in Chapter 1. Patterns of behavior were explained as the consequence of a subset of beliefs within the ideational code we call Tibetan culture. Moreover, the elements of that subset exemplified all five key properties of culture as it is conceptualized today, including, in the case of the monomarital principle, a social history of more than thirteen hundred years. In this way, the Tibetan case study amply confirmed the validity and utility of the explanatory dimension to cultural analysis.

Explaining Beliefs

This effort to explain behavior led directly to the second main problem addressed in the chapter, namely, How do we then explain the beliefs behind the behaviors? Specifically, we went on to ask (1) Why did the thongpa generally adhere to a monomarital principle ($M = 1$) and not to its obvious alternatives ($M = 2, 3,$ or 4)? and (2) What accounts for the persistence of this belief through at least thirteen hundred years of Tibetan social history? In answer to these questions we then considered two hypotheses: that the monomarital principle had persisted through space and time because of its perceived and valued consequences for the thongpa (Hypothesis 4); and that these valued consequences, in turn, enhanced thongpa survival and reproduction in the special social and natural environment of Tibet (Hypothesis 5).

The next several sections of the chapter offered tests of these hypotheses. First, we saw that the monomarital principle does indeed have perceived and valued consequences for the thongpa: when it fails, they assert, the end result "may so impoverish a household that its members simply cannot sustain themselves." (Levine 1977: 245.) Moreover, the thongpa maintain that these consequences are not recent in origin but that they have been recognized and valued for generations by their fore-bears—forebears who also confronted, according to the best of our information, a fundamentally similar social ecology. While caution is always in order when an analyst attempts to infer past effects from present circumstances (see discussion in App. A.2.4)—a point underscored by the current Chinese occupation of Tibet—such an extrapolation appears reasonable within the time frame and context examined in this study.

Second, the survival and reproduction implications of alternative marriage principles ($M = 1, 2, 3$, etc.) were tested with a computer simulation based upon actual fertility, mortality, and land tenure data for Tibetan populations in Nepal. The results clearly supported Hypothesis 5: under the assumption of constant land constraints, a sustained belief in the monomarital principle soon produces more surviving descendants per household than any of its alternatives. This finding was then extended in a second set of computer simulations designed to investigate the impact of occasional, temporary relief from the land constraints (as when one household inherits a second estate following an extinction). Here the simulations asked, in effect, When does it "pay" in terms of surviving descendants for a thongpa household to initiate a one-time-only partition? The results suggested that the exceptions, too, might generally be carried out in a way that is reproductively advantageous for the thongpa.

My arguments concerning the explanation of beliefs may therefore be summarized as shown in Fig. 2.4, a figure whose axis labels have been kept deliberately general in order to suggest the broader applicability of this approach. Panel A shows what I have called the ecological consequences of adherence to each of the existing "variant beliefs." In the thongpa case, the Y axis may be thought of as measuring a household's net economic productivity per heir after some number of generations, j (not shown), of partitioning according to the variant marriage principles on the X axis ($M = 0, 1, 2$, etc.). As I have argued, the thongpa's ecological consequence function is optimized at $M = 1$; because of land and labor constraints, economic productivity falls off sharply on either side of this variant (the slopes get steeper with j, assuming constant technology). Panel B shows the relative rates of social transmission of the same set of variant beliefs. The arrows labeled V represent the influence of the value system on the rates at which alternative variants are taught and learned in the population: as shown, cultural values cause the differential transmission of alternative marriage principles in rough proportion to their ecological consequences, so that the monomarital principle is transmitted more frequently than any of the alternatives.

Finally, panel C depicts the relative reproductive success, after three or more generations, of thongpa women and their co-husbands who adopt and transmit to their offspring the various cultural alternatives. As shown, the monomarital principle (Variant 1) leads to the highest reproductive success. The covariation of this curve with that in panel B illustrates Hy-

Panel A

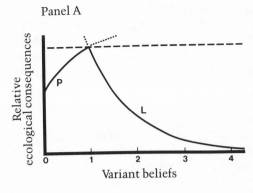

Relative ecological consequences

P

L

Variant beliefs

0   1   2   3   4

Panel B

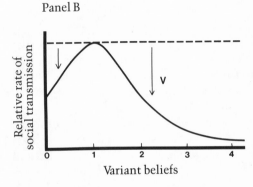

Relative rate of social transmission

V

Variant beliefs

0   1   2   3   4

Panel C

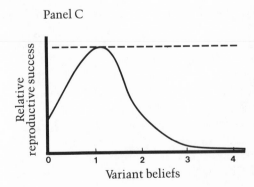

Relative reproductive success

Variant beliefs

0   1   2   3   4

Fig. 2.4. A model of preservation by preference in cultural evolution. These three panels summarize my argument for the persistent social transmission of the monomarital principle among the thongpa serfs of ethnic Tibet. Using curves smoothed to facilitate interpretation, the panels illustrate how value-guided decision making can favor cultural variants with reproductive advantage. Panel A shows the relative ecological consequences of behavior guided by each member of a set of "variant beliefs" numbered 0 to 4 (the number of variants shown is hypothetical; in actual cases the number will vary as a function of other variables, including social and cultural constraints). Here, adherence to the monomarital principle (Variant 1, as in *M* = 1) is associated with the highest per capita economic productivity among the heirs of a thongpa estate. The consequence function has two main components as shown: a labor productivity component, *P*, which reflects the constraint on economic productivity from the shortage of household labor; and a land area component, *L*, which reflects the constraint on productivity arising from the partitioning of household land resources. Panel B shows the relative rates of social transmission of the variant beliefs within a thongpa population. The influence of traditional cultural values concerning land holdings and agricultural production is shown (arrows labeled *V*) to reduce the relative rates of social transmission of the variants *M* = 2, *M* = 3, etc. and to favor the teaching and learning of the monomarital principle. Finally, panel C shows the relative reproductive success associated with adherence to each of the variant beliefs. As in Figs. 2.2 and 2.3, reproductive success is measured by the average number of surviving descendants in some future generation (here unspecified for simplicity) of married and fertile thongpa women, a quantity equal to the average of the summed reproductive successes of their co-husbands. The curve summarizes the results of the computer simulations described earlier: optimal long-term reproductive success is achieved by adherence to the monomarital principle.

pothesis 5: Beliefs with valued consequences enhance the reproductive success of their carriers. The covariation of all three panels in Fig. 2.4 illustrates how a belief like the monomarital principle can be both reproductively advantageous and yet preserved by local preferences that are described in other terms.

Culture and Reproductive Success

The final problem addressed by this chapter concerned the one remaining unexplained marriage form, the "conjoint marriage" of the Nyinba. Following the earlier analysis of Nancy E. Levine (1977), I argued that four additional beliefs of the Nyinba were necessary and sufficient for the cultural explanation of this marriage form: (1) the special per stirpes inheritance rule; (2) the reproductive interests of co-husbands; (3) the principle of sibling solidarity; and (4) the reproductive interests of co-wives. Although these additional beliefs (especially the per stirpes rule) are to some extent unique to the Nyinba case, they underscore in a very vivid way the more general concern for survival and reproduction that exists among the thongpa in all of the communities we have considered. To a great extent, *all* thongpa marriages seem to be conducted in a way that enhances the long-term reproductive success of the parents.

Fig. 2.5 illustrates the point by recasting part of the domestic economy theory in terms of reproductive success. As shown in the figure, the average reproductive success, S, of fertile thongpa women varies hypothetically as a complex function of the number, N, of their economically active co-husbands. On the one hand, S tends to decrease with N if one considers only the probability of partitioning and subdivision of household lands, the curve labeled L in the figure. On the other hand, S tends to increase with N when one focuses on total household economic production, whether in one of the more productive areas of ethnic Tibet (represented by the curve P_b) or in one of the less productive areas (P_w). When both L and P considerations are taken into account simultaneously, the number of co-husbands for optimal reproductive success will be a compromise of these two influences, that is, the N-value where the curves cross in the hypothetical examples shown.

At first glance, these refinements may seem to do little more than translate the domestic economy theory into another idiom; indeed, the predicted optimum number of adult males is the one that minimizes the likelihood of partition while simultaneously maximizing household production, just as we predicted earlier. On the other hand, formulating the theory in terms of reproductive success allows one to offer additional predictions. If, for example, thongpa parents truly do arrange the marriages of their children in a manner that promotes long-term reproductive success, then Fig. 2.5 would lead us to predict both more polyandrous marriages and more brothers per marriage (after controlling for fertility and mortality) in the less favorable environments of the Tibetan plateau, even

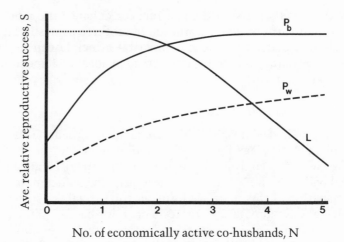

No. of economically active co-husbands, N

Fig. 2.5. Reproductive success as a function of marriage configuration according to the domestic economy theory. Under the assumption that the marriage principle is held constant at $M = 1$, but also that family disharmony increases the probability of eventual partition, the average reproductive success, S, of fertile thongpa women will vary as a two-component function of the number, N, of their economically active co-husbands (whose summed reproductive success also equals S). One component, labeled L for "land," shows how, other things being equal, S varies hypothetically with N because of the risk of partitioning and erosion of household agricultural land. The other component, represented here by two curves labeled P, shows how, other things being equal, S varies hypothetically with N because of household economic production. The curve P_b relates S to N in a "better," more productive environment; similarly, P_w relates S and N in a "worse" environment, with lower returns to labor. According to this model, the number of co-husbands for optimal reproductive success is given by the N value with the highest S when both components are taken into account. For the example shown, optimal reproductive success requires two co-husbands in the better environment and four co-husbands in the worse environment.

though the probability of partition there is also higher.[52] Such a prediction would be difficult to make unless the outcome of the component hypotheses could be measured in terms of the same variable.

In conclusion, my point is simply that the various hypotheses of this chapter are all consistent with the view that the values and beliefs of the thongpa act as effective guides to successful survival and reproduction. The beliefs governing thongpa marriage share with other Tibetan beliefs what Sherry B. Ortner (1978: 160) calls "experiential aptness," and in this case actual adaptive significance. Within the very real social and ecological constraints of the thongpa environment, the values, ideas, and beliefs we have examined appear to guide behavior in directions that are reproductively advantageous. This is particularly true of the monomarital principle and the age-old value bestowed upon land and sustained agricultural production. The evidence suggests that their effects are neither neutral nor opposed to the survival and reproduction of their carriers.

[52] It should be noted that there exists considerable support for this hypothesis. Thus according to Carrasco (1959: 47) "[polyandry] is everywhere prevalent in the [west-central] province of Tsang; one reason given by the Tibetan informant of Bell [1928] is that in Tsang

Four implications of this finding deserve emphasis. First, our analysis implies that cultural evolution in the thongpa context caused the selective retention of an ideational entity, the monomarital principle, that had genuine adaptive significance for its carriers. This means not only that cultural evolution can be a selective process, but also that its selectivity can run parallel to genetic selection (see Chapter 3). Beliefs, like genes, can be favored when they confer reproductive advantage upon their carriers. Of course the processes of differential transmission are quite distinct in the two cases: in one of them, "nature" does the choosing; in the other, people. Nevertheless the results, in terms of net effect on reproductive success, can be the same.

Second, we have also seen that it is the cultural value system of the thongpa that guides differential transmission in this case. Although the extinction of whole households does sometimes contribute to the social transmission advantage of $M = 1$, the value-guided choices of the thongpa appear to have played a more important role. The implication is that culture, through socially transmitted values, is capable of directing its own evolutionary dynamics. When the products of those dynamics are found to enhance reproductive success, this can mean that cultural values have favored the social dissemination of variants with net reproductive benefit. In this manner, culture is capable of guiding its own evolution in ways that have adaptive significance for the carriers who make the choices.

The third implication concerns a remaining unanswered question: with behavior explained as a product of beliefs, and beliefs explained as a product of value-guided evolutionary dynamics, we must still ask, What explains the particular values that characterize thongpa culture and cause its adaptive selectivity? For example, what accounts for the traditional value placed on arable land and economic productivity? How did these values themselves become culturally prominent and so capable of enhancing reproduction? To this point, it might have appeared that our analysis was complete, and that Tibetan marital diversity needed to be explained solely in terms of information in the cultural system, without reference to information in the genetic system. However, the important

---

the soil is poorer than in Ü [an east-central province] and the holdings are larger, requiring more persons to look after them, and making polyandry well suited to the province." (The same conclusion is reached in Prince Peter 1963: 415; Baber 1886: 97.) The converse of Tsang may well be the lower and more fertile province of Spiti at the western fringe of Tibetan-speakers. As Carrasco has noted, "in Spiti, polyandry is not practiced among the regular landholders since only the eldest son marries and his brothers become lamas." (1959: 36; see also Das 1893: 9.) Similarly, polyandry is not found today among the Tamangs, another group of Tibetan-speakers who live adjacent to the Sherpas, just south of the Khumbu area of Nepal. Although local tradition traces their origin to the Tibetan plateau, they live today at the relatively productive altitude of 5,000 to 9,000 feet where they grow a wide variety of grain crops including millet, wheat, and maize (see Fricke 1986). The Tamang case appears to be a fitting "natural experiment" in support of Fig. 2.5. According to Fürer-Haimendorf (1955–56: 171), the Tamangs still use the same kin term, *tsang*, for a man's brother's wife and for his son's wife; this is probably a "survival from a time when polyandrous marriages of the Tibetan type were customary."

choice-guiding values of this case clearly have their own cultural evolutionary history. In that history, the information of the genes—specifically, their instructive effects upon the human brain, the senses, and the connecting nervous system—is likely to have played an important contributory role. I shall return to this topic in later chapters. For now, I wish only to imply that the values governing the selectivity of cultural evolution in this case have themselves descended with modification from earlier forms, and that the information of the genes has surely played an influential role in that descent.

Assuming that there is some truth in this, the fourth and final implication is that our findings call into question the adequacy of the dichotomy between "ultimate" and "proximate" explanations introduced in Chapter 1. In a very real sense, our cultural explanation of Tibetan marital diversity is neither as ultimate as genetic evolutionary explanations, such as the sociobiological hypothesis described above, nor as proximate as arguments concerning ontogeny and physiology. True, I have argued that the behavior of the thongpa functions in specific ways to promote the long-term reproductive success of the parents. But I have not argued, as in ultimate explanations, that this behavior is the product of historical changes in the "genetic program" of Tibetans; nor have I argued, as in proximate explanations, that the behaviors are explained by "the individual's history and present circumstances," that is, the "decoding" of the genetic program (Mayr 1982: 68). Instead, I have argued that the behaviors of the thongpa are the product of a special, conceptual "cultural program" with its own evolutionary history. Working from specific ideational elements of that program, my explanation of Tibetan marital diversity is neither ultimate nor proximate in the conventional sense of those terms. Instead, it constitutes a third form of causal analysis, one that truly is "intermediate."

GENES AND HUMAN

DIVERSITY: A Case Study of

Sickle-Cell Anemia in West Africa

Tropical West Africa is a large and ethnically diverse region southwest of the Sahara Desert. There, among its human populations, great variation exists in the frequencies of several congenital hemoglobin diseases, or "hemoglobinopathies." The best known of these diseases is sickle-cell anemia, an often fatal disorder named for the distorted shape of red blood cells in its victims. In some West African populations, this particular hemoglobinopathy remains unknown or is, at most, very rare; in others it occurs today at some of the world's highest frequencies. Moreover, these differences can be traced deep into the history and cultural evolution of the region. In the high-frequency populations, for example, long years of experience with sickle-cell anemia have prompted the linguistic evolution of specific vernacular names for the condition, names like *chwechweechwe, nwiiwii, nuidudui,* and *ahotutuo* (among the Ga, Fante, Ewe, and Twi peoples of Ghana respectively), whose onomatopoeia reflects "the relentless and repetitive gnawing pains in the bones and joints characteristic of the disease." These same peoples recognize not only that the disease tends to "run through families" but also that, "in the vast majority of cases, parents of *chwechweechwe* children [are] not different phenotypically from normal healthy adults." (Konotey-Ahulu 1974a: 611.) In addition, many of these same populations utilize traditional folk remedies, such as "limb-girdle tattoos" to relieve the pressure on tissue and joints that sickling causes (see Konotey-Ahulu 1969, 1973), and it has even been suggested that traditional beliefs in reincarnation are related to the high incidence of the disease in this group of populations.[1] In short, sickle-cell anemia in West

[1] The possibility of a link between West African beliefs in "repeater children" and sickle-cell anemia has been explored by James Onwubalili (1983) and Stuart Edelstein (1986). In some parts of Nigeria, for example, Onwubalili noted that "children born to particular families suffered chronic ill health and failed to thrive, and most died before their tenth birthday, many before their fifth. Some children were thought to be later reborn in the same family to the same or subsequent generations, and to die again and repeat the cycle. The reincarnate child was normal at birth, but from early childhood it suffered growth retardation, recurrent

Africa offers a second benchmark example of human diversity—one of physiological differences and their derived cultural correlates.

In this chapter I would like to explore the leading genetic explanation for these physiological differences. My argument, which roughly parallels the cultural explanation in Chapter 2, has four goals: first, to review the evidence linking differences in the phenotypes associated with sickle-cell anemia to differences in the code—here, the genetic code—that instructs their formation; second, to relate contemporary differences between populations in the frequencies of these phenotypes to corresponding differences in the frequencies of their genes and genotypes; third, to inquire about the Darwinian evolution of these genetic differences, illustrating along the way some useful concepts and tools of analysis from the field of population genetics; and fourth, to review and test the "malaria hypothesis," which purports to explain the organic evolution of existing diversity through reference both to endemic malaria and to the culturally guided activities of human populations that have affected its prevalence. The malaria hypothesis is widely regarded as "the single most important piece of professional research and theory construction" concerning the relationships of genes and culture (Bennett 1976a: 200). Largely, however, because of the paucity of suitable data, a number of its key arguments had gone for years without systematic testing. Happily, this situation has now changed, particularly for well-studied regions like West Africa. Today we are in a good position not only to review this important example of human diversity, but also to conduct empirical tests of key arguments along the way.

At the outset, let me urge readers who are new to molecular biology or to population genetics, or who would like a brief refresher course on these subjects, to read App. B before continuing. The appendix provides brief, nontechnical introductions to both the role of genes in protein synthesis and thus their "instructive effect" on phenotypes (section B.1), and to selected basic principles of population genetics, including the kinetics of gene-frequency change under genetic selection (section B.2). The remainder of this chapter assumes familiarity with the terms and concepts reviewed in that appendix. In a similar vein, readers already well versed in

---

febrile illness, convulsions, body aches and pains, protuberant abdomen, and sometimes yellow eyes. . . . This pattern of features was known by various tribal names, including *Ogbanje* (Igbo tribe) and *Abiku* (Yoruba tribe), which literally means 'a child destined to die and be born repeatedly to the world'." (p. 504.) Onwubalili concluded with the hypothesis, "It is most probable that the 'reincarnate' child had sickle-cell anaemia, since this disease would explain all the clinical features and natural history of 'reincarnation'." (p. 503.) Edelstein went on to test this hypothesis on a sample (admittedly small) of thirteen *ogbanje* Igbo children and eight of their parents. He found not only that none of the *ogbanje* children had sickle-cell anemia but also that six of the eight parents were not even carriers of the gene for the disease, which precluded the possibility that sickle-cell anemia was the cause of death among the *ogbanjes'* deceased siblings. He concluded that the link is, at best, "imprecise" and suggested that more research is needed on the topic (see 1986: ch. 4).

genetic evolutionary theory may find it convenient to skim quickly through to the section headed "The Malaria Hypothesis."

Sickle-Cell Anemia: A "Molecular Disease"

Sickle-cell anemia was first described in the Western medical literature in 1910 by the Chicago physician James B. Herrick. One of Herrick's patients was a black student from the West Indies, twenty years old, who complained of recurrent joint pains, fevers, and dizziness. When the patient's blood was examined under the microscope, Herrick found "peculiar elongated and sickle-shaped" erythrocytes (red blood cells) amidst the more usual biconcave cells. In addition, the patient's total red blood cell count proved to be unusually low. He subsequently suffered "bilious attacks" with severe nausea, epigastric pain, and what he described as muscular rheumatism. Unfortunately, the patient stopped seeking medical assistance soon thereafter, and Herrick was left to conclude that "the question of diagnosis must remain an open one." Nevertheless, his report ended with the provocative suggestion that perhaps "some unrecognized change in the composition of the corpuscle itself may be the determining factor." (1910: 520–21.)

In the years since 1910, the efforts of literally hundreds of investigators have combined to produce a fairly comprehensive picture of the causes and consequences of sickle-cell disease (see App. A.3.1 for a review of historical highlights). Our understanding today includes the following key elements.

1. Herrick's suggestion was correct: sickle-cell disease *is* caused by a change in the composition of corpuscles. We now know this change to be a biochemical alteration in the structure of hemoglobin, the oxygen-carrying globular protein that normally accounts for 95 percent of the dry weight of each erythrocyte. Normally, the major hemoglobin in adult human beings is the complex molecule called hemoglobin A (abbreviated to Hb A). Generally speaking, this molecule is densely but evenly dispersed throughout the cytoplasm of mature erythrocytes.

2. In individuals with sickle-cell anemia, Hb A is replaced by hemoglobin S (Hb S), a molecule with different chemical properties (for details, see App. A.3.1). Under certain conditions this chemical difference allows Hb S to crystallize into long strands, distorting the shape of the cells in which it is housed. The difference between Hb A and Hb S has in turn been traced to molecular variation in the DNA of the gene that contains assembly instructions for one of the main subunits of the hemoglobin molecule. By convention, the variants of the gene coding for Hb A and Hb S are therefore called, respectively, the "A allele" and the "S allele." Today, the S allele is recognized as only one of more than several hun-

dred different alleles that affect the hemoglobin molecule's structure and function.[2]

3. Because the genetic material of an individual normally contains two copies of each gene, a condition known as "diploidy," we recognize three genotypes and three phenotypes with respect to sickle-cell anemia, as follows.

Genotypes	Phenotypes (hemoglobin characteristics)
AA	"Normal" (Hb A only)
AS	Sickle-cell trait (Hb A and Hb S mixed)
SS	Sickle-cell anemia (Hb S only)

For our purposes, individuals of the homozygous AA and SS genotypes may be regarded as having pure Hb A and Hb S respectively, whereas individuals of the heterozygous AS genotype have a mixture of both. Under normal physiological conditions, the hemoglobin A present in the erythrocytes of AS individuals is sufficient to inhibit or "mask" the sickling propensity of Hb S. Therefore AS individuals normally suffer no adverse effects from their genotype, and many are completely unaware that they are carriers.[3] On the other hand, some sickling can be induced in AS individuals under special conditions, as in a laboratory, so AS individuals have sometimes been called "sicklers" and their phenotype "sicklemia."

4. Although some crystallization of Hb S is thought to exist at all times within erythrocytes of SS individuals, the tendency of the molecules to aggregate is greatly enhanced by low partial pressures of oxygen, such as may be encountered in the capillary beds of the body's tissues and organs. Under such conditions, Hb S crystallizes rapidly, stretching the red cells into the characteristic sickle shape. This process, in turn, often leads to serious complications at the physiological level. Sickled cells often do not flow as rapidly or smoothly as normal ones; indeed, sometimes they do not flow at all. The resulting oxygen deficiency causes

[2] In order to reduce the complexity of this chapter, my presentation follows the lead of Ayala (1982) and others and largely ignores the co-alleles of S at the beta-globin locus. Although expedient, this means that the quantitative theory described below should be regarded as a first approximation. For expositions of theory where the C allele has also been included, see Cavalli-Sforza and Bodmer (1971) and Templeton (1982). Note, however, that the C allele is taken into account in the empirical analysis described later in the chapter (but even there, I was forced by the data to treat all non-S and non-C alleles as if they were A alleles).

[3] There is, however, some debate on this point. The literature contains infrequent, scattered reports of clinical pathologies, even death, among AS individuals; see, for example, the reports of sickling crisis and death in a 23-year-old AS individual of West Africa (Edington and Lehmann 1955), and in four apparently healthy AS recruits to the U.S. Army (Jones et al. 1970). These have prompted a number of authors, among them Song (1971), Lehmann and Huntsman (1974), and Heller (1974), to suggest that additional longitudinal analysis is needed. Nevertheless, the relative infrequency of these effects in most environments, despite substantial representation of the AS genotype in corresponding populations, indicates that S generally behaves as a true recessive allele.

more Hb S to crystallize in adjoining cells, leading to further circulatory impairment and setting off the "vicious cycle" of erythrocyte destruction (Harris and Kellermeyer 1970: 201). This cycle may then lead to impairment of circulation and damage to vital organs, including the brain, lungs, heart, spleen, and retina of the eye. Finally, sickling also causes premature aging and death of red blood cells, reducing their mean life expectancy by over 80 percent. This, of course, results in the chronic anemia first observed in Herrick's patient, a condition often associated with bone-marrow enlargement, heart dilation, and impaired mental or physical functioning.

5. Although it is possible for any or all of these effects to occur singly and in isolation, any type of physiological stress—strenuous physical exercise, rapid temperature variations, or even a pathogenic disease—may trigger several reactions at once. The result can be a painful "sickle-cell crisis" (the "bilious attacks" of Herrick's patient) that often leads to irreversible damage and, eventually, death. Because such stress is a normal part of life in most environments, fatality is by far the most common consequence.[4] The accepted generalization in the biomedical literature is that SS individuals, in the absence of advanced medical care, rarely survive the first years of life.[5]

In short, we know today that the salient phenotypic differences between individuals with sickle-cell anemia, sickle-cell trait, and normal red blood cells can be traced to the level of one small biochemical change in the DNA instruction set for hemoglobin synthesis. The S allele there-

[4] The seriousness of sickle-cell anemia has been underscored by reports from physicians and geneticists working in tropical areas where the S allele is particularly prevalent. Reviewing the literature on Central Africa, for example, A. C. Allison (1965: 368) noted that many years of medical experience in Uganda had failed to produce even a single case of homozygous sickle-cell disease among adults. In addition, a complete population survey of over 33,000 individuals in one province of the Congo revealed not one SS genotype over twenty years of age despite large numbers of AS's and a high prevalence of the S allele. From these case reports and others Allison concluded, "Hence there is little doubt about the extensive and early mortality of sickle-cell disease under [Central] African conditions." (See also Lehmann and Raper 1956; G. Jacob 1957; Attah and Ekere 1975.)

[5] Although there is no reason to question this generalization, it is also true that some SS individuals do survive to adulthood, a fact that has been apparent since Herrick's report in 1910. Indeed the first four cases of sickle-cell anemia reported in the medical literature were all of individuals twenty years of age or older. As the years went by, these came to be seen as "anomalies" or "rare exceptions" in light of the evidence coming in from overseas locations like Central Africa. Eventually, however, enough data accumulated to suggest regional variations in SS seriousness: see, for example, the relatively benign cases of sickle-cell anemia in Ghana described by Edington and Lehmann 1955 and Konotey-Ahulu 1974b, and in Jamaica by Serjeant et al. 1968 and Serjeant 1973. One implication of these findings is that the SS genotype has a variable "norm of reaction," that is, the same genes are said to "react" or express themselves differently under varying conditions such as differences in diet (Bertles 1973; Nurse 1979), climatic conditions, rates of pathogenic disease, and presence of "modifying factors" in their genetic environment (Dover et al. 1981; Embury et al. 1982; Mears et al. 1983). In short, sickle-cell anemia seems to be more environmentally labile than originally thought.

fore offers a good example of the way in which genes can influence human diversity, in this case physiological diversity. The phenotypic property of this example is clearly "genetically variable" or "subject to genetic variation": changes in the coded information of the genes are causally related to changes in observable function.[6] With reasonable care, these insights can be extended to the study of differences in the observable attributes of whole populations. At this level, the relevant questions are three. First, how much variation exists between human populations in the frequencies of the phenotypes associated with sickle-cell anemia, and how is that variation geographically distributed? Second, to what extent are these differences in phenotype distributions due to underlying differences in the distributions of genotypes? Third, what then accounts for such differences in genotype frequencies? In particular, why are the genotypes that contain the S allele relatively common in some populations and quite rare in others? With these questions, we are interested in explaining the diversity that exists *between* populations.

Fortunately, enough is known about the molecular basis of the sickling phenotype and about the "norms of reaction" of the AA, AS, and SS genotypes to supply an answer to Question 2 at the outset. There is reason to believe that virtually *all* of the differences between populations in these particular phenotype distributions can be accounted for by associated differences in genotype distributions. In this rather special case, we may therefore conclude that genetic diversity is the cause of phenotypic diversity, but only if we remind ourselves that this inference cannot, without good reason, be generalized to other human phenotypic properties.[7] With this cautionary note well in mind, we can therefore focus our attention on Questions 1 and 3. In due course, these questions will bring us back to the subject of relationships between genes and culture and to the particular concerns of evolutionary anthropology.

Geographical Distribution of the S Allele

During the 1940's and 1950's, at the same time that work was under way to elucidate the biochemical basis of sickling in SS erythrocytes, an impressive body of literature began to accumulate concerning the geographical distribution of the sickle-cell trait in human populations around the world.[8] One of the investigators to make best use of this new informa-

---

[6] The oft-repeated phrase "genetically determined" is misleading and should not be used in this connection. Environmental conditions external to the genes play a key role in the formation of phenotypes, all the way down to the level of transcription and translation (see App. B).

[7] Unwarranted assumptions of just this kind, as discussed in Chapter 1, have fueled the better part of the sociobiology debate.

[8] That literature was impressive both in quantity and in quality: in quantity because literally hundreds of articles offered estimates of sickling prevalences in different populations; and in quality because the studies often contained large sample sizes (1,000 or more subjects was not unusual) and because they quickly adopted the best available assay procedures—

tion was Frank B. Livingstone, an anthropologist who had himself worked on the distribution of sickling in Liberia, and who summarized the emerging global pattern as follows.

Frequencies of more than 20 percent of the sickle-cell trait have been found in populations across a broad belt of tropical Africa from the Gambia to Mozambique. Similar high frequencies have been found in Greece, South Turkey, and India. At first it appeared that there were isolated "pockets" of high frequencies in India and Greece, but more recently the sickle-cell gene has been found to be widely distributed in both countries. . . . Moreover, between these countries where high frequencies are found, there are intermediate frequencies, in Sicily, Algeria, Tunisia, Yemen, Palestine, and Kuwait. Thus, the sickle-cell gene is found in a large and rather continuous region of the Old World and in populations which have recently emigrated from this region, while it is almost completely absent from an even larger region of the Old World which stretches from Northern Europe to Australia. [Livingstone 1958: 533]

At the same time, the gene and its associated trait were absent from all New World populations sampled by that time, except for populations that included descendants from affected areas of the Old World.

These data raised an important analytic question: What process or processes had been responsible for this genetic differentiation between human populations? More specifically, why was the S allele relatively common in some parts of the Old World and "almost completely absent" from others? Indeed, why was it concentrated "across a broad belt of tropical Africa" in stark contrast to areas farther north and south, such as Europe and Australia? And why was it lacking altogether in Native American populations?

Several early attempts to answer these questions focused on a hypothesis of migration and interbreeding, the idea being that genetic differences could spread in regular patterns by population movement and nonrandom reproduction. The suggestion was useful as far as it went, but, as Livingstone pointed out, such attempts raised a number of "additional and striking problems" when viewed from the vantage point of genetic evolutionary theory.

Since persons who are homozygous for the sickle-cell gene very rarely reproduce, there is a constant loss of sickle-cell genes in each generation. In order for the gene to attain frequencies of .1 to .2, which are equivalent to about 20 to 40 percent of the sickle-cell trait, there must be some mechanism which is compensating for the loss. In other words, there must be some factor which is tending to increase the number of sickle-cell genes in the population. [1958: 533]

Historically, the elucidation of this "factor" proved to be a fascinating challenge in the study of human genetics and evolution. On the basis of the random changes introduced by mutation, one could readily explain a frequency of the S allele in a population on the order of one in a million or

---

including, by the 1950's, electrophoresis (see, for example, the early compilation in Beet 1949).

even one in a hundred thousand, but not frequencies four or five orders of magnitude greater. A good deal of research in the late 1940's and 1950's therefore came to focus on the question, Why is S so common in certain areas of the world? The question brings us back to the subject of genetic evolution as briefly introduced in Chapter 1, and to theories concerning the genetic differentiation of populations through time.

Genetic Evolutionary Theory

In his impressive treatise on the (cultural) evolution of biological thought, Ernst Mayr (1982: part II) argues that genetic evolutionary theory has come to recognize two distinct categories of evolutionary processes. One, called "transformation," refers to the changes of form through time within a population, a species, or a "phyletic line." This, says Mayr (p. 400), is the "vertical" and "usually adaptive" component of genetic evolution, or what is often called "microevolution." Guiding this component are a number of processes through which specific genes either increase or decrease in prevalence through time within a given population.

The second or "horizontal" component, called "diversification" or "macroevolution," refers to the multiplication of species and the branching of phyletic lines. Here the focus is on change in species composition within lineages as caused by speciation—that is, the formation of new species—and extinction. Speciation, in turn, may proceed in either of the two ways alluded to in Chapter 1. First, speciation can occur through transformation, the cumulative but slow vertical change within each of two or more newly isolated "sister populations." This kind of change is the phyletic gradualism of Darwin's "Great Tree of Life" (Fig. 1.1, panel A). Second, and more commonly according to some authors (see Eldredge and Gould 1972; Gould 1982b), speciation can occur through abrupt change in initially small, peripheral isolates of a larger parent population. Here we are dealing with the punctuated equilibria model of Fig. 1.1, panel B (the small initial size of peripheral isolates presumably allows their rapid genetic divergence; see Gould 1980a). Either way, Mayr's point is that the theory of genetic evolution should be viewed as a pluralistic theory, one that features patterns and processes of change on at least two levels (see also Vrba and Eldredge 1984).

Accordingly, one could reasonably include both levels of analysis in the study of the "descent with modification" of human hemoglobins. Thus at the macro level one could attempt to analyze the phylogenetic trends among related avian and mammalian hemoglobins. In particular, one could focus on the branching events suggested by the "sudden" appearance of gene duplications in a phyletic line, for example, or by the accumulation of specific, localized changes within single genes (that is, of nucleotide replacements). Studies of this kind show diversification to have been an important component of hemoglobin evolution during the last 500 million years (see, for example, Czelusniak et al. 1982; Jeffreys et al. 1983). However, it is not yet clear how much of that diversification has been punctuational as opposed to gradual. In addition, macrolevel studies establish that hemoglobins do not necessarily change during speciation—for example, the Hb A of human beings and chimpanzees is chemically *identical*—and they imply that important evolutionary changes have also occurred within phyletic lines (for a review of hemoglobin macroevolution, see Dickerson and Geis 1983: ch. 3).

Similarly, one could also attempt a microevolutionary analysis of human hemoglobin, focusing on transformational changes in the molecule within and between populations, all subsequent to the first appearance of our species. Because the subject of concern in this chapter is precisely the interpopulational diversity within our species, I follow such a microevolutionary approach in the sections that follow. Compared to its macro counterpart, this approach also has the advantage of a more advanced quantitative theory, allowing both more rigorous definitions of terms and concepts, and the possibility of quantitative tests of hypotheses. Let us therefore turn to look more closely at the theory and mechanisms of microevolution as they are understood today.

The Conceptual Structure of Microevolutionary Theory

Many of the basic features of microevolutionary theory were alluded to in Chapter 1. There, drawing on Lewontin's conceptualization, we said that evolution could be described as the sequential transformation of a system through time. In principle, therefore, the challenges to any evolutionary theory are, first, to provide an adequate representation of the state of "the system" at any given time; and, second, to provide a satisfactory description of the laws that govern its transformation.

State variables. In genetic microevolutionary theory (also called "genetic microtheory"), the system is generally defined as a population of living organisms delimited in time and space by frequent intermating. Accordingly, the state of this system is represented by two distributions: the distribution of phenotypes in the population (usually defined with respect to some particular trait of interest), and the distribution of genotypes that carry DNA-based instructions for those phenotypes. A hypothetical example of these distributions is shown in Fig. 3.1 for the phenotypes and genotypes associated with sickle-cell anemia. As can be seen in panel A, the phenotypes of sample individuals form three distinct clusters: 0 percent Hb S, 20 to 50 percent Hb S, and 80 to 100 percent Hb S. Although there is some additional within-group variance, each cluster clearly corresponds to a distinct genotype—as can be seen in comparison with panel B, a corresponding example of the distribution of genotypes within a population. The percentage of Hb S is therefore a "genetically

Panel A

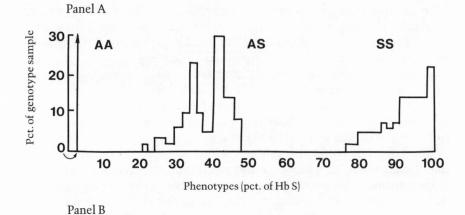

Phenotypes (pct. of Hb S)

Panel B

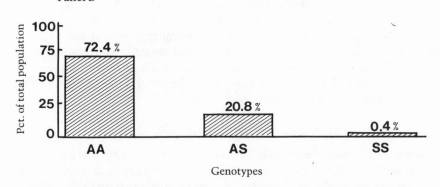

Genotypes

Fig. 3.1. Sample distributions of the phenotypes and genotypes associated with sickle-cell anemia in human populations. Panel A shows the distribution of phenotypes in three distinct samples, one for each of the genotypes AA, AS, and SS. The phenotype scale (X axis) measures the proportion of Hb S in the red blood cells of individuals of a given genotype. The Y axis measures the proportion of individuals within a given genotype sample who have the specified percentage of Hb S (the proportions sum to 100 percent for each genotype). Three distinct phenotypic clusters are visible: a "normal" cluster associated with AA genotypes; a sickle-cell trait cluster associated with AS genotypes; and a sickle-cell anemia cluster associated with SS genotypes. The clear separation of the clusters indicates that genotypic variation explains most of the phenotypic variation contained within these data. Adapted from Allison 1955: 241. Panel B shows the distribution of the three genotypes AA, AS, and SS in a pooled sample of West African populations. Even though 72.4 percent of the sample have the AA genotype, the S allele is still present at one of the world's highest frequencies because of the relatively large proportion of AS individuals. (Another 6.4 percent of the sample, not shown, have genotypes that include the alternative C allele, another variant of the A gene.) Data from Livingstone 1967 and 1973, pooling 29 samples from the yam-cultivating subgroup of Kwa-speakers in West Africa (for details, see App. A.3.2).

variable" phenotypic attribute; in other words, there is clear covariation between the genotypes and phenotypes of this case (for a statistical assessment of this covariation, see Nance and Grove 1972).

In essence, genetic microtheory interrelates, for a given population, changes through time in these two kinds of distributions. On the one hand, a change in the distribution of phenotypes during a given generation (as caused, for example, by their differential survival) can mean a change in the distribution of genotypes during that generation, and thus a change in the genes available to form the genotypes of the next generation. On the other hand, a change between generations in the distribution of genotypes can produce, through the instructional effect of genes upon protein synthesis, a corresponding change in the population's distribution of phenotypes. Indeed, organic microtheory can be described as a genetic theory of evolution for this very reason: for every significant movement in what Lewontin (1974) calls the "phenotype space" of a population, the theory assumes an accompanying, explanatory movement in its "genotype space." Because this one-to-one correspondence is assumed by the theory, many authors in fact define organic evolution to be the sequential transformation of genotype distributions in a population.[9] The point of the theory, though, is to relate phenotypic change across space and time to genotypic change. Again, it is to *interrelate* the two sets of state variables.

Laws of transformation. The task of interrelating these state variables through time in an evolving population is more complex and challenging than it may at first seem. Again, let us follow the lead of Lewontin (1974) and examine what he has called the "structure" of microevolutionary genetics, summarized in Fig. 3.2. If we represent the distribution of genotypes in a population at the start of a given generation *i* as G_i, and similarly the initial distribution of phenotypes as P_i, then the point of genetic microtheory is to interconnect changes in G_i with those in P_i as time and generations pass. This interrelationship, simplified for purposes of presentation, may be said to involve four sets of transformations during the course of each generation:

1. The interaction of the genotypes in G_1 with their environment gives rise to a distribution of phenotypes P_1. Guiding the process $G_1 \rightarrow P_1$ are what Lewontin calls the "epigenetic laws" of transformation, T_1. T_1 continues to influence P_1 throughout the time interval of generation 1. A single arrow represents this transformation for the whole generation because the genotypes of individuals do not change during their lifetimes.

2. During the course of generation 1, the distribution of phenotypes P_1 changes to P_1' (read "P_1 prime") as individuals migrate in or out, enter the effective breeding population or do not, reproduce with variable success, and die. The laws governing this transformation are designated T_2.

3. The genotypes of the individuals in P_1' constitute G_1', a distribution inferred by T_3 or what Lewontin (1974: 13) terms "an immense set of epigenetic relations that allow inferences about the distribution of genotypes corresponding to the distribution of phenotypes."

4. Finally, the fourth transformation maps the set of genotypes G_1' into the array of genotypes G_2 of the next generation. This set of laws, T_4,

[9] For example, Dobzhansky et al. (1977: 9) write that "organic evolution is a series of partial or complete and irreversible transformations of the genetic composition of populations, based principally upon altered interactions with their environment."

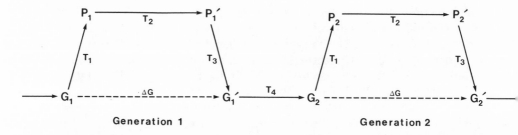

Generation 1   Generation 2

Fig. 3.2. The conceptual structure of genetic microevolutionary theory. A hypothetical population of organisms is represented by two principal "state variables": G_i, representing the distribution of genotypes within the population during generation i, and P_i, representing the corresponding distribution of phenotypes. In genetic microtheory G_i and P_i are interrelated through the laws of transformation, T_1 to T_4, in the course of each generation. The distribution of genotypes at the start of generation 1, G_1, instructs the formation of the initial phenotypes of the population, P_1; P_1 is subsequently transformed to P_1' as organisms differentially survive and mate over the course of the generation; associated with P_1' is a new distribution, G_1', effectively the distribution of genotypes among parents of the next generation; G_1' is transformed through mating and Mendelian principles to G_2, the distribution of genotypes at the start of generation 2. The dotted lines labeled ΔG represent the net genetic change, if any, during a given generation, effectively summarizing the genetic consequences of the laws of transformation, T_1 to T_3. As the diagram makes clear, genetic microevolution occurs within a population when changes in the distribution of phenotypes are related to changes in the distribution of genotypes. Adapted from Lewontin 1974: 14. Copyright © 1974 Columbia University Press. Used by permission.

includes the Mendelian principles governing genetic inheritance (see, for example, Olby 1985).

The new distribution of genotypes, G_2, then provides instructions for a new generation of phenotypes, P_2, and the whole process begins anew. The two distributions, genotype and phenotype, are therefore interrelated by four sets of transformations in each and every generation.

According to the theory, then, *genetic evolution occurs if and only if a change in the genotype distribution, $\Delta G_{1,2}$, accompanies a change in the phenotype distribution, $\Delta P_{1,2}$.* When this condition is met, $\Delta G_{1,2}$ helps to explain $\Delta P_{1,2}$; it may or may not explain all of that change since the environment may also contribute by way of T_1 and T_3 and so might culture (in ways to be described in Chapter 4). But the important consequence is that the distribution of genotypes has changed, and with it the genetic instructions for future generations of phenotypes. In short, the theory of genetic evolution accounts for changes in P_i in terms of changes in G_i.

As we have seen, it appears highly probable that most, if not all, of the variation between populations in the frequency of sickling hemoglobin can be traced to underlying variation in the prevalence of its instructing gene, the S allele. We have also seen that the transformations T_1, T_3, and T_4 are too constant in space and time to account for these differences. Thus, the problem before us can be rephrased as a problem of understanding the differential consequences of the laws of transformation, T_2, as they have operated in different human populations. We must therefore turn our attention to T_2 in order to explain how, with the passing of generations, the distributions of sickling phenotypes in human populations could have been modified in such divergent ways.

Fortunately, because of the constancy of T_1, T_3, and T_4 in this special case, we can take another step toward conceptual simplification of the problem. Essentially, that step is to concatenate the set of transformational laws T_1 to T_4 into one abstract process, a T_0 if you will (the dotted line in Fig. 3.2), that focuses exclusively on evolutionary changes in genotype distributions through time. In other words, we will treat the evolution of phenotypic diversity in this example as if it were a simple matter of explaining the evolution of genotypic diversity. This simplification allows us to draw upon the quantitative microtheory of population genetics.

The Perspective of Population Genetics

As a subfield of evolutionary biology, population genetics focuses on the fate of specific alleles in populations, or on what we can call genefrequency dynamics. The critical assumption, again, is that the evolutionary change of phenotypes in a population is accurately represented as the product of simple change in the frequencies of genes and genotypes. In other words, P_i's are assumed to "descend with modification" as a direct and exclusive consequence of sequential transformations in the distributions G_i. Where this assumption is valid, as in the case of sickle-cell anemia, evolutionary change can be represented by the elegant and precise quantitative formulations developed by population geneticists.[10]

Gene Pools and Gene Frequencies

From this perspective, genetic evolution can be represented schematically as shown in Fig. 3.3. The diagram depicts transformational change through time in the "gene pool" of a hypothetical breeding population (or "deme"), using small circles to represent the genotypes of individual organisms alive at time 1 (left side) and time 2 (right); under the assumption of diploidy there are two alleles per genotype.[11] As can be seen from

[10] Born of the intellectual fusion of Darwin's theory with Mendel's principles of inheritance, population genetics underwent rapid cultural evolution in the early decades of this century (see Provine 1971; Mayr 1982: ch. 12). Leading the way were Ronald A. Fisher (1930), J. B. S. Haldane (1932), and Sewall Wright (1921a, 1933), whose idea it was to study the fate of specific genes, Mendel's "elements" of inheritance, in whole populations of reproducing organisms. Although the early formulations have been justifiably criticized as "beanbag genetics" (Mayr 1976b) for their simplifications, many of their theoretical insights remain central today (see Haldane 1985).

[11] In human populations the boundaries of a deme are often demarcated culturally (as, for example, in the case of the neighboring villages Barkhang and Teya, described in Chapter 2) as well as ecologically and geographically. In many cases, the deme coincides with recognizable ethnolinguistic groupings in an area.

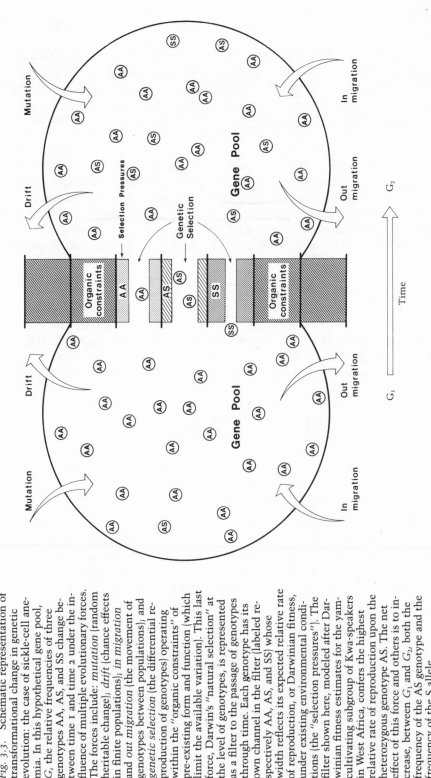

Fig. 3.3. Schematic representation of transformational change in genetic evolution: the case of sickle-cell anemia. In this hypothetical gene pool, *G*, the relative frequencies of three genotypes AA, AS, and SS change between time 1 and time 2 under the influence of multiple evolutionary forces. The forces include: *mutation* (random heritable change); *drift* (chance effects in finite populations); *in migration* and *out migration* (the movement of genotypes between populations); and *genetic selection* (the differential reproduction of genotypes) operating within the "organic constraints" of pre-existing form and function (which limit the available variation). This last force, Darwin's "natural selection" at the level of genotypes, is represented as a filter to the passage of genotypes through time. Each genotype has its own channel in the filter (labeled respectively AA, AS, and SS) whose width reflects its expected relative rate of reproduction, or Darwinian fitness, under existing environmental conditions (the "selection pressures"). The filter shown here, modeled after Darwinian fitness estimates for the yam-cultivating subgroup of Kwa-speakers in West Africa, confers the highest relative rate of reproduction upon the heterozygous genotype AS. The net effect of this force and others is to increase, between *G₁* and *G₂*, both the frequency of the AS genotype and the frequency of the S allele.

the figure, the genetic composition of the population changes substantially, from G_1 at time 1 to G_2 at time 2. In particular, the frequency of the AS genotype has noticeably increased and with it q, the gene frequency of the S allele.[12] Remembering that human populations generally have frequencies of S far lower than that shown for G_1 and that even West Africa's high frequency populations must once have had low frequencies, let us take Fig. 3.3 to represent the special evolutionary change that lies behind the phenotypic diversity of the region. Some populations have remained with frequencies as low as G_1 or lower; others have undergone the transformation to G_2 and have done so, apparently (on the basis of evidence reviewed below) in the last one to two hundred generations. The questions, then, are two: (1) Why has q increased in some populations and not others? and (2) Where changed, why has q increased at such a seemingly high rate? In the terms of the "key questions in evolution" posed in Chapter 1, these are variants of Question 4, the transformation question. A major goal of population genetics is to provide answers to this kind of inquiry.[13]

The Hardy-Weinberg law. With the rediscovery early this century of Gregor Mendel's famous breeding experiments, it became important to know whether or not the simple mechanisms of gene sorting and shuffling during germ cell formation could cause genetic evolution in a population. Was heredity itself a force causing gene-frequency change? Historically, this question proved difficult to answer because of the confounding influence of nonrandom, assortative mating patterns in a given population.

The problem was independently studied and resolved between 1903 and 1908 by no fewer than four authors (see Provine 1971). In essence, all four asked the following question: What will happen through time to gene frequencies in a gene pool where heredity alone is at work? To make the question tractable, they assumed (1) that two co-alleles, like A and S in our example, are present at initial frequencies p and q among both the males and females in the population; (2) that mating is truly random with respect to the alleles in question (and thus that the phenotypic effects of the alleles are subtle, inobvious, or otherwise noninfluential in assortative mating); (3) that Mendel's laws of inheritance are obeyed; and (4) that none of the other, established forces of organic evolution (like natural selection or migration) are in operation. Under these conditions, the investigators noted, the germ cells (or "gametes") of the parent generation

---

[12] Technically speaking, such frequencies should be called "allele frequencies" but convention dictates otherwise.

[13] In fact, after one has made all the assumptions and simplifications needed to get to this level of abstraction, evolution is sometimes *defined* as "any change in gene frequency in a population" (see, for example, Wilson and Bossert 1971: 20; Mettler and Gregg 1969: ch. 3). Although I agree that this is a useful, diagnostic aid within the confines of population genetics, I hasten to remind the reader that (1) not all evolution is genetic, particularly in the human context (see also Chapter 4 on this point), and (2) not all genetic evolution results from simple gene-frequency change within populations; there is also diversification and macroevolution as discussed earlier.

would combine in direct proportion to their frequencies in the population to form the fertilized cells (or "zygotes") of the next generation. More specifically, with p eggs and sperm bearing the A allele and q eggs and sperm bearing S, random mating would create the genotypes of the next generation in the proportions p^2 of AA, $2pq$ of AS, and q^2 of SS, as predicted by the expansion of $(p + q)^2$. But in this next generation, the investigators showed (see App. B for details), the new gene frequencies of A and S would equal p and q respectively, that is, they would be precisely equal to their starting frequencies in the parents' generation. In other words, the calculations showed that heredity itself does not produce changes in gene frequency and therefore does not cause genetic evolution. This principle has come to be known as the Hardy-Weinberg law, after two of its authors.[14] A gene pool under these conditions would remain in a gene-frequency equilibrium through time—the so-called Hardy-Weinberg equilibrium—unless and until other forces intervened. In short, the answer to our question of why the S allele has increased over time cannot be found in the mechanics of genetic transmission.[15]

Candidate forces of gene-frequency change. The logical place to look for evolutionary forces is in the set of conditions that could disrupt a gene pool from Hardy-Weinberg equilibrium. Among the more salient possibilities would be forces causing an alteration of zygotes from their initial chance frequencies of p^2, $2pq$, and q^2. Over the years, population geneticists have identified four major candidates, each shown schematically in Fig. 3.3.

One of these forces is mutation, that is, random heritable change in the chemical code of DNA molecules. Generations of biochemical change converting the A allele to the S form could conceivably lie behind some of the increase in S that we believe has taken place in the last one or two hundred generations. However, mutation cannot provide a complete explanation for two reasons. First, mutation rates are normally quite low, on the order of 10^{-5} or 10^{-6} mutations per egg or sperm per generation, and this is far too low to explain the emergence of a frequency like 10^{-1} (or 0.1) in the case of the S allele. Second, for many genes (including the A and S alleles), "back mutations" may also occur. This means that for every so many conversions of A to S there is another number, though smaller, of reverse conversions of S to A. While mutation is certainly a potential source of evolutionary change in populations, it cannot account for the successful genetic history of the S allele.

Migration to or from other populations, or what is sometimes called "gene flow," is another potential force of genetic evolution. The idea here

[14] It should be emphasized that the Hardy-Weinberg law is *not* "the law that $p^2 + 2pq + q^2 = 1.0$," as is so often claimed. That equation holds true *whenever* $p + q = 1.0$, regardless of whether or not the observed genotype frequencies occur in the proportions p^2 of AA, $2pq$ of AS, and q^2 of SS, which is the true concern of the law.

[15] Although the mechanisms of genetic transmission cannot themselves cause evolutionary change, this is not true of cultural transmission, as we will see in Chapter 4.

is that the S allele could potentially increase in frequency over time in a given gene pool as a consequence of the arrival of S-carrying migrants from other regions and populations. Unfortunately, as Livingstone noted, migration is also not sufficient to explain evolutionary change in this context. It simply begs the questions of how S got to such substantial frequencies in those other places, and why so many S carriers migrated away.

A third candidate force is "genetic drift," sometimes also called "sampling error." This force arises from the chance events of gene transmission in finite populations, particularly in small populations in which random change can have a big impact. Although genetic drift cannot be completely ruled out as a contributory cause of high S frequencies in West Africa, it is unlikely to be a major part of the explanation because of three considerations. First, the size and territorial expanse of some high-frequency populations today suggest that at least a number of them have been relatively large for many years, large enough for chance events to have played only a minor role. Second, chance events would have to have been of tremendous magnitude to counter the systematic loss of S alleles at each generation owing to the generally lethal consequences of sickle-cell anemia. Finally, one can turn the probability argument around by noting how unlikely it is for the effects of chance to produce high S frequencies in so many populations at once and over such a broad geographical area. The very fact that Livingstone was able to point to patterns in the world distribution of S calls into question any explanation on the basis of drift alone.

The fourth candidate force, natural selection (already discussed briefly in Chapter 1), has the most intuitive appeal for explaining our sample case of genetic diversity. Proposed by Darwin as the "predominant Power" (1964 [1859]: 43) in organic evolution, this is the force that arises in a given environment from the reproductive advantages of "favourable variations" and the reproductive disadvantages of "injurious variations."[16] (p. 81.) Given the clearly injurious phenotypic effects of the SS genotype, it seems very likely that natural selection has somehow been involved in the historical emergence of S-frequency diversity. The question is, How?

[16] In *On the Origin of Species*, when (as in 1964 [1859]: 81) Darwin defined natural selection in terms of the preservation and rejection of variants, it was clearly preservation *by reproductive advantage* that he had in mind. This can be seen, for example, in his emphasis on biological descent and descendants, in his attention to the "doctrine of Malthus" and the "struggle for existence," and in his insightful anticipation of the concept of evolutionary fitness, which he described (p. 62) as "success in leaving progeny." In this and later chapters, I therefore use the term "natural selection" only where preservation is a consequence of actual reproductive advantage. It should be noted, however, that in a later publication, *The Descent of Man and Selection in Relation to Sex*, Darwin generalized the concept of natural selection to include preservation through differential social transmission. Most notably, he praised a remark by the linguist Max Müller that, in the "struggle for life" among a language's words and grammatical forms, "the survival or preservation of certain favored words . . . is natural selection." (1981 [1871]: 61.) While, as I shall argue in later chapters, there are

Evolution by Genetic Selection

For reasons described in Chapter 1, I use the term "genetic selection" to refer to natural selection at the level of genotypes. This definition nicely captures the spirit of Darwin's concern with the procreative differential of what he called "variations," and it has the advantage of greater rigor and clarity. It ties the concept of reproductive advantage directly to genotypes, paving the way for the elucidation of genetic laws of transformation.

The basic idea of genetic selection is shown schematically in Fig. 3.3 (p. 116). Prevailing environmental conditions are represented as a kind of filter through which alternative genotypes must pass. The number of alternative genotypes—here three are shown, namely, AA, AS, and SS—as well as the nature and magnitude of their phenotypic effects, are all limited by "organic constraints" inherent in the genetics and development of the organism (on which see Mayo 1983; Maynard Smith et al. 1985). Within these constraints, each available genotype has its own filter channel as shown, an opening whose size reflects the relative reproductive success of that genotype. A genotype that is relatively successful in surmounting such environmental selection pressures as competition, disease, and climatic conditions—what Darwin (1964 [1859]: 70) called nature's "limiting checks"—will pass through the filter with relative ease, increasing its representation in the gene pool of future generations; it will be "selected for." By analogy with the decision-making processes explored in Chapter 2, this, too, can be seen as a kind of "choice," only here "nature" does the choosing among variants—and does so on the basis of their actual reproductive performance. As a logical consequence, the alleles comprising the "chosen" or positively selected genotypes will tend to increase in frequency, at least until some new form of equilibrium is reached. The result, therefore, is that genetic selection operating through different pressures in different environments is fully capable of creating—and maintaining—substantial gene-frequency differences between populations. The question before us, then, is this: Could genetic selection have created the patterns of S-frequency diversity that we find among contemporary human populations? More specifically, What environmental selection pressures would have favored relatively high frequencies of S? Could variations in the severity of these pressures account for the patterns we observe today in the prevalence of S?

Genetic selection against recessive homozygotes. Let us begin with a look at the population genetics of natural selection in perhaps its simplest context, the case of selection against recessive homozygotes like SS. Here we are interested to know what would be the fate of the S allele in human populations were sickle-cell anemia the sole source of differ-

clear parallels between the two processes, important disanalogies between genes and culture, plus the need for unambiguous labels, argue against this generalization.

Panel A

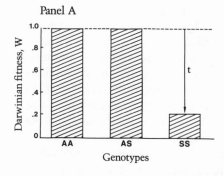

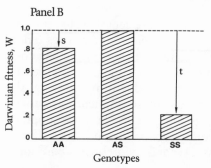

Fig. 3.4. Fitness diagrams representing genetic selection among the three human genotypes AA, AS, and SS. In both panels, the *Y* axis measures *W*, the Darwinian fitness, or relative reproductive ability, of the three genotypes arrayed along the *X* axis. Panel A represents a hypothetical case of selection against the homozygote recessive genotype. Here the Darwinian fitnesses of genotypes AA and AS are assumed to be 1.0 in contrast to that of the victims of sickle-cell anemia, which is shown to be about 0.20. The selection coefficient *t*, which measures the magnitude of the selection pressure against SS, is therefore 0.80. Panel B represents a hypothetical case of selection against both homozygotes, AA and SS. The heterozygote has the highest relative fitness because of the operation of two selection pressures in the deme, one against each homozygote. The selection coefficient *s*, which measures the selection pressure against AA, is shown with a value of 0.20, and the corresponding coefficient *t* for the SS genotype is shown with a value of 0.80.

ential reproduction among the AA, AS, and SS genotypes. As noted above, the intuitive prediction is that the S allele should then be ubiquitously rare. Population genetics gives us the opportunity both to check and to quantify that intuition.

Consider a hypothetical human gene pool containing at least a few individuals of all three genotypes. If we assumed for the moment that the anemia of SS individuals is the exclusive source of differential reproduction in that gene pool, then the "Darwinian fitnesses" of the three genotypes (that is, their expected relative rates of reproduction during a given generation) would be as shown in panel A of Fig. 3.4.[17] The Darwinian fitness of AA, often designated W_{AA}, would be 1.0, as would that of AS. In contrast, the fitness of the SS genotype would, as discussed above, be much less than this in all known environments; indeed, it would be virtually 0.0 in many areas. With these values in mind we can now ask, What would be the fate of the S allele in a hypothetical population subject to this form of genetic selection?

The answer constitutes one of the laws of evolutionary transformation

[17] The "Darwinian fitness" of a genotype, conventionally designated *W* (after the geneticist Sewall Wright), can be measured by its relative change of frequency in a gene pool during one generation's worth of genetic selection. Thus W_{AA} for the genotype AA, for example, can be estimated from the ratio: (AA's frequency in generation *i* after selection)/ (AA's frequency in generation *i* before selection). By convention, the genotype with the highest such ratio is assigned the fitness value of 1.0 and the ratios of the other genotypes are scaled proportionately on a scale of 0.0 to 1.0 (negative Darwinian fitness is not possible

derived from population genetics, a law best described by a so-called Δq (read "delta q") equation. As explained in App. B, Δq equations express the change in the frequency of a recessive allele like S during a single generation of genetic selection. Here the appropriate Δq equation (namely, Eq. B.4b of App. B) states that under the action of sickle-cell anemia alone, the S allele will always *decrease* in frequency, no matter what its initial value. It also states that the higher the starting frequency of S, the steeper its initial rate of reduction and that even then, in theory, it takes an infinite number of generations of selection for S frequency to be reduced all the way to zero. It follows that selection against homozygote recessives simply cannot account for the evolutionary increases in S frequency that we seek to explain.

This finding clearly confirms one's intuition: Were genetic selection to proceed through sickle-cell anemia alone, the S allele would always tend to decrease in frequency through time. The reduced fitness of the SS genotype cannot possibly be the only reason for the evolutionary increase in the frequencies of the S allele to levels observed today in many tropical populations. When, in the course of the 1940's, these implications came to be fully appreciated, researchers began to look for one or more supplementary selection pressures that could counteract or "balance" the effect of the anemia. Behind this reasoning was a second theoretical prediction from population genetics, as follows.

Genetic selection against both homozygotes. A slightly more complicated form of genetic selection occurs in the hypothetical situation of two selection pressures, one operating on each of the two homozygous genotypes. This situation, shown graphically in panel B of Fig. 3.4, leads (as one would expect) to a new, slightly more complicated Δq equation (namely, Eq. B.5a in App. B), one that predicts a more variable fate for the S allele. For high initial frequencies of S, this equation predicts negative values for Δq and thus decreases in S frequency, much as in the previous case of selection against recessive homozygotes. But for low initial frequencies of S, the equation predicts that Δq can be positive, suggesting evolutionary increase, albeit slow, in the frequency of the S allele. The implication is an important one: even when sickle-cell anemia is assumed to be lethal to victims in their prereproductive years, S frequency can increase through time from low initial values because of the balancing effect of selection against the AA genotype. In other words, the combined action of the two selection pressures could, in theory, account for elevated frequencies of S in particular human gene pools.

In addition, the more complex Δq equation implies the existence of a new gene-frequency equilibrium in gene pools affected by these balancing pressures. Whether S frequency begins at a high level and subsequently decreases, or begins at a low level and subsequently increases, the rates of

---

as we use it here). Note again that W is a *relative* measure; it corresponds to the expected relative rate of reproduction of a given genotype in a given environment.

evolutionary change, provided that the two selection pressures remain constant, will eventually level off to zero and leave S at the same intermediate frequency, a number often called $\hat{q}$ (read "q hat"). Because this is a new equilibrium—known as a "selectional equilibrium" to distinguish it from the Hardy-Weinberg equilibrium discussed earlier—S will remain at $\hat{q}$ until one of the balancing selection pressures changes or some new source of differential reproduction emerges. Indeed, it can be shown that the magnitude of $\hat{q}$ is given by a special ratio formula of the selection pressures operating against the two recessive homozygotes (see Eq. B.5b in App. B).

Thus, in the case of genetic selection against both homozygotes, we do have an evolutionary transformation that is capable of generating an increase in the frequency of the S allele. The condition required for this transformation is, again, that the heterozygote be the genotype of highest Darwinian fitness. This condition, called "overdominance" or "heterozygote advantage," means that neither allele can completely eliminate the other from the gene pool; the fittest genotype requires both alleles at once. Both, therefore, will persist at frequencies greater than could be expected by mutation alone. Following Darwin's reference to "polymorphic species," E. B. Ford (1940) termed this situation a "polymorphism." If and when a selectional equilibrium of this type is reached, both alleles will persist in what is called a "balanced polymorphism." In conclusion, this body of theory indicates that a pair of simultaneous selection pressures could well explain the evolution of the substantial S frequencies we observe today in many parts of the world. The two remaining questions are then, What causes the selection pressure against AA—the kind of pressure labeled s in panel B of Fig. 3.4—to which AS is relatively immune? and, Does this selection pressure actually explain the existing gene-frequency variation of the S allele in contemporary West African populations? Let us take up each of these remaining questions in turn.

The Malaria Hypothesis

Among the first to propose a balancing selection pressure to explain hemoglobin polymorphisms was the geneticist J. B. S. Haldane. In the course of a brief discussion of another hemoglobin disorder, alpha thalassemia (or "thalassemia major"), he pointed out that an unusually high mutation rate would be required for mutation alone to explain the frequencies of the disorder observed in some Mediterranean populations. For example, if the heterozygote for the thalassemia gene

had normal viability, equilibrium would be secured by a mutation rate of 4×10^{-4}. On the other hand if the heterozygote had an increased fitness of only 2.1% there would be equilibrium without any mutation at all. . . . I [therefore] believe that the possibility that the heterozygote is fitter than the normal must be seriously considered. . . . It is at least conceivable that [the erythrocytes of thalassemia het-erozygotes are] more resistant to attacks by the sporozoa which cause malaria, a disease prevalent in Italy, Sicily, and Greece, where the gene is frequent. [1948: 270–71]

This suggestion, now called the "malaria hypothesis," was soon gener-alized to sickle-cell disease and other hemoglobinopathies. In essence, it proposes that interpopulational differences in the frequency of S (and other variant hemoglobin genes) are the product of genetic selection through the agency of malaria. More specifically, it holds that one or more forms of malaria within a population, particularly the virulent species *Plasmodium falciparum*, can create substantial reproductive differentials between resistant and nonresistant genotypes.[18] If S (or some other allele) confers a measure of resistance upon heterozygotes, then these reproduc-tive differentials can increase, within limits, the frequency of that allele. The predicted result is that the nonzero frequencies of S will covary with the severity of endemic malaria.

Unbeknownst to Haldane in 1948, there was already some evidence in support of the argument from an analysis by E. A. Beet (1946), an officer of the British Colonial Medical Service who examined the frequencies of sickle-cell trait among the Lunda and Lovale peoples of southern Africa. Unfortunately, Beet failed to pursue the evolutionary implications of his findings. Eight years later, however, A. C. Allison offered both experi-mental and geographic evidence that "the severity of malaria is a very im-portant factor in determining the frequency of the sickle-cell trait." (1954b: 316.) In the years since 1954, evidence of four kinds has continued to accumulate in support of the malaria hypothesis.[19] The first comes from further analysis of geographical correlations between the distri-butions of *P. falciparum* malaria and the frequency of the S allele. A num-ber of authors have compiled regional or even world-level comparisons with striking results (Motulsky 1960; Allison 1961a, 1961b; Bodmer and Cavalli-Sforza 1976: 310–11). But even better support has come from de-tailed "micro-geographic" analyses. Studies in Ghana (Ringelhann et al. 1976), Togo (Bienzle et al. 1972), and Greece (Stamatoyannopoulos and Fessas 1964), among others, have found close, local-level correlations be-tween malarial infection rates and the prevalence of sickle-cell trait, a correlation specifically predicted by the malaria hypothesis.

[18] *Plasmodium falciparum* is the most virulent of four distinct species of single-celled protozoans known to cause malaria in human populations; the others are *P. malariae*, *P. ovale*, and *P. vivax*. Each is transmitted between human hosts by the bites of females of at least one vector species of mosquito. On the biology of malaria and its vectors, see Hackett 1937; Boyd 1949a, b, c; Holstein 1954; Colbourne 1966; Kreier 1980; and Bruce-Chwatt 1980, 1987. For a nontechnical, historical account see G. Harrison 1978. On the economic and social effects of malaria, see J. May 1958 and references in Sotiroff-Junker 1978.

[19] In contrast, conclusive evidence remains elusive for many of the other hemoglobino-pathy genes such as C, D, E, and G-6-P-D–deficiency (see, for example, reviews in World Health Organization 1966; Miller and Carter 1976; Luzzatto 1979; Vogel and Motulsky 1979; Livingstone 1971, 1983).

A second line of evidence comes from what may be called agricultural correlations as predicted by Livingstone (1958). His argument was based upon the observation that *Anopheles gambiae*, the principal mosquito vector of *P. falciparum*, requires warm, sunlit ponds of fresh water for its reproduction. But such a habitat, Livingstone noted, is normally quite rare in dense-canopy tropical forests, an environment otherwise ideally suited for malarial transmission. On these grounds Livingstone argued that "it is only when man cuts down the forest that breeding places for *A. gambiae* become almost infinite" (p. 554); and that therefore, in many locations, "the spread of [slash-and-burn] agriculture is responsible for the spread of the selective advantage of the sickle-cell gene, and hence for the spread of the gene itself." (p. 555.) This argument, which can be called the Livingstone hypothesis, predicted strong correlations between the genetic and cultural evolution of human populations in this specific case, with the causal arrow leading from agricultural change to changes in gene frequencies.[20] Accordingly, Livingstone was able to document that the "clines," or gradients, of S frequency in West Africa closely correspond to geographical patterns in the spread of yam-based agriculture in the south and of rice-based agriculture in the east. His support for the malaria hypothesis was later reconfirmed by Stephen L. Wiesenfeld (1967) in a study showing a correlation between the prevalence of S in African populations and the degree of their dependence on agriculture for subsistence.[21]

A third kind of support for the malaria hypothesis has come from epidemiological analysis in populations still exposed to recurrent malaria (see reviews in Livingstone 1971, 1983). One of the most thorough of such studies was the six-year Garki Project, named after Garki District of Kano State, Nigeria, an area of Sudan savannah where the study was conducted

[20] More specifically, Livingstone's argument suggested that culture modified the selection pressures acting among human genotypes—a relationship that I call cultural mediation (see Durham 1982 and Chapters 4 and 5 of this book). Now called "a classic in human population genetics" and "the first clear and detailed example of the close association between culture, biology, and the disease process" (Johnston and Low 1984: 224), Livingstone's 1958 paper is appropriately seen today as a pioneering effort in evolutionary anthropology.

[21] Wiesenfeld's argument proposed a ratchet-like feedback effect betwen genetic and cultural change, so that "where a socioeconomic adaptation causes a change in the environment, the frequency of a gene will change in proportion to the survival value the gene confers on the carriers in the new ecosystem. . . . The gene frequency and the socioeconomic adaptation continue to develop in a stepwise fashion until either the limit of the gene frequency or the limit of the socioeconomic adaptation is reached." (1967: 1137.) Although a provocative hypothesis, the whole notion that "malaria blocks development" has been seriously challenged in more recent analyses, such as Brown 1979. Moreover, I was unable, using the West Africa sample described below, to duplicate Wiesenfeld's correlation between agricultural dependence (as coded in Murdock 1967) and the S allele. I did obtain a significant positive correlation (vaguely resembling his fig. 1), but only when I plotted data for the forest-dwelling yam cultivators of the south together with data for the Fulani herders of the northern Sudan savannah on the same plot. To do that, however, is to compound dramatic differences of climate and ecology with the key variable, dependence on agriculture. Unfortunately, Wiesenfeld did not identify the "60 communities" of his study except to say (p. 1135) that they were drawn from "east and west Africa."

(Molineaux and Gramiccia 1980; see also Molineaux et al. 1979; Cornille-Brøgger et al. 1979). The study compared blood samples from children of AA and AS genotypes and found both lower frequencies and lower densities of *P. falciparum* parasites in the latter, particularly in the dry season. In addition, although AS and AA genotypes did not differ in fertility, 29 percent more of the AS genotypes survived, presumably because they were more resistant to malaria. Although studies in other areas have sometimes failed to find correlations between human genotypes and rates of malarial infection or mortality, the great majority of epidemiological surveys do point to some degree of malarial protection associated with the AS genotype.

Biochemical studies have contributed the fourth category of supporting evidence. Researchers in this area have established, first, that AS erythrocytes, which normally do not sickle under physiological conditions, do show a dramatic sickling propensity when infected by malarial protozoans (Luzzatto et al. 1970; Roth et al. 1978). Second, studies by Milton J. Friedman and his colleagues (see especially Friedman 1978; Friedman and Trager 1981) have shown that the sickling process itself causes a loss of intracellular micronutrients, especially potassium, and eventually the death of the parasite inside AS cells. Because AA cells are incapable of sickling, this biochemical defense mechanism is a special adaptive advantage of the AS genotype.

Taken together, these studies constitute reasonably strong support for the malaria hypothesis. However, it is still true that, as the geneticist Arno G. Motulsky noted (1975: 279), "there is no single set of data which is convincing by itself." Moreover, most of the evidence is indirect with respect to gene frequencies. There remain few, if any, direct tests of the malaria hypothesis since Allison's—tests that would specifically measure the proportion of interpopulational variance in the frequency of S (symbolized, it will be remembered, by q) that is explained by differences in the severity of malaria.[22] As originally articulated by Allison (1954b: 314),

[22] The study by Hiernaux and Froment (1976) stands out as one exception. They included statistics for S frequencies among their "coefficients of correlation between 5 climatic variables and 31 anthropobiological variables," calculated for 219 populations of sub–Saharan Africa. Because (as we shall see) malarial transmission is strongly affected by weather, the authors say (p. 764) "there is little doubt that these correlations [with S frequency] are the product of the selective power of falciparum malaria," as is shown by the following table (p. 759).

Variable correlated with S frequency	r	r^2
Mean annual rainfall	+.20	.04
Mean humidity mixing ratio of wettest month	+.14	.02
Mean humidity mixing ratio of driest month	+.19	.04
Mean maximum temperature of hottest month	−.01[a]	.00
Mean minimum temperature of coldest month	+.23	.05

[a]Insignificant at 0.05 level.

the hypothesis specifically proposes that the "proportion of individuals of sickle-cell trait in any population, then, would be the result of a balance between two factors: the severity of malarial infection, which would tend to increase the frequency of the gene, and the rate of elimination of sickle-cell genes in persons dying of sickle-cell anemia."[23]

Designing a Test of the Malaria Hypothesis

Motivated by the lack of direct tests despite the accumulation of almost 30 years of genetic data, I undertook a statistical assessment of Allison's hypothesis. Because of the demanding nature of the task of data collation, I decided early on to focus the effort on a single geographical area, and chose West Africa for a number of compelling reasons. First, its great ethnolinguistic diversity provides an appropriately large number of demes within a single, well-defined geographical area. Second, the region has been relatively well studied by ethnographers, linguists, geographers, and historians. The work of linguists, for example, particularly my colleague Joseph H. Greenberg (1966a), indicates that the populations of the region can be divided into three major language groups, Congo-Kordofanian, Nilo-Saharan, and Afroasiatic, and further subdivided into linguistic families and subfamilies as shown in Fig. 3.5. Because the S allele was almost certainly introduced into West Africa after these linguistic groups began to diverge (Livingstone 1958: 544), one may attempt multiple tests of the malaria hypothesis in the different linguistic stocks of the region. Third, studies of agricultural production in the region point to the existence of three sharply delineated agricultural zones in West Africa, each with a fairly distinctive climate and ecology: the yam zone, the rice zone, and the sorghum-and-millet zone, as shown in Fig. 3.6. Fourth, *P. falciparum* and the group of vectors commonly referred to as *A. gam-*

But, as we can see from the low r^2 figures, surprisingly little of the variance in q was explained by these climatic variables. Indeed the proportions were still lower when the sample was reduced to those 194 populations with nonzero S frequencies. The crude scale of the weather maps, source of the data for the independent variables, was no doubt partly responsible for the low correlations.

[23] As stated by Allison and others, the malaria hypothesis assumes that the heterozygote advantage of the AS genotype derives simply from its resistance to malarial infection. However, the Ghanaian physician Felix Konotey-Ahulu (1970, 1973) points out that some AS males in a population will have additional motivation to marry polygynously when their first wives are also of the AS genotype and some of their offspring are SS's and die young (a one-in-four probability for each pregnancy); "one of the reasons that Africans acquire more wives," he added, "is the death of children born to the first wife." (1973: 36.) A higher frequency of polygyny among AS males could indeed enhance their fitness above and beyond any malarial advantage. By the same logic, however, one would think that childhood deaths from malaria, too, might motivate males to seek additional wives. In that event, though, males of the AA genotype would statistically have the greater motivation, because children of AS males would be more likely to have malarial resistance and thus to survive. Ironically, this force would counter the one proposed by Konotey-Ahulu. Clearly his proposal deserves further study and modeling, but for present purposes it can be viewed as a source of additional, unexplained variation in the data analyzed here.

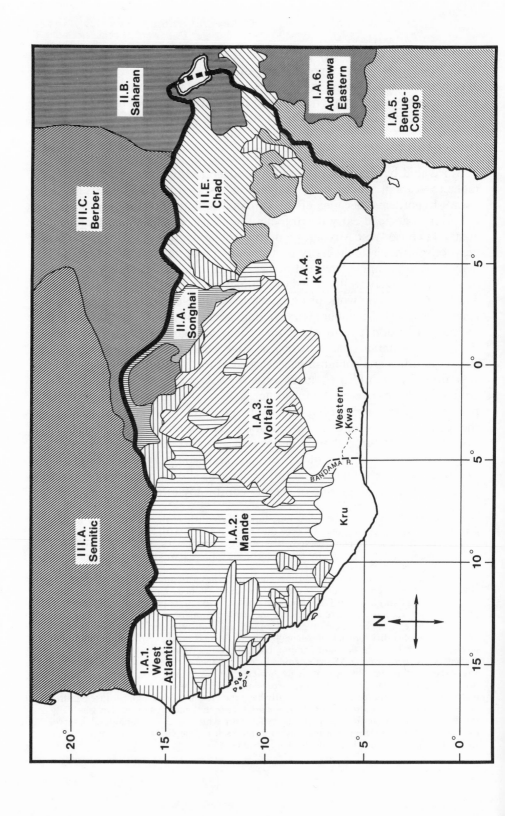

biae are both widely distributed across the landscape of West Africa. Another malarial parasite, *P. malariae*, and its primary vector, *A. funestus*, also occur widely throughout West Africa, although the amount of information about them is considerably less than for the previous pair. These ranges allow for broad comparative study and for the elucidation of key variables at work in the genetic differentiation of the region. Fifth, as we shall see, the data on major hemoglobinopathies in West Africa are excellent by comparative standards; in fact, they embrace nearly the full world range of frequencies of the sickle-cell gene.

Finally, a direct test of the malaria hypothesis in West Africa seemed particularly appropriate since many of the best indirect assessments of that hypothesis have been conducted in the region. Of particular value in this respect have been Livingstone's detailed analyses including the 1958 paper discussed in several earlier sections. It was Livingstone who, in that paper, first emphasized the importance of comparative study of gene frequencies among the diverse language groups of the region and who first pointed out the importance of migration and gene flow as contributors to the regional diversity of q (Livingstone 1958).[24] West Africa, then, was the obvious choice. Ably assisted by a team of dedicated Stanford students, graduate and undergraduate (J.G., P.I., E.L., T.S., and R.W.), I was then challenged to design a tractable test of the hypothesis and to assemble and collate the requisite data. The first step was to formulate specific, testable predictions that follow from the principles of population genetics discussed earlier.

[24] Livingstone (1969a, 1976) has had considerable success in replicating some major gene-frequency clines of West Africa using computer-based simulations of gene flow. The simulations chart the "advancing wave" of S frequency as the gene arrives via migration and "inoculates" new demes at greater and greater distance from an ancestral homeland. Although these models demonstrate very clearly that time and migration can be important factors in the evolution of human genetic diversity, their value is limited, in my view, by the unrealistic assumption that the same set of fitness values applies to all climates and habitats along the simulated transects. Diversity is thus attributed to gene flow alone; in contrast to the arguments of his earlier work (see, for instance, 1958: 541), no allowance is made for variation in the intensity of selection. Given dramatic intraregional differences in rainfall, drainage, and cropping patterns (see the maps in, for example, Morgan and Pugh 1969), it is reasonable to ask not only what migration and gene flow but also what genetic selection contributes to genetic diversity in West Africa.

Fig. 3.5 (opposite). The distribution of language groups in West Africa. Roman numerals designate major linguistic divisions: I. Congo-Kordofanian; II. Nilo-Saharan; III. Afroasiatic. These are subdivided into families, represented by capital letters, such as: I.A. Niger-Congo; II.A. Songhai; II.B. Saharan; III.E. Chad. The families are further subdivided into subfamilies, represented by Arabic numerals, such as I.A.1 West Atlantic; I.A.2 Mande; and I.A.3 Voltaic. Unnamed language areas, which appear here as "islands," have been shaded according to their family or subfamily; two unnumbered subgroups of languages of the subfamily Kwa are shown, the Kru (west of the Bandama River; but see note 27) and the "Western Kwa" (in the delta region of the Bandama River). This linguistic diversity provides multiple opportunities for testing the malaria hypothesis in greater West Africa (the area bounded by the heavy black line). Adapted by permission of the publisher from Durham 1983a: 48. Copyright 1983 by Elsevier Science Publishing Co., Inc.

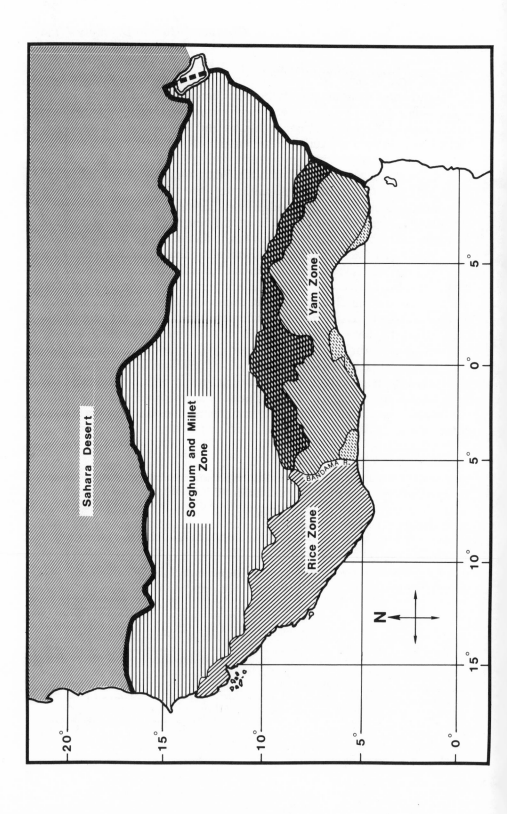

Predictions from Population Genetics

There is one unfortunate parallel between the cultural evolutionary analysis of Chapter 2 and the genetic evolutionary analysis here before us: in both cases, detailed data on the history of stasis or change in key variables are simply unavailable. In other words, there is again no "fossil record" of the changes that one assumes took place as S evolved to higher and higher frequencies in particular West African populations. Whereas I attempted to work around this problem in the last chapter by using a computer simulation, here I have little choice but to resort to synchronic comparisons—that is, to comparisons between populations at one point in time—and to the match between predicted values, which assume a certain evolutionary history of change, and contemporary observed values.

Using this strategy, then, and Allison's formulation of the malaria hypothesis, the frequency, q, of the S allele is expected to be a function of three key variables: (1) the "selection coefficient," s, which measures the magnitude of malarial selection against the unprotected AA genotype as compared to the reproductive fitness of AS (see Fig. 3.4, panel B); (2) a second selection coefficient, t, which measures the Darwinian fitness reduction caused by sickle-cell anemia in the SS genotype as also compared with the AS genotype; and (3) the time, T, that these selection pressures have had to operate within a given gene pool. If we use the selectional equilibrium model, as already discussed in the section on population genetics, these three variables can be combined to form an expected distributional pattern for the gene frequencies of S.

Consider, first, the predicted relationship if T were very large and uniform among a sample of distinct West African populations. Let us further assume that the selection coefficients s and t have been relatively constant through time within each population of this sample, but that they have also been widely variable between populations as some groups were exposed, for example, to higher rates of malarial mortality. Under these conditions, the q values of the various populations would have evolved to levels approaching those of the corresponding selectional equilibria, $\hat{q}$, in accordance with Eq. B.5b. A range of $\hat{q}$ values of this kind is shown by

Fig. 3.6 (opposite).   The major agricultural zones of West Africa. The "primary yam zone" (shaded diagonally from top right) represents the area in which *Dioscorea* yams have been the major staple of human diet since the advent of agriculture in the region. Just to the north of this zone, extending to approximately 10 degrees north latitude, is the "secondary yam zone" (crossed shading), encompassing areas where yams are an important but secondary food crop. To the south of the primary yam zone are three small pockets of land (dashed shading) that are either too dry, as is the center one, or too wet for yam cultivation. The rice zone (diagonal shading from top left) begins abruptly at the Bandama River of Ivory Coast and extends up the west coast of the region into Senegal. Sorghum and millet are the principal staples across the broad band of Sahel savannah to the north (horizontal shading). Redrawn by permission of the publisher from Durham 1983a: 49. Copyright 1983 by Elsevier Science Publishing Co., Inc.

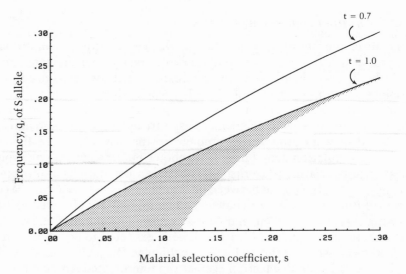

Fig. 3.7. The expected distributional pattern of S allele frequencies (shaded) in a sample of populations subject simultaneously to genetic selection and gene flow. The curves labeled $t = 0.7$ and $t = 1.0$ represent theoretical equilibrium frequencies of S ($\hat{q}$ values) that vary as a function of the selection coefficients s and t, which are defined as in Fig. 3.4. Because s values may vary within populations through time, and also the lapsed time under genetic selection may vary between populations, actual present-day frequencies of S are expected to deviate from these curves in a pattern resembling the shaded portion of the figure. For the sake of simplicity, only one shaded distribution is shown, that corresponding to a fixed t of 1.0. In principle, however, the t values within populations may also vary through time to as low as $t = 0.7$. In that event, the expected distribution of S frequencies would expand to include the full area between the two curves. Based on Eq. B.5b. Redrawn by permission of the publisher from Durham 1983a: 52. Copyright 1983 by Elsevier Science Publishing Co., Inc.

curved lines in Fig. 3.7. In the figure, s ranges from 0.0 to 0.30 (a function of the severity of malarial infection and the level of immunity in a population), while t has sample values of 1.0 or 0.7 (fitness estimates of the SS genotype in West Africa rarely exceed 0.30).[25] It must be emphasized that values of q on or near these lines are expected only after many generations of selection at constant s and t. So, for example, Luigi L. Cavalli-Sforza and Walter F. Bodmer (1971: 139) show that a T of 60 generations is adequate for the frequency of S to increase in a hypothetical population from the low initial value, $q_0 = 0.00001$, to selectional equilibrium at $\hat{q} = 0.23$ when $s = 0.20$ and $t = 0.67$. A T of only 40 generations is required, they indicate, to reach an even higher $\hat{q}$ of 0.31 when s is instead 0.30.

In the actual context of West African history, however, the three key variables are difficult to estimate with any precision. This is particularly true of the variable T. From the uneven distribution of the S allele among Bantu-speaking populations (who are closely related by descent to the

[25] Sample W_{SS} values from the literature on West Africa include 0.208 (Allison 1955: 251), 0.20 ± 0.11 (Cavalli-Sforza and Bodmer 1971: 163), and 0.225 (calculated from Fleming et al. 1979: 165).

Kwa), Livingstone (1976: 497) has argued that S would have attained polymorphic proportions only after the Bantu migration was under way, an event that probably began some two to three thousand years or roughly one to two hundred generations ago (see Phillipson 1975). The argument is further substantiated by recent biochemical analyses of chromosome segments from different regions of Africa, each containing the S allele (see, for instance, Pagnier et al. 1983, 1984). The molecular differences found in these studies indicate that the S allele of central and southern African populations is not of West African origin but is, instead, an independent "Bantu mutation" of the A allele. For that matter, they also indicate that the S allele of populations along the Atlantic seacoast of West Africa is yet a third independent mutation (see Livingstone 1989, however, for a different interpretation). But even with this information, we can still only estimate an approximate upper limit to T for central West Africa, a limit of about one to two hundred generations. Sadly, the same kind of uncertainty characterizes our knowledge of s and t as well. There has been no systematic study of the way in which s varies from place to place in West Africa. In most studies, t is simply assumed to be 1.0.

Any test of the malaria hypothesis in West Africa must therefore begin with a modified version of the selectional equilibrium model—one that sacrifices the formal precision of population genetics for a gain in realism and generality (another example of the "modeler's dilemma," as in Levins 1966). What we can reasonably expect of the data, in other words, is not a close match to the actual isoclines of Fig. 3.7, but a broader distribution of gene frequencies resembling the shaded portion of the figure. That portion represents an approximate expected distribution of S frequencies for West African samples under two assumptions: that the lapsed time under selection, T, varies between demes; and that the selection coefficient due to malaria, s, varies over time but generally in the upward direction. It also reflects the fact that the number of generations required to reach equilibrium decreases as s increases. Thus, after a given interval of time under selection, more variation in q is expected at the lower end of the s scale compared to the upper end.

The overall width of the expected distribution or "shadow" will also vary, generally increasing with the range of T values (selection intervals) among sample populations. In other words, the effect of gene flow and the relatively uneven arrival time of the S allele in a sample of populations will show up here as greater variance in the expected distribution.[26] Moreover, "isolated enclaves" of peoples with delayed introduction to the S allele should be recognizable, at least in the higher ranges of s, as discrete clusters off to the underside of the expected distribution. Finally, it should be noted that the shaded region of Fig. 3.7 assumes a constant $t =$

[26] Populations sharing a more or less uniform T will cluster into a narrower pattern, and populations with highly variable T's will form a wider scatter. In a statistical sense, gene flow may be expected to create additional variance left unexplained by the analysis of variance due to selection.

1.0 over the interval of selection. If this, too, had varied historically to as little as $t = 0.7$, as shown, then the shaded distribution of today's q's would include the full area between the isoclines. The effect, once again, would be to add variance to the gene-frequency pattern, variance that cannot be explained by malarial selection alone.

In summary, the malaria hypothesis should be tested in West Africa not against the immediate expectation of precise isoclines generated by constant s and t and unlimited selection periods. Instead, the hypothesis may be examined by comparing observed S-allele frequencies with an expected distributional pattern that allows for spatial and temporal variation in s, t, and T between sample populations. In the analysis below, I therefore rely on the statistical procedure known as "analysis of variance." This procedure allows one to estimate the proportion of the total variation in S frequencies that can be ascribed to s, that is, to selection caused by differential mortality through malaria. If Haldane and Allison were correct, this test should generally indicate that a large proportion (though surely not all) of the variation in q among sample populations is explained by variation in s.

Predictions from the Livingstone Hypothesis

When these predictions of population genetics are combined with the Livingstone hypothesis, it becomes possible to formulate specific predictions about the effects of malarial selection among the linguistic subfamilies of West African peoples. Consider, first, the Kwa-speaking peoples of the southern forest-belt of West Africa (see Fig. 3.5), the group that includes the majority of West Africa's yam cultivators. According to Livingstone's historical reconstruction, the S allele appears to have been carried westward from south-central Nigeria by an expanding wave of these populations pushing ever farther into the forest habitat. Given the antiquity of yam cultivation by Kwa-speakers (see Posnansky 1969; D. Coursey 1976a), this process would have allowed well over two thousand years of genetic selection and gene flow. We would therefore expect to find a gene-frequency distribution among the yam-growing Kwa like that of Fig. 3.7. In this subsample, we would further predict relatively low variance in the distributional shadow of the S frequencies because of the comparatively long elapsed time T under selection.

In the same analysis, we should expect to find much lower frequencies of S among two subgroups of Kwa-speakers at the west end of the Kwa range, namely, the Kru (to the west of the Bandama River, see Fig. 3.5) and a subgroup I will call the Western Kwa (the inhabitants of the so-called lagoon region of the Ivory Coast, an area around the delta of the Bandama River). According to Livingstone, these two subgroups remained hunters and gatherers much longer than other Kwa and were pushed farther and farther into the southwestern forests by their yam-cultivating brethren. Because of the relative scarcity of breeding grounds for *Anopheles* in this habitat, the Kru and Western Kwa should, in this test of the malaria hypothesis, appear as relative genetic isolates.[27]

A second group of populations whose S frequencies are predicted to match the pattern of Fig. 3.7 are the populations of the West Atlantic subfamily of languages (subgroup I.A.1 of Fig. 3.5). Livingstone's (1958) review of the historical material available for these peoples led him to the conclusion, first, that the sickle-cell gene had spread by "mixture" through this area, rather than, as in the Kwa case, through large-scale migration; and second, that the timing of the spread of S coincided with the diffusion of rice agriculture through this language group (see p. 553). From the research of Roland Portères (1976), we now know that rice cultivation was, in turn, introduced to this zone from the inland Niger "delta" area of what is now Mali, a "primary center" of domestication (as Portères calls it) that has produced rice since 1500 B.C. or earlier. The diffusion of this technology gave rise to a "secondary center of varietal diversification" on both sides of the coastal Gambia River in the West Atlantic language area; from archaeological evidence, Portères (1976: 445–46) estimates that this had already occurred by 800 B.C. The implication here is that gene flow and genetic selection have had no fewer than 2,700 years to influence S frequencies among West Atlantic–speakers. Again, if the malaria hypothesis is correct, we should expect to find an association between q and s resembling the "shadow" of Fig. 3.7. From Livingstone's argument about mixture, however, we should expect to see more variance or "scatter" in the correlation because of the comparatively greater variation here in T.

As in the case of the Kwa-speakers, there is reason to anticipate some number of genetic isolates among the West Atlantic–speakers. We may reasonably expect to find anomalously low S frequencies among island inhabitants of the region (for example, the Bijago who live off the coast of Guinea-Bissau) and among a number of groups apparently regarded by their neighbors as "beyond the pale," a likely cause of genetic isolation if there ever was one (Reeve 1912, cited in Livingstone 1958: 545). Aside from these few exceptions, however, the malaria hypothesis would predict a strong correlation of s and q throughout the sample data. If the "hostilities" between mosquitoes, malaria, and man (G. Harrison 1978) have had a similar history throughout the region, these general patterns should be repeated in data for Mande-, Voltaic-, Afroasiatic-, and Nilo-Saharan–speaking peoples.

[27] Since this analysis was completed, Ruhlen (1987: ch. 3) and other linguists have suggested that the Kru language may well belong not to the Kwa subfamily, which Ruhlen renames "South Central Niger-Congo," but to the alternative "North Central Niger-Congo" subfamily. According to Ruhlen, the latter also contains the Voltaic languages (labeled I.A.3. in Fig. 3.5) as well as the Adamawa-Eastern languages (I.A.6.). If correct, this reclassification implies that the Kru are more closely related to these other populations than they are to the Kwa. Although they would still be genetic isolates relative to the Kwa, this scheme implies that their S allele frequencies would no longer offer a good test of the Livingstone hypothesis: any differenes between Kwa and Kru could then be traced to variables other than agriculture.

Mosquitoes, Malaria, and Monthly Rainfall

In order to test these predictions, I proceeded with the help of student assistants (J.G., P.I., E.L., T.S., and R.W.) to derive measures for key dependent and independent variables from data available in published sources. S frequencies, to begin with, were calculated separately for each ethnolinguistic population included among Livingstone's compilations (1967, 1973). We used a conservative estimation technique designed to provide a value of q based upon the largest possible sample for each population (see details in App. A.3.2). We also calculated frequencies of a second hemoglobinopathy gene, the C allele, which is co-allelic with S but reaches appreciable proportions only among populations of the Voltaic language subfamily and their neighbors. Our hope here was to explore a possible, if geographically limited, association between the C allele and endemic malaria. The procedure generated a data base of 157 different population samples, representing among them the hemoglobin types of more than 111,000 individuals. The sample thus obtained was large and diverse enough to permit comparative analyses among the major linguistic and agricultural subdivisions described above.

Data for the critical independent variable, the selection coefficient s arising from the severity of *P. falciparum* malaria, were much more difficult to obtain. As valuable as they are, malarial survey data for the area are either too highly localized or too regional and too coarsely aggregated for these purposes. I therefore looked for a reliable surrogate variable among the meteorological measures, one with known effect on the parasite or on its principal vector, *A. gambiae*. In this task, I was guided by arguments that precipitation is a key factor limiting malarial transmission in West Africa and elsewhere. As mentioned above, *A. gambiae* depends upon warm, sunlit freshwater ponds for its reproduction. Moreover, the age-specific survivorship rates of mature mosquitoes (and therefore their vectorial capacity) increase sharply with relative atmospheric humidity. It therefore seemed reasonable to look for correlations between rainfall and malaria rates in the pre-DDT malaria and mosquito research in West Africa from the 1920's and 1930's.

With my assistants' help, I was able to track down and correlate monthly measures of rainfall, humidity, mosquito densities, and malaria rates from two relatively early studies in different regions of West Africa. The first site, in the vicinity of Lagos, Nigeria (the "yam zone" of Fig. 3.6), was studied between November 1929 and October 1930 by M. A. Barber and M. T. Olinger (1931). These investigators found that despite a bimodal pattern of precipitation in the rainy season, common in tropical areas, there was but a single peak of *Anopheles* density beginning in the month of June. In August and September, an abrupt and severe "little dry season" in the midst of the rains (as discussed, for example, in Ireland 1962; Walter 1967; Ojo 1977) acted as an ecological bottleneck from which the *Anopheles* population did not recover even with the return of the rains in October. The data from this study therefore suggested that the maximum monthly rainfall ought to serve as a good predictor of the peak rates of malaria transmission and therefore of malarial selection.

A similar seasonal pattern of rainfall and mosquito densities was reported at about the same time (1930–31) for a site near Freetown, Sierra Leone, in the rice zone in the westernmost part of the region (Gordon et al. 1932). The data indicated that the total annual rainfall was substantially higher there than in Lagos, but also that it was concentrated into a single peak (Fig. 3.8, panel A). Much as in Lagos, a steep increase in the *Anopheles* densities followed on the heels of the maximum monthly rainfall (panel B). Once again the implication is that that maximum should be a good predictor of the magnitude of the seasonal wave of malaria transmission.[28] From these observations, it appeared that maximum monthly rainfall would serve as a reliable surrogate for the intensity of selection caused by *P. falciparum*. I then proceeded to match each of the 157 ethnolinguistic populations with its nearest weather station from the network of 86 West African weather stations that were part of the World Meteorological Organization's (WMO's) regular reporting service in the 1950's and 1960's (see App. A.3.2.).

By combining these analytic procedures I was able to conduct four separate statistical tests of the malaria hypothesis and thus of the connections between genes and culture in this special case of human diversity. As described below, three of the four tests produced statistically significant correlations between q and the surrogate for malarial severity, maximum monthly rainfall, but the strength of that association varied widely.

Genes, Culture, and Sickling Diversity

Consider, first, the results from the yam-cultivating Kwa speakers, shown in Fig. 3.9 (solid circles). The figure reveals a close curvilinear association between S allele frequencies and maximum monthly rainfall and thus provides strong support for the malaria hypothesis. The central tendency of the data closely corresponds to the equilibrium lines of Fig. 3.7, and there is remarkably little "shadow variance" within the sample. Other authors, most notably Allison (1956b: 433) and Cavalli-Sforza and Bodmer (1971: 153), have argued that malarial selection began early enough in West Africa for there to have been more than enough time to reach the balanced polymorphism of S and A. The results shown here agree with that prediction.

In order to measure the proportion of the total variability in q accounted for by the malarial surrogate, I performed a second-order polynomial regression analysis on these data. This procedure is designed both

---

[28] The data for Sierra Leone indicate that for this zone annual rainfall would also be a reasonable surrogate for malarial intensity since there is no mid-season "little dry." Nevertheless, maximum monthly rainfall best captures the buildup of the *Anopheles* population, and it also allows for comparisons with the data of the yam zone as well as other areas. (Additional annual mosquito cycles are given by Holstein 1954, for the sorghum and millet zone.)

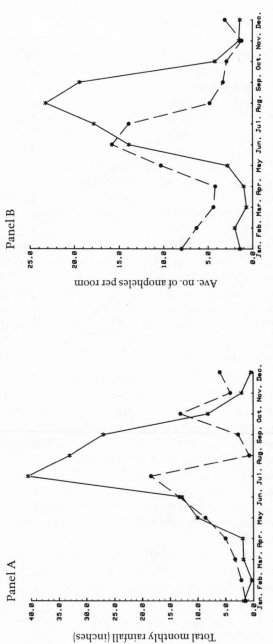

Fig. 3.8. A comparison of monthly rainfall levels and *Anopheles* mosquito counts for sites near Freetown, Sierra Leone (solid lines), and Lagos, Nigeria (broken lines). As panel A shows, monthly rainfall figures for Freetown generate an annual total that is not quite double that of Lagos, and Freetown has no midsummer "little dry season." Still, both areas have the same continuous stretch of dry months followed by a gradual increase to peak monthly rainfall levels in July. Panel B shows that monthly mosquito counts (the average number of *Anopheles* per room of human habitations) have a similar "single-wave" pattern of malaria vectors. Because there is no midsummer break in the Freetown rains, mosquito densities there continue to climb to a peak in August. In contrast, the mosquito densities near Lagos fall off drastically in August, demonstrating that the little dry season is an ecological bottleneck for this population. These curves suggest that the rainfall levels of the wettest month can be used as a reasonable surrogate for the peak rates of malarial transmission and therefore for the malarial selection coefficient, *s*. Panel A redrawn by permission of the publisher from Durham 1983a: 58. Copyright 1983 by Elsevier Science Publishing Co., Inc. Data for panel B from Gordon et al. 1932; Barber and Olinger 1931.

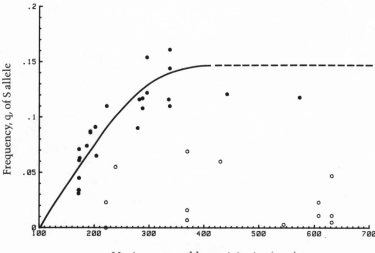

Fig. 3.9. A test of the malaria hypothesis among the Kwa-speakers of West Africa. The close, curvilinear association between S allele frequencies and maximum monthly rainfall levels among populations of yam-cultivating Kwa-speakers (solid circles) provides striking confirmation of the malaria hypothesis. As expected, the frequency of the sickle-cell gene increases rapidly as a function of the malarial surrogate to a plateau value averaging close to 0.15. A second-order polynomial regression curve (solid line), extended linearly at its apex (dotted line), explains 78.2 percent of the variance in q (the right-half of the fitted regression curve, not shown, returns symmetrically to zero). Among populations of rice-cultivating Kwa-speakers (represented by open circles), who have apparently adopted agriculture only in the last few centuries, there is no statistically significant correlation between their S frequencies and rainfall. Living in a remote, closed-canopy rain forest environment, with fewer breeding places for *Anopheles* mosquitoes, these populations appear to have experienced a late introduction of the S allele and/or little or no malarial selection. Redrawn by permission of the publisher from Durham 1983a: 61. Copyright 1983 by Elsevier Science Publishing Co., Inc.

to fit a curve of the form $y = a + bx + cx^2$ to the data and also to assess the magnitude of the residual variance (a function of the square of the distance between all points and that curve). The resulting parabola, half of which is shown by the solid line of Fig. 3.9, explains a total of 78.2 percent of the interpopulational variance in S. This statistic constitutes striking confirmation of the malaria hypothesis. In addition, the data suggest an upper limit to the maintenance of S by malarial selection in this region, a limit shown by the dotted line. Above this quantity of rainfall, there appears to be little increase in the relative selective force of malaria. All in all, the data of the Kwa-speaking yam cultivators show a very close fit to our theoretical expectations. The steepness of the regression curve emphasizes the importance of malarial selection in the evolution of genetic diversity among these peoples.

The data from the rice-growing Kru- and Western Kwa–speakers (Fig. 3.9, open circles) also conform to our expectations; the populations lie well below the distributional "shadow" of the yam-zone data. For example, the cluster of populations near 600 mm of monthly rainfall experiences one of the wettest of West Africa's humid tropical environments during the summer months, and yet their S frequencies lie very near to the figure's X axis. In sharp contrast to the polynomial regression for the yam growers, the best second-order fit to these data produces regression coefficients that are not statistically different from zero. In short, the data from the Kru- and Western Kwa–speakers stand in dramatic contrast to the central tendency among yam-growers. They appear to represent gene pools relatively isolated from their neighbors to the east, and relatively exempt from the genetic selection pressures of malaria operating there. Given the climatic and linguistic controls built into this comparison (but see note 27), these data would seem to offer statistical support for Livingstone's earlier argument that these gene-frequency differences trace to cultural differences between these groups. More specifically, it would seem that agricultural differences, through their influence on the local density of mosquito vectors, are responsible for the variable course of genetic evolution in these two groups of populations.

In an attempt to check the robustness of this analysis, I repeated the same statistical procedure using a number of different humidity surrogates for malaria compiled from the indices and weather stations used by Juan Papadakis (1966) in his study of crop zones in the region. One such index, called "water surplus" or "leaching rainfall," offers an especially appropriate check on my use of the rainfall surrogate for malarial selection, s. This index was calculated by Papadakis as the total rainfall of the "big rains" in an area (that is, the rains before the bottleneck), minus the potential evapotranspiration of the area for the same period.[29] This quantity is therefore a "puddling index": it measures the tendency of water to accumulate in excess of what a habitat can be expected to recycle within a certain period. Given the importance of freshwater pools to the life cycle of *A. gambiae*, we should expect to find another close curvilinear association between S frequencies and this measure. Fig. 3.10 may therefore be seen as confirming support for the malaria hypothesis. The pattern is strikingly similar to that of Fig. 3.9: once again the Kru and Western Kwa subgroups fall well outside the distributional pattern of the yam-zone data, confirming the hypothesis that malarial selection has been a far weaker force in the genetic evolutionary history of these peoples.[30] Considering, again, the difference in agricultural history between these subgroups, this contrast offers additional solid support for the malaria hypothesis. We may reasonably conclude that evolution by genetic selection, operating

[29] For some number of (unspecified) sites with relatively minor "little dry" months, Papadakis calculated water surplus for the full interval of the rainy season, a procedure that is probably responsible for some of the additional unexplained variance in the results below (see Papadakis 1965).

[30] The results for another Papadakis variable, maximum monthly "humidity index" (the monthly quotient of rainfall divided by potential evapotranspiration), were qualitatively and quantitatively similar to those reported here for "water surplus."

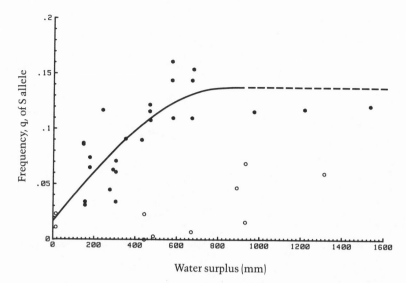

Fig. 3.10. Another test of the malaria hypothesis among the Kwa-speakers of West Africa. Again there is a close, curvilinear association between S frequencies and a second surrogate for malarial selection, seasonal "water surplus," among populations of yam-cultivating Kwa-speakers (solid circles). Developed by Papadakis (1965) as a measure of rainfall accumulation, water surplus is calculated as the difference between rainfall levels and potential evapotranspiration during the rainy season. Once again there is no significant association between S frequencies and water surplus values for the rice-cultivating Kru and western Kwa populations (open circles). Redrawn by permission of the publisher from Durham 1983a: 62. Copyright 1983 by Elsevier Science Publishing Co., Inc.

through sickle-cell anemia on the one hand and varying degrees of malarial selection on the other, explains most of the variation in the sickle-cell polymorphism among West Africa's Kwa-speaking populations.

Fig. 3.11 summarizes a parallel analysis of the data on West Atlantic–speaking populations.[31] Again, there is a curvilinear central tendency indicating that the frequency of S does tend to increase with the intensity of malarial selection. However, the figure also reveals substantially more unexplained or residual variance than was found in Fig. 3.9, and a good proportion of this variance appears to arise from a second cluster of genetic isolates. In this instance, the isolates are a cluster of rice-cultivating populations who appear on the plot inside the dashed enclosure between 500 and 700 mm of maximum monthly rainfall. Many of these populations were among those described by their neighbors as being "beyond the pale," and thus presumably cut off from interbreeding and gene flow. I

[31] In order to utilize the largest possible data set for this analysis, I lumped together the three main agricultural subgroups of West Atlantic–speakers: groups that are today rice cultivators, sorghum and millet cultivators, and nomadic herders, namely, the Fulani. The resulting plots (see Fig. 3.11) indicate that the basic pattern of association between *q* and *s* is consistent across the subgroups; thus the sorghum and millet populations appear simply to extend the same curve to a lower (that is, drier) point on the *X* axis.

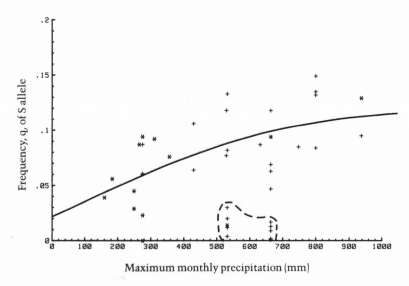

Fig. 3.11. A test of the malaria hypothesis among the West Atlantic–speakers of West Africa. The plot shows the association between S allele frequencies and maximum monthly rainfall, a surrogate for malarial selection intensity, for both rice-cultivating West Atlantic–speakers (the +'s) and sorghum-and-millet-cultivating West Atlantic–speakers (the *'s). The dotted line separates presumed genetic isolates from the populations used in the statistical analysis. A second-order polynomial regression analysis of the remaining data produced the curved line, which accounts for 38.9 percent of the variance in S frequencies. Redrawn by permission of the publisher from Durham 1983a: 64. Copyright 1983 by Elsevier Science Publishing Co., Inc.

therefore treated these groups as analogous to the Kru and Western Kwa above and deleted them from further statistical analysis.

I then calculated the second-order polynomial regression equation for the remaining populations of the West Atlantic subgroup. The resulting curve is shown in Fig. 3.11; the equation accounts for about half as much of the variance in q (i.e., 38.9 percent of the total) as does its counterpart among the yam-cultivating Kwa. Again the general distributional pattern matches our predictions for populations subject to both malarial selection and gene flow. However the width of the distributional shadow here indicates that gene flow has played a substantial role in the evolution of diversity among West Atlantic–speakers, a greater role than implied in the case of the Kwa. This finding is wholly consistent with Livingstone's argument, noted above, that S appears to have spread throughout this language group by mixture rather than by migration. Nevertheless, the distributional pattern confirms that a significant role has been played by malarial selection. It is exceedingly unlikely that the other evolutionary forces of Fig. 3.3 would have produced so consistent a correlation between S frequencies and rainfall.[32]

[32] By definition, drift and mutation can affect gene frequencies only by way of chance events and these, presumably, are unaffected by precipitation levels. Similarly, an explanation primarily in terms of migration or "mixing" would require both that S had been intro-

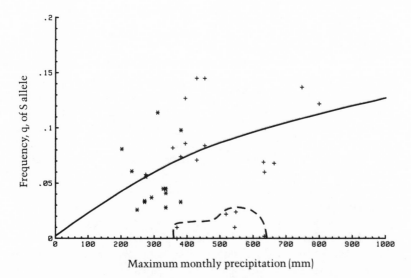

Fig. 3.12. A test of the malaria hypothesis among the Mande-speakers of West Africa. As for the Kwa and West Atlantic populations (see Fig. 3.11), there is again a curvilinear association between S frequencies and maximum monthly rainfall levels among rice-cultivating Mande-speakers (+) and sorghum-and-millet-cultivating ones (∗). The dotted line separates populations known to be genetic isolates from the populations used in the statistical analysis. In this case, however, the second-order regression curve (solid line) accounts for only 23.9 percent of the variance, which suggests that evolutionary forces in addition to selection by *P. falciparum* malaria have probably been involved. (Note that one of the +'s at 385 mm of precipitation falls directly on the *X* axis.) Redrawn by permission of the publisher from Durham 1983a: 66. Copyright 1983 by Elsevier Science Publishing Co., Inc.

The association between S frequencies and maximum monthly rainfall among the Mande populations is very similar to that of their West Atlantic neighbors. Just as in the West Atlantic case, I found a small cluster of low-frequency genetic isolates among the Mande, that is, among precisely those populations (Mano, Gio, Dan, Guro, and others) identified by Livingstone (1958) as the isolated "Mande Fu" subgroup and assigned linguistically today to the "southern group, eastern branch" of Mande-speakers. Their extremely low S frequencies despite substantial rainfall values, together with Livingstone's suggestion that these were peripheral peoples pushed farther into the forest by the expansion of more powerful neighbors, prompted their deletion from statistical calculations of central tendency. I then repeated the plotting and regression analysis procedures as before and obtained the results shown in Fig. 3.12. Once again, a significant curvilinear association was found. The regression has a very similar general appearance to that of Fig. 3.11, but in this case only 23.9

duced from some outside location and that the migrants had preferentially sought out the wetter environments. Even setting aside the issue of habitat preference, the first requirement can be dismissed on the basis of the recent molecular evidence, discussed earlier, for an independent origin of S in the region. Migration and mixing have surely played some role, but genetic selection through the agency of malaria is the force most likely to have elevated S frequencies in the wetter environments.

percent of the variance can be ascribed to the effect of malarial selection. Gene flow, drift, or selective forces of other origin appear to have played a prominent role among the Mande groups.

A similar analysis was repeated separately on the remaining linguistic subdivisions of the data set: Voltaic, Afroasiatic, and Nilo-Saharan. The results were similarly negative in all three cases. For example, the data for the Gur-speaking (Voltaic) peoples are shown in Fig. 3.13 (note that frequencies of both S and C alleles are depicted on this plot, by asterisks and x's respectively). The graph is qualitatively different from all the preceding ones: there is virtually no covariation between S frequencies and maximum monthly rainfall. Instead the populations group together in a relatively small cluster. The same pattern is found among the Afroasiatic and Nilo-Saharan populations.

Fig. 3.13 provides ample demonstration that maximum monthly rainfall, although useful in the case of the peoples who speak Kwa, West Atlantic, and Mande, has little or no explanatory power in these Sudanic regions of West Africa. The surrogate simply does not appear to represent

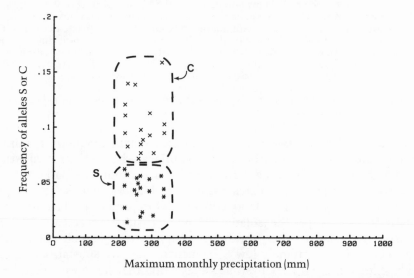

Fig. 3.13. A test of the malaria hypothesis among the Voltaic-speakers of West Africa. In contrast to the plot in previous figures, this one indicates that there is no statistically significant association between S frequencies (shown by the *'s) and maximum monthly rainfall in these populations, nor indeed is there such an association for the alternative C allele (shown by the x's). One reason for this is surely the narrow range of rainfall variation in the zone, which may subject all the groups to similar densities of *Anopheles* and to similar rates of *P. falciparum* parasitism. Another reason may be that maximum monthly rainfall is not a reliable surrogate for the other major malaria in this zone, *P. malariae*, with its vector, *A. funestus*. Indeed, it seems possible that the C allele offers greater protection against *P. malariae* than does S, for C is the more common allele in this language subgroup. In any event, further research is clearly needed to explain S and C gene frequencies in this cluster of populations. Redrawn by permission of the publisher from Durham 1983a: 67. Copyright 1983 by Elsevier Science Publishing Co., Inc.

the important evolutionary forces that have acted on the sickle-cell allele in these populations. Indeed, the operation of other forces is also suggested by the especially high prevalence in this region of the C allele, a geographically localized alternative to S. At the same time, however, this finding cannot be construed as an out-and-out refutation of the malaria hypothesis. Other species of *Plasmodia* or other parasite vectors may be involved in an interaction with climate that follows qualitatively different patterns compared to those observed in other areas. Instead, this analysis emphasizes the importance of additional efforts to identify the special dynamics of malarias and mosquitoes in the Sudan savannah of West Africa. It is likely that both more appropriate and more illuminating surrogate variables can be found.

Genetic Analysis: Explanation and Evolution

Before turning to conclude this chapter with some general remarks about genetic selection and organic evolution, let me first offer a brief summary of our findings in this case analysis. First and foremost, these tests of the malaria hypothesis offer an assessment of the role of malarial selection in the evolution of West Africa's sickle-cell polymorphism. Through the use of a surrogate variable for malaria, maximum monthly rainfall, we have seen that the selective action of the parasite accounts for a substantial proportion of the diversity in S allele frequencies among the Kwa, West Atlantic, and Mande language groups. More specifically, a polynomial regression analysis relating S frequencies to rainfall levels was able to explain 78.2 percent, 38.9 percent, and 23.9 percent, respectively, of the variance in the dependent variable in these populations. In each instance, the curves closely resemble the frequency distributions expected of populations subject to the simultaneous influence of both natural selection and gene flow. The analysis therefore provides a new and more direct form of support for the malaria hypothesis as formulated by J. B. S. Haldane and A. C. Allison.

At the same time, the analysis here also reveals two classes of exception to this finding within the West African data set. The first class concerns relative genetic isolates, populations with low S frequencies that appear to have been marginal demes, isolated from the spread of S, during the last several thousand years of West African history. In the graphic analysis, these isolates were all found to lie well below the distributional pattern of S frequencies found for other groups in the sample. Believing this pattern to have arisen as a consequence of impeded gene flow (and hence impeded selection), I omitted these cases from statistical treatment. The second class of exceptions concerns three language groups, the Voltaic (Gur), Nilo-Saharan, and Afroasiatic language groups of West Africa. Among these samples, I found no consistent pattern of covariation between S frequencies and the rainfall surrogate. In retrospect, this finding is not altogether surprising given the differences in climate and habitat between the locations of these peoples and the others of the sample. As argued above, the negative results obtained for these populations do not constitute a refutation of the malaria hypothesis. Instead, they suggest the importance of additional research on the malarias and mosquitoes of these regions.

The third finding of importance for our purposes is the evidence that culture, specifically the know-how of slash-and-burn agriculture, has played an instrumental role in the genetic evolution of West African populations. Our analysis indicates large and statistically significant differences between the S frequencies of populations with a long cultural tradition of cultivation and those who have adopted this technology much more recently. In some cases (most notably the Kwa's), this cultural difference is associated with a difference of 10 to 12 percentage points in q. The implication is that culture has played a major role in defining or redefining the selection coefficients acting on the genotypes (a subject that will be pursued further in Chapter 5). While this suggestion is certainly not a new one—whole volumes (for example, Montagu 1962; Garn 1964) have been assembled on the general theme in addition to Livingstone's specific arguments on this case—the tests of the malaria hypothesis presented here offer a particularly clear demonstration of the impact of culture. In West Africa, the fate of genetic instructions for sickling hemoglobin has covaried with the cultural environment.

The Genetic Explanation of Diversity

For a number of reasons, these tests of the malaria hypothesis provide fitting conclusion to this case study of the genetic explanation of human diversity—here, human physiological diversity. First, they bring us back to an argument made at the point of departure: a genetic evolutionary explanation of human diversity is valid if and only if there is a causal link between underlying genotypic differences and the phenotypic differences of concern. Fortunately, in the early sections of this chapter, we were able to draw upon evidence establishing a link of just this kind. In particular, at the level of individual phenotypes, we were able to trace differences in the percentage of sickling hemoglobin (Hb S) to differences in the genetic instructions (the A and S alleles) that direct the biosynthesis of different hemoglobin molecules. Similarly, at the level of populations, we were able to relate differences in the frequency distributions of these phenotypes to differences in the frequency distributions of their corresponding genotypes. Although there are a number of obvious differences, the analysis here has roughly paralleled the use in Chapter 2 of the cultural code as an explanation for the behavioral diversity of Tibetan marriages.

Second, these tests of the malaria hypothesis have illustrated in almost exemplary fashion the utility of genetic microtheory for explaining the organic evolution of a human polymorphism. As we have seen, a major goal of genetic microtheory is to provide explanations for the historical changes in gene and genotype frequency that lie behind contemporary genetic diversity. Here we drew on a portion of that theory, namely the selection equations of population genetics; our purpose was to generate a set of predictions about the expected range and form of genetic diversity among a group of populations that had experienced genetic selection for many generations. When these predictions were compared with the actual patterns of genetic diversity among certain West African populations, the close match of theory and observation provided substantial support for the genetic explanation. In other words, the phenotypic diversity of the sickle-cell polymorphism in West African populations today appears to be the result of genetic evolutionary forces in the past, an argument that is, again, parallel in a number of respects to the cultural evolutionary argument of the last chapter. As in that chapter, synchronic correlational evidence is certainly no substitute for a detailed historical record of change. Nevertheless, in the absence of such a record, the multiple independent tests of the malaria hypothesis performed here allow us to have some measure of confidence in this genetic evolutionary explanation. As James Bowman (1964: 161) has succinctly summarized, "the lack of another reasonable explanation for the high frequency of [Hb S and other hemoglobin variants] is, perhaps, the best evidence for the malarial selective effect."

Third, this study has also illustrated the efficacy of genetic selection in its role as the "design architect" of organic evolution. We have inferred that the distribution of phenotypes in certain West African populations (the P_i's of Fig. 3.2) changed over time as a consequence of changes in the genotype distributions (the G_i's), and that the genotype distributions were in turn modified through the differential reproduction of component genotypes in malarial environments. In this way, genetic selection made an important contribution to the laws of transformation (T_2) operating in this case. Its transformational effect appears to have varied with the intensity of malarial parasitism, giving rise to the genetic differences of the populations we have studied. The result, if this account is correct, has been the evolution of phenotypic diversity through the statistical accumulation of one allele at the expense of another—a case of gradualistic "descent with modification." We have also found evidence that gene flow, mutation, and drift have contributed to the process, singly or in combination, adding still more diversity to the populations. But, true to Darwin's words, the regressions imply that this is a case where "Natural Selection has been the main but not exclusive means of modification." (Darwin 1964 [1859]: 6.)

Fourth, this study has also produced evidence that the sickle-cell trait, the phenotype of mixed Hb A and Hb S, constitutes a bona fide organic adaptation to the malarious environments of the region. As discussed in Chapter 1, the term "organic adaptation" should be reserved for the features of organisms that both promote reproductive fitness and were historically favored by genetic selection because of their current role or function. Such features should be distinguished from organic "exaptations," or characters that evolved for other reasons and acquired their current function after the fact (see Gould and Vrba 1982). In the case at hand, the evidence of this chapter leaves little doubt that sickle-cell trait is an organic adaptation in the proper sense. As we have seen, there is both clinical and biochemical evidence that the sickling of erythrocytes in response to malaria has a protective function.

Moreover, the West African genotype-frequency data indicate that the AS genotype does have an appreciable fitness advantage over AA and SS genotypes. Among the Kwa-speakers of the yam zone, for example, I estimate that the AA and SS genotypes have only 90.1 and 29.3 percent, respectively, of the fitness of the heterozygotes (using the fitness estimation technique of Cavalli-Sforza and Bodmer 1971: 162–63 on the data set prepared for this case study). In addition, the results of our statistical analysis suggest that the trait was historically favored by genetic selection because of its protective value. This inference was clearest and strongest from the comparison of yam-cultivating and non-yam-cultivating Kwa-speakers. There we found the S allele to be present in substantial frequency today only where the heterozygote genotype would have had a long-standing protective function—in and around the fields of slash-and-burn agriculture.

Genetic Selection and Organic Evolution

At the same time, however, this study raises a number of cautionary points about the role of genetic selection in organic evolution. Let me conclude this chapter with brief comments on three of them. First, the preceding case study emphasizes that the processes of organic evolution do not relentlessly promote a universal optimization of phenotypes. Although there may well be some popular misconception on the subject— misconception that Gould and Lewontin (1979) call the "adaptationist programme" and the "Panglossian paradigm"—our analysis clearly demonstrates that neither genetic selection nor the other evolutionary forces of the case can be credited with "the best of all possible solutions" to West Africa's malaria. To be sure, genetic selection *does* seem to favor the AS genotype, as we have seen, and that genotype, according to the best of our information, *is* adaptive in malarious environments. However, as a consequence of heterozygote advantage, genetic selection simultaneously guarantees the persistent recurrence of suboptimal AA and SS genotypes. In fact, when genetic selection causes an increase in the frequency of the S allele in a population, it causes a proportionately greater increase in the preselection frequency of the SS genotype (that is to say, in the frequency of zygotes of the SS genotype formed at the start of the next generation; see App. B.2.6). Paradoxically, this means that the process of genetic adaptation to malaria actually propels an increase in the frequency of maladaptive genotypes. The "best solution" genetic selection has been able to achieve in these circumstances is, in fact, a cold, cruel compromise (see also Templeton 1982).

Apart from genetic selection, our analysis has also indicated that other, nonoptimizing evolutionary forces have been at work on the frequency of S in West Africa. Among these other forces, migration (gene flow), drift, or both have been implicated as significant sources of variability. To these Lewontin (1979b: 13) adds "a number of evolutionary forces that are clearly nonadaptive and which may be correct explanations for any number of actual evolutionary events." His list includes, for example: (1) the role of chance in the evolution of one phenotype out of multiple "selective peaks"; (2) the role of "pleiotropic gene action," which means that all phenotypic effects of a gene may change when one of them causes selection; (3) the role of "allometric growth," that is, the evolutionary growth of a given attribute arising as an incidental by-product of selection for an increase in some other feature; and (4) the role of biological "random noise processes"—that is, chance events at the cellular and molecular level during an organism's development. Given all of these mechanisms, it is important to reiterate a point not lost on Darwin over a century ago but sometimes forgotten today: natural selection at the level of individual organisms (or what we would call today the level of genotypes) is not the sole author of evolutionary change, and adaptation is not its sole product.

A second cautionary note is in order concerning the place of the population genetics presented here within the greater scheme of evolutionary biology. The Δq equations we have applied here are but a small, though crucial, part of microevolutionary theory, the study of evolutionary processes within populations of a single species (for more see Hartl 1980; Falconer 1981). In turn, as we have seen, microevolutionary theory is itself but part of the greater scheme of genetic evolutionary theory. Given the rapid development of speciation and macroevolutionary theory today, it must be remembered that microevolution is only a fraction of the full story. It is an important fraction, to be sure; but it is nevertheless incomplete.

Gould (1980a, see also 1982b), among others, has pointed out two dangers inherent in forgetting this fact and in viewing "adaptive allelic substitution" as an adequate representation of the whole of organic evolution. The first is a tendency to overlook the hierarchical organization of life, including the hierarchy of both the genetic material—nucleotides, genes, chromosomes, genomes, gene pools—and of the living forms that carry it, such as individuals, social groups, populations, species, and communities. Genes do not exist as independent, freely interchangeable particles as microtheory so often implies. Instead, they exist as integral parts of this hierarchy—as "holons" in the terminology of T. F. H. Allen and Thomas B. Starr (1982: chs. 2, 7)—subject to its properties and its constraints. Since a process of selection by differential reproduction is conceivable on each of these levels, not just at the level of individuals and genotypes, we must give heed to evolutionary events and forces throughout the hierarchy. Change at different levels of the hierarchy will have different properties (Brandon and Burian 1984; Vrba and Eldredge 1984; Arnold and Fristrup 1984).

The second danger comes from ignoring or downplaying the role of so-called structural influences in organic evolution—the "organic constraints" of Fig. 3.3—compared to the role of the "functional" influences, most notably genetic selection. If the evolution of an organism were simply a matter of allelic substitutions governed by genetic selection, Gould argues, the organism could be regarded as a sphere, ready to roll in any direction and always subject to changes over which its current form had little or no influence. Thus to view evolution solely in terms of classical population genetics would be to view organisms as "billiard balls, struck in a deterministic fashion by the cue of natural selection, and rolling to optimal positions on life's table." A more appropriate metaphor, he suggests, is that of the organism as a polyhedron whose facets constrain the course of evolution.

[These] facets are constraints exerted by the developmental integration of organisms themselves. Change cannot occur in all directions, or with any increment. . . . When the polyhedron tumbles, selection may usually be the propelling force. But if adjacent facets are few in number and wide in spacing, then we cannot identify selection as the only, or even the primary control upon evolution. For selection is channeled by the form of the polyhedron it pushes. [Gould 1980a: 129]

There are those who feel that Gould overstates his case (cf. Stebbins and Ayala 1981; see also, in reply, Gould 1982a). But the general point is a good one. As the blocked filter channels of Fig. 3.3 are meant to illustrate, the current design of an organism does impose real limits upon the "choice," or sorting process, of genetic selection. As the organism evolves, the constraints, too, will change, sometimes providing more latitude for selection and sometimes less. Either way, however, adaptive allelic substitutions are clearly not the whole story. Selection can thus be carried out at many levels and affected by many constraints.

Third and finally, it is important to return to a point made earlier in Chapter 1: although genetic selection may well be "the only acceptable explanation for the genesis and maintenance of [organic] adaptation" (Williams 1966: vii), the process is surely *not* the cause of nor the "only acceptable explanation for" all recognized forms of adaptation. The present analysis, for instance, has provided confirming evidence that sickle-cell trait is a true organic adaptation. But that evidence clearly does not make this phenotype the exclusive form of human adaptation to malaria in West Africa—particularly since its benefits are enjoyed by, at most, a small fraction of the affected populations. On the contrary, there is evidence throughout the region for supplementary cultural adaptations to malaria, that is to say, for adaptations based upon socially transmitted information and shaped by cultural evolutionary processes like those we explored in Chapter 2.

Moreover, these cultural adaptations have at least the potential to reduce the likelihood of malarial infection for all or nearly all members of a local population. Consider, for example, the "ritual cleansing" of villages that takes place during the rainy season among the Yoruba, one of the Kwa-speaking groups of southern Nigeria. At one Yoruba location, the

Ẹ̀bì festival is a rite for the general spiritual cleansing of the community. A kind of symbolic action accompanies the rite. At noon on the appointed day, every adult in the community gets an òfọ̀nràn (burning firebrand) and with this he or she chases evil spirits and calamity out of every corner of [every] house into the streets and from the streets into the bush and from the bush into an appointed flowing stream. . . . As the firebrands sink into the river and are carried away, so evil spirits, losses and sickness are believed to be carried away from the community. . . . The idea is that once evils have been swept away in this dramatic way, peace will come back and remain in the town." [Awolalu 1979: 153–54]

If we remember that *Anopheles* mosquitoes normally spend the hot and bright hours of the day perched in shady recesses (Holstein 1954: ch. 5), it is not surprising that Yoruba see this "symbolic action" as driving away "their human miseries, diseases, sores and death" (Awolalu 1979: 155). Nor is it surprising that, among the culturally related Igbo peoples nearby, similar "measures are taken to prevent 'flying' sickness from entering a village and, at intervals, stipulated ceremonies are fulfilled and sacrifices offered for 'driving out' sickness," again in daylight and with firebrands (see Basden 1966 [1938]: 50–51; Henderson 1972: 310–11).[33] Although a systematic study of these rites and their variations has obviously been beyond the scope of this present chapter, I suspect that they do represent bona fide cultural adaptations, having been shaped by parallel selective processes of cultural evolution to which we return in Chapter 4. For now, my point is simply that the differential reproduction of genotypes is neither the cause of nor the explanation for these adaptations.

---

[33] Basden describes a second intriguing cultural adaptation to malaria among the Igbo: "In some badly infected areas, mosquito-proof houses are built specially for sleeping quarters. The roof consists of very thick thatch which rests solidly on the walls. There are no windows and the one small door is made to fit closely. At bedtime, the family, accompanied by fowls, goats, and dogs, retire to this apartment and stay there until dawn appears [at which time mosquito activity levels drop precipitously; see Holstein 1954: ch. 5]. It must be dreadfully stuffy for, in barring out mosquitoes, every breath of air is also excluded. Yet it is the only way to have a moment's peace after nightfall in some districts." (1966 [1938]: 154.) Other West African cultural adaptations to malaria include the folk remedies described in Ajose 1957; a purported folk remedy for sickle-cell anemia itself is discussed in Sofowora and Isaacs 1971. On cultural adaptations to malaria in other places, see J. May 1954, 1958; P. J. Brown 1979, 1981a, 1986; N. Etkin 1979, 1981; N. Etkin and Ross 1983.

To return to the case at hand, it is therefore important to underscore the two key inferences on which our analysis of the sickle-cell polymorphism was based. The first one concerns the relationship of phenotypes to genotypes. In this analysis, information available from molecular genetics permitted us to make a crucial "inference of genetic covariation," that is, we had reason to believe that the different phenotypes of our study were, in fact, associated with different genotypes. In terms of the structure of evolutionary genetics, as shown in Fig. 3.2, this inference established the transformation T_1 and allowed us to offer a genetic explanation for the evolutionary change in phenotypes.

On a more general level, the point is that an inference of genetic covariation is logically required of *any* attempt to use the process of natural selection among genotypes as an explanation for phenotypic change. The reason, as Ronald A. Fisher (1958) reminded us, is that natural selection is, at this level, a "genetical theory"; the differential reproduction of genotypes can explain evolutionary changes of form if and only if the phenotypic differences in a population are correlated with genotypic differences. As David Barash, writing in *Sociobiology and Behavior*, has expressed it, genetic selection "will produce evolutionary change only if the difference between the phenotypes of those individuals that are reproductively favored (selected) and those that are not is due to differences in the genotypes between individuals of these two groups." (1982: 14; see also Dawkins 1982a: 21; Sober 1984b: 42.) If, in fact, differences in phenotypes are not correlated with differences in genotypes, then, obviously, the natural selection of genotypes cannot be the mechanism that causes change in the phenotypes, nor can any other process of genetic transformation.[34]

The second inference of importance to this analysis followed on the first: it was the inference establishing the natural selection of genotypes as the principal genetic mechanism behind the evolution of high frequencies of S. This was an "inference of specific mechanism." Information about the other possible causes of gene-frequency change (mutation, migration, and drift) allowed us to infer their lesser role, in general, in the evolution of the sickle-cell polymorphism. This inference allowed us to focus on the mechanism of genetic selection, guiding our attention to-

[34] Admittedly, there are a number of reasons for confusion about the role of natural selection in evolutionary change. One of them, alluded to in Chapter 1, is that authors use the term "natural selection" in very different ways. These range from any process that sorts among living variants by differential birth and death (a definition that can make speciation a form of natural selection; see Vrba and Eldredge 1984) to a process, such as "the natural selection of cultural variation" (as in Boyd and Richerson 1985), that also sorts among nonliving variants. Because of this problem, I prefer to use the term "genetic selection" for the differential reproduction of genotypes. Another reason for confusion, explained more thoroughly in Chapter 4, is that there are times when the differential reproduction of genotypes can be credited with an *indirect* role in phenotypic change that it has not produced. This situation can occur when change is caused not by the *process* of genetic selection, but by the *products* of genetic selection, that is to say, by biochemical and neurophysiological mechanisms of individual learning.

ward testable predictions of S-frequency change in response to various hypothetical selection coefficients. Both historically, in the developments of the 1940's leading to the malaria hypothesis, and in this case study of physiological diversity in West Africa, the inference helped to predict the nature and form of the transformation T_2 from among the vast array of possibilities. It paved the way for a tractable test of a specific genetic hypothesis. If, in other contexts, a specific mechanism cannot be inferred from the start, one must be careful not to assume a priori that genetic selection has been the main guiding force. Mutation, migration, and drift must also be considered.

In light of these cautionary notes, I believe that the genetic analysis of human diversity must be approached with some care. If this case study has been successful in explaining certain human differences, it is because we were able to make these inferences, and thus to provide a genetic explanation within an evolutionary framework. Given that these inferences do not automatically apply to other instances of human diversity, particularly to behavioral diversity where cultural causes may also be involved, this analysis must surely emphasize the need for scrutiny and caution in the application of genetic theory to the human context.

4 /   THE RELATIONSHIPS OF
GENES AND CULTURE

In previous chapters we have seen that both genes and culture constitute systems of organized information; that both exert profound influence on human phenotypes; and that both are capable of evolutionary transformation through space and time. In addition, we have seen that evolutionary change in both systems exhibits the properties of multiplicity—that is, the existence of multiple causal forces of transformation—and selectivity, or the propensity for non-random differential transmission of variants. Given this array of shared properties, it is little wonder that attempts to relate genes and culture take one or the other of two theoretical stances: either culture is viewed as a product or expression of the genes, or else it is considered to be a distinct but parallel second channel of information inheritance. In the latter case its properties are seen as roughly parallel to those of the genetic system because the cultural system depends upon organically evolved features of the human organism.

In this chapter, I will briefly summarize and compare the leading theoretical arguments of each kind. Of necessity, my review will focus on recent formulations, particularly on those to appear since the start of the sociobiology debate of the 1970's.[1] But first I should mention one important assumption that is shared by all of the models we will discuss. The

[1] For a brief discussion of three earlier formulations, see App. A.4.1; for other recent formulations outside the scope of this review, see Blum 1978; Plotkin and Odling-Smee 1981; Swanson 1983; Lopreato 1984; de Winter 1984; Rindos 1985, 1986a; Barash 1986; Schmid and Wuketits 1987; Tooby and Cosmides 1989. On the history of evolutionary theory in the social sciences, see Van Parijs 1981, Peters 1982, and Ingold 1986. Following Geertz (1973: 144), I distinguish between "culture"—that is, "the framework of beliefs, expressive symbols, and values" of a population—and "social system," its actual "pattern of social interaction." Thus my review does not include recent theories about the evolution of social systems of generally increasing size and complexity—so-called "social evolution"—even where this is equated with cultural evolution by its authors (as in Flannery 1972; Schmookler 1984; Hallpike 1986; Johnson and Earle 1987). I do lay some groundwork for studying the linkages between social and cultural change, but I leave its expansion and development to future work.

assumption is simply that human beings have a so-called capacity for culture that has evolved under the influence of genetic selection during the last three million years or so of our phylogenetic history. In other words, these models assume genetic covariation and adaptive origins for the "hardware" of the cultural system—for the structures and functions of the brain (particularly the neocortex), the supralaryngeal tract, the vocal cords, and arguably bipedal locomotion itself (for specific arguments see Spuhler 1959a; Geertz 1962, 1965; Holloway 1969, 1975b, 1981; Lieberman 1975, 1984; Rindos 1986a, 1986b). Thus both of the caveats at the end of Chapter 3 are covered: genetic selection, working through the covariation between genotypes and phenotypes, is assumed to have been the principal mechanism behind the evolution of these human features. For convenience, I will call this the assumption of "natural origins" (after Boyd and Richerson 1985: 13).

While reasonable, this assumption immediately prompts two further questions: first, How does this organically evolved "hardware" relate to culture's "software" (its ideational content) and to changes through time in that "software"? and second, What does the genetic history of the hardware imply about the influence of the software on human phenotypes? The theoretical models described below provide a range of different answers to the first question; let me defer answering the second until Chapter 8.

Models of Gene-Culture Relations

Theories, like species, continually evolve. This makes it difficult—indeed unwise—to impose rigid classification schemes on current forms. On the other hand, a rough preliminary framework can help both to organize diversity and to clarify salient distinctions, whether in species or theories, even if these later prove to have been transient. In this spirit, I propose a three-way classification of the recent models of gene-culture relations (for other schemes, see Lumsden and Wilson 1981: ch. 6; Boyd and Richerson 1985: 158, table 5.5). My classification is derived from the issues in evolutionary anthropology discussed in Chapter 1. In particular, it emphasizes two questions involved in the "distinction issue": (1) Is culture a second inheritance system? and (2) What are the best units to use in the study of cultural transmission? Looking over the recent literature, I find three different kinds of answer to these questions. It is no coincidence that they have appeared in approximate chronological order.

The first kind (Category A), which I will call "models without dual inheritance," pays heed to the concept of culture but does not distinguish it as a second inheritance system. Theories in this category discuss phenotypic change in human populations in terms of a single fitness principle, namely, reproductive fitness in one of its guises. The arguments do not recognize units with evolutionary fitness in the cultural system; instead, culture is conceptualized as part of the phenotype.

The second kind (Category B) is "models with dual inheritance and trait units." It, too, conceptualizes culture as part of the phenotype, in terms of "cultural traits" or "cultural behaviors," but answers yes to Question 1. Culture is viewed as a second, nongenetic inheritance system whose units are defined as culturally heritable aspects of phenotype. These units are recognized as having their own measure of fitness within the cultural system, a measure for which the expression "cultural fitness" is generally used. In Category B formulations, the differential transmission of traits or behaviors within a population constitutes cultural evolution.

The third kind of answer (Category C) includes the model of gene-culture relations that I propose in these pages. In this category, "models with dual inheritance and ideational units," the answer to Question 1 is again yes, but the answer to Question 2 is not in terms of traits or other phenotypic units. Rather, culture is conceptualized in terms of ideational units. In these models, culture is portrayed as a separate "track" of informational inheritance, but one with a number of features that are more or less analogous to the features of the genetic "track." In these renderings, culture evolves through the differential transmission of ideas, values, and beliefs in a population.

Category A: Models Without Dual Inheritance

The first category or "genus" of gene-culture models can be subdivided into two related species, as described below. Although there are differences between these species, they have one important common property: they do not include an evolutionary theory of cultural change.

Sociobiology I

The first model, which I will call Sociobiology I, represents the relationship between genes and culture inherent in the attribution of human behavioral phenotypes to evolution by genetic selection, the differential reproduction of genotypes. As discussed in Chapter 1, it is a relationship implied by much of the early literature of sociobiology, particularly in the years 1975 to 1978, wherein one reads hypotheses of "selection for" this or that attribute, or arguments that "selection would have favored" a given form of human social behavior. Its hallmark is the attempt to explain human behavior in terms of the *process* of genetic selection. By this reasoning, a cultural belief is a cognitive "self-interpretation" of natural propensities (as in Bischof 1972: 29), or the articulated message of our "whisperings within" (as in Barash 1979). Either way, the hardware specifies the software.

Arguments like this one assume a relationship between genes, culture, and behavior that is sometimes called "genetic determinism." Whether intentional or not, they presuppose a one-to-one correspondence between phenotypes and underlying genotypes. As we saw in Chapter 3, the process of genetic selection can favor a phenotype p_1 *if and only if* it differs from alternative states, say p_2 and p_3, as a consequence of DNA differences between corresponding genotypes. Consequently, in Sociobiology I, human diversity is given genetic explanation: phenotypes differ because genotypes do.

In my view, two fundamental problems are apparent here. One is the implied generality of an isomorphic "epigenetic law" that translates genotypes into phenotypes in a one-to-one fashion (as if the T_1 of Fig. 3.2 were deterministic). The second is the assumption that the process of genetic selection is responsible for any phenotypic diversity for which it can be made to seem responsible. Although it is true that genetic selection does favor the evolution of adaptive phenotypes, Chapter 2 has suggested that cultural evolution can do the same. If so, then the adaptiveness of a phenotype tells us nothing about whether it evolved genetically or not.

Sociobiology II

The second model, which I will call Sociobiology II, can as well be called a "genetic influence model" because it views genes as contributing to the explanation of behavioral differences rather than as completely specifying such differences in final form. In this model, genetic differences account for "a substantial fraction of human behavioral variation," in the words of Edward O. Wilson (1978: 43), a leading proponent of this view. Here, genes have a probabilistic influence.

Wilson's *On Human Nature* (1978) suggests two ways in which genetic influence can come about. The first is in setting limits: "Rather than specify a single trait [as in Model 1 above], human genes prescribe the capacity to develop a certain array of traits. In some categories of behavior, the array is limited and the outcome can be altered only by strenuous training—if ever. In others, the array is vast and the outcome easily influenced." (pp. 56–57.) But often, says Wilson, the genes do more than merely limit the arrays. They may also add developmental probabilities so that "we inherit a capacity for certain traits, and a bias to learn one or another of those available." (p. 60.) He explains this developmental "bias" (which is in fact an epigenetic transformation rule, shown as T_1 in Fig. 3.2) by using the metaphor of a ball rolling down the contours of a landscape, an image derived from the geneticist C. H. Waddington. Compared to the "developmental landscape" of a mosquito, for example, Wilson notes that

the developmental topography of human behavior is enormously broader and more complicated, but it is still a topography. In some cases the valleys divide once or twice. An individual can end up either right- or left-handed [as one example]. If he starts with the genes or other early physiological influences that pre-dispose him to the left hand, that branch of the developmental channel can be viewed as cutting the more deeply. If no social pressure is exerted the ball will in most cases roll on down into the channel for left-handedness. But if parents train the child to use the right hand, the ball can be nudged into the shallower channel for right-handedness. [p. 61]

One attractive feature of this model is its allowance for extra-genetic in-fluences on human diversity. For example, Wilson argues that "the imag-ery of the developmental landscape must be altered subtly as increasing amounts of learning and culture come to prevail on the downward slopes. In the case of language, dress, and the other culturally sensitive categories of behavior, the landscape dissolves into a vast delta of low ridges and winding oxbows." (p. 63.) On the other hand, the developmental processes can be steeply "canalized" by the genes, causing this model to grade into Model 1.[2]

My criticisms of this model are two. First, Wilson and other propo-nents have not offered predictive hypotheses concerning the relative steepness of these developmental landscapes of human behaviors. With-out such predictions it becomes difficult to test the model, since all be-havioral phenotypes will fit *somewhere* between the steepest of valleys and the flattest of oxbows. It also becomes difficult to tell how much of a role culture has, and when. Again we are back to the problem of Wilson's "leash" (p. 167), as introduced in Chapter 1. The landscape model makes clear that we must see the relationship of genes and culture as one with many different leashes, some short and tightly constraining (the steep val-leys) and some very long and functionally ineffective (the winding ox-bows). The idea of the leash itself is uninformative, except insofar as customary usage implies certain lengths and constraints: we need to know when—for what phenotypes—the leashes are short and when they are long.[3]

Second, given that leashes can be very long, we need to know how cul-ture finds its way alone. This question is clearly raised by the landscape metaphor, for surely something must shape the "vast delta" and guide the ball till it stops. However, the image of "winding oxbows" imparts the quality of aimless meandering to cultural change, a view that is strikingly

[2]As an example of deep canalization, consider Wilson's description of the role of genes behind human inbreeding avoidance, a topic to which we will return in Chapter 6. "The manifestations of inbreeding pathology [i.e., genetic defects among inbred progeny] consti-tute natural selection in an intense and unambiguous form. . . . So powerful is the advan-tage of outbreeding that it can be expected to have carried cultural evolution along with it. . . . Natural selection has probably ground away along these lines for thousands of genera-tions, and for that reason human beings intuitively avoid incest through the simple auto-matic rule of bond exclusion." (E. Wilson 1978: 37–38.) Here the "developmental land-scape" is steep and deeply canalized: human beings are "guided by an instinct" (p. 38) to avoid brother/sister inbreeding.

[3]Van den Berghe (1983: 101) makes a related point concerning the strength of genetic and cultural "pulls" on the leash. "We can legitimately argue," he says, "about . . . whether we are dealing with a Great Dane held by a toddler, a Chihuahua held by a Sumo wrestler, or some more likely pairing in between."

antithetical to the ordered, goal-oriented marriage system we found earlier among the Tibetans. There is obviously much more to culture and cultural change than this model reveals.

Culture as a Second Inheritance System

Sociobiological models bring us to the heart of the issue raised by Question 1, namely, Is culture a second inheritance system? There are really two issues here. First, is the influence of culture on phenotypes truly distinct from the influence of genes? Second, if so, does culture also warrant distinction from "environment"? Are Flinn and Alexander right in claiming that "no rationale has ever been advanced for regarding the influence of culture on the development and expression of behavior as other than a special subset of the environment"? (1982: 391.) For reasons given below, my argument is that culture does constitute a bona fide inheritance system in its own right, a system characterized by both its own particular form of information transmission and by its own dynamics of transformation through time. I argue that culture must therefore be distinguished from both genes and environment.

Consider first the distinction between genes and culture. I submit that culture deserves recognition as a distinct inheritance system by virtue of its conceptual reality and social transmission—two of culture's most basic properties, as described in Chapters 1 and 2. Because of these features, culture provides informational guides to behavior that are shared within populations, but are not passed through DNA. Yet, as the Tibetan case shows, these guides can and do exert a powerful influence on human behavior. The result is an effective "second channel" of information transfer within human populations, a second inheritance system.

It bears emphasis that this information channel is distinct from the genes both in content and in mechanism. In terms of content, we have seen that culture consists of learned information that is received and processed within the brains and nervous systems of its carriers. Although the molecular machinery for receiving, housing, and activating that information is not fully understood at present, one thing *is* certain: socially transmitted information is not incorporated into the biochemical code of the genetic inheritance system. It does not cross "Weismann's barrier," that is, the barrier to the flow of information from the soma, or body, to the germ line, or genes (for which see, for example, Mayr 1982: ch. 16). Thus the monomarital principle remained perpetually in the cultural system of the thongpa, being coded in language and passed from one generation to the next through teaching and learning rather than being somehow encoded in DNA and then passed through gametogenesis (gamete formation) and syngamy (fertilization). Consequently, these two forms of information—one housed in brains, the other in genes—remain biochemically distinct throughout the lifetime of each and every culture-carrying individual. They may both act as guides to behavior and, as we will later see, they may well share some number of other properties. Nevertheless, they *coexist* as distinct and separate forms of information.

Another point made by the Tibetan example is that the mechanism by which cultural information is passed along is also qualitatively different from the mechanism of genetic transmission. Among the many consequences are differences in the tempo, mode, and ratio of the transmission. The tempo of cultural transmission is highly variable because of the social nature of the process, but learned information certainly has the potential for much more rapid dissemination than the intergenerational process of genetic transmission. The modes of cultural transmission are also more variable than the vertical transmission of genes from parent to offspring. In particular, cultural information is often conveyed "horizontally" (among peers) and "obliquely" (from nonparental elders; see Cavalli-Sforza and Feldman 1981: 54). Furthermore, what I call the "ratio" of the transmission—the proportion of learners to teachers—is also highly variable in culture. In addition to the one-to-one ratio of the genetic system, cultural transmission can also be many-to-one and one-to-many. In short, both the mechanisms and the contents of genetic and cultural inheritance differ substantially.

Turning now to the question of whether culture warrants distinction not only from the genes but also from "environment," I would say that it does, but only because Flinn and Alexander are, at once, both right and wrong. First, they are surely right in viewing culture as part of the "environment" of the genes. By definition, *anything* outside the genetic material itself—"all non-genetic circumstances that influence the phenotype" (Falconer 1981: 100)—qualifies as part of that environment; indeed, molecular geneticists sometimes speak of one gene as being part of the "environment" of another. Second, the argument is also right in regarding culture as a "special subset" of that environment, for as we have seen, culture exhibits no fewer than five basic properties that are unusual among the other members of that environment set.

At the same time, however, their argument is surely wrong in suggesting that culture has more properties in common with other elements of "environment" than it does with the genetic inheritance system. My argument is actually just the reverse. In my view, culture shares with the genes a number of special features that are not exhibited in the aggregate by any other subset of the genes' environment. Indeed, it can be argued that the human capacity for culture evolved by genetic evolution to its present degree of influence precisely because the cultural system has these very special features (a point we will return to later). It is therefore my view that genes and culture should *both* be differentiated from "environment." For the human animal, a trichotomy makes more sense here than a dichotomy.

Chief among my reasons for this perspective are two observations. First, I maintain that culture, like genes, consists of information that informs or instructs phenotypes, particularly behavior. In this sense, culture and the genes have similar form and function: they both offer guides to behavior in an "environment." Second, culture also evolves in a selective manner. In culture as in genes, variant instructions are not all transmitted through space and time at equal rates. Indeed, "environment" has a major influence on the transmission differentials in both systems. The point is then that genes and culture stand in symmetrical relationship to "environment." If we conceptually distinguish genes from environment, surely we should also distinguish culture from environment. The next category of models reflects this distinction.

Category B: Models with Dual Inheritance and Trait Units

The incorporation of culture as a selective second channel of information inheritance requires the identification of two kinds of entities, one genetic and one cultural, each with its own kind of fitness. Models with dual inheritance usually identify genotypes, on the one hand, and their relative reproductive fitnesses as discussed in Chapter 3. On the other hand, they also identify some cultural entity and a measure of its relative fitness for social transmission in a given human population. In particular, the models of Category B identify cultural "traits" as the pertinent second entity, and characterize them as having some sort of differential "cultural fitness." The differences between such models stem from the forces each one uses to explain cultural fitness differentials, and from the more general relationship each describes between genetic and cultural change.

The Cultural Transmission Model

In a series of papers and monographs extending from 1973 onward, my Stanford colleagues Luigi Cavalli-Sforza and Marcus Feldman have developed a model of cultural transmission with the following features. They define the units of cultural transmission as "cultural traits," that is, "traits that are learned by any process of nongenetic transmission, whether by imprinting, conditioning, observation, imitation, or as a result of direct teaching." (1981: 7, 73.) The definition tidily distinguishes the means of transmission from the genetic inheritance process, and it paves the way for developing a cultural theory roughly parallel to genetic microtheory. One can then ask, What are the forces that change the relative frequencies of traits through time in human populations?

In answer to this question, they offer no fewer than five potential forces:

The cultural differences between human groups can, in terms of our model, be regarded as the outcome of the balance of several evolutionary forces: (1) *mutation*, which is both purposive (innovation) and random (copy error); (2) *transmission*, which is not as inert as in biology [i.e., conveyance may also be horizontal and oblique]; (3) *cultural drift* (sampling fluctuations); (4) *cultural selection* (decisions by individuals); and (5) *natural selection* (the consequences at the level of Darwinian fitness). . . . [1981: 351]

Notice that the list includes "natural selection" as a force of *cultural* change, by which they mean the differential survival and reproduction of trait carriers, not the differential reproduction of genotypes (see 1981: 101). Notice also that they distinguish the force of transmission, which is caused by the tempo, mode, and ratio of social conveyance, from the force of cultural selection, which is caused by individual choice.[4]

The third key element of their framework is supplied by the matrices of "transmission coefficients" giving the probabilities or frequencies that specific traits will be conveyed from "transmitters" (be they parents, older-generation teachers or models, or fellow age-mates) to "receivers." Under various sets of assumptions, these matrices then allow Cavalli-Sforza and Feldman to calculate the effect that differences in the modes of transmission (vertical, horizontal, oblique, and various combinations) or in the intensities of "natural selection" have upon the frequency of a given trait in a hypothetical model population.

The procedure shows a number of resemblances both to epidemiological theory (culture is treated as if it spreads contagiously, like disease) and to population genetics, except that Cavalli-Sforza and Feldman have chosen here to measure the frequency of traits, not the frequency of underlying informational units. Thus, to take one example, they calculate the fate under vertical transmission of a trait H that has the properties (1) that it is always culturally transmitted upon exposure (thus the transmission coefficient is 1.0) but (2) that it invariably reduces the survival and reproduction of its carriers (a model they call the "Kuru case," for which see Chapter 7). By their calculations H can actually eliminate "up to (but not more than) 50 percent of its carriers and still spread through the population from an initially low frequency." (1981: 105.)

To date, the approach has proven to have great value. Among other accomplishments, the cultural transmission model was the first quantitative model of cultural evolution, the first to articulate the distinction between oblique, horizontal, and vertical pathways of transmission, and the

---

[4] The term "cultural selection," which was probably derived from "natural selection" by way of Keller's (1915) "societal selection," has been used over the years with a number of different meanings. One of the first definitions I know of is Baker's (1960: 11), wherein cultural selection actually refers to genetic selection (i.e., the differential reproduction of genotypes) caused by "cultural standards of beauty" (see also Kuttner 1968 [1960]: 288; Tobias 1961: 33–36). Carneiro gives a definition more like Cavalli-Sforza and Feldman's, calling it "the cultural equivalent of natural selection"; he sees it as caused either by trait competition, in which "two or more variants of a trait compete for the same 'cultural slot'," or by societal competition, in which "selection operates not on the culture trait as such but the society bearing it." (1970: iv; a similar distinction of levels is made by Lenski and Lenski 1982: 60–81.) Ruyle (1973: 203) speaks not of cultural selection per se but of "cultural design," which he defines ideationally as "the differential replication of ideas by individuals." Corning (1974: 278) suggests that cultural selection can also be called "human selection": the "selection of cultural forms by individuals, groups, or 'authorities'" based upon "the relative economies or utilities involved." In earlier papers (reviewed in the next section), I used a definition similar to Corning's.

first to allow systematic study of the influence of social structure—specifically, the structure of transmission—on cultural dynamics. Moreover, Cavalli-Sforza and Feldman were among the first authors to specify two units with fitness and thus two *kinds* of fitness in culture-carrying populations.[5] As noted at the start of this section, this is a key conceptual ingredient of any dual inheritance theory. Noting that some cultural traits may spread even though they do not "appreciably alter the probability of surviving or having children," Cavalli-Sforza and Feldman point out that the "probability of acceptance as a measure of *cultural selection* must be clearly differentiated from the *Darwinian* or *natural selection* due to the cultural trait." (1981: 15–16.) This measure of cultural selection they call "cultural fitness."

Finally, this was also the first model to show that cultural inheritance does not conform to the cultural equivalent of the Hardy-Weinberg law. As discussed in Chapter 3, that law establishes that the Mendelian mechanics of genetic inheritance do not themselves cause gene-frequency changes in a population. In contrast, Cavalli-Sforza and Feldman's calculations show that variability in mode and ratio enables cultural transmission to cause trait frequencies to vary over time in the absence of other forces. In essence, this is because two or more cultural variants can have equal "probabilities of acceptance" within a population and still change in frequency provided that one of them has a ratio advantage (i.e., a higher average ratio of receivers to transmitters), a mode advantage (i.e., more pathways of transmission, for example a combination of horizontal and vertical modes), or both. It is therefore legitimate to speak of "transmission forces" as one potential cause of cultural evolution.

Despite these advantages, however, the model is not as useful as it might be. The key reason, in my view, stems from one of its deliberate simplifications: in the interest of mathematical tractability, the authors lump together, into a single "transmission coefficient," the combined effects of transmission forces and cultural selection (see 1981: 102, 349). Consequently, the model confounds structural forces of evolutionary change—that is to say, the forces arising from context and constraint—and functional forces of acceptability and perceived advantage. The authors rationalize this simplification with the argument that the role of decision making is often tightly "circumscribed," resulting in the "pervasiveness" of direct, invariant transmission (pp. 64–65).[6] This is particu-

[5] Explicit discussion of two kinds of fitness can be traced to Cavalli-Sforza's 1971 paper, wherein he differentiates between the Darwinian fitness of genotypes in organic evolution and the (unnamed) fitness of ideas in "sociocultural evolution": the latter is defined as the "probability of acceptance by [a] susceptible individual or group." (p. 540.) A related measure, "the efficacy with which a [cultural] trait propagates itself," was then dubbed "cultural fitness" by Boyd and Richerson (1976: 254). Before Cavalli-Sforza's definition, two kinds of fitness were implicit in the dual inheritance arguments of Keller (1915), Medawar (1960), Waddington (1961), Dobzhansky (1962: ch. 1), Blum (1963), Mather (1964: ch. 7), Campbell (1965), Lenski (1970), Masters (1970), and Monod (1971).

[6] Cavalli-Sforza and Feldman offered a second rationalization as follows. "Lest we be accused of 'transmissionism,' we hasten to add that the use of summary transmission coeffi-

larly true, they point out, "in situations in which some knowledge or behavior is spread in the population at the command of a religious or political leader. . . . Here acceptance could be called obedience and is determined not by true cultural selection (that is, a true persuasion that the requested behavior is good or adaptive), but by the acceptance of the authority of the leaders." (p. 64.) The general point is well taken: surely there are many situations in which individuals have little or no choice in the course of cultural transmission (we considered one of these in the discussion of imposition in Chapter 2). But it also follows that choice, when it does occur, is a very different force from "obedience," and one that can steer cultural evolution in a very different direction. The very fact that structural and functional forces like these are "often conflicting," as Cavalli-Sforza and Feldman are the first to admit (p. 65), suggests to me the importance of specifically differentiating their effects. Among other consequences, this would allow the recognition and analysis of power relations and conflicts of interest that would otherwise lie concealed within unitary transmission coefficients.

But there is yet another reason for distinguishing the structural forces of cultural evolution from the functional ones. Such a procedure promises to help resolve what I call the "cultural transmission paradox," namely, how it is that the human capacity for culture can have had both a substantial potential for maladaptive consequences (a potential clearly emphasized by the Cavalli-Sforza and Feldman models) and "natural origins" in genetic selection. As Chapter 3 has shown, the assumption of natural origins requires every innovation in the capacity for culture (or more precisely, the genotypes behind every such innovation) to have had a persistent and adaptive net effect for at least some of its inheritors. If it is true that cultural transmission has so great a potential to act counter to genetic selection, then what happens to ensure that "harmony between the two is expected on average," as Cavalli-Sforza and Feldman put it (p. 341), for at least some culture carriers?

An Early Coevolution Model

My own first efforts to answer this question began with premises similar to those of Cavalli-Sforza and Feldman but proceeded in a different direction. My starting point was the observation that "for many years, biologists and anthropologists have realized that the organic and cultural evolution of human beings have been interdependent, mutually comple-

---

cients in the theory is not intended to indicate that the process cannot be subdivided. These coefficients are conveniences in terms of which correlations between certain types of individuals are simply expressed and vice versa. . . . It is much more likely that transmission as a whole can be measured than the components of which it is made." (1981: 349.) Although it may sometimes be necessary to measure the coefficients of "transmission as a whole," this procedure should not be followed uncritically. It can also preclude our obtaining insight on important analytic issues, such as on the question, discussed in a later section, of the relative importance of imposition versus choice behind a given cultural tradition.

mentary processes. . . ." (1976b: 89.) It seemed to me that scholars had not taken full advantage of the implications of this argument.

I therefore proposed that the case for a fully complementary theory would be strengthened if the benefits of culture could be "measured in the same terms and at the same level as the usual benefits of [features molded by genetic] selection. . . . Unless it can be shown that cultural evolution has somehow run consistently counter to the trends of genetic selection (an unlikely proposition, see Alexander 1971), it is not likely that individual humans generally act in opposition to their own inclusive fitness." (1976a: 386.) People, I went on to suggest, "tend to select and retain from competing variants those cultural practices whose net phenotypic effect most enhances their individual inclusive fitness." I saw this process, which I called "cultural selection," as both independent of and complementary to genetic selection.

Drawing on the earlier schemes of George Peter Murdock (1971 [1956]) and Donald Campbell (1965), both of which are discussed in App. A.4.1, I went on to outline a theory of cultural evolution based upon this mechanism of cultural selection. As I conceived of it at the time, the theory consisted of three principal hypotheses, two corollary arguments, and a series of implications for a larger, more general theory, which has since become the subject of this book.

Briefly stated, the hypotheses were as follows. First, I proposed that "cultural evolution results in large part [but not invariably] from the interindividual selective retention of cultural attributes." (1976b: 96.) Second, I proposed that inclusive fitness has been one important general criterion of selection, acting through closely correlated cultural values and beliefs (such as concern for the welfare of descendants and close kin) in local populations.[7] At the same time, I pointed out that cultural selection "can best be viewed as a multicriterion process and that at least some nonfitness criteria are important in and of themselves." (pp. 105–6.) Third, I suggested a number of "biases" that would tend to keep people from selecting maladaptive forms (1979b: 44–46). One kind of bias I de-

---

[7] The correlation between conscious human goals and inclusive fitness has also been emphasized by Irons (1979a, 1979b, 1983) who notes that "[organic] evolution, of course, has not produced a conscious striving for fitness. Rather it has produced a conscious striving for intermediate goals—such as a good diet or sexual satisfaction—which in past environments enhanced fitness." (1983: 200.) Though expressed in different terms, this mechanism is equivalent to cultural selection at the conscious level. As Irons puts it, "it is clear that people do consciously weigh the probable consequences of alternative behaviors, and choose those which they evaluate as probably producing the most desirable consequences. The view expressed here assumes that what is consciously evaluated as desirable would equate with the biologically optimal in the environments in which human beings evolved." (1979b: 9.) Why, then, is there such "harmony" (to use Cavalli-Sforza and Feldman's term again) between human desires and reproductive fitness? Says Irons, this is because "the evaluations of consequences flowing from different behaviors are ultimately determined by preferences which are universal traits of human beings." (p. 36.) Here, too, our answers are similar, except that I prefer to think of the "universal traits" as organically evolved neurophysiological *biases* on choice (see Durham 1979b: 45–46) rather than as determinants.

scribed—and one we will return to later in this chapter—results from socialization to the traditional norms and values of a given society. My argument was that these norms and values produce individual-level selectivity in cultural transmission, a "selectivity in the adoption of new forms, on the basis of what is held to be adaptive and 'for [one's] own good'." (p. 45.)

The corollaries dealt with the variation that could be expected from the general trend predicted by these hypotheses. The first corollary suggested that "the importance of inclusive fitness to our understanding of human behavior will be conditionally dependent on the degree to which any [given] behavior taxes the highly variable amount of time and energy available to an individual." (1976b: 105.) My reasoning here was simply that many, if not most, cultural practices involve extremely low fitness costs and/or benefits for their carriers. When the options differ hardly or not at all with respect to inclusive fitness, the spread and perpetuation of cultural practices are likely to be better explained in other ways (see 1976b: 102–5).

The second corollary pointed out that whereas the proposed mechanism of cultural selection would normally result in adaptive phenotypic attributes,

it is actually easier to conceive of cultural influences getting "off track" in the evolution of a phenotype than it is for [genetic] influences. Maladaptive cultural practices *can* be maintained at substantial frequency in a population, particularly when the biases previously mentioned are overridden or prevented from functioning by force, threat, misinformation, or restrictions on alternatives. Maladaptive behaviors can also recur through the conscious or deliberate choice of individuals to behave counter to their reproductive interests for whatever reason, but I am suggesting that this behavior is not likely to become a long-lasting cultural tradition. [1979b: 48]

Finally, it seemed possible that this approach could lead to a general theory relating the separate but interacting influences of genes and culture in the evolution of human phenotypes. If it were indeed true that organic and cultural evolution generally result from mechanisms of selection that operate at the same level or range of levels and effectively with the same criterion, that is, the criterion of inclusive fitness, then genetic and cultural change would be truly complementary. They would act as parallel, "co-equal" influences on human phenotypes, *both* tending to enhance the inclusive fitnesses of individuals. I therefore called this suggestion a theory of "coevolution."[8]

[8] The term "coevolution," a logical extension of Darwin's term "coadaptation" (see, for example, 1964 [1859]: 60, 109), was originally coined by Paul Ehrlich and Peter Raven (1964) to refer to interdependent genetic evolution in two species, as in the coevolution of butterflies and their host plants (see Futuyma and Slatkin 1983 for discussion and examples). I use the term to describe the parallel action of cultural selection and genetic selection in the evolution of human phenotypes, especially behaviors. As I describe later in this and subsequent chapters, genetic change and cultural change in human populations are sometimes

But there were problems in this formulation. First, it was pointed out to me independently by several colleagues—Eric A. Smith, George Collier, and the late Michelle Rosaldo—that there were fundamental problems in my conceptualization of culture as socially transmitted behaviors or "traits" rather than as the socially conveyed information behind them.[9] Second, my arguments suffered from insufficient attention to social structure. Unlike the cultural transmission model, my model did distinguish, in mechanism and in outcome, a number of structural forces from their functional counterparts (see, for example, the discussion of manipulation in Durham 1976b: 109). I also pointed out that the process of cultural selection would create group-wide adaptive optimization only under special conditions (1976a: 394), and that "not everyone need directly benefit from an activity for it to be perpetuated in society." (1976b: 109.) But like the cultural transmission model, my model still did not adequately describe how asymmetrical power relations would affect the direction and rate of cultural selection. The absence of that description was misleading and could be construed, despite disclaimers, as promoting the "Panglossian paradigm" (for which see Gould and Lewontin 1979).[10] There remained a need for a theory of cultural evolution that would integrate structural and functional themes, and allow cultural evolution to be linked interactively with concurrent evolutionary change in social structure.

The Social Learning Model

Another dual inheritance model of gene-culture relationships was proposed by Richard Alexander in 1979 (see also MacDonald 1984). Called the "social learning model," this formulation links "the traits of culture" to the influence of the genes through the reinforcing feedback of social learning.

Alexander's argument begins with the suggestion that cultural change can be studied in a fashion parallel to genetic evolutionary change, from

---

interdependent and sometimes not. I subdivide interdependent change into two modes of "interactive" relations between genes and culture, and further identify three modes of "comparative" relations that do not entail interdependent change. See also note 15.

[9] Smith's argument was that although a trait could be *culturally variable*, calling it "cultural" (particularly to contrast it with traits likewise labeled "genetic" or "biological") has the effect of imposing a nature/nurture distinction on a property that most likely depended to some extent upon genes and environment as well as culture. In earlier formulations, I sometimes spoke of the coevolution of human "biology" and culture when I should have said *genes* and culture (as pointed out, for example, by Flinn and Alexander 1982). Collier and Rosaldo emphasized that an analytic focus on traits and culture as behavior had the effect of isolating my arguments from the important developments in ideational culture theory (as discussed in Chapter 1), thus preventing some potentially valuable cross-fertilization.

[10] Indeed Lopreato (1984: 252) accuses me of just that, despite my arguments and a case study to the contrary (Durham 1977, 1979a). The point is that the structural features of society must be *explicitly* related to the model of cultural selection. This has the additional benefit, it seems to me, of enabling bridges to be built between the study of cultural evolution and political economy.

which he borrows five major processes (1979a: 73–74, citing Murdock 1971): "inheritance" ("the traits of culture are heritable through learning"); "mutation" ("like the genetic materials, culture is also mutable"); "selection" ("some traits of culture in some fashion, by their effects, reinforce their own persistence and spread; others do not and eventually disappear for that reason"); "drift" ("traits of culture can also be lost by accident or 'sampling error'"); and "isolation" ("different human societies become separated by extrinsic and intrinsic barriers; they diverge, and they may contact and reemerge or continue to drift apart").

Using this conceptual framework, Alexander then argues that "the important question about cultural evolution is: Who or what determines which novelties will persist, and how is this determination made? On what basis are cultural changes spread or lost?" (1979a: 76.) In answer to this question, Alexander proposes a specific learning mechanism that both guarantees the persistence of adaptive "cultural traits" and provides for "the link" between genes and culture. The proposal is offered as part of a critique of other models, still to be reviewed, some of which view the transmission of cultural information (so-called cultural instructions or cultural replicators) as uncoupling genetic selection and cultural change. Instead, says Alexander,

there is every reason to expect a correlation between cultural change and inclusive-fitness-maximizing. . . . To whatever extent the use of culture by individuals is learned—and if this is not the rule then one is at a loss to explain how any special human capacity to use and transmit culture could have evolved—*regularity of learning situations or environmental consistency is the link between genetic instructions and cultural instructions which makes the latter not a replicator at all, but in historical terms, a vehicle of the genetic replicators.* [1979a: 78–79, emphasis in the original]

Alexander's two main points are that culture must generally change in the direction of improved adaptation for its carriers, and that the social environment of learning is "the link" that makes this happen. His suggestion is that the positive and negative reinforcement deriving from social situations constitutes the chief selective force that causes "the continued *coupling* between culture and the genes." (1979a: 81.) The coupling, moreover, has already been guaranteed by genetic selection, which has favored "the accumulation of genes causing us to be positively reinforced according to the number and intensity of physiologically or socially 'pleasant' interactions with particular individuals (and we could also be *negatively* reinforced by the opposite)."[11] (1979a: 110.) This he calls the "social learning mechanism."

[11] As a primary confirmation of his argument, Alexander, like Wilson (1978; see note 2 above), cites "the clear evidence that the basis for avoidance of sexual relations between very close relatives such as siblings (i.e. incest avoidance) is not their genetic relatedness as such but the fact that they are consistently reared together, thus socially intimate while prepubertal . . . the learning of incest avoidance occurs in a specific and narrow direction that is advantageous to genetic reproduction." (Alexander 1979a: 79.) At the same time, al-

The model has a number of attractive features: the mechanism is plausible and logically consistent, it relates genes and culture without genetic determinism, and it accurately views social life as an important environment of learning. Moreover, it provides a mechanism whereby human social behaviors can be consistent with the predictions of Darwinian theory without having themselves evolved in every case by the differential reproduction of genotypes.[12] The fates of "cultural traits" are influenced by past *products* of genetic selection (namely, the neural system of pleasure and pain), thus avoiding the fallacy (which plagues the sociobiology models) that correlation implies causation.

At the same time, I have reservations about Alexander's fairly restrictive concept of "social learning." In the Tibetan example of Chapter 2, it was clear that individuals acquired the monomarital principle through learning, and through learning in a social context. However, it was also clear that the learning process there differed in two key respects from the process as described in Alexander's model. First, the evidence indicated that the positive reinforcement of social interactions was *not* important in keeping the monomarital principle in place; instead, the principle was a lesser evil, maintained because its perceived ecological benefits outweighed the social difficulties it caused. Second, the principle was learned not from *personal* experience in most cases, but from the social transmission of information about other people's experience. Moreover, it seems to me that Alexander goes too far in arguing that "social learning may be *the only general or widespread mechanism* whereby individuals acquire the ability to behave in evolutionarily appropriate ways toward genetic relatives." (1979: 192, emphasis added.) No doubt Alexander's "social learning" is one general mechanism to have this effect, but it is surely not the only one, as the Tibetan case makes clear. The arguments and evidence presented below lead me to suspect that Alexander's model is, in fact, a special case of a still more general and more influential process.[13]

---

though "in general, multiplicity, intensity, and pleasurableness of social interactions with others of opposite sex" form the prelude to increasing intimacy, "with regard to incest—and only incest—the precise opposite is true: those with whom we are most socially intimate and most pleasurably stimulated are the very individuals with whom sexual activities and marriage commitments would be most disadvantageous." (p. 196.) In the case of cosocialized children, the "multiplicity, intensity, and pleasurableness of social interactions" result in a *negative* reinforcing effect on sexuality later in life (see Chapter 6 of this book).

[12] Alexander's arguments have sometimes been called "sociobiology" (see, for instance, Barash 1980). There is certainly some overlap between Alexander's model and Sociobiology I and II; indeed, there is some overlap between all the models outlined in this chapter. Nevertheless, for reasons explained in Chapter 1, the "social learning model" does not qualify as sociobiology since it can explain "how cultural change can occur without genetic change, while nonetheless maintaining a structure consistent with the maximizing of inclusive fitness by individuals." (Alexander 1979a: 194–95.)

[13] In a subsequent paper, Flinn and Alexander (1982: 394) argue "that the critical issue before culture theorists is: What are the evolved proximate mechanisms upon which adaptive learning is based?" Their answer ignores the social learning mechanism altogether and turns to the argument that genetic selection "must have favored abilities continually to reprogram the mind's analysis of cultural traits (i.e. learning)." As examples, they

The Gene-Culture Transmission Model

The last major model in Category B is the "gene-culture transmission" model of Charles Lumsden and Edward O. Wilson. The model can be seen as an evolutionary outgrowth of Wilson's earlier "genetic influence" model, but one that has been significantly enhanced by a number of new definitions and formal derivations. The authors describe it as "the first attempt to trace development all the way from genes through the mind to culture," and as one stimulated by "the remarkable fact that sociobiology has not taken into proper account either the human mind or the diversity of cultures." (Lumsden and Wilson 1981: ix; see also 1983, 1985; Lumsden and Gushurst 1985.)

Their model begins with three definitions. First, they define the basic unit of culture to be a "culturgen," which is any member of "an array of transmissible behaviors, mentifacts, and artifacts" in a population.[14] To take their examples, an array of culturgens might be "an assortment of food items, an array of carpenter's tools, a variety of alternative marriage customs to be adopted or discarded, or any comparable array of choices," so long as the alternatives are "equally accessible for both teaching and learning." (p. 7.)

Second, the culturgens are "processed" through a sequence of "epigenetic rules," or "genetically determined procedures that direct the assembly of the mind." The rules "comprise the restraints that the genes place on development (hence the expression 'epigenetic'), and they reflect the probability of [an individual's] using one culturgen as opposed to another." (p. 7.) They further distinguish "*primary epigenetic rules*," which are "the more automatic processes that lead from sensory filtering to perception," from secondary ones, which include "the evaluation of perception through the processes of memory, emotional response, and decision

suggest such "shortcuts and cues" as: "(1) imitating those who appear successful; (2) behaving oppositely or differently from those who appear unsuccessful (anti-imitation?); (3) accepting advice and instruction from those with an interest in one's own success . . . (4) viewing skeptically advice and instructions given by an individual with interests that conflict with one's own in regard to the topic being instructed. These simple mechanisms provide many possibilities for explanations of cultural phenomena." (1982: 394–95.) Each of these would seem to be a value-based decision rule, rather than a reinforcement from pleasant interactions.

[14] Lumsden and Wilson (1981: 27) give "culturgen" a more formal definition as "a relatively homogeneous set of artifacts, behaviors, or mentifacts (mental constructs having little or no direct correspondence with reality) that either share without exception one or more attribute states selected for their functional importance or at least share a consistently recurrent range of such attributes within a given polythetic set." (A "polythetic set" refers to a collection of entities in which each exhibits some large number of the attributes defining the group.) Lumsden and Wilson assert that this unit "is the equivalent of the artifact type employed in archaeology . . . and *is similar in variable degree* to the mnemotype of Blum (1963), idea of Huxley (1962) and Cavalli-Sforza (1971) . . . instruction of Cloak (1975), culture type of Boyd and Richerson (1976), meme of Dawkins (1976), and concept of Hill (1978)." (p. 7, emphasis added.) But their unit includes artifacts and behaviors as well as ideational phenomena, and the ideational phenomena identified are said to have "little or no direct correspondence with reality."

making through which individuals are predisposed to use certain culturgens in preference to others." (p. 36.) Finally, they define "bias curves" (or "epigenetic curves") to represent the "probability distributions of the [adoption and] usage of various culturgens" (p. 55), a concept that reflects Wilson's (1978) arguments about "developmental bias" in the Sociobiology II model reviewed under Category A.

Using these definitions, Lumsden and Wilson proceed to differentiate "the three conceivable classes" of culturgen transmission that are shown in Fig. 4.1. In the first, "pure genetic transmission," the same culturgen is selected each time; in the second, "pure cultural transmission," all the available culturgens are assumed to have an equal probability of transmission; and in the third, "gene-culture transmission," at least two culturgens have different probabilities. According to Lumsden and Wilson, the second hypothesis is the one that "appears to be the prevailing view" (p. 10) among social scientists today. In their view, however, the third one, gene-culture transmission, "appears to be the most likely mode of inheritance for all categories of culturgens, in the human species and in all other imaginable species in which the capacity for culture evolves." (p. 11.)

The next component of their model, "gene-culture translation," is defined as "the effect of the genetically determined epigenetic rules of individual cognition and behavioral development on social patterns." (p. 100.) In other words, "translation" refers to the expression at the societal level of the cumulative effects of the transmission process at the individual level. The results of this process are represented by hypothetical "ethnographic curves" that portray the frequency distributions of human societies according to the proportion of their members to use a given culturgen or culturgens. Finally, they discuss the "coevolutionary circuit" that ties all the various pieces of the model together.[15] The "genetically-determined epigenetic rules" influence individual choices, are translated into societal patterns, and then form part of the selecting environment of the genes. The societal patterns and individual genotypes then determine individual inclusive fitnesses which, in turn, lead to changes in gene frequency and thus to changes in the epigenetic rules themselves (see p. 348). The circuit essentially iterates the steps of their argument into a process of interdependent genetic and cultural change through time.

In short, the Lumsden-Wilson model is an important contribution to

[15] Although gratifying, Lumsden and Wilson's use of the expression "gene-culture coevolution" is admitted to be substantially different from my own. "In the strict usage of biology," as they put it, "the word coevolution means genetic change of one species in response to the evolution of a second species, which in turn changes in response to the first species [see note 8] . . . We stretched the term to include the reciprocal effects of genetic and cultural change within the human species. Our usage is also different from that of William Durham. . . . By coevolution Durham means parallel but unlinked changes in genes and culture." (Lumsden and Wilson 1983: 206; see also 1981: 257.) As I argue later in this and subsequent chapters, there are considerable advantages to a conceptualization of gene-culture relations that *permits but does not require* the effects to be reciprocal and interactive in every instance.

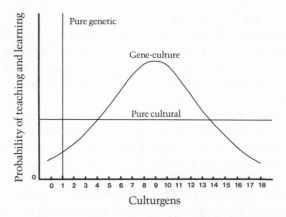

Fig. 4.1. The "gene-culture transmission" model of Charles Lumsden and Edward O. Wilson. The graph shows three hypothetical "bias curves" governing the spread of an array of cultural elements ("culturgens") in a given human population. In "pure genetic" transmission, "the development of individual members of the society is genetically constrained in such a way that the same culturgen is selected each time" from the array of possibilities (Lumsden and Wilson 1981: 9). In "pure cultural" transmission, all of the available culturgens are assumed to have equal probabilities of transmission within the population. Finally, in "gene-culture" transmission, "at least two culturgens differ in the likelihood of adoption because of the innate epigenetic rules." (p. 11.) The authors argue that gene-culture transmission is the most likely mode of inheritance in cultural evolution. Redrawn with permission of the publishers from figure 1-3 from Lumsden and Wilson 1981: 9, Harvard University Press, copyright © 1981 by the President and Fellows of Harvard College.

gene-culture theory. Nevertheless, I have a number of problems with it, problems that range from picky to profound (see also the reviews included in Lumsden and Wilson 1982). One picky problem concerns the model's terminology: there is an unfortunate insistence here upon an entirely new vocabulary for the concept of cultural selection, which already had a cultural tradition of its own among scholars working in the field. Concerning more profound problems, I find two of particular significance. First, there is the problem of what it is in society, or more specifically in *culture*, that needs to be explained. For instance, when Lumsden and Wilson deal with inbreeding avoidance—that is, the behavioral avoidance of mating between consanguineous relatives—they introduce the subject in a discussion of incest taboos, which are obviously *cultural* rules (1981: 85–86; see also Chapter 6 of this book). But at the stage of "gene-culture translation" they use their theory only to predict the number of individuals in each society who will *behaviorally* avoid brother-sister matings. They offer no explanation for the rules themselves; culture, in a word, has been left out.[16] What then has been explained? Remembering that all people are assumed at the start to have a "strong intrinsic preference" to

[16] A major portion of the problem here can be traced to two conceptual errors. First, the pertinent culturgens are defined as behavioral, rather than ideational, alternatives: "the culturgen c_1 is incest avoidance and c_2 is the incestuous relationship." (Lumsden and Wilson 1981: 151.) Second, the word "incest" is used when "inbreeding" is meant, giving the illusion that culture is nevertheless involved. As discussed in Chapter 6 of this book, "incest" is

avoid brother-sister inbreeding (p. 151), how surprised can we be by "ethnographic curves" predicting brother-sister mating to be rare in samples of existing societies?

The second problem concerns the conceptualization of gene-culture transmission and translation. Like the three earlier models of Category B, Lumsden and Wilson's model appropriately focuses on the social transmission of cultural variants within human populations and asks, in effect, What explains the differential transmission of alternative forms (the "culturgens")? Like the others, the gene-culture transmission model also emphasizes individual decision making as the leading force of cultural change, and thereby heavily weights the functional side of evolutionary process. And like the others, the model explicitly recognizes the biasing effects of the organically evolved structures and functions of human neurophysiology. Indeed, Lumsden and Wilson elevate to central importance the neurophysiological biases that other authors have called "satisfaction," or sensory reinforcement, and of "learning canalization." The problem lies in the argument that, when cultural options are not equiprobable, this is "because of the innate epigenetic rules" and "genetically determined procedures." (Lumsden and Wilson 1981: 11, 7.) Part of the difficulty stems from simple terminology. Thus, when they use the words "innate" and "genetically determined," surely Lumsden and Wilson mean something more like "genetically variable" or "subject to genetic modification" (see also Cloninger and Yokoyama 1981).

More importantly, however, when tracing causation "from genetically determined epigenetic rules to the final ethnographic curves" (Lumsden and Wilson 1981: 101), their model admits evaluational input from epigenetic rules alone (see, for example, fig. 4.1, p. 101). This means that bias curves are treated as the product of "genetically directed learning" and individual development (p. 96); no weight is given to the socially transmitted values already in the cultural system.[17] Once again, at a critical step, culture has been left out. To take a concrete example, I suggested in Chapter 2 that alternative marriage principles were formerly transmitted among the thongpa with a "bias curve" that strongly favored the monomarital principle ($M = 1$). I argued that the thongpa had a conscious preference for that principle and that it had, in fact, been adaptive. But there was no evidence to suggest that the preference was "innate," or even that

conventionally defined as sexual behavior that is specifically prohibited by one or more cultural rules.

[17] Culture is therefore seen as "the product of myriad personal cognitive acts that are channeled by the innate epigenetic rules. The 'invisible hand' in this marketplace of culturgens has been made visible [in the model] by characterizing the epigenetic rules at the level of the person and translating them upward to the social level through the procedures of statistical mechanics." (Lumsden and Wilson 1981: 176.) The authors recognize that the conscious mind relies upon "simple heuristics" (p. 87) and "cognitive shortcuts" (p. 89) when choosing between culturgens. Yet they fall short of identifying the more important of these as socially transmitted values with cultural evolutionary histories of their own (see 1981: 86–92). Consequently, the model portrays culture as shaped exclusively by "biologically grounded individual cognition." (p. 177.)

it had been derived from epigenetic rules during individual development. Instead, the preference was, by all indications, the product of age-old cultural values concerning land, wealth, and agricultural production.

It would be a small matter if the issue here were semantic or a matter of emphasis, but there are several reasons why I am not persuaded that it is. First, gene-culture transmission is defined at the outset by Lumsden and Wilson to refer to transmission differentials caused by "genetically determined" rules (ch. 1, passim). Second, in their "coevolutionary circuit," genetic selection is the *only* force identified as shaping the bias curves. Third, Lumsden and Wilson dismiss as "cultural determinism" the suggestion (like mine concerning Tibet) that cultural patterns emerge "as the outcome of conscious choices made according to culturally acquired rules of inference and evaluation." (p. 56.) Here their argument stereotypes both sides of the regrettable dichotomy between genetic and cultural determinism, and overlooks the fertile fields between. Finally, they try too hard to sweep aside cultural influences, not to mention environmental influences, on the shaping of peoples' preferences. In their view, "habitat and economic strategy are not necessarily the prime movers [of cultural change]. They represent *boundary conditions* whose selection is influenced by the epigenetic rules and which constrain rather than direct the choices made by individual members of society." (1981: 56, emphasis added.) While I would agree that Tibetan economic strategy has been *influenced* by Lumsden and Wilson's "epigenetic rules," I cannot agree that thongpa habitat and economic strategy "constrain rather than direct" the choices made by individuals. Nor do the data suggest that the alternative marriage rules "differ in the likelihood of adoption because of the innate epigenetic rules." As we have seen, there is simply much more to it than that.

In my view, the gene-culture transmission model points clearly to the need for a theory of cultural change that explicitly integrates the influences of genes, environment, *and* pre-existing culture on the differential transmission of cultural forms.

Category C: Models with Dual Inheritance and Ideational Units

The third and final category comprises models with ideational units of cultural transmission. These models are fewer in number than trait-based models, probably because traits are relatively easy to observe and study, and are among the more tangible units to show the influence of culture (artifacts being another example).[18] Ideational units do not offer these immediate advantages; still I think their benefits outweigh their costs.

[18] Ernst Mayr (1982: 736) reminds us that "prior to about 1910 the silent assumption was made almost universally that there is a 1:1 relation between genetic factor (gene) and character. Hence, when one spoke of a unit character, it did not really matter whether one meant

One clear benefit to ideational models we have already touched upon, namely, the benefit of avoiding a unit of analysis that pits nature against nurture. By focusing on ideas, values, and beliefs rather than on behaviors, these models avoid the confusing and misleading implication that a given trait is "cultural" and therefore free of all genetic influence. But there is a second, if less obvious, advantage: ideational units can greatly simplify the analysis of cultural transmission. This is both because a given unit of information may influence many different kinds of traits, and because such a unit, depending on the circumstances, may instruct many different forms of the same trait.

Consider, for example, the unnecessary complexity that would have been introduced into our analysis of the Tibetan marriage system had we taken "form of marriage" as the unit of cultural transmission. What we were able to interpret as the diverse behavioral consequences of a few fairly simple beliefs would have generated, instead, an absolutely bewildering array of trait transmission probabilities. Worse still, this matrix of probabilities would have varied greatly from place to place and from time to time. In contrast, as Chapter 2 makes clear, the relevant transmission is not of traits, but of beliefs and principles that, depending on family circumstances, create a wide array of traits. The beliefs appear to be fairly uniform among the thongpa throughout Tibet; indeed, they help to explain the evident variation of "traits" from place to place and from time to time.

Finally, there is also an advantage to ideational models in terms of levels of analysis. The models discussed above, whether in Category A or B, share the common property of being *microevolutionary* in scale. Each is based on a theory of cultural change through "trait substitution," the analog of allelic substitution in genetic microevolution. Alternative traits, like alleles, are viewed as interchangeable parts whose frequencies vary because of differential rates of transmission. In these formulations, cultural evolution is simply the shifting frequency of independently varying traits within a population.

In recent years, this approach has been criticized by the proponents of a *macroevolutionary* view of cultural change, that is, of a view that the important temporal changes of culture involve a form of "quantum adjustment" (see, for example, P. Diener 1980; P. Diener et al. 1978). According to this approach, change occurs through "a form of cultural speciation that involves changes in the regulatory or control constraints governing the

---

the underlying genetic basis or its phenotypic expression. . . . With the rapidly increasing genetic activity after 1900, the need arose for a technical term designating the material basis of an independently heritable character. The Danish geneticist W. L. Johannsen . . . proposed in 1909 to adopt a shortened version of [the earlier term] pangen—*gene*—for the material basis of a hereditary character." Of course one could always object that the case is not parallel: some years later, the "material basis" of the gene was confirmed, and it seems clear that no such transmitted substance will be found for culture. On the other hand, that a unit of information is ideational and not "material" does not make it any less "real" or influential (see Popper 1976: 180 ff. on this point).

internal cohesion of the culture and its 'genome' and that alters its political and economic functioning." (P. Diener 1980: 427.) In much the way that genes are not independent in either a physical sense (because of chromosomes and linkage) or a functional sense (because of regulatory genes and genic interaction or epistasis), so too is cultural information interconnected in complexes and "self-descriptive systems" (like religions, for example).[19] When culture changes at this level of complexity, "evolutionary leaps" may result, a process considerably different from the piecemeal substitution of individual traits. Analogous to the theory of organic evolution by punctuated equilibria discussed in Chapter 1, this process can give rise to whole new cultural systems in short periods of time.

The point is well taken. At the same time, however, macroevolutionary arguments have sometimes implied that cultural transformation is a process of purely internal, systemic reorganization, and therefore somehow removed from the interests and manipulations of its human culture carriers.[20] The ensuing debate has been productive (see, for example, P. Diener 1980), and has helped to stir new interest in the patterns and processes of cultural change. But it may also have sidetracked the discussion. It remains possible that, in culture, micro- and macrochange are in effect two poles of a more general process, one that applies consistently at both extremes and at all possible levels in between.

This would seem to be another advantage to ideational theory: it has the potential for adequate generality. By virtue of a focus on the transmission of information rather than traits, ideational theory does not require some uniform and invariant "unit of culture," whether micro *or* macro in scale. Judging from the properties of culture outlined in Chapter 1, an appropriate ideational unit will necessarily be variable in size (that is, in quantity of information) and in organization. Moreover, it must have the properties of a "holon," that is "a dual tendency to preserve and assert its individuality as a quasi-autonomous whole, *and* to function as an in-

[19] With respect to the conceptualization of culture, the macroevolution model of Diener, Nonini, and Robkin (1978, 1980) certainly qualifies as a Category C model. Following John von Neumann's theory of self-reproducing "automata," Diener and his colleagues view culture as an information system capable of "self-description" and, under appropriate conditions, of self-reproduction. It contains all of the descriptive information needed for the design and function of a complete social system. The model is clearly on the right track, as it were, with respect to state variables. Regrettably, however, deficiencies in the model's laws of transformation as described to date preclude its inclusion in my Category C listing. First and most importantly, the model fails to describe the directions of change predicted from its mechanism. Second, the model assumes that these changes, however they occur, are necessarily unrelated to their consequences in a given environment (see Diener, Nonini, and Robkin 1978: 21). Thus the model not only fails to provide specific laws of transformation but also eliminates by assumption the possibility of laws of transformation based upon the consequences of culture for its carriers.

[20] As a case in point, Diener (1974: 611) argued that the rise of Anabaptism among marginalized peasants in sixteenth-century Europe represented cultural evolution at the level of an entire ideology. He also indicated that this was "not a philosophical movement, but primarily a pragmatic one." Thus, the unit was clearly "macro," but the process—by Diener's own description—was still one of differential social transmission according to consequences.

tegrated part of (an existing or evolving) larger whole." (Allen and Starr 1982: 9.) In principle, these properties can easily be accommodated within an ideational model of cultural change. With this list of advantages in mind, let us now complete our survey of models.

The Social Selection Model

Proposed in 1915 by Albert G. Keller of Yale University, the social selection model warrants inclusion here because of its explicit parallels with the Darwinian theory of natural selection, and because of its influence on more recent models by way of a well-known paper by the psychologist Donald Campbell that appeared in 1965. Building on the earlier work of William Graham Sumner (1907; see also Sumner and Keller 1927), the model attempts to provide evolutionary explanations for the myriad social traditions or "folkways" of human populations.

Keller's model is based on the notion of human mental changes or "brain adaptations" said to take the place of the "bodily adaptations" formed through genetic natural selection and to render them unnecessary. These mental changes "emerge in the form of ideas," said Keller (1915: 19); they are then "materialized or realized" in behavior, specifically in the "folkways" of a people. The result is that human beings have a way "of escaping the fatal sweep of natural selection." (p. 22.) The mode of evolution is therefore changed in culture, Keller was fond of pointing out, but "the process [of adaptation] goes on."

Keller defended this theory of what he called "societal evolution" on the grounds that the salient conceptual features of Darwin's theory, namely, variation, selection, and heredity, had counterparts in the realm of ideas, social mores, and mental processes. Anticipating charges that he was "reasoning from analogy," Keller claimed to "find something in the social field which *is* variation, whether or not it may be *like* what is called variation in the organic field; similarly social selection *is* selection and not merely *like* it." (p. 15; see also Childe 1951: 175–79.) Indeed, Keller recognized two forms of social selection of which only the first relied on a simple analogy to Darwin's "survival of the fittest." He called it "automatic" or "societal" selection, and pointed out that "the contest is not between ideas but rather their adherents or exponents"; the result was "selection of the mores through the annihilation of their bearers." (p. 71.) In contrast, the second form of selection was called "rational"; ideas and mores were viewed as differentially propagated on the basis of some judgmental evaluation "performed in the light of knowledge." (p. 96.) Even so, "the primitive touchstone for the mores was the sensation of pleasure and pain, or to put it more generally, the degree of satisfaction experienced." (p. 103.) In Keller's view, both forms of social selection tended to produce adaptation. He was therefore not surprised to find that contemporary mores showed adaptation: this simply betrayed "selection still at work." (p. 92.)

The Programmed Learning Model

Although largely by coincidence, H. Ronald Pulliam and Christopher Dunford have presented a model that reads like an updated extension of Keller's thesis.

With the advent of social learning, the evolution of behavior begins to run on two tracks, genetic and cultural, which are interdependent but nevertheless separable. Both genetic and cultural evolution depend on transmission of information from one generation to the next. Genetic transmission is by reproduction. Cultural transmission is by learning from others. . . . A genetic trait spreads in the population because it enhances relative fitness. . . . Is the same true of a cultural trait? [Pulliam and Dunford 1980: 8]

According to Pulliam and Dunford, the answer to this question depends on two variables, "the [reproductive] fitness of individuals who adopt the trait" and "the probability that the trait is learned by other individuals." (p. 9.) It is the closer look at these variables that produces some similarity to Keller's argument.

Consider the reproductive fitness argument first. Pulliam and Dunford suggest that ideas, as units of cultural information, are sometimes selected out of the cultural system by the reproductive failure of their carriers. In this instance, ideas disappear by "natural" or "Darwinian subtraction" (p. 106), a process similar to that of genetic selection (and equivalent to Cavalli-Sforza and Feldman's "natural selection of culture"). As in Keller's automatic selection, the contest here is not between ideas but between their carriers: ideas will change in frequency as their perpetrators, individuals or groups, reproduce or die out.

Second, the fitness of an idea is also affected by the rate at which it is positively evaluated and thus socially transmitted by the members of a population. Here Pulliam and Dunford draw on learning theory and decision theory to argue that the evaluation of a variant depends upon feedback from primary and secondary "reinforcers." Much like Keller's "primitive touchstone for the mores," the primary reinforcers are described as genetically evolved neural structures that classify some sensations as pleasant or satisfying and others as unpleasant or frustrating (p. 25). Similarly, secondary reinforcers are stimuli that become associated in the brain with primary neural feedback, and thus constitute additional guides to learning. Pulliam and Dunford's point, then, is that human beings, like other learning animals, have been "programmed" by genetic evolution operating on the nervous system to accept these socially transmitted ideas "that increase pleasure, reduce pain, reduce anger, reduce fear or increase cognitive consistency." (p. 66.) For the most part, such information would produce adaptations just as Keller argued.

Overall, the programmed learning model is a big step in the right direction. In the first place, Pulliam and Dunford are among the first of the modelers to appreciate the ideational nature of culture.

We want to make clear the importance of distinguishing human behavior from human ideas about behavior [or other things]. This distinction is crucial to understanding the evolution of human behavior. Our actual behavior may directly affect our Darwinian fitness, in terms of chances for survival and reproduction, but our ideas *cannot* do so *directly*. Ideas affect fitness only when they motivate behavior. . . . Unfortunately for parsimonious explanations, the evolution of human cultural behavior is bound to the evolution of human ideas. [1980: 107–8]

Second, I believe they correctly identify two of the main pathways through which cultural variants may achieve high cultural fitness. Third, they make the important point that rational selection is based on a "learning program" that features, as fundamental evaluation criteria, the primary reinforcers of the nervous system. Finally, I think they are right when they note that "secondary reinforcers may vary between human cultures, but . . . all humans are anchored to the same emotions by the same primary reinforcers, which are universal [genetically variable] traits of our species." (1980: 43–44.)

My one major criticism is simply that Pulliam and Dunford did not go further with what they had. As we shall see, the groundwork is laid here for a much more useful general theory. They agree that there should be a theory of cultural selection, to complement the theory of natural selection, but modestly decline to join in the debate about it. Sadly, then, we are left in the end with the same nagging problem we faced at the start, "to specify how ideas are eliminated from human cultures and how this process relates to Darwinian fitness." (p. 108.)

Darwinian Culture Theory

Robert Boyd and Peter Richerson have proposed another recent model of gene-culture relationships, one they call a "Darwinian theory of the evolution of cultural organisms." (1985: 2; see also Richerson and Boyd 1978, 1984, 1989.) The theory is designed to answer two basic questions: What are the implications of different patterns of socialization—the "structures of transmission"—for the fate of cultural variants in a population? and, What are the ecological conditions under which such structures could have been favored by organic evolution through genetic selection?

The model has many features to recommend it. First, as required for inclusion in Category C, the model both postulates dual inheritance—indeed, the term was coined by Boyd and Richerson (1976)—and begins from an ideational conceptualization of culture, which is defined as "information acquired by imitating or learning from other individuals and able to affect an individual's phenotype, usually behavior." (1984: 430.) Second, for reasons similar to those already given, the model makes an appropriate distinction between genes, culture, and environment. In particular, it describes culture as one of the "evolving properties" of a population and contrasts it with environment, "those processes in the physical and biological realm that . . . are somehow external to the population itself." (1985: 4–5.) Moreover, it tidily identifies the main structural differences between genetic and cultural inheritance: the cultural "mating system" is different (that is, receivers or "cultural offspring" can have many "cultural parents"); the cultural "generation length" is more variable; and the cultural "transmission events" can take place at any time in the life cycle, or even sequentially for that matter. Third, the model makes good use of genetic evolutionary theory, including population genetics, as "a source of analogies and formal mathematical machinery with which to build a theory of the evolution of culture." (p. 4.) But the most important of its contributions is surely the elucidation and analysis of five different forces of cultural evolution, which the authors divide into three classes: random forces, decision-making forces, and natural selection acting directly on cultural variation (1984: 430).

Understandably, the first class of forces receives relatively little attention, consisting as it does of the familiar cultural analogs of mutation (force 1) and drift (force 2). The decision-making forces, however, are more interesting. Here Boyd and Richerson subdivide the decision-based "programmed learning" model into two contrasting mechanisms. The first (force 3) is called "guided variation," or "the cultural transmission of the results of learning." (1985: 174.) This force derives from the impact that "ordinary individual learning" can have on the frequency of cultural variants when decisions, or "favored variants," in one generation are socially transmitted to the next. Hence variation is "guided": choices made in generation X can, by virtue of their social transmission, influence the variation available at the start of $X + 1$. It is, in effect, a form of Lamarckian inheritance: preferred "acquired forms" are passed along sequentially from teachers to learners. Boyd and Richerson show that this force increases the frequency of variants favored by individual learning to the point where the phenotype they instruct is the "average phenotype" in the population (see 1985: ch. 4).

The second decision-making force, "biased transmission," comes into play "when naive individuals exposed to a variety of models preferentially imitate some rather than others." (1984: 430.) In contrast to guided variation, biased transmission is assumed to involve learners who choose only from existing variants; they do not invent or modify alternatives on their own. But this force is also more complicated, being divided into three different forms: "direct bias" (force 4a), according to which "people may adopt some cultural variants rather than others based on their judgments about the properties of the variants themselves" (1985: 10); "frequency dependent bias" (force 4b), according to which they choose their variant on the basis of its frequency in the population at large (for example, by choosing the majority opinion); and "indirect bias" (force 4c), which can occur when "naive individuals prefer some models over others . . . and [then] use such preferences to determine the attractiveness of that model for other characters." (p. 243.) Through the use of mathematical models for each of these mechanisms, Boyd and Richerson demonstrate that rigorous adherence to a frequency criterion or an indirect criterion can act to "increase the frequency of cultural variants that have lower [reproductive] fitness than other variants." (p. 166.) In other words, strict adherence to these decision rules can be maladaptive.

Importantly, this same outcome is also predicted by their model of force 5, the remaining one, which is "the natural selection of cultural variation." Unlike forces 4b and 4c, this force does not depend on decision making or on the use of external criteria of desirability. Instead, it derives from differential modeling—that is, from "all the things that happen to an individual [that] affect the probability that the individual will be available as a model for naive individuals." (p. 200.) One of those things, which I will call force 5a, is true Darwinian natural selection—that is, the selective preservation of cultural variants as a consequence of actual reproductive differentials (coupled with parent-offspring social transmission; for an example, see Boyd and Richerson 1985: 177–78). A second cause of differential modeling, which I will call force 5b, is better termed "role selection," the preservation of cultural variants as a consequence of interpersonal competition for influential roles in society. A hypothetical belief in belligerence or "fierceness," for example, could spread through a tribal population if ever fierceness were to make males more likely to become village headmen and thus important behavioral models for others. Even if success in the headman role required reproductive sacrifice, so Boyd and Richerson would argue, the differential cultural influence of that position could still cause the evolutionary spread of fierceness. This argument is an important one, and we will return to it in Chapter 7.

The Boyd and Richerson approach is in many ways a useful extension of Donald Campbell's (1965) arguments about mechanisms (see App. A.4.1), and also a timely answer to Davydd Greenwood's (1984) call for a theory of culture that shows the full impact of Darwinian thinking. Yet I have reservations. First, despite an appropriate starting definition of culture, the models are built on a surprisingly impoverished conceptualization of it. The models assume, for example, that "culture is acquired by directly copying the phenotype"—that is, by directly imitating observable behavior (1985: 9). The premise appropriately emphasizes the difference between genetic and cultural transmission, but it also distances the authors' models from the ideational nature of, and meaning in, cultural systems. What is important in their approach, in other words, is not what one thinks or believes but simply what one does.

Contributing to this impoverishment are some trivializing examples of cultural transmission, such as the "homebodies and hellraisers" example of chapter 2 (1985), and Boyd and Richerson's centerpiece diagram of "the evolutionary process of a cultural species" (1985: 6; © 1985 by The University of Chicago), which is based on Richard Lewontin's "structure of population genetics theory" (1974: 12; see also Fig. 3.2 of this book):

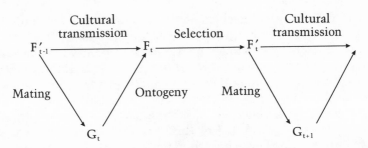

In this diagram, G_t and G_{t+1} refer to the distribution of genotypes in a given population at times t and $t + 1$, and similarly the F_t's refer to the distribution of phenotypes before (F_t) and after (F_t'), a period of "selection." Consistent with Boyd and Richerson's emphasis on a "dual inheritance" view of phenotypic change, the schema does indeed imply a distinct track for the genes (as might be extended from G_t to G_{t+1}). But there is no track for culture: their second "system of inheritance" has been wholly subsumed within phenotype distributions.

In my opinion, this omission has three unfortunate consequences: first, it conceals the symmetry of influence that exists between genes and phenotypes on the one hand, and between culture and phenotypes on the other; second, it portrays cultural transmission as a discontinuous, intergenerational process, broken up by intermittent periods of "selection" acting on phenotypes; and third, it contributes to the persisting misimpression that culture can fairly be treated as an aspect of phenotype. In effect, these authors define culture as one thing (information) but treat it as another (behavior). As a result, its extrasomatic, conceptual existence disappears.

My second reservation concerns social structure, the "actually existing network of social relations" within human populations (Geertz 1973: 145). As in almost all of the previous models, Darwinian culture theory is based on a premise of so-called radical individualism: cultural change is viewed as the statistical outcome of vast numbers of choices by the individual members of a society. There are virtually no structured asymmetries or power relations, and coercion, when Boyd and Richerson mention it at all (as in 1985: 229–30), is treated as individually delivered "punishment of noncooperators" (and is shown to be an unlikely course of action for atomistic maximizers at that). In the genetic track, of course, one can often get by with such simplifications, if only because the transmission of genes is a closed, bi-parental affair that is relatively impervious to third-party interventions. But surely the situation is different in the cultural track: certain nonparental individuals or groups are often able to impose their own preferred transmission upon many recipients. In cultural systems, in other words, significant evolutionary forces can and do arise from unequal social relations; to ignore these forces is to ignore what may often be the leading cause of transformation. It is also to ignore the interaction between cultural evolution and changes in the social organization of a population, or what can be called its "social evolution" (as in Hallpike 1986; see also Johnson and Earle 1987).

Last but not least, I have reservations concerning one of Boyd and Richerson's most important conclusions about cultural process. In their attempt "*to amend* neo-Darwinian theory" to accommodate cultural inheritance (1985: 9, emphasis added), the authors have perhaps taken the abstract genetic analogy a bit too far. Ironically, their pursuit of "Darwinian culture theory" leads them to a conclusion that is strongly anti-Darwinian. As they put it, "if we start with [the assumption of natural origins], but still show that cultural transmission leads to the evolution of genetically maladaptive traits, then we have the strongest indication that the forces of genetic and cultural evolution are not always coincident [and] that the existence of culture causes human evolution to be *fundamentally different* than that of noncultural organisms." (p. 99, emphasis added.) In the sections that follow, I propose a theory that shares a number of features with the Boyd and Richerson model, but in which culture does not cause human evolution to be "fundamentally different."

A Coevolutionary Theory

Despite their differences, the three categories of models just described represent significant progress toward understanding gene-culture relations in human populations. Nevertheless, several major problem areas remain. Generally speaking, the models suffer from greatly oversimplified conceptualizations of culture, from insufficient attention to structural forces of cultural change, and from poorly defined causal priority among hypothesized mechanisms. Concerning the latter, I think it is fair to say that we now have a decent idea of the range of possible mechanisms; what we lack is a clear sense of what is important.

In an attempt to address these problems, let me now propose a remodeled version of coevolutionary theory. It is useful to begin by drawing a distinction between two categories of cultural evolutionary processes, a distinction that parallels Ernst Mayr's arguments about organic evolution (1982: 400; see also Chapter 3 of this book). The first category, "transformation," includes all processes that cause change through time within established cultural systems. This category of processes is illustrated schematically in Fig. 4.2, panel A, which shows a hypothetical culture undergoing two sequential transformations. The second category, "diversification," includes all processes by which a given cultural system branches through time into two or more distinct cultures. For comparison, diversification is depicted in Fig. 4.2, panel B.

Using these terms, let me now summarize two basic propositions that are shared, implicitly or explicitly, by virtually all efforts at evolutionary

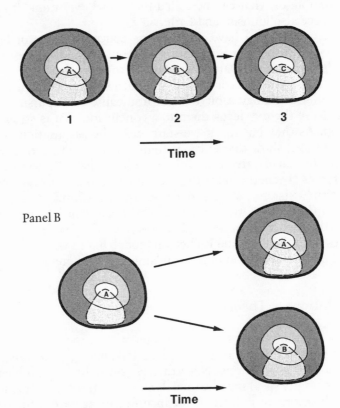

Panel A

1   2   3

Time

Panel B

Time

Fig. 4.2. Two categories of cultural evolutionary process. In this diagram, a hypothetical cultural system—represented as a hierarchically arranged conceptual space (with lighter shading at higher levels)—undergoes two different kinds of evolutionary change. Panel A illustrates "transformation," or sequential change within the system. Some portion, *A*, of the conceptual space at time 1 is transformed to a variant form, *B*, at time 2, and on to form *C* at time 3, where *A*, *B*, and *C* differ in their information content. Panel B illustrates "diversification," the branching or splitting of a cultural system into two or more "daughter" cultures and their subsequent differentiation. In the hypothetical example shown, a common ancestral culture splits into two daughters, one characterized by the novel variant, *B*, and the other by the persisting ancestral form, *A*. Note that outside this region of difference, the two daughter cultures illustrate the "unity of type" that is caused by common descent (after Darwin 1964 [1859]: 206). For purposes of illustration, the cultural variants—*A*, *B*, and *C*— of both panels are shown as large and hierarchically complex regions of conceptual space (as would be needed, for example, to represent whole cultural subsystems such as religion, kinship concepts, or subsistence strategy). They are also shown as constant in size and shape through time. In reality, however, these ideational "units of culture" vary widely in scope and complexity from case to case; within a given case, they may also vary through time.

culture theory (see also Durham 1990): (1) *Although also related in other ways (by diffusion, for example), all human cultures are related by historical derivation or "descent"*; and (2) *The descent with modification of cultural systems is always a product of the two kinds of processes, transformation and diversification.* Taken together, these propositions imply that any portion of the evolutionary phylogenies of contemporary cultures, whether more "treelike" (as in Fig. 1.1, panel A) or more "bushlike" (as in Fig. 1.1, panel B), are explicable by some combination of transformation and diversification. Because diversification is itself the product of isolation—that is, of some relative impediment to social transmission between groups of people—plus subsequent transformation of the isolates, I have chosen to focus on the leading causes of cultural transformation in the remainder of this chapter.[21] Involved in both components of evolutionary change, transformation is arguably a more basic category of evolutionary process.

A central question is, then, What are the most important causes of transformation in cultural evolution? What, in other words, are the principal processes by which cultural systems change through time, and how do these processes relate to the dynamics of change in the corresponding genetic system of inheritance?

The Conceptual Structure of Coevolution

Earlier in this chapter, under "Culture as a Second Inheritance System," I argued that genes and culture exist in a symmetrical relationship with respect to *both* human phenotypes and the environment. In other words, they share the same basic properties of instructing phenotypes and of being transformed sequentially through replication in a given environment. My contention is that an adequate theory of gene-culture relations must build upon both of these symmetries.

Fig. 4.3 summarizes the general conceptual structure of the theory I propose.[22] In the figure, the genes, G_i, and culture, C_i, of a hypothetical human population in generation i are represented as distinct though interacting systems or "tracks" of inheritance. Both tracks are subject to se-

---

[21] This is not to deny the importance of isolation in the evolution of cultural systems, an importance highlighted, for example, by Hill (1971). Without isolation, there would probably be but one culture in the world today, just as, in the parallel case of organic evolution, there would probably be but a single species of living organisms (see Chapter 1). By the same token, however, isolation does not produce cultural evolution in the absence of transformation; both are clearly required.

[22] For other related schemas see Maynard Smith (1961: 87), Pollitzer (1970: 84), T. Williams (1972: 68, 82), Blum (1978: 35), Ruse (1979: 180), Diener et al. (1980: 12), Plotkin and Odling-Smee (1981: 228), Baldwin and Baldwin (1981: 21), Cavalli-Sforza and Feldman (1981: 291), Lewontin (1982: 28), Swanson (1983: 8), Dyson-Hudson (1983: 8), Ingold (1986: 361), and Gordon (1988: 434). Of these models I believe my own is the first to portray the special kind of symmetry that exists between genes, culture, and phenotypes, all within a variable environment and social system. Still needed, however, is a schema that shows in detail how "social evolution," or change through time in the social system, affects the dynamics of genetic and cultural change.

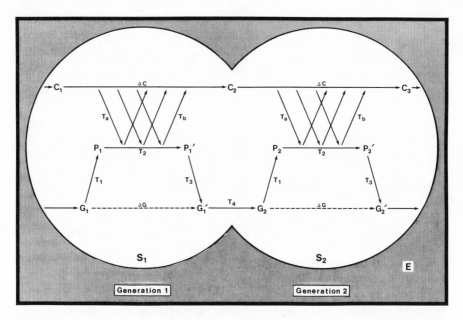

Fig. 4.3. The conceptual structure of coevolutionary theory. The distribution of phenotypes, P_i, within a population changes through time in response to evolutionary transformations, T, in both the genetic instructions, G_i, and the cultural instructions, C_i, of the population (i denotes generation number). These transformations are specific both to the existing social system, S_i, of the population, which also varies through time, and to other features of the environment, E, represented by the plane of the diagram. Genes and culture are thus represented as two evolving "tracks" of informational inheritance, each with an influence on the phenotypes of the population. In the lower half of the figure, genetic evolution within the population is subdivided into the four major transformations (T_1 to T_4) that interrelate changes in the genotype and phenotype distributions (as in Fig. 3.2). Similarly, in the upper half of the figure, cultural evolution interrelates changes in the cultural system and the phenotype distribution of the population. Two types of cultural transformation are shown: T_a, representing the various processes by which cultural instructions influence phenotypes (and are thus learned or "adopted" by their carriers); and T_b, representing the ways in which the phenotypes have reciprocal influence upon cultural transmission (through such processes as teaching and modeling). The net effect of these various transformations—T_1 to T_4, T_a and T_b—is to cause evolutionary change in the distribution of phenotypes through genetic change (the dotted line, ΔG, at bottom), cultural change (the solid line, ΔC, at top), or both.

quential transformation under the influence of the environment, E (represented by the plane of the diagram), which includes the existing social system, S_i. Evolution in the genetic system, shown in the lower part of the diagram, includes all of the components discussed earlier in Chapter 3 (and is thus comparable to Fig. 3.2). Evolution in the cultural system is shown as a roughly parallel process in the upper half of the figure. There, a pool of ideational instructions, analogous to the pool of genotypes (and discussed further in the next section), is shown undergoing sequential transformation, ΔC, from distribution C_1 to C_2 to C_3. Guiding that transformation are the sets of laws T_a and T_b, representing the changes introduced by learning and imitation, T_a, and those introduced by teaching and dissemination, T_b. In contrast to the genetic laws, these laws of cultural transformation are represented by multiple arrows in each generation in order to emphasize that cultural instructions to the phenotypes can be "inherited" continuously throughout life and that they can also change during people's lifetimes. In addition to T_a and T_b, however, the laws T_2 may also be directly involved in cultural evolution. Here, too, they may cause transformation via differential reproduction—the actual natural selection of cultural variation.

Several implications of Fig. 4.3 warrant special mention. First, its structure emphasizes that culture is a parallel or "paragenetic" transmission system (after Waddington 1961: 72), a system whose influence on phenotypes is symmetric with respect to that of the genes. Among other things, this means that changes in either the genetic information, the cultural information, or both can cause evolution in the phenotypes of the population. Phenotypes are thus subject to the *coevolutionary* influences of genes and culture. Again, the "co-" emphasizes that genes and culture constitute symmetrical inputs to the phenotypes and that, as pointed out by Cavalli-Sforza and Feldman, their influences are expected to show a certain "harmony" on average, at least for those persons who direct the course of cultural evolution (I shall return to the subject of harmony in later sections and in Chapter 7). Second, the various laws of transformation in the figure, T_1 to T_4, T_a, and T_b, are all specific to the particular social system and environment of a given population. Through these transformations, in other words, the framework incorporates social structural forces of cultural change, including imposition (discussed briefly in Chapter 2 and described in more detail below). Finally, Fig. 4.3 also reminds us that any general theory of cultural evolution will necessarily resemble organic evolutionary theory to some degree. As Donald Campbell has emphasized (see App. A.4.1), these resemblances are neither coincidental nor are they the product of our wishful thinking. Instead, they are inherent properties of any evolving system, not to mention an organically derived evolving system, where there is both variation among the replicated units and selective retention of some variants at the expense of others. As he puts it, in what I like to call Campbell's rule, "the analogy to cultural accumulations [is not] from organic evolution per se; but rather from a general model [of evolutionary change] . . . for which organic evolution is but one instance." (1965: 26.)

Key Components of Cultural Evolutionary Theory

Let me turn now to examine some of the principal analogous features of cultural evolutionary theory as I envision them. The first challenge, of course, is to identify the units of the system that are capable of replication and thus of sequential transformation.

Units of culture. Convinced of the value of an ideational unit for culture theory, I conducted a literature search of precedent examples with the help of students A.C. and M.D.[23] Not surprisingly, the commonest unit we found is the obvious candidate, "idea" (as suggested, for example, by Huxley 1962; Cavalli-Sforza 1971; Pulliam and Dunford 1980). This unit has a number of attractive features; for example, ideas have conceptual reality, they are socially transmitted, and they can be organized and structured into full, coherent systems of thought. In addition, provided they are successfully transmitted through time, ideas can acquire their own social history. But the problem is that "idea" is really too general. The term encompasses more than the shared conceptual phenomena of our concern (including, for example, strictly individual perceptions, thoughts, and even fantasies), and it entails a number of inappropriate connotations, such as "ideal," "essence," or "pattern." Although the unit we seek needs to be ideational, it must also connote the sense and specificity of a shared cultural instruction.

But even though "idea" was the commonest unit in the literature, we found an abundance of alternative suggestions: for example, "belief," "thought," "rule," "value," "principle," "premise," "postulate," "instruction," and "concept." In my view, little is to be gained by adding still more terms to this list, or by arguing over which word constitutes the best name. The point is rather to identify the major theoretical properties such a unit must have and then simply to choose an appropriate descriptor. As a minimum set of properties, I propose that a useful "unit of culture" will (1) consist of information that actually or potentially guides behavior; (2) accommodate highly variable kinds, quantities, and ways of organizing information (that is, with variable amounts of hierarchy and integration);[24] and (3) demarcate bodies of information that are, in fact, differentially transmitted as coherent, functional units.

Using these features as criteria, I found that most of the cultural units proposed in the literature could be eliminated outright. Among the ones surviving this test, two seemed most appropriate: "symbol," when defined, as by Gerhard and Jean Lenski (1982), to be any vehicle for the transmission of socially meaningful information; and "meme," when defined, as by Richard Dawkins (1982a), to be the unit of information that is conveyed from one brain to another during cultural transmission.[25]

[23] Copies of our compilation are available from the author on request.

[24] The importance of a unit of variable size and complexity is suggested by the range of levels at which cultural evolution is possible in language. There, sequential transformation can occur at the level of individual units of sound (phonemes), units of meaning (morphemes), units of writing (graphemes), rules of syntax, grammars, dialects, and indeed whole languages. Unnecessary confusion and controversy would surely arise if "the unit" of linguistic change were too closely identified with any one of these levels.

[25] I had hesitations about three other reasonable suggestions: "theme" (Opler 1945), "concept" (Hill 1978), and "culture-type" (Richerson and Boyd 1978). "Theme," a higher-order "organizing principle" according to Opler, is too specific and too fixed in the hierarchy of culture to serve as a general unit. "Concept" is also given too specific a definition in my view—namely, "the idea of a class of objects," expressed as "oppositions of two or three elements abstracted from the whole" (Hill 1978: 378–79)—and "culture-type" has too many connotations from previous use in anthropology (as in Steward 1955, for example). In

After some debate—both terms have their advantages and disadvantages—I have chosen to use the term "meme," for two main reasons. First, meme is not a term with a priori connotations from common usage as is "symbol" (it is, if you will, a better symbol for these purposes than "symbol").[26] Second, meme has appropriate, if sparse, antecedent usage. For example, the related word "mneme" was used by Richard Semon (1921: 12) to refer to the general capacity for memory in living systems, including the (cultural) system, which he called "practice and habit." Similarly, "mnemotype" was used by Harold Blum (1963, 1978; see also Durham 1982) to refer to "all the kinds of information that may be stored in the brain, whether relating to action, behavior, beliefs, aesthetic concepts or whatsoever." (1963: 36.) Finally, meme is closely related to the terms "mnemon" and "neme" used by some neurophysiologists and computer scientists to represent a basic unit of memory or association (see, for example, Young 1978: 86 and Minsky 1986: 200, 211).

This antecedent history suggests that "meme" is a reasonable name for the functional unit of cultural transmission. At the same time, the relative unfamiliarity of the word will help to emphasize that I take it to represent actual units of socially transmitted information, regardless of their form, size, and internal organization. The point is that whenever culture changes, *some* ideational unit is adopted and one or more homologous alternatives are not. That unit I will call a "meme"; its alternative forms or manifestations I will further subdivide into two categories. The first and more inclusive group consists of *all* variants of a given meme—its "holomemes"—whether they are actually acted upon or not. Holomemes, in other words, represent the entire cultural repertoire of variation for a given meme, including any latent or unexpressed forms. The second and more important group for our purposes, "allomemes" (a deliberate parallel to the term "allele" in genetic theory), refers to the subset of holomemes that are actually used as guides to behavior by at least some members of a population in at least some circumstances. Examples of allomemes would include the alternative marriage principles used by the thongpa, including the monomarital principle and its variants ($M = 2$ and $M = 3$, for example); differing techniques or strategies for procuring sub-

---

contrast, "meme," as introduced by Dawkins (1976) and revised by him in 1982, is "regarded as a unit of information residing in a brain. . . . This is to distinguish it from its phenotypic effects, which are its consequences in the outside world." (1982a: 109.) With this clarification, the term meme can be unencumbered of the meme/model duality described by Mundinger (1980: 198). Culture is then the system of memes characterizing a population at a given time.

[26] Sherry Ortner, for example, writes that "the term 'symbol' still tends to call to people's minds things in relation to which (other—of course) people have irrational reactions—unicorns, national flags, crucified saviors—rather than anything 'which serves as a vehicle for a conception' (Geertz 1966: 5). Rather than 'symbol,' I prefer terms taken from more formal jargons—'model,' 'map,' 'programme,' 'template.'" (1975: 133.) An alternative point of view, which explicitly defends the use of "symbol" as an analog of "gene," is given by Emerson (1956: 147), Masters (1970: 300), and Geertz (1973: 92).

sistence resources; alternative schools or sects of religious thought co-existent within a population; differing conceptions about the length of a postpartum sex taboo; or variable definitions of a word or label, such as variations in the wavelengths of light described by a given color term (an example we will return to later in this chapter). Note especially the variation in information content that is implied by these examples.

State variables. With this terminology, then, the principal state variables of cultural evolution can be described as the distribution of phenotypic variants in a population at a given time, P_t, and the distribution of allomemes, C_t, believed to inform or instruct those variants. Accordingly, the goal of cultural evolutionary theory is to explain patterns of historical change in P_t in terms of sequential transformations through time in C_t.[27] Just as in genetic evolutionary theory, the assumption is that any given movement in the "phenotype space" of the population is caused partially or completely by a corresponding movement in its "cultural" or "ideational space." Such a change may well happen independently of genetic change, and thus represent what some authors have called "pure" cultural evolution, or it may be confounded with genetic change, and therefore constitute "biocultural evolution" (as in Katz 1982 and D. Ortner 1983). Either way, the point of cultural evolutionary theory is to interrelate the C_t's and P_t's as they change through space and time.

Laws of transformation. Since the potential sources of change in C_t are many and varied, a complete theory of cultural evolution must also be pluralistic with regard to mechanisms. Many of these mechanisms can be appreciated from the analogy with the genetic system, a point not lost on the authors of the models described above. Thus one reads of cultural processes analogous to the classic forces of gene-frequency change: mutation, migration, drift, and genetic selection (as in Fig. 3.3). As Campbell's rule suggests, these are reasonable comparisons, particularly since sequential transformation in both systems occurs through replication. The problem, however, is that there are more ways for cultural variants to be replicated—and thus *differentially* replicated—than there are for genetic variants.

One way to start toward an understanding of the laws of transformation in culture is simply to ask, In what ways can a given allomeme X increase in frequency through time within a given population and cultural system? Here, let me simply mention some of the more salient possibilities, which I will group into two main categories. Belonging to Category A, which I will call the "nonconveyance forces," are all the things that can happen to increase the frequency of X without its actually being

---

[27] Here I use the variable P_t (where t represents "time") rather than P_i as in Fig. 4.3 (where i represents "generation number") to emphasize the possibility of continuous cultural change within generations. In general, P_t is the more appropriate variable for cultural evolution because demographically defined generations are not the natural time units for cultural change that they are for genetic change.

transmitted between members of the population. So, for example, X can increase in frequency through recurrent innovation (the analog of mutation), migration (either the immigration of people carrying X or the emigration of noncarriers), or cultural drift (the loss of non-X variants through such chance events as random memory lapses or random deaths). The transformational effects of these forces, which obviously vary with their individual rates of recurrence, will generally be additive. Belonging to Category B, the "conveyance forces," in contrast, are the various ways by which X may increase in frequency through social transmission. These forces, too, will generally have additive influence. They include, first, the familiar force of natural selection: X will increase in frequency over time if and when X's carriers both produce a greater-than-average number of offspring and also transmit X successfully to most or all of them. In addition, X may also increase in frequency via the transmission forces discussed earlier, namely, the forces that arise from social conveyance's potential for violating the analog of the Hardy-Weinberg law. For example, X may simply be conveyed with a ratio advantage, that is, a ratio of receivers to transmitters that is higher than that among other, equally attractive allomemes. In the genetic system, in contrast, such transmission forces appear to be influential only in special cases (see, for example, Crow 1979).

But there are two additional conveyance forces that lack exact counterparts in genetic evolution and that deserve special attention. The first of these is choice, the operation of discrimination or selectivity on the part of both transmitters and receivers. This selectivity is tantamount to parents being able to determine which of their particular genes and chromosomes they want to transmit to their offspring, and to the offspring being able to decide which genes and chromosomes they want to accept. True, the possibility does exist for a less direct form of choice in the genetic track of inheritance; for example, females in some species are believed to choose mates on the basis of phenotypic correlates of "good genes"—an example of sexual selection (see, for example, Dawkins 1976: ch. 6). In principle, however, the cultural track offers the possibility both of choosing one's "inheritance" directly, for one's self, and even of changing that inheritance, if desired, during one's lifetime. This possibility may or may not be fully exploited, of course, depending upon socialization practices and the politico-legal system of the population in question. Indeed, some social systems seem almost completely intolerant of change through choice, particularly those with a powerful elite whose political and economic interests would thus be endangered. And even in societies that are more open and democratic, cultural tradition may include many, many ideational elements that cannot be rejected by individuals at will. Still, the potential is there for choice to have far greater importance in cultural evolution than it has in organic evolution. Moreover, the example of the thongpa marriage system makes clear that this potential is at least sometimes realized.

By the same token, however, cultural change is rarely, if ever, a simple matter of *free* choice among multitudinous options; there are always constraints. The cultural constraints are analogous to the "constraints of inherited form" in the genetic system (as in Fig. 3.3); the social constraints originate in the interventions of third parties in the social transmission process—interventions that have no counterpart in the closed, vertical pathway of genetic transmission. Of central importance, in my view, are the social constraints, called "imposition" in Chapter 2, that force compliance with someone else's choice. I believe that imposition, although still based on a decision-making mechanism, warrants distinction as a second main force of cultural evolution because its directions and rates of change can differ drastically from those expected as the result of unbridled local discretion. For example, it is possible that the post-1959 impositions of the Chinese in Tibet have now interrupted the thongpa's preservation by choice of the monomarital principle, thereby bringing a rapid end to their age-old marital system.

A Theory of Evolution by Cultural Selection

In the following sections I propose to integrate the forces of choice and imposition into a general theory of cultural evolution. Paralleling its genetic counterpart, the theory interrelates changes in the distributions of phenotypes, P_t, in a human population with changes in the frequency distributions of allomemes, C_t, within the cultural system. And like its genetic counterpart, the theory explicitly recognizes the multiplicity of forces that can affect C_t (and thus P_t), but goes on to assign causal priority to a small subset of those forces.

My proposal, however, differs from genetic microtheory in at least three key respects. First, because the cultural system changes—or does not—as people differentially adopt, sustain, and transmit existing ideational variants, the theory focuses on differential social transmission rather than on differential reproduction. Although the latter, as noted above, may surely contribute to the differential replication of allomemes, I believe choice and imposition are generally far more important. Second, because cultural variants are socially conveyed, differential replication is not necessarily decided at the individual level. Allomemes can also be adopted and rejected through the collective decisions of social aggregates of various sizes. Finally, cultural evolutionary change need not arise "by the accumulation of innumerable slight variations" or "by the shortest and slowest steps." (Darwin 1964 [1859]: 459, 194.) As noted earlier, the functional units of cultural transmission can vary widely in the quantity and organization of their information content. Although change may sometimes be slow and gradual as in Darwin's theory, it can also be fast and episodic; in this formulation, culture *can* take a leap. I begin with the following assumptions and definitions.

Key Assumptions and Definitions

First, let us assume a collection in space and time of individuals who have similar capacities for culture, each conforming to the assumption of "natural origins" (that is, of having evolved under the guiding influence of genetic selection), and each having similar access to a given pool of cultural information. For now, let us call this group a "subpopulation"; our purpose in doing so is simply to acknowledge that the provision of similar access to cultural information will often partition a full ethnolinguistic population into a number of subunits. Second, let us assume that this pool of information can itself be subdivided into memes that are transmitted across space and time as coherent units. For the sake of simplicity, let us focus on one such meme, and further assume that innovation (whether by deliberate invention, pure chance, or some combination of the two) and/or diffusion have created several variants of that unit—several allomemes—that effectively constitute rivals in the social transmission process. Finally, let us also assume that these allomemes have some specific influence or "instructive effect" upon the observable phenotypic properties of their carriers.

Meme selection. Under these assumptions, virtually any force that causes change in the distribution of allomemes within the subpopulation will cause some amount of evolution in its phenotypes. For that effect to have major evolutionary significance, however, the change per unit of time in the distribution of allomemes must either be large—so-called "quantum adjustment" (as in P. Diener 1980, after Simpson 1944)—or else small but cumulative over time (as was change in Darwin's theory). Either way, the conveyance forces of Category 2 have causal advantage: because they allow change to be socially disseminated, they are more likely to have a major impact upon C_t than are the nonconveyance forces. Conveyance forces, in short, have the advantage of causing the differential social transmission of allomemes, or what can be called "meme selection."[28] This advantage has been fully appreciated by proponents of the "dual inheritance" models described earlier in this chapter (model Categories B and C); indeed, they all seem to agree that meme selection is the most important cause of cultural evolutionary change in human popula-

---

[28] Defined in this way, meme selection is the analog of so-called genic selection in organic microtheory—that is, natural selection at the level of alternative alleles (Williams 1966: 96; not to be confused with the genetic selection of alternative genotypes). In recent years there has been considerable debate over the organic evolutionary potential of genic selection (see, for example, Brandon and Burian 1984). The reason, of course, is that genes usually cannot be transmitted independently of the reproduction of their carriers. This constraint obviously does not apply to memes.

tions. Put another way, they all imply that differential social transmission plays the same central role in cultural evolutionary theory that differential reproduction plays in genetic evolutionary theory: it sorts among existing variants. Again, this is not to deny nonconveyance forces a part in cultural evolution; rather, it is to suggest that, in most circumstances, they are less important.

Cultural fitness. This definition of meme selection suggests, in turn, the utility of a measure of relative "transmission success" among the allomemes of a cultural system, a measure analogous to the reproductive success of individuals or genotypes in the study of genetic evolution. I employed such a measure in Chapter 2; it was called "the relative rate of social transmission" (that is, of Tibetan marriage principles). As we saw there, any number of alternative marriage principles ($M = 2$, $M = 3$, and so on) have been considered and tried by the thongpa. Yet only one of those variants, the monomarital principle, has enjoyed the highest overall rate of transmission and use generation after generation. It has had an evolutionary success of its own that requires explanation.

Building on my own earlier arguments (especially Durham 1982) and those of Cavalli-Sforza and Feldman (1981), let me therefore define the "cultural fitness," F_c, of an allomeme to be its overall suitability for replication and use within the cultural system of a given subpopulation. More formally, cultural fitness can be described as an allomeme's expected relative rate of social transmission and use within a subpopulation, where the "expected rate" can be defined, following Philip Kitcher (1985: 51), as "the probabilistically weighted average of the possible values." For analytic purposes, cultural fitness can be estimated by a measure I will call "replicative success," or R, an allomeme's relative empirical rate of social transmission and use within a subpopulation.[29] Defined in this way, R closely parallels its counterpart in the genetic track of inheritance, namely, the reproductive success of an individual or genotype. As with estimates of reproductive fitness, let us assign the standardized maximum value, 1.0, to the variant or variants most successfully conveyed (and used) during a given interval, and then scale the replication rates of the other variants accordingly. Thus, in the Tibetan example, the monomarital principle would have an R value of 1.0.

By extension, let me also define the "cultural fitness function" to be the F_c values of the full set of allomemes existing in a given subpopula-

[29] The cultural fitness advantage of one variant over another will be *expressed* as a difference in actual rates of social transmission. But it should not be *defined* by that difference, for to do so would be to set up a "survival of the fittest" tautology, a mistake that has sometimes been made in the analogous definitions of reproductive fitness (see discussion in Gould 1977: 42). Instead, the cultural fitness of an allomeme should be defined, as it is here, in terms of its suitability for replication, or "replicability," within the given cultural system. For reasons explained below, I believe that the single most important determinant of replicability is an allomeme's evaluation according to the pre-existing cultural values within that system.

Panel A

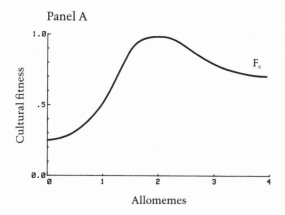

Panel B

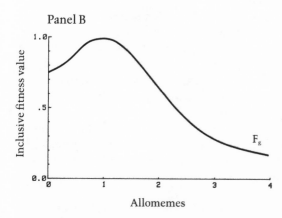

Fig. 4.4. Two key measures of fitness in coevolutionary theory. Panel A illustrates F_c, the cultural fitness or "suitability for replication and use," for each of the available allomemes, o to 4, in a hypothetical human subpopulation. Using a continuous curve for clarity, this plot summarizes the expected relative rates of social transmission per unit of time for each of the variants, including the "null allomeme" o, that is, the absence of any form of the given meme. Allomemes are numbered for identification only; they need not differ quantitatively from one another. Panel B illustrates F_g, the "inclusive fitness value" for each of the same allomemes, o to 4. Again using a continuous curve for clarity, this plot summarizes the average relative inclusive fitness of all culture carriers in the subpopulation whose behavior is guided by a given allomeme. In this hypothetical example, allomeme 2 shows the highest cultural fitness (panel A), whereas allomeme 1 confers the highest average inclusive fitness upon its carriers (panel B).

tion at a given time. A hypothetical example of such a function, smoothed for clarity, is shown in panel A of Fig. 4.4, where allomeme 2 is shown to have the highest F_c value.[30] Note that the cultural fitness function merely summarizes the F_c differences among allomemes; it specifically does not reveal *why* variant 2 is the most readily transmitted and used. Note also that a time unit is not specified for measuring F_c; in cultural transmission there is no relatively fixed interval equivalent to the "generation time" of population genetics. For analytic purposes, however, an operational "cultural generation time" can be defined as the average, over all members of a

[30] This figure has been reworked to correct misimpressions from my earlier rendition (see Durham 1982: 293). Here F_c varies among allomemes (not phenotypes, as before); in this respect, the plot resembles the "usage bias curves" of the gene-culture transmission model (Lumsden and Wilson 1981) discussed under Category B above. In an attempt to simplify notation in this and subsequent chapters, I use "F_c," depending upon the context, to refer either to the cultural fitness of individual allomemes or to the cultural fitness function of all such values for an array of allomemes. Similarly, I use "F_g" (defined below) to refer either to one allomeme or to a full set.

subpopulation or sample, of the interval between (1) the time of each individual's adoption of one allomeme or another, and (2) the average time of adoption of that variant among all persons he or she subsequently influences or "transmits to."

Inclusive fitness. Although subsequent sections focus largely on differences in cultural fitness and their causes, it will be useful here to draw upon another measure of fitness, namely, W. D. Hamilton's (1964: 8) "inclusive fitness of individuals." My purpose is to compare the direction of change in cultural evolution with the direction of change in organic evolution by genetic selection. More specifically, I will use a measure of the impact of different allomemes upon the relative reproductive fitnesses of culture carriers themselves—that is, upon the effectiveness of their overall "designs for reproductive survival" (Williams 1966: 158; see also Chapter 1 of this book).

As we saw in the Tibetan example, allomemes are sometimes characterized by large and conspicuous differentials in this regard, some variants enabling a carrier's descendants to thrive for many generations and others causing them to perish in short order. But, as we also saw in Chapter 2 when discussing the special case of the Nyinba, behaviorally significant allomemes can also have subtle and finely tuned effects on individual reproductive survival. If to these observations we now add the implication from genetic microtheory that reproductive survival is best measured in terms of gene propagation (see Chapter 3), it seems reasonable to differentiate allomemes on the basis of their net inclusive fitness effects. In other words, let us compare cultural variants on the basis of their expected impact upon the relative contribution of carriers' genes to future generations.

Let me therefore define the "inclusive fitness value," F_g, of a given allomeme to be the average of the individual inclusive fitnesses of all members of a subpopulation who act on the basis of that allomeme as compared with others. For analytic purposes, this value can be estimated from the average of the actual reproductive successes of a given allomeme's carriers and their relatives, standardized (according to the highest of such values) to the usual 0.0 to 1.0 scale.[31] F_g is thus a measure of an allomeme's

---

[31] As in the definition of cultural fitness in note 29, I distinguish here between *design* for reproductive success—that is, inclusive fitness proper—and actual reproductive *performance*. The distinction is appropriate in this context not only for the reasons given by Williams (1966: chs. 2 and 6) but also because people may very well switch during their lifetimes between allomemes with different reproductive implications. The latter is a special feature of culture; generally speaking, one does not change genotypes. If we follow M. J. West Eberhard (1975: 6), F_g can be estimated in terms of "offspring equivalents" averaged over all of the individuals who act on the basis of a given allomeme. In principle, one begins with the number of offspring actually born to each such person; from this one subtracts the estimated number of offspring equivalents that derive from the individual's interactions with consanguineous relatives; then one adds the number of offspring equivalents that accrue through the lifetime sum of the person's effects on the reproduction of his or her relatives. The numbers so obtained can then be standardized to the conventional 0.0-to-1.0 scale.

effect upon the reproductive fitnesses of its carriers. By extension, let us define the "inclusive fitness function" of a set of allomemes to be the array of their F_g values; a hypothetical example is shown in panel B of Fig. 4.4. Note that these definitions bring us to a total of three distinct fitness measures for use in the study of human evolution, one for genotypes (W) subject to genetic selection, one for allomemes (F_c) subject to cultural selection, and a second for allomemes (F_g) that can be used to compare the directions of genetic and cultural change.

The Determinants of Cultural Fitness

We can now rephrase what Alexander (1979a: 76) called "the important question" about cultural evolution and ask, Who or what gives an allomeme its cultural fitness within a subpopulation? More specifically, what does it take for a variant to have high suitability for replication and use in a given cultural system, and why are other variants less culturally fit? (For earlier formulations of the same question, see Harris 1960: 63; Ruyle 1973: 202; Dawkins 1976: 208.)

This is one question, I submit, whose answer can be found neither in the analogy with genetic evolution nor in the analogy with disease transmission. Consider, again, the genetic analogy. As we saw in Chapter 3, the Darwinian fitness differentials of genetic theory reflect differences in the reproduction of organisms as they confront nature's "limiting checks." Thus, when selection occurs, as B. F. Skinner (1984) reminds us, it is "selection by consequences." Genotypes are favored or not by virtue of their own reproductive output.

But this is not true in cultural evolution, or at least it is not exclusively true, Skinner's own arguments notwithstanding (see Skinner 1984: 478). In the first place, cultural fitness differentials are not necessarily tied to procreation. As noted earlier, meme transmission may be virtually continuous rather than generational and from many sources in addition to biological parents. Therefore, although procreation and child rearing are certainly among the avenues of cultural transmission, cultural fitness is not in any way limited to rates of intergenerational transmission. Second, memes can be selected for or against by their *carriers* long before they are selected by their *consequences*. A meme that is mildly disadvantageous to its bearers, for example, can sometimes be eliminated through judgments about its deleterious effects long before it is eliminated through those effects themselves. Equivalent selection cannot happen to a gene (or at least not yet).

Similarly, human choice creates problems for the analogy between cultural transmission and disease transmission. Surely there *are* circumstances in which memes do spread as if by contagion or "contact transfer." But just as surely there are other circumstances where judgment and choice intervene, as in the diffusion of technological innovations (see, for instance, Rogers 1983; Rogers and Shoemaker 1971; Cancian 1979). Imagine the changes that would be needed in epidemiological theory, for example, if people sometimes had free choice about the diseases, or strains of diseases, that they host; alternatively, imagine the changes that would be required if diseases were commonly imposed upon some by the choices of others (as indeed they are in "biological warfare"). Yet it seems to me that these are precisely the kinds of changes required by an evolutionary theory of culture.

What seems to be lacking, then, in both the genetic and the disease analogies of cultural transmission is attention to the role of human beings as decision makers. Provided they are given both a range of options and an opportunity to choose, people can participate in the transmission process as selecting agents. In other circumstances, where options and choice are largely pre-empted, cultural evolution may still be guided by human decisions—that is, by the imposed decisions of powerful, external individuals or groups. But either way, culture changes under *human* direction; people, not "nature," do most of the selecting. In my view, cultural evolution is more likely to occur "according to consequences" than it is "by consequences."

Cultural selection. Let me therefore define "cultural selection" as the differential social transmission of cultural variants through human decision making, or simply as "preservation by preference." Note that cultural selection is thus one form of meme selection, a form in which differential social transmission results specifically from human decisions (other forms of meme selection include natural selection and transmission forces). Let me also explicitly define the two principal modes of cultural selection, which can be thought of as the idealized poles of a decision continuum. At the relatively less constrained end is "selection by choice" or simply "choice," the preservation of allomemes through election or free decision making by individuals or groups ("free," that is, within the cultural constraints of mental habit and existing technology). At the other end is "selection by imposition" or simply "imposition," the preservation of allomemes by compliance with the decisions of others. Following the sociologist Steven Lukes (1974), we can subdivide imposition by the four forms of power used to secure compliance: "coercion" (in which compliance is induced by threat of sanction or deprivation); "force" (in which compliance is secured by eliminating or precluding choice); "manipulation" (in which compliance is secured by controlling the values and desires of others); and "authority" (in which compliance follows because another's command is reasonable in terms of one's own values).

Choice and imposition are illustrated in Fig. 4.5. In panel A, the "modal allomeme" of a subpopulation—that is, the allomeme of highest frequency in the pertinent distribution, C_t—is shown to change over time (from C_0 to C_4) as a consequence of free decision making within cultural constraints. In panel B, cultural evolution follows the same hypo-

Panel A

Panel B

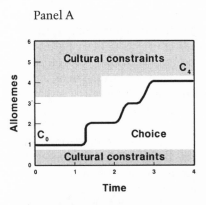 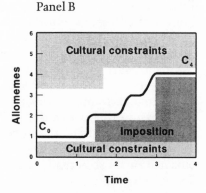

Time

Time

Fig. 4.5. The two principal modes of cultural selection. Panel A represents selection by choice, the preservation of allomemes through election or free decision making on the part of individuals or groups within a human subpopulation. For the hypothetical case shown, a cultural system changes through time, from C_0 to C_4, as people preferentially transmit and use different allomemes from the array of possible choices (the state of the system C_t at time t is represented by the most common, or modal, allomeme in the subpopulation). Note that some options are blocked by cultural constraints such as preconceptions, prejudices, and technological capabilities; in this rendering, allomeme 4 becomes available to choice near time 2, as may happen through technological change, for example. Panel B represents selection by imposition, the preservation of allomemes through compliance with the decisions of others. Here the cultural system changes from C_0 to C_4 as culture carriers are required by external agents to shift from their initial preference, allomeme 1, to allomeme 2, and eventually on to allomeme 4 (along the way, choice is temporarily exercised in the culture carriers' adoption of allomeme 3). Imposition may be viewed as a second layer of constraint—one of social rather than cultural origins—that further reduces the range of options available for choice.

thetical pathway, but does so largely as a result of imposition, a force that effectively reduces the range of options available for choice. To facilitate comparison, cultural evolution in both panels follows the same path; as noted earlier, however, choice and imposition are generally expected either to guide cultural evolution toward different modal allomemes, or to push it along at different rates, or to do both. But whether by choice or imposition, cultural selection always involves some kind of comparative evaluation of variants according to their consequences. We must therefore ask, What governs the outcome of this process? How do the pertinent decision makers evaluate their options and by what criteria do they decide?

Primary and secondary values. In my view, the key to answering these questions lies in some of the earlier insights of George E. Pugh (1977) and of Pulliam and Dunford (1980), who describe the "value-driven decision system" located in the human brain.[32] This system endows

[32] In Pugh's description, this system is said to have the following component parts: (1) a data collection subsystem, namely the nervous system and its peripheral sensory receptors, "to supply information needed to define the environment" as it affects cultural options (p. 54); (2) a mental model of the local environment "to project or estimate the probable out-

people with two decision-making capabilities that are crucial to the dynamics of cultural evolution. First, the system provides them with the ability to make decisions based upon actual experience with the consequences of different options. This ability, in turn, depends upon their perceiving at least some of the consequences of each option, upon associating different consequences with different options, and upon evaluating the options in terms of one or more decision criteria. Second, the system also provides them with the ability to pretest different options by anticipating their effects in a "symbolic model of the problem environment." (Pugh 1977: 56.) In both cases, the system assesses consequences—those expected or those actually experienced—according to one or more decision criteria, and then searches for the optimal decision, that is, for the alternative(s) with the best overall evaluation. Although the quality of the decisions produced by such a system is known to depend upon a number of factors, including the accuracy of both the mental model and the optimization procedure, the outcome, as Pugh notes, is typically most sensitive to the specified decision criteria or "values."

For our purposes, this last observation is particularly important because human values are influenced by both the genetic and the cultural inheritance systems. On the one hand, notes Pugh, it is possible to speak of the "primary values" that are designed into any decision system by the designer, in this case by organic evolution via genetic selection.[33] According to Pugh (p. 112), these values generally take the form of "valuative sensations [that] are experienced as *intrinsically* good or bad, pleasant or unpleasant." They include feedback from the senses, from the internal reward system of the brain, and from organically evolved cognitive processes (on which see Konner 1982; Cosmides and Tooby 1987). They develop within each individual out of the interaction between ner-

---

comes of different courses of action [or memes]" (p. 56); (3) a number of procedures for pretesting "action alternatives" and estimating their consequences (p. 54); (4) "a method for assigning values to the estimated consequences" (p. 54); and (5) "a decision mechanism for selecting the alternatives that show the best value." (p. 54.) Pugh (1977: ch. 6) locates each of these parts within "nature's system design" for the human brain. Inevitably, the structure and function of such a system will impart a degree of intrinsic bias or "psychological selection" to the decision process. Dawkins (1976: 212), to take one example, suggests that "the idea of hell fire is, quite simply, *self-perpetuating* [in Western religious tradition], because of its own deep psychological impact." In the interest of parsimony, I include such psychological biases in the "primary values" (defined below) of the decision system. Recent work by evolutionary psychologists (e.g., Cosmides and Tooby 1987; Tooby and Cosmides 1989) suggests that such biases are many and varied, being specific to particular domains of cognition. Complex and multifaceted, the human decision system clearly warrants further study and elucidation.

[33] I disagree with Pugh's statement that the "evolutionary design objective" of the human decision system was "survival of the species" (see 1977: 29–31). Although group-level selection may well have played an important role in human evolution (see discussion in Durham 1976a), Pugh errs when he calls group benefit "a straightforward and unchanging objective that has been constant throughout biological evolution." I also disagree with Pugh's characterization of primary values as "innate" and "instinctive." As he is the first to point out, primary values "respond to physical and social stimulation in accordance with complex built-in rules." (1977: 30.)

vous system and environment, and they characteristically require no input from social transmission. When they hold sway in a given decision between two or more allomemes, let us call this form of cultural selection "primary value selection"—that is, choice or imposition governed by primary or "developmental" values.

On the other hand, Pugh argues, human decisions are also influenced by a set of derived "secondary values" that stem not from individual experience and ontogeny, but from collective experience and social history. These include the "rules of thumb, wise proverbs, social conventions, moral or ethical principles, and even habit" that people use as "a practical aid in making decisions, [helping] the decision system to make decisions more efficiently or more reliably." (p. 33.) Revising Pugh's formulation slightly, I take a value to be secondary if its persistence in a population is dependent upon social transmission.[34] Although both kinds of values may surely be involved in any one evaluation, let us use the term "secondary value selection" to refer to decisions—whether choices or impositions—where secondary values hold sway. Defined in this way, primary and secondary value selection form a continuum—a "second axis" of cultural selection, if you will—that is perpendicular to the axis of choice and imposition (Fig. 4.6).

Importantly, these secondary values are cultural: they exist as socially transmitted ideational phenomena and they form an integral part of local cultural systems. Note that there is some similarity between them and the "secondary epigenetic rules" of Lumsden and Wilson; however, my usage makes explicit the fact that these values have their own cultural evolutionary histories. In the terminology advanced here, secondary values are thus bona fide memes, and this fact endows the cultural inheritance system with an interesting and important property: it can be *self-selecting*.

Self-selection in culture. I use the term "self-selection" to refer to the capability of the cultural system to influence the direction and rates of its own evolutionary change. This capability stems from the influence that memes can have as secondary values in the human decision system. By serving as criteria for the evaluation of other cultural phenomena, existing memes can create F_c differentials that would otherwise not obtain. In this way, culture can share in the causation of its own dynamics.

Consider, for example, the hypothetical case where the evaluation feedback from one or a set of secondary values parallels the input from the primary value system (for example, an array of allomemes could be similarly rank-ordered by the two sets of criteria). In such a case, the net

[34] As one example of a secondary value (discussed further in Ch. 6), consider the criterion governing marriage decisions among Nuer pastoralists of Africa: any union that bears healthy children is divinely blessed (see Hutchinson 1985: 630). The persistence of this value—not to mention its meaning and persuasive force—clearly depends upon the social transmission of cultural information. Because this is a defining feature, all secondary values will show "descent with modification" within and between human populations (see "The Evolution of Secondary Values," below).

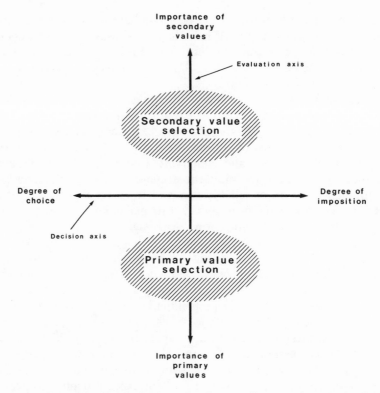

Fig. 4.6. Key forms of cultural selection. This diagram illustrates the conceptual subdivision of cultural selection into secondary value selection (the area above the horizontal axis, defined as decision making governed by socially transmitted values) and primary value selection (the area below the horizontal axis, in which decisions are governed mainly by primary or "developmental" values). The vertical, or "evaluation," axis of the figure measures the relative importance of primary and secondary values in a given decision. The horizontal or "decision" axis represents the continuum between choice and imposition, that is, between relatively free decision making and compliance with the decisions of others. Thus, depending upon the weight given to the different kinds of values, a given instance of selection by choice would qualify as either secondary value selection (upper left quadrant) or primary value selection (lower left quadrant). A similar subdivision applies to selection by imposition (upper right vs. lower right quadrants).

evaluation from the decision system would preserve the ranking of alternatives made by the primary system, but the input from the secondary values could have the effect of accentuating the relative desirability of the preferred variant(s). In this case, then, cultural values would augment the F_c differentials expected from primary evaluation alone. In a similar fashion, cultural values could conceivably create F_c differentials between allomemes valued evenly by primary criteria and could even reverse a set of primary rankings—a point to which we will return. Although the decision system's integration of value assessments is probably quite complex, I will assume here, as a first approximation, that primary and secondary values have an additive influence on F_c differentials. Thus, I will assume that we may speak of "partial cultural selection coefficients" (or "partial coefficients" for short), one each for primary and secondary values, whose contributions are additive to the overall cultural fitness function. In these terms, then, cultural self-selection occurs whenever there is a nonzero partial coefficient for secondary values.

An example from our own Western scientific process may help to illustrate the idea of self-selection. Although Western science is arguably not representative of cultural change in all its aspects, in my opinion it does epitomize this notion of self-selecting evolution. The memes of science—principles, concepts, and hypotheses, for example—are differentially transmitted over time according to their consequences, particularly their success in explaining phenomena according to socially transmitted standards.[35] Today, these standards include the convention of "critical values" for statistical tests, such as that a null hypothesis should not be rejected unless the correlation of observation and prediction is expected fewer than five times per hundred by chance. Memes that meet or exceed this standard or others are socially transmitted among scientists with far greater success than are rivals that do not. Note, however, that the standards are all memes themselves. Indeed, in this special domain, there is a deliberate attempt to minimize the influence of primary values on cultural fitness. According to Van Potter (1964: 1020), for example, the whole point of the scientific method is to assure "that the correctness of an idea is not determined by how good the idea makes us feel at the moment of illumination."

I therefore regard this example as one good illustration of the force that pre-existing memes can have in guiding cultural evolution (other examples are given in subsequent chapters of this book; see also App. A.4.1 for a discussion of Hoebel 1954 on this point). In a very real sense, a cultural system may set its own standards for the evolutionary fitness of allomemes and thus directly affect its own dynamics of change. But secondary values are also important in another way. As measures of "the differential standing of a given object in a system of meaningful relationships" (Sahlins 1976b: 36), I believe cultural values provide a crucial link between the meaning of cultural phenomena and their evolutionary per-

[35] For fuller discussion of Western science as a value-driven evolutionary process, see Popper (1963, 1972, 1984), Toulmin (1961, 1967, 1972), Campbell (1960, 1970, 1974), and reviews in Shrader (1980), Ruse (1986), and Radnitzky and Bartley (1987). To take one example, Toulmin argues that "in the evolution of scientific ideas, as in the evolution of species, change results from the selective perpetuation of variants. . . . For every variant which finds favor and displaces its predecessors, many more are rejected as unsatisfactory. So the question 'What gives scientific ideas merit, and how do they score over their rivals?' can be stated briefly in the Darwinian formula: 'What gives them survival-value?'" (1961: 111.) The answer, Toulmin suggests, lies in the set of standards "by which such scientific variants are judged and found worthy or wanting. . . . Two rival hypotheses may [even] be so closely related that their relative merits are positively computable [by] 'significance tests'." (pp. 110–12.) Toulmin's arguments epitomize the rational choice model of the evolution of science; in my opinion, they also underestimate the influence of imposition in science.

sistence. Simply put, cultural values can be expected to bias cultural change toward variants that match or "fit" the existing web of local meanings. They may thus be seen as a kind of conceptual bridge between the subject matter of symbolic or interpretive anthropology, which focuses upon what I have called the "horizontal dimension" of cultural analysis (see Chapter 1), and the subject matter of evolutionary anthropology, with its emphasis on the temporal dimension.

The Main Force of Transformation

Having discussed both the state variables and the transformational forces of the cultural system, it remains for me simply to hypothesize the general causal priority of cultural self-selection, a proposition I will call the Hypothesis 1 of coevolutionary theory. Following Darwin's lead, I therefore propose that *secondary value selection is the main but not exclusive means of cultural evolutionary change.* In other words, I suggest that the single most important force of cultural transformation derives from the secondary-value-driven decisions of culture carriers. Where the pertinent decisions are largely a matter of free choice, I would expect the relative rates of social transmission of the various allomemes—their F_c's—to covary with their evaluation in terms of the prevailing secondary values of the subpopulation itself. Alternatively, where the pertinent decisions are socially imposed from outside the subpopulation, I would expect cultural fitness differentials to reflect the external secondary value preferences of the imposers.[36] But under either set of conditions, choice or imposition, cultural variants would be differentially transmitted on the basis of a predominantly cultural evaluation by the effective decision makers; successful variants would be preserved by their preference.

Some implications of this hypothesis can be appreciated if we compare it with the principal hypothesis of the Darwinian theory of organic evolution, namely, that natural selection, or "preservation by reproduction," is the main source of genetic transformation within populations. To be sure, there are a number of strong parallels: both hypotheses describe selective mechanisms that cull or filter variants rather than create them; both operate through some process of differential replication; and both are capable of cumulative long-term effects. But there are also important differences, particularly with Darwinian theory as recast in terms of population genetics. Unlike genetic selection, for example, secondary value

[36] Under conditions of imposition, even secondary values themselves can be imposed upon a subpopulation by a dominant external group, often as part of efforts to disseminate an ideology or worldview that is favorable to their interests. As Steven Lukes (1974: 23) puts it, "*A* may exercize power over *B* by getting him to do what he does not want to do, but he also exercizes power over him by influencing, shaping, or determining his very wants. Indeed, is it not the supreme exercize of power to get another or others to have the desires you want them to have?" The achievement of cultural leadership through value manipulation and ensuing consensus is also referred to as hegemony or hegemonic authority (see Bocock 1986).

selection can operate on a collective as well as individual level—indeed at *any* level where decisions are made within a subpopulation. It can also operate across the full range of size and complexity of allomemes, from small, slightly varying alternatives (analogous to those described by Darwin) to entire religions, philosophies, or worldviews, provided that variation is available at this level. By implication, this one causal mechanism of secondary value selection can cause both gradualistic and punctuated cultural change, as well as many combinations and intergradations thereof. In addition, it can proceed on the basis of anticipated consequences, creating what Christopher Boehm (1978) calls "rational preselection," as well as on the basis of experienced consequences. Finally, secondary value selection is an intentional or goal-directed process, depending as it does on willful human agency within social and cultural constraints. Yet even with these differences, there remains a fundamental similarity in outcome: both genetic selection and cultural selection tend to favor those variants, whether genotypes or allomemes, with the best existing "design for replication"—that is, the highest fitness—within their respective systems.

Modes of Relationship Between Genes and Culture

If Hypothesis 1 is correct and secondary value selection is the predominant force of cultural transformation, then one would expect to find a whole array of different forms or "modes" of gene-culture relationships in human populations. The reason is simply that, under this hypothesis, it is possible for secondary values to favor cultural variants that either improve, or reduce, or do not affect the reproductive fitnesses of their carriers. I therefore offer what I will call Hypothesis 2 of coevolutionary theory: *There exist no fewer than five distinct modes of relationship between genes and culture, namely, two "interactive" modes, in which genes and culture act as each other's "selecting environment," and three "comparative" modes, in which culture changes through secondary value selection.* I call the last of these the "comparative modes" because we should then be able to compare the cultural fitness of allomemes, F_c, with their inclusive fitness consequences, F_g.

Interactive Modes

Consider first the two "interactive" modes of relationship. In these modes, genotypes and allomemes influence each other's fitness values directly: culture may thus "mediate," or modify, the differential reproduction of genotypes, and genes may similarly "mediate" the cultural selection of alternative allomemes. Let us take culture first. The existing distribution of allomemes at any given time may be viewed as a feature of the environment that affects the survival and reproduction of genotypes. The role of culture may be to augment the Darwinian fitness differentials among the various genotypes (as in the case of sickle-cell disease, discussed in Chapter 3), or it may be to reduce or eliminate such differentials (so-called "relaxed selection" as, for example, in Post 1971). Either way, this relationship of genes and culture can be called "cultural mediation," that is, a relationship in which culture redefines the selection coefficients operating among alternative genotypes. The effect of culture can thus be to alter the direction and/or rate of genetic evolution. The cultural instructions capable of such an effect include, but are not limited to, memes associated with technology, subsistence strategy, marriage and kinship patterns, and social structure. Chapter 5 will explore the idea of cultural mediation in more detail.

As for the genetic causes of cultural evolution, or what I will call "genetic mediation," this mode of relationship may be said to exist whenever primary values—the representatives of the genes in matters of decision making—contribute to the comparative evaluation of allomemes. Because such a contribution is surely very common, if not universal, I find it helpful to distinguish between "major" genetic mediation, in which primary values are the main determinants of cultural fitness differentials, and "minor" genetic mediation, in which primary values do have input but secondary values hold sway. It follows as a direct consequence of Hypothesis 1 above that I do not view primary value selection as the main means of modification in cultural evolution, and therefore that I do not expect major genetic mediation to be a common mode of relationship in human populations. By the same token, however, the major form is of greater theoretical significance than the minor form (witness its role in the "gene-culture transmission" model described earlier), and I do consider it to be important in special cases, one of which is discussed in the final section of this chapter. In the pages that follow, I will therefore use the term "genetic mediation" to refer to the major form unless indicated otherwise.

Comparative Modes

Because of culture's potential for self-selection, the relationships between genes and culture are more complicated than mediation alone. As I have already argued, existing memes can serve as the main criteria by which people evaluate other memes. In this way they create cultural fitness values different from those that would have resulted from primary value selection alone. The process of secondary value selection thereby creates the hypothetical possibility of three more modes of relationship between genes and culture, modes that may be described as "enhancement," "neutrality," and "opposition."

Enhancement will be considered in more detail in Chapter 6. In essence, the idea is that the cultural values of a population may confer the highest cultural fitness, F_c, on the allomeme or allomemes with the highest inclusive fitness consequences, F_g, thereby promoting a genuine cultural adaptation. Neutrality, in turn, refers to any situation in which an array of allomemes is adaptively neutral, that is to say, in which the allomemes' behavioral consequences are closely matched in terms of F_g. Nevertheless, secondary value selection may still create substantial cultural fitness differentials among the variants, a possibility we will consider further in Chapter 7. Finally, opposition may exist in circumstances where cultural values bestow high cultural fitness upon allomemes with suboptimal inclusive fitness consequences. In other words, secondary value selection may favor the spread or persistence of variants whose net effects are deleterious to the survival and/or reproduction of their carriers. This mode of gene-culture relationships will also be considered in Chapter 7.

In short, Hypothesis 2 predicts that there is much more to gene-culture relationships, and thus to coevolutionary theory, than simply reciprocal interaction. Yet other authors define "coevolution" in precisely these terms; to Lumsden and Wilson, for example, coevolution means "any change in gene frequencies that alters culturgen frequencies in such a way that culturgen changes alter gene frequencies as well." (1981: 372; see also 1982, 1985.) To prevent confusion in terminology, I will therefore refer to the interactive modes of relationship—that is, to genetic and cultural mediation—as "coevolution in the narrow sense." I will continue to use the word "coevolution" or, for emphasis, the phrase "coevolution in the broad sense" to refer to the full set of five hypothetical modes of relationship, including the three comparative modes just described.

The Evolution of Secondary Values

Given the central role of cultural self-selection in the theory I propose, it becomes important to understand the evolutionary history of secondary values, or what Pugh calls their "value derivation." This brings us back to the question asked at the conclusion of the Tibetan case study of Chapter 2, namely, What explains the origin and persistence of cultural values themselves? How do these influential decision criteria evolve to cultural prominence in the first place?

Let me begin by returning to two observations made by Pugh in his 1977 treatise. First, he points out that primary values are, after all, "simply surrogates or substitutes" for the real evolutionary criterion of genetic selection, namely, reproductive fitness. In other words, primary values are themselves "simply the best compromise the [organic] evolutionary process has been able to produce" for guiding decisions toward that end (1977: 31). Second, however, Pugh notes that part of this compromise was the inclusion, indeed the elaboration, of the secondary value subsystem. From all indications, this subsystem also emerged and was improved through an "iterative process" involving genetic selection; indeed a key support structure of this subsystem, the human brain, roughly trebled in size as the iterations proceeded (see Chapter 1, Fig. 1.2), not to mention the structural changes it must also have experienced. The implication is an important one: secondary values must generally have returned judgments "evaluated as 'good' when measured in terms of the *primary* value structure." (p. 32.) In other words, they must have acted as true "surrogate values," helping the system to make decisions more efficiently or more reliably, but still in general agreement with what was effectively the decision criterion of genetic selection.[37]

But this argument has two further implications of importance to our discussion. First, not just any value will work as a true surrogate in this sense; as a general rule, cultural values that promoted decisions with maladaptive, F_g-reducing consequences for their makers must themselves have been weeded out. Evidently the human decision system has long been able to promote the cultural evolution of reproductively advantageous secondary values. Today, then, we may expect to find a general, if imperfect, congruence between evaluations by primary and secondary values in human populations—an important generalization that I will call the "principle of congruence." Second, the argument implies that the evolution of cultural values was itself achieved primarily through value-guided decision making. In other words, secondary values emerged as products of the very same decision system that they then went on to direct. Early in human prehistory, of course, the effective criteria in these evaluations must have been the primary values. But eventually, as the value subsystem grew, secondary values must have been increasingly assessed by other secondary values. The result, as Pugh summarized, is that human judgment has come to be based on "extensive networks of derived values." (p. 63.) Logically the iterations of value derivation can proceed at ever greater removes from primary values, but they will continue smoothly only so long as they do not oppose the primary values and hence the decision criterion of genetic selection. This is because the feedback of the primary values is always present in the system, even if that feedback is relatively unimportant in the selection of higher-order surrogates. Should an opposition of values emerge, however, while primary values remain fully functional (and thus not blocked or impeded in some

---

[37] A number of authors have made similar arguments. For example, Symons (1979: 46) suggests that "emotions might be considered to be the genes' closest representatives in the mental processes of learning and decision making." Pulliam and Dunford (1980: 3–4) compare the genes to "investors who cannot change or cancel their original instructions to their stockbrokers. . . . the investor's instructions emphasize strategy rather than details," leaving the latter to the decision maker. Similarly, Dawkins (1976: 64) pictures the genes, because they dictate "the way survival machines and their nervous systems are built," as exerting "ultimate power over behavior. But the moment-to-moment decisions about what to do next are taken by the nervous system. Genes are the primary policy-makers; brains are the executives."

way, a point we will return to in Chapter 7), their feedback will automatically tend to favor the preservation of any variant more consistent with the effective criterion of genetic selection.

On the basis of this argument, therefore, I propose Hypothesis 3 of co-evolutionary theory: *The main but not exclusive effect of the human decision system is to promote a general pattern of positive covariation between the cultural fitnesses of allomemes and their inclusive fitness values for the "selectors" (i.e., those who actually decide).* More specifically, I suggest that culture carriers faced with a choice of allomemes will generally confer the highest rates of social transmission ($F_c = 1.0$) upon one or more of the variants of highest relative inclusive fitness value ($F_g = 1.0$), although not necessarily upon all such variants. Likewise, I suggest that persons in a position to choose will generally confer low rates of social transmission upon allomemes offering them low inclusive fitnesses. Under conditions of imposition, on the other hand, there will still be a general pattern of positive covariation; however, it will be a positive type of covariation between rates of social transmission of allomemes and their inclusive fitness values for the imposers, not for those imposed upon.

My suggestion here generalizes another argument from the Tibetan case study, namely, the hypothesis that allomemes with valued consequences tend also to confer high reproductive fitness on those who choose (or impose) them. But notice that the hypothesis carries no specification about the nature or form of these consequences. In theory it does not matter whether the consequences are manifest in terms of land and labor (as in the Tibetan case), in terms of "pleasant interactions" with relatives (as in Alexander's social learning model), or in terms of freedom from a disease like malaria, for example. This is one reason why I prefer the general label "ecological consequences" for describing these diverse phenomena. What matters is that the consequences, however they may manifest themselves, should translate into potential inclusive-fitness benefit.

In later chapters, we will explore a number of the implications of Hypothesis 3. For now let it suffice to point out that while Hypothesis 2 states that three comparative modes of gene-culture relations are possible—namely, enhancement, neutrality, and opposition—Hypothesis 3 states that they are not all equally likely under any given set of social conditions. Within subpopulations free of substantial imposition, for example, Hypothesis 3 implies that secondary value selection (i.e., choice) will most often, though not always, result in the relationships of enhancement and neutrality. An opposing relationship—that is, one where allomemes of high F_c cause low F_g—may also result from secondary value selection under these circumstances; but this is expected only where cultural values do not, for some reason, perform their general duties as surrogates for the primary values. Within subpopulations affected by imposition (or "preservation by force") on the other hand, Hypothesis 3 implies that secondary value selection will often result in opposition. Under such conditions, enhancement and neutrality may well lack the potential F_g benefits that imposition offers to powerful outside individuals or groups.

Conscious and Unconscious Cultural Selection

Before turning to the subject of genetic mediation, let me simply point to two implications of the theory outlined above. The first concerns the question of consciousness in the process of cultural selection. It should be apparent from the previous discussion that cultural selection can surely proceed on a conscious level, with individuals making deliberate, conscious choices according to recognized criteria. This process has the advantage of being rapid and relatively efficient. In its most obvious manifestation, the process is sometimes called "rational choice" (as, for example, in Simon 1955; A. Cohen 1974; Heath 1976; Elster 1979), "rational preselection" (Boehm 1978), or simply "problem solving."

At the same time, cultural selection can proceed quite unconsciously. Although it is slower, unconscious selection can nevertheless be quite effective, proceeding through the reinforcement that follows from a given variant, either unrecognized or simply not causally associated. For example, cultural selection can surely proceed through unconscious operant conditioning (see Jones 1971; Alland 1972c; Reyna 1979). A meme that is adopted, even accidentally, can be reinforced by its consequences at a subconscious level, becoming part of an accepted cultural tradition. Should that meme be singled out subsequently, its carriers may be at a complete loss to explain its existence. For example, it seems possible that the correlation between subsistence dependence upon maize in New World populations and their possession of an alkali processing technique, such as presoaking or cooking with lime, ashes, or lye, resulted from unconscious conditioning (see Katz, Hediger, and Valleroy 1974). The practice certainly seems to be adaptive, enhancing as it does the balance of essential amino acids and the freeing of otherwise unavailable niacin (thereby preventing pellagra, among other consequences). However, when contemporary populations are asked about the alkali-processing meme, the treatment is usually described as a way of softening the tough outer kernel (p. 770). Cultural selection in this case and many others may have proceeded largely at an unconscious level, through the reinforcing assessment of primary and/or secondary values.

Reference Groups

A second implication of this theory is that the relevant social unit of cultural evolution, the "reference group" if you will, is a unit defined by the functions F_g and F_c. More specifically, the reference group should be the collection of individuals in space and time that shares *both* the same inclusive fitness function *and* the same cultural fitness function. In other words, it is a group of individuals who face more or less the same set of options, who experience more or less the same set of consequences, and who respond with more or less the same pattern of transmission rates. In the Tibetan case study, for example, my arguments about the evolutionary persistence of the monomarital principle pertained, as noted in Chapter 2, not to "all Tibetans" nor even to "all rural Tibetans." Instead, they applied to the much more homogeneous reference group of thongpa serfs who appear to have faced fundamentally similar opportunities and constraints during the cultural evolution of the beliefs that support their marriage system.

My reason for singling out reference groups is simple: within any given population, I would expect cultural evolution to be driven by different forces, or proceed in different directions, or both, within each of the subpopulations defined in this manner. Consider, for example, what would happen if the range of available allomemes were to vary within a hypothetical population such that the F_g-maximizing variant were available to one politically dominant, "autonomous" reference group—that is, a reference group in which individual selectors are free to adopt allomemes by their own volition—but not, because of imposition, to another group (which is therefore nonautonomous). Cultural selection would produce two different traditions within these groups, and tradition in the second would be relatively maladaptive. If an analyst were then to ignore the social constraints on that group, he or she could well get the false impression that maladaptation had been the product of choice and the group's own doing. Consequently, because of asymmetrical power relations, it will often be essential—particularly in complex societies—to subdivide large ethnolinguistic populations into the appropriate number of smaller and more homogeneous reference groups, and to look at the forces and directions of change within each of them. Culture may well be a "population-level phenomenon," as Boyd and Richerson (1985: 6) emphasize, but it often reflects the special interests, desires, and impositions of smaller subgroups within the whole. To identify reference groups is to acknowledge the simple fact that cultural evolution is an intrinsically political process.

The Genetic Mediation of Cultural Evolution

Let us now take a closer look at the first of the five modes of relationship between genes and culture, namely, genetic mediation. Genetic mediation may be said to exist whenever the cultural fitnesses of allomemes vary within or between reference groups as a function of their genotype frequency distributions, G_i, and do so because of genotype-specific differences in primary values. It is, in other words, a relationship in which a genetic change within one reference group, or a genetic difference between two groups, causes a difference in the corresponding phenotype dis-

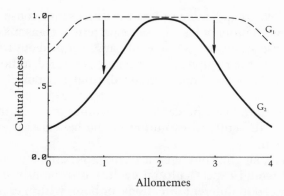

Fig. 4.7. A theoretical framework for major genetic mediation. In this hypothetical example, the relative cultural fitnesses, or F_c's, of an array of allomemes vary as a function of primary value assessments, and thus of genotype frequency distributions G_1 and G_2, in two reference groups (or in one reference group at two different times). Within the group with frequency distribution G_1, allomemes 1, 2, and 3 are evaluated more or less equally by the primary values, and therefore show similarly high rates of social transmission per unit of time (the broken curve). In contrast, within the group characterized by G_2, allomeme 2 is favored by primary values to such an extent that it alone has the highest F_c (as shown by the solid curve). The difference between these cultural fitness functions (indicated by arrows) is evidence of genetic mediation: genetic differences cause the evolution of cultural differences. (This diagram is similar in several respects to Fig. 4.1, the Lumsden-Wilson model of gene-culture transmission.)

tributions that (1) changes the primary value assessments of alternative allomemes by some individuals, and so (2) also changes the allomemes' rates of social transmission. If, as noted earlier, these primary value assessments are the most important cause of F_c differentials, then we may refer to the relationship as "major" genetic mediation.

A hypothetical version of major genetic mediation is shown in Fig. 4.7. The broken curve represents a hypothetical cultural fitness function for an array of allomemes transmitted among the members of a reference group with the genotype distribution G_1. A relatively wide range of variants are assumed, for this illustration, to show similar rates of social transmission. A different genotype distribution, G_2, causes primary values to bestow substantially different rates of social transmission (the solid line) upon all but allomeme 2 of the array. In this hypothetical example, genes mediate the direction and rate of cultural evolutionary change; they effectively change the "selecting environment" and redefine the quantity $(1.0 - F_c)$ for each allomeme—the quantity that I call its "cultural selection coefficient."

Because it describes the genetic causes of cultural change, this mode of relationship has received considerable attention in the years since the start of the sociobiology debate. For example, genetic mediation was highlighted by David Barash (1979) in *The Whisperings Within*, and was given more formal, mathematical treatment in the Lumsden-Wilson model of gene-culture transmission (1981) described earlier in this chapter. It bears emphasis, however, that genetic mediation and its logical counterpart, cultural mediation, are only two of *five* modes of relationship that are predicted by the hypotheses proposed here. My argument, then, is not that these earlier formulations were wrong in what they proposed, for I believe that symmetrically interactive relationships do exist. Instead, I view these formulations as being seriously incomplete. As a general rule, much more goes into determining the cultural fitnesses of allomemes than the "whisperings within" of our primary values. I believe that the interactive modes of relationship must therefore be supplemented by the comparative modes made possible by the self-selective property of cultural systems.

That said, let us return to genetic mediation and to the case study that I view as the best of available evidence today for the role of genetic mediation in the cultural fitnesses of a set of memes. The memes of the case are descriptive verbal labels for the experience of color. The genotypes of the case are those responsible for the pigment-based system of light absorption in the eye, on the one hand, and for the neurophysiological processing of sensory input to the brain, on the other. The example is particularly apt, first because it is amenable to experimental testing and empirical verification; and second, because in the opinion of many, "language is the best approximation of pure culture."[38] (Gerard et al. 1956.) If the relevance of genetic mediation can be established in the realm of "pure culture," then we will have grounds for believing its effect may extend into other, "less pure" realms of culturally influenced behavior.

The Cultural Evolution of Basic Color Terms

In 1969, the anthropologists Brent Berlin and Paul Kay published an influential monograph on the subject of basic color terms in human languages. The book described their attempts to test the hypothesis (taken as doctrine by some) called "extreme linguistic relativity." According to this hypothesis, Berlin and Kay noted, "each language performs the coding of experience into sound in a unique manner. Hence each language is semantically arbitrary relative to every other language." (1969: 1–2.) In such a view, there would be no semantic universals; different languages would subdivide human experience into very different descriptive categories.

Before 1969, this hypothesis was widely accepted by linguists as the

[38] For these and other reasons, the color-terms example has been discussed by many previous authors (see, for example, Bornstein 1973a and b, 1975; Rosch 1973; Ratliff 1976; Lloyd 1977; Witkowski and Brown 1977; Bolton 1978; Kay and McDaniel 1978; Von Wattenwyl and Zollinger 1979; Zollinger 1979; Lumsden and Wilson 1981, 1983; Durham 1982; Lumsden 1985; MacLaury 1987). My summary will therefore be selective and brief.

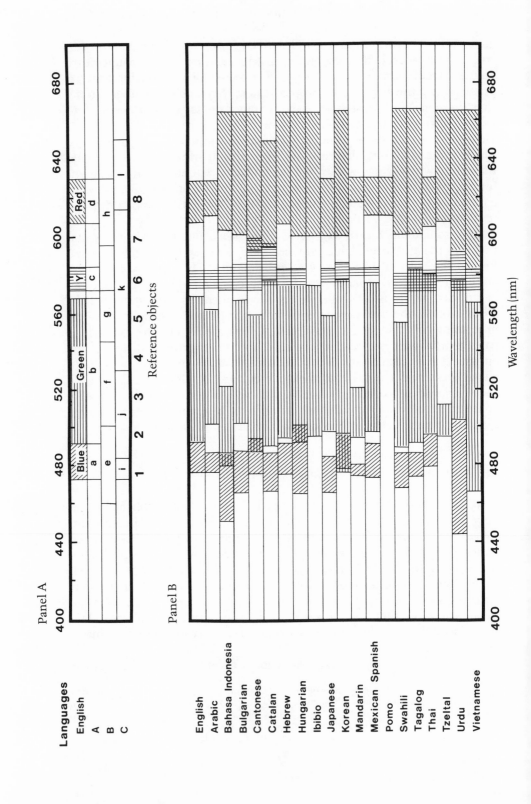

Panel A

Languages

English

A

B

C

Reference objects

Panel B

English
Arabic
Bahasa Indonesia
Bulgarian
Cantonese
Catalan
Hebrew
Hungarian
Ibibio
Japanese
Korean
Mandarin
Mexican Spanish
Pomo
Swahili
Tagalog
Thai
Tzeltal
Urdu
Vietnamese

Wavelength (nm)

explanation for interlanguage differences in color terminology. Indeed, color terms were often used in basic texts to exemplify the arbitrary semantic structure of languages. One commonly cited case in point was Verne F. Ray's study of the color-naming systems of some sixty linguistically and culturally distinct groups of native American Indians (1952, 1953). Presenting informants with a preselected array of "color samples," or pigmented swatches, Ray found great and seemingly arbitrary variation in the way colors were described or "encoded" in these languages. He wrote: "I conclude that there is no such thing as 'natural' division of the spectrum. The color systems of man are not based upon psychological, physiological, or anatomical factors. Each culture has taken the spectral continuum and has divided it upon a basis which is quite arbitrary except for pragmatic considerations [like preventing confusion]." (1953: 104.)

The findings by Ray and other researchers were generalized and abstracted to the form shown in panel A of Fig. 4.8. This panel illustrates the "spectral continuum" Ray spoke of, that is, the variation of lights according to their wavelength (from 400 to 700 nanometers, or nm), a variable we often describe as "hue." Now suppose that eight objects (or even better, eight monochromatic lights), numbered 1–8 in the figure, were shown to speakers of four languages, listed as English and the three hypothetical languages A, B, and C. Ray's argument is that there will be, in general, great discordance between the languages in the use of labels used to describe these objects. Consider object 7 for example, an object reflecting light with a dominant wavelength of 590 nm. Language B would describe this object by its word "h," the word most clearly corresponding to our term "red." Language C would describe the object as "k," which, in this hypothetical case, also includes wavelengths we would describe as "green." From this perspective, the cultural labels for color are viewed as arbitrary.

Fig. 4.8 (opposite). Cross-cultural similarities in the wavelength boundaries of basic color terms; wavelength ("hue") is measured in nanometers (nm). Panel A illustrates the hypothesis of extreme linguistic relativity, which constitutes a formal statement of the null hypothesis. The basic color terms of the world's human languages are expected to show arbitrary partitioning of the physical spectrum and substantial discordance of meaning (in terms of the wavelengths referred to). Thus, English and three hypothetical languages A, B, and C, as shown, would exhibit unpredictable variation in the range of wavelengths to which specific color terms (a, b, c, etc.) apply. Panel B, in contrast, which is based on data collected by Berlin and Kay (1969), shows striking concordance between the wavelengths referred to by basic color terms in a sample of twenty languages. For example, all the sample languages except Pomo have a basic color term closely corresponding to the English word "green." As can be seen in the figure, this term generally applies to a wide range of wavelengths, overlapping in some cases with the ranges of "yellow" and/or "blue." But there is not a single case where this term overlaps with the range of "red." This concordance of meanings allows us to reject the null hypothesis. Panel A adapted from Lyons 1968: 57; panel B prepared from data in Appendix I of Berlin and Kay 1969, with dominant wavelength values from Munsell Color Co. 1976b.

The Semantic Coding of Color

In the research described in their 1969 book, Berlin and Kay sought to test—and by their own admission to reconfirm—the hypothesis of extreme linguistic relativity using a broader sample of languages than Ray's and also a better set of color standards. Their color standards were drawn from the *Munsell Book of Color* (Munsell Color Co. 1976a), which is a systematic assortment of color swatches or "chips" based on three principal dimensions of color perception. One dimension is the familiar one also utilized by Ray, namely, hue—the property of light that varies as a function of wavelength. A second dimension, "brightness," refers to the amount of light reflected by a chip, and a third, "saturation," to the relative purity of a color, that is, its departure from neutral, grayish hues. Berlin and Kay drew a large array of 329 chips from this collection, 320 of various chromatic colors and 9 neutral chips (black, white, and various grays). The 320 chromatic chips formed a grid of 40 equally spaced hues (or, more accurately, hue-categories such as red, yellow-red, and green) classified by eight degrees of brightness, and all selected at the maximum available saturation.

Berlin and Kay then assembled a sample of native speakers of each of 20 different languages, given in panel B of Fig. 4.8, and asked two tasks of each: first, to provide the basic color words of their native language, using various criteria designed to screen out words that did not fit that description; and second, to locate on the grid of color chips both the focal point, or "best, most typical example" of a given term, and the outer boundary of acceptable referents that it described. Again, the authors' expectations were for widely scattered focal points and for great discordance in outer boundaries.

Their results formed a striking contrast to the hypothesis of extreme linguistic relativity. First, they found a very high degree of concordance or correlation among the boundaries of the basic color terms. This concordance is best seen in terms of the range of dominant wavelengths of the chips that were included within the boundaries for each basic color term. From data supplied by the Munsell Company (1976b), two student assistants (P.I. and E.L.) and I plotted the ranges for terms corresponding with "blue," "green," "yellow," and "red" in English, and obtained the results shown in panel B of Fig. 4.8. The figure demonstrates that the boundaries are actually quite similar with respect to wavelength. Moreover, when overlap occurs (as when the range of "yellow" overlaps with "green" and/or "red"), it is of a special pattern. There is no overlap in any of the languages between terms corresponding to green and red, or to blue and yellow. Both of these results run directly counter to the relativity hypothesis represented in panel A.

Second, as shown in Fig. 4.9, Berlin and Kay found a tight clustering of

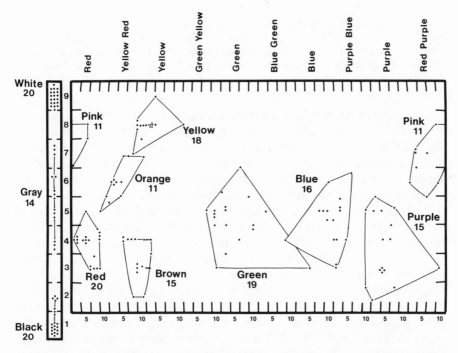

Fig. 4.9. Cross-cultural similarities in the focal points of basic color terms. Lines enclose clusters of color-term foci from the twenty languages studied by Berlin and Kay (1969) and listed in Fig. 4.8. Foci were determined by asking native speakers of each language to point out the best example or examples of a given basic color term on a stimulus array of 320 Munsell chromatic colors (represented here by the large rectangle, subdivided into 40 columns and 8 rows of color chips) and 9 neutral colors (represented here by the narrow rectangle at left). Each plotted point represents the "center of gravity" of the focus area designated by informants for one term of one language. Each cluster is labeled with the corresponding English term and the number of sample languages included in the cluster. From these data, Berlin and Kay conclude that "color categorization is not random and the foci of basic color terms are similar in all languages" (p. 10). The numerals and labels along the border of the chart refer to the Munsell system of color notation. Hue varies horizontally, brightness or value varies vertically, and all chips represent the peak saturation level available in the Munsell system. Redrawn from Berlin and Kay 1969: 9, fig. 3.

the focal points rather than a culturally arbitrary scatter. Informants' choices showed an impressive concordance that held up no matter how many basic color terms were included in their native color "lexicons," or vocabularies. These results pointed to a very basic set of eleven focal categories as the universe of basic terms for all languages. These categories were white, black, red, green, yellow, blue, brown, purple, pink, orange, and gray. To their surprise, Berlin and Kay also found that

if a language encodes fewer than eleven basic color categories, then there are strict limitations on which categories it may encode. The distributional restrictions of color terms across languages are: (1) all languages contain terms for white and black; (2) if a language contains three terms, then it contains a term for red; (3) if a language contains four terms, then it contains a term for either green or yellow (but not both); (4) if a language contains five terms, then it contains terms for both green and yellow; (5) if a language contains six terms, then it contains a term for blue; (6) if a language contains seven terms, then it contains a term for brown; (7) if a language contains eight or more terms, then it contains a term for purple, pink, orange, grey, or some combination of these. [1969: 2–3]

Berlin and Kay were able to confirm the existence of this "implicational hierarchy" in a larger sample of languages. Out of a logically possible 2,048 different lexicons built from the 11 basic color categories, they found no more than 22 in their expanded sample. Finally, they proposed that "there appears to be a fixed sequence of evolutionary stages through which a language must pass as its basic color vocabulary increases." (p. 14.)

In the years since Berlin and Kay's publication, a great deal of new work has been carried out on color terms, most of it confirming or slightly revising their original findings (see reviews by Conklin 1973; Collier 1975; Collier et al. 1976; Kay and McDaniel 1978; Burgess et al. 1983; Baines 1985; MacLaury 1987). This work has shown, for example, that the early stages of lexical expansion represent not the sequential encoding of new foci as Berlin and Kay had implied, but the successive differentiation of pre-existing broad categories. Thus, according to Kay and Chad McDaniel (1978: 638–40) and Robert MacLaury (1987), color lexicons begin with the composite categories "light-warm" and "dark-cool" instead of "white" and "black." Then, in an orderly sequence of stages, these composite categories appear to be successively decomposed into words for their six "primary constituents," namely black, white, red, yellow, green, and blue. Once all six primaries are differentiated in this way, subsequent stages add terms for colors that represent particular combinations of the primaries. Findings like these do offer important refinements and extensions of the original Berlin and Kay conclusions. But they do not, to date, contradict them. In terms of the theoretical framework introduced earlier in the chapter, we can therefore conclude: (1) that basic color terms are a special kind of meme with considerable cross-cultural regularity; (2) that compared to other descriptors of color, known or imaginable, these appear to have especially high cultural fitness in human populations; (3) that when new memes are added to the set, they enter in a specific and highly constrained fashion. It is proposed, then, that regularities in the linguistic encoding of color result from regularities in the neural coding of color in the brain, with the implication that this is a case of genetic mediation.

The Neural Coding of Color

Recent advances in the neurophysiology of color vision provide strong support for the hypothesis of genetic mediation in this special context. Evidence available from the comparative study of human and nonhuman primate visual systems indicates that the nervous system codes spectral

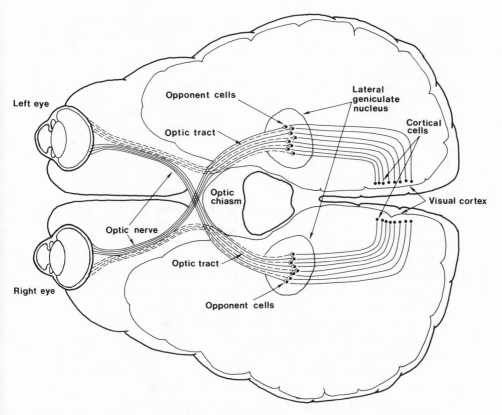

Fig. 4.10. The human visual pathway (viewed from below). The neural coding of color begins in the retina of the eye, where incoming light is absorbed to varying degrees by rods and three kinds of cones. The nerve-impulse activity so generated is transmitted to other retinal neurons (bipolar and ganglion cells) before passing on up the optic nerve, through the optic chiasm (a chi-shaped nerve crossing), to the lateral geniculate nucleus (LGN). After being processed in the LGN, the nerve-impulse patterns contain coded information regarding the hue, brightness, and saturation of the stimulus light. This information, in turn, is relayed to the visual cortex where further processing results in the perception of color contrast, among other things. Adapted from Pettigrew 1972: 85.

radiation according to its wavelength in a way that creates a kind of biological categorization of the spectrum. It seems likely, then, that color-term memes whose foci and boundaries correspond to these neurophysiological categories tend to be the memes of highest cultural fitness. The evidence may be summarized as follows.

Three major stages in the neural coding of color are often distinguished both functionally and anatomically (see Fig. 4.10). The first stage occurs in the retina of the eye, where radiant energy is captured within specialized receptor cells—the rods and cones—and converted into nerve-impulse energy. Human and other primate retinas contain three types of color-sensitive cones, each with a different photosensitive pigment (Wald 1964;

Nathans 1987).[39] The receptors, however, are not genuinely color-specific, for all three types of cones are stimulated by any radiation in the visible band; instead, their spectral sensitivities are "broadly tuned" and only quantitatively different. Nevertheless, the variation in the magnitude of their response rates provides the neurophysiological basis for what is called the "trichromacy," or three-color, theory of human vision. As observed by Helmholtz over a century ago, any color stimulus can be matched by an appropriate mixture of three chromatic lights such as blue, green, and red.

But the processing of color stimuli only begins in the receptors. Information about the wavelength of light can be obtained in the nervous system only by the comparison of outputs from two or more receptors of different pigments and spectral sensitivities (De Valois and De Valois 1975). In other words, wavelength information is conveyed to the brain as a comparison of cone activation levels. This comparison begins in the retina and is only completed at a higher center in the visual pathway called the lateral geniculate nucleus, or LGN (see Fig. 4.10). In the LGN, a special category of nerve cells receives nerve impulses transmitted from mixtures of the various cone types. These cells have the property of responding positively to certain ranges of wavelength and negatively to others. Four such cell types are known: two of them respond positively to red light and negatively to green, or vice versa; and two display the same basic pattern for yellow and blue light (De Valois et al. 1966). Significantly, any given cell responds positively to only one color of light in each of the pairs (e.g., to red but not green, etc.). The implication is that the nervous system treats these as discrete, graded categories. These "spectrally opponent response processes," as they are called, do not create the intermediate perceptual categories of reddish green and bluish yellow, and indeed, as noted earlier, we do not find words for these in the basic color vocabularies of the world.

The third and final stage of neural coding takes place in the visual cortex, where the information is received from the LGN (Fig. 4.10). The input of the LGN appears to go in two directions in the visual cortex: into cells that respond only to certain wavelengths of light; and into cells responsible for color contrast (see Livingstone and Hubel 1984). This higher center appears to integrate the wavelength information of the LGN cells into a coherent visual image containing information on hue, brightness, and saturation.

[39] These visual pigments, like many other features of the human visual pathway, have long been known to be genetically variable (see reviews in Kalmus 1965; Boynton 1979; Jacobs 1981; Zrenner 1983). Recently, however, their detailed molecular genetics have been elucidated, "verifying the hypothesis that the three human cone pigments and the rod pigment rhodopsin form a single family of homologous proteins encoded by the corresponding members of a family of genes"—all related by descent (Nathans et al. 1986a: 201–2). Indeed, it has now been shown that inherited variations in color vision, such as red-green "color blindness," are caused by modifications in the genes that encode the various visual pigments (Nathans et al. 1986b).

Correlations of Semantic and Neural Coding

Working from this information, two groups of researchers have pointed to close similarities in the neural and linguistic coding of color. The first group includes the linguistic anthropologists Kay and McDaniel (1978) mentioned earlier. Among other things, their work demonstrates that the universal lexical sequence discovered by Berlin and Kay represents a specific pattern in the coding of but six "fundamental neural responses." Early stages in the sequence contain composite semantic categories ("dark-cool," "light-warm," "warm," or "cool") representing what have been called "fuzzy set" unions of two or three of these responses. The later stages of the sequence reflect additions to the lexicon of terms that correspond to the fuzzy-set intersections of fundamental neural responses (for example, brown is the fuzzy-set intersection of black and yellow, and pink is the intersection of red and white).

In short, the implied lexical sequence can be matched to a neural response model. The pattern is constrained and orderly, its categories behave like model neural processes, its transitions are physiologically intelligible, and it appears to apply cross-culturally with few exceptions. And this is just what we would expect for a case of genetic mediation, in which all sample populations had similar distributions of the pertinent genotypes and phenotypes. The evidence suggests that the neural response patterns—dependent as they are on genetically variable properties of the visual pathway—function as an influential set of primary values that govern the fate of alternative color-term definitions. Out of the broad range of possible definitions, each with different boundaries and foci, only certain variants have achieved high cultural fitness in each of the sample populations. These favored variants have properties that closely match the neural response pattern. The match suggests that their cultural fitness derives mainly from primary value assessment.

The second group of researchers to point out these similarities is that of psychologists and neuroscientists. Their evidence leads to the same general conclusion but from a slightly different route (for details, see App. A.4.2). First, the color-naming studies of Robert Boynton and James Gordon (1965) have provided a detailed, quantitative picture of the semantic coding of color by native speakers of one language, namely, English. In their tests, people were shown monochromatic lights of different wavelengths and were asked to describe them in one or two words: "blue," "green," "yellow," or "red." When the responses were converted to point scores and plotted by wavelength, the meaning of each term was found, again, to be a fuzzy set. In particular, the point scores for each term showed a broad distribution by wavelength, each with its own special shape and single, mid-range focus.

Second, Russell De Valois and colleagues (1966) have devised a technique for summing the total neural response output by wavelength from the spectrally opponent cells of the LGN (using data from the macaque

LGN, believed to be a reasonably good model for the human one). Their results show striking similarities to those of Boynton and Gordon: color by color, the response curves are parallel and the foci are closely matched (see also De Valois and De Valois 1975). But even more interesting is the close correlation between the wavelengths of the original Berlin and Kay focal points and the LGN response pattern: for example, "green" shows the broadest distribution in both coding schemes, and "yellow" and "blue" the sharpest.[40] Given the complete independence of the data bases, and the great improbability of such a correlation by chance, these findings, too, suggest that primary value selection has been a key force in the cultural evolution of basic color terms. This case would seem to be a good example of genetic mediation.

Primary Values and Cultural Fitness

The most convincing evidence of all for genetic mediation comes from an experiment by the psychologist Eleanor Rosch (1973) on color-term learning among the Dani people of highland New Guinea. From earlier work Rosch knew that the Dani language had only two basic color terms: one for "light" or "white" and the other for "dark" or "black." The experiment therefore consisted of teaching groups of Dani schoolchildren eight completely new color words using three sets of Munsell chips as reference categories. Group 1 learned from a set presumed to represent "natural prototypes": for each new word, students were shown one focal chip from a Berlin and Kay cluster together with two chips of equal brightness that reflected light of slightly longer and slightly shorter wavelengths. Group 2 students were taught from deliberately "nonnatural prototypes" consisting in each case of one chip from the center of an area *outside* the Berlin and Kay clusters, flanked by chips reflecting slightly longer and slightly shorter wavelengths. And finally, group 3 students were taught from stimuli that resembled the natural prototypes except that each focal chip was accompanied by two chips reflecting longer wavelengths. All three groups were taught to associate familiar noncolor words (Dani descent group names, in fact) with each of these color categories; Rosch kept track of each student's successes and failures at recalling the correct color term.

This study can be viewed as a clever experimental test for the kind of difference shown in Fig. 4.7. Hypothetically, the Dani—or any other human population—could have a distribution of genotypes like G_1 in the figure, whose associated primary values confer equal F_c's upon a broad range of alternative color-term definitions. In Rosch's terms, the "natural structure" of the color space of such a population would then be "un-

---

[40] See App. A.4.2 for supporting analysis. See also Bornstein (1973a: 260), Bornstein et al. (1976: 201), and Lumsden (1985: 5807) for related discussions; the latter, for example, compares Berlin and Kay color term foci with the perceptual categories of hue among human infants.

differentiated." (1973: 331.) Alternatively, the Dani could have a distribution of genotypes, like G_2 in the figure, whose associated primary values create "natural hue categories" and thus a much narrower range of allomemes with high F_c.

Not surprisingly, Rosch's study provides strong evidence for the latter. The three groups of Dani schoolchildren showed large and statistically significant differences in the ease with which they learned the different color concepts. Group 1 children learned the new color terms fastest and showed the fewest errors per attempted recall; in contrast, group 2 had the greatest difficulty learning the nonnatural prototypes. Because teaching and learning are obviously prerequisite for successful social transmission, Rosch's data show that primary value assessments can sometimes be the main cause of differences in cultural fitness, in this case of color terms (for further discussion, see Witkowski and Brown 1982).

Coevolution

In this chapter, I have outlined a general theory for relating genetic and cultural evolution in human populations. Called "coevolution," the theory focuses on evolutionary change in human cultural systems and on its relationship to the dynamics of genetic microevolution. The theory has a number of important features that bear emphasis in this concluding section.

First, the theory is based on three main hypotheses. Hypothesis 1 concerns the causal priority of transformational mechanisms in cultural change; it proposes that secondary value selection—that is, decision making governed by cultural values—is the main but not exclusive means of cultural evolutionary change. In other words, this hypothesis predicts that the evolutionary fitness of cultural entities—their "suitability for replication and use" within a given population—is largely governed by their relative appeal to persons in a position to choose or impose them. Other forces, including any ratio advantage (i.e., a normally high ratio of "receivers" to "senders" during social transmission) and/or reproduction advantage, may surely contribute to high cultural fitness and may be most important in special cases. But, as a general rule, I predict that the secondary value assessment by decision makers is the most important determinant of success in social transmission. By implication, this importance accrues also to cultural selection, or "preservation by preference"—the more general category of processes including primary as well as secondary value selection.

Hypothesis 2 interrelates the dynamics of genetic and cultural change. It proposes that there exist no fewer than five distinct modes of relationship between genes and culture: two "interactive" modes of relationship—genetic mediation and cultural mediation—which refer to the reciprocal causal effects of genetic and cultural change; and three "comparative" modes—enhancement, neutrality, and opposition—in which culture changes primarily through secondary value selection, and does so with directions and rates that can be compared to what would be expected under similar conditions in genetic evolution. The first two modes of relationship constitute what I call "coevolution in the narrow sense"; the last three modes, which I believe to be both more common and more analytically useful, are included in "coevolution in the broad sense," or simply "coevolution" as I use the term here.

Hypothesis 3 concerns the directions and rates of cultural evolutionary change in the comparative modes of relationship. It predicts that the human decision system promotes a general pattern of positive covariation between the cultural fitnesses of allomemes (that is, their suitability for social transmission in a given population) and their inclusive fitness values for those who decide. Remembering that inclusive fitness assesses the "effectiveness of design for reproductive survival," the prediction here is that cultural variants with more potential to improve the reproductive fitness of their selectors will spread through a population by choice or imposition at the expense of alternative variants with less of that potential. Put differently, the hypothesis predicts the eventual elimination of cultural variants that offer the effective decision makers lower-than-average inclusive fitness. When this hypothesis is added to the other two, the resulting theory relates genes and culture in a way that is at once compatible with organic evolutionary theory and yet not reductionistic or deterministic, as some earlier models of gene-culture relations have been.

I should re-emphasize here that the unit of culture in this model is an ideational unit, potentially highly variable in size, complexity, and configuration. Called a "meme" after Dawkins (1976, 1982), with variants called "allomemes," the unit embraces cultural instructions ranging from the most "micro" to the most "macro." Memes are viewed as informational guides to behavior; their relationship to human phenotypes parallels that of genotypes, creating a second "track" of inheritance.

By this theory, then, the consequences of a set of memes will vary not only in space and time (as ecological conditions vary) but also within large and/or heterogeneous populations. Analytically, it is therefore important to differentiate "reference groups" for whom memes have recognizably similar consequences and ranges. According to the hypotheses proposed here, the dynamics of cultural transmission within such groupings should show a fairly uniform pattern. If I am correct, then the cultural fitness function F_c of a given set of allomemes (not to mention their inclusive fitness function) will covary in space, time, and subgroup with their consequences. Cultural fitness should not, therefore, be regarded as an invariant property of the memes themselves.

Further, this conceptualization regards people as decision makers and active participants in cultural change. It assumes (1) that they actively compare and choose among options, provided they are free to do so; and (2) that they base their evaluations on estimates of the consequences of the alternatives. Concerning (1), it should be remembered that there are two kinds of constraints or "structural forces" that limit the choice of allomemes: there are the cultural constraints of pre-existing form, analogous to their counterparts in genetic evolution; and there are the imposed constraints that arise from social intervention in the transmission process. As argued in later chapters, I consider such constraints to be an important force behind the cultural evolution of maladaptive traditions. As regards (2), cultural selection requires familiarity with the consequences of alternative allomemes. Because people cannot be assumed to have perfect knowledge of those consequences, adaptations may sometimes be slow to emerge even where there is freedom of choice.

Finally, this theory of cultural evolution is "content-oriented," that is, the major force of change depends upon the information content of the variants. The information is evaluated on the basis of its phenotypic consequences and these, in turn, are assessed by primary and secondary values of the human decision system. In my usage, secondary values are themselves cultural, thus providing the cultural system with the capacity for "self-selection." The implications of this important property, especially for the comparative modes of gene-culture relations, are explored in subsequent chapters.

In the last few sections of the chapter, we turned to examine a mode of relationship between genes and culture called "genetic mediation." As defined, the relationship implies (1) that genetic differences between human populations (in genotype-frequency distributions) may sometimes give rise to cultural differences (in ideas, values, and beliefs); and obversely (2) that the genetic similarity of populations may sometimes cause their cultural similarity. The evidence reviewed in this chapter strongly suggests that color encoding is an example of (2).

CULTURAL MEDIATION:

The Evolution of Adult

Lactose Absorption

The study of basic color terms in Chapter 4 offered a provocative test case of genetic mediation, one of the five modes of relationship I have proposed to describe the interplay of genes and culture in human populations. In this chapter, we will examine the logically symmetrical mode called "cultural mediation." In this mode, the configuration of cultural instructions in a population directly affects the differential reproduction of genes and genotypes. After a brief look at a theoretical framework for cultural mediation, we will undertake a case analysis of adult lactose (milk sugar) absorption in human populations. The genetic evolution of this rather specialized physiological capability will illustrate the important ways in which culture contributes to the evolution of human genetic diversity.

The Cultural Mediation of Genetic Evolution

The relationship I call cultural mediation may be said to exist whenever (1) a cultural change within a population or (2) a cultural difference between two populations causes some difference in the rate and/or direction of genetic evolution. More specifically, cultural mediation occurs whenever a cultural difference in memes within or between populations creates a behavioral difference that, in turn, causes a difference in the reproduction of genotypes. In such a situation, the distribution of memes may be viewed as part of the "selecting environment" of the genes, contributing to the relative reproductive success or failure of particular gene combinations. The nature and frequency of the memes are responsible for altering the selection coefficients acting on the genotypes. As in the case of genetic mediation, the important point is that a difference in the *frequencies* of one kind of instruction causes a difference in the *fitnesses* of the other kind. In cultural mediation, differences in meme frequency cause differences in the rates of gene replication.

This mode of relationship is represented schematically in Fig. 5.1. The

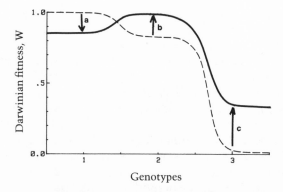

Fig. 5.1. A theoretical framework for cultural mediation. Shown here are three hypothetical genotypes (1, 2, and 3) undergoing differential reproduction, with the initial Darwinian fitnesses shown by the dashed curve. Cultural mediation refers to any change in the relative fitnesses of genotypes in a population (as shown by arrows *a*, *b*, and *c*) caused by either a cultural change within a population or a cultural difference between two populations. For the purposes of illustration, the Darwinian fitness functions shown here are approximately those pertaining to the genotypes of the sickle-cell anemia example discussed in Chapter 3, so that genotype 1 = AA, 2 = AS, and 3 = SS. Redrawn from Durham 1982: 300.

figure illustrates how a hypothetical change in the distribution of memes within a population, or a hypothetical difference in the distributions of memes between populations, affects the relative Darwinian fitnesses of three genotypes under selection. The dashed curve shows Darwinian fitnesses before a cultural change—that is, a change in the distribution of memes—and the solid curve depicts the new fitnesses after that change. The arrows *a*, *b*, and *c* indicate the direction and magnitude of fitness changes for the three genotypes in this example. In a diallelic situation (one in which three genotypes are formed from combinations of two alleles) such changes may enable one allele to achieve fixation, or at least predominance, at the expense of the other, or the effect of culture may be to create a genetic polymorphism. Either way, culture will affect the course of genetic change.

The hypothetical example of Figure 5.1 closely corresponds to the proposed role of culture in the evolution of the sickle-cell gene frequencies of West Africa, as already discussed in Chapter 3. Genotypes 1, 2, and 3 correspond to AA, AS, SS in that example, and the arrows reflect the changes in fitness hypothesized for the prehistoric shift from hunter-gatherer subsistence to widespread yam cultivation among the Kwa-speakers (see Fig. 3.4, panel B, and Fig. 3.5). The cultural mediation arising from agriculture in the yam zone would have reduced the relative fitness of the AA genotype because, as discussed in Chapter 3, AA's lack the biochemical resistance of the AS's to the falciparum malaria that was encouraged, we believe, by cleared fields. Simultaneously, that same mediation might also have increased the relative fitness of the SS genotype through a more abundant and more stable food supply, a change that would have benefited all genotypes but especially the SS's, which are prone to sickling under physiological stress. As we saw in Chapter 3, the result of these changes was to promote higher frequencies of the S allele among West African agriculturalists than among their nonagricultural and more recently agricultural neighbors.

To date, cultural mediation remains the most likely explanation for the balanced polymorphism of West Africa's A and S hemoglobin genes. Nevertheless, this example stands out as a bit unusual or extreme in two ways. First, the S allele is noteworthy because of its phenotypically serious consequences. One would like to show that cultural mediation is capable of affecting a range of genotypes far broader than the special case of lethal recessives. Second, *P. falciparum* malaria is also a particularly virulent pathogen. It would be helpful to demonstrate that culture can influence genetic evolution through consequences not quite so deadly as tropical malaria. In the pages that follow I therefore present a second case study involving cultural mediation—a case that is more general and much more mundane.

Human Diversity in Adult Lactose Absorption

Most North Americans are surprised to learn that a great many of the world's adults lack the physiological ability to digest fresh milk. Living in "a culture strongly committed to the concept that milk is an ideal food" (Kretchmer 1981b: 6), we tend to think of adult milk consumption as a perfectly normal and healthy dietary habit, indeed a very "natural" thing. This cultural ideology is reinforced by such common dairy association advertisements as "Everybody needs milk" and "You never outgrow your need for milk." It seems almost incomprehensible that many adults in the world need, if anything, an *absence* of milk in their daily diets, and that they do indeed outgrow their need for this food just as they also—and quite naturally—outgrow their ability to digest it.

Part of the reason for this surprise can be traced to the history of Western science. It was only in 1965 that biomedical researchers began to recognize that systematic variation exists in the milk-digestion physiology of adults. In that year, Pedro Cuatrecasas, Dean Lockwood, and Jacques Caldwell published a study reporting that fresh milk could not be digested by 30 of 41 (73 percent) black teenagers and adults tested in Baltimore, Maryland, in contrast to a high frequency of "normal" digestion in their sample of whites (16 of 19, or 84 percent). A much rarer inability to digest milk had been recognized among infants since the early 1900's, a condition characterized by "severe fermentative diarrhea" following milk ingestion and called "congenital lactose intolerance." Only after the Baltimore study did physicians and social scientists begin to realize, first, that many of the world's adults share these same symptoms of intolerance; and second, that an even greater number of adults, in fact the clear majority, have as part of their normal phenotype the inability to digest key nutrients in milk. Apparently this entire dimension of human diversity was "hidden" from medical research for many years by a successful behavioral adjustment of nondigesters: they tend to avoid it (Bayless 1981: 120).

The discovery of this dimension of human diversity in the 1960's immediately raised a number of practical and theoretical issues. On the practical side, the discovery came in the midst of an era of increasing U.S. food aid, a substantial portion of which was being sent abroad in the form of powdered milk averaging forty to fifty percent lactose. As the anthropologist Robert McCracken pointed out in 1971, the practice amounted to nutritional ethnocentrism. Quite literally unable to absorb our food aid, intended beneficiaries were commonly forced to find other ways to dispose of the substance. In some places, the milk powder found its way into whitewash for buildings; in others, people doled it out in small quantities as a laxative. Worse still, our generosity may actually have backfired in populations where the substance was more readily consumed. For reasons I shall explain shortly, the ingestion of substantial quantities of milk by malabsorbers can upset the normal digestive processes of the gut, speeding the passage of undigested matter, and reducing the absorption of nutrients from other foods. Ironically, the effect of our "food aid" may sometimes have been to *increase* malnutrition.

On the theoretical side, the questions raised were again those of interpreting a particular dimension of human diversity, namely, why is it that only a small portion of the world's population can fully digest milk as adults? What historical or evolutionary forces lie behind the emergence of this specialized physiological capacity? And what have been the contributions of genes and culture along the way? In an attempt to work toward answers to these questions, let us begin with a look at the physiology of fresh milk consumption.

The Digestion of Lactose

The chemical compound responsible for these problems of milk digestion in both infants and adults is lactose, the principal solid and sole sugar in most mammalian milks.[1] Like other disaccharide sugars, lactose is synthesized from two simple sugars, or monosaccharides, that are enzymatically bonded into a single larger molecule.[2] Although the process

[1] Another class of milk digestion problems results from physiological intolerance and/or allergy to milk proteins (see, for instance, Walker-Smith 1984). These are clinically and analytically distinct from the problems of lactose absorption discussed here.

[2] In particular, lactose is synthesized from the monosaccharides glucose and uridine diphosphate galactose. The synthesis is catalyzed by an enzyme, galactosyl transferase, which is itself "specified," or activated, by another constituent of milk, α-lactalbumin (for more details see Leloir and Cardini 1961; Nickerson 1974; Kuhn, Carrick, and Wilde 1980). The amino acid sequence of α-lactalbumin is remarkably similar to lysozyme, another of the body's proteins, whose function is to break apart the cell walls of bacteria. According to Gould and Vrba (1982: 9), α-lactalbumin diverged from lysozyme during the evolution of mammals, and therefore became an "exaptation" (defined in Chapter 1 of this book); origi-

of synthesis is basically similar among all mammals, the lactose concentrations of milk vary from approximately 7.0 percent of the volume of human milk to 2.5 percent of reindeer milk, and on to 0.0 percent in the milk of the Pacific pinnipeds (seals, sea lions, and walruses, for example)—the only milk lacking lactose altogether (Palmiter 1969; Patton 1969; Kretchmer 1972). A principal function of the lactose, of course, is to provide energy for the newborn; in the Pacific pinnipeds, the reduced lactose is compensated by a higher fat content in the mother's milk.

Curiously, all lactose-bearing milks present a problem for mammalian digestion: the disaccharide molecules of lactose are not readily absorbed through the membranous lining of the small intestine. For complete digestion, lactose must be broken back down into the simple sugars from which it was synthesized.[3] An interesting evolutionary paradox suggests itself immediately: How is one to interpret the evolution of the mammalian genetics behind this enzyme-regulated synthesis when its product, lactose, must promptly be broken back down for efficient absorption and use? And why did genetic selection apparently eliminate the enzymes of the synthesis pathway, and thereby eliminate lactose, from the milk of the Pacific pinnipeds, of all mammals? We shall return to these questions later.

In humans, the digestion of lactose takes place primarily in the jejunal region of the small intestine (see Fig. 5.2, panel A). There, a class of enzymes called lactases are synthesized within the mucosal cells that line the many small absorptive protrusions of the jejunal wall.[4] The lactases cause the enzymatic hydrolysis of lactose back into its constituent monosaccharides, glucose and galactose, which are then quite readily absorbed across the cell membranes of the intestinal wall and may be transported on to the bloodstream. One of the lactases involved, called "neutral lactase" or lactase I, accounts for over 90 percent of the lactose digestion of the small intestine; it is this particular enzyme that appears to be lacking in adults unable to digest milk (Harrison 1975). At least two other lactases have been identified, but their role is secondary in the process of lactose absorption.

Early in the life of most mammals, lactase I is produced in the jejunum in sufficient quantity to convert virtually all of the lactose ingested with mother's milk. Before long, however, the production of the enzyme normally begins a dramatic decline, resulting in low levels of lactase activity

---

nally shaped by genetic selection for one function (lysing bacteria), it has been co-opted for another (specifying lactose synthesis).

[3] Lactose and other disaccharides are not readily absorbed as intact molecules in the small intestine because the lipid bilayer of mucosal cell membranes acts as an effective chemical barrier to their passage. In contrast, the monosaccharides (such as glucose and galactose) that make up these larger sugars are readily absorbed by way of molecular transport mechanisms built into the cell membranes (see Moog 1981).

[4] Lactases are also called "β-galactosidases" in the technical literature, in reference to their ability to cleave the chemical bond—called a "β 1,4 glycosidic linkage"—between the component monosaccharides of lactose (see, for example, Nickerson 1974).

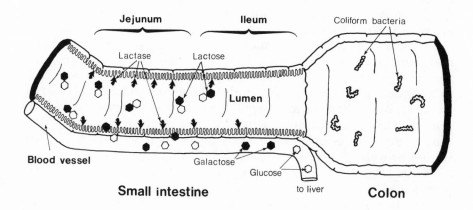

Panel A   Lactose absorber

Jejunum   Ileum   Coliform bacteria

Lactase   Lactose

Lumen

Blood vessel

Galactose

Glucose

Small intestine   to liver   **Colon**

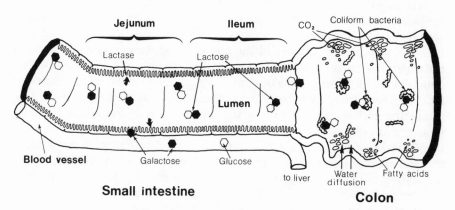

Panel B   Lactose malabsorber

Jejunum   Ileum CO_2 Coliform bacteria

Lactase   Lactose

Lumen

Blood vessel   Galactose   Glucose

to liver   Water diffusion   Fatty acids

Small intestine   **Colon**

Fig. 5.2. The anatomy of lactose absorption and malabsorption in simplified cross section. Panel A shows the fate of lactose molecules in the intestines of a lactose absorber. Lactose molecules (enlarged for clarity) arrive in the jejunum, where they are enzymatically split by lactase (dark arrows) and are readily absorbed through the intestinal membranes. Few, if any, molecules of lactose survive the trip through the jejunum and ileum (greatly foreshortened for illustration) to arrive in the colon of a lactose absorber. Panel B shows the contrasting fate of lactose molecules in the intestines of a malabsorber: because of low levels of lactase activity, the molecules pass right on through the jejunum and ileum and arrive in the colon, where they are digested by coliform bacteria (also not to scale). The resulting accumulation of water and bacterial waste products (CO_2 and fatty acids, as shown) can cause fermentative diarrhea, characteristic of "lactose intolerance." The reaction is not always so serious, however, and malabsorption may have consequences no more detrimental than the loss of the food value of milk sugar. Adapted from Zihlman 1982. Copyright © 1982 by Coloring Concepts, Inc. Reprinted by permission of Harper & Row, Publishers, Inc. Additional data from Kretchmer 1972; Moog 1981.

from about the time of weaning onward. This general mammalian pattern appears to hold for the majority of human beings as well, although there is considerable variation in the timing of the decline in lactase activity (see Simoons 1980a).[5] For this reason, most human beings in their postweaning years are called "lactose malabsorbers" and are said to have the phenotype of lactose malabsorption (LM).[6] In such persons, the remaining, "residual" lactase activity, caused in large part by lactase II, is insufficient to break down any substantial quantity of ingested lactose. This insufficiency serves as the basis for one of the main clinical tests for malabsorption (see Flatz and Rotthauwe 1977; Torún et al. 1979; McGill 1983). In contrast to dairy association advertisements, then, most people in the world—as well as most other mammals of *all* species—actually do outgrow their need for milk (but see Katz 1981 for the dairy council perspective).

Many lactose malabsorbers also suffer from "lactose intolerance" (LI), a distinctly negative reaction by the body (symptoms include flatulence, intestinal cramps, diarrhea, nausea, even vomiting) caused by the failure of lactose subdivision in the jejunum. In this instance, most of the lactose molecules continue on down the gut to the ileum and the colon, which are largely lacking in lactase activity. There, the effect of the lactose is to increase the particle density of the gut, causing water to be drawn from the surrounding tissues by osmotic action (as shown by the arrows labeled "water diffusion" in Fig. 5.2, panel B). Eventually, any undigested lactose is fermented by naturally occurring coliform bacteria in the colon, producing carbon dioxide, fatty acids, and gaseous hydrocarbons. The result, commonly, is the same "fermentative diarrhea" that characterizes congenital lactose intolerance among infants. Adult intolerance should therefore not be confused with malabsorption per se, even though the two are statistically correlated (this was a frequent mistake in the older literature; see Johnson, Cole, and Ahern 1981; Ferré 1982). The implication is either that many lactose malabsorbers have enough residual lactase activity to prevent symptoms or that they have intestinal bacteria that can

[5] On the basis of this general mammalian pattern, Lieberman and Lieberman (1978) propose that progressive lactase deficiency evolved early in the history of mammalian evolution, perhaps 75 million years ago. They hypothesize that it evolved by genetic selection because it facilitates weaning—presumably by causing gastrointestinal distress in older sucklings—and foreshortens the period of conflict between parent and offspring over lactation (see also Rozin 1982: 240). In a related argument, Farb and Armelagos (1980: 187) suggest that "the loss of the enzyme is obviously [a genetic] adaptation. . . . Its absence prevents adults from competing with infants, who can digest only milk." Others (Holmes et al. 1976) argue that the onset of lactase deficiency has had selective advantage as a defense mechanism against intestinal infections.

[6] Lactose malabsorption is sometimes further divided into "primary" LM, when onset occurs gradually with age, and "secondary" LM, when onset results from disease or injury to the intestinal membranes. The focus of the analysis in this chapter is on primary adult lactose malabsorption, or what Flatz (1987: 5) calls "low lactose digestion capacity (low LDC)." Although sympathetic with Flatz's critique of "malabsorption"—a term which, if taken literally, misidentifies the problem as one of absorption rather than hydrolysis and mislabels it a disease or abnormality—I use the conventional nomenclature in order to minimize confusion with all other literature on the subject.

metabolize lactose without causing the symptoms of intolerance, or both (see Alpers 1981; Hill 1983; R. Johnson et al. 1987).

There are two exceptions to the general pattern of declining lactase activity with age: the Pacific pinnipeds, again, with virtually no lactase activity at any age; and the unusual human populations of adult lactose absorbers. In the latter case, lactase I continues to be produced in the jejunum at physiologically active concentrations straight through into adulthood in most people (see Welsh 1981 for sample data). Such people are able to derive full caloric benefit as adults from the consumption of fresh milk.

The Distribution of Adult Lactose Absorption

Since the scientific community discovered adult lactose malabsorption in 1965, many studies have been undertaken to assess the reactions of the world's adult populations to ingested lactose. In order to take advantage of standard field-testing procedures, most of these studies have focused on absorption and malabsorption rather than on intolerance. This growing body of data has been reviewed on numerous occasions (see, for instance, J. Johnson et al. 1974; Harrison 1975; Flatz and Rotthauwe 1977; Torún et al. 1979; Flatz 1987; Scrimshaw and Murray 1988). But the first comprehensive compilation—and the one available as I began this study—is that of the geographer Frederick J. Simoons of the University of California at Davis. Simoons (1978a) has summarized the results of 197 population studies from around the world, conducted in societies ranging from band-level hunter-gatherers to industrialized nation-states. The study populations are grouped into seven categories, according to features of their subsistence economies, with the sample data for each on the prevalence of lactose absorption (LA). Simoons's compilation points both to the range of human diversity in lactose-absorbing ability—literally from 0 to 100 percent among the peoples investigated—and to a pronounced pattern in the distribution of LA. Simoons concluded that

high prevalences of LM, from about 60–100% of the persons studied, are typical of the overwhelming number of ethnic groups around the world . . . including all American Indians and Eskimos studied so far, some New World Mestizos, most sub-Saharan African peoples and their relatively unmixed overseas descendants, most Mediterranean and Near Eastern groups, most subjects whose origins are India, all peoples of Southeast and East Asia, as well as the two Pacific groups, New Guineans and Fijians, who have been studied. Low prevalences of LM (from 0 to 30%), on the other hand, typify a minority of the world's peoples, primarily northern and western Europeans and their overseas descendants, but also certain peoples of the Mediterranean and Near East, three pastoral groups of Africa (Tussi, Hima, and Fulani), and several groups living in the western parts of the Indian subcontinent. There are some groups who have intermediate prevalences of LM (30–60%), but they are few, and almost all have a mixed absorber/malabsorber ancestry. Thus, the relatively unmixed ethnic groups of the world seem to fall into two population categories: lactose absorbers (0–30% prevalences of LM) and malabsorbers (60–100% prevalences). [1978a: 964]

TABLE 5.1

Indicators of Genetic and Cultural Diversity in Sixty Populations
Tested for Adult Lactose Absorption, 1966–1978,
Categorized by Subsistence and Location

Category and population	Percentage of lactose absorbers	Approximate latitude	Total milk consumption (liters/person/year)	Cheese production (% of milk production)
Category A. Hunter-gatherers (traditionally lacking dairy animals): $N = 4$				
1. Eskimos of Greenland	15.1%	69.2 N	0.0	—
2. Twa Pygmies of Rwanda	22.7	1.6 S	0.0	—
3. !Kung Bushmen	2.5	19.6 S	0.0	—
4. ‡huâ Bushmen of Botswana	8.0	23.0 S	0.0	—
Average	12.6% [a]			
Category B. Nondairying agriculturalists: $N = 5$				
5. Yoruba	9.0%	6.3 N	4.5	16.0%
6. Ibo	20.0	4.4 N	4.5	16.0
7. Children in Ghana	27.0	5.3 N	0.6	12.0
8. Bantu of Zaire	1.9	4.2 S	0.2	37.4
9. Hausa	23.5	12.0 N	4.5	16.0
Average	15.5% [a]			
Category C. Recently dairying agriculturalists: $N = 5$				
10. Kenyans (mainly Bantu)	26.8%	1.2 S	67.5	0.3%
11. Bantu of Zambia	0.0	15.3 S	8.8	12.1
12. Bantu of South Africa	9.7	26.1 S	92.1	10.2
13. Shi, Bantu of Lake Kivu area	3.6	1.6 S	7.3	0.0
14. Ganda, other Bantu of Uganda	5.7	0.2 N	29.8	0.0
Average	11.9% [a]			
Category D. Milk-dependent pastoralists: $N = 5$				
15. Arabs of Saudi Arabia	86.4%	24.4 N	NA[b]	NA[b]
16. Hima pastoralists	90.9	1.0 S	NA	NA
17. Tussi, in Uganda	88.2	0.2 N	NA	NA
18. Tussi, in Congo	100.0	4.1 S	NA	NA
19. Tussi, in Rwanda	92.6	1.6 S	NA	NA
Average	91.3% [a]			
Category E. Dairying peoples of North Africa and the Mediterranean: $N = 16$				
20. Jews in Israel	40.8%	32.1 N	203.6	40.1%
21. Ashkenazic Jews	20.8	32.1 N	203.6	40.1
22. N. African Sephardim	37.5	33.4 N	28.5	10.7
23. Other Sephardim	27.8	37.0 N	120.1	18.0
24. Iraqi Jews	15.8	33.2 N	38.3	38.4
25. Other Oriental Jews	15.0	35.4 N	71.1	33.8
26. Arab villagers in Israel	19.4	32.1 N	203.6	40.1
27. Syrian Arabs	5.0	33.3 N	81.0	36.3
28. Jordanian Arabs	23.2	31.6 N	15.8	54.3
29. Arabs (Jordan, Syria, etc.)	0.0	31.6 N	15.8	54.3
30. Other Arabs	19.2	33.3 N	81.0	36.3
31. Egyptian fellahin	7.1	30.0 N	48.5	54.9
32. Greeks (mostly mainland)	52.1	37.6 N	181.1	48.8
33. Greek Cretans	44.0	35.2 N	181.1	48.8
34. Greek Cypriots	28.4	35.1 N	141.2	56.4
35. Ethiopians/Eritreans	10.3	13.0 N	21.8	5.4
Average	38.8% [a]			

TABLE 5.1 *(continued)*

Category and population	Percentage of lactose absorbers	Approximate latitude	Total milk consumption (liters/person/year)	Cheese production (% of milk production)
Category F. Dairying peoples of northern Europe (over 40°N): $N = 12$				
36. Danes	97.5%	55.4 N	1032.8	9.0%
37. Swedes	97.8	59.2 N	393.1	24.4
38. Finns	85.1	60.1 N	677.9	8.1
39. Northwest Europeans	87.3	51.3 N	283.3	15.0
40. French	92.9	48.5 N	580.3	21.2
41. Germans from Central Europe	85.5	52.3 N	390.2	23.0
42. Dutch (living in Surinam)	85.7	52.2 N	828.1	13.7
43. Poles (living in Canada)	71.4	52.2 N	516.6	15.4
44. Czechs (living in Canada)	82.4	50.1 N	391.5	20.2
45. Czechs (Bohemia, Moravia)	100.0	49.1 N	391.5	20.2
46. Spaniards	85.3	40.2 N	171.2	19.6
47. North Italians (Ligurians)	70.0	44.2 N	210.9	37.6
Average	91.5%[a]			
Category G. Populations of "mixed" (dairying and nondairying) ancestry: $N = 13$				
48. Iru	61.5%	0.2 N	29.8	0.0%
49. Hutu	49.0	1.6 S	7.3	0.0
50. Hutu/Tussi mixed persons	45.5	1.6 S	7.3	0.0
51. Fulani/Hausa	33.3	12.0 N	4.5	16.0
52. Yoruba/European mixed persons	55.8	6.3 N	4.5	16.0
53. Nama Hottentots	50.0	26.0 S	81.6	0.0
54. Eskimo/European mixed persons	62.0	69.2 N	21.6	—
55. Yemen Jew/Arab mixed persons	55.6	32.1 N	203.6	42.0
56. Skolt Lapps in Finland	39.8	69.5 N	677.6	8.1
57. Mountain Lapps in Finland	62.7	69.0 N	677.6	8.1
58. Fisher Lapps in Finland	74.5	68.0 N	677.6	8.1
59. Mountain/Fisher Lapps	66.3	69.5 N	677.6	8.1
60. Rehoboth Basters	35.0	26.1 S	92.1	10.2
Average	56.2%[a]			
OVERALL AVERAGE	62.0%[c]			

SOURCE: Lactose absorption data from Simoons 1978a; dairying data for 1978 derived from United Nations, FAO 1979a and 1979b, based on population data for the same year from UNESCO 1982.

NOTE: For fuller discussion of the procedures used to generate this table, see App. A.5.1.

[a] Weighted by the sample sizes (see App. A.5.1) for each population in the category.

[b] National-level statistics are not applicable to specialized pastoralists.

[c] This figure must be used with caution because northern Europeans are greatly overrepresented in the subsample.

A reasonably good idea of this diversity in LA/LM frequencies is provided by Table 5.1, a subsample of 60 of the populations from Simoons's compilation. Prepared with the help of student assistants (E.L. and P.I.) according to procedures outlined in App. A.5.1, this subsample was designed to represent the full range of LA diversity in human populations while providing a data set of manageable proportions. It preserves both

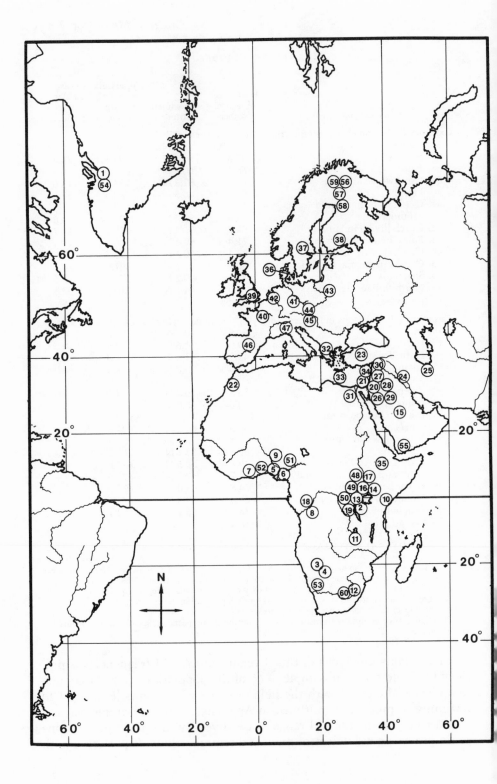

the diversity of subsistence modes represented in Simoons's compilation, from hunter-gatherers to milk-dependent pastoralists, and the full range of habitats and latitudes included in the original list. In addition, it includes 13 groups of "mixed" ancestry (Category G) in which substantial intermarriage has occurred between absorbing and malabsorbing populations. The geographic location of each population is given by its subsample number (1–60) in Fig. 5.3.

The data of Table 5.1 are thus representative of existing group differences in lactose absorption and malabsorption among contemporary human populations. As shown, LA frequencies vary all the way from 0.0 percent among the Bantu of Zambia (number 11) to 100.0 percent among Tussi pastoralists in the Congo basin (number 18). Not surprisingly, LA frequency is low among hunter-gatherers in the sample (12.6 percent overall), nondairying agriculturalists (15.5 percent), and recently dairying agriculturalists (11.9 percent). It is high among dairying populations of northern Europe (91.5 percent overall) and among milk-dependent pastoralists (91.3 percent). Interestingly, LA is relatively uncommon among dairying populations of the Mediterranean region (38.8 percent) and intermediate in the subsample populations of mixed ancestry (56.2 percent).

Candidate Hypotheses

A number of hypotheses have been advanced since 1965 to account for this variation in human digestive physiology. Once again, Simoons provides a concise statement of the four principal contenders (1978b; see also 1969, 1978a):

(1) *the disease hypothesis*, which suggests that the differences in question are not primary but are secondary to disease [e.g., dysentery or protein-calorie malnutrition], that some groups have greater prevalences of intestinal diseases which damage the intestinal mucosa; thus . . . LM is more prevalent among them; (2) *the hypothesis of dietary inhibition*, which holds that some groups may consume food or drugs [like spicy foods or betel nut] that inhibit lactase activity and lead to high prevalences of LM among them; (3) *the induction hypothesis*, which contends that continued consumption of milk after the normal time of weaning induces lactase activity in the intestine and keeps the milk drinker a lactose absorber; by this hypothesis, differences in the prevalence of LM are mainly reflections of milk consumption patterns; and (4) *the genetic hypothesis*, by which

Fig. 5.3 (opposite). Locations of the human populations included in the analysis of adult lactose absorption. From the total sample of human populations previously tested for LA frequencies, I compiled information on a subsample of 60 populations whose homelands lie between 60 degrees west longitude and 60 degrees east, as shown here. Some clustering of populations is apparent, because of geographic constraints on and predilections of researchers. Nevertheless, the subsample includes the full range of subsistence strategies, habitat types, and longitudinal dispersion featured in the larger sample. Data from Simoons 1978a. For fuller discussion of procedures used to generate the subsample, see Appendix A.5.1.

the differences are viewed as resulting from genetic contrasts [i.e., from different distributions of genotypes] among the groups involved. [1978b: 19, emphasis added]

In the years since these arguments were first advanced, sufficient information has accumulated to cast doubt upon the general applicability of three of them. First, disease may surely be a contributory factor in individual cases (see, for example, Johnson, Cole, and Ahern 1981). At the same time, it does not suffice as a general explanation for observed group differences. Many lactose malabsorbers are healthy individuals with no unusual medical history, with no evidence of jejunal abnormality, and with no difficulty in absorbing other disaccharides. Similarly, the dietary inhibition hypothesis remains unsubstantiated. No one has yet been able to identify a consistent foodstuff or set of foodstuffs that would cause malabsorption so widely in the many diets, subsistence systems, and environments of the malabsorbing populations. Third, the induction hypothesis (as proposed, for example, in Bolin and Davis 1970) has also been called into question despite the fact that lactase is, in bacteria, "the classic example of an inducible enzyme." (Lehninger 1975: 978.) A number of experimental attempts to induce absorber-like levels of lactase among malabsorbers, including studies in the United States, Nigeria, Israel, and Thailand (see reviews in G. G. Harrison 1975; J. Johnson 1981), have all failed. Indeed, there is now abundant evidence that the biochemical models of enzyme induction in bacteria do not apply to more complex organisms (see, for example, Hawkins 1985: chs. 6 and 7). It would thus appear that "evidence for major [induced] changes in intestinal lactase activity, particularly in man, is not available." (Johnson 1981: 15.) What little induction *is* achieved through sustained lactose exposure after weaning may instead explain why milk *tolerance* is relatively common among malabsorbers.

In contrast to the first three hypotheses, the genetic hypothesis has received increasing support from the accumulating data. Today, two lines of evidence support an inference of genetic covariation, that is, that genetic differences are largely responsible for the phenotypic difference between absorbers and malabsorbers. First, populations of "mixed" ancestry, like those of Category G in Table 5.1, generally exhibit absorption prevalences intermediate between those of the parent populations. So, for example, the subsample population of Yoruba-Europeans (number 52) is characterized by 55.8 percent LA, about halfway between "proper" Yoruba (number 5, 9 percent LA) and the European average (Category F, 91.5 percent LA). The same is true for the other populations listed in Category G, and for a detailed analysis of lactose absorption among the Pima Indians of Arizona (not in Table 5.1; see J. Johnson et al. 1977). Unlike the sample "pureblood" Pima and Pima-Papago individuals at 95 percent LM, subsamples of mixed European-Pima ancestry had rates that varied by proportional

TABLE 5.2

Genealogical Evidence for the Genetic Inheritance
of Adult Lactose Absorption and Malabsorption

Parental phenotypes	Number of families[a]	Number of progeny	Progeny with LM	Observed proportion of LM	Expected proportion of LM[b]
LA × LA	10	31	8	0.258	0.250
LA × LM	60	196	101	0.515	0.500
LM × LM	76	220	208	0.945	1.000

SOURCE: Table reprinted with permission from Johnson et al. 1977: 1303. Copyright 1977 by The American Gastroenterological Association. Table notes adapted by W. H. D.

[a]"The majority of the families represented in this table are of Mexican, Nigerian, Jewish, or Pima descent. Also represented are small numbers of families of Asian or northern European extraction." (Johnson et al. 1977: 1303.)

[b]The expected proportions of LM are based on the assumptions (1) that lactose absorption is inherited as a single dominant allele and (2) that all lactose absorbers in the sample populations are heterozygotes. The latter assumption is justified, according to Johnson and his coworkers, because most of these data come from populations with low frequencies of the LA phenotype. In such populations, homozygous dominant absorbers would be quite rare.

admixture: "1/16 Anglos" were 100 percent LM, "1/8 Anglos" were 76 percent LM, and "1/4 or 1/2 Anglos" were 39 percent LM.

The second line of support for the genetic hypothesis comes from the study of genealogical patterns in the transmission of lactose absorption. The study of the Pima cited above, for example, concluded that "the results of our family studies are generally consistent with the notion that adult lactose absorption is inherited as an autosomal dominant trait (and lactose malabsorption as an autosomal recessive trait)." (p. 1302.) The study went on to review a broad sample of data from families of diverse ancestry (Mexican, Nigerian, Jewish, Pima, Asian, and Northern European) with similar results. As summarized in the last two columns of Table 5.2, the composite data show a close match to the proportions expected if lactose absorption were inherited as an autosomal dominant characteristic.[7]

As of this writing, however, more genealogical studies and a better understanding of lactase production at the molecular level are needed to clarify the genetic basis of lactase activity patterns. In the terminology of Chapter 3, the nature of the transformation T_1, from genotypes to phenotypes, is still poorly understood in this case. The possibility has been suggested that there are one or more regulatory genes for lactase biosynthesis, and that they are similar to the ones regulating the time course of hemoglobin production (see, for instance, R. Herman 1981; Flatz 1983).

[7]G. G. Harrison (1975), Kretchmer (1981a), and Flatz (1983, 1987) review other data supporting this conclusion. Ferguson and Maxwell (1967), Sahi et al. (1973), and Ho et al. (1982) go so far as to propose single-locus genetic models. A note of caution concerning single-locus arguments, however, has been raised by Johnson, Cole, and Ahern (1981) who point out that the offspring of cross-ethnic matings show generally higher proportions of LM than would be expected from single-locus control.

But to the best of my knowledge, such a mechanism has not been documented and so the inference of genetic covariation must remain tentative for now. With some reservation because of that uncertainty, I will nevertheless follow the lead of others (e.g., Flatz and Rotthauwe 1977; Sahi 1978; Flatz 1983), and treat the LA/LM difference as a bona fide human lactase polymorphism.

That tentative conclusion, then, leads us to a familiar question in the study of human genetic diversity: What explains the polymorphism? How and why would adult lactose absorption have evolved in some human populations and not others? More specifically, what evolutionary forces are responsible for the special genetics of adult lactose absorbers?

The Culture Historical Hypothesis

In the late 1960's two scholars, Frederick Simoons, author of the data compilation described above, and the anthropologist Robert McCracken independently identified a correlation between the frequency of LA and the cultural history of dairying in human populations. Simoons (1969), for example, noted that populations lacking traditions of dairying exhibited consistently low levels of LA. Thus, peoples of the tropical forest belt of Africa who did not herd dairy cattle because of tsetse-borne "sleeping sickness" showed characteristically low proportions (0–20 percent) of LA. Similarly, the peoples of mainland and insular East Asia were mostly both nonmilkers and nonabsorbers. On the other hand, virtually every population classified as an "absorbing population" (that is, with 60–100 percent LA) had a history of dairying that could be traced back for at least several millennia. This observation, too, held for populations as distinctive in other ways as the French and the Tussi pastoralists of Central Africa.

The apparent association of dairying and lactose absorption suggested a hypothesis to Simoons and McCracken that has come to be called the "geographic" or "culture historical" hypothesis.

By that hypothesis, in the hunting and gathering [period], human groups everywhere were like most other land mammals in their patterns of lactase activity. That is, in the normal individual lactase activity would drop at weaning to low levels, which prevailed throughout life. With the beginning of dairying, however, significant changes occurred in the diets of many human groups. In some of these, moreover, there may have been a selective advantage for those aberrant individuals who experienced high levels of intestinal lactase throughout life. That advantage would have occurred only in certain situations: where milk was a specially critical part of the diet, where the group was under dietary stress, and where people did not process all their milk into low-lactose products such as aged cheese. Under those conditions, most likely to occur among pastoral groups, such aberrant individuals would drink more milk, would benefit more nutritionally as a result, and would enjoy increased prospects of survival, well-being, and of bearing progeny and supporting them. In a classical [Darwinian] way, then, the condition of high intestinal lactase activity throughout life would come to be typical of such a group. [Simoons 1981a: 29; see also 1970a, 1978a]

Two features of the culture historical hypothesis deserve special mention in this context. First, the hypothesis clearly emphasizes the role of culture in the genetic evolution of lactose absorption. Essentially, the idea is that *agriculture*, specifically dairying, provided new selective pressures within the affected gene pools—pressures that conferred highest Darwinian fitness on the genotype(s) of lactose absorption. In populations that continued without dairying, chance mutations giving rise to "aberrant" lactose absorbers would not have achieved the same reproductive advantage. There, the gene or genes for absorption would have remained at low levels, interpretable as the product of recurrent mutation and/or drift. In contrast, the frequency of LA genes in dairying populations would have increased through time as a direct function of the cultural context of human survival and reproduction. Dairying would have selected for the LA genotypes. The hypothesis put forward by Simoons and McCracken thus includes the concept of cultural mediation at its very core, since the hypothesized fitness advantage of LA genotypes would have depended upon the presence of socially transmitted values and beliefs that supported dairying.

Second, the hypothesis proposes that the selective advantage of LA genotypes derived from what Simoons calls "the general nutritional advantage" of fresh milk consumption. In other words, LA genes would have conferred the highest reproductive fitness upon people who lived in populations subject to recurrent food shortage and dietary stress, conditions that would have been at least partially alleviated by the addition of fresh milk to the food supply. Today, then, adult lactose absorption should be found in populations where (1) fresh milk from domesticated animals has been available for many generations, and where (2) hunger was once a common and serious problem.

The strength of this argument lies in its generalizability: these conditions may obtain in human populations living in a wide variety of climates, habitats, and social systems. Of course, the case is particularly compelling for groups of pastoral nomads, like those of Category D in Table 5.1, whose dependence upon fresh milk and fresh milk products is virtually complete. Adult lactose absorption would there confer an indisputable selective advantage, provided that culturally transmitted techniques for processing lactose, to be discussed later in this chapter, were not always used by these peoples, as one study (Flatz and Rotthauwe 1977: 230) suggests they were not. However, the culture historical hypothesis should apply equally well to nutritionally stressed populations of other subsistence means, provided LA made available otherwise useless or harmful nutrients during times of food scarcity. Simoons (1981a) is therefore critical of alternative explanations that postulate more specific advantages to adult lactose absorption.[8]

Correlational Evidence for the Hypothesis

Two kinds of correlational evidence lend support to the Simoons-McCracken version of the genetic hypothesis. First, there is evidence to suggest that sufficient time has elapsed since the advent of dairying to allow for the genetic evolution of lactose absorption. According to archaeological evidence from Greece and the Near East, cattle (the species *Bos taurus*) were first domesticated between 9000 and 7000 B.C. Before its domestication, the wild ancestral aurochs (*Bos primigenius*) had been successfully hunted for thousands of years across much of Europe, Asia, and North Africa (see, for example, Isaac 1970: 78 ff.; Zeuner 1963). The evidence suggests that the use of cattle principally for meat continued through the first few millennia of domestication. It was only later, perhaps between 4000 and 6000 B.C., that evidence for dairying entered the record in North Africa, Europe, and the Near East, as part of what Andrew Sherratt (1981) has termed "the secondary products revolution."[9] Yet even with this delay, milk and milk products have been an important component of some human diets for over 6,000 years, or somewhere between 200 and 300 generations.

As noted, then, by L. L. Heston and I. I. Gottesman, there has been "plenty of time" (1973, from Simoons 1978a: 972) for the genetic evolution of lactose absorption among the descendants of early dairyers. Their conclusion is supported by computer simulation studies, such as the one by Walter Bodmer and Luigi Cavalli-Sforza (1976: 278 ff.; see also Cavalli-Sforza 1973: 85–86), in which genetic selection can be shown to increase the frequency of a hypothetical LA allele from the status of a rare mutant, with frequencies on the order of 0.00001, to the contemporary frequencies of southern and central Europe, which are about 0.5.[10] The

[8] For example, he criticizes an argument by Cook and Al-Torki (1975: 135; see also Cook 1978) that LA first evolved to high frequency in the Arabian peninsula in response to a selective advantage "associated with the fluid and calorie content of camel's milk, which is important for survival in desert nomads." Whatever the merits of their case for the Arabian deserts, however, such an advantage is clearly insufficient to explain the high frequencies of LA in other areas, like northern Europe. Moreover, I see little value in the "conjectural possibility" that "the high [LA] gene frequency in northern Europe also had its origin in Arabia." (Cook 1978: 423.)

[9] The evidence that milking was a part of this trend comes from several sources: Neolithic artistry, such as Saharan rock paintings (4000–3000 B.C.), Egyptian funerary pots (ca. 3100 B.C.), and Mesopotamian friezes and cylinder seals (ca. 2900 B.C.; see Simoons 1971); Neolithic and Bronze Age pottery vessels for liquids, with "uncanny resemblances" (Sherratt 1981: 280) between areas as distant as northwest Europe and the Balkans; and wooden pots and tools apparently fashioned for milk processing, some from Switzerland (Milisankas 1978: 81), and some from the northern plain of Poland (Bogucki and Grygiel 1983).

[10] These simulations are based upon a simplifying assumption that there are but three genotypes with respect to lactose absorption, LL, Ll, and ll, with relative fitnesses (before standardization) of $1 + s$, 1, and $1 - s$, respectively, where s is a selection coefficient similar

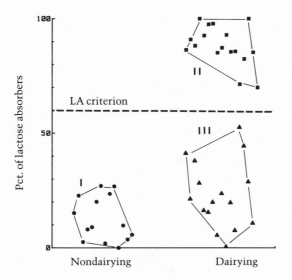

(N = 47 out of 47 "nonmixed" populations)

Fig. 5.4. The association between adult lactose absorption and dairying history in sub-sample populations. This scatterplot depicts the LA frequencies and dairying histories (treated as a categorical variable) for each of the 47 "nonmixed" populations of Table 5.1. Cluster I includes all "nondairying" populations of the sample (that is, populations of Categories A, B, and C, lacking long cultural histories of dairying), each of which is represented in this and subsequent figures by a solid circle. In line with the culture historical hypothesis, all populations of this cluster have fewer than 30 percent adult lactose absorbers and may thus be classified as malabsorbing. Cluster II is the opposite: it contains dairying populations that are also absorbers (having 60 percent or more of the LA phenotype, as shown by the dotted line), each represented by a solid square. This cluster contains all populations of Categories D and F of Table 5.1. Cluster III populations, belonging to Category E of the table, are dairyers with low frequencies of LA; each is represented by a solid triangle. All but four populations of this last cluster may be classified as malabsorbers by the 30 percent criterion. Data from Table 5.1.

antiquity of dairying in the Old World is thus consistent with the idea of a culturally mediated evolution of adult lactose absorption in human populations.

The LA-frequency data of Table 5.1 provide additional evidence in support of the culture historical hypothesis. Consider, first, Fig. 5.4, which

to those described in Chapter 3. In other words, each copy of the L (absorber) gene is assumed to add the quantity s to the genetic fitness of the average carrier. Under these assumptions, Bodmer and Cavalli-Sforza showed that a selection coefficient as low as 0.015 to 0.04 would be sufficient to propel the evolution of L to the frequencies observed today in absorbing-dairying populations. Moreover, the two values of s were obtained in simulations that assumed a single original mutant in breeding populations ranging from 5 persons (where s could be as low as 0.015) to 50,000 (where s could be as low as 0.04). It is probable that the size of the actual deme or demes in which the L mutation first increased through genetic selection was intermediate between these numbers. Therefore a selection coefficient on the order of 0.02 to 0.03 would have sufficed—a number far less than the selection coefficient attributable to malaria in the sickle-cell anemia example of Chapter 3. (See Aoki 1986 and Flatz 1987 for further discussion and testing of these inferences.)

plots the subsample data (without Category G, the groups of mixed ancestry) according to two characteristics: the cultural history of dairying and the prevalence of adult lactose absorption. The figure cleanly separates the subsample populations into three distinct, analytical clusters, I, II, and III. Cluster I shows that all nondairying populations in the subsample (including five "recently dairying" groups) can be categorized as malabsorbers. Cluster II shows that all absorbing populations in the subsample (i.e., those exceeding 60 percent LA) have a cultural history of dairying. In other words, the genetic and cultural features of subsample populations in these two clusters *do* covary, just as the culture historical hypothesis predicts. The figure may be taken as evidence that dairying conferred a genetic selection advantage upon the genotypes of adult lactose absorption.

A critical problem, however, is apparent in Cluster III: not all dairying populations are lactose absorbers. Indeed Cluster III is composed of 16 dairying populations—nearly half (48.5 percent) of all dairyers in the subsample—each of which fails to meet the 60 percent criterion. All but four of them, in fact, qualify as malabsorbing populations. In a statistical sense, Cluster III reduces the covariation between dairying history and frequency of lactose absorbers. In a logical sense, Cluster III raises an important challenge to the culture historical hypothesis, namely, Why has there been no selective advantage to absorption in these dairying populations? How were Cluster III peoples able to avoid the selection pressure or pressures that operated so clearly, it would seem, in Cluster II?

A Cultural Solution to Lactose Malabsorption

Simoons and McCracken have long recognized the questions raised for their hypothesis by Cluster III populations, and they have proposed tentative answers. One possibility is that Cluster III populations have simply not experienced the same severity or duration of dietary stress as have the peoples of Cluster II, presumably because of more favorable climates or more efficient subsistence techniques.[11] But to my knowledge no one has documented, with evidence independent of LA/LM frequencies, the kind of consistent differences in dietary stress that would be necessary to account for the genetic differences between these populations. Such documentation would seem to be particularly important since dairy animals, too, would likely suffer from the same circumstances that caused food shortages for humans.

A more convincing answer to these questions lies in the suggestion by

[11] This possibility is hinted at by Simoons (1978a: 965), when he contrasts Cluster II populations, described as "peoples, including some of pastoral tradition, who have consumed amounts of milk and lactose-rich dairy products for a long historical period and have lived under conditions of dietary stress," with Cluster III populations, described as "peoples who have used milk since antiquity but who do not meet conditions of strong selective pressures against LM." (p. 967.)

Simoons and McCracken that populations in Cluster III have simply had another way to obtain the postulated general nutritional benefit in milk, one that circumvents the lactose issue. They propose that these populations adopted a *cultural* solution to the lactose problem, "short-circuiting" the selection pressure that otherwise would have favored LA genotypes. The argument is that these peoples routinely processed fresh milk into one or more of the "soured" and fermented milk products common in the Old World—for example kefir, maconi, kurt, yogurt, dahi, chal (from camel's milk), or koumiss (from mare's milk)—or into aged cheese (for a more complete list and discussion, see Kon 1972). With these techniques, lactose concentrations are reduced by one or more of three mechanisms. (1) Lactose may be *externally predigested* by lactic acid bacteria (*Lactobacillis bulgaricus*) and yeast (McCracken 1971: 480). (2) Lactose may be *autodigested* by lactase from the bacteria within the processed milk, effectively substituting for intestinal lactase (Kolars et al. 1984). (3) Lactose may be *physically drained away* with the separation of cheese curds from lactose-rich whey (McCracken 1971: 480). In any of these ways, the problem of lactose digestion is minimized or even eliminated.

These processing techniques, reminiscent of maize-processing procedures among New World Indians (Katz et al. 1974), are clearly based upon cultural instructions that have been transmitted socially through space and time. Yet their effect at the molecular level of digestion is quite similar to the phenotypic effect of LA genotypes: either way, complex disaccharide molecules are rendered absorbable. In short, McCracken and Simoons propose that milk processing evolved culturally in populations of Cluster III as an alternative solution to the problem of lactose digestion.

This argument, which I will call the "milk-processing corollary," has much to recommend it from the coevolutionary perspective. First, the relevant cultural instructions are associated with consequences of potential benefit to all the malabsorbers in Cluster III populations. These memes would thus have had inclusive fitness benefits for many individuals, particularly if some form of dietary stress were also a problem in these populations. Second, the instructions have certainly had high cultural fitnesses as well. The aforementioned processing techniques are, in most cases, ancient and possibly even go back to the origins of dairying. Cheesemaking, for example, is thought to have originated in southwestern Asia as early as 6000 B.C. (Kosikowski 1985: 88) and to have spread as far as northern Poland by 4300 B.C. (Bogucki and Grygiel 1983: 111). Although the specific memes have surely changed in the interim, it is not likely that they have changed toward a process less technologically efficient or less biochemically effective at lactose hydrolysis. The implication is then that these memes have both high cultural fitness and high inclusive fitness value.

In addition to the case for cultural mediation in Cluster II, then, the milk-processing corollary proposes another kind of relationship between genes and culture in the populations of Cluster III. In particular, the theoretical framework of Chapter 4 suggests two likely candidates. First, these populations may exhibit "enhancement," a relationship in which cultural selection effectively complements genetic selection (as discussed in more detail in Chapter 6). In that case, the memes for milk processing would have high cultural fitness as a result of secondary value selection, that is, as a result of a positive, largely cultural evaluation of their consequences within each population. Alternatively, these populations may exhibit genetic mediation, a relationship already examined in Chapter 4. Under that scenario, the milk-processing memes would have high cultural fitness because of primary value selection, perhaps including a postulated "innate lactose aversion" (a possibility discussed, for example, in Lumsden and Wilson 1981: 69). Either way, milk processing would be maintained as part of the cultural traditions of Cluster III populations.

Although I must leave a comparative test of these two possibilities for another time and context, the point remains that processing techniques have provided a way for milk to become valued and used within malabsorbing populations. Of course there are some malabsorbing populations, particularly the nondairyers, for whom milk remains uninteresting or unacceptable even when converted to low-lactose products. Simoons (1970, 1979) notes, for example, that some malabsorbing populations have shunned milk and its processing techniques even though they have been repeatedly introduced to them through contact with milk-processing neighbors. And some malabsorbers in East Asia, particularly the Chinese, show considerable disdain for cheese to this day—even more than they show for fresh milk—in some areas regarding it as "the putrefied mucous discharge of an animal's guts." (Anderson and Anderson 1977: 341.) Such cases emphasize that, whatever the role of primary values in the evolution of milk-processing traditions, a favorable view of low-lactose milk products is certainly not a universal correlate of LM genotypes.

Cultural Diversity in Milk Production and Consumption

Restated in a different form, the milk-processing corollary of Simoons and McCracken proposes that dairying populations classified as malabsorbers should tend to show a relatively high degree of dependence on milk-processing procedures. Culturally influenced patterns of milk consumption and use in these Cluster III populations should contrast substantially with the same patterns in dairying populations classified as absorbers (Cluster II).

This proposition can be tested on the subsample populations of Table 5.1 by means of indirect indicators of cultural differences regarding milk production and use. Unfortunately, reliable data of this nature are difficult to obtain, particularly for the small, nonstate societies that under-

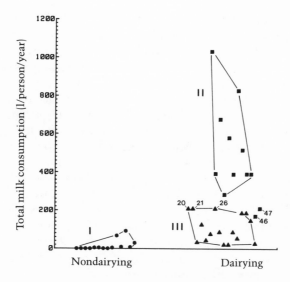

(N = 42 out of 47 "nonmixed" populations)

Fig. 5.5. The association between fresh milk consumption (including milk used to make butter) and dairying history in subsample populations. With only two exceptions (populations 46 and 47 at lower right), the same three clusters are formed in this scatterplot as in Fig. 5.4. Not surprisingly, lactose absorbers do drink substantially more milk per person per year than malabsorbers, although there is considerable within-cluster variance. The figure implies that Cluster III populations consume much of their dairy production in some form other than fresh milk. Data from Table 5.1.

standably collect few statistics about themselves. McCracken (1971), however, suggests the use of the *FAO Production Yearbook* statistics on milk and cheese production as general indicators of aggregate tendencies and cultural variation.[12] With the aid of student assistants (E.L. and P.I.), I have followed his lead and compiled the pertinent FAO figures for the populations of Table 5.1.[13]

One prediction of the milk-processing corollary is that the dairying-malabsorber populations of Cluster III should exhibit substantially lower levels of annual fresh milk consumption per capita than the dairying-absorber populations of Cluster II. This prediction is tested in Fig. 5.5

[12] Using these data, McCracken calculates that Greek Cypriots, for example, use over 84 percent of their fresh milk production to manufacture cheese, which "explains how a population can be [malabsorbing] and still produce and utilize large quantities of milk." (p. 494.)

[13] The problems inherent in this use of FAO statistics are readily acknowledged by McCracken and by me. For instance, national-level aggregate statistics are often little more than informed guesses, particularly for developing nations, and they conceal any variability in milk-use practices between ethnolinguistic subgroups of a country. Nevertheless, these data are about the most reliable and standardized ones available for comparative analysis. Indicator variables were derived from statistics published by FAO for the homeland county of each population shown in the table. For the nation-state populations of the subsample (for example, those designated as French, Italians, Finns, Swedes, etc., by Simoons 1978), the FAO-derived indicators are probably reasonably accurate. But for the smaller ethnolinguistic populations (the Yoruba, Ibo, Kikuyu, and Egyptian fellahin, for example), these figures can

with the implied fresh milk consumption data of Table 5.1; as before, the populations are separated into nondairying and dairying. Just as expected, the same three clusters are apparent. The nondairying populations of Cluster I show, not surprisingly, little or no per capita consumption. The dairying-absorbing populations of Cluster II show relatively high and variable consumption rates (the exceptions being populations 46, Spaniards, and 47, North Italians) and, as predicted, the dairying-malabsorbing populations (Cluster III) show generally low rates. Considering the global range in milk consumption within the sample, the range of the *Y* variable among Cluster III populations is, once again, not much greater than the range obtained for Cluster I. Moreover, the three highest values of the cluster (corresponding to populations 20, 21, and 26 in Table 5.1) are all populations in Israel, a country whose milk-use patterns have been influenced by Jewish immigrants from Cluster II populations.

A second prediction of the milk-processing corollary is that Cluster III populations should process much of their fresh milk into low-lactose milk products, a procedure unnecessary for the populations of Cluster II and out of the question for the populations of Cluster I. Fig. 5.6 shows a test of this prediction according to the data on cheese production in Table 5.1.[14] The plot shows the percentage of total milk production dedicated to cheese manufacture as a function of the categorical variables, dairying and nondairying. Again, three clusters are apparent. The populations of Cluster I, as expected for nondairying and recently dairying peoples, generally produce little milk and little cheese. Cluster II populations consume much more fresh milk and therefore use relatively low percentages of milk for cheese, the only exception being 47, North Italians, with 37.6 percent. And Cluster III populations, also as expected, generally use a high percentage of their milk for cheese production. Given that Fig. 5.6 represents cheese production alone, ignoring yogurts, kefirs, sour cream, and other low-lactose products, the conclusion seems inescapable. With few exceptions, the milk-processing corollary is confirmed: populations that remain malabsorbers despite millennia of dairying do indeed process the bulk of their milk into low-lactose forms.

This finding, together with the archaeological evidence for the antiquity of milk processing, would seem to "save" the culture historical hypothesis from any counterindication by Cluster III. However, the analysis does raise a second, more serious challenge. If, as postulated, the evolutionary advantage of adult lactose absorption were truly its general nutri-

---

at best be taken as first approximations. For this analysis I used 1978 as the base year, the same year as Simoons's compilation of the LA data. In order to ensure the generalizability of the comparisons, I checked the 1978 figures against FAO statistics for 1970 and 1980, recalculating all of the indicators. Since the overall trends in the data were consistent across this time period with only minor deviations, I based the analysis upon the 1978 figures. For further discussion of methodology, see App. A.5.1.

[14] Cheese is not the only low-lactose product potentially available to populations of Cluster III, but it is the only one for which FAO reports adequate data.

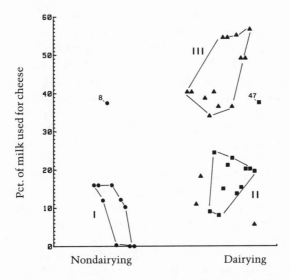

(N = 38 out of 47 "nonmixed" populations)

Fig. 5.6. The association between milk-use patterns and dairying history in subsample populations. When the proportion of fresh milk converted to cheese is plotted as a function of dairying history, three clusters are once again apparent. In this case, however, the positions of Clusters II and III are reversed. Thus Cluster II, the dairying-absorbing populations, convert milk to cheese in just about the same proportions as do traditional nondairying peoples (the exceptionally high data point for nondairyers, population 8 in Table 5.1, is based on data for Zaire, a country that produces very little milk to begin with). Most populations of Cluster III convert high percentages of their milk production to cheese before consumption (the exceptions are populations 22, 23, and 35). Data from Table 5.1.

tional benefit, then why did the milk-processing solution not work for the populations of Cluster II? Why would milk processing not have eliminated the Darwinian fitness advantage of LA genotypes in all populations? In other words, why was the adaptation of Cluster II peoples not the cultural one—with potentially greater speed and effectiveness—rather than the genetic one?

In my view, these questions seriously embarrass the culture historical hypothesis, particularly its claim that adult lactose absorption has a general nutritional advantage. To begin with, we cannot assume that Cluster II populations were ignorant of all efficacious milk-processing procedures throughout the genetic evolution of their high LA frequencies. The archaeological record is admittedly scanty on the subject, but such evidence as there is indicates that Cluster II populations have long been familiar with the basic techniques. For example, milk-processing utensils and the remains of what may well have been curdling agents have been found in Polish and Swiss Neolithic sites dating back to earlier than 4000 B.C. (Bogucki and Grygiel 1983: 111; Milisankas 1978: 81), and these are areas surrounded today by lactose absorbers.

But even without such evidence, it would still be difficult to assume that Cluster II populations were historically unaware of lactose-reducing remedies. A number of the standard processing procedures require minimal equipment or technology aside from leakproof vessels, and some are, in a manner of speaking, automatic with milk's aging; sour milk, for instance, has a low lactose content, and its preparation requires "no special skill" (Flatz and Rotthauwe 1977: 230). Thus, as dairying spread across Europe and Africa from its probable origins in North Africa or the Near East, it is likely that milk-processing know-how spread right along with it.

Today there is certainly no lack of milk-processing activity within Cluster II populations, and the cultural fitnesses of these memes can hardly be a recent phenomenon. Not only do many of the world's most renowned cheese varieties trace to origins in Europe, where many of the world's lactose absorbers reside (the list includes the French cheeses Roquefort, Cantal, and Beaufort, which have been manufactured since at least Roman times; see O'Keefe 1978), but Cluster II populations also exhibit high contemporary levels of per capita cheese consumption, higher in fact than do the populations of Cluster III. As Fig. 5.7 shows, the dairying-absorbing populations generally consume an average of more than twice as much cheese per person per year as do their dairying-malabsorbing counterparts—even though this represents a substantially lower proportion of their total milk production. The exceptions are the Finns (38), Spanish (46), and inhabitants of the United Kingdom (39), with unusually low levels of cheese consumption for absorbers, and the Israelis (20, 21, 26), Greeks (32, 33), and Cypriots (34), with unusually high per capita consumption for malabsorbers.

The implications of the preceding discussion are three. First, we may assume that Cluster II's ancestors have had low-lactose processing techniques available to them for virtually as long as they have practiced dairying. It does not seem likely that, in the past, these people had either to drink fresh milk or suffer dietary stress. As Norman Kretchmer (1977: 67) has noted, we would therefore "not be justified in making the assumption that the advent of dairying automatically created a selective pressure in favor of lactose digestors as opposed to nondigestors." Second, the idea of fresh milk consumption has nevertheless acquired high cultural fitness in Cluster II populations. This is indicated by the impressive levels of per capita milk consumption today and further suggested by the evidence of elevated LA gene frequencies in these same populations. Third, it does not seem likely that this cultural fitness was achieved as a consequence of people, largely malabsorbers in early periods, turning from low-lactose dairy products to milk drinking only to obtain essentially the same "general nutritional advantage." The implication is that direct milk consumption must have had some other, special benefit.

These arguments all point to a key weakness in the culture historical

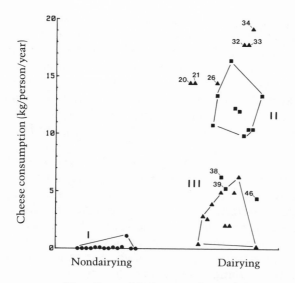

(N = 42 out of 47 "nonmixed" populations)

Fig. 5.7. The association between cheese consumption and dairying history in subsample populations. Even though Cluster II populations process relatively little of their milk into cheese, they generally consume more cheese than their Cluster III counterparts. These data, together with the antiquity of cheesemaking among the peoples of Cluster II, suggest that dairying-absorbing populations have long had available to them the same *cultural* solution to lactose malabsorption as Cluster III populations. Data from United Nations, FAO 1979a and 1979b; cheese consumption estimated as explained in App. A.5.1.

hypothesis: it fails to provide convincing motivation for the spread of milk *drinking* at the expense of milk *processing* in Cluster II populations. This problem is implicit in the arguments by Simoons, McCracken, and others, but research to date has focused largely on the genetic aspects of lactose absorption and has tended to ignore concomitant evolution in the cultural realm.[15] In essence, the culture historical hypothesis must assume a special and unprecedented cultural configuration for the populations of ancestors to Cluster II. Unlike the first dairying peoples who, it is argued, relied heavily upon techniques of milk fermentation (see, for

[15] In a 1973 paper, for example, Simoons argued that "milk likely would have been available to the first dairying peoples only in small amounts. Such amounts would not bring on symptoms of intolerance and people thus would be able to consume available milk products without difficulty." In addition, since (he believes) processing techniques had been available to dairying populations since the very earliest days of documented milking, "even if people did develop symptoms, they could have continued to consume dairy products, such as butter, cheese, and yogurt and other fermented milks in which the lactose had been largely eliminated by washing, or broken down by bacterial lactase." (1973: 88.) But Simoons went on to note that "none of the above [dairy products] would give any selective advantage to the aberrant individual who could consume large amounts of lactose. A high prevalence of lactose [absorption] probably developed *only after certain human groups had large amounts of milk available but did not process it into low-lactose products*, and had other foods inadequate in amount and quality of protein and perhaps other nutrients." (p. 88, emphasis added.)

example, Kretchmer 1977), the first populations to undergo genetic selection for LA must have relied instead upon fresh milk. The culture-
historical hypothesis does not explain how and why such cultural change
came about, and this is all the more problematic because a change from
milk-processing procedures would have caused discomfort to many resident malabsorbers. The crucial question then is this: given both the availability of processing techniques and high initial frequencies of malabsorption, why would cultural traditions ever have come to favor fresh milk
consumption?

In a manner reminiscent of the sickle-cell analysis in Chapter 3, what
began as a straightforward problem in human genetic diversity has led us,
on closer inspection, to important questions concerning the patterns and
processes behind cultural diversity. In this instance, the available evidence suggests that the memes behind milk consumption attained high
cultural fitness because of some special advantage in Cluster II populations, an advantage available only through fresh milk consumption. This
advantage, in turn, would have favored the genotypes of lactose absorption over those of malabsorption, to whom the benefit would be precluded. It thus seems reasonable to look for some benefit to milk drinking
and adult lactose absorption other than the postulated general nutritional
benefit. Let us turn now to explore two possible candidates.

The Ancestral Pastoralism Hypothesis

One alternative to the culture historical hypothesis, first proposed by
R. Shatin (1966, 1968), may be called the "ancestral pastoralism" hypothesis. By this hypothesis, high frequencies of adult lactose absorption
are expected today among the descendants of early pastoral peoples who
themselves evolved high frequencies of LA before milk-processing techniques were fully developed. Andrew Sherratt, author of the arguments
on the "secondary products revolution" (1981), is one of the proponents of
this alternative. He suggests that adult lactose absorption first evolved
among agricultural populations who took up pastoralism in marginal,
semiarid areas of the Near East before 4000 B.C.

As agricultural communities expanded to the edges of the Fertile Crescent, they
encountered extensive semiarid areas which supported large mobile animal populations. Because of the uncertainty it involved, in areas without alternative resources, hunting was not a viable economy. With a product like milk which could
be continuously obtained, and especially with the added mobility given by
draught- and riding-animals, such areas could be exploited by pastoralism. Because of the easier alternative methods of increasing subsistence, especially by
small-scale irrigation, this pattern was slow to evolve. The evolution of lactose-
tolerant populations removed an important brake on the development of such systems, which could themselves develop techniques of milk processing (initially for
storage) which rendered it usable by nontolerant populations. The adaptation
could thus spread more rapidly than its genetic basis. [Sherratt 1981: 287]

According to this hypothesis, LA had a special advantage over LM in a setting of population growth and land competition. In suboptimal habitats it enabled a viable economy based partly, or even entirely, on pastoralism. Moreover, the hypothesis proposes that milk-processing procedures were first developed by absorbers after technology could no longer erode LA's selective advantage, and that they later spread to malabsorbers, an argument counter to the suggestions by Simoons and others above.[16]

This hypothesis is subject to the same logical criticism as the culture historical hypothesis: it must assume that malabsorbing pastoralists were reproductively disadvantaged even though milk processing was available and effective—and indeed, processing is used quite successfully by such contemporary herders as the Nuer (Evans-Pritchard 1940: ch. 1) and the Yakut (Jochelson 1906). However, it is also possible to assess its strength empirically. One test that suggests itself is a comparison of the geographical distribution of lactose absorption in contemporary Old World populations with the documented routes of expansion and migration of their pastoralist ancestors (see, for example, Gimbutas 1970, 1977). Following the arguments of P. Menozzi, A. Piazza, and L. Cavalli-Sforza (1978), one might therefore expect gradients in LA frequencies along these routes arising from the diffusion of ancestral pastoralist LA genes out of their Near Eastern homeland. The analysis of Menozzi et al., based upon a total of 38 independent alleles from ten genetic loci (not including LA), revealed a principal "cline," or gradient, of just this sort, originating in the Near East and fanning out to levels of lower and lower genetic similarity across central and northern Europe. The pattern parallels archaeological evidence for the spread of agriculture (see Ammerman and Cavalli-Sforza 1984) and suggests "a slow and gradual migration of farmers from the Near East into Europe." (Menozzi et al. 1978: 788.)

By the ancestral pastoralism hypothesis, a similar pattern should exist in the LA frequencies of the descendants of early pastoralists. Populations closely related by migration should show high genetic similarity (that is, a high prevalence of LA), and the frequency of LA should diminish with geographical distance from the pastoralists' original homelands. An argument along these lines has been made by Simoons, who considers pastoralists a special case of the culture historical hypothesis.

The ancient Indo-European homeland is believed by many to have been in the Pontic and Caucasian steppes and, when the Indo-Europeans first gained prominence, they were pastoralists. From there, Indo-European peoples are believed to have pushed onward, with some reaching northern Europe about 2300 B.C. . . . and others entering what is now Pakistan about 1500 B.C. That Indo-Europeans in

[16] The chronology of this hypothesis is attractive because it helps to account for the three to five millennia between the origins of cattle domestication and the first appearance of artifacts associated with dairying. Presumably this was the time during which genetic selection favored increases in LA frequency among emergent pastoralists, before the elaboration of diverse secondary products.

regions as far apart as Pakistan, Scandinavia, and Spain should have low prevalences of LM, leads to the question whether selection against LM may have begun in their ancient homeland. [1978a: 973]

If the LA genes were largely spread throughout Europe, Asia, and Africa by Indo-European pastoralists in this manner, then we should expect to find a specific geographical pattern of LA prevalences today. The highest frequencies would be expected along the principal pathways of their expansion. According to Marija Gimbutas (1977), these so-called Kurgan peoples, or Indo-European steppe pastoralists, spread in waves from their Eurasian steppe homeland adjoining the Black and Caspian seas out along the Danube basin into southern Europe, on the one hand, and southeastward toward what are today Iran, Iraq, and Pakistan on the other. In her model, the first wave spread into prehistoric southern Europe between 4400 and 4300 B.C., reaching the lower Rhine in Germany sometime between 3400 and 2900 B.C. In other models, such as that of Colin Renfrew (1988, 1989; see also Mallory 1989: ch. 6), the early Indo-European peoples were agriculturalists from central Anatolia (today part of Turkey), not pastoralists from the southern steppes, which means that they would be lacking high LA frequencies. But if Gimbutas is right, then we would expect highest frequencies of LA today in southern and central Europe, southern Russia, Iran, and Iraq, the areas most immediately and most directly infiltrated by the Indo-European immigrants. The ancestral pastoralism explanation can thus be tested with respect to the contemporary distribution of LA, a comparison I shall attempt after examining a second hypothesis.

The Calcium Absorption Hypothesis

A second alternative to the culture historical hypothesis was put forth in 1973 by Gebhard Flatz and Hans Werner Rotthauwe, the geneticists cited above who first spoke of "human lactase polymorphism." Flatz and Rotthauwe propose that milk consumption and lactose absorption after weaning have, under proper conditions, specific physiological advantages for the calcium metabolism of the body. Not only, they observe, is milk a relatively abundant source of calcium (especially nonhuman milks, which average over 1.2 parts per thousand of the mineral), but the lactose of fresh milk is also known to act physiologically like a vitamin D supplement, facilitating the absorption of calcium from the small intestine (see review in Allen 1982; Williams 1986).

Their argument, the "calcium absorption" hypothesis, therefore proposes that LA evolved to high frequencies in certain populations because of a specific calcium-absorption advantage from fresh milk consumption. They reason that because calcium ions, Ca^{++}, are crucial to so many physiological and biochemical processes, there could be a substantial reproductive benefit to making calcium easier to absorb by drinking milk, particularly in populations that are deficient in vitamin D. Importantly, this benefit would accrue only to lactose-absorber genotypes. Experimental studies have shown that lactose substantially increases the permeability of the intestinal wall to calcium ions, but only in the jejunum and ileum—the same sites where lactase is produced—*and only in LA individuals* (see, for example, Condon et al. 1970; Schaafsma and Visser 1980; Cochet et al. 1983). It appears that this effect of lactose is clearly associated with the organism's capacity to digest it.

Lactose and Vitamin D

By this argument, then, the genotypes of postweaning lactose absorption would attain particular selective advantage in environments associated with chronic vitamin D deficiency. Provided that there has been ample and consistent opportunity for genetic selection, one would then expect the LA frequencies of contemporary populations to vary inversely with the historic availability of that vitamin.

This prediction links the calcium-absorption hypothesis to the burgeoning literature on the biochemistry and physiology of vitamin D, and leads, I believe, to a fairly robust test of its predictions. The test is suggested by a number of developments in vitamin D research that warrant brief summary here (for a thorough review of these and related topics, see DeLuca 1979, 1986; Norman 1979, 1985; Holick 1985; Haussler et al. 1988).

1. Since the pioneering work of Sir Edward Mellanby in the 1920's on rickets, it has been recognized that vitamin D (called simply the "antirachitic factor" at the time) can be procured dietarily. Mellanby, for example, substantiated the older folk belief that cod-liver oil is a potent antirachitic agent. Today the list of recognized dietary sources has been expanded to include other fish and fish livers, mammalian livers, shellfish, and egg yolks.

2. More recent research, however, indicates that human beings do not require a steady dietary supply of the "vitamin." Rather than a true vitamin, it is recognized as a kind of steroid hormone, officially called a "seco-steroid," that is both synthesized and activated by nearly all human genotypes under the proper conditions.

3. The physiologically most active form of vitamin D, called D_3, can be synthesized from a precursor "provitamin" in the human epidermis via a reaction that requires ultraviolet radiation (UV). The optimal UV light for the reaction is known to be of wavelength 295 to 300 nanometers, or what is referred to as ultraviolet B (UV-B) radiation.

4. Photosynthesized vitamin D_3 is routinely transported by the blood stream to the liver and kidneys, where it is chemically converted to its biologically active form. The amount of activated D_3 is, in turn, moni-

tored and partially regulated by the parathyroid gland, which helps to maintain a proper balance of circulating calcium and its close metabolic associate, phosphorus.

5. The biologically active form of D_3 is carried in circulation to the intestines, bones, and kidneys, where it has a number of effects on mineral metabolism. The most important of these for our discussion takes place in the upper portion of the small intestine, just above the jejunum, where activated D_3 is absorbed into the mucosal cells lining the intestinal wall.

6. There, vitamin D_3 is believed to activate the synthesis of a specific polypeptide, called "calcium binding protein" (see Norman 1979; Wasserman 1981). This protein, in turn, plays an active role in helping the mucosal cells absorb the Ca^{++} ions—a role very similar in function, if not in biochemical detail, to that played by lactose in the jejunum and ileum of lactose absorbers.

7. Significantly, young children and suckling rats remain insensitive to these effects of activated D_3 for as long as they consume mother's milk (see De Luca et al. 1982). Yet they are also able to maintain normal levels of circulating calcium (even from mothers deficient in vitamin D) because the lactose facilitates their Ca^{++} uptake. This indicates that lactose plays a truly vital role in calcium metabolism among preweaning mammals, essentially taking the place of vitamin D. Viewed in this light, the calcium absorption hypothesis proposes simply that genetic selection favored, in populations deficient in vitamin D, a *prolongation* of the existing lactose-based mechanism for absorbing calcium.

8. There is abundant evidence that conditions arising from vitamin D deficiency can make a difference to survival and reproduction. The bone disease rickets, for example, causes the skeletal structures of children to remain soft and malleable during growth. The pelvic deformities that result from rickets are particularly detrimental for females since the size of the birth canal may be reduced to as little as 56 percent of normal (Eastman 1956; see also Shorter 1982: 22–28).[17]

9. A second such disease, osteomalacia (the decalcification of mature bone), contributes to bone fractures and deformities among adults and has also been linked to survival and reproduction (see, for example, Mankin 1974).[18] Other pathologies that result from vitamin D deficiency include

[17] As Neer (1975: 411) has summarized, vitamin D–related deformities like this "significantly reduce reproductive efficiency" by making vaginal delivery still more difficult than normal, or impossible. In the absence of modern techniques for caesarean section, total fetal mortality in such cases is at least 50 percent higher than average, and maternal mortality is often higher still. Data from Parisian maternity hospitals in the nineteenth century, for example, show that the percentage of mothers dying in childbirth increased from an overall average of 6 percent to between 19 and 49 percent, depending upon the contraction of the pelvis (Shorter 1982: 89). "To this reproductive disadvantage," Neer points out, "must be added an additional evolutionary disadvantage due to the increased incidence of brain damage in viable infants delivered through a contracted pelvis (Eastman 1956)."

[18] Lactose malabsorption has also been implicated in some cases of osteomalacia (Birge et al. 1967; Newcomer 1978; Marcus 1982). The seriousness of both osteomalacia and rickets

hypertension (linked to Ca^{++} deficiency; see McCarron et al. 1982), neuromuscular disorders (as serious as tetany and convulsions), and a number of psychological syndromes. One of the latter, called *pibloktoq* or "arctic hysteria" has been linked to hypocalcemic stress in certain northern Eskimo populations, but there is no direct evidence of its affecting survival and reproduction.[19]

In summary, these findings support two important inferences for our analysis of adult lactose absorption. First, they suggest an answer to the evolutionary enigma raised earlier in this chapter, namely, Why would genetic selection favor genotypes capable of lactose synthesis when their product must promptly be broken back down for absorption? The answer would appear to lie in the special ability of lactose absorption to enhance intestinal calcium uptake at a time in development before other agents, particularly vitamin D, are available or active.

The importance of this function of lactose is further emphasized by two findings: human milk is sufficient in all required vitamins *except* vitamin D; and no unfortified milk supplies enough vitamin D for the needs of infants and young adults (Kon 1972: 9). Nevertheless, breast-fed infants rarely develop rickets before weaning. Indeed, they are less susceptible than are infants fed on cow's milk, even though the latter generally contains higher concentrations of both vitamin D and calcium.[20] Back in 1932, this observation led the nutritionist Harriette Chick (1932: 381) to conclude, "It would appear as if some other protective factors, at present unknown, must be operating in human milk." Key among these factors, we know today, is lactose, one of the few nutrients present in greater concentration in human milk than in cow's—about 50 percent greater, in fact (Hambraeus 1984). I find it ironic that this information has been used in the past not to foster a recognition of the beneficial consequences of lactose for calcium absorption in children and other absorbers, but to urge commercial milk producers to add supplemental vitamin D to

---

is suggested by the findings of Danish scientists who excavated a former Viking colony at Herjolfsnes, Greenland. The only skeletal remains of females to be found were those of young women and among them were cases of serious, birth-impairing deformities. Maxwell concluded that "rickets and osteomalacia played their part—possibly a most important one—in the extinction of the Herjolfsnes colony." (1930: 640.)

[19] A number of alternative theories have been advanced on the origins of *pibloktoq* (see discussion in Foulks 1972), but acute hypocalcemic stress related to vitamin D deficiency is a probable cause (see Wallace and Ackerman 1960; Wallace 1961; Katz and Foulks 1970; Foulks and Katz 1975). More recently, Kehoe and Giletti (1981) have proposed that deficiencies in calcium and vitamin D, particularly among females, may relate on a more global scale to the tetany and altered consciousness that characterize "spirit possession," but there is little specific data to support their argument, or to suggest that it creates reproductive differentials (see also Lewis 1983; Bourguignon et al. 1983).

[20] These observations would also seem to answer the concern of Räihä (1981: 220) that "lactose is specific for milk, yet its evolutionary advantage remains obscure." We can now appreciate that milk contains not only the essential mineral calcium but also an absorbing agent for that mineral that functions independently of, and developmentally prior to, vitamin D.

their product. Physiologically speaking, the result is redundant—literally superfluous—for the vast majority of milk drinkers who are also lactose absorbers.

The second important conclusion of research on vitamin D and lactose is that, for human populations, the availability of vitamin D may be expected to vary both by diet and by average rates of biosynthesis in human skin. Accordingly, wherever dietary resources of D_3 are not sufficient for calcium absorption, the availability of the vitamin and thus of calcium will vary with the energy levels of incident UV-B radiation. These levels, in turn, vary over the earth's surface. The basic pattern is shown in Fig. 5.8, which uses, for illustration, the total global solar radiation of wavelength 307.5 nm received, including cloud cover, for the populations given in Table 5.1 and Fig. 5.3. The data show a pronounced UV-B radiation gradient with respect to latitude, from high values near the equator to roughly one-fourth of those values up near the Arctic Circle.[21] Especially noteworthy here is the high UV-B "plateau" that extends from 25 to 30 degrees south latitude to 25 to 30 degrees north, a by-product of the earth's axial tilt. We may infer that there exists a great potential for vitamin D photosynthesis in this equatorial region, but that this potential drops off drastically, almost hyperbolically, with latitude below 30 degrees south or above 30 degrees north. To make matters worse, temperature also drops off sharply with latitude. As a result, of course, additional clothing is needed and there is still further reduction in UV-B exposure, especially in winter.

The implication is that the potential for vitamin D photosynthesis is sharply reduced at higher latitudes. If so, and if lactose does act like a vitamin D supplement, then we might predict that the genetic selection intensity for adult lactose absorption would covary inversely with the UV-B trend. According to that prediction, we would expect to find the highest frequencies of LA today among populations living at high latitudes, that also (1) evolved years ago, by cultural means, a set of values, ideas, and beliefs encouraging the consumption of fresh milk after weaning; (2) produced, from the same early time, sufficient quantities of milk from dairy animals to allow substantial consumption after weaning; and (3) procured, meanwhile, insufficient dietary sources of vitamin D. By this hypothesis, populations meeting these criteria and living at intermediate latitudes would undergo selection of intermediate intensity, and would therefore be expected to have intermediate LA frequencies today.[22]

[21] This gradient has been described by Caldwell and his coworkers as "the result of a natural latitudinal gradient in total atmospheric ozone column thickness [which very effectively absorbs UV-B], prevailing solar angles at different latitudes, elevation above sea level [controlled in the figure], and an optical amplification effect, which results from a combination of highly wavelength-dependent radiation attenuation in the atmosphere and the pronounced wavelength dependence of biological action spectra." (1980: 600.) In addition, the UV-B values of Fig. 5.8 include the estimated effect of cloud cover, which is also a correlate of latitude.

[22] This prediction makes the reasonable assumption that the time available to genetic selection (the variable T, as in Chapter 3) has generally been insufficient for fixation to

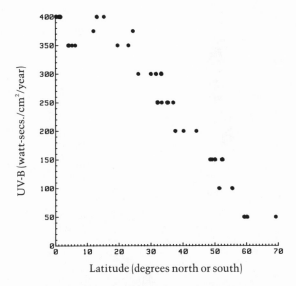

(N = 47 out of 47 "nonmixed" populations)

Fig. 5.8. The steep latitudinal gradient in ultraviolet B radiation at the earth's surface. This plot shows the average annual energy (direct beam plus diffuse) received from light of a 10-nm bandwidth centered at 307.5 nm at the homeland location of each of the populations in Table 5.1 and Fig. 5.3 (omitting "mixed" populations, Category G). The values are controlled for elevation and include the estimated effect of cloud cover. Note that the curve levels off to a plateau of 350 to 400 watt-seconds per cm² per year below 25 degrees north or south latitude. Outside that region, UV-B levels diminish rapidly with latitude to an average of only 50 watt-seconds per cm² per year at 60 to 70 degrees north or south. Given the importance of UV-B for vitamin D biosynthesis, this plot dramatically illustrates the potential for vitamin D deficiency at high latitudes. Data from Schulze and Gräfe 1969; see also Williams 1979: 230; Bener 1972.

The resultant pattern is virtually opposite to the prediction of the ancestral pastoralism hypothesis: the gradient of LA frequencies should run from low values between 30 degrees north latitude and 30 degrees south to high values at high latitudes. Among subsample populations that conform to these assumptions, one should find relatively low prevalences in the Near East and southern Europe in contrast to high prevalences in Scandinavia.

The Parallel Case of Skin Depigmentation

Before turning to a direct test of the calcium absorption hypothesis, it will be useful to review other evidence from human populations showing not only that vitamin D deficiency *can* act as a selection pressure, but that it actually has. The evidence comes from the comparative study of

occur, that is, for the LA gene or genes to reach a frequency of 1.00. Supporting this assumption is the observation that very few of the human populations tested for adult lactose absorption show 100 percent of the LA phenotype (in Table 5.1, for instance, only 2 populations of 60).

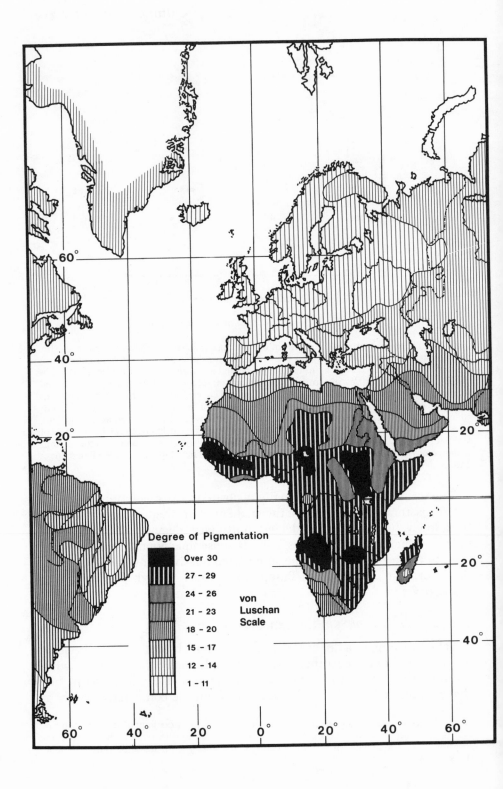

Degree of Pigmentation

Over 30
27 – 29
24 – 26
21 – 23
18 – 20
15 – 17
12 – 14
1 – 11

von
Luschan
Scale

human skin color, a complex phenotype whose variability stems, in part, from the instructions of genes quite unrelated to adult lactose absorption.

As first proposed by Frederick G. Murray (1934; see also App. A.5.2.), there are both theoretical arguments and reasonably good empirical data to suggest that much of the variation in human skin pigmentation is a genetically evolved adaptation to ambient UV-B levels. More specifically, "constitutive melanization" (the average density of the skin pigment, melanin, in the absence of exposure to sunlight, and hence of tanning) appears to have evolved by genetic selection in response to two pressures. First, at low latitudes, selection probably operated by way of biochemical damage, such as mutation and skin cancer, induced by UV-B. In these regions, genetic selection would have favored genotypes that instructed phenotypes to form a dense, absorptive layer of epidermal melanin. Second, at higher latitudes, the selection pressure would have reduced this protective melanization. There, selection would have favored genotypes whose associated phenotypes allowed enough UV-B through the epidermis to synthesize adequate quantities of vitamin D. The result, by this theory, would be a close geographical correlation between UV-B levels and the degree of human skin pigmentation.

Support for Murray's "vitamin D hypothesis" is shown in Figures 5.9 and 5.10, which attempt to reconstruct the geographic variation in human skin color before the era of global migrations. The figures show close correspondence with the predicted pattern including, as in Fig. 5.10, an "equatorial plateau" of heavy pigmentation out to at least 20 degrees north and south latitude. This correspondence, confirmed also by skin reflectance studies (see App. A.5.2), implies that vitamin D deficiency has operated as a powerful agent of genetic selection, one whose magnitude varies directly with latitude and inversely with UV-B intensity.[23] It thus

[23] Still further support for this hypothesis is provided by studies of two additional genetic polymorphisms: an analysis of PKU (phenylketonuria) in European populations (McCulloch 1978; Kaufman 1983); and a worldwide study of group-specific component (Gc) allele frequencies (Mourant et al. 1976). PKU is a lethal metabolic abnormality that may result from homozygosity for a gene involved in the synthesis of epidermal melanin. McCulloch hypothesized that classical PKU, which is characterized by significantly lightened skin pigmentation, is the by-product of a balanced polymorphism much like sickle-cell anemia (see Chapter 3 of this book), caused by the "inability of the heterozygote to synthesize normal amounts of melanin." At high latitudes, as he pointed out, the same deficiency would allow more sunlight to penetrate the skin and activate the production of vitamin D, thus enhancing the heterozygote's Darwinian fitness (1978: 231). In an analysis of European heterozygote frequencies as a function of incident midwinter sunlight, McCulloch obtained re-

Fig. 5.9 (opposite). Relative skin pigmentation of human populations in the subsample area. This is an approximate reconstruction of the geographic distribution of epidermal melanization, as measured on the von Luschan scale, before 1492. The von Luschan scale consists of skin-colored ceramic tiles in a numbered array, from 1 (least pigment) to 36 (most pigment); the tiles are used for matching to the underside of subjects' forearms. By grouping von Luschan numbers and shading as shown, the map reveals a general correlation between melanization and latitude. Adapted from Biasutti 1959: fig. 4.

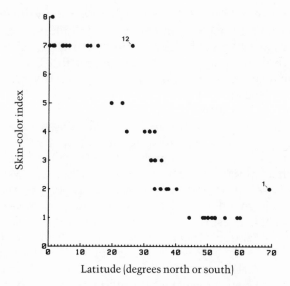

Latitude (degrees north or south)

(N = 47 out of 47 "nonmixed" populations)

Fig. 5.10. Relative skin pigmentation of subsample populations as a function of latitude. The skin-color index refers to Biasutti's condensation of the von Luschan scale, as in Fig. 5.9 ("1" refers to von Luschan numbers 1–11, "2" to von Luschan numbers 12–14, etc.). This curve shows close correlation with the UV-B curve of Fig. 5.8, suggesting that latitudinal depigmentation is largely an evolutionary response to vitamin D deficiency. Two exceptions to the trend are Eskimos of Greenland, at 69.2 degrees north latitude (population 1 of Table 5.1), an exception discussed in the text; and Bantu of South Africa at 26.1 degrees south latitude (population 12), who are recent immigrants from a more equatorial homeland. Data from Biasutti 1959: fig. 4.

seems a reasonable candidate for the evolution of greater or lesser levels of adult lactose absorption.

One could always argue, on the other hand, that depigmentation at high altitudes has largely resolved any vitamin D problem. It is, after all, conceivable that relatively depigmented skin completely compensates for the UV energy gradient at the earth's surface, thus eliminating any further advantage to genotypes that absorb calcium efficiently. But while a theoretical possibility, this argument runs against considerable human experience. R. Ted Steinbock (1976) and Rebecca Huss-Ashmore and her colleagues (1982) describe the fragmentary archaeological evidence for

gression equations "very similar to estimate equations comparing skin color . . . to latitude and environmental conditions." (p. 234; see also App. A.5.2.) Gc alleles, of which only Gc[1] and Gc[2] have been found in all populations tested, instruct the synthesis of a particular alpha-globulin protein of human blood plasma that binds and stabilizes vitamin D in circulation (Daiger et al. 1975). In their study of the geographical distributions of these alleles, Mourant and his colleagues found that "frequencies of Gc[2] are low in areas of high insolation and high where there is little sunshine." (1976: 311.) Thus PKU heterozygote frequencies, Gc[2] frequencies, and epidermal depigmentation all vary as an inverse function of UV-B levels, just as one would expect from genetic selection caused by vitamin D deficiency.

rickets in Neolithic, Iron Age, and medieval Scandinavia. But other evidence suggests continuing and even increasing health effects of vitamin D deficiency at high latitudes, particularly in northern Europe.[24] In short, evidence from both the study of skin color and the persistence of rickets suggests that vitamin D deficiency has been at least an intermittent health problem and selection pressure, and one whose magnitude has varied sharply with latitude. The question remains, Can this pressure also explain the observed patterns of variation in adult lactose absorption?

A Test of the Hypotheses

Thus we are left with three alternative hypotheses, each with at least some degree of plausibility, for explaining the genetic diversity of adult lactose absorption. First, the culture historical hypothesis proposes that LA genes evolved to high frequencies by virtue of a general nutritional advantage within dairying populations that were subject to dietary stress. The argument would seem to be most compelling for those milk-dependent pastoral groups (if any) that have historically lacked milk-processing procedures; for other populations this hypothesis begs the question of why the age-old techniques of lactose treatment would not confer the same advantage on all genotypes.

Second, the ancestral pastoralism hypothesis proposes that high frequencies of LA first evolved between 5000 and 3000 B.C. among Eurasian steppe pastoralists, before efficient processing treatments had been developed. From these peoples, the LA genes would have spread by migration and diffusion, creating a gradient from peak frequencies near an ancestral homeland in southern Eurasia to progressively lower proportions southeastward toward India and northeastward toward central and northern Europe.

Third, the calcium absorption hypothesis proposes that genetic selec-

[24] Fifteenth- and sixteenth-century paintings from Germany and the Netherlands—Hans Burgkmair's 1509 *Virgin and Child*, for example—often depicted young children as rachitic (see Cone 1980; Foote 1927). Rickets was already well known before physicians began to write about it in the seventeenth century, and the origins of the term are probably too old to trace (see Ihde 1974; LeVay 1975). The incidence of rickets is known to have increased rapidly in Britain after the Industrial Revolution, possibly because smoke from coal fires reduced sunlight (Loomis 1970), but also because of behavioral changes and an urban diet lacking in fresh milk and milk products (Drummond and Wilbraham 1939: 193 ff.; Wallace 1977). Later, after World War I, rickets again reached epidemic proportions during the winter months in Vienna and other areas with seriously disrupted food supplies (Chick 1932: 382). More recently, a comparative study by Kloster of children in Lapp, Norwegian, and Finnish villages in the 1930's found a high incidence of rickets throughout the locality but especially in a village of prosperous and fair-skinned Finns. Although their diet included some milk and meat, the Finns consumed much less fish and fish-liver oil than did other inhabitants, particularly the darker-skinned Lapps (Saami). This last study shows quite clearly that vitamin D deficiency was not fully resolved by skin depigmentation; the crucial factor was dietary vitamin D from fish and fish-liver oils (Kloster 1931).

tion for LA has operated primarily through the agency of vitamin D deficiency; this, as we have seen, increases sharply in seriousness with latitude. According to this hypothesis, we should find that LA prevalences today vary inversely to the gradient of incident UV-B, from lows in the "equatorial plateau" to highs in Scandinavia. The only exceptions to this rule should be populations with large dietary sources of vitamin D or populations of pastoralists who fit the special assumptions of the culture historical hypothesis. The general latitudinal trends predicted by Hypotheses 2 and 3 form a striking contrast, suggesting a simple and direct test.

With the help of student assistants E.L. and P.I., I performed that test on the subsample data of Table 5.1, with the results shown in Fig. 5.11. The figure plots the frequency of adult lactose absorbers in each of the 47 nonmixed populations as a function of its homeland latitude. It identifies a clear central tendency among the data points and at the same time documents two kinds of exceptions, labeled IV and V in the figure. Consider, first, the central tendency (we will return to the exceptions below): the data conform most closely to the calcium absorption hypothesis. The fig-

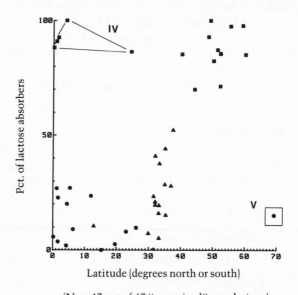

(N = 47 out of 47 "nonmixed" populations)

Fig. 5.11. The association between adult lactose absorption and latitude in subsample populations. The sampled frequency of adult lactose absorption is plotted as a function of homeland latitude for each of the populations of Table 5.1. A general latitudinal trend is apparent: the prevalence of LA increases dramatically with latitude above a low-frequency plateau from about 0 to 25 degrees. These data provide strong support for the calcium-absorption hypothesis. There are, however, two clusters of exceptions. Cluster IV is made up of milk-dependent pastoral peoples of East Africa and Saudi Arabia who exhibit high LA frequencies regardless of latitude—a result consistent with the culture historical hypothesis. Cluster V represents Eskimo (Inuit) populations of Greenland who live at 69 degrees north latitude without dairy animals, but with a diet that, until recently, protected them from the ravages of vitamin D deficiency. Data from Table 5.1.

ure reveals a steep increase in the proportion of lactose absorbers with latitude, but only outside the margins of an equatorial plateau extending to between 25 and 30 north or south latitude. The curve closely resembles the UV-B plot of Fig. 5.8 flipped upside down; the resemblance extends even to a slight tendency for the slope to flatten out above 50 degrees latitude. As predicted by the Flatz and Rotthauwe proposal, LA and latitude are *positively* correlated, the r value being 0.37 ($p < .01$) for all 47 non-mixed populations; not surprisingly, the association between LA and incident UV-B is an inverse one, and even stronger, -0.49 ($p < .01$).[25]

This pattern, we may infer, provides little or no support for the ancestral pastoralism hypothesis. LA frequencies are relatively low in southern Europe—Greece and Italy, for instance—precisely where the impact of Indo-European pastoralists would have been earliest and most direct. Likewise, the frequencies are highest in northern Europe and Scandinavia, areas that would have been peripheral to the Kurgan infiltration. To make matters worse for the pastoralism argument, more recent investigations in Iran and Afghanistan reviewed in Simoons (1981; not represented in Table 5.1) suggest that LA genes did not spread at particularly high frequency to the south and east of the steppe homeland either. A study of 21 Iranian adults found only 3 (14 percent) to be absorbers, for example, and in Afghanistan only 13 to 24 percent prevalences of LA were found among 270 persons from various ethnic groups. Additional research may support the idea of demic diffusion in special cases, including India as Simoons suggests (1981: 32–33; see also Flatz 1987: 54–55). But, in the present study, the ancestral pastoralism hypothesis contributes very little to the explanation of variance.

Overall, the results of this test provide striking confirmation of the calcium absorption hypothesis. There are, however, exceptions to the rule. The first group, designated Cluster IV in Fig. 5.11, are the milk-dependent pastoralists of Table 5.1, Category D. Their frequencies of LA are high, it would seem, regardless of latitude.[26] These data, as well as studies completed since the subsample data base was prepared (Bayoumi et al. 1981, 1982; Hussein et al. 1982), do suggest that a general nutritional advantage

[25] The plot of LA frequencies as a function of UV-B shows an LA-frequency threshold at about 300 watt-seconds per cm^2 per year. Below 300, adult lactose-absorption frequency rises dramatically to peak levels, attained at 150 watt-seconds per cm^2 or less. Unfortunately, without specific information concerning the timing of the introduction of LA genes to high-latitude populations, it is impossible to say whether this low UV-B plateau represents another "threshold" of selection intensity, or whether the pattern is due to variation in the period of exposure to selection. Timing is no doubt a source of additional variance in the results of Figure 5.11. However, the general sequence of events in the spread of dairying provides a bias, if anything, *against* the calcium-absorption hypothesis. The time available for genetic evolution to occur was substantially greater at lower latitudes, leaving little doubt that the gradient of Fig. 5.11 does reflect actual selection intensities.

[26] In a plot of LA frequencies by UV-B levels, the populations of Cluster IV are grouped tightly together at the upper end of the UV-B range. With an average of 350 to 400 watt-seconds per cm^2 each per year, it is very unlikely that they suffer from chronic vitamin D deficiency.

accrues to LA genotypes among pastoral peoples. Moreover, the non-Arab pastoralists of Cluster IV are all of Nilotic stock and therefore unrelated to the Proto-Indo-Europeans of the ancestral pastoralism theory (Lincoln 1981). According to some scholars (see, for example, Simoons 1970: 706), these populations are the modern descendants of ancient Saharan pastoralists who began using milk by at least 4000 B.C. It thus appears that the selective mechanism of the culture historical hypothesis may be responsible for these exceptional cases.[27] That argument may thus be said to *contribute* to the explanation of LA frequencies in this subsample. But since the pastoral populations of Cluster IV are few in number and specialized in subsistence, that contribution is comparatively minor.

The second group of exceptions, designated Cluster V in Fig. 5.11, represents the Eskimos (Inuit) of Greenland, a people who survive and reproduce successfully at a latitude of 69 degrees north and who, for obvious reasons, lack a cultural history of dairying. How, we might ask, do they circumvent the devastating effects of bone disease in that environment—the fate that befell the Viking colonies (see note 18)? Their situation is all the more noteworthy because of their skin pigmentation, which is relatively dark for these latitudes and is classified the same as Mediterranean populations' (see Fig. 5.9), and because of the climate, which requires extensive clothing most of the year. Dark skin, heavy clothing, low and periodic UV radiation, and in addition no lactose supply after weaning—the circumstances would certainly seem to warrant chronic and pervasive bone disease. Yet, until recently, rickets and osteomalacia occurred among Eskimos with "extreme rarity," even among pregnant and lactating women with extra calcium requirements (Wallace 1961: 376).

The exceptional case of Cluster V peoples was first addressed by F. G. Murray, as part of his early argument relating the evolution of skin-color differences to vitamin D deficiency. Realizing the challenge that this case offered to his theory, Murray proposed that the heavier melanization of the Eskimos could be attributed to their "subsisting almost exclusively on a fish oil and meat diet. Cod liver oil, as has been stated, is fully as efficient as sunlight in preventing rickets. Now the daily diet of the Eskimo calculated in antirachitic units of cod liver oil equals several times the minimum amount of cod liver oil [and vitamin D] needed to prevent rickets." (1934: 441.) By this suggestion, repeated by Loomis (1967: 504), So (1980: 73), and others, the Eskimos' dietary provision of vitamin D would greatly reduce or even eliminate the selection coefficients favoring demelanized genotypes. Therefore, continued Murray,

[27] But the milk-processing techniques of pastoralists (as described, for example, in Evans-Pritchard 1940: ch. 1) remain a problem for the culture historical hypothesis. Other advantages of LA should therefore be considered in Cluster IV populations, including the proposal of Cook and Al-Torki (1975) and Cook (1978) that, in arid regions, the selective advantage of LA "might in fact have been more directly related to water and electrolytes than to a [general] nutritional advantage." (Cook 1978: 425.)

they "probably [have] the same pigmented skin with which [their ancestors] arrived in the far north ages ago." Presumably then, even if dairying *had* been successfully established in the Arctic, and even if the LA genes *had* been introduced early on, one still would not observe today high levels of adult lactose absorption. Here, again, there is evidence for a culturally based "solution" to a chronic problem of adaptation (although the occurrence of arctic hysteria among Eskimos in other areas suggests continuing, if acute, shortages). The "exception" here is almost a logical converse to the culturally transmitted solution offered by milk processing for lactose malabsorption. According to Murray, the Eskimo case helps test the rule.[28]

The exceptional circumstances of the Eskimos also suggest an answer to one of the puzzling questions about lactose raised at the start of this chapter, namely, Why, in the Pacific pinnipeds of all mammals, has there evolved a lactose-free milk? The elevated vitamin D concentrations of fish and pinnipeds in the Eskimo diet offer a provocative clue. Adult Pacific pinnipeds consume marine fishes almost exclusively, and many of these fishes are thought to be capable of enzymatic, light-free synthesis of vitamin D (Loomis 1970). Effectively shielded from UV-B by sea water, different species of marine fish contain vitamin D concentrations that range from a low of some 44 international units per 100 grams—equivalent to the amount in two egg yolks, for example—to as high as 1,500 units. Moreover, the raw livers of such fishes, considered almost a delicacy by some human populations, may contain many times these levels.

Consequently, one would expect to find that Pacific pinniped milks are unusually high among mammals in their average vitamin D content, obviating any physiological advantage to the calcium absorption of LA genotypes. Should this prove to be the case—and I simply do not know at present—then the puzzle of no-lactose milk would become understandable: selection coefficients for lactose-producing genotypes would be relaxed within populations that have access to generous quantities of the vitamin. Indeed, the selection pressures would probably work *against* LA because of its link to intestinal disease (as pointed out by Holmes et al. 1976) and its general "wastefulness" (because it continues the biosynthe-

[28] Arne Høygaard's carefully documented study (1941) of the diet of Angmagssalik Eskimos of eastern Greenland provides noteworthy support for Murray's claim (see also Holm 1914, on the Angmagssalik; and Draper 1977, 1980, on the Wainwright Eskimos). Høygaard monitored the daily consumption of all major foodstuffs by a family of seven. With the help of an able student assistant (F.H.), I estimated from these data the average daily adult consumption of both vitamin D and calcium within the family. We found daily calcium consumption levels to average about 1.5 times the level recommended by the World Health Organization, which is 400–500 mg per person per day, and we found vitamin D levels generally more than *ten* times the recommended level (100 international units per day). We found the dietary consumption of both nutrients to be especially high during the winter months, when photosynthesis of the absorbing agent is virtually out of the question. Even after allowance has been made for personal eating habits and outside influences on Eskimo culture, it seems likely that traditional foodways were responsible for the low incidence of bone disease among Eskimo groups, which scarcely knew rickets until, in some areas, they were converted to European diets by well-meaning missionaries (Loomis 1970).

sis of lactase to no avail). The high concentrations of vitamin D in marine fishes may thus explain two very different kinds of exceptions in the evolution of lactose production and consumption: the health of the Eskimos with low LA frequencies at high latitudes, and the existence of pinniped milks with low lactose at all latitudes.

To return to the analysis at hand, then, we have seen that milk-dependent pastoralists and arctic Eskimos can be viewed as special cases in the evolution of adult lactose absorption. By far the greater proportion of diversity in LA frequencies can be accounted for by the calcium absorption hypothesis. The prevalences of LA vary just as we might expect of a genetic adaptation to low levels of UV-B radiation and so of vitamin D synthesis. Unfortunately the data remain insufficient to tell us whether the frequencies of LA genes are still changing at mid- and high-latitude locations, or whether some new genetic equilibrium has been attained, one that varies with latitude in much the way that the equilibrium frequencies of the sickle-cell gene vary with malarial selection as discussed in Chapter 3. For now, the one strong inference that can be drawn is that genetic selection has generally increased the frequency of LA genes in direct proportion to latitude and in inverse proportion to UV-B. In fact, if we omit from the calculations the exceptional cases described above, and the nondairying populations of Table 5.1, which leaves the dairying populations of North Africa, the Mediterranean, and Europe, the correlation coefficients, r, become an impressive 0.88 for LA and latitude, and -0.90 for LA and UV-B.

But an important question remains to be addressed: Does this example genuinely constitute cultural mediation? Can we legitimately infer, as implied by these data, that culture helped to shape the course of genetic evolution? Did the prevailing ideology of dairying, as we may call it, join with calcium absorption to create the selection pressure for LA genotypes? If so, can we also interpret some of the *cultural* variability of this example in terms of the calcium absorption hypothesis? If not, what other forces have shaped the variations in milk use and consumption indicated by Figs. 5.5, 5.6, and 5.7? And what then explains the geographic distribution of LA? Clearly, important aspects of cultural diversity remain to be explored in this example, and it is to this subject that we now turn.

Culture and the Evolution of LA Diversity

At the start of this chapter, I described cultural mediation as the mode of relationship between genes and culture in which the memes of culture affect the selection coefficients that act among alternative genotypes. Where this relationship persists within culturally diverse populations for enough years for genetic evolution to occur, a correlation will be created between the prevalence of cultural forms and the frequency of genes under selection. In order to establish that the diversity of LA frequencies may, as hypothesized, be a product of mediation, we must be able to demonstrate (1) that the values and beliefs concerning milk use show a comparable latitudinal gradient among the subsample populations, encouraging the consumption of fresh milk at high latitudes; and (2) that this has been the case for many, many generations.

This task first appeared a formidable one. The challenge was to come up with indicators of the variability in memes related to dairying, indicators that were sufficiently sensitive for a convincing acceptance or rejection of the null hypothesis of no latitudinal variability. With the help of student assistants (E.L., J.G., N.M., P.I.), I tried two approaches. The first was to assess the role of milking in the traditional mythology and folklore of dairying populations—its nutritive role among mythical figures, its symbolic qualities and associations, and the implied lessons or morals, if any, for the makers and bearers of myth. The second was to test the milk-use patterns of contemporary populations in a more quantitative way, using aggregate behavioral measures as an indication or reflection of underlying cultural differences.

The Role of Milk in Mythology

Early in the project, I decided to focus on the myths of peoples speaking Indo-European languages. I had two main reasons: the documentation seemed most systematic and extensive for these peoples, and their current homelands span a large portion of the latitudinal range in the lactose subsample. A search through the literature revealed that common bovine themes pervade these mythologies and, more importantly, that these themes vary in a particular nonrandom fashion. The roles of dairying and milk drinking in the myths vary strikingly from place to place and, indeed, as a function of latitude. Moreover, there is good reason to believe that many of the variants are related by descent to a common ancestral stock and are thus true cultural homologs.

My thinking about this case of cultural "descent with modification" was greatly aided by an important recent synthesis of Indo-European myth in the work of the anthropologist Bruce Lincoln (1975, 1981). Lincoln's interpretation, based on the comparative study of Indo-European creation myths, provided both additional mythological material related to dairying and a general evolutionary framework with which to tie together some otherwise disparate observations from the literature. His arguments, together with some of my own extensions and elaborations, are described more fully in App. A.5.3, but the basic outline of the case is summarized here (see also Lincoln 1986).

Building on the approach of Georges Dumézil and what has been called the "genetic model" of Indo-European mythology (see also Littleton 1973; Larson 1974a,b), Lincoln documents an impressive array of correspondences among myths about the origins and peopling of the world. He uses

TABLE 5.3

Cultural Evolution of Indo-European Mythology: Correspondences in the Myth of First Sacrifice

Source mythology	First priest (*Manu)[a]	First king (*Yemo)[a]	First bovine	Fresh milk production	Fresh milk consumption	First sacrifice	Creation
1. Old Norse	Odin (god)	Ýmir (giant)	Auðhumla[b] (female)	Yes (abundant)	Adults (gods and giants)	Giant	Earth, mountains, sea and waters, sky
2. Gaelic	Lugh/ Ioldanach (god)	Balor (giant)	Gray cow (female)	Yes (abundant)	Adults (gods and giants)	Giant	Mountains, lakes, and rivers
3. Roman	Romulus (man)	Remus (man)	(She-wolf) (female)	Yes	Infants	Man	City of Rome
4. Greek	Zeus (god)	Cronos (titan)	Amalthea (female goat)	Yes	Infants	Giants	Humanity
5. Iranian	Ahriman (demon)	Gayōmart (man)	"Sole-created ox" (male)	No	No	Man and ox	Plants, animals, humanity, metals
6. Indic	Gods	Puruṣa (man/bull)	Puruṣa (male)	No (processed)	No	Man/bull	Animals, social classes, earth, sky

SOURCE: Data for Old Norse, Roman, Iranian, and Indic myths are from Lincoln 1981; for the Gaelic myth they are from E. Hamilton 1940 and Graves 1960 (see App. A.5.3).

[a] Asterisks denote the reconstructed Proto-Indo-European term for these mythical figures.
[b] The mythical cow who fed Ýmir with "streams" of milk.

these correspondences, structural as well as linguistic, to reconstruct the outline of the ancestral "Proto-Indo-European" creation myth. That myth centers around what he calls the first or primordial sacrifice, a sacrifice that both created the world and served as the mythical prototype of all sacrifice in traditional Indo-European religion; indeed, it served as prototype of all creative action. In the original myth, "the world begins with a pair of [anthropomorphic] twins: *Manu, 'man,' and *Yemo, 'twin.' *Yemo is the first king and *Manu is the first priest, and in the course of the myth *Manu kills his brother, thus performing the first sacrifice. As a result of this act, the world is created and *Manu fashions the earth and the heavens as well as the three social classes [priests, warriors, and commoners] from his brother's body." (Lincoln 1981: 87.) Also offered in the first sacrifice with *Yemo (the asterisk denotes a reconstructed form) is the "first bovine," which Lincoln believes from comparative study to have been an ox.

The basic elements of this myth—a first priest, a first king, a first bovine, a first sacrifice, and then creation—are found by Lincoln throughout his survey of ancient texts from locations as diverse as India, Iran, Rome, Ireland, and Scandinavia. But the different versions show systematic latitudinal variation in the nature and role of the first bovine, and corresponding variation in references to milk and milk drinking. Table 5.3 summarizes the major features of this variation as organized by source mythology and arranged in latitudinal order from north to south. To the correspondences described by Lincoln, I have added two further entries from my own reading of Greek and Gaelic mythology.

To begin with, the table shows that a recognizable version of the "myth of the first sacrifice," complete with corresponding personages and structurally similar roles, can be found in all six Indo-European mythologies studied. In each case a *Manu–first priest figure slays a *Yemo–first king figure who is, in most cases, either a twin or another close genealogical relative. A first bovine is also a part of each of the myths, although the sex of the bovine and its mythical role vary as shown in the compilation. From the first sacrifice, involving either the *Yemo figure alone or the *Yemo and first bovine together, are created various aspects of the world and its human population.

Table 5.3 indicates that the roles of bovines and milk drinking in Indo-European creation myths do vary with latitude in a pattern notably consistent with the predictions of the cultural mediation hypothesis. In the northernmost examples, Old Norse and Gaelic, the first animals or first bovines are female; they produce milk in great quantity; milk is consumed directly and fresh by anthropomorphic figures; although those figures, whether giants or gods, are clearly adult, milk for them is the most basic staple or even the sole source of food; this diet of milk is associated with their great size, strength, and physical stamina; and, finally, the first bovine is not sacrificed in the act of creation, but continues in a nurturant capacity thereafter.

The themes of the southernmost variants stand in striking contrast. The bovines are male (bulls and oxen); they are part of the first sacrifice; and there is no mention of milk production or consumption. Rather than continuing on into the creation in a nurturant capacity, the dismembered bovines are converted at the sacrifice into other plants, animals, and varied resources. The only mention of milk in the creation tale at all is a reference to a processed by-product, "curdled butter." The Mediterranean variants, in turn, may be seen as intermediate between these extremes. The "bovines" are neither prolific cows nor powerful bulls but she-wolf and goat; their role is clearly nutritive, but the milk is consumed conspicuously by infants.

These differences suggest an early evolutionary divergence in the mythology of the Proto-Indo-Europeans, giving rise to two distinct ancestral stocks. One became Indo-European mythology, founded upon a creation myth that featured female bovines in a nurturant role and a sacrificial battle between gods and giants. The other became Indo-Iranian mythology, founded upon a creation myth in which both a man-giant and a male bovine are offered together as the first sacrifice. Lincoln noted these differences, and proposed that they "may be easier to understand when we recall that the Europeans were an agricultural society for whom the chief value of cattle was the milk-giving ability of the cow. The pastoral Indo-Iranians, however, esteemed their animals in a much broader sense and described their productive value in the mythical image of the primordial ox from whose body numerous goods stream forth." (1981: 87; see also 1986: ch. 3.) Further diversification resulted in appropriate refinements. In the case of the Mediterranean tradition, the refinements were appropriate to dairying populations that had not evolved (and would not evolve) high levels of adult lactose absorption. But more importantly, the northernmost refinements were appropriate, I submit, to an environment of chronic vitamin D deficiency.

From the perspective of evolutionary anthropology, these findings have two important implications. First, they imply that some force or forces of nonrandom selectivity guided the cultural evolution of Indo-European mythology. We can infer both that there were sources of variation in the content of myths and, more importantly, that the variants were subject to some systematic process of differential transmission within regional populations. Let us agree with Larson (1974a: 1) that "myth articulates the basic self-understanding of a people and thereby operates as a kind of charter for the total cultural life." It is therefore likely that different forms had, in conjunction with other beliefs and values related to dairying, different consequences for people, depending upon their social and ecological setting. Those consequences would have provided various kinds of positive or negative feedback, such as better or worse food supply and better or worse health and survival.

In terms of the arguments of Chapter 4, my hypothesis would be that this feedback was the leading cause of differential transmission among the variants. Such a result could have occurred in a number of ways: through the actual differential reproduction of myth carriers, that is, through the "natural selection of cultural variation" (after Boyd and Richerson 1985); through primary value selection, that is, through choice or imposition governed by a primary value assessment of consequences; through secondary value selection, that is, choice or imposition governed by a cultural evaluation of consequences; or through some combination of these forces. As proposed in the last chapter, my hypothesis would be that secondary value selection has been the most important of these forces, and that the variants favored by it are those that best enhance the survival and reproduction of the selectors. In other words, I hypothesize that the patterned variation in Indo-European mythology constitutes evidence for enhancement, one of the comparative modes of gene-culture relations (discussed further in Chapter 6). By this line of reasoning, the differences between Indo-European variants would not be accidental, neutral, or opposed to the inclusive fitnesses of their carrier-selectors. Instead they would be a product of the cultural selection of variants that had adaptive significance for those who perpetuated them. Although time and space preclude a full test of these suggestions, at least the data are consistent with my hypothesis.

For our purposes in this chapter, however, it does not matter just how the "myth of the first sacrifice" evolved or even if it is an example of enhancement or not. What matters is the second implication of the findings described above, namely, that for generations of Indo-European history there existed a latitudinal pattern of variation in cultural beliefs and values about milk. The traditional values coded in these ancient texts are of precisely the kind that would be required if culture mediated the genetic evolution of LA.

But while key features of the myths do seem to vary in the right direction, the data points are few in this analysis, the scale is crude in terms of latitude, and these are, after all, memes rather than behavior. What evidence is there that these memes and others have actually influenced human behavior in appropriate ways? Is it really true that dairying populations at low latitudes habitually process most of their fresh milk into low-lactose forms? And do their high-latitude counterparts actually have traditions of high per capita consumption of fresh milk? One way to answer these questions is to look again at recent patterns of dairy production and milk use in the sample populations of Table 5.1. Although these data obviously do not stand for all time, they can at least tell us whether recent trends are consistent or not with the hypothesis.

Patterns in Contemporary Milk Use

In order to provide a more direct quantitative test of the mediation hypothesis, I therefore undertook a statistical analysis of contemporary milk-use patterns using the 1978 FAO data of Table 5.1. The analysis is based on two assumptions. First, I assume that variations in milk-use behavior (that is, in actual patterns of milk consumption and processing) reflect underlying cultural differences in the values and beliefs that people attach to milk. Essentially, I assume that we can, in this instance, "measure backwards" from behavior (customary milk use) to culture (the socially transmitted memes regulating consumption). A population that actually consumes a high proportion of its total milk production as fresh milk is assumed to "place value on" fresh milk or to "have a preference for" dairy production in that form. I assume that such values and preferences are transmitted socially, although, as I shall explain, this does not rule out some influence from the genetic composition of the population.

My second assumption is that the general trends revealed by this study of 1978 data are not entirely of recent origin. Certainly the *magnitude* of the cultural indicators of Table 5.1—per capita rates of milk consumption, for example—will be subject to annual vagaries of climate, trade relations, price subsidies, and a whole host of factors extrinsic to cultural rules and preferences about milk use per se. Moreover, each of these indicators has its own growth curve subject to what may be very idiosyncratic dynamics in population growth, economic development, standard of living change, and many other factors. Still, I believe that if we focus not on the absolute values of the statistics but on comparative trends, the differences we observe will be more than spurious or ephemeral.[29]

Given these assumptions, it is possible, by using three partially independent measures available from the FAO data, to test for latitudinal variation in cultural preferences regarding milk use. To substantiate the mediation hypothesis, we should expect three findings. (1) The number of dairy cows per thousand people should increase sharply with latitude above 30 degrees north or south.[30] (2) The consumption of fresh milk per person should also increase sharply with latitude, particularly above 30 degrees north or south where UV-B radiation diminishes rapidly and where LA frequencies begin their rapid latitudinal ascent. (3) Cheese production should be increasingly de-emphasized with latitude. Concerning this last prediction one may reasonably expect a high net conversion of milk to cheese in low-latitude areas where both LA frequencies are low and warm climates make the storage properties of cheese an advantage.

[29] Insofar as possible, I have checked this assumption against earlier data. I repeated the analysis on 1970 and 1980 FAO data and, where possible, I examined time-series trends in milk use (see, for example, Drummond and Wilbraham 1956: 430) on United Kingdom food supplies from 1880 to 1954. I found the overall patterns to be reasonably consistent.

[30] Since raising cows for meat is not as efficient as raising steers, this statistic may be taken as a measure of the subsistence emphasis given dairying in the sample populations. Ideally, one would include the sheep, goats, and buffalo that are also important milk producers in some areas, but the FAO statistics do not distinguish the females from the males of these species.

But one would also expect high conversion rates at high latitudes if fresh milk consumption were not a preference in those regions. The existence of a milk-processing gradient with latitude (from high conversion to low) would thus constitute good evidence for an inverse gradient in the preference for fresh milk.

The FAO data collected in this study confirm all three of these hypotheses. As shown in Fig. 5.12, the number of cows per thousand people increases sharply beginning at about 25 degrees north or south latitude. The central tendency rises from an average baseline of some 20–30 cows per 1,000 inhabitants in populations near the equator to as much as seven times that number in European populations, the highest point corresponding to population 36, Danes. The figure also shows considerable unexplained variance in the dependent variable (the correlation coefficient is 0.59 with latitude and −0.64 with UV-B, both of $p < .01$). However, a substantial portion of the residual variance arises from just three exceptions to the general trend, with more than 80 cows per 1,000 people despite latitudes under 15 degrees. But each of these populations (number 10, Kenyans; number 14, Ganda and other Bantu of Uganda; and number 35,

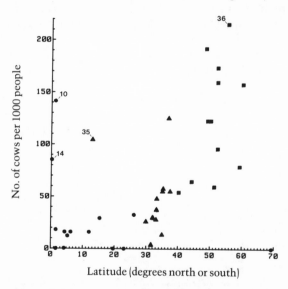

Latitude (degrees north or south)

(N = 42 out of 47 "nonmixed" populations)

Fig. 5.12. Subsistence emphasis on dairying in subsample populations as a function of latitude. The total number of dairy cows per thousand inhabitants is used as a measure of the importance of dairying in each of the populations of Table 5.1. Aside from the three notable exceptions below 15 degrees latitude—all populations that include dedicated pastoralists—the general trend is the familiar steep increase above 25 degrees north or south latitude. These data suggest a gradient in the cultural evaluation of dairying, a gradient that surely reflects both the relative ease and productivity of dairying at high latitudes and the special nutritional value of milk in environments with low levels of UV-B radiation. Data on cows from United Nations, FAO 1979a; on population from UNESCO 1982 (see App. A.5.1).

Ethiopians and Eritreans) includes a sizable number of milk-dependent pastoralists who are *expected* to lie above the central tendency. Much of the remaining variability in Fig. 5.12 can be attributed to land area, soil conditions, profit margins, and the like—that is, to factors outside the scope of this analysis. Still, the figure makes clear that the importance of dairying to diet increases generally with latitude, just as we would expect from the cultural mediation hypothesis.

Similar confirmation is found in the data on the second cultural indicator, total per capita consumption of milk. As shown in Fig. 5.13, fresh milk consumption increases from a baseline of almost 0 liters per person per year at low latitude to as high as the Danish figure of 1,033 (which includes milk converted to butter). Importantly, the increase begins at about 25 degrees of latitude, resulting in an overall correlation coefficient of 0.72 with latitude and of −0.77 with UV-B. There can be little doubt but that, as expected, milk consumption patterns covary with latitude.

Finally, Fig. 5.14 confirms that the pattern of milk consumption in the subsample reflects actual preferences for fresh milk over processed forms at higher latitude. With few exceptions, milk processed into cheese decreases from highs of 30 to 60 percent in North Africa and southern Europe to lows on the order of 10 to 20 percent in central and northern Eu-

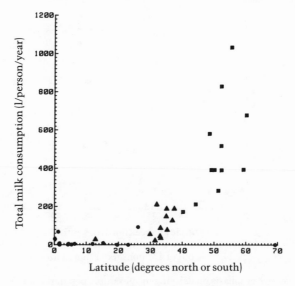

(N = 42 out of 47 "nonmixed" populations)

Fig. 5.13. Total milk consumption as a function of latitude among subsample populations (not including the populations of Category D, milk-dependent pastoralists, for whom comparable dairying statistics are not available). The number of liters of fresh milk (from cows, goats, sheep, and/or buffalo) consumed per person per year increases in another steep latitudinal gradient above 25 degrees north or south. This trend closely resembles the latitudinal gradient in LA frequencies (Fig. 5.11), suggesting coevolution between the genes for persistent lactase activity and the memes promoting adult milk consumption. Data from Table 5.1.

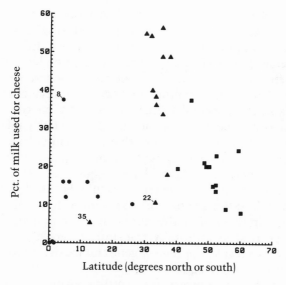

Latitude (degrees north or south)

(N = 38 out of 47 "nonmixed" populations)

Fig. 5.14. The conversion of milk to cheese in subsample populations as a function of latitude. This graph plots the percentage of all milk (from cows, goats, sheep, and buffalo) that is converted to cheese of one form or another by the populations of Table 5.1. Because high-latitude populations clearly have the option of processing more of their milk to cheese, these data suggest the cultural preferences for fresh milk increase directly with latitude above 30 degrees north. The only exceptions among the dairying populations of North Africa, the Mediterranean, and Northern Europe (represented by solid triangles and squares) are the two populations at low levels of milk conversion: population 35, Ethiopians and Eritreans, at 13 degrees north latitude; and population 22, North African Sephardim, at 33.4 degrees north latitude. Low levels of milk conversion are also found among most nondairying populations (the exception being population 8, Bantu of Zaire) and their recently dairying counterparts, all shown by solid circles; this finding indicates that the production of cheese is not a universal response to milk-storage problems at low latitudes. Data from Table 5.1.

rope. The correlation coefficient, calculated for categories E and F of Table 5.1, is −0.59 ($p < .01$). We may therefore conclude that fresh milk consumption is the preferred form of milk use in northern Europe, just as required by the cultural mediation hypothesis. In addition, the populations of categories B and C (the nondairying populations) are characterized by low levels of milk conversion despite their low-latitude locations. This finding suggests that cheese making for storage is not automatically the preferred treatment of milk in all warmer regions. I submit, therefore, that the cheese-making propensity of Mediterranean populations reflects its "nonaccidental appropriateness" for peoples who have long-standing cultural traditions of dairying, and who derive no special benefit from the calcium-absorbing action of lactose. If anything, fresh milk consumption has *dis*advantages at this latitude.

In summary, we may reasonably conclude that a latitudinal gradient does exist in the cultural evaluation of fresh milk for human consumption. This evidence from contemporary behavioral trends points in the same general direction as does the previous analysis of milk-and-bovine symbolism in ancient myths. Both investigations of cultural diversity indicate that memes promoting fresh milk consumption by adults persist at high cultural fitness in precisely the same regions where vitamin D deficiency has long been a chronic problem. Because the evidence used in the two studies is so fundamentally different, as are their time frames and methods of analysis, I believe this conclusion to be fairly robust.

There is therefore reason to believe that pertinent cultural differences have existed in the subsample region for many years, long enough in fact to mediate the genetic evolution of LA frequencies. At low latitudes, fresh milk consumption has offered no particular benefit to human beings after weaning; indeed it may often have caused the harmful effects of lactose intolerance. In this region, the "problem" of adult malabsorption has been largely resolved by culturally transmitted procedures for external processing and, as a result, the gene or genes for persistent lactase activity have not evolved to high frequency.

At high latitudes, in contrast, fresh milk consumption has had substantial benefits. Chief among them, I propose, have been the health benefits of enhanced calcium absorption, particularly since milk contains both generous concentrations of calcium salts and the lactose with which to absorb them. These benefits would then have had two principal results in the north.

First, the health effects of milk consumption would have reinforced the idea of milk as a healthy and nutritious food for consumption after weaning. As we have seen, this idea appears with prominence in the age-old creation myths of northern Europe that directly link milk consumption to physical size, strength, and stamina. Moreover, in some areas, milk came to be regarded as a cure-all or "tonic" for ill-health or during convalescence. In England, for example, a common folk belief dating back to at least the Middle Ages held that donkey's milk was especially good for children and invalids (see Drummond and Wilbraham 1958: 124)—a milk second only to human milk in lactose content.[31] Of course, not all of the milk in northern diets was imbibed directly, fresh and whole. It was also an important ingredient of other foods, particularly porridge. In addition, whey (the lactose-rich by-product of cheese manufacture) was widely consumed as a staple drink of northern peasants (Slicher Van Bath

[31] A similar belief existed in sixteenth-century France, where donkey milk was "quite the fashion. . . . Apparently it was valued for medicinal purposes because King Francois I took it for his health." (Chasan 1983: 73.) But I would disagree with Chasan when he adds, "It is unclear what Francois I thought he was getting from asses' milk since its only distinguishing feature seems to be remarkably low (1.4 percent) fat content." A significant distinguishing feature is its unusually high lactose content; in fact, lactose and fat content are inversely correlated for mammals in general (see, for example, Palmiter 1969). There is also evidence from other areas, such as China, that peoples who do not regularly drink fresh milk "nevertheless recognize its value for giving strength and good health to specified individuals." (Simoons 1970b: 553.)

1963: 288). Consequently, the diet was rich in lactose, and there is little doubt but that this helped substantially to reduce rickets. I submit that milk, whey, and whey cheese (including the notoriously sweet Gjetöst of Norway and Mysöst of Sweden, made respectively from goat's-milk and cow's-milk whey) deserve to be added to the list of such antirachitic folk practices in northern Europe as Icelandic "halibut-oil cocktails" (Stefansson 1960: 37) and the more general custom of fish on Friday (Loomis 1970: 91).

Second, the health benefits of milk use at high latitudes would have played a direct role in the natural selection of LA genotypes. The maintenance of herded bovines bred for dairy production together with an explicit ideology of adult milk consumption would have contributed to a sizable reproductive advantage for lactose absorbers. The analysis of cultural diversity in the subsample thus unravels the enigma of Fig. 5.4 as to why dairying populations have differentiated genetically in the first place. One way or another, the positive health effects of lactose at high latitudes appear to have reinforced a different pattern of milk use in that region, and this pattern, in turn, has acted jointly with vitamin D deficiency to create the selection pressure for LA. In time, LA gene frequencies were increased in proportion to latitude as a consequence of cultural mediation.

The Influence of Culture on Genetic Evolution

This analysis of the genetic diversity of adult lactose absorption in human populations has led to two major conclusions. First, using data obtained from samples of human populations in Europe, Greenland, western Asia, and Africa, we have seen that the prevalence of adult lactose absorption covaries with latitude in a pattern just opposite to that of incident UV-B radiation. This finding, together with other evidence concerning the physiology of mineral metabolism, supports the hypothesis that the genes responsible for adult lactose absorption have evolved to high frequencies in populations that (1) have a long-standing tradition of dairying and fresh milk consumption; and (2) live in environments of low ultraviolet radiation where vitamin D and metabolic calcium are chronically deficient.

Populations lacking Condition 1, but meeting Condition 2, exhibit low levels of adult lactose absorption. Groups of this nature include Eskimo and Lapp populations, who live above or near the Arctic Circle, but whose diet, rich in vitamin D, largely circumvents the problems of rickets and osteomalacia. In like manner, populations lacking Condition 2 but meeting Condition 1 exhibit low frequencies of adult lactose absorption. This category includes a number of populations who inhabit the Mediterranean climates of southern Europe and who circumvent the difficulties of lactose absorption by the use of external milk-treatment processes. The milk-dependent pastoralists among the sample populations constitute an exception to this general rule. These peoples show high prevalences of adult lactose absorption regardless of their homeland latitude—a result consistent with the culture historical hypothesis. In these populations, LA genotypes may well have been favored by genetic selection for their general nutritional advantage during times of food stress. Alternatively, they may have been favored because of the advantage to tapping an additional source of water and electrolytes in hot, arid environments (see note 27). Either way, by far the greater share of variance in the LA prevalences examined here is explained instead by the calcium-absorption hypothesis.

This conclusion points directly to the role of culture in the evolution of adult lactose absorption. The evidence of this chapter indicates that culture mediated in the historical evolution of LA genes by defining the nature and magnitude of existing selection pressures. Wherever a cultural history of dairying was lacking, or wherever a cultural preference existed for processed milk, we find today low levels of adult lactose absorption. It must be emphasized, therefore, that the genetic variability of human populations in this case is culture-dependent. We find high prevalences of LA today only in populations with (1) comparatively high rates of per capita fresh milk consumption at present; and (2) a traditional mythology, dating back centuries, that both records and encourages adult fresh milk consumption. The importance of the selective effect of culture is further emphasized by the fact that it is only in humans, of all mammalian species (including even the domestic cat; see Hore and Messer 1968), that we find some populations maintaining into adulthood what is otherwise a physiological capability of infants alone.

The second major conclusion of this analysis is that cultural aspects of dairying and milk use also vary with latitude in a way that helps to compensate for the trend in UV radiation. Our analysis of Indo-European mythology indicated that an ancient prototypical myth of first sacrifice underwent evolutionary transformations in a latitudinal pattern. In the north, a symbolism of heavy emphasis on cows, milk, and nurturance replaced the earlier and more southerly themes of male bovines, slaughter, and sacrifice. In addition, the study of FAO statistics shows that annual per capita milk consumption increases with latitude, whereas the proportional manufacture of cheese, a product with little or no lactose, displays the reverse trend. The implication is that cultural beliefs actively encourage fresh milk consumption at high latitudes, and have for quite some time.

I have also suggested that the cultural emphasis on milk drinking in northern areas is an example of enhancement, that is, of a relationship between genes and culture in which cultural selection, guided by traditional values, is functionally complementary to natural selection operating on genes. This inference is based on several considerations. First, it is reasonable to infer that primary value selection, as defined in Chapter 4, originally had little or no positive effect in promoting the idea of milk drinking. Instead, there are grounds for assuming that the senses fueled an *aversion* to milk drinking by adults as dairying spread from early sites in southeastern Eurasia. Simoons (1979a, 1981a), for example, argues that such an aversion blocked the spread of dairying to much of China and East Asia (see also Farb and Armelagos 1980: 186 ff.; for generalizations to the greater "psychobiology" of food selection see Barker 1982). In order for milk-drinking memes to have reached high cultural fitness in northern Europe, some perceived and valued consequence must have overcome any earlier beliefs *against* milk consumption that persisted by virtue of primary value selection. Of course, any such selection against milk drinking would have declined as genes for LA increased in frequency. However, this genetic change would only have *allowed* milk drinking to achieve higher cultural fitness. There is nothing about adult lactase production that would *compel* high replicative success among milk-consumption memes.

Second, the available evidence suggests instead that a key force behind the persistent transmission of these memes has been the positive evaluation of their own healthful consequences in UV-B deficient environments. To be sure, other forces may have played some role. Perhaps one such force was the natural selection of variants through the differential reproduction of their carriers. Another may have been the "indirect bias" of imitating the milk-drinking ways of mythical heroes or influential leaders who were respected (and thus culturally valued) for some other reason. Nevertheless, there is evidence that milk drinking did have beneficial health effects at high latitudes; that these effects were positively evaluated by local populations; and that this evaluation contributed in important ways to the stability and persistence of the underlying memes. Perhaps the most telling data in this regard come from the comparative analysis of creation myths; the latitudinal variation summarized in Table 5.3 is otherwise difficult to explain. In short, I propose that the most important cultural evolutionary mechanism was secondary value selection.

Third, this hypothesis does not require conscious understanding or "rational preselection" (as in Boehm 1978) for milk drinking, although that, too, may have played some role. Instead, it simply requires that, early on, milk-drinking memes had consequences that were valued positively according to the cultural values in effect (including, for example, the value given to healthy, tall, or strong children), and that this feedback had a conscious or unconscious reinforcing effect upon the transmission of the memes. Such evidence as we have suggests that the feedback was often *un*conscious. For example, recent reviews of the history of rickets and rickets therapy (Loomis 1970; Ihde 1975) imply that the antirachitic effects of fresh milk were not widely recognized, although they were recognized in the case of cod-liver oil, a much more concentrated source of calcium-absorbing agent. Instead, milk drinking was valued and reinforced in much vaguer terms, evidenced, as we have seen, by folklore linking milk consumption to a very general notion of good health. In some areas, the cultural evaluation of milk may have come close to a conscious recognition of benefits, as where myths speak of culture heroes and giants raised on milk. But more generally, milk drinking probably had a strong but unrecognized effect and merely came to be accepted as a natural part of life: when people drank it, they thrived.

Fourth, in this instance of enhancement, there is a strong inference concerning the inclusive fitness value of the memes behind milk drinking at high latitudes. The concomitant evolution of adult lactose absorption provides convincing evidence that the cultural changes associated with dairying directly enhanced human survival and reproduction in these areas. In the past, we may conclude, the memes associated with dairying and milk use made a positive contribution to the reproductive fitnesses of their bearers—a contribution parallel to that of their genetically selected counterparts, the LA genotypes, and interdependent with it. Considering the evidence for both their functionality, then, and their history of preservation by cultural selection, we may conclude that the memes supporting milk drinking in high-latitude populations represented a true cultural adaptation.[32]

The Coevolution of Dairying and Adult Lactose Absorption

On these grounds, I submit that the memes of dairying and the genes of adult lactose absorption *coevolved* as a function of latitude, and that they did so through two simultaneous forms of gene-culture relationships. On the one hand, we have found evidence for cultural mediation, an interactive mode of relationship and a form of what I have called (in Chapter 4) coevolution "in the narrow sense." We have seen how a cultural difference in meme frequencies—in this case, a difference arranged latitudinally—can cause a difference in the selection coefficients acting on a set of genotypes. The lactose case is thus an example of what Frank Livingstone (1980) has called "cultural causes of genetic change." Although this mode of relationship has, of course, been recognized for years and credited with an important role in human evolution (see, for example, Montagu 1962; Garn 1964), I believe it is fair to say that we have here a particularly clear example.[33]

---

[32] This conclusion does not, of course, mean that the milk-consumption values and beliefs of these peoples necessarily remain adaptive today; indeed, there is some evidence for overconsumption and maladaptation in recent years. Lest such evidence be taken incorrectly as a counter to the arguments in this chapter, let me emphasize that (1) this analysis has a retrospective time-frame (i.e., the pertinent memes were those at high frequency during the generations of genetic evolution of LA); and that (2) cultural selection can, under certain circumstances explored in Chapter 7, cause the retention of maladaptive memes and thus create opposition.

[33] In Chapter 7 of his 1985 book, *Good to Eat*, the anthropologist Marvin Harris provides a condensed and popularized review of many of the arguments of this chapter, drawing on and citing an early draft of my manuscript. Although Harris's discussion is generally suppor-

On the other hand, there is also some evidence here for enhancement, which is one of the comparative modes of relationship and an integral part of coevolution "in the broad sense." I have already suggested that cultural values governed the differential transmission of memes related to milk use, and did so in a way that conferred the highest rates of social transmission, F_c, on the memes of greatest inclusive fitness benefit for their selectors. Although cultural mediation has deliberately been the focus of this analysis, we have also considered some evidence for the preservation by preference of milk-drinking memes, and have found both historical and contemporary cultural variation to be consistent with this mechanism and with the comparative mode of enhancement.

Given, then, these two modes of relationship, one governing genetic change and the other governing cultural change, the question naturally arises, How were they interrelated in space and time? Let me conclude this chapter with the further suggestion that coevolution here resembled the evolution of the proverbial chicken and egg: as genes for LA were favored at high latitudes, more people could drink milk after weaning, thereby spreading the benefits of milk production and improving the local cultural evaluation of the memes behind the practice. The increased availability of milk, in turn, would have continued the genetic selection of LA genotypes, thereby augmenting the frequency of adult lactose absorption, the benefits of milking, the cultural preference for milk, and so on in perpetuity.

Although the connection is difficult to prove, logic suggests that the cycle may have started as a continuation of routine infant feeding practices. Early on, the milk of dairy animals may have been tried as a supplement to mothers' milk, increasing the volume of lactation, its duration, or both. By virtue of the (initially rare) LA genotypes, some recipients would have maintained lactase sufficiency beyond its normal lapse, continuing to drink milk and thereby avoiding rickets in their early years. On

---

tive and complimentary, let me correct two mistakes in his review that I might have prevented had I known of his interest in this work. First, Harris's comment that lactose molecules are "too complex" to be absorbed in the small intestine (1985: 133) is a mistake, similar to my own mistake in earlier drafts that the molecules are "too large." As an anonymous reviewer of this manuscript pointed out to me, the problem instead resides in: (1) the polar properties of saccharides, whether complex or simple, large or small, which inhibit their free passage through the lipid bilayer of cell membranes (see note 3 in this chapter); and in (2) the specificity of receptor sites in the transport proteins that do offer a membrane shuttle service, but only for monosaccharides (see Moog 1981). Second, Harris's concluding discussion of coevolution (1985: 153) is also mistaken. He writes, "The 'coevolution' of lactophilia [i.e., fondness for fresh milk] with the genetic basis for lactase sufficiency is highly instructive . . . because it is so different from the evolution of most foodways. There is no evidence that similar genetic changes accompanied or facilitated the evolution of vegetarianism, the pork and beef taboos, [and so on]." The passage erroneously equates my use of the term "coevolution" with simultaneous interactive change in genes and culture. As I have been at some pains here to point out, this is only the "narrow-sense" meaning of the term. Had Harris obtained and read other chapters of this work, he might have learned that the comparative modes of coevolutionary change are even more useful to his analysis of what is good to eat.

the average, these recipients would have attained higher inclusive fitness than their malabsorbing counterparts. In particularly rachitogenic areas, the advantage to fresh milk consumption would have extended into adolescence and adulthood. Assuming that milk yields could be made to suffice, actual adult consumption would have had the further benefit of reduced osteomalacia. The sequence I suggest is, of course, speculative. But it is also matched by the pattern of milk production and use coded in ancient Western mythologies.

If I am correct in this proposal, then there would have been a ratchet-like interplay of genetic and cultural change within populations where LA prevalences were evolving. The pattern would resemble Wiesenfeld's suggestion (1967: 1137) of stepwise evolution between agriculture and sickle-cell gene frequencies in East and West Africa. Here, an incremental increase in the milk consumption of a population at high latitudes would be followed by an incremental increase in LA frequency, which would, in turn, promote another increment in milk consumption and so on.[34] If this stepwise dynamic had occurred throughout the subsample, limited at each location by the genetic selection pressures of its latitude, then we should find today a close pattern of covariation between per capita milk consumption and the frequency of LA.

As Figures 5.11 and 5.13 suggest, such a pattern does indeed characterize the subsample data. In a polynomial regression analysis on the data of Table 5.1, I found that a second-order equation accounts for 79.5 percent of the variance.[35] Although such a pattern is consistent with other hypotheses (the induction hypothesis, for instance, or the idea of genetic mediation by LA genes), these arguments have already been called into question on other grounds. The data may thus be said to support the hypothesized interrelationship of cultural mediation and enhancement.

It occurs to me, however, that the most convincing argument for the coevolution in the broad sense between dairying and adult lactose absorption may be the intrinsic symmetry of the analysis presented here. Although we began the chapter with a look at genetic diversity and moved from there to cultural diversity, the argument could readily have been made in the reverse direction. We could well have begun with an analysis of variation in the creation myths of Europe and the Middle East, or with a look at contemporary patterns of milk consumption and use. Motivated in either case by the desire to explain salient *cultural* differences, we

---

[34] The stepwise evolution of this example, however, would not entail the positive feedback effect hypothesized by Wiesenfeld in the evolution of sickle-cell hemoglobin. A rise in the prevalence of LA at high latitude would probably not intensify the selection pressure against LM in the same way that an increase in S frequency, in Wiesenfeld's argument, increases (by way of slash-and-burn cultivation) the selection coefficient against the AA genotype. (See p. 125, note 21.)

[35] The full regression equation is: estimated percent LA = $8.130 + 0.239C - 0.0002\,(C^2)$, where C = milk consumption.

would then have been led to prevalences of adult lactose absorption and on to the calcium-absorption hypothesis. Clearly, in this example at least, analyses of genetic diversity and cultural diversity cannot be conducted apart. Reversibility of explanation is the hallmark of interdependent feedback processes like those proposed here.

6 /   E N H A N C E M E N T : The Cultural

Evolution of Incest Taboos

In the last two chapters, we have looked at relationships between genes and culture in which each acts
as a kind of selecting environment of the other. We have considered both
genetic mediation, as suggested by cross-cultural similarities in the meanings of basic color terms, and cultural mediation, as suggested by the
covariation between dairying practices and prevalence of adult lactose absorption. In this chapter, I would like to turn from mediation to enhancement, the third proposed mode of gene-culture relationships and the first
of three modes we will examine that involve what I have called the self-
selective property of cultural evolution.

Enhancement: A Comparative Relationship

Consider an autonomous reference group in which conditions permit
selection by choice among a given set of allomemes.[1] By the arguments of
Chapter 4, the relative rates of social transmission of these allomemes
are expected to vary as a function of three main additive components:
(1) the "natural selection of cultural variation," that is, the preservation
of certain variants through the reproductive advantage of their carriers
(coupled with subsequent *social* transmission from parent to offspring);
(2) "primary value selection," the differential social transmission of allomemes according to their evaluation by primary, or developmental, values; and (3) "secondary value selection," the differential social transmission of variants governed by the cultural evaluation of their consequences.
I use the term "enhancement" to refer to the relationship between genes
and culture that exists whenever components (1) and (2) do not fully ac-

[1] Although this chapter includes some discussion of imposition, its focus is on enhancement resulting from choice. As described in Chapter 4, choice and imposition are conceptualized here as intergraded processes. Indeed, imposition may be viewed as setting socially
determined boundaries to the set of options available for choice.

count for the cultural fitness differentials among allomemes and yet the variants of highest F_c are nevertheless those that promote the highest inclusive fitness value, F_g, for their carriers. For there to be enhancement, cultural self-selection must contribute to the F_c differentials among allomemes, and must do so in a way that promotes human survival and/or reproduction, and therefore individual inclusive fitness.

The term "enhancement" is appropriate for this relationship because, as shown in Fig. 6.1, cultural selection here enhances not only the individual inclusive fitnesses of culture carriers but also the cultural fitness differentials among allomemes. Panel A shows a hypothetical inclusive fitness function for a range of alternative memes, numbered 0 to 4, that exist in a human population. In this example, the highest F_g accrues to individuals who act on the basis of allomeme 1. Panel B shows the cultural fitness function, F_c, for the same set of allomemes and its three additive components: the component arising from differential reproduction (DR), that from primary value selection (PV), and that from secondary value selection (SV). A comparison of the two graphs illustrates enhancement: allomeme 1 confers the greatest survival and reproduction advantages to its carriers and is, at the same time, the variant most favored by cultural selection. As the solid curve in panel B shows, the effect of cultural self-selection is to increase the cultural fitness advantage of allomeme 1 substantially over what it would be under differential reproduction and primary value selection alone. When, for a given allomeme or range of allomemes, the SV component is the largest of the three, the relationship qualifies as what I call "major" enhancement for that allomeme or range; otherwise, when the SV component is present but smaller than one or both of the other components, I call it "minor" enhancement.

Fig. 6.1 assumes that the three components behind the F_c curve are one hundred percent complementary in favoring the same allomeme of the set. Although such complementarity, as I have argued, has probably been very common in human history, exceptions can and do occur. In a given context, for example, primary value selection might play little or no role, or it might even favor different allomemes from those promoted by cultural self-selection.[2] But either way, so long as secondary values augment the cultural fitness advantages of F_g-enhancing allomemes, the relationship of genes and culture is appropriately considered enhancement.

Enhancement is thus a comparative mode of relationship, one whose rates and directions of change are governed by the self-selectivity of culture. It therefore has two additional noteworthy features. First, in enhance-

[2] One possible example of evolutionary tension between primary and secondary value selection was suggested in Chapter 5. In some northern European populations, memes promoting fresh milk consumption were historically favored during cultural evolution. This occurred despite initially high frequencies of the genes responsible for malabsorption and, presumably, for some aversion to milk. Unfortunately, aversion on the part of malabsorbers has not been carefully studied. At least one investigator, the psychologist Paul Rozin (1976: 60) suggests it is a learned response to gastrointestinal symptoms.

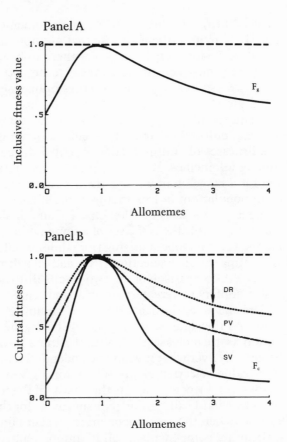

Fig. 6.1. A theoretical framework for enhancement through selection by choice. Panel A shows the inclusive fitness function, F_g, for an array of hypothetical allomemes arbitrarily numbered o to 4; as in earlier figures, o represents the "null allomeme," the absence of any form of the given meme. The F_g curve indicates that the average survival and reproduction of individual culture carriers is maximized through behavior guided by allomeme 1. Panel B shows the cultural fitness function, F_c (solid curve), for the same array of allomemes. Here, too, allomeme 1 has the highest value, indicating that it is expected to show the highest rate of social transmission within the population. But there are three additive components to the net F_c differentials as shown. The first component, represented by the dotted curve, summarizes the differences in social transmission expected from the actual differential reproduction of culture carriers (together with subsequent parent-offspring social transmission). The arrow labeled *DR* illustrates the contribution of this force to selection against allomeme 3; *DR* can be thought of as a "partial cultural selection coefficient" (or "partial coefficient" for short). The second component of F_c differences, represented by the next curve down, adds the influence of primary value selection. As before, the arrow labeled *PV* designates the partial coefficient against allomeme 3 from this source. The third component, caused by secondary value selection, increases the cultural fitness differentials to the values summarized by the solid F_c curve at bottom. Again, *SV* designates the contribution of secondary value selection to the total cultural selection coefficient working against allomeme 3. The resultant F_c curve illustrates enhancement: secondary value selection enhances the relative cultural fitness advantage of allomeme 1 and, in so doing, causes cultural evolution to favor the variant that most enhances the average inclusive fitnesses of its culture carriers.

ment (unlike genetic mediation) cultural phenomena themselves contribute to the cause of cultural change. More specifically, the course of cultural evolution depends here upon cultural values; a change in cultural values within a population, or a difference in cultural values between two populations, will cause a difference in the rates and/or directions of cultural change. Second, in enhancement, the influence of culture on human phenotypes will be to produce adaptations that appear as though they could equally have evolved by the natural selection of alternative genotypes. Through enhancement, in other words, cultural evolution can mimic the most influential of all processes in genetic microevolution. The implications of this argument are important and will be discussed more fully below.

With this theoretical framework in mind, let us now turn to a case analysis of incest taboos, one of the oldest and most widely debated of all topics in social science. It is my belief that valuable new insights can be gained on this topic with the theoretical perspective proposed here. Although the limitations of time and space prevent this from being an exhaustive test, data presented below support the preliminary conclusion that enhancement has played an important if not ubiquitous role in the cultural evolution of these particular memes.

The Nature of Incest Taboos

It will be helpful to start with a definition. Following Dorothy Willner (1983), I take the incest taboo of a population to be any rule or set of rules that prohibits sexual activity among kin (see also White 1948; Schneider 1976a; Rubin and Byerly 1983).[3] Three features of this definition deserve emphasis at the outset.

1. As the definition makes clear, "the defining feature of incest is the existence of prohibitions against it" (Willner 1983: 134). This means, among other things, that incest and inbreeding must be viewed as different (see Fig. 6.2); there can be both nonincestuous inbreeding (as when sexual intercourse between certain categories of kin is not prohibited) and noninbred incest (as when prohibitions apply between parents and their adopted or step children).

[3] Technically speaking, the rules prohibiting sex among kin may take many forms or intergradations of forms in a population. They may range from taboo proper, defined by Hoebel (1954: 260) as "a social injunction that is sanctioned by supernatural action" (see also Radcliffe-Brown 1965: ch. 7), to more formalized law that is sanctioned by society or by authorized persons acting in behalf of society. It is, however, conventional usage in anthropology to refer to all such rules as incest taboos. Formerly, it was common to speak of "*the* incest taboo" as if the same prohibition applied to all populations. Because the rules are now believed to be "neither unitary nor universal" (Willner 1983: 135), the plural form seems more appropriate.

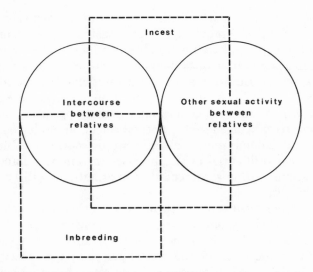

Fig. 6.2. Schematic diagram of the relationship between "incest" and "inbreeding." Incest refers to any form of sexual activity between relatives that is formally or informally prohibited within a given society. "Relatives" include persons related by consanguinity, marriage, adoption or fosterage, or by local conventions of so-called fictive kinship. Inbreeding refers to sexual intercourse between actual consanguineal relatives. By these definitions, sexual activity between relatives is not always incest; similarly, sexual intercourse between relatives is not always inbreeding.

2. The definition takes as incest *any* form of sexual activity that is prohibited between kin in a population, including "activities that cannot possibly result in offspring" (p. 136), because there is considerable variation between populations in this regard (Schneider 1976a). Ideally, one should treat the nature and range of forbidden activity in a population as part of the data to be explained.[4] The incest taboo is (or should be) what the natives say it is.

3. The definition implies that incest taboos can be at once *variable* and *comparable* between populations. As we will see, the rules also vary widely with respect to both the range of relatives who are prohibited from sexual activity, and the kinds and severities of sanctions that follow from violations. Nevertheless, as Willner points out, there is common meaning in the prohibition of sex among relatives, a common meaning that calls

[4] In actual practice, however, ethnographers have rarely been systematic in collecting data on the full *range* of forbidden activity. The taboo has largely been focused on the prohibition of sexual intercourse among kin or, indeed, on the prohibition of marriage per se. Sometimes this focus is also the native view; for example, Irving Goffman reports that, among the Cubeo of Amazonia, "one informant told me that it was not improper for brother and sister to indulge in external coitus. According to this man, it was intromission that constituted incest." (1963: 181.) But in the ethnographic record, one cannot always tell. Most authors therefore find it necessary to adopt a more restrictive definition of the incest taboo, such as Melvin Ember's "the prohibition of familial mating and its extension to first cousins," with mating defined as "sex and/or marriage." (1975: 255.)

for "some attempt at explanation that goes beyond the particularity of culturally specific constructions of reality." (p. 139.)

Memic Properties of Incest Taboos

Defined in this manner, incest taboos are but a special subset of the general category, "cultural rules," that we first encountered in the analysis of Tibetan marital diversity in Chapter 2. Accordingly, incest taboos exhibit all of the basic properties of memes; indeed, they may be viewed as prototypical examples of those units. Five points in particular need to be emphasized.

First, like all other aspects of culture, incest taboos exist as conceptual phenomena in the minds of human beings. They consist of information handed down through generations by social transmission, constituting part of a people's shared understandings or "ethos." This information is clearly intended to have a guiding influence upon human behavior but it is not, properly speaking, behavior itself. Accordingly, the taboos must not be confused with behaviors or behavioral tendencies and dispositions (for which the words "inbreeding," "outbreeding," and "inbreeding avoidance" are more appropriate).

Second, incest taboos are socially transmitted. They comprise an integral part of the "cultural heritages" of human populations and are passed along through the generations formally or informally, implicitly or explicitly, and with or without modifications.[5] Their preservation clearly depends upon the processes of social learning. Because they are rules, however, their conveyance involves more than "directly copying the phenotype" (as Boyd and Richerson 1985: 8, among others, would have it).

Third, incest taboos have an important symbolic dimension. The acts of incest defined by the rules often symbolize the transgression of proper social relationships and the very desecration of major cultural values. As summarized by David Schneider (1976a: 166), for example, incestuous acts are variously associated with cannibalism, with witchcraft or shamanism, with acting "as an animal," with "eating blood," and with other symbols of desecration "special to that particular system of symbols and meanings, the culture, that is, in which [they are] embedded." (For a noteworthy example, see the discussion of incest on Yap in App. A.6.3.)

Fourth, the restrictions on sex among kin are only a small, though basic, part of the larger system of rules governing kinship and social or-

---

[5] The social transmission of incest taboos, a subject taken for granted in much of the literature, is clearly in need of additional empirical research. Only occasionally does one read specific accounts of the transmission process, such as that described among the Lepchas of Sikkim (of the Tibetan language family) by Lindholm and Lindholm (1985: 158). There, "sex is forbidden with a partner related back at least seven generations on the father's side and at least four on the mother's. . . ." But because it is also considered incestuous "to sleep with [any] woman one's father has had sex with," transmission requires fathers to "instruct their young sons early as to their permitted and prohibited sexual partners."

ganization in human populations. As is often the case with cultural rules, incest taboos both contribute to the greater organization of social relations in a given population and, at the same time, are reinforced and legitimized by that system.[6] Some analysts go so far as to claim that "questions about the incest prohibition . . . cannot be separated from questions about the whole kinship system of which it is an integral part." (Schneider 1976a: 158.)

Fifth, incest taboos do have social histories, reflecting their own potential for cultural evolutionary change. On the one hand, incest taboos do not form spontaneously each generation, nor for that matter are they acquired through personal experience or trial and error. Instead, they derive from pre-existing memes and from ideational descent. On the other hand, their social histories need not be identical with that of the surrounding "full systems" in which they are nonetheless embedded. There are both theoretical reasons why incest taboos *may* show semi-independent variability in space and time, and considerable empirical evidence that they do.

On the theoretical side, to begin with, it should be noted that the taboos frequently apply to all or nearly all members of a population. As Eugene Hammel and his colleagues (1979) have emphasized, these restrictions may, by themselves, entail considerable social costs both to individuals (who may therefore have difficulty finding a mate) and to their social units (which may have lowered fertility and growth). In theory, at least, such costs may be perceived as a problem, even when the system as a whole provides no motivation for change. In addition, given that incest taboos apply specifically to sexual *acts* rather than to institutionalized *relationships* (marriage) between individuals, there would seem to be ample opportunity for evolutionary change in these rules even within relatively fixed structures of marriage and kinship. It is said that the British social anthropologist Maurice Freedman (cited in Fox 1980: 9) was fond of emphasizing this point, asking why people could not have "a sexual free-for-all within the family and still marry out of it."

Furthermore, there is also empirical evidence that incest taboos can be "singled out" from cultural systems and changed semi-independently. For example, it is reported that the incest taboo of the San Blas Kuna of Panama has changed considerably in the recent past, most likely in response to their migration and settlement (since 1850) on small Caribbean islands, even though other features of Kuna culture have been unaffected or less affected (see Nordenskiold 1938: 34; for other examples, see Pospisil

---

[6] To take one example, many cultures feature a logical and mutually supportive relationship between the rules restricting *sex* between relatives in a population (incest taboos) and the rules restricting *marriage* between relatives (what are called rules of exogamy, or "marriage out"). Indeed they are often so closely "embedded" that there has been "a consistent, almost overwhelming confusion between sexual intercourse and marriage" in the anthropological literature (Schneider 1976a: 152; see also Fox 1983: ch. 2; van den Berghe 1980, 1983).

1958: 165–66, 282–83; Schwerin 1980; Goody 1983; Hutchinson 1985). Similarly, there is evidence for evolutionary change and diversification in the incest taboos of closely related populations in the Caroline Islands (Smith and Kennedy 1960) and Marshall Islands (Kiste and Rynkiewich 1976) of Micronesia. To take an example closer to home, there is also some movement today to relax or repeal altogether the specific incest prohibitions of Sweden and the United States (see Y. Cohen 1978; De Mott 1980).

In all five respects, then, incest taboos are similar to the other memes of cultural systems. There are, however, a number of special properties that give incest taboos unusual significance in the study of cultural diversity. Several of these properties were succinctly described by the anthropologist George Murdock in his 1949 publication, *Social Structure*. I will therefore draw upon Murdock's conclusions for this summary.[7]

Special Features of Incest Taboos

The first and most widely cited of Murdock's conclusions posited the universality of incest prohibitions within the nuclear family. As Table 6.1 shows, data from his cross-cultural sample indicated that sexual activity (in this case, pre- and postmarital intercourse as well as marriage) was prohibited without exception between opposite-sex members of the nuclear family aside from husband and wife. The few exceptions were "in each instance too partial to appear in the table. . . . By their special circumstances or exceptional character these cases serve rather to emphasize than to disprove the universality of intrafamily incest taboos." (1949: 12–13.)

Recent investigations, however, point to more substantial exceptions in both number and kind, and seem to require that we back off to a claim of "near universality" (see, for example, R. May 1979; Willner 1983). One of the more detailed and carefully documented of these concerns brother-sister marriage among commoners in Egypt during the Roman period (about 30 B.C. to A.D. 324). Analysis of papyrus texts from the period, described by Jaroslav Cerny (1954) and Russell Middleton (1962), and a meticulous study of surviving census returns by Keith Hopkins (1980), establish beyond reasonable doubt that commoners "often practiced brother-sister marriage," including full and unabashed sexual relations (Middleton 1962: 606).[8] Nevertheless, current evidence indicates that

---

[7] Murdock's study compared the incest taboos of the 85 societies then represented in the files of the Cross-Cultural Survey of the Institute of Human Relations at Yale University, augmented by 165 societies of his own choosing to a total sample of 250 societies. From this comparison he came to a total of eight "factual conclusions" from which I have extracted those I consider most important. See Ember (1975) for additional discussion of the special features of incest taboos.

[8] Hopkins (1980) was the first to estimate the frequency of brother-sister marriage among commoners, finding in a total sample of 113 no fewer than 9 indisputable cases (8.0 percent). Hopkins, moreover, considers this to be a *conservative* estimate since the tally increases to

TABLE 6.1

Prohibition of Sex Between Members of the Nuclear Family
in Murdock's Sample of Human Populations

	Nature of sexual activity[a]					
	Premarital intercourse		Postmarital intercourse		Marriage	
Potential partners	Total cases	Percent prohibited	Total cases	Percent prohibited	Total cases	Percent prohibited
Brother-sister	109	100%	106	100%	237	100%
Mother-son	76	100	74	100	184	100
Father-daughter	—	—	81	100	198	100

SOURCE: Adapted from Murdock 1949: 12.
[a]Defined with respect to the male's marital status (hence the blanks for father-daughter premarital intercourse).

Murdock was guilty of only slight overstatement. For our purposes, what is especially noteworthy is that incest taboos of one form or another have achieved high cultural fitness in virtually every one of the natural and social environments inhabited by humanity. In my view, this remains the most important special feature of these memes.

A second special feature of incest taboos, also documented by Murdock (1949), is their great interpopulational variation in extent. On the one hand, Murdock noted, the prohibition of sex is rarely limited to nuclear family relationships, but applies to at least some more distant relatives. On the other hand, to whom it applies among those relatives is highly variable: "incest taboos do not apply universally to any relative of opposite sex outside of the nuclear family." (p. 285.) Ethnographic data on the subject tend to be scattered and fragmentary. But even so, said Murdock, they are conclusive: he could find "no relative outside of the nuclear family with whom intercourse or marriage is not allowed in at least one of our 250 societies."[9] (p. 285.)

---

23 (20.4 percent) when half sibs and ambiguous cases are included. In addition, his study of other surviving documents indicates that brother-sister marriages "were declared openly, not only in family matters but also in business" (p. 323), and that they were often characterized, like other matrimonies of the period, by love, caring, and affection. Other exceptions to Murdock's first conclusion have been summarized in recent reviews by van den Berghe (1980, 1983). According to him, some of the best known and most frequently cited exceptions involve brother-sister inbreeding in the royal lines of Hawaii, the Incas, and Egypt (see also van den Berghe and Mesher 1980). He adds, however, that "in only 8 societies is there any evidence of incest being tolerated among commoners." (van den Berghe 1983: 99.) It remains true that *most* exceptions involve privileged ranks or classes that exhibit Murdock's "special circumstances or exceptional character," and that few, if any, of them also condone sexual relations between father and daughter or mother and son.

[9]Murdock also argued that "incest taboos, in their application to persons outside of the nuclear family, fail strikingly to coincide with nearness of actual biological relationship. . . . Very commonly, in fact, incest taboos exempt certain close consanguineal kinsmen but apply to adoptive, affinal, or ceremonial relatives with whom no biological kinship can be traced." (1949: 286–87.) Much of Murdock's evidence for this conclusion came from rules governing actual marriage among kin (exogamy). The problem here, as discussed by van den

The third major feature of incest taboos to be noted here is their considerable variation in severity. Although there is some evidence for interpopulational variability in this regard, the most striking pattern is intrapopulational.[10] To begin with, compared to other sex-related prohibitions (menstrual taboos, for instance, or those against adultery or fornication), Murdock (p. 288) found the taboo against sex among nuclear family members to have a "peculiar intensity and emotional quality" in most populations, often taking the form of a "grisly horror" that was associated with a high frequency of the death penalty. At the same time, Murdock found that

incest taboos tend to apply with diminished intensity to kinsmen outside of the nuclear family, even though they are [often] designated by the same kinship terms as primary relatives. From the point of view of a male Ego, the prohibitions against sexual intercourse and marriage with an own mother, sister, and daughter are the strongest of all taboos. Other relatives may fall under an equally severe ban, but analysis of our data reveals no instance where a relative outside the nuclear family is more stringently tabooed than one within it. The reverse, however, is often the case . . . the taboos apply more strongly to own than to "classificatory" sisters, to half sisters than to cousins, to first than to second or remoter cousins, and so on. [p. 286]

This gradation, Murdock added, is certainly not uniform or parallel in all directions, such as patrilateral/matrilateral, among ego's relatives, but neither is it increasing or even constant as a function of kinship distance in *any* direction.

Murdock's final conclusion is also of importance in this regard: "Despite the strength of cultural barriers and their internalization in the con-

Berghe (1980, 1983), is that the rules prohibiting marriage are sometimes distinct from the rules prohibiting sex in lineage-based societies. Moreover, according to Irons (1981), the prohibition of marriage is motivated to some degree by distinct social forces. In addition, Alexander (1979a: 178–82) has pointed out that in societies permitting or prescribing sororal polygyny, cross cousins (children of siblings of different sex) and parallel cousins (children of siblings of the same sex) will often be genetically related to *different* degrees, so that asymmetric rules with regard to the marriage of first cousins are, in fact, correlated with matching asymmetries in genetic relatedness. Although one might be tempted to attribute this finding to parallel asymmetry in the genetic consequences of inbreeding among first cousins, P. Bateson (1983b: 502) has pointed out that in "a polygynous society, the parallel cousins will [also] be much more likely to grow up together than the cross cousins," and so be more likely to develop the type of sexual aversion discussed later in this chapter. Additional research is clearly called for. Nevertheless, when the taboo is defined specifically in reference to sexual activity, Murdock does still have a point: incest taboos do not show perfect correlation with genealogical distance. We shall return to this point later.

[10] Interpopulational variation in severity was not addressed by Murdock except indirectly, but it has been emphasized by van den Berghe, for instance, who points out that incest in many societies "is considered absurd, more the object of ridicule than opprobrium." (1983: 92; see also Fox 1980.) Related to this variation in emotional intensity is also considerable variation from society to society in the sanctions, if any, that enforce the incest prohibition. Murdock noted that in many societies there exists "an invariable death penalty for this breach of the mores," while in others "the act is considered simply unthinkable, and, if it occurs . . . its punishment [is] left exclusively to inexorable fate or divine vengeance." (p. 288.) Schneider (1976a) and Fox (1980) have also pointed to this aspect of variation in incest taboos, the latter calling some sanctions "lax" and others "fierce."

sciences of individuals, sporadic instances of incestuous intercourse are reported in most of our sample societies for which ethnographers have investigated the subject." (p. 289.) In other words, violations do occur in spite of the rules and their consequences, and they occur so often that it is not unusual for informants to know of plural instances, either proven or suspected, within their own lifetimes and local communities. Incest taboos are therefore not some highly abstract and imaginative creation of capricious minds, but are instead rules of importance to real—and surprisingly common—human behavior.

To summarize up to this point, then, Murdock's study raised three main questions about incest taboos: (1) What explains their impressively high cultural fitnesses? (2) Why do they vary so much in extent? and (3) Why do they vary so much in severity?[11] In the years since Murdock's work, evidence has accumulated for two more of his "factual conclusions" (1949: 289) that should be taken into account here: the genetically deleterious effects of inbreeding in human populations, and the evidence for aversion-based inbreeding avoidance in both humans and other animals. Let us review the factual evidence in some detail before turning to examine the leading theories of explanation.

The Genetic Consequences of Inbreeding

In the last several decades, thanks to progress in both genetic theory and empirical documentation, Western scientific knowledge of the genetic effects of inbreeding has advanced substantially. It is now recognized that inbreeding effects are governed by two key variables: the number of deleterious recessive alleles that have accumulated in a given gene pool, expressed as the average number of "lethal gene equivalents" per individual; and the actual degree of genetic relationship between two inbreeding individuals. Because it is an unusual human population that has not accumulated a substantial number of deleterious recessives, inbreeding generally does have detrimental effects in humans: as I will show below, the likelihood of congenital abnormality among inbred offspring grows sharply with the relatedness of their parents. Inbreeding therefore tends to reduce individual inclusive fitness.

The Theory of Inbreeding Depression

The central argument of inbreeding theory today is that the mating of close relatives tends to reverse the individual-level genetic benefits de-

[11] One could, of course, add to this list the question, "Why and in what circumstances are incest taboos so frequently violated?" The question is certainly pertinent, but is directed more at incest behavior than at incest prohibition. In the interest of time and space, I have chosen to focus here on questions concerning the cultural diversity of the prohibitions themselves. For an approach that focuses more on incest behavior, see Arens 1986.

rived from sexual reproduction.[12] Genetically speaking, inbreeding negates sex. It has the effect of approximating both parthenogenesis (reproduction without the conjunction of gametes) and self-fertilization
(reproduction with the conjunction of gametes from the same bisexual
parent): inbred progeny are predicted to be genetically more similar to
each parent—and to each other—than would otherwise be the case. Why
this is detrimental can best be seen in light of current arguments about
the two main selective advantages to sexual reproduction (see, for example, Maynard Smith 1984; Blute 1984; Bellig and Stevens 1988; Michod
and Levin 1988).

First, sex promotes genetic variation *within individual organisms*. Because sexual organisms generally have at least two copies of all autosomal
genes (the term for all their genes except the ones on the sex chromosomes), sex allows a beneficial allele inherited from one parent to "complement," or mask, a deleterious allele inherited from the other parent.
Maynard Smith (1978) argues that this may well have been the original
evolutionary advantage of diploidy ("two copies") and sexual reproduction (see also Darwin 1889 [1876]: 462). At the same time, sex also allows
for heterozygosity at any given autosomal locus, and so for the "heterozygote advantage" discussed in Chapter 3. In both of these ways, sexual
reproduction can engender a distinct reproductive fitness advantage.

Second, sex also promotes genetic variation *among related individuals*. In the words of the sociologist Marion Blute, "the consequence of sex
is to produce offspring which combine in a single individual the genes of
two parents. Such offspring are both genetically different from the parents
(creating diversity temporally in a descent line) and genetically different
from their siblings (creating diversity spatially within a sibship)." (1984:
193.) This variation arises both through the simple reshuffling of genes
between generations and through genetic recombination, which is the
physical exchange of chromosomal material during germ cell formation
that results in new combinations of alleles. According to current thinking, this interindividual variation translates into microevolutionary advantage under two conditions. First, there may be selective benefit to
genetic dissimilarity (and thus phenotypic variation) among related individuals who inhabit a spatially or temporally heterogeneous environment, as in the case of a population faced with genetically coevolving
competitors, predators, or pathogens (see Bell 1982; W. D. Hamilton 1982;
Tooby 1982). Second, there may also be a selective benefit to within-
family variation even in uniform environments, if and when it reduces

---

[12] Sexual reproduction also appears to have evolutionary benefits at the species level—
what Maynard Smith (1978, 1984) terms the "long-term advantages of sex"—namely, the
acceleration of evolution in sexual lines compared with asexual ones and the ability of sexual organisms to prevent the accumulation of deleterious mutations (see also Stanley 1979:
ch. 8). Because we are interested here in the intraspecific effects of inbreeding, this chapter
requires a microevolutionary focus.

Generations   **Hypothetical genealogy**

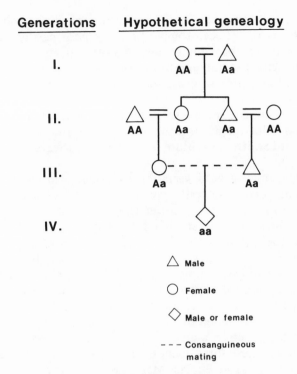

Fig. 6.3. The genetic consequences of inbreeding, as illustrated by the mating of first cousins. In a hypothetical case, **a** is a rare recessive allele that has deleterious phenotypic effects in its human carriers. It is present only in the heterozygous "great-grandfather" of generation I. However, with a probability of 1 in 4, it is possible for *both* of his progeny, the "grandparents" of generation II, to inherit the **a** allele in a masked, heterozygote state. It is then possible, again with 1 in 4 probability, for both of these individuals to pass along the identical **a** allele to their offspring, the first cousins shown in generation III. If these cousins then inbreed, the probability will again be 1 in 4 that any given child in generation IV will be homozygous and thus exhibit the deleterious phenotypic effects of the **a** allele. Thus, the total probability that any given offspring of generation IV will be homozygous for **a** (or for any other allele present in generation I) will be the product of these separate probabilities, or 1 in 64. In this way, inbreeding brings together rare recessives that are identical by descent from a common ancestor. It thus promotes "identical homozygosity."

competition between siblings. Either way, theory suggests, it is possible for sex to increase the reproductive fitnesses of individuals.

The fitness costs of inbreeding. Against this background, the genetic effects of inbreeding can readily be appreciated. The mating of relatives, by reducing both forms of genetic variation, robs sex of its microevolutionary functions and jeopardizes the reproductive fitnesses of its practitioners. The way this happens is illustrated in Fig. 6.3. In the figure, **a** is a rare recessive allele that, like the vast majority of new mutations (according to Fisher 1958 [1930], Crow and Kimura 1970, among others), has deleterious phenotypic effects in the homozygote state. Although present in only a single individual in generation I, **a** can be passed to both of his progeny in generation II, and again to both of his grandchildren in generation III, each time with a probability of 1 in 4. If these grandchildren (who are themselves related as first cousins) should inbreed, then there is again a 1 in 4 probability that the two rare and deleterious **a** alleles, identical by descent from the grandfather, can be brought together in a homozygous great-grandchild (generation IV). In this way, inbreeding promotes homozygosity: it allows any given allele, including a deleterious recessive allele as shown, to be inherited simultaneously through both the maternal and paternal sides of a genealogy.

Now were the two parents in generation III not related, they could still conceivably produce an **aa** homozygote, although chances of the simultaneous transmission of the **a** allele would be minute, since it is assumed to be rare in the population. Such an offspring would be called an "independent homozygote" because the **a**'s would have been passed along from independent (or essentially independent) origins in the two sides of the family. On the other hand, since in our hypothetical example the parents are related, a homozygote offspring is much more likely; indeed the chances are $1/4 \times 1/4 \times 1/4 = 1/64$ for *any one* of the four alleles present in the individuals of generation I, or 1 in 16 overall. Such an offspring can be called an "identical homozygote"; the **a** allele is identical by descent from a common ancestor. In this manner, inbreeding replaces the (relatively minute) probability of independent homozygosity by the (relatively great) probability of identical homozygosity.

Three further aspects of inbreeding's genetic consequences deserve emphasis. First, by negating the microevolutionary advantages of sex, identical homozygosity reduces an individual's Darwinian fitness. At one stroke, it reduces both the variation within each of an individual's offspring, preventing complementation and heterozygote advantage (a common problem, for instance, in the inbred royal houses of Europe), and the variation among an individual's offspring, causing disadvantage in heterogeneous or changing environments and more competition between siblings. Inbred offspring are therefore predicted to be less vigorous, less healthy, and less reproductively successful than their noninbred counterparts. Second, these genetic consequences have an even greater impact in terms of individual inclusive fitness (as defined in Chapter 1). The reason is simply that the inbreeders are, by definition, relatives with a considerable degree of genetic similarity. Consequently, an inbreeder's inclusive fitness loss includes not only the direct loss of personal reproductive success but also the indirect loss from detrimental effects on the reproduction of the related mate. In other words, the full cost of inbreeding entails the loss of individual Darwinian fitness plus the loss of additional genetic "offspring equivalents" that could accrue, in the absence of inbreeding, through ego's positive effects on the reproduction of the given relative.[13]

---

[13] In a sense, inbreeding not only negates sexual reproduction, it also negates reproductive nepotism (that is, behavior assisting the reproduction of close kin). Alexander (1979a:

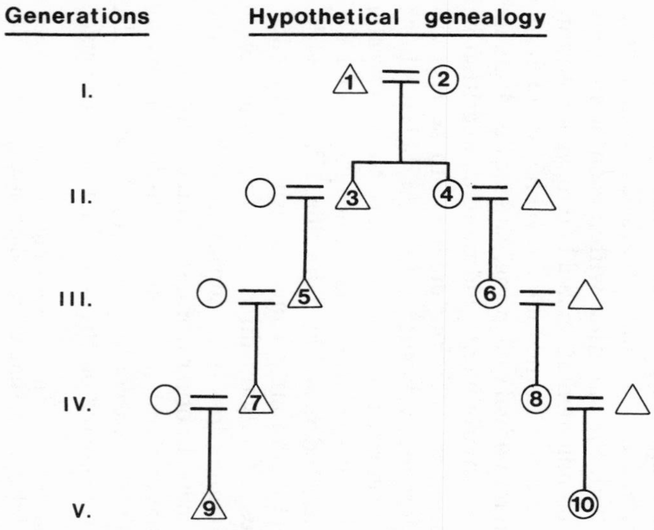

Generations	Hypothetical genealogy	Individuals	Potential mates	r	F
I.		1-2	Unrelated parents	0.000	0.000
II.		1-4, 2-3	Parent-offspring	0.500	0.250
		3-4	Siblings	0.500	0.250
III.		3-6, 4-5	Uncle-niece, aunt-nephew	0.250	0.125
		5-6	First cousins	0.125	0.062
IV.		5-8, 6-7	First cousins once removed	0.062	0.031
		7-8	Second cousins	0.031	0.016
V.		7-10, 8-9	Second cousins once removed	0.016	0.008
		9-10	Third cousins	0.008	0.004

Fig. 6.4. Values of the coefficient of relationship, *r*, and of Wright's inbreeding coefficient, *F*, as functions of genealogical relationship. As shown, *F* falls off quickly with the genealogical distance between relatives. These values of *F* assume no "global," or generalized, inbreeding in the population, in which case $F = (\frac{1}{2})r$. Adapted from Hartl 1983: 478, fig. 14.10. Copyright © 1983 by Harper & Row, Publishers, Inc. Reprinted by permission of the publisher.

Third, these effects of inbreeding are probabilistic, not deterministic, and their likelihood varies sharply with the degree of consanguinity between the parents. Back in the 1920's, Sewall Wright developed a way of estimating these probabilities, now called "Wright's inbreeding coefficient," symbolized by F (see Wright 1921b, 1922, 1969: ch. 7; also Shields 1982). Wright reasoned that the probability of homozygosity in an offspring at any given locus would vary as a function of the coefficient of relationship, r, between its two inbreeding parents.[14] More specifically, he came to two conclusions.

1. For children produced by a single generation of inbreeding, Wright showed that

$$F = \frac{r}{2}(1 + F_o) \qquad (6.1)$$

where F_o represents the level of "global," or generalized, inbreeding in the parental population (it is effectively 0.0 in large, noninbred populations). This index, F, also represents the average proportional increase in homozygosity at all loci in a given inbred individual compared with the homozygosity expected among the offspring of random mating.[15] Sample values of r and F (with $F_o = 0.0$) for a single generation of inbreeding are shown in Fig. 6.4.

2. Wright also showed that if inbreeding is a regular and repeated event, homozygosity rapidly accumulates in subsequent generations. In other words, if consanguineous relatives were to reproduce routinely in a human population, then F would continue to increase through time as shown in Fig. 6.5. The figure indicates that 50 percent of all heterozygosity would be lost within three generations for repeated full-sibling matings, within five generations for half-sibling matings, and within eight generations for double-first-cousin matings.

Calculating inbreeding depression. The impact of this homozygosity on an individual's reproductive fitness can be estimated in terms of "inbreeding depression," i, which is a measure of the actual reduction in the viability of inbred offspring. Moreover, because i includes only direct losses in Darwinian fitness, it provides a conservative, minimal estimate

---

195–96) suggests that inbreeding may be "the only social act" that is regularly "disadvantageous not only to one's own reproduction but to the reproduction of all one's closest relatives as well, and both things are true whether the [inbreeding] is committed by one's self or by one's close relatives."

[14] The coefficient r expresses the average proportion of all genes that are identical by descent in two relatives. For example, brothers and sisters having the same parents will have identical genes at an average of 50 percent of their loci, so that $r = 0.50$.

[15] There are a number of equivalent ways of defining the inbreeding coefficient. Thus "F may be considered to express the probability that two alleles at a locus are derived from a common ancestral allele. Alternatively, F may be viewed as measuring the proportionate decline of the average number of heterozygous loci in an individual, compared to the average number in its ancestors, or the average decline in population heterozygosity at all loci." (Lerner and Libby 1976: 370.)

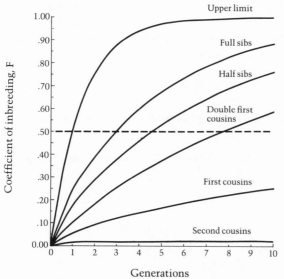

Fig. 6.5. Increases in Wright's inbreeding coefficient, *F*, through consecutive generations of consanguineous mating. Homozygosity continues to accumulate with repeated inbreeding, although the rate of increase tapers off with the passing of generations. Calculated from equations in Wright 1921a, 1921b, 1933.

of inbreeding's total effects on inclusive fitness. The biologist Robert May (1979) has proposed a particularly insightful technique for estimating *i* in terms of *F* and the expected fitness-reducing effects of identically homozygous genes. The latter, May noted, can be approximated by a measure called the "lethal gene equivalents," *n*, obtained "by adding up for all deleterious recessive genes, the average probability of their occurrence times the decrease in fitness they produce in the homozygous state; in this accounting one recessive lethal is equivalent to 10 recessives that each produce a 10 percent decrease in the fitness of a homozygote (for example, 1 in 10 such individuals dies)." (R. May 1979: 194.) This index will vary from population to population as a function of the number of accumulated deleterious recessives, sometimes called the "genetic load."

In populations with high values of *n*, the genetic effects of inbreeding will be particularly detrimental. Such values are expected in large and randomly mating populations where deleterious recessives can accumulate to relatively high equilibrium frequencies (though generally not as high as those we encountered in the special case of sickle-cell anemia). This is because random mating and large population size assure that any given rare recessive will normally occur in the heterozygous state, masked (where dominance is complete) by an alternative allele. In principle, then, the frequency of this recessive can increase until random mating results in enough independent homozygotes for there to be a stabilizing counterforce from genetic selection (Shields 1982: 55).

Although human populations rarely show truly random mating (in part *because of* incest taboos), the point remains that human *n* values are likely to be largest in relatively large, noninbred populations. For such populations, notes May (1979: 193–94), "a classic estimate of the average number of lethal equivalents per person [produced an] n in the range 3 to 5." In other words, individuals in such populations carry genes whose effect when expressed would be adequate to reduce their individual Darwinian fitness to zero three to five times over.

In contrast, notes Shields, values of n are expected to be lower in small, nonrandomly mating populations. In principle, the genetic load may even approach zero in populations characterized by continuous close inbreeding (see also Livingstone 1969b; Sanghvi 1975). There, "a deleterious mutant is not masked and dispersed throughout the breeding group, rather it is quickly reassorted into [homozygotes] . . . and immediately placed at selective risk. If inbreeding is intense enough, a recessive behaves in the same manner as a detrimental dominant. . . . The mutant's equilibrium frequency will be the lowest compatible with its recurrence rate [from mutation and/or migration] and its selective advantage." (Shields 1982: 55.) Not surprisingly, relatively low estimates of n have been obtained in small, isolated, and relatively inbred human populations. So, for example, the mean number of lethal equivalents among such endogamous South Brazilian Indian populations as the Caingang and Guaraní has been estimated as roughly 1.5 per individual (Salzano et al. 1962), and as "about two" among the isolated and highly inbred Kota of South India, whose total population is 1,200 (Ghosh and Majumder 1979: 206).

For purposes of presentation, and to make the case as generalizable as possible, it seems reasonable to use the conservative baseline figure of $n = 2.2$ (from Cavalli-Sforza and Bodmer 1971: 364–65). As May (1979: 194) points out, this figure is "heavily weighted with data from Japanese populations, and it may be low." It can therefore be used with some confidence.[16] If and when some fraction of these 2.2 gene equivalents are expressed in an inbred offspring, they will predictably reduce reproductive fitness. Using these two measures, F and n, and assuming that all genes included in n were independently inherited, May estimated the average depression of individual Darwinian fitness caused by one generation of inbreeding as follows:

$$i = 1 - \frac{1}{e^{nF}} \qquad (6.2)$$

Values of i as a function of genetic relationship are shown in Fig. 6.6 (a second curve for $n = 5.0$ is included for comparison). Here, it can be seen that a value of 2.2 lethal gene equivalents predicts a fitness reduction of 42 percent from nuclear family incest (corresponding to $r = 0.500$). In other words, as May (p. 194) noted, "about 42 percent of the offspring of sister-brother or parent-offspring matings die before reproductive age,

[16] Although incest taboos may themselves reduce inbreeding (and thus contribute to a high n), they are not alone in this role but are often joined by mechanisms and rules of dispersal (see, for example, Bischof 1975; Shields 1982; Read and Harvey 1988), and, as we shall see later in this chapter, by a neurophysiological aversion to sex that develops between cosocialized individuals. If anything, these "inbreeding barriers" probably predated the cultural emergence of incest taboos.

compared with the offspring of other similar but unrelated parents." The conclusions are inescapable: even one-time inbreeding can have a significant negative effect upon reproductive success; and generations of repeated inbreeding will sharply increase the average depression of fitness as a consequence of increases in F as shown in Fig. 6.5.

The latter conclusion is illustrated in Fig. 6.7 with, again, the conservative estimate of 2.2 lethal gene equivalents. This figure has two particularly important implications for understanding the genetic consequences of inbreeding. First, it shows that the additional mortality caused by inbreeding would surpass 50 percent beginning with (1) the second generation of full sibling (or parent-child) inbreeding, (2) the third generation of half-sibling inbreeding, and (3) the fifth generation of double-first-cousin inbreeding. On theoretical grounds alone, this information challenges an old but widely held misconception that, in the words of the anthropologist Yehudi Cohen (1978: 73), "genetic disadvantages are not frequent enough to justify a prohibition."

Second, the figure implies that the effects of repeated inbreeding would quickly surpass the severity of most other health problems in human populations. Compare, for example, the fitness differentials of Fig. 6.7 with the differentials we encountered in the earlier cases of sickle-cell anemia and adult lactose absorption. One generation of inbreeding at the level of first cousins ($r = 0.125$) or higher creates fitness differences already greater than those implied for calcium deficiency and adult lactose absorption (which are on the order of 2 to 4 percent), and certainly not less than those created by malaria (on the order of 8 to 15 percent), thought to be among the most deadly of all diseases. Moreover, four or five successive generations of nuclear family inbreeding would create fitness dif-

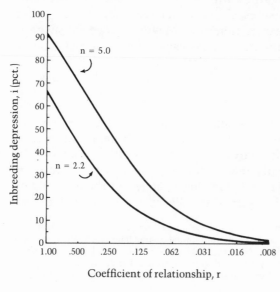

Fig. 6.6. Inbreeding depression, i, as a function of the coefficient of relationship, r. The plot gives two estimates of the reduction of Darwinian fitness among parents related by r (shown with special scaling for clarity), one estimate based on the conservative value of 2.2 "lethal gene equivalents," n, and one on an n value of 5.0. In both sets of estimates, i represents the average decreased proportion of children who will survive to reproductive age compared to the number produced by unrelated parents. The plot assumes that this is first generation inbreeding. As a conservative estimate, nuclear family incest ($r = 0.500$) is thus expected to result in 42 percent fewer viable offspring than are the matings of unrelated individuals. Calculated from Eq. 6.2 (after R. May 1979).

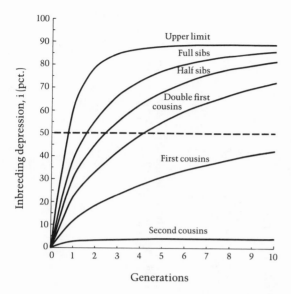

Fig. 6.7. Increases in inbreeding depression, *i*, through consecutive generations of consanguineous mating. Reproductive impairment grows ever more serious owing to the continued accumulation of homozygosity. The estimates shown here are based on the conservative value of 2.2 lethal gene equivalents. Calculated from Eq. 6.2, with Wright's formulas for *F* (Wright 1921a, 1921b, 1933).

ferentials as great as those estimated for sickle cell *homozygosity* (SS) in West Africa. Not only have these effects been calculated on the basis of a fairly conservative *n* value, 2.2, but they also seriously underestimate losses from sterility and subfecundity (see discussion in Bengtsson 1978); again, they do not include the "offspring equivalents" component of inclusive fitness. In short, genetic theory predicts fairly devastating fitness effects from inbreeding, particularly sequential inbreeding, in large and normally outbreeding populations. Let us now compare this prediction with the evidence.

Empirical Evidence for Inbreeding Depression

With the help of a computer-based literature search and a diligent student assistant (M.D.), I found three particularly useful empirical studies of morbidity and mortality among the children of consanguineal matings. Let me briefly summarize the findings and implications of these studies according to the coefficients of relationship, *r*, of their inbreeding parents (summarized in Table 6.2).

Nuclear-family inbreeding (r = 0.50). The most extensive study to date of nuclear-family inbreeding is one by the Czech geneticist Eva Seemanová (1971). From the records of district courts, maternity homes, children's homes, and hospitals, Seemanová collected information on 161 children of incest: 88 from father-daughter incest (54.7 percent), 72 from brother-sister incest (44.7 percent), and one from mother-son incest (0.6 percent). In addition, Seemanová's sample also contained its own control group, namely, 95 children born to the same mothers from other matings with unrelated partners.

The findings of this study are a close match to the theoretical expecta-

TABLE 6.2

A Comparison of Predicted and Observed Inbreeding Depression as Estimated from Data on Death and Major Defects in Three Studies of Inbreeding in Human Populations

| Consanguineal mating | r | Location | Percent death-plus-major-defect | | Observed[a] i | Predicted[b] i | Reference |
			Inbred children	Control children			
Nuclear family	0.500	Czechoslovakia	50.09%	9.76%	44.69%	42.30%	Seemanová 1971
Uncle-niece	0.250	Israel	34.19	17.53	20.20	24.04	Fried and Davies 1974
First cousins	0.125	Japan	13.47	6.60	7.36	12.85	Schull 1958
1½ cousins[c]	0.062	Japan	9.13	6.60	2.71	6.64	Schull 1958
Second cousins	0.031	Japan	6.60	6.60	0.00	3.38	Schull 1958

SOURCES: Data from references in column 8.

[a] Estimated inbreeding depression was calculated from the formula $i = 1.0 - W$. W, an estimate of average individual Darwinian fitness, was calculated in turn from the formula $W = (100 - d_i)/(100 - d_c)$ where d_i and d_c represent the percentage of death-plus-major-defect in inbred children and control children respectively.

[b] Calculated from the equation proposed by May (1979), $i = 1 - (1/e^{nF})$, where n is the estimated number of lethal gene equivalents, here assumed to be 2.2, and F is Wright's inbreeding coefficient, $F = r/2$.

[c] First cousins once removed.

tions for inbreeding depression. Concerning mortality, Seemanová found that 15 of 161 children of incest (9.3 percent) were stillborn or died by age one compared to 5 of 95 control children (5.3 percent). Concerning morbidity, Seemanová found that 53 of 130 children of incest (40.8 percent) had congenital malformations and other serious abnormalities such as cleft palate and deaf mutism. In contrast, only 4 of 86 control children (4.5 percent) were found with similar abnormalities, and no cases of multiple congenital malformations were found in this group.[17]

In Table 6.2, line 1, I have compiled Seemanová's morbidity and mortality statistics under the assumption that the abnormal children constitute fitness losses roughly equal to those caused by child mortality. Calling this statistic "death-plus-major-defect" (after Adams and Neel 1967), I obtained a total value of 50.09 percent among the children of incest compared with 9.76 percent among the control children. This differential converts to an average inbreeding depression among the parents of approximately 44.69 percent, which corresponds closely to the expected *i* value of 42.30 percent.[18]

Uncle-niece inbreeding (r = 0.25). Inbreeding effects at the level of *r* = 0.25 were studied by K. Fried and A. M. Davies (1974) among Moroccan Jewish immigrants in Israel. This study had the advantage that uncle-niece inbreeding is considered fully legal and nonincestuous among Moroccan Jews, an aspect that certainly reduces what Morton S. Adams and James V. Neel (1967) have called the "special psychic factors" of incest, factors that could well affect the course of morbidity and mortality following pregnancy. A total of 131 children from 27 uncle-niece marriages were examined and compared with 134 children from 27 unrelated control marriages.

Again in this case, morbidity and mortality were significantly higher

[17] Patrick Bateson (pers. comm., 1986) points out that Seemanová's figures may slightly exaggerate the genetic effects of inbreeding in the nuclear family. The children of incest were in most cases firstborns and were delivered while the mothers were still very young and therefore prone to birth complications (see Seemanová 1971: 112–15). Even though these variables may very well have affected some of the reported congenital malformations, they were probably not a factor in the majority of cases. In addition, it seems to me likely that genetic effects and mother's-age effects are commonly compounded in inbred children (particularly given the relative frequency of father-daughter inbreeding in many societies; see J. Herman 1981). If so, these effects may still be fairly counted as part of inbreeding depression; the exaggeration is only in calling them *genetic* effects.

[18] A similar study of nuclear family incest by Adams and Neel (1967) found a frequency of death-plus-major-defects among 18 children of incest of 33.3 percent compared to 5.6 percent among the controls, producing an estimated *i* value of 29.3 percent. Although this is lower than the *i* of Seemanová's study (44.7 percent), it should be noted (1) that Adams and Neel had a much smaller sample size (*N* = 18 compared with *N* = 161); and (2) that Adams and Neel's controls were not a subsample of the incestuous women, as were Seemanová's, but rather women matched "as closely as possible" with respect to age, ethnicity, weight, stature, intelligence, and socioeconomic status. For these reasons, I put greater confidence in the Czech data. Another study, with the advantage that inbred children "were referred as a matter of policy and not because of signs or symptoms" (Baird and McGillivray 1982: 855), reported 42.9 percent in the "death-plus-major-defect" category among 21 children of nuclear-family incest. This figure falls midway between those of Seemanová and of Adams and Neel; unfortunately, the study included no control group.

among the inbred children than among the controls. From the data of Fried and Davies, I calculated a "death-plus-major-defect" differential of 34.19 percent as shown in Table 6.2, line 2. This differential converts to an average inbreeding depression of 20.20 percent, a figure that very closely matches the predicted value of 24.04 percent.

Cousin-cousin inbreeding (r = 0.125 and less). One of the most thorough and painstaking of all assessments of inbreeding is the monumental study *The Effects of Inbreeding on Japanese Children*, by the geneticists William J. Schull and James V. Neel (1965; see also Schull 1958). Initiated as a study of the delayed biological effects of exposure to ionizing radiation from atomic bombing, this project included large samples of offspring born to first cousins ($r = 0.125$), to first cousins once removed ($r = 0.062$), and to second cousins ($r = 0.031$), all of which are permitted marriages in Japanese society. The authors' data also included information on more than sixty thousand control children born to unrelated parents.

The best subsample of their data for estimating i values is that from the city of Hiroshima. Here, Schull and Neel were able to keep track of child mortality up to age eight, which allowed them a better estimate of inbreeding depression than they could have made from neonatal mortality figures alone. Their results, converted to an estimate of "death-plus-major-defect," are shown in Table 6.2, lines 3 to 5, together with i values for these degrees of consanguinity. In each case, the inbreeding depression estimate is close to the predicted i value, but some 3 to 5 percent below it. The discrepancies are not unreasonable, particularly given the early cutoff age of the mortality statistics. These results, then, may also be seen as confirming the expected trend.

In summary, on the subject of inbreeding depression in human populations, theory and expectation are closely matched.[19] To these observations could be added literally scores of comparable inbreeding effects reported in the literature on nonhuman animals and plants, a literature that ex-

[19] Considerably higher i estimates for this range of consanguineal matings can be derived from Scott-Emuakpor's (1974) study of inbreeding in Yoruba families in southwestern Nigeria. This study offers two advantages for making such estimates: "the population practices polygamy and preferentially includes both consanguineous and unrelated spouses within each household" (p. 674), thus providing built-in controls; and there is greater diversity of types of marriage at some of the r values. The one major disadvantage is the population's high overall level of mortality, caused in part by malaria, which increases sampling error and renders comparison with Table 6.2 difficult. Nevertheless, the data summarized below indicate that the i values expected from inbreeding theory are by no means exaggerations.

| r | Percent death-plus-major-defect | | Observed i | Predicted i |
	Inbred children	Control children		
0.250	39.72%	24.99%	19.64%	24.04%
0.125	32.50	13.69	21.80	12.85
0.062	35.04	17.20	21.54	6.64
0.031	23.40	11.70	13.25	3.38

tends from Darwin (1889, 1890) to the present (see, for example, Ralls et al. 1979, 1988; Shields 1982). Suffice it to say that inbreeding has a demonstrably adverse effect on reproductive fitness. The magnitude of that effect varies with the genetic relationship of the parents, r, and with the accumulated load of deleterious recessives, n, that has built up within a population. But it is expected to be genetically deleterious in any population with an n value greater than 0.0.[20]

Let us now turn to the second of the additional "factual conclusions" that should be taken into account in our discussion of inbreeding and incest taboos.

Aversion and Inbreeding Avoidance

In 1891, the Finnish sociologist Edward Westermarck (whose writings on polyandry we encountered in Chapter 2) suggested that a psychological *aversion* to sexual intercourse develops between human beings who have been reared in prolonged and intimate childhood association. According to Westermarck, "the existence of an innate aversion of this kind has been taken by various writers as a psychological fact proved by common experience; and it seems impossible otherwise to explain the feeling which makes the relationship between parents and children, and brothers and sisters, so free from all sexual excitement." (1891: 321.) Unfortunately, Westermarck did not provide concrete evidence for this aversion despite his confidence in it. He mostly cited the inferences of other authors, many of whom had no better evidence than he.[21] Instead, as we shall see, Westermarck attempted to use the "psychological fact" of aversion in ex-

[20] There is a long and unfortunate history of confusion on this point in the social science literature, a confusion reflected in Murdock's statement that "modern developments in the science of genetics . . . cast doubt on the assumption of the biological harm of close inbreeding itself." (1949: 290). The misunderstanding traces back in the literature to Alfred H. Huth whose monograph, *The Marriage of Near Kin* (1875), originated the belief that inbreeding's genetic effects could go either way, "for good or for evil." (p. 305.) Partly because genetics and heredity were then poorly understood, this belief prospered for some few decades. Contributing to the problem was great sloppiness in classification by the proponents of the "injury theory"; thus whooping cough, croup, goiter, leprosy and, yes, common rickets were attributed to inbreeding (see Huth 1875: 254). Also to blame was the lack, until Sewall Wright's work of the 1920's, of a probabilistic theory of inbreeding depression that was capable of explaining why the harmful effects were sometimes, but not always, observed. May's equation, discussed earlier in this section, implies both that Huth was wrong and that Murdock was right *only* when the accumulated n of a population is essentially zero. Note, however, that the conditions required for near-zero n are fairly stringent: a population must be small as well as closely and continuously inbred; it must also receive negligible migration from other populations (for further discussion and a likely example see Rao 1984). More importantly, perhaps, there are at least two forces that will tend to drive n upwards: the aversion to sexual relations that develops between cosocialized children (discussed in the next section); and the interest of individual parents in the health of their own offspring. Consequently, I believe near-zero n must be the exception, not the rule.

[21] For example, one of the authors Westermarck cited in the passage above was a certain Mr. Mathew who spoke, in fact, of "an instinctive hankering after foreign women." (1891:

plaining the incest taboos and rules of exogamy of human populations. Consequently, he failed to convince the social scientists of his time, and of several generations thereafter, that this aversion was indeed a phenomenon to be reckoned with in incest theory.

Today, however, there is much stronger evidence for the "Westermarck effect." In contrast to the old adage that "familiarity breeds contempt," there is now reason to believe that "familiarity does not breed." Let me briefly review the evidence of the three most carefully documented cases (for other reviews see van den Berghe 1983; Shepher 1983: ch. 5; Arens 1986: ch. 5).

Children of Israeli Kibbutzim

Quite unintentionally, a quasi-experimental test for the Westermarck effect was initiated some years ago in the communal villages or kibbutzim of Israel. There, for several generations, children have been raised collectively and in prolonged intimate association as members of an age-graded peer group called the *kevutza*. For the most part, these intimate childhood companions are neither genetically related nor are they taught to think of sexual relations within their group as incest. Nevertheless, three separate studies have found a pronounced pattern of avoiding intercourse and/or marriage among members of the same *kevutza*.

First, Melford Spiro (1958: 347) found in his study of one kibbutz that "in not one instance" did two members of the same *kevutza* have sexual intercourse or marry. Second, Yonina Talmon studied 125 second-generation couples from three kibbutzim and found, again, "not one instance in which both mates were reared from birth in the same peer group." (1972: 140.) Third, Joseph Shepher's (1971, 1983) later study of still another kibbutz revealed "not a single case of erotic behavior between children reared in the same educational group." (1983: 57.) Still more impressive were the data Shepher obtained on 2,769 marriages from 211 kibbutzim throughout Israel in which "there was not a single case in which spouses born on a same kibbutz had been socialized together without interruption." (p. 59.)

Looking back over these three Israeli studies, Shepher (1983: 59) concluded that "[in the kibbutzim] we seem to have a strong case for Westermarck's instinctive avoidance theory. In a large population from all over Israel which shared a system of socialization, there were no marriages between people who had been continuously reared together for their first 6 years. This avoidance and aversion could not be attributed to prohibition or taboo. My fieldwork proved what Spiro and Talmon had thought: there is no marriage between second generation kibbutzniks yet there is no taboo against such marriage." Moreover, noted Shepher, this emotional property appeared without any obvious extrinsic stimulation such as

---

321.) Mr. Mathew's remark is not so much about aversion to local women as it is about attraction to unfamiliar women.

punishment for childhood sex play or guilt instilled by teachers and care-takers. Indeed, elders often expressed their *preference* for marriages be-tween kibbutzniks as one way to keep close kin from moving away. Never-theless, unambiguous avoidance behavior resulted, behavior strongly suggestive of Westermarck's developmental aversion (but see Kaffman 1977 for a dissenting view).

Minor Marriage in Taiwan

A second, highly suggestive case for aversion was documented by my Stanford colleague Arthur Wolf during the course of five years of field-work in the Haishan region of northern Taiwan (Wolf 1970, 1976; Wolf and Huang 1980). Among the inhabitants of this region, Wolf found five recognized forms of marriage, including two virilocal forms of particular interest. One of the principal differences between them was the age at which bride and groom became intimately acquainted.

The preferred and predominant form of virilocal marriage was what Wolf terms "major marriage." In this arrangement, brides and grooms were fully mature adults (median ages of about 19 and 23 years respectively) who, because of a local preference for village exogamy, were seldom even acquainted until the night of their wedding. Then, in the space of one day, "the bride leaves her natal home and relinquishes membership in her family of orientation; she steps over the threshold of the groom's home and becomes a member of his household; and she is presented to the groom's ancestors and thereby acquires the status of wife." (1966: 883.)

The alternative form of virilocal marriage was structurally equivalent; the same ceremonial procedures were carried out and the same social relationships established. However, in this kind of matrimony, what Wolf calls "minor marriage," the change in residence was separated from the marriage by as much as ten to fifteen years, since "the bride enters her future husband's home as a child. She is seldom more than three years of age and often less than a year. On entering the home as a bride, the girl becomes a member of the household and a daughter-in-law, but in this case she is not immediately presented to the family's ancestors. This last phase in the marriage process does not take place until she is old enough to fulfill the role of wife." (p. 884.) In this case, the *sim-pua* ("little daugh-ter-in-law") and her future husband were reared together in "intimate and prolonged childhood association." Such marriages were particularly com-mon in the first couple of decades of this century, according to Wolf's data, with the result that "forty percent of all first marriages united a boy and girl who had been raised together from early childhood as intimately as any brother and sister." (1976: 227.)

In a fashion similar to the Israeli kibbutzim, the Chinese custom of major and minor marriages provided a fitting natural experiment in which to test for the aversion Westermarck proposed. In this case, the comparison could be made between the sexual attraction of marriage partners cosocialized as siblings and those brought together as unfamiliar adults. But more than this culturally shaped "experimental design" worked in Wolf's favor; also available were unusually reliable, if indirect, demographic measures of sexual interest and aversion.[22]

All the measures, behavioral and demographic, in Wolf's data pointed to an aversion in adulthood between the partners in a minor marriage. The most telling indicators were the statistics on adultery, divorce, and fertility: women in minor marriages were more than twice as likely to be involved in extramarital relations and nearly three times as likely to be divorced; they also had some 20 to 30 percent fewer children (Wolf and Huang 1980: chs. 11–13).[23] Some idea of what these statistics mean in the daily lives of Taiwanese peasants can be gained from Wolf's field observations and informant reports. Concerning the consummation of minor marriages at maturity, for example, he was told by one old man "that he had to stand outside of the door of their room with a stick to keep the newlyweds from running away; another man's adopted daughter did run away to her natal family and refused to return until her father beat her; a third informant who had arranged minor marriages for both of his sons described their reactions this way: 'I had to threaten them with my cane to make them go in there, and then I had to stand there with my cane to make them stay.'" (Wolf 1970: 508.)

While Wolf describes these as the more exceptional cases of aversion, most of his informants had heard of similar accounts involving minor marriage partners. The local inhabitants may well be oblivious to some of the demographic consequences of minor marriage (Wolf, pers. comm. 1983), but they are fully aware of the general problem: when asked whether they had heard of a father's beating the bride and groom of a *major* marriage to keep them in the same bedroom, informants simply laughed at the question (p. 508).[24]

[22] For the years between 1906 and 1945 the Japanese colonial government maintained meticulous statistical registers on each household in the district of Haishan (as well as elsewhere), providing detailed data on the composition and demography of each family unit (see Wolf and Huang 1980: ch. 2). The Japanese officials not only kept careful track of major and minor marriages but also required the registration of demographic "events" (births, deaths, marriages and the like) within ten days of occurrence, and double-checked them yearly.

[23] Other findings by Wolf and Huang point to the specifically developmental nature of the disinclination. From the Japanese registers, they were able to calculate the age of future husbands at the time that the *sim-pua* were adopted, and then to calculate divorce rates and marriage incompletion rates as a function of that age. If an aversion did truly develop out of childhood association as Westermarck argued, then divorce rates and marriage incompletion rates should vary inversely with the age of the husband at *sim-pua* adoption (that is, the lower the age, the higher the rates). This is precisely what the household data reveal: as the husband's age increases from birth to 14 years, the percentage of marriages ending in divorce drops from an average of 20.2 to 9.7 (see Wolf and Huang 1980: 187), and the percentage of uncompleted marriages drops from 36.0 to 18.4 (p. 198). Additional information from the analysis allowed the authors to cast doubt upon alternative explanations for this set of observations, and the most parsimonious conclusion is that an intimacy-based aversion was at work.

[24] In the Taiwan case, one can always argue that any sense of aversion between childhood associates was confounded by the incest taboo itself, in the sense that the maturing minors may have internalized the rule as applying to them. This argument has been advanced as a

In both cases—the Israeli kibbutzim and northern Taiwan—the childhood associates under study were generally not consanguineal relatives at all. However, under most other kinds of household circumstances, kinds that do not, as Pierre van den Berghe says, "fool mother nature" (1980: 154), this same emotional response would presumably come to characterize the relationships of close kin. Aversion would therefore result in inbreeding avoidance, a situation exemplified by the third case study.

Patrilateral Parallel Cousins in Lebanon

In a 1983 article, the anthropologist Justine McCabe described a field study of marriage practices in a rural Lebanese community of farmers and wage-laborers. Her sample of 117 marriages included 23 unions between a man and his father's brother's daughter, often called "FBD marriage," or the marriage of patrilateral ("father's side") parallel cousins.

These FBD marriages offer another good opportunity for testing Westermarck's purported "fact proved by common experience." Because of a local "penchant for siblings, especially brothers, to live in close proximity within the village" (McCabe 1983: 58), patrilateral parallel cousins grew up in an association "as close as that of siblings." Behaviorally, the patterns of play and intimacy were nearly the same between first cousins of opposite sex as they were between brothers and sisters, even to the level of heterosexual exploration and play. So close were the cousins that McCabe actually had difficulty in identifying the true natal households of the children in the community. Lending still more value to this study is the fact that patrilateral cousin marriages are considered perfectly acceptable in Lebanese society (that is, like all marriages between cousins, they are not proscribed by rules of incest and exogamy). Indeed, there is a cultural *preference* for such unions, freeing them, we may presume, from any taint of the incest taboo.

Following the precedent of Wolf's analysis in Taiwan, McCabe derived relatively unobtrusive indicators of sexual dissatisfaction from her census of the Lebanese community. Her first measure, the divorce rate, revealed four times as many divorces among patrilateral parallel cousin marriages as among all non-FBD marriages. Significantly, her sample included 26 "other cousin" marriages, *none* of which ended in divorce. Her second measure was marital fertility. McCabe found the total fertility of FBD marriages to be some 20 percent lower than that of all non-FBD marriages, a figure strikingly close to Wolf and Huang's comparison of minor

---

general problem in Westermarck's contention (Lévi-Strauss 1969: 16–17), and Wolf himself admits that "although the *sim-pua* marriage is culturally recognized and socially acceptable, the impression we were given by many villagers was that they privately regard it as something very like incest." (1964: 194.) On the other hand, minor marriage partners describe their own feelings in terms of "overfamiliarity," not guilt or shame (see Wolf 1966, 1970). Moreover, it is not clear how internalizing the taboo would cause the developmental trends that Wolf observes in his data (for example, the finding, cited in note 23, that divorce and marriage incompletion rates vary with the husband's age at the time of adoption). Still better evidence on this point comes from McCabe 1983, discussed in the next section.

and major marriages in Taiwan.[25] Moreover, this differential applied across all years of marriage for which the sample sizes were 10 or more, and it held when FBD marriages were compared with all other forms of cousin marriage. In short, McCabe found patrilateral parallel cousins to be both closer in childhood and less successful in marriage than cousins of any other type.

Unanswered Questions

The data of Israeli, Taiwanese, and Lebanese studies add up to a convincing demonstration that an emotional aversion to sexual relationships does develop out of prolonged and intimate childhood association. But two important questions remain unanswered.

First, does this developmental aversion apply to intergenerational relations as well? In all three of the empirical cases described above, the data concern cosocialized individuals of roughly the same age category. To date, there is little or no concrete evidence indicating an intergenerational extension of the aversion, although such an extension was hinted at by Westermarck (1922 [1891], 2: 194) and has been argued by van den Berghe (1983). It remains possible that other forces are involved in intergenerational relationships in addition to, or in place of, the aversion. Second, is the emotional response implied by these data an evolutionary *adaptation*, favored by the forces of organic evolution because of its current adaptive function, or is it better described as an *exaptation*, that is, as a by-product of features of the nervous system that evolved for other reasons? It is tempting to suggest the former, particularly given the apparent magnitude of close inbreeding depression in many populations.[26] On the

[25] In an effort to eliminate the confounding influences of inbreeding depression, McCabe defined fertility to include all pregnancies (that is, live births plus miscarriages, abortions, and stillbirths). Her measure of "total fertility," then, denotes the average number of pregnancies per married woman per 5-year interval of marriage, summed over five such intervals. The data would be still more convincing in this respect if married women of unproven fertility had been deleted from her samples. But in any case, it appears likely from her figures that the cultural preference for FBD marriage is an example of the relationship between genes and culture that I call opposition (see Chapter 7). McCabe tells us that "among the four types of first cousin union, FBD marriage is statistically more popular than any other type, yet still produces significantly fewer children and more divorce than any other marriage." (1983: 63.) The minor marriage custom of the Chinese may or may not involve opposition since it seems not to be the preferred form of marriage except where other options are blocked. Yet both of these examples would seem to warrant closer study in that regard.

[26] Westermarck (1922 [1891], 2: 236–37) was explicit in assuming "that in this, as in other cases, natural selection has operated, and by eliminating destructive tendencies and preserving useful variation has molded the sexual instinct." Similarly, writing even before Westermarck, Darwin suggested: "It seems possible that men during primeval times may have been more excited by strange females than by those with whom they habitually lived. . . . If any such feeling formerly existed in man, this would have led to a preference for marriages beyond the nearest kin, and might have been strengthened by the offspring of such marriages surviving in greater numbers." (1890, 2: 104.) According to these arguments, then, the aversion was an explicit adaptation (Westermarck, however, apparently had second thoughts; see 1934: 159). In contrast, a number of more recent authors, notably Kortmulder (1968), Parker (1976), Demarest (1977), and Bateson (1983a and b) have proposed neu-

other hand, current information is simply not sufficient for a fair test of the hypotheses. It therefore seems prudent to leave the question open at this time.

At this juncture, let us return to the list of questions raised by Murdock's study of incest taboos. According to that list, we need to explain not only (1) the high cultural fitnesses of incest taboos but also (2) their wide variation in extent and (3) in severity. To the list we may now add two more questions: (4) What is the relationship of incest taboos to the phenomenon of inbreeding depression? and (5) What is their relationship to the sexual aversion that develops from childhood association? These five questions constitute the main analytic challenge before us. For the moment, we shall lump the first three of them together as one group. Our task can then be seen as one of providing a theory that "coordinates three parallel groups of facts which seem intrinsically to belong together: the [incest] rules [with their various properties], the aversion to sexual intercourse between persons living together from childhood, and the injurious consequences of inbreeding." (Westermarck 1922 [1891], 2: 239.)

As I looked over Westermarck's "facts" at an early stage of this research, it occurred to me that all three might well be "coordinated" by a theory proposing the cultural evolution of incest taboos through meme selection—the differential social transmission of variant forms. It seemed to me that Westermarck's apt summary identified both a powerful set of consequences (inbreeding depression and the aversion, each affecting human reproduction) and a set of cultural entities (the rules) whose properties seemed to exhibit considerable nonrandom selectivity. Could these phenomena have been causally related through some selective process of social transmission? If so, what would have been the main causal mechanism? In particular, how might such consequences have guided the evolutionary descent of the taboos? Would we have here a case of the "natural selection of cultural variation," for example, or of primary value selection, secondary value selection, or some combination of all three? And if a combination, which process would have been most influential?

The anthropologist Robin Fox has noted that, as with other such arguments, "to say that incest has [even] dire consequences does not *necessarily* explain why it is tabooed or avoided"; one must go on to bridge what he terms the "explanatory gap" between the mere statement of such consequences and the reasons why taboos were instituted and why they persist (1983 [1967]: 59). It occurred to me that all three of these cultural evolutionary forces may have been involved. My hunch, however, was that, because of the combined "dire consequences" of inbreeding depression *plus* aversion, secondary value selection would have been the most important. This hunch, in turn, called for a review of contending theories and a comparative test of hypotheses, subjects to which we now turn.

---

rophysiological mechanisms for aversion that depend upon very general features of the nervous system.

Current Theories

Although untold numbers of theories have appeared in the history of social science for explaining the properties of incest taboos, only a small subset remain in contention today. Cultural selection in this special context—the differential persistence of alternative theories on the basis of their explanatory power—has left, according to most reviewers, no more than five viable arguments (see, for example, Aberle et al. 1963; Ember 1975; Shepher 1983; Arens 1986).

1. *"Family harmony"* or *"family disruption"* theory. Incest taboos have high cultural fitness because of their advantages in preventing competition and disruptive tensions within the principal units—families—upon which stable social orders are built. (Malinowski 1955 [1927]; Aberle et al. 1963.)

2. *"Group alliance"* or *"cooperation"* theory. Incest taboos persist because they promote beneficial cooperation, alliances, and/or exchange between families, and as Tylor (1888: 267) argued in a famous passage, because "again and again in the world's history, savage tribes must have had plainly before their minds the simple practical alternative between marrying-out and being killed out." (See also White 1948; Lévi-Strauss 1969.)

3. *"Psychoanalytic"* or *"incestuous impulse"* theory. Incest taboos protect against universal "incestuous wishes," one of "the oldest and most powerful of human desires," that would otherwise be a challenge to the social order (specifically to the mating interests of older males, as in Freud 1950 [1938]: 32) or to the health and viability of the social group (Lindzey 1967; Spiro 1982).

4. *"Aversion and moral disapproval"* or *"Westermarckian"* theory. Westermarck (1891) first proposed that "the fundamental cause" of incest prohibitions is the aversion to heterosexual relations that develops between persons reared together from an early age, an aversion that expresses itself in moral disapproval, custom, and law.

5. *"Inbreeding"* or *"bad stock"* theory. Incest taboos have high cultural fitness because they limit inbreeding in a population and thereby reduce its genetically deleterious consequences (Morgan 1985 [1878]; Burton 1973; Ember 1975).[27]

Although these theories are regarded as the leading contenders, not one of them has escaped criticism. Consider, first, theories 1 and 2. Both are

[27] Many authors, following the arguments of Miriam Slater (1959), add a sixth or "demographic" theory to this list. Early in human prehistory, Slater claims, "ecological conditions independent of cultural rules" (p. 1048) caused high mortality rates and thus necessitated marriage outside the nuclear family. Later, when "people became capable for the first time of forming childrearing alliances within the family [inbreeding] was not permitted because it would have been disruptive to an already existing system." (p. 1048.) Although this is a novel account of the origins of outbreeding *behavior* (and one criticized by Ember 1975 among others), when it comes to our concern here, the origins and persistence of incest taboos, it becomes, as Slater admits, indistinguishable from theory 1 of the list.

"functionalist" theories, as Fox (1983 [1967]: ch. 2) and others point out, because they relate the origins and persistence of taboos to their consequences, specifically to their social consequences. In principle, they are therefore generally compatible with a theory of "selection according to consequences," and indeed the social functions of these arguments deserve our attention in these pages. As explanatory theories, however, they are subject to two criticisms, the first of which I will call "the problem of alternative solutions." The family harmony theory, to begin with, has been challenged on the grounds that a lifelong incest prohibition is not required by the function it purportedly serves. Other possible rules, like one permitting brother-sister relationships at maturity, could "achieve the same desirable consequences of acceptance of parental authority and integrity of the family as a social unit." (Ember 1975: 253.)

The group alliance theory has been similarly criticized as constituting a better theory of exogamy, or marriage outside a kin group, than of prohibitions against sex per se. In a matrilineal society (that is, one in which membership in kin groups is passed through the female line), it may well be strategic practice for a man in one descent group to take his wife from another, but that does not explain why sex is forbidden with his own daughter. Malinowski, on encountering this problem among the Trobriand Islanders, noted (1955 [1927]: 69) that "the daughter is not actually tabooed by the laws of exogamy, yet sexual intercourse between the two is considered in the highest degree reprehensible, though it is never given the name of *suvasova*, which means breach of exogamy." The point is simply this: if it were true that incest taboos had evolved culturally according to the consequences stipulated in theories 1 and 2, we might today expect to find alternative solutions—in other words, different rules.[28]

A second criticism of theories 1 and 2 concerns what I will call "the problem of exclusive functions." Each theory assumes that one social function, or closely related set of social functions, is adequate by itself for explaining the cultural evolution of incest taboos in all contexts and social formations, however diverse. The possibility of additive benefits to different social functions is not considered, nor indeed are additive benefits of other kinds, such as the contribution to avoiding genetic homo-

---

[28] The family harmony and group alliance theories can also be criticized for certain of their historical assumptions now known to be invalid. Thus, the starting premise of Lévi-Strauss's group alliance theory is his view of incest prohibition as "a kind of remodelling of the biological conditions of mating and procreation (which know no rule, as can be seen from observing animal life) compelling them to become perpetuated only in an artificial framework of taboos and obligations. It is there, and only there, that we find a passage from nature to culture, from animal to human life, and that we are in a position to understand the very essence of their articulation." (1971 [1956]: 350.) Recent research in animal behavior has revealed that nonhuman animals ranging from frogs, to prairie dogs, to anthropoid primates *do* systematically avoid inbreeding (see, for example, Bischof 1972, 1975; Packer 1979; Pusey 1980; Murray and Smith 1983). Incest prohibition is not, therefore, a wholesale "remodelling" of mating and procreation as Lévi-Strauss assumed. At best it seems to represent a cultural *improvement* over the avoidance mechanisms of nonhuman animals.

zygosity, for example. The presumption of these theories is, as Maynard Smith (1978: 142) puts it, that "the origin and maintenance of these prohibitions has nothing to do with the biological effects of inbreeding." This seems particularly unfortunate for two reasons: (1) there can be genetic benefits to outbreeding at the same time as there are social benefits to family harmony, group alliance, *or both*; and (2) although these social benefits may, as noted, be obtained through other kinds of rules, it is conceivable to me (for reasons discussed more fully below) that rules requiring outbreeding may be the only reliable way to curb the genetically deleterious consequences of inbreeding.[29]

The psychoanalytic or incestuous impulse theory suffers from another set of problems. First, the assumption behind the theory of a "near-universal motivation to incest" in mammalian species (Spiro 1982: 147) has been called into question in recent years by evidence that many mammalian species avoid close inbreeding, sometimes through specific mechanisms of kin recognition and avoidance (see, for example, Bischof 1972, 1975; Holmes and Sherman 1983; Read and Harvey 1988). Second, the theory has difficulty explaining the variation in the extent and severity of incest taboos, particularly given a motive force that is assumed to be constant and universal. Although one might be tempted to dismiss this variation as, say, "random noise," there is some evidence that it is ordered and systematic (see Ember 1975 and discussion below), and that taboos do change in a distinctly nonrandom fashion (see, for example, Hutchinson 1985). Third, there is a logical inconsistency in at least some variants of the theory: one cannot assume both an ancient and effective incestuous impulse on the one hand and taboos whose function is to reduce inbreeding depression on the other. If the "incestuous wishes" had ever been effective, before or even during the cultural emergence of the taboos, attendant inbreeding would have caused genetic selection against deleterious recessives, and this would have undermined the presumed functional consequence of the rules.

In my view, the family harmony, group alliance, and psychoanalytic theories are critically weakened by these objections. This leaves us with two remaining contenders, both of which have been criticized, but each of which also has more potential than the ones so far discussed.

The Aversion and Moral Disapproval Theory

In his monumental treatise *The History of Human Marriage*, Westermarck (1922 [1891], 2: ch. 20) offers one of the two surviving theories. He

[29] In his comparative review of contending theories, Ember (1975: 251) put the case more strongly than I, suggesting that incest taboos are "the only possible solution to the [genetic] problem of inbreeding." Westermarck's aversion seems to me to offer another *possible* solution to the problem, but one that is not always reliable, because close consanguineous relatives are not invariably reared together (on this point, see Fox 1980 and discussion in the next section of this chapter).

TABLE 6.3

*A Comparison of Westermarck's and Burton's Theories
Concerning Incest Taboos*

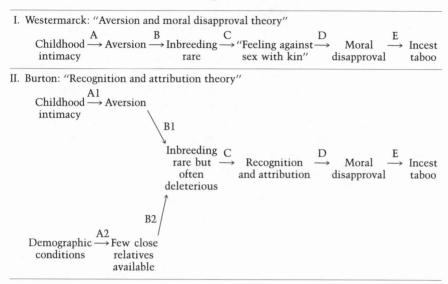

I. Westermarck: "Aversion and moral disapproval theory"

$$\underset{\substack{\text{Childhood}\\\text{intimacy}}}{\text{Childhood}} \xrightarrow{A} \text{Aversion} \xrightarrow{B} \underset{\text{rare}}{\text{Inbreeding}} \xrightarrow{C} \underset{\text{sex with kin"}}{\text{"Feeling against}} \xrightarrow{D} \underset{\text{disapproval}}{\text{Moral}} \xrightarrow{E} \underset{\text{taboo}}{\text{Incest}}$$

II. Burton: "Recognition and attribution theory"

$$\underset{\substack{\text{Childhood}\\\text{intimacy}}}{\text{Childhood}} \xrightarrow{A1} \text{Aversion}$$

B1

$$\underset{\substack{\text{rare but}\\\text{often}\\\text{deleterious}}}{\text{Inbreeding}} \xrightarrow{C} \underset{\text{and attribution}}{\text{Recognition}} \xrightarrow{D} \underset{\text{disapproval}}{\text{Moral}} \xrightarrow{E} \underset{\text{taboo}}{\text{Incest}}$$

B2

$$\underset{\substack{\text{Demographic}\\\text{conditions}}}{\text{Demographic}} \xrightarrow{A2} \underset{\substack{\text{relatives}\\\text{available}}}{\text{Few close}}$$

proposes, first, that there develops a sexual aversion, as we have seen, between intimate and prolonged childhood associates; and second, that this aversion creates a moral community, disapproving of inbreeding, that expresses itself in each human population in the form of an incest taboo.[30] Technically speaking, the first of these propositions constitutes an "aversion hypothesis" by itself and so, to avoid confusion, I prefer to call the full argument the "aversion and moral disapproval theory."

Westermarck's propositions are diagrammed as Theory I of Table 6.3. As shown, the argument begins with the proposition that intimate childhood association causes, in some fashion, a "normal want of inclination for sexual intercourse between persons who have been living closely together from the childhood of one or both of them." (p. 194.) This "want of inclination" or "sexual indifference" becomes a stronger, positive aversion (arrow *A*) if ever sexual relations are considered, let alone forced upon associates as in the case of Chinese minor marriage. Low frequencies of actual inbreeding (arrow *B*) are predicted, therefore, because of the simple fact that close genetic relatives are generally reared together— what Robin Fox (1980) calls nature's "rule-of-thumb" approach.

At the next step (arrow *C*), the aversion to sex with close childhood

---

[30] Instead of "incest taboos" Westermarck uses the term "exogamous prohibitions," reflecting his view that "exogamous prohibitions do not apply to marriage alone, but to sexual intercourse in general; the few exceptions to this rule have reference to remoter kindred only." (1922 [1891], 2: 239.) He therefore treats "rules against sex" as equivalent to "rules against marriage."

associates is expressed as a feeling against sex with persons near of kin.[31] This "transition" takes place, says Westermarck, because the aversion is only one of "an immense group of facts which, though ultimately depending upon close living together, have been interpreted in terms of kinship." (p. 205.) The feeling against sex with kin, then, gives rise to moral disapproval of that act (arrow *D*) because "aversions which are generally felt readily lead to moral disapproval." (p. 198.) Finally, says Westermarck, this disapproval is formalized over time into an explicit de jure incest taboo (arrow *E*): "the law expresses the general feelings of the community and punishes acts that shock them." (p. 204.) By this chain of reasoning, what begins as an internal, individual reaction (aversion) eventually "displays itself in custom and law as a prohibition to intercourse between near kin." (p. 193.) Patrick Bateson (1983b: 501), one of several recent authors to employ Westermarck's theory, suggests that "fear of the unusual" prompts the majority to prohibit actions to which they feel averse.

One attractive feature of Westermarck's argument is its plausibility; the argument is able to provide reasonable answers to all five of our analytic questions, as follows.

1. *High cultural fitness.* Incest prohibitions are maintained within and between generations by the emotional force of the aversion. Spatially, a "moral community" supportive of an incest taboo exists wherever young children are permitted intimate and prolonged associations; temporally, the renewal of the aversion each generation guarantees community support for the rule.[32]

2. *Variation in extent.* "The extent to which relatives are forbidden to intermarry is nearly connected [i.e., is closely correlated] with their close living together." (1922 [1891], 2: 207.) For example, relatively extensive marriage prohibitions should be found in populations with large households or other large socialization units.[33]

3. *Variation in severity.* Within populations, the variation in the severity of the taboo should correlate with the strength of moral disapproval in

---

[31] To reduce confusion, I will use the term "aversion" to refer only to the disinclination to sex among those cosocialized as children and not to its transformed expression regarding sex among close kin, as did Westermarck (for example, 1922 [1891]: 204). In early editions of *The History of Human Marriage*, Westermarck also used the term "instinct" for these feelings, but in 1922 he wrote "I now prefer to avoid this term." (p. 197.)

[32] Violations would of course occur, but even these could be explained by Westermarck's argument that "the sexual interest is so powerful that when it cannot be gratified in a normal manner it may seek abnormal gratification." (1922 [1891], 2: 201.) According to Westermarck, the small number of the violations is more remarkable than the fact that they occur.

[33] Unfortunately, Westermarck modified this argument to a weaker form and one more difficult to test through what he called the "law of association" (1922 [1891], 2: 216). Through this law, the "feelings of intimacy and kinship" from close physical association are transferable, he argued, to nonintimate acquaintances. As a result, "the [incest taboos], though in the first place associated with kinship because near relatives normally live together, have come to include relatives who do not live together—just as social rights and duties connected with kinship, although ultimately depending upon close living together, have a strong tendency to last after the local tie is broken." (p. 214.) Facilitating this transfer, in Westermarck's account, are symbols, especially names, that "come to stand for blood-relationship." On the one hand, this does help to generalize Westermarck's contentions be-

the community, presumably a function of aversion and propinquity (p. 206). Between populations, stronger affect and stricter rules should occur in populations with greater childhood intimacy.

4. *Relation to inbreeding depression.* The injurious effects of inbreeding have caused Darwinian processes to favor the organic evolution of a nervous system capable of sexual aversion, whether as an adaptation, as Westermarck proposed (see note 26 of this book), or (as discussed earlier) an exaptation.

5. *Relation to aversion.* The aversion is obviously a central part of Westermarck's formulation. The theory predicts a "moral community" approximately co-terminous with the aversion, and an incest taboo that expresses the sentiments of that community.

On a priori grounds, therefore, the theory is a strong contender. Moreover, it is also an example of primary value selection, discussed earlier in this chapter, and of the gene-culture relationship I call genetic mediation (for which see the case history of basic color terms in Chapter 4). As natural selection presumably "molded" the properties of the aversion in our ancestors, the changes in genotype frequencies would have affected the F_c's of alternative memes, favoring those that expressed the common sentiment.

Westermarck left open the question of whether the cultural changes were contemporary with the genetic changes or came along later, after the aversion had evolved to more or less its present character state. But he did make clear that this theory, in his view, "explains a world-wide institution [incest prohibitions] by a mental characteristic which may be presumed to be common to all [human populations]." (p. 239.) Because of this, his argument has been widely praised in the sociobiological literature. Ironically, however, most recent theorists have used the aversive force in different ways from Westermarck, suggesting that its role warrants careful reconsideration. In particular, the arguments of Robin Fox (1962, 1980) and Pierre van den Berghe (1980, 1983) raise some question about the strength of the aversion as Westermarck describes it.

Fox (1980: 23) claims that the most common feeling among cosocialized children is simply a "lack of inclination"; in his view, there is simply not enough strength in this indifference for it to maintain a strict incest taboo or evoke "grisly horror." Instead, Fox predicts that in "permissive" societies, where intense physical interaction among siblings is allowed or encouraged, we should find "low anxiety about incest, a minimal interest in the subject, and fairly lax treatment of offenders who nevertheless will be pulled into line in some mild way, because it just 'isn't done'."[34] (1980:

---

yond those specific cases where childhood intimacy is obvious and readily established. On the other hand, the expanded form of the argument makes it much more difficult to test. The resulting prediction, that "the extent of the prohibited degrees is closely associated with social intimacy, whether combined with actual living together or not" (p. 216), can be fairly tested only if "social intimacy" is carefully and independently defined.

[34] Stern prohibitions and grisly horror are more likely to be found, says Fox, in "puritanical" societies that preclude physical intimacy even among cosocialized youngsters. In

27.) This argument may itself be an overstatement judging from Wolf's evidence from Taiwan, where the cane-wielding fathers-in-law come immediately to mind. However, it does suggest that the truth may lie somewhere in between.[35] Does a feeling that reduces but does not prevent minor marriage in Taiwan truly have the strength to explain the high cultural fitnesses of incest taboos the world over?

In addition, Fox argues that the aversion is actually countermanded in many instances by other cultural rules whose effect is to keep close relatives apart. Paradoxically, when incest taboos prohibit intimate contact from an early age, the development of intersibling aversion can be cut short by the taboos themselves.[36] But the same effect is achieved more commonly by other rules, Fox continues, including the rules of postmarital residence (as introduced in Chapter 2). Indeed, residence rules of various kinds can preclude whole categories of consanguineal relatives from the close and prolonged interaction required for aversion formation. This is another case of "fooling mother nature," only here what gets fooled is the prophylactic effect of childhood intimacy.[37]

---

these societies, "the young male goes into an inhibitory reaction against his own hostile impulses [regarding the older men and their free access to the women]: or rather, he is easily triggered into doing so because he is easily made guilty about them." (1980: 163.) This emotional mechanism, Fox adds, will only be activated if the "natural avoidance of the sister" has *not* been developed through childhood intimacy. Building on Freud's *Totem and Taboo* (1950 [1938]), he sees the mechanism as strongest in young males. I call this proposal by Fox, and related arguments by van den Berghe, the "cultural substitution" theory: incest taboos are viewed as functionally equivalent to the aversion (or "natural avoidance") in their effect on inbreeding, even taking the latter's place where children are reared in separation (see van den Berghe 1983: 98). The effort to reconcile Freud and Westermarck is certainly valiant, but it inverts the latter's theory, and fails to account for the variation in the extent of incest prohibitions among societies with formal ("stern") taboos (see Spain 1987 for a reconciliation that is fairer to Westermarck).

[35] Even with an aversive reaction, Wolf and Huang found that earlier this century, "more than 80 percent of all [minor] matches led to marriage." (1980: 196.) If we remember that these completed minor marriages would have on the order of 70 to 80 percent of normal fertility rates, it is evident that many couples united in this fashion would, if consanguineous, go on to experience appreciable inbreeding depression. To judge by these data, the genetic problems of inbreeding are far from completely solved by an aversion based on intimacy. Pulliam and Dunford (1980: 94) make a similar point when they say, in discussing Seemanová's study (1971) of incest in Czechoslovakia, that "the very fact that such large numbers of children born from [nuclear family] incestuous matings are available for scientific study indicates to us that active prohibition might be necessary to prevent far more incestuous matings."

[36] Such a provision is often called an avoidance rule. In the Trobriand Islands, for example, "the taboo on incest begins to act at an early age, and the boy is removed from any intimate contact of this sort with his mother and above all his sisters." (Malinowski 1929: 55). This rule takes effect just about "as soon as any intimacy in play or in childish confidences might spring up," with the result that "any natural impulses of infantile tenderness are as systematically repressed from the outset as other natural impulses are in our children, and the sister becomes thus 'indecent' as an object of thought, interest and feeling, just as the forbidden things do for our children." (Malinowski 1955 [1927]: 68–69.) Consequently, notes Fox (1980), the development of an intersibling aversion or indifference is cut short by the taboo itself.

[37] Fox's argument is an effective reply to Wolf's "that under the conditions of intimate and early association propinquity does annihilate sexual desire, and that *there is therefore no need to be concerned with the social or biological advantages of the incest taboo*. We will

To make matters worse, there is little or no direct support for Westermarck's "moral disapproval" step.[38] First, of the three studies already cited as supporting Westermarck's argument about intimacy and aversion, not one shows evidence for a moral disapproval expressive of that emotion. In the kibbutzim, to begin with, an aversion may well prevent cosocialized children from marrying, but at the same time society does not express this sentiment with an intra-*kevutza* taboo. Quite to the contrary, Shepher reports (1983: 60) "that such marriages were *preferred* by parents and other members of the kibbutz." Similarly, minor marriage partners in Taiwan may sometimes have to be forced into a bedroom to consummate marriage, but the father-in-law wields his cane simply in order to keep them in there, not to express any moral disapproval or community concern. Last, but not least, McCabe reports evidence for sexual dissatisfaction following FBD marriage, but the very opening line of her report acknowledges that "one of the most salient features of marriage in the Arab Middle East is the *preference* for a man to marry his patrilateral parallel cousin." (1983: 50, emphasis added.) Any one of these cases might be taken as exceptional, and therefore dismissed from concern. But it is hard to accept that argument for all three, especially since the most familiar of all potential partners are not prohibited. In effect, the available evidence says, "Aversion, yes—moral disapproval, no."

Second, and still more enlightening in my opinion, is the folk historical material Westermarck presents regarding the cultural history of incest taboos. Instead of offering suggestive evidence for steps C and D in the chain of his argument, nearly every single folk tale speaks to the al-

---

have to seek an explanation of the taboo elsewhere." (1966: 897, emphasis added.) Fox's point is that there exist institutionalized barriers to the aversion mechanism, barriers whose significance can be inferred, for example, from the statistical distribution of postmarital residence rules in Murdock's *Ethnographic Atlas* (1967). Thus, Pasternak (1976: 44) found that 68.5 percent of 858 populations have patrilocal residence rules, 13.1 percent have matrilocal residence rules, and 4.7 percent have neolocal residence rules (where newlyweds set up their own independent households). All of these rules will result in considerable reduction of the efficiency of the aversion, and in some "skewing" of the aversion toward one group of relatives but not another. Consequently, aversion offers incomplete protection from inbreeding depression in no fewer than 86.3 percent of all human populations.

[38] In support of this step Westermarck originally claimed that "an abundance of ethnographical facts . . . prove that it is not, in the first place, by the degrees of consanguinity, but by the close living together that prohibitory laws against intermarriage [or sex] are determined." (1891: 321). As a general statement this was mistaken, and Westermarck eventually came to realize that fact: in later editions of the book, the sentence was replaced by the admission that "prohibitory rules . . . frequently refer to the marriage of kindred alone." (1922 [1891]: 207). In fact, in the words of the anthropologist Paul Kirchhoff, "*there is no clear report of any such people*, whose only marriage restriction would consist in the demand of 'local exogamy' [i.e., marriage with a partner from outside the coresidential group]." (1931: 93, emphasis added; translation for me by Thomas Baker.) Westermarck later claimed that the "moral disapproval" link in his incest theory was simply one example of how "aversions which are generally felt lead to moral disapproval and prohibitory customs or laws," adding that this was "as I have pointed out in another work." (1922 [1891], 2: 198.) The cited other work, *The Origin and Development of the Moral Ideas* (1906–8) shows signs of having been modeled after his earlier theory about incest prohibition. Even a few ethnographic cases showing clearly how moral disapproval stems from aversion and not from other origins would greatly have aided his cause.

ternative "inbreeding" or "bad stock" theory. Space requires that I quote but part of his list.

> The Dieri of the Lake Eyre basin [of Australia], according to Mr. Gason, have a tradition that after the creation fathers, mothers, sisters, brothers, and others of the closest kin intermarried promiscuously, until the bad effects of these marriages became manifest. A council of the chiefs was then assembled to consider in what way the evil might be averted, and the result of their deliberations was a petition to the Muramura, or Good Spirit. In answer to this he ordered that the tribe should be divided into branches, and distinguished one from the other by different names . . . and that the members of any such branch should be forbidden to marry other members of the same branch.
> The Achewa, a Nyanja-speaking tribe in the Nyasaland Protectorate, have a very similar legend about the origin of the exogamy of their totemic clans. . . . The Fanti of the Gold Coast, again, attribute the institution of their exogamous totem clans to a wise seer of old, and they are said to consider the practice of exogamy "of the greatest benefit for the improvement of the species"; whereas the children of parents who belong to the same totem clan are believed not to live long. . . . Speaking of the custom prevalent among the mountain tribes in South Africa of a man marrying the daughter of his father's brother, Mr. McCall Theal observes that there is nothing else in their customs "that creates such disgust as this intermarriage does in the minds of the coast natives. They attribute to it the insanity and idiocy which are prevalent in the mountains, and they say the Basuto deserve to have idiots for children, as their marriages are like the marriages of dogs." [1922 (1891): 171–72]

To the best of my knowledge, Westermarck's summary remains to date the single best compilation of native accounts to support an inbreeding theory of the incest taboo (another useful but shorter compilation is given in Sumner and Keller 1927: 1585–87).[39] Although these tales and legends cannot, of course, be taken as an actual record of history, I do give significance to the fact that not one of them includes mention of the aversion as a contributory force. Perhaps the native accounts are telling us that even a strong aversion has less emotional impact then does sterility, death, and deformed children. Let us therefore turn to consider the alternative theory.

Inbreeding Theory

Writing in 1877, Lewis Henry Morgan was among the first authors to propose an inbreeding theory of incest taboos (see Aldridge 1951 for a discussion of other early formulations). The theory was included as part of Morgan's justly criticized unilinear scheme of cultural evolution (from Savagery to Barbarism to Civilization), in which the institution of the human family was depicted as developing through a uniform sequence of universal stages. Morgan assumed that the original family type was a "consanguine family," a union composed of biological brothers and sisters as well as cousins. His argument was that this family type evolved

---

[39] With so extensive a list linking injurious effects to the origins and persistence of incest taboos, why did Westermarck discredit the natives' own explanations of the taboos? The reasons he gave were three. First, he said "in some cases it is quite obvious that the belief in the injurious effects on the offspring is sheer superstition." (1922 [1891], 2: 174.) In "some

into the next higher type, the "Punaluan family," by the deliberate elimination of biological brothers and sisters from the list of acceptable mates.

> The transition from one into the other was produced by the gradual exclusion of own brothers and sisters from the marriage relation, the evils of which could not forever escape human observation. . . . Commencing, it may be supposed, in isolated cases, and with a slow recognition of its advantages, it remained an experiment through immense expanses of time; introduced partially at first, then becoming general, and finally universal among the advancing tribes, still in savagery, among whom the movement originated. It affords a good illustration of the operation of the principle of natural selection. [1985 (1877): 424–25]

Nearly every single aspect of this argument has been criticized by more recent anthropologists (for example, see M. Harris 1968; Sahlins 1976b). The unilinear scheme of social evolution was clearly wrong, the original "consanguine marriage" is clearly a fiction, and Morgan should have spoken of "cultural selection" or its equivalent, not natural selection, since he seems to have meant the differential transmission of the idea of exclusion, not the differential reproduction per se of its carriers. Nevertheless, modern scholars have had cause to reconsider the inbreeding argument in Morgan's passage. A number of reasonable reformulations of the idea have appeared in recent years, prompting R. Rubin and G. Byerly (1983: 94) to call inbreeding theory today "one of the most common explanations of the incest taboo."

Burton's recognition and attribution theory. In my view, the most complete of these formulations is the theory proposed by the psychologist Roger Burton (1973). In the course of an attempted cross-cultural study of "resistance to temptation," Burton received "the impression that the most common reason given in both primitive and modern societies for the incest taboo is that it [inbreeding] produces bad stock." (p. 505.) The evidence inspired his formulation of a cognitive "folk theory" of in-

---

cases," Westermarck is clearly correct, but it is not surprising that peoples without a genetic theory of inbreeding would intermingle genetic effects and spuriously correlated misfortunes of other kinds; after all, Western science before 1900 did the same (see note 20). Second, Westermarck claimed "that among the lower races the exogamous rules, especially those relating to the nearest relatives, are generally so strictly observed that no genuine knowledge could possibly be based on the few instances in which they are transgressed." (1922 [1891], 2: 178.) But this criticism equally applies to his own theory: if the transgressions are that scarce, how could they then sustain the indignation of the moral majority? Third and finally, Westermarck insisted that "even if savage men everywhere had discerned that children born of marriage between closely related persons are not so sound and vigorous as others, we could certainly not be sure that they everywhere would have allowed this knowledge to check their passions." (pp. 178–79.) But here one must note, first, that it is not simply "knowledge" that would provide the check to passions; presumably the check would come also from the taboo, a *prohibition* derived from "knowledge" and buttressed by the threat of convincing sanctions, social as often as supernatural. Second, though Westermarck treats knowledge and aversion as alternative causes, why could it not be that "savage men" both feel aversive, in general, to sexual relations with close relatives and also notice harmful effects among the children born to the few such unions that do occur? And in fact, toward the end of his life, Westermarck was apparently dissuaded of his own objections to inbreeding theory. According to Lévi-Strauss (1969: 16–17, footnote 3), he came to believe "that the ultimate origin for the prohibition was to be sought in a vague awareness of the harmful consequences of consanguineous unions."

cest taboos, a theory based upon the implications of recent theoretical and empirical research on the genetics of inbreeding depression.

In essence, Burton's theory contains two hypotheses. The first, which I will call the "recognition" or "bad stock" hypothesis, proposes that native populations *recognize* in some form the deleterious consequences of inbreeding. Second, the "attribution" hypothesis proposes that people then formulate a folk explanation for this phenomenon in which they interpret injurious effects as a form of supernatural punishment. Burton puts it this way:

> With a probability of at least 50% visibly deleterious effects [from nuclear family inbreeding], even nonscientific, non-record-keeping people would perceive the bad results of such close inbreeding and would want to control it. Even for societies lacking an understanding of the connection between copulation and conception, a high frequency of defective infants born to women who had sexual relations with father, brother, or son could lead to and reinforce a belief that the gods were punishing that behavior. If production of defective children was attributed to supernatural causes, it is likely that the observers of the defective offspring would see the event as some kind of punishment or immanent justice. The rarity of intrafamilial incest would make this behavior likely to be noticed as different from what people usually do and thus likely to be considered the act that displeased the supernatural. It is this belief that would account for the intense, affective horror attached to incest. Furthermore, the transmission of such beliefs could occur without every member of the society personally observing the event. [1973: 507–8]

In support of this argument, Burton gives two reasons why inbreeding would have been both rare and dramatically deleterious when it occurred in the ancestral human poulations where these folk theories supposedly began. First, as Slater (1959) argues, demographic conditions alone would have reduced the general frequency of inbreeding. Because of delayed maturity and presumed short life spans, says Burton, "early humans mated out, 'not in order to survive, but in order to mate at all'." (1973: 509, citing Slater.) Second, Burton also acknowledges the Westermarck effect, pointing out that the "revulsion" for sex with close childhood associates would generally reduce inbreeding even where demography permitted. Under these conditions, Burton notes, there would be "a high absolute level of risk for incestuous matings" and "a sharp contrast in risk [of inbreeding effects] between incestuous and other matings."[40] (p. 508.)

Burton's argument is summarized as Theory II of Table 6.3, where a couple of its special properties can be seen. First, part of the argument (arrows A_1, B_1, C, D, and E) closely parallels Westermarck's theory, except that "recognition and attribution" replace "feeling against sex with kin." In this way, Burton's proposal builds on the logical and empirical strength of the aversion part of Westermarck's argument, while also challenging the argument that moral disapproval is based on feelings of disinclina-

[40] Independently, J. T. Burnham has proposed a similar theory. Like Burton, he suggests that inbreeding avoidance from the aversion must have predated the incest taboo, and that the taboo would have been "positively reinforced by the production of subvital and hereditarily defective offspring by violators of the proscription." (1975: 96.)

tion. Instead, says Burton, disapproval stems from the "belief that the gods were punishing" sexual relations among kin (p. 508). Second, Burton's proposal places great weight on the perceptive and analytic skills of human populations (arrows *C* and *D*). On the one hand, this feature makes the theory falsifiable: either populations "recognize and attribute," or they don't. On the other hand, it also invites native views and "folk theories" into the discussion as bona fide data. As Burton (p. 514) puts it, "folk theory should be carefully and thoroughly investigated before being rejected as superstitiously based and replaced by hypotheses that appear more scientifically sophisticated."

Just as we found in the case of the "aversion and moral disapproval theory," Burton's argument also provides plausible answers to our five main questions.

1. *High cultural fitness.* Incest taboos will have high cultural fitness in any population where inbreeding has had observable deleterious effects and where supernatural agents are regarded as capable of inflicting corporal punishment as a sign of their displeasure.

2. *Variation in extent.* Although not addressed specifically by Burton, the extent of the incest taboos should covary with the extent of detectable inbreeding effects, itself a function of such things as (a) the number of lethal gene equivalents, n, built up in a population; (b) the sample sizes of inbred offspring for each degree of inbreeding; and (c) the "background" levels of mortality (that is, of mortality not related to inbreeding in a given environment).

3. *Variation in severity.* Within populations, severity should vary in rough proportion to the likelihood of progeny with congenital abnormalities. Between populations, it should vary with n and with local beliefs about the retributional powers of supernatural agents.

4. *Relation to inbreeding depression.* The genetic effects of inbreeding are part of the feedback to or reinforcement of incest taboos. The role of inbreeding depression here is not its usual biological one (that is, of genetic selection); rather, it is one of differentially rewarding or punishing those who adopt alternative beliefs.[41]

5. *Relation to aversion.* The "Westermarck effect" was an important feature of the early social environments of humanity; it did promote outbreeding, high n values, and the recognition of inbreeding as unusual. But it was *not* the principal force in the cultural evolution of incest taboos.

In short, we have here a second theory that seems able to "coordinate the facts" of the case.

[41] Burton is very explicit on this point, suggesting that inbreeding depression would "lead to and reinforce a *belief* that the gods were punishing [close inbreeding] behavior." (1973: 508, emphasis added.) The crucial unit of selection is here the meme itself, not the carriers of the meme (although some "natural selection" could also take place through inbreeding depression). Burton envisioned a process of cultural evolution guided by genetic effects—yet another case of differential transmission according to consequences.

The main point of contrast between Westermarck's and Burton's theories, then, lies not in what questions they can, in principle, answer. Rather, the difference lies in *how*, in fact, they answer them. Where Westermarck speaks of aversion and argues for cultural change via primary value selection, Burton proposes cultural self-selection: the consequences of nascent "taboo variants" would be comparatively evaluated within populations in terms of pre-existing values for normal, healthy offspring, and in terms of beliefs concerning the powers of supernatural agents. Burton acknowledges the idea of aversion-guided primary value selection. But he argues that, because of the aversion, "it is likely that any incestuous union would have been noticed, not because it was considered wrong or was yet a taboo, but because such unions tended not to be the way persons satisfied their sex drive. *Even so, the tendency for such conditions to occur seems insufficient to account for the establishment of a taboo.* These unions, however, would provide just the conditions necessary for familial incest to produce the high rate of visibly deleterious effects presented in the genetic data." (p. 511, emphasis added.) In other words, the aversion is regarded as having "insufficient" force for guiding the cultural selection of taboos. The predominant evolutionary force would be the differential transmission of memes that pleased the gods and produced healthy children. The proposal therefore suggests both cultural evolution guided by secondary value selection and an enhancing mode of gene-culture relations. Existing values and beliefs would favor the cultural selection of incest prohibitions that enhance the individual inclusive fitnesses of their bearers.

Although my search of the incest literature was unrewarding with respect to specific criticisms of Burton's proposal, two general categories of comments would seem to apply. First, Burton's argument should be scrutinized for the standard weaknesses anthropologists have found in previous inbreeding theories. Drawing on Murdock (1949), Burton himself summarizes these criticisms, as follows.

[1] Primitive peoples may not have understood the facts of physical paternity since even some primitive societies in this century have not understood the physical basis of procreation; [2] extensions beyond the nuclear family do not follow the degree of consanguineous relationship involved; [3] awareness of inbreeding effects would not account for the intensity of affect attached to the taboo; and most important, [4] the evidence of genetics suggested that inbreeding produced positive effects as often as undesirable ones so that, "if the alleged biological harm of inbreeding is not a fact, then primitive peoples could not have discovered or recognized it." [1973: 505, citing Murdock 1949: 290]

Having had the benefit of these comments as he developed his argument, Burton gives these responses to three of the four arguments: (1) understanding physical paternity is unnecessary so long as aversion makes close inbreeding stand out as the unusual act that displeases deities; (3) if inbreeding effects are the work of angry gods, this would account for the special emotional intensity of the taboo; and (4) the "evidence of genetics" is simply not as Murdock suggested. Although Burton does not specifically address point 2, some of the variability in taboo extensions outside the family could be accounted for by allowing for asymmetric coefficients of relationship among collateral relatives where pertinent (see note 9). Consequently, the standard objections do not stand in the way of this formulation.

There are, however, a number of nonstandard objections that could be raised against Burton's theory. Ironically, the first of these is the suggestion that inbreeding depression may not be a full measure of the fitness reduction that is entailed by sexual relations with close kin. For example, there can be indirect "social effects" of genetic deformity that are not normally included within the definition or measurement of inbreeding depression. Thus Shozo Yokoyama (1983: 61) and others have found a powerful social reaction to congenital abnormalities that can sometimes stigmatize whole families, with the result that the reproductive fitness of a *normal* relative is "reduced as much as that of the affected individual." In addition, Willner (1983: 141) points out that sexual activity imposed by an older relative "may influence reproduction and subsequent generations independently of the genetic effects of inbreeding." From the clinical literature on incest in Western societies, especially the father-daughter form, she infers that "children severely damaged by incest are less likely to become parents than [are children from] the population at large" because of psychoses, suicidal tendencies, and other mental disturbances and/or subsequent fear or avoidance of sex, fear of parenting, and a tendency toward certain kinds of homosexuality. In addition, "if they do become parents, they are more likely to become abusive in their turn."

In terms of Burton's argument, this observation may be significant in two respects. First, on the theoretical side, it indicates that inbreeding depression functions, or i curves (as in Fig. 6.6), should be augmented by the estimated fitness effects of the psychological consequences of inbreeding. One can well imagine circumstances under which these effects become a significant component, or even the most important component, of the fitness costs of sexual activity with relatives. Second, with respect to explanation, these costs will no doubt help to account for both the prohibition of forms of sexual activity that cannot possibly produce pregnancy, and for the extension of incest prohibitions to nonconsanguineous kin as, for example, to stepparents and stepchildren. Indeed, "if sexual abuse by a father surrogate or familiar male is no less destructive than incest imposed by a father or older brother, this might be an element underlying the extension of kinship categories and incest taboos to most or all adults of small local communities in tribal societies." (Willner 1983: 141.)

A second criticism of Burton's argument harks back to a criticism of Westermarck as well: Burton produces little concrete evidence for his argument, not even the list of supporting cases Westermarck had previously compiled. He chooses instead to argue by analogy from other instances of "folk theory" with seemingly adaptive benefit: for example, from informants' explanations of Eskimo dog-rearing practices, male initiation rites, and the correlation of long postpartum sex taboos and polygyny (see Whiting 1964). In fact, the only ethnographic evidence he refers to is that of the "cross-cultural study of incest myths" by Leslie Segner (1968).[42]

Two problems inhere in this procedure. First, some of the purportedly analogous examples of folk theory are themselves contested (for a review of arguments on postpartum taboos and polygyny, for example, see Page and Lesthaeghe 1981), and even those that are not contested are far from being truly analogous. Second, there may have been problems of sample bias in the Segner study. Based on an examination of myths in the Human Relations Area Files for 57 societies, the study is often cited as documenting that "in roughly one-third of the myths involving incest, deformed offspring or infertility were a consequence of the union" (Lindzey 1967: 1052), which would indeed be supportive of the recognition hypothesis. However, my attempt (described later in this chapter) to duplicate Segner's results using a stratified random sample of world societies produced a much more ambiguous fraction, one-eighth. Thus, despite its plausibility, Burton's hypothesis remains essentially untested.

A third and final criticism pertains to the role of "recognition" in the argument. Burton proposes that his theory "would account for both the *origin* [of incest taboos], owing to the likelihood of early humans becoming aware of the bad results of intrafamilial breeding, and, as suggested by Aberle et al. (1963) the *persistence*, owing to the adaptive value of the incest taboo[s]." (1973: 511, emphasis added.) The problem concerns persistence: once the idea is established that inbreeding displeases the deities, belief in other forms of incest punishment, such as purgatory or torture in an afterlife, can compete for cultural fitness with the "bad stock" meme. The more effective these alternative beliefs, the less common the inbreeding in the population, and the less important the reinforcing effects of inbreeding depression. In this way, the cognitive link between the harmful consequences of incest and its prohibition could eventually be broken: a taboo that originated through recognition and attribution could come to be maintained by forces that appear to negate Burton's theory.[43]

The point, then, is that the influence of recognition need not be continuous, as Burton implied, to be also significant in the cultural evolution of

---

[42] Burton actually referred to an unpublished manuscript coauthored by Segner and Alfred Collins. The results of that study, however, are fully described in Segner 1968: 27–38.

[43] This criticism occurred to me in the course of a brief visit in 1980 to the San Blas Kuna, one of three major indigenous populations of Panama. Living in small, endogamous island villages, the Kuna are reported to have the highest frequency of albinism in the world (see Keeler 1953, 1964, 1970). Albinism is a phenotype characterized by little or no epidermal melanin, a product of autosomal recessive inheritance (Witkop et al. 1983). Although Kuna mythology both links albinism (and other deformities) to inbreeding and makes clear that the "Great Father" strongly disapproves of incest, the recurrence of this phenotype today is not regarded as a sign of the deity's displeasure. Instead, the incest taboo appears to be reinforced by mythical tales of the *other* ways in which the Great Father punishes offenders, including purgatory. In future publications, I will explore the Kuna example in more detail.

incest taboos. The importance of this fact can be seen in the social history of incest taboos in Western civilization. Although most of us would probably not cite inbreeding depression as the salient force behind our own incest prohibitions, there is ample evidence that recognition and attribution have helped to shape both canon and civil law. Consider, for example, the evidence for "recognition and attribution" in Catholic tradition, manifest in late-sixth-century correspondence between Augustine, the first archbishop of Canterbury, and Pope Gregory the Great, as translated and discussed by the anthropologist Jack Goody (1983: ch. 3; see also Muller 1913).[44] Among other questions, Augustine reportedly asked, "'Within what degree may the faithful marry their kindred?' [Pope Gregory replied] 'A certain secular law in the Roman State allows that the son or daughter of a brother and sister, or of two brothers or two sisters may be married. But we have learned from experience that the offspring of such marriages cannot thrive. Sacred law forbids a man to uncover the nakedness of his kindred. Hence it is necessary that the faithful should only marry relations [at least] three or four times removed.'" Prior to this exchange, notes Goody, certain forms of cousin marriage "must have been common in English, and indeed German, society. But [with this pronouncement] they are forbidden, the arguments against them being framed partly in physical terms (the likelihood of infertility) and partly in religious ones." (p. 36.) Years later, if followers of Catholicism do not normally give a "physical" explanation for the prohibition of inbreeding, we would still be wrong to conclude that recognition and attribution have played no role.[45]

Although these criticisms of the Burton theory imply, by themselves, the need for a revised and expanded inbreeding argument, the case for such a theory can be made still stronger when other reproductive costs and benefits are factored in. In the following section, let me describe some of these additional costs and benefits, and then outline a new kind of inbreeding argument.

An Optimal Outbreeding Theory of Incest Taboos

Consider, first, the striking fundamental similarity between the genetic effects of inbreeding, the psychological effects of sex between rela-

---

[44] Although there is some question concerning the authenticity of the exchange as recorded, there is no doubt, Goody (1983: 35) notes, about its impact and historical importance: "The document is preserved in more than 130 versions which were distributed very widely, in northern Italy, Gaul, Switzerland, Germany, Denmark, as well as England."

[45] A complementary, second example comes from the early history of civil law. In the *Capitularia Regum Francorum*, compiled by Charlemagne (768–814) and his descendants, "it is stated as a matter of fact that from marriages among relatives come blind, crippled, and deformed offspring, and those affected with blear eyes." (Sumner and Keller 1927: 1590.) It is possible that Charlemagne also had a religious motive in forbidding incest (see, for example,

tives, *and* the Westermarck effect of prolonged childhood association: all three are capable of substantial, independent reduction of individual inclusive fitness. To judge from the Lebanese data, in fact, the reduced marital fertility of sexually averse first cousins can have an even greater impact on individual inclusive fitness than would their direct inbreeding depression (assuming the applicable n value to be 2.2 or more). Following the logic of Burton's arguments, then, one would think that "recognition" might be broadened to allow for harmful effects from all three sources.[46]

Second, the interpretive act of "attribution" might also be broadened. Rather than assume a uniform "belief that the gods were punishing this behavior" (Burton 1973: 508), one can imagine any number of ways to interpret or "make sense" of the negative feedback from inbreeding. Particularly where the local pantheon is, for instance, uninvolved in embryogenesis, or is incapable of corporal retribution, one would sooner expect other kinds of folk explanation, such as the belief that the "blood" of close kin does not "mix" properly for normal procreation. But rather than attempt to second-guess even the range of native responses, it seems wiser simply to hypothesize that the locals supply some appropriate interpretation of inbreeding consequences, where "appropriate" denotes both "locally meaningful" and "negatively valued." Among other advantages, this extension of Burton's argument—which I will call the "interpretation hypothesis"—allows direct linkages here between the symbolic and evolutionary dimensions of cultural analysis. As Willner (1983: 142) has noted, "Widespread beliefs that incest and inbreeding can adversely affect those subjected to them [are] far from incompatible with culturally specific constructions of incest as 'desecration.'"

Third, even with these broadening provisions, the Burton theory still

---

Ganshof 1971: 61). Still, our own cultural history clearly refutes the common preconception that "*there is no evidence at all* that hereditary disadvantages to such close inbreeding gave rise to the incest prohibition, even though the prohibition may have some biological survival value." (Ford 1960: 232, emphasis added.) A third example, from Greek mythology, is that of Perseus, the young warrior who set out to slay Medusa, one of the Gorgons. Along the way, Perseus had to defeat the Graeae, who were "sisters of the Gorgons and, like them, malevolent bogies. . . . They were born [already] old women, the progeny of Phorcys and Ceto, a brother and sister whose union also produced Nereus, the father of the Harpies, Scylla, the Sirens, Echidna, Chimaera, and the Sphinx. Their relatives declare their character." (Halliday 1933: 134). In the end, Perseus was successful in his quest, but even that does not detract from the story's clear "message" about inbreeding.

[46] No one seems to have studied the ethnographic record for the "folk wisdom" about aversion and its effects on fertility. Yet the literature is sprinkled with suggestive evidence, much of it from the local incest taboos themselves. Among the Ga of Ghana, for example, "children brought up in the same women's compound and 'who have sucked the same breast, slept on the same mat and eaten from the same dish are brothers and sisters' [and therefore prohibited from sexual relations] in spite of the fact that they may not be blood relations." (Manoukian 1950: 77; see also Schappera 1963: 111.) Among the San Blas Kuna of Panama, for another example (see note 43), the incest taboo includes a provision against sex or marriage between "step siblings *if reared together in the same household.*" (Stout 1947: 27, emphasis added.)

suffers from the problem of exclusive functions. Reproductive impairment, whatever its cause, is certainly one important consequence of sexual relations with relatives; indeed I would go so far as to call it the most basic consequence because it applies no matter what the other implications are of such activity in a particular context. But it is also not unique. It would seem particularly desirable to formulate a theory that would also allow one to include the various *social* consequences of incest (such as family disruption, or the loss of alliances). Thus, to follow Burton's logic once again, one can well imagine the hypothetical case of a people who prohibit sex with relatives on the grounds that it is both reproductively harmful *and* politically unwise.

Fourth, although the Burton theory is explicit about the "costs" of inbreeding, it fails to take into account the very real, simultaneous costs of outbreeding—again, costs of both genetic and social origin (on the genetic costs, see especially Shields 1982). For example, as Richard Alexander (1977: 330) points out, "Restricting one's sexual or marriage partner to increasingly distant relatives involves increasing costs. Thus, fewer individuals are available, greater distances may have to be traveled to locate them, and greater risks may be involved in securing them; deleterious partitioning of reproductive resources [or indeed their forfeiture] may also result." In addition, when outbreeding requires a change of residence, there may also be a loss of benefits associated with social position in kinship and descent systems, for example, or in local political and economic organizations. As a result, Alexander notes, the costs of inbreeding do not necessarily imply "that only the most distant possible relatives, or nonrelatives, are suitable marriage or sex partners." (p. 330.) Indeed, an optimal balance may be struck somewhere in between: mates representing the lowest *total* costs are likely to be neither the closest of kin nor complete outsiders.

A Cost/Benefit Model

Taken together, these arguments suggest an expanded inbreeding theory of incest taboos, a two-part proposition that I will call "optimal outbreeding theory."[47] The first part is simply a cost/benefit model of optimal mating strategy, a model modified from the earlier formulations of Alexander (1977), Norbert Bischof (1972), and Patrick Bateson (1983a). The model requires the additional assumption that the individual-level costs and benefits of inbreeding and outbreeding can be measured on a scale of individual inclusive fitness. That is to say, we will assume that all

[47] This paradoxical name follows from Patrick Bateson's (1983a) "optimal outbreeding model" of mate choice. The underlying logic is that one mates *out* to varying degrees in order to avoid the harmful effects of mating *in*. Frankly, were it not for this terminological convention, the arguments presented here could be called an "optimal *inbreeding* theory" of incest taboos and mean exactly the same thing. After all, inbreeding and outbreeding are both matters of degree along the same continuum.

Panel A

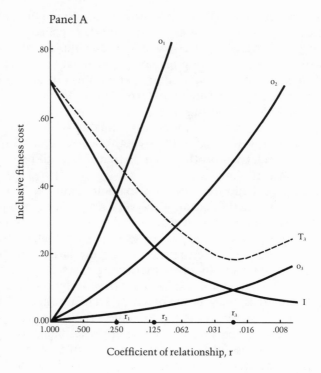

Panel B

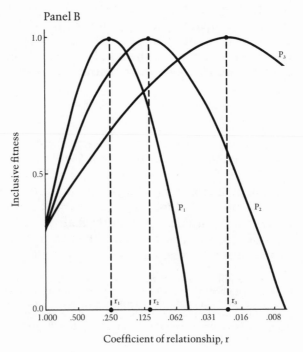

costs, social *and* reproductive, of inbreeding and outbreeding can be assessed in terms of F_g (however else they might also be measured).

The first part of the theory, a graphic model of optimal outbreeding, is summarized in Fig. 6.8. Panel A shows the average total inclusive fitness costs of inbreeding (that is, the average total cost of all consequences, reproductive and social) and of outbreeding as a function of r, the coefficient of relationship between mates, in each of three hypothetical populations. To facilitate comparison, the inbreeding costs, I (which include but are usually greater than i) are assumed constant in the three populations, while outbreeding costs vary; the curves O_1, O_2, and O_3 represent high, medium, and low outbreeding costs respectively. In principle, the reproductively optimal mates within each population will be the ones that minimize the additive costs of inbreeding and outbreeding (for example, the additive costs from curves I and O_3 are shown by the dotted curve, T_3). Panel B shows how the average inclusive fitness of individuals within each population will then vary as a function of the r value between mates. The resulting curves define reproductively optimal mates within each population: for example, in the population with low outbreeding costs (curve O_3 of panel A) optimal mates will be related by the coefficient r_3. As the figure indicates, an increase in outbreeding costs (for example, a shift from O_3 to O_2, or from O_2 to O_1), with inbreeding costs held constant, will cause a shift in optimal mates toward a higher coefficient of relationship (for example, from r_3 to r_2 or r_2 to r_1). A similar shift could occur through a reduction of inbreeding costs (that is, through a change to lower values of I) with outbreeding costs held constant. In short, this model predicts that optimal outbreeding in any given population will depend upon the balance of situation-specific costs to inbreeding and outbreeding. Where the costs of outbreeding are high (as in O_1) reproductively optimal mates are predicted to be close relatives.

Fig. 6.8 (opposite). A model of optimal outbreeding. In theory, reproductively optimal outbreeding occurs when individuals choose mates whose coefficient of relationship, r, minimizes the additive inclusive fitness costs of inbreeding and outbreeding. Panel A shows the total costs of inbreeding (I) and outbreeding (O) as functions of r for three hypothetical populations, each with a different level of outbreeding costs $(O_1, O_2,$ and $O_3)$. To facilitate comparison between populations, the inbreeding cost curve, which summarizes reproductive impairment from all sources (genetic, social, and psychological), is assumed constant. In any given population, optimal outbreeding occurs at the value of r with the lowest sum of I and O values; in population 3, for example, the sum of O_3 plus I, represented by curve T_3, indicates that optimal mates are related by the value of r_3 as shown. Similarly, the relationship between optimal mates in populations 1 and 2 is r_1 and r_2. Panel B shows average individual inclusive fitness as a function of r for each of the populations $(P_1, P_2,$ and $P_3)$ represented in panel A. The fitness values for each population have been standardized on the usual 0.0 to 1.0 scale after subtracting the total of inbreeding and outbreeding costs shown in panel A. Highest relative fitness occurs at the r values of lowest total cost. The model confirms intuitive expectations: when the costs of outbreeding are high, as when nonrelated mates are geographically distant, optimal mates may be quite closely related (e.g., r_1 is equivalent to the mating of double first cousins). Panel A adapted from P. Bateson 1983a: 258, fig. 11.1, published by Cambridge University Press.

The Forces of Evolutionary Change

The second part of the theory adds a cultural evolutionary framework to the model of Fig. 6.8. In particular, let us consider the hypothetical cultural dynamics of an autonomous reference group whose beliefs include a range of different variants of an incest taboo. Let us further assume that these variants are subject to various forces of cultural evolutionary change, but that selection by choice is the single most important means of modification. For purposes of discussion, let us also assume that the taboo variants differ only in their extent; that is to say, we will assume that the variants, or allomemes, can be arranged along the X axis scale of Fig. 6.8 according to the r value of the genealogically most distant consanguine with whom sex is prohibited (this assumption, too, can be relaxed later to accommodate variation in severity). These assumptions allow us now to view one of the curves of Fig. 6.8, panel B, as the relevant inclusive fitness function for our set of allomemes. For purposes of discussion, let us assume that P_2 applies; in this way panel B of Fig. 6.8 becomes the equivalent, for this hypothetical case, of panel A of the general framework for enhancement, Fig. 6.1.

Let us now consider the cultural fitness function for this same array of allomemes. My proposal is that the F_c curve, too, will resemble its counterpart in Fig. 6.1, panel B. More specifically, I hypothesize (1) that various forces of cultural selection will operate under these conditions; (2) that the most important single force will be secondary value selection; (3) that the guiding cultural values of that process will tend to favor variants of lowest total F_g costs of inbreeding and outbreeding; with the result (4) that F_c will commonly be maximized for reproductively optimal variants of the incest taboo. I propose, in short, that secondary value selection will enhance the cultural fitness advantage of the reproductively optimum taboo well above its F_c value created by other forces. If I am correct, then the relationship between genetic and cultural evolution in this case will constitute an example of enhancement.

Consider, first, the natural selection of cultural variation within our hypothetical reference group. It stands to reason that differential reproduction can play a nontrivial role in this case: taboo variants can achieve an advantage in social transmission simply by virtue of their reproductive consequences for carriers, whether as individuals or as groups.[48] This

---

[48] Indeed, one of the most common suggestions in the literature is that incest taboos have culturally evolved through societal selection, that is, through natural selection at the level of whole social groups. Consider, for example, Lindzey's argument (1967: 1051–52): "A human group practicing incest operates at a selective disadvantage in competition with outbreeding groups. . . . [Over time] natural selection would lead to the preservation of societies that practiced outbreeding [because they had incest taboos] and elimination of those societies that favored, or were neutral to, the practice of incest." (For other examples, see Frazer 1910, 4: 166; Sumner and Keller, 1927: 1593; Mather 1964: 109; Ember 1975: 256; Melotti 1981: 629, 1984: 87; Fox 1983: 65.)

force includes, for example, what H. R. Pulliam and C. Dunford (1980: 95) call the "natural subtraction" of variants caused by the resultant inbreeding depression of their carriers. Considering the implications of Fig. 6.7, this force would give an F_c advantage, however small, to the taboo variants that optimize the average inclusive fitnesses of their carriers. Differential reproduction, in other words, would tend to favor an optimizing rule.

Now consider primary value selection, in this case the evolutionary role of Westermarck's aversion. Again, we may assume that it does have some influence: individuals who, from their own childhood associations, have strong feelings against sex with kin are likely to play an active role in the social transmission of taboo variants. It is reasonable to expect them to be both receptive to taboo variants that reflect their disinclinations and to feel motivated to participate in the further social transmission of those variants. To some extent, then, "formal incest taboos are the cultural reinforcement of the automatic inhibition" that affects cosocialized children (Ruse and Wilson 1986: 184)—or at least, the inhibition contributes to the preservation of such rules. And because of the simple rule of thumb that cosocialized children are often among the closest of relatives, this force would tend to give F_c advantages to variants that lowered the costs of inbreeding.

By the same token, however, I would not expect the aversion to bring about the evolutionary "fine tuning" of the incest taboo, that is, to mold it optimally to local circumstances. One reason is the developmental source of the aversion, intimate and prolonged childhood association, which is presumably insensitive to site-specific outbreeding costs. In order to get optimal outbreeding, then, people would have to manipulate the extent of childhood association in inverse proportion to the costs of outbreeding—to create, for example, less aversiveness where outbreeding costs are high and inbreeding is relatively desirable. Another reason harks back to the "fooling of mother nature": where residence rules or other cultural phenomena restrict the intimacy of close kin, aversiveness to sex can hardly vary in close proportion to inbreeding costs, even if one invokes Westermarck's wildcard "law of association" (1922 [1891]), 2: 216; see also note 33). In short, although the aversion is almost certainly a contributory force, I do not believe it shows us that "a tight and formal connection can [here] be made between biological evolution and cultural change." (Ruse and Wilson 1986: 184.)

Instead, I believe it reasonable to suggest that secondary value selection is the most important of these forces of cultural evolutionary change. I also believe it is the one most likely to explain such fine tuning as may exist within the variation of incest taboo extensions. I suggest that people do recognize the major costs of inbreeding and outbreeding, including inbreeding depression and/or aversion where these are significant; that they interpret these costs in locally meaningful ways, including, but not limited to, the displeasure of supernaturals; and that they evaluate them accordingly, in terms of locally evolved cultural values. Further, I propose that these cultural evaluations contribute significantly to the F_c differentials among taboo variants with the result that, at least in autonomous reference groups, the favored allomemes are generally the ones that promote a reproductively optimal degree of outbreeding. In short, I would expect this process to favor the cultural evolution of taboos that prohibit the mating of kin who are more closely related than the F_g optimum.

A priori, this optimal outbreeding theory would seem at least as plausible as the Westermarck and Burton theories. With respect to autonomous reference groups, it offers the following answers to our five main questions.

1. *High cultural fitness.* Incest taboos will have high cultural fitness in any population where there are substantial reproductive costs to inbreeding, including inbreeding depression, sexual aversion between childhood associates, and any psychological effects. Although the recognition and interpretation of reproductive impairment are not logically required for taboos to attain high F_c, they are nevertheless predicted to provide a major force of cultural selection in most populations.

2. *Variation in extent.* What Westermarck called the "extent of the prohibited degrees" (1922 [1891], 2: 216) is expected to vary within and between populations according to the r value of reproductively optimal mates, itself a function of local costs of inbreeding and outbreeding. Between populations of roughly equal inbreeding cost curves, for example, more extensive taboos are expected where outbreeding cost curves are lower.[49]

3. *Variation in severity.* Variation in severity within and between populations should reflect the relative magnitude of the inclusive fitness consequences of sex with close kin. Within populations, one would expect severity to rise sharply with r; between populations, severity should vary with reproductive and social costs.

4. *Relation to inbreeding depression.* The genetic effects of inbreeding are built into the theory as one of the main sources of reproductive impairment and thus of inbreeding cost. They contribute to the natural selection of cultural variants and, when recognized and interpreted, to the cultural self-selection of those variants as well.

5. *Relation to aversion.* The "Westermarck effect" is important both

[49] Optimal outbreeding theory may also help to explain why incest taboos "fail strikingly to coincide with nearness of actual biological relationship." (Murdock 1949: 286; see also note 9 of this chapter.) In any given population, inbreeding and outbreeding costs can both be asymmetrically distributed among one's matrilateral and patrilateral kin. To take but one example, in a population with a patrilocal residence rule or preference, the sexual aversion from childhood association among patrilateral parallel cousins (the children of brothers) could add a level of inbreeding cost not incurred between the children of brother and sister. Other things being equal, this could cause an evolutionary extension of the incest taboo to the averse cousins alone; the taboo would then, as Murdock noted, "fail strikingly to coincide" with r.

as a source of inbreeding costs and as a cause of primary value selection. It is viewed as a contributing force of cultural evolutionary change, but not as a force capable of fine-tuning taboos to their specific social and ecological contexts.

I therefore submit that this theory, too, can coordinate the facts of the case.

One Specific Example

Before turning to a systematic test of this proposal in comparison to the others, let me briefly summarize a particularly revealing ethnographic example of secondary value selection at work. The example comes from a study by Sharon Hutchinson (1985) of changes during the last half century in "the scope and relative intensity of various categories of incest [and thus of incest taboo] and exogamy" (p. 625) among the pastoral Nuer peoples of Sudan, East Africa. Hutchinson bases her observations on the earlier ethnographic descriptions of E. E. Evans-Pritchard who noted that, in the 1930's, marriage was prohibited "if relationship can be traced between a man and a woman through either father or mother . . . up to six generations." (1963: 85.) Sexual relations within that limit were said to be *rual* (incest), a term that connotes not only forbidden sexual activity but also the subsequent hardships and misfortunes attributed to it, including the "illness, abnormality and early death" of the inbred children (Hutchinson 1985: 630).

In recent years, however, the limits have been changing, particularly among the Eastern Nuer. There, people "now argue that a lapse of only three generations is sufficient to avoid risk of *rual.*" (p. 629.) Significantly, this "gradual easing of exogamic prohibitions" has proceeded, despite the opposition of conservative local courts, by a process locally known as "feuding" and called "pragmatic 'fecundity testing'" by Hutchinson (p. 637).

It is not at all uncommon for a couple frustrated in their desire for marriage by official decrees of *rual* to run off together shortly after the trial. If the union then proves fruitful and the child thrives, the couple can later return to their families confident that some sort of marriage arrangement will be made. If not, the lovers usually separate voluntarily. . . . [This is called "feuding" because] the lovers "feuded for each other" . . . that is, they defied public opinion and eventually overcame their families' reluctance by eloping and bringing forth a healthy child. . . .

The reason why this mode of "feuding" is so often effective is that most Nuer, Easterners and Westerners alike, regard any union that proves fruitful as divinely blessed, and thus consider it to be in some sense free of *rual.* . . . It is the fortune or misfortune of such couples, closely watched and commented upon by all, that is later cited as evidence for or against the validity of a particular exogamic [and incest] prohibition. [pp. 629–30; for a parallel example, see Kiste and Rynkiewich 1976: 223–24]

In short, the effects of inbreeding are recognized and appropriately interpreted; indeed, they are "attributed" along the lines of Burton's original suggestion. As befits selection by choice, a widely held cultural value ("any union that proves fruitful [is] divinely blessed") has even greater influence upon cultural fitness than do the official decrees of the local chief's court.[50]

Three further aspects of Hutchinson's account are of particular interest here. First, although this evolutionary change in the Nuer incest taboo has clearly been stimulated by recent outside influences, there is reason to believe that the *mechanism* of cultural change is an old one. As Hutchinson (p. 630) puts it, "of course this method of testing the limits of 'divine tolerance' in matters of incest and exogamy is nothing new. The existence and relative severity of different categories of *rual* have long been revealed to Nuer through the experience and interpretation of affliction," in other words, through the cultural evaluation of consequences. Second, the whole process of "grappling with the logic, nature, and meaning of *rual* itself" has also been influenced by the very real *social* costs to the Nuer of inbreeding and outbreeding. Indeed, the current wave of cultural selection was undoubtedly provoked by changes in the social costs, such as the recent "undermining [of] the importance of extended political alliances" (p. 632), which would tend to lower the total costs of inbreeding, and the "contraction of patterns of bridewealth distribution" (p. 636), which would tend to lower the costs of outbreeding.

Finally, although selection by choice is clearly the main means of modification at work, Hutchinson suggests that there is also some change by imposition. In particular, she describes the concurrent "hardening" of one facet of the Eastern Nuer incest taboo—the prohibition of sex between a man and his father's sister's daughter—as "an injunction directed primarily at the sons of the influential" (p. 638) not to challenge the latter's privileged position in society. It is a challenge because, in Nuer society, wealth, influence, and "procreative power" all accrue to a man with many "children of girls," that is, with many children born to his father's sister as well as his own sisters and daughters (p. 634). If his son were then to initiate sexual relations or marriage with a sister's daughter, this would effectively "deny the integrative and procreative potential" (p. 635) of his position, including an important payment of bridewealth. According to Hutchinson, this particular facet is deliberately "insulated from the pub-

[50] A striking example of the strength of this cultural value comes from Hutchinson's account of two "cattleless orphans," full brother and sister, who began "living together openly as husband and wife." Lacking cattle, family, and thus prospects of proper marriage, "the two reasoned that 'since they were dead anyway,' they had nothing to lose if they were later killed by *rual* and that by taking the risk involved they might succeed in bringing forth children. . . . Eventually they were summoned to chief's court, but only after having brought forth a healthy child. Upon examining the couple's situation, and hearing the reasoning behind their decision, the elders of the court are said to have actually blessed the union." (1985: 637.)

lic rethinking and questioning of *rual* limits" (p. 637); it is, however, also in the economic, political, *and* reproductive self-interest of the imposers.[51]

Testing the Theories

We are left with two alternative theories: the Westermarck aversion and moral disapproval theory; and an improved inbreeding argument called optimal outbreeding theory. Both offer plausible answers to our five main questions and both are supported by empirical evidence at key points. The difference between them, though perhaps small in terms of theory structure, is important in terms of gene-culture relations: the Westermarck theory identifies the leading causal process as primary value selection; the outbreeding theory sees it instead as secondary value selection. Which provides the better explanation of the facts?[52]

Fortunately, in the attempt to answer that question, we may be guided by the earlier comparative analysis of the anthropologist Melvin Ember (1975), an analysis that makes three important contributions to the study of incest taboo theories. The first is Ember's inspiration to focus on Question 2 in our list of analytic questions, namely, What explains the cross-cultural variation in the extent of incest taboos? Reasoning that "it is difficult to design a test of theory when the condition to be explained [the nuclear family taboo] is invariant," or close to it, Ember chooses as his

[51] As a general rule, when the cultural evolution of incest taboos is guided by imposition, one would expect the extent of the taboo and its severity to deviate from reproductive optima in ways that have real or potential reproductive benefit to the imposers. An excellent example, from the history of our own incest prohibitions, is offered by Goody (1983). Beginning with the letter of Pope Gregory to the first Archbishop of Canterbury late in the sixth century A.D. (discussed above, in the section "Inbreeding Theory"), the prohibition of marriage (and presumably of sex) among close kin became a matter of "prime significance" for the Church. "Not content with the prohibition on first cousins," notes Goody (p. 56), the Church then extended the ban in the sixth century to the third canonical degree (that is, to second cousins), then to the fourth degree (third cousins), and eventually, by the eleventh century, to the *seventh* canonical degree (sixth cousins). In Goody's analysis, these changes—often justified by the church on the grounds "that the fertility of the mother or the health of the children might be endangered" (p. 57)—actually "constituted ways of alienating property [from the populace] that were introduced by the Church largely for its own benefit." (p. 46.)

[52] Ideally, of course, one would like to test these theories against the detailed social histories of incest taboos—histories like Hutchinson's (1985) but with greater time depth—in a substantial sample of human populations. With such data, it would be possible to separate examples of selection by choice from examples of imposition. Within each category, one could then attempt to assess the actual historical role of various cultural evolutionary forces. The problem, however, is that such data are quite scarce; there are precious few studies, like Goody's (1983), of even the social history of our own incest prohibition. We are forced to settle for second best, namely comparative analysis, while hoping that anthropology's new "rapprochement with history" (Ortner 1984: 159) will soon help to fill the gap. In this compromise, though, as a partial validity check, we may follow the lead of both Westermarck and Burton and pay close attention to the natives' own "folk theories" about incest taboos.

dependent variable the prohibition of first cousin marriages (1975: 249; see also note 4).

His second contribution is a test of the contending theories that uses the largest comparative data base available, Murdock's *Ethnographic Atlas* (1967) of some 800 world populations. From codes in the atlas describing cultural rules for cousin marriage, Ember was able to categorize societies as either prohibiting all first cousin marriages or permitting one or more types of such unions (Ember 1975: table 1, p. 259).

But Ember's third contribution is the most important one: he formulated a set of predictions concerning cousin marriage that permit empirical tests of rival theories.[53] The predictions are based on two key variables: (1) degree of community exogamy, as a predictor of the familiarity or intimacy between cousins; and (2) deme size, a variable that would affect both the frequency of cousin marriages and the visibility of subsequent inbreeding depression. Particularly helpful to us here is Ember's argument about community exogamy. He predicts

> that those societies with *endogamous* communities [i.e., with a preference for marital partners from within the co-resident population] should be the most likely to prohibit all cousin marriage (because all of one's cousins would be living in the same community and therefore would be likely to be known to each other), that those societies with *agamous* communities [i.e., no formal rule] should be less likely to prohibit all cousin marriages (because some of one's cousins would be living in other communities and [would] therefore be less familiar), and that those societies with *exogamous* communities should be the least likely to prohibit all cousin marriage (because aside from one type of parallel cousin [e.g., patrilateral parallel cousins in virilocal societies] most of one's cousins would be living in other communities and would therefore be quite unfamiliar). [1975: 258–59, emphasis added]

However, although intimacy *is* surely precluded by rules of local exogamy, one cannot be sure that it is simultaneously *promoted* by rules of endogamy. As a partial correction for this problem, Ember suggests that community size could also be taken into account in endogamous societies. Again from the Westermarck theory, one would expect that, because cousins in smaller endogamous communities are more likely to know each other well, such communities should be less likely than larger endogamous communities to allow first cousin marriage.

In contrast to these predictions, Ember offers a second set of hypotheses based upon inbreeding theory. These hypotheses stem from the argu-

---

[53] Ember was much more generous than I have been, admitting into his predictions and tests the psychoanalytic theory, the family harmony theory, Slater's (1959) demographic theory, and the group alliance theory. At the same time, however, I feel that Ember overstated the case for the inbreeding theory, saying it "seems to be *the only theory* which postulates an advantageous effect that only the incest taboo (of all possible mating rules) could produce." (1975: 257, emphasis added.) The Westermarck theory also postulates an advantageous effect that only an incest taboo could produce: by reducing the occurrence of incest in a given population, the taboo reduces the shock and retributive emotions that would otherwise be felt by the moral majority.

ment that, before prohibition, cousin marriages—*and* their harmful genetic consequences—are likely to be more frequent in small demes, whether endogamous or exogamous, because of the relative shortage of alternative mates. But frequent cousin marriages, in turn, provide more opportunity for a prohibition to spread either by natural selection (that is, by virtue of its demographic consequences), or by diffusion in response to the observation of harmful effects, or by both of these mechanisms (see 1975: 256). Ember thus predicts that the smaller the deme or breeding population, the more likely it is to prohibit first cousin marriages. In an attempt to assess the validity of these predictions, Ember cross-tabulated the societies of the *Ethnographic Atlas* by the dependent variable (prohibition or not of first cousin marriage) and each of the independent variables (community exogamy and deme size), using average local community size and the number of political jurisdictional levels as indicators of deme size. His principal results may be summarized as follows. First, the community exogamy test on 717 populations failed to support the Westermarck theory: first cousin marriages were actually prohibited with *greater* frequency in societies where most cousins are routinely precluded from childhood intimacy by rules of exogamy. Second, the endogamy–deme size test also failed: the smaller endogamous demes failed to show a significantly higher proportion of cousin prohibitions than did the larger demes.

On the other hand, Ember's test results are uniformly consistent with his formulation of inbreeding theory. Using the full world sample once again, Ember found that populations with smaller demes are more likely to prohibit first cousin marriage than are their counterparts with larger ones. Not only does the correlation hold for both measures of deme size, but even the exceptional cases can be explained. In fact, most of the small-deme populations who do permit the marriage of cousins have also experienced significant depopulation in the last 400 years, a situation which may have prompted the relaxation of earlier cousin prohibitions (see 1975: 263–69). Ember concluded that a selective, cultural evolutionary process "appears to favor the extension of the incest taboo to first cousins more [often] in lower density than in higher density societies, just as inbreeding theory would predict." (p. 263.)

As the first systematic analysis of interpopulational variation in incest taboos, Ember's study was clearly a milestone. Nevertheless, the study also leaves a number of important questions unanswered. First, because different combinations of variables were used to test different hypotheses, one is left to wonder what would happen if inbreeding theory and Westermarck's propositions were compared using the same set of variables. Would inbreeding theory still have the greater explanatory power? Second, although Ember's arguments place appropriate emphasis on the reproductive costs of inbreeding, they also ignore, by and large, the countervailing reproductive costs of outbreeding. (The one exception is Ember's depopulation argument, wherein a reduced pool of potential mates raises the costs of outbreeding and thereby encourages mating between closer kin.) Does cross-cultural variation in the extent of incest prohibitions also reflect differences in the costs of mating out? In other words, is there evidence that the incest taboos of autonomous reference groups really do serve as guides toward the choice of reproductively optimal mates? Third and finally, although Ember discusses two distinct evolutionary mechanisms for the spread of incest prohibitions—one being natural selection and the other being, in my terms, "cultural selection" or "preservation by preference"—he explains variation in the data solely in terms of natural selection. Is natural selection truly sufficient to explain existing taboo variation, or is there evidence for a major contribution from human decision making? More specifically, do incest taboos support my general claim that secondary value selection has been the main but not exclusive means of cultural evolutionary change? Do we have here a case of enhancement or not?

A "Sixty Cultures" Test

In a first attempt to answer these questions, and to retest the Segner mythology study (1968) cited by Burton, I turned to the Human Relations Area File (HRAF) world probability sample called "Sixty Cultures" (Lagacé 1977). While certainly far from perfect, the sample does offer these advantages for comparative study: (1) it consists of 60 populations selected by stratified random sample from all major world "culture areas" (see App. A, Table A.6.1, for a list of all populations included); (2) it provides coded *access* to the ethnographic information of these populations, not coded data; (3) it contains a number of rare sources and translated documents that would otherwise be unavailable.

As I began this study, I had two sets of objectives. The first and most general of these was simply to repeat the analyses of Segner and Ember with a random sample of world populations and with textual data (including folk theory, where it existed), as well as quantitative codes. My predictions at this level were simply these: (1) if Segner was correct about the evidence for inbreeding depression in myth, then about one-third of the populations with incest myths in the Sixty Cultures sample should show evidence of genetic consequences in their mythologies; (2) if Ember was correct, then more finely tuned measures of the variation in incest taboos should confirm the explanatory advantage of our revised inbreeding theory over the Westermarck theory; and (3) if incest taboos have been shaped and maintained largely through cultural self-selection, then one should find abundant evidence in a random sample to bolster Westermarck's earlier list of societies that recognize the deleterious effects of sex with close relatives and prohibit such behavior for that reason.

My second set of objectives was to attempt a preliminary test of the optimal outbreeding theory of incest taboos. Following Ember's lead, I thought it reasonable to focus on variation in the extent of the prohibitions and to attempt to explain that variation in terms of the costs of inbreeding and outbreeding. But that immediately created the challenge of finding appropriate cross-cultural indicators of costs. Here, too, Ember's example pointed the way. First, I decided to use his variable "deme size" as a measure of relative inbreeding costs because of its direct correlation with levels of inbreeding depression. As discussed in the earlier section "Calculating Inbreeding Depression," the number of lethal gene equivalents, n, is likely to attain high values, and thus cause high levels of inbreeding depression (by Eq. 6.2), in large, noninbred populations. Similarly, n and i are likely to have considerably lower values in small, inbred demes where genetic selection more efficiently eliminates deleterious recessives. Thus deme size, although not an all-inclusive measure of inbreeding costs, can be counted on to represent at least the "basic cost" of inbreeding depression.

Second, it occurred to me that Ember's surrogate variable for childhood intimacy, namely, community endogamy, might also work as an index of relative outbreeding costs. My reasoning here was based on a number of cases in which it was apparent that (1) an existing rule of community endogamy was itself a deliberate strategy to minimize the appreciable economic costs (to both individuals and communities) of marrying out; and (2) there can be outbreeding costs, such as economic penalties and added stigma, *because of the rule*. Thus it seemed reasonable to hypothesize that Ember's three levels of local exogamy—namely, endogamy, agamy, and exogamy—could serve as indicators of high, medium, and low outbreeding costs, roughly corresponding to curves O_1, O_2, and O_3, in Fig. 6.7. In other words, an increasing degree of community exogamy, like an increase in relative inbreeding costs, should also cause optimal mates to be less closely related.

If valid, these arguments have one further advantage: they allow a direct, comparative test of the two rival theories (see Table 6.4). If it is true, as Ember argued, that aversion between consanguines has the greatest opportunity to develop where relatives spend their full lives in the same small community, and if it is also true that prohibitions express the general feelings of a population, then Westermarck's theory (row 1 of the table) would predict the most extensive taboos in small, locally endogamous demes. By the same token, the hypothesized "correlation between close living together and the prohibited degrees of relationship" (Westermarck 1922 [1891], 2: 209) would lead us to expect the least extensive taboos in large, locally exogamous demes.

But now compare these predictions with their counterparts from optimal outbreeding theory (row 2 of the table). By that theory, the most extensive taboos are expected where *both* inbreeding costs are high, as in large populations with high n values, *and* outbreeding costs are low, as in populations preferring or requiring local exogamy. Conversely, the least extensive taboos are expected in small, locally endogamous demes; there,

TABLE 6.4

A Comparison of Predictions from the Aversion
and Moral Disapproval Theory and the Optimal Outbreeding Theory

	Predicted conditions for:	
Theory	Least extensive taboos[a]	Most extensive taboos[b]
Aversion and moral disapproval theory	Large, locally exogamous demes	Small, locally endogamous demes
Optimal outbreeding theory	Small, locally endogamous demes	Large, locally exogamous demes

SOURCE: After Ember 1975: 259–63.
[a]Taboos that prohibit sexual relations among relatives with high r values only.
[b]Taboos that extend to relatives with low r values.

inbreeding costs are low, because small inbred populations evolve low n values, and outbreeding costs are high. In short, the predictions of the two theories are truly orthogonal. A retest of Ember's analysis using a world probability sample and improved measurement of key variables should directly support one theory or the other.

Procedures. Assisted by a team of talented Stanford undergraduates (F.H., J.B., P.S., M.H., C.S., and D.G.), I compiled information on four topics for each population in the Sixty Cultures sample: (1) the occurrence of incest in recorded myths; (2) the nature and extent of incest prohibitions; (3) patterns of local endogamy or exogamy and postmarital residence; and (4) inbreeding and its effects, when reported for that population.

A major part of our effort (which is described in detail in Apps. A.6.1 and A.6.2) was dedicated to defining the incest taboo of each population as accurately as possible. Whenever the literature permitted, we therefore kept track of differences between prohibiting consanguineal marriage and prohibiting sex per se, and of differences between prohibitions pertinent to lineage mates and those pertinent to other, non-descent-group relatives. We also developed a series of quantitative measures of taboo extent based upon the coefficient of relationship, r. These variables, listed in Table A.6.1 and discussed more fully below, were defined to measure an ego's most distant prohibited relative of a given kind or category, as described in HRAF documents.[54] Finally, with the aid of student assistants (F.H. and B.C.), these data were tabulated and analyzed, where appropriate, on a Hewlett-Packard 9845B minicomputer with the manufacturer's cross-tabulation program. Our results may be summarized as follows.

The "incest myth" hypothesis. First, after literally months of effort, we found ourselves unable to duplicate the results of the study by Segner

[54]The meaning of our measures of extent may be visualized as follows. Imagine an abstract "kinship space" for a particular person, "ego," in which each of his or her consanguines is represented by a point separated from ego (at center) by a distance commensurate with the r-value of their relationship. For a given kind or category of relative, our measures of extent are equal to the radius of the smallest sphere that includes *all* such relatives "covered" by the taboo and thus prohibited from sexual relations (or, alternatively, from marriage).

(1968) that advocated the "incest myth" hypothesis. In the first phase of this effort, using HRAF files alone for the universe of information (as did Segner), we did find myths of incestuous motif for 23 of the 60 populations (38.3 percent). However, among those myths, we found reference to "inferior offspring or infertility" in only 3 cases: the African Dogon, and the South American Cagaba and Guaraní. This finding, equivalent to 13.0 percent of the incest myth total and 5.0 percent of the grand total, contrasts sharply with Segner's results (32.3 percent and 17.5 percent respectively).

Not to give up easily, and spurred by Clyde Kluckhohn's remark that "there is no corpus of mythology that I have searched carefully where this motif [incest] does not turn up" (1960: 47), we expanded the search procedure and the universe of sources in a second phase of this study, as explained in App. A.6.1. This brought the total to 56 incest myths, distributed among 33 populations, but still only 5 of the sample populations had myths specifying deleterious genetic effects (15.2 percent of those with incest myths and 8.3 percent of the total). A far greater number of cases (23 myths in 20 societies) featured incest myths with neutral to beneficial consequences, such as the birth of culture heroes or giants of super strength.

In short, if one takes as Segner's hypothesis the statement that an encoding of inbreeding depression in the myths of "almost one-third" of the sample populations "is probably a minimal estimate" (1968: 33), our test is an unambiguous rejection. I can only conclude that Segner's sample was seriously biased in the first place.

The recognition hypothesis. Second, we studied the consequences of taboo violations, real or hypothetical, as they were described by the natives to the ethnographers represented in HRAF. Our results are given in the last three columns of Table A.6.1, here summarized as Table 6.5, where the following tallies can be seen: (1) we found at least one reported consequence of incest in 40 of the 60 populations of the sample; (2) of these 40, we found mention in 29 cases (72.5 percent of the subtotal) that a *social* sanction, most commonly death, followed against one or more of the guilty parties; and (3) in 16 cases, some of which overlapped with (2), there was mention of a *supernatural* sanction, most commonly disease or death.

But the most important finding was (4): in a full 20 populations—one-half of all unambiguous cases with some reported consequence or other—we found mention of a "bad stock" argument. In other words, of all the populations that could, with these data, be said to have recognized the harmful effects of inbreeding, a full 50.0 percent were found to have done so.[55] Many of the citations were frustratingly brief; understandably, in-

[55] These totals are based only on information contained in HRAF. Thus, I have not included the case of the San Blas Kuna even though other sources suggest some form of recognition (see, for example, Segner 1968: 50). I have also not included the Trukese of the Central Caroline Islands of Micronesia even though there is solid evidence for recognition in

TABLE 6.5

Reported Consequences of Incest Among Populations in the "Sixty Cultures" Sample

Occurrence within the "Sixty Cultures" sample	Reported consequences of incest[a]			Total[b] (any reported consequence)
	Social sanction	Supernatural sanction	Inbreeding depression	
Unambiguous cases[c]				
Number of populations	29	16	20	40
(Percent of total)	(72.5%)	(40.0%)	(50.0%)	
Total cases				
Number of populations	29	16	23	42
(Percent of total)	(69.0%)	(38.1%)	(54.8%)	

SOURCE: Table A.6.1.

[a] Social sanctions include ostracism, beating, and death; supernatural sanctions include chaos, disease, and death; inbreeding depression includes physical and mental defects as well as infertility.

[b] This number is not the simple sum of row entries because multiple consequences are reported for some populations.

[c] Refers to populations for which there is an unambiguous report of the given consequence. (For the ambiguous cases, see note 55.)

breeding effects are not always in the forefront of attention among recording ethnographers. For example, among the Lapps of Scandinavia, the report is that incest "makes insanity and bad blood"; among the Tlingit native to North America, that "the children are likely to be deformed"; among the Kapauku of Papua New Guinea, that through incest "their vital substance will deteriorate"; and among the Tucano of South America, that with incest, "we will not have children or . . . the children will die." But several of the descriptions, including some recorded well before the genetics of inbreeding depression were understood in the West, bordered on virtual theories of what one might justly call "ethnogenetics."

Three features of the tabulation in Table 6.5 are especially noteworthy. First, we found more reports claiming inbreeding depression (abnormal offspring or sterility) as a consequence of incest (20 populations) than reports of supernatural sanctions like death and disease (16 populations), once thought to be *the* defining feature of incest prohibitions. Second, this total of 20 populations is more than two-thirds of the equivalent total (29 populations) for which we found evidence for any social sanction. Third, our impression, confirmed by simple statistical measures, was that the number of "positive" cases was limited largely by the mere quantity of ethnographic material available.[56] In short, the data from this world

---

other nearby, closely related populations of the region, such as the Ulithians and Yapese (see App. A.6.3). In addition, I have not counted three ambiguous cases, namely the Azande, the Somali, and the Libyan Bedouin. For the Azande we are told only that "the reason for this prohibition is the danger of mixing blood" or the "danger in encountering the blood of a relative in mating"; for the Somali, that "no Somali ever marries a girl of his own tribe for fear of consanguinity"; and for the Libyan Bedouin, only that incest is "dangerous." Because the nature of the dangers was unspecified, I include these only in the bottom row of Table 6.5.

[56] As one check on the implications of this tally, we correlated the total number of pages coded in the HRAF category 582 ("regulation of marriage"), a crude measure of the relative

probability sample, incomplete though they are, indicate that a majority of the world's human populations do recognize the deleterious phenotypic effects of inbreeding.

The interpretation hypothesis. At the same time, however, these data do not permit a systematic test of the interpretation hypothesis, that is, the hypothesis concerning the natives' efforts to make sense of any inbreeding depression that they notice. Instead, the data require a more focused examination of a few specific cases in which the reporting ethnographers obviously pursued the topic in some detail. Although this procedure limits the generalizations that can be drawn, the evidence is, in some ways, still more persuasive than that already presented. These cases suggest, for instance, that in at least some populations: (1) incest does recur with sufficient frequency to ensure periodic reinforcement of local taboos, even in the face of aversion and moral disapproval; (2) people do take more than casual, passing interest in the harmful phenotypic consequences of inbreeding; and (3) the repetition of such consequences through time has prompted their appropriate local interpretation. Far from being the projections or fabrications of Western scholars, as some authors have suggested, folk understandings of inbreeding effects can be an integral part of locally evolved "systems of meaning." Moreover, these cases show that the consequences of inbreeding are not always viewed as the work of angry gods; sometimes they are interpreted simply as physical incompatibilities. Let me briefly describe two particularly revealing cases from our findings in the Sixty Cultures study (see App. A.6.3 for additional examples drawn from the greater ethnographic literature).

According to Raymond Firth's classic study, the incest taboo of the Polynesian Tikopia is comprised of "a series of bans of decreasing intensity, the prospect of breaking the rule and substantiating one's conduct becoming the greater as the kinship tie becomes less close." (1957 [1936]: 330.) The intensity decreases from nuclear family relationships ("viewed with extreme repugnance"; "would probably be banished or driven to suicide") to the unions of first cousins ("not actually prevented, [but] are viewed with disgust by the people at large"), and on to second cousins, who are "free to do as they wish." (pp. 330–31.)

Curiously, notes Firth, the disapproval of sexual relations among close kin is usually "carried no further than verbally." The reason, he continues, "lies in [the belief] that unions of close kin bear with them their own doom, their *mara* . . . [meaning] failure, or ill luck, misfortune. The idea essentially concerns barrenness." (pp. 333–34.) But this barrenness is not complete biological infertility. It "consists not in the absence of children, but in their illness or death, or some other mishap [such as periodic

---

quantity of incest-related data available for a given society, with the number of pages where we found mention of an inbreeding "folk theory." We obtained a correlation coefficient of $r = 0.29$ $(p < .05)$ in the full sample, and of $r = 0.51$ $(p < .05)$ in the subsample of 21 populations with community endogamy. Quality of information aside, with simply a greater quantity of documentation we would expect to find more folk theories.

lunacy]. . . . The idea that *the offspring of a marriage between near kin are weakly and likely to die young* is stoutly held by these natives and examples are adduced to prove it." (p. 334, emphasis added.) But notice that this statement is close to what the genetic theory of inbreeding depression would predict. Tikopians not only recognize that inbreeding is harmful; they also appreciate the probabilistic nature of that harm as well as its variable manifestations—illness, death, or lunacy—in the offspring. Indeed, Tikopians substantiate their views with examples from living memory. At the same time, they offer an interpretation of these effects along the lines of Burton's attribution hypothesis. Their belief, says Firth, "is not of the nature of a biological theory that inbreeding is injurious per se, but it is a belief in the operation of supernatural forces. These are [believed to be] an expression of the resentment of the parents of the guilty pair, who in life have suffered the union, but after death vent their accumulated spleen on the offspring." (p. 334.) By this folk theory, it is the spirits of deceased parents or other ancestors who return to bewitch and torment the offspring of the incestuous couple. Cases of the death of such children were said to be "known to everyone," forming "the empirical basis for the common opinion." (p. 335.)

The Tikopia case shows quite clearly that a folk theory of great affective strength can persist at high cultural fitness even in the absence of reinforcing social sanctions. It is this theory that, as Firth explains, "helps to explain why the Tikopia seem so apathetic about taking action in regard to [incest]. They disapprove, they sneer, but they put no other physical barrier in the way of the union of closely related lovers. . . . For sooner or later the incestuous pair will have to pay for their disregard of custom." (pp. 335–36.) It may be that a folk theory lacking in additional, socially imposed consequences is especially likely among populations with high "global inbreeding" (i.e., F_o substantially greater than 0.0 in Eq. 6.1), such as the insular Tikopia. Nevertheless, the case demonstrates that the intrinsic negative reinforcement of inbreeding depression can be sufficient to maintain the belief through space and time.[57]

The case also demonstrates the "absolute" quality of the moral code legislated by the spirits, which is more than the product of their personal displeasure or anger; rather, it "exists in the absolute, independent of the gods." (p. 335.) That moral law is, I suggest, the cultural equivalent of our Western genetic law of inbreeding depression.[58] If followed faithfully, it

[57] An interesting parallel to the Tikopian case is that of the Zulu of southern Africa, whose reactions to incest are said by Krige to "vary according to the closeness of the relationship of the people concerned. If a man were to commit incest with his own sister or with a young wife of his father, his own people would rise up and kill him in horror. . . . If, however, the relationship is less close and a relative such as the father's sister's child is married, people will be angry and the culprit might be forced to flee from public opinion, but he would not be put to death. *It is believed, however, that the ancestral spirits themselves will inflict punishment, and that the offspring of an incestuous relationship will be a monster.*" (1936: 224, emphasis added.)

[58] Firth was apparently not convinced of the link between genetics and the "absolute" moral law of the Tikopia. He favored a "sociological basis of the incest ban," because in-

will prevent the vengeful effects of the spirits. But the law is also much more than a simple translation of principles; it is an integral part of the greater Tikopian system of understandings and meanings. As part of that system, one suspects that the law is especially convincing for the locals, indeed far more convincing than would be our Western genetic analog, in part because it is viewed as "absolute." In Tikopia, "the spirits [too], just as men, respond to a norm of conduct of an external character." (p. 335.)

A second noteworthy folk theory is that of the Toradja, an Indonesian population living in the center of Sulawesi (Celebes) that was studied by the Dutch ethnographers Nicolaus Adriani and Albert Kruyt earlier this century. According to the Toradja, the incest taboo rests on the incompatibility that arises when "a man and a woman have physical characteristics (*oea ngkoro*) that come into conflict with each other when they marry." The children of such a marriage will be "weak, sickly, or idiotic and quickly die. *Therefore a marriage with a person too closely related is considered unsuitable* (*bare'e raposioea,* literally, not corresponding in physical characteristics); *their children are then not healthy and do not live long.*" (Adriani and Kruyt 1951, 2: 181, in HRAF "Toradja," OG11: 263.) Here, then, is a population that clearly recognizes the deleterious effects of inbreeding, that clearly attributes them to a regular and systematic cause, and that clearly sustains a marital prohibition on that account. But the attribution is to something more like a principle of ethnogenetics (the "conflict of physical characteristics") than it is to the displeasure of the supernatural. The Toradjans view the consequences of incest as evidence that "nature was thrown into confusion." (Adriani and Kruyt 1950, 1: 219, in HRAF "Toradja," OG11: 325.)

Importantly, the Toradjans' argument reportedly caused objections to marriage only in the case of individuals related in a direct line. For example, Adriani and Kruyt report that "many object to a marriage between cousins out of fear that such a union will remain childless; or that the children resulting from it will not have viability, [or] will be idiotic or crippled." (1951, 2: 284, in HRAF OG11: 412.) On the other hand, if the blood relationship of marriage candidates is more distant, objections can be brushed aside so long as certain rites of expiation are observed. In this way, the probabilistic nature of inbreeding depression is handily accommodated; the expiation often "works" among distant consanguines—and the children of the marriage are often healthy.

The Toradja case is also interesting for its evidence that incest does occur despite proscription.

---

cest "creates difficulties in the working of the kinship group." (1957 [1936]: 336–37.) "I am prepared to see it shown," he added, "that the incest situation . . . has very little to do with the prevention of sex relations as such, but that its real correlation is to be found in the maintenance of institutional forms in the society as a whole, and of the specific interest of groups in particular." (p. 340.) Although I am persuaded of these *additional* consequences, not one of them can explain the supernatural sanction, the *mara*, as described by Firth's informants.

There are many stories about men and women who supposedly married a tree spirit. There are women who say that they are visited every night by a *bela*. Many become pregnant from such intercourse. . . . [Some of] the children who are said to result from a marriage with a spirit are described as "light of skin with blue eyes and white hair." This refers to albino children. . . . So-called spirit-children do not live long, because their fathers take them in order to bring them up themselves. [1951, 2: 56–57, in HRAF OG11: 82–83]

The description of these "spirit-children" amounts to an accurate folk account of the effects of inbreeding, complete with an explanation for common premature mortality.[59] The fact is not lost on Toradja chiefs and elders, several of whom assured the authors "that women claimed to have been made pregnant by a tree spirit when their condition was the result of intercourse with a member of her kin group whom she was not permitted to marry." (p. 57, in HRAF p. 82.) I find it particularly revealing that the chiefs consider inbreeding effects to be *diagnostic* of such concealed, illicit unions. One could scarcely ask for better evidence of recognition.

A test of the cost/benefit model. Although the Sixty Cultures study has offered reasonably strong support for optimal outbreeding theory, the evidence has not so far permitted us to compare its success with that of Westermarck's proposal. Such a comparison is made possible by a test of the cost/benefit model (Fig. 6.8) using the various measures already described. In particular, it becomes possible to examine the conditions of deme size and local endogamy or exogamy under which incest taboos reach their greatest extension, thus prohibiting sexual relations among kin out to small values of r.

For this purpose, I find it useful to define the variable r_s to be, for any given population, the r value of the most distant consanguineous relative with whom sex is forbidden, not including lineage mates.[60] (See Table A.6.1 for the r_s values obtained for each population of the Sixty Cultures sample.) Thus a value of r_s equal to 0.125 would indicate that, in a given society, the incest taboo extends to at least one "kind" of cousin (for example, to the children of two brothers, or so-called patrilateral parallel

---

[59] Relatively high frequencies of albinism are reported for many small and globally inbred populations. For example, the San Blas Kuna (population number 50 of the sample; see also note 43) are reported to have the world's highest frequencies (see Keeler 1953, 1964, 1970). Albinism is also known among the Tikopia (number 47), where it was described to Firth (1957: 16–17) as "running in families" and as causing short life span.

[60] For some of the populations in the Sixty Cultures sample, incest taboos are defined in the literature solely in terms of marriage as opposed to sexual relations. In such cases (designated in Table A.6.1 by square brackets around the r_s values), I substituted for r_s the values of another variable, r_m, representing the most distant consanguineous relative with whom marriage is forbidden, not including lineage mates. These r_m values, in turn, were obtained from yet other measures as follows. First, r_{dg} was defined as the r value of the most distant relative of ego's descent group to be included in the prohibition of marriage. Second, r_{pat} and r_{mat} were defined as the r values of the most distant patrilateral and matrilateral relatives prohibited as marriage partners, setting aside descent group members. Third, r_m was then defined as a summary of the marriage prohibition, designating the higher r value of the two, r_{pat} and r_{mat}. It indicates that at least one relative at the next lower r value is an eligible marriage partner.

cousins), and that relatives at the next smallest r value, 0.062—for example, first cousins once removed—are eligible partners for sexual relations. In terms of r_s, then, one would predict that if Westermarck's aversion were the principal force in the shaping of incest taboos, then r_s should tend to be smaller (that is, the taboos should tend to be more extensive) in small endogamous communities. In contrast, if the costs of inbreeding and outbreeding hold sway, then r_s should be larger in such communities.

Tests of these predictions are summarized in Tables 6.6 and 6.7. Here the Sixty Cultures populations are cross-tabulated according to degree of community exogamy and their value of r_s. Table 6.6, tabulated from the full sample (minus five cases with missing values), reveals a striking general trend: as community exogamy increases, and so the costs of outbreeding (presumably) go down, r_s values also decrease dramatically. Thus, the high average r_s of endogamous societies, 0.245 (meaning that, on average, persons are prohibited from sexual relations only with nuclear family members and uncles or nieces), is replaced by the lower average of 0.074 among exogamous societies (meaning that sexual relations are prohibited, on average, with relatives as distant as first cousins once removed).

The association is a statistically significant one: locally endogamous populations do tend to be more accepting of close relatives as sexual partners than do their locally exogamous counterparts.[61] But, if we assume that these endogamous societies also provide opportunity for more relatives to share intimate childhood association, and thus to have a feeling against sexual relations, these findings run counter to the predictions of the Westermarck theory. At the same time, they do provide solid support for the optimal outbreeding argument: local endogamy implies high outbreeding costs, which are predicted to cause optimal mates to be more closely related. This matches the pattern of Table 6.6.

But does the correlation of r_s and endogamy hold when average local community size is taken into account? As we have seen, there is reason to believe that relatives in societies with smaller communities "should be more familiar than [relatives] in the ones with larger communities" (Ember 1975: 260) and thus that, according to Westermarck, taboos should extend farther in the more intimate circumstances. But as we have also

[61] With a discrete scale for degree of exogamy (1 = endogamy, 2 = agamy, 3 = exogamy), the Pearson correlation coefficient for Table 6.6 has the value -0.58 ($p < 0.01$). The correlation is negative, implying that low values of r_s (denoting extensive taboos) are generally associated with a high degree of exogamy. When both r_s and exogamy are treated as discrete variables (such that r_s is recoded to 1 for the value 0.500, 2 for 0.250, 3 for 0.125, and so on), a nonparametric correlation coefficient, Kendall's τ, has the value $+0.37$ ($p < 0.05$; the correlation is positive as a consequence of the recoding). The one endogamous society at $r_s = 0.031$ is population number 52, the Aymara of Bolivia. Not surprisingly, I obtained very similar results using the variable r_m, a measure indicating the most distant consanguine with whom *marriage* is forbidden (see note 60), instead of r_s. In that case, the Pearson correlation coefficient, is -0.55.

TABLE 6.6

The Correlation Between Community Exogamy and Extent of Incest Prohibition
in All Populations of the "Sixty Cultures" Sample

(number and percent of sample populations with a given r_s)

Degree of community exogamy	Extent of incest prohibition								Row totals	Row averages[a]
	0.500	0.250	0.125	0.062	0.031	0.015–0.008[a]	0.004–0.002[a]	0.001[b]		
Exogamous (Row %)	0 (0.0)	2 (11.1)	4 (22.2)	3 (16.7)	4 (22.2)	2 (11.1)	1 (5.6)	2 (11.1)	18 (100.0)	0.074
Agamous (Row %)	2 (11.1)	7 (38.9)	7 (38.9)	1 (5.6)	1 (5.6)	0 (0.0)	0 (0.0)	0 (0.0)	18 (100.0)	0.207
Endogamous (Row %)	3 (15.8)	10 (52.6)	5 (26.3)	0 (0.0)	1 (5.3)	0 (0.0)	0 (0.0)	0 (0.0)	19 (100.0)	0.245
Column totals (Column %)	5 (9.1)	19 (34.5)	16 (29.1)	4 (7.3)	6 (10.9)	2 (3.6)	1 (1.8)	2 (3.6)	55[c] (100.0)	0.177

$\chi^2 = 25.4$ (p < 0.01).

SOURCE: Data from the Human Relations Area Files (see Table A.6.1).

[a] Aggregate categories of r_s; the midrange values were used in calculating row averages.

[b] Used for prohibitions described as applying to all recognized consanguines.

[c] This total omits five populations with missing values.

TABLE 6.7

The Correlation Between Community Exogamy and Extent of Incest Prohibition in Populations with Small Communities (<400) in the "Sixty Cultures" Sample

(number and percent of sample populations with a given r_s)

Degree of community exogamy	Extent of incest prohibition								Row totals	Row averages [a]
	0.500	0.250	0.125	0.062	0.031	0.015–0.008 [a]	0.004–0.002 [a]	0.001 [b]		
Exogamous	0	0	2	2	4	2	0	2	12	0.044
(Row %)	(0.0)	(0.0)	(16.7)	(16.7)	(33.3)	(16.7)	(0.0)	(16.7)	(100.0)	
Agamous	1	4	4	0	1	0	0	0	10	0.203
(Row %)	(10.0)	(40.0)	(40.0)	(0.0)	(10.0)	(0.0)	(0.0)	(0.0)	(100.0)	
Endogamous	2	3	3	0	0	0	0	0	8	0.266
(Row %)	(25.0)	(37.5)	(37.5)	(0.0)	(0.0)	(0.0)	(0.0)	(0.0)	(100.0)	
Column totals	3	7	9	2	5	2	0	2	30	0.156
(Column %)	(10.1)	(23.3)	(30.0)	(6.7)	(16.7)	(6.7)	(0.0)	(6.7)	(100.0)	

$\chi^2 = 21.5$ (p < 0.01).

SOURCE: Community size data from Murdock 1967; other data from the Human Relations Area Files (see Table A.6.1).

[a] Aggregate categories of r_s; the midrange values were used in calculating row averages.

[b] Used for prohibitions described as applying to all recognized consanguines.

seen, small endogamous communities are expected to have, if anything, *lower* inbreeding depression and lower inbreeding costs, and therefore optimal partners of higher r than larger endogamous communities. With this second variable included in the tabulations, then, which theory provides the better fit to the facts?

The answer, as shown in Table 6.7, remains the same: the correlation between the degrees of prohibition and exogamy is still more pronounced here, among societies with average local community size under 400, than it is in Table 6.6.[62] Indeed, the average r_s of the small endogamous communities, 0.266, is, as expected by outbreeding theory, slightly higher than the already high value in Table 6.6, 0.245, and no endogamous population in Table 6.7 prohibits relatives more distant than first cousins. In short, the overall pattern corroborates Ember's findings on first cousin marriage. It also fits with Austin Hughes's (1980) report that, of all 97 societies in Murdock's *Atlas* that prefer or actually prescribe some form of first cousin marriage, 72.2 percent have an average community size of less than 200. As optimal outbreeding theory predicts, small endogamous populations do seem to have less extensive incest taboos than do their exogamous counterparts.

In short, the results of these tests on the Sixty Cultures sample confirm and extend Ember's (1975) earlier findings. They indicate that inbreeding theory, supplemented by a consideration of outbreeding costs, accounts for more of the variance in incest taboos than does the aversion and moral disapproval theory. On the one hand, this implies that aversion-based primary value selection must have been a relatively weak force in the cultural evolution of incest taboos, if indeed it has been a force at all. On the other hand, these results suggest that secondary value selection has been much stronger. We have seen, first, that many societies do recognize and negatively value one or more of the consequences of inbreeding. The data are compelling on this point despite (1) their obvious gaps and uneven quality; (2) a certain prejudice against this conclusion on the part of many anthropologists (see, for example, White 1948: 418); and (3) my own deliberately conservative requirement that, to be counted, each society had to have its own independent report of recognition. Because Table 6.5 ignores reports from other cultural systems closely related by descent to those in the Sixty Cultures sample, the tally here should be viewed as a minimum estimate of recognition. Second, we have seen how in the case of two particular societies—Tikopia and Toradja— people interpret the consequences of inbreeding and react against them and their behavioral causes. This reaction, in turn, does two things: it reinforces the social transmission of the memes prohibiting such behavior; and it causes, in effect, valued-based cultural selection against more permissive variants. Third, we have seen that this cultural evolutionary pro-

---

[62] If we follow the procedures described in note 61, the correlation coefficients for Table 6.7 are −0.70, r, and +0.48, τ—both substantially greater than their counterparts for Table 6.6. When r_m is substituted for r_s, the value of r is −0.65.

cess may well generalize. Indeed, the evidence presented here does not rule out the provocative evolutionary hypothesis that all existing incest taboos are related by descent to one, or a few, ancestral prohibitions that were based on recognition and interpretation. For all we currently know, these ubiquitous memes may all be cultural homologs—locally refined variations on the same ancestral theme.

I conclude that the evidence of our cross-cultural analysis is consistent with the hypothesis that secondary value selection has been, in most societies, the principal guiding force in the cultural evolution of incest taboos. In fact, judging from the correlations shown in the tables, incest taboos appear to offer fairly reliable guidance when it comes to balancing the costs of inbreeding against the costs of mating out. The implication is that the taboos are generally adaptive, and therefore that the relationship of genes and culture here *is*, in most cases, enhancement. This conclusion does not, of course, rule out imposition as an important contributory force or even as the main mechanism in particular cases. But overall it does suggest that selection by choice, guided by cultural values, has been the predominant power.

Enhancement and Evolution

To conclude this case study of human incest taboos, let me briefly summarize what I see as the two central arguments of this chapter, one an argument about mechanism and one an argument about relationship.

Secondary Value Selection

Consider, first, the argument about mechanism. In this chapter I have, in essentials, retraced the logical footsteps of my argument in Chapter 2 about the mechanism of cultural evolution among the thongpa serfs of Tibet. The phenomena I have sought to explain here are, of course, very different from those of the Tibetan case, and so are the specific features of the theory I have offered to account for them. Yet the basic logic of that theory runs closely parallel. I have suggested that incest taboos, like the monomarital principle, may be viewed as memes that have been kept "alive" in cultural pools largely through the positive cultural evaluation of their consequences.

More specifically, the evidence presented in this chapter suggests that the ecological consequences of taboo variants—consequences broadly defined to include various costs of inbreeding and outbreeding—have had a major feedback effect on their differential social transmission. I have argued that this feedback effect is governed by the cultural evaluation of the consequences. That evaluation, in turn, promotes decisions against memes that allow or encourage mating with the closest of relatives and in favor of memes that direct mate choices toward more distant (and more reproductively beneficial) kin. Moreover, the evidence indicates that cultural selection has often been conscious and deliberate, guided by a recognition of inbreeding effects together with a folk theory of their causation by supernatural agents or inferred natural laws. People have commonly "figured out" that inbreeding is deleterious, and have reacted accordingly.[63]

In incest taboos, then, I believe we have another example of the differential social transmission of memes according to their consequences. In mechanism, the example is similar to other cases we have considered. But there are two distinguishing features of this case. First, the valued ecological consequences of this example are particularly close correlates of individual inclusive fitness. At issue here are effects still more direct than the life-sustaining resources of agricultural estates, or the severity of calcium deficiency diseases; the effects here are human fertility and mortality themselves. Moreover, because of the very nature of inbreeding, their effect on inclusive fitness is automatically compounded. Nevertheless, it is again the case that people are motivated and guided in their choices neither by abstract scientific notions nor by an intuitive concept of inclusive fitness (a point also made by Firth 1957 [1936]: 334, as noted earlier), but by local values and a system of meanings that render the case against inferior options particularly convincing to them.

A second distinguishing feature concerns the range of environmental conditions under which these ecological consequences are presumably realized. In earlier chapters, the reinforcing effects of selected memes were highly condition-specific; for example, in some locations, human populations can and do obtain both calcium and vitamin D without drinking fresh milk. Similarly, there appear to be any number of environments where parents manage to provide for their children in blissful absence of a monomarital rule. In contrast, there are few human environments, if any, that preclude or mask the deleterious effects of inbreeding.[64] It seems to me likely that this property of human incest taboos, together with their direct impact on inclusive fitness, helps to explain their ubiquitously high cultural fitness.

Incest Taboos as a Case of Enhancement

On these grounds, I submit that incest taboos exemplify an enhancing relationship between genes and culture in most of the populations where

[63] Pulliam and Dunford offer a similar argument, suggesting that the recognition of inbreeding effects provides a mechanism for cultural selection quite apart from "natural subtraction": "perhaps someone would see that the custom of incest led to malformed children and would persuade the family members to change their ideas about incest. In this case, the custom would cease because the ideas that motivated it would be shown to be inconsistent with the desired goals of the individuals. At any rate, whether by cognitive inconsistency or by natural subtraction, the custom would decline and eventually disappear." (1980: 95.) This "cognitive inconsistency" is what I have called cultural selection: the influence of value-guided decisions on cultural evolution.

[64] An exception that tests the rule was suggested by van den Berghe and Mesher (1980). They point out that the persistent inbreeding of some royal families—Egyptian pharaohs, Incan emperors, Hawaiian kings—was accompanied by extensive noninbred polygyny. In

they exist. I suggest that (1) there are substantial inclusive fitness costs both to close inbreeding and to distant outbreeding in most if not all human populations; (2) these costs have generally been recognized and culturally evaluated as the basis for the cultural selection of variant incest taboos; and (3) incest taboos have therefore evolved in the direction of properties, such as greater versus lesser extent, that tend to enhance human survival and reproduction. Additional functions have sometimes been added (as when incest taboos grade into lineage exogamy), and the taboos are clearly part of larger systems of kinship rules and regulations. Nevertheless, the data presented in this chapter suggest that they constitute a cultural evolutionary response to the problems of optimal outbreeding.

Let me summarize, then, why I believe the cultural selection of incest taboos to qualify as examples of enhancement.[65] As discussed at the start of this chapter, the defining features of enhancement are two: first, the culturally selected allomemes must have the highest inclusive fitness consequences for their carriers; and second, the influence of cultural values must be to augment the cultural fitness advantages of the allomemes in question over what those advantages would otherwise be. The evidence I have presented suggests that both features commonly apply to the cultural selection of incest taboos. First, cross-cultural variation in the range of prohibited relatives matches the pattern one would expect of memes that promote optimal reproductive success among their carriers. Second, close inbreeding is widely considered detrimental to reproduction and is often said to be prohibited for that reason. It is true that much of the evidence is only correlational, that the sample is rather small (particularly when subdivided to control for community size or other variables), and that more refined measures and tests are certainly called for. Nevertheless, the overall pattern is suggestive, particularly in light of detailed ethnographic cases of "pragmatic fertility testing," of incestuous unions that "bear with them their own doom," of "physical characteristics that come into conflict," and the like.

The implication is that value-guided cultural selection has been the principal mechanism of change in the evolutionary descent of incest taboos. This does not, of course, imply that other forces of cultural evolution have been insignificant. Quite to the contrary, we have seen that there is ample potential both for the natural selection of taboo variants and for their primary value selection under the influence of sexual aver-

---

principle, this social arrangement could provide for high inclusive fitness (and royal succession) even when the inbred unions were themselves subject to serious inbreeding depression.

[65] A number of previous authors have come to the same conclusion; for example, Ray Bixler points out that through incest taboos "culture *enhances* the avoidance of inbreeding depression beyond that achieved by other species." (1981b: 281, emphasis added.) While I agree with Bixler on this point, I use the term enhancement with a broader meaning. With respect to incest taboo variants, for example, I suggest that culture also enhances differences in the rates of social transmission.

sion. But it is also clear that these are unconscious, imprecise, and relatively slow forces, and that their operation may be thwarted by common circumstances—like the physical separation of related children—in human social life. As a result, I agree with Wolf (1966: 897) that although intimate childhood association, for example, does create an aversion to sexual relations and marriage, this fact "does not explain the incest taboo, nor does it explain the associated and sometimes independent rules of exogamy." Primary value selection and differential reproduction may play some role, but they are not sufficient explanation.

Probably, it seems to me as I look back over this analysis with the 20-20 vision that comes from hindsight, the results of comparing the Westermarck and Burton theories should not have been surprising. Given our capacity for culture, a belief in the deleterious effects of inbreeding is virtually bound to have a greater influence than an aversion, no matter how strong that aversion may be. In the first place, the belief carries the weight of a greater sanction: it warns of defective children to follow, not simply uncomfortable feelings. Second, the belief can readily be linked to other ideational phenomena, including superstitions about additional consequences (see, for example, Frazer 1910, 4: 165–66) and the whole panoply of religious beliefs and meanings. Indeed, it can even be linked to a recognition of the aversion itself, which, after all, has fitness consequences similar to inbreeding depression. Finally, the belief can also prevent the recurrence of inbreeding depression caused by arrangements for child rearing that, in effect, "fool Mother Nature" (van den Berghe 1980: 154) and keep close relatives apart. In all of these ways, it seems likely that the belief would be more efficient than the feeling in performing the very same function.

If this analysis of incest taboos is correct, then secondary value selection truly can favor cultural instructions whose net phenotypic effects mimic the results of genetic selection. In this way, cultural evolution can shape bona fide adaptations in the absence of genetic change.[66]

---

[66] For other candidate examples of an enhancing relationship between genes and culture see, for example, Bailit 1968, on betel-nut chewing in the Solomon Islands; Neumann 1977 and Paque 1984 on salt taboos in North America and Morocco; McDonald 1977 and Ross 1978 on food taboos in Amazonia; S. Katz 1982 on selected food processing techniques among American Indians, Africans, and Chinese; Burchard 1975, 1976, and 1980, Bolton 1976 and 1979, and Fuchs 1978 on coca-leaf chewing at high altitude in South America (but see Bray and Dollery 1983). In addition, Rabin et al. 1965 describe a meme that has helped to combat congenital hip disease among the Navaho of the southwestern United States; however, because the meme was apparently preserved for other reasons, the case appears to be a cultural exaptation, not an adaptation.

NEUTRALITY AND

OPPOSITION: From Cultural

Reason to Cannibalism

The case studies of Chapters 5 and 6 confirm that culture can provide a powerful and effective means of improving human adaptation. Yet many of the same properties that allow culture to work so well at enhancing reproductive fitness can also encourage the spread of less beneficial memes, namely, (1) memes that have little or no adaptive consequence, and (2) memes that have genuine maladaptive effects. In this chapter, I would like to examine these last two possibilities. Called here "neutrality" and "opposition," they represent two additional comparative modes of relationship between genes and culture in human populations.

The Cultural Evolution of Nonadaptive Traditions

Adaptation is guaranteed a central place in genetic evolutionary theory as long as the differential reproduction of individuals can be considered the "predominant Power" (Darwin 1964 [1859]: 43). This argument, however, does not apply to an evolutionary theory of culture. Because cultural variants are spread by differential social transmission—a process that, as we have seen, is not limited to differential reproduction—the operation of natural selection does not itself guarantee a central place for adaptation in culture theory. In the words of the anthropologist Philip Burnham (1973: 95), since culture is "learned and not genetically transmitted, differential reproductive rates do not necessarily act as [important] selective forces in the modification of culture." In fact, some of the forces that are important in the modification of culture, including selection by choice and by imposition, operate through mechanisms that are independent of reproduction. Therefore, *if* adaptation does warrant a central position in culture theory (a question to which we return in the next chapter), its importance must derive from a different set of principles.

Mechanisms of Nonadaptive Change

For the present, let us turn to examine two kinds of mechanisms, both independent of reproduction, that can and do promote the cultural evolution of nonadaptive traditions. These two special forms of cultural selection, which I call "imposition" and "imperfect choice," are, I believe, the most important of all causes of nonadaptive change in cultures.

Imposition. Because the ideas, values, and beliefs in culture are socially disseminated, they can also be controlled and manipulated in a number of devious, self-interested ways. Among other possible outcomes, the cultural system of a population can be co-opted to the advantage of some members with little or no benefit to others, or indeed with considerable cost to them. Through imposition—that is, through the use of authority, manipulation, force, or coercion to alter the course of cultural selection—what is enhancement for one reference group in a population may result in neutrality or opposition for another.

This point was impressed upon me in unusually vivid terms in the course of fieldwork on the rugged, infertile slopes of the hinterlands of El Salvador and Honduras in Central America (see Durham 1979a). Engaged in a study of ecological pressures behind local and regional conflict, I was led inevitably to the countryside where, other authors claimed, "a ravenous scourge of peasants is virtually devouring the land." (Ophuls 1977: 51.) At first glance, that description seemed valid: the landscape, particularly in El Salvador, was littered with telltale signs of maladaptation. Slopes of forty or fifty degrees, or more, were being cultivated in perpetuity with age-old technology, no capital improvements, and steadily declining yields. Corn was cultivated in rock outcrops, animals were grazed in steep gulleys, and the erosive force of tropical rains carried off ever more of the leached and worn-out topsoil. Sewers, sanitation facilities, and supplies of fresh, clean water were unknown, and children with distended bellies and discolored hair—the unmistakable signs of protein-calorie malnutrition—could be seen everywhere. It was an ecologist's nightmare.

The origin of the problem was not to be found in local peasant culture, nor for that matter in the peasants' "lack of education" or "lack of concern" for improving the conditions of life. Rather, it was the self-interested manipulation of national land tenure policies by the landed elite in the nineteenth century, and the more recent institutional support for export agriculture at the expense of traditional food producers, that had increasingly squeezed the peasants from the productive lands of these countries (Durham 1979a: chs. 2 and 4). I came away convinced that the situation *was* hopelessly maladaptive, being opposed, particularly in the long run, to the survival and reproduction of the very cultivators and their descendants who lived and worked under such conditions. But I was also convinced that the situation was not a product of their own choosing. It had been imposed upon them by force, for the economic and social benefit of others. This was a clear case of "imposed opposition" (for further discussion of this example, see Durham 1979a: ch. 2; Browning 1971: ch. 5).

Imperfect choice. A second feature of culture that allows for neutrality and opposition stems from what I have called its "self-selecting capability." In earlier chapters I have argued that secondary values, themselves culturally evolved, can have a major influence upon cultural evolution through their role in the evaluation of allomemes as they undergo selection by choice or imposition. More specifically, I have proposed that secondary values themselves evolve under the influence of primary values; that they therefore generally evolve toward functional appropriateness for local conditions; and that they go on to aid culture carriers in the many evaluations and decisions that life entails. In autonomous reference groups, I have suggested, the usual result is a culturally guided mechanism of change—secondary value selection—that tends to promote human survival and reproduction, and does so with considerably greater efficiency than does natural selection.

But this does not mean that the system is perfect even when choice is permitted. Far from it, for the routine dependence of the decision system on secondary values, surrogate criteria that they are, entails a number of side effects that are potentially maladaptive. For one example, consider the interval of time and human experience that may be required for the cultural evolution of effective secondary values. Although this interval is surely far less, on average, than that required for the genetic evolution of primary values, there is nevertheless the possibility of "value disequilibrium," or what William Ogburn (1950 [1922]: 200–213) called "cultural lag": in changing environments, yesterday's cultural values may be markedly inappropriate and maladaptive for today's circumstances. For another example, consider the potential for damage as a result of "value generalization": though perhaps useful and adaptive for choices faced in one set of circumstances, a given cultural value can be transferred to other circumstances where its feedback may be dangerously misleading.

As a result of these and other "imperfections of choice," there is considerable potential for the cultural evolution of maladaptive traditions. Organically evolved because of its *generally* adaptive consequences, the human decision system can and does have other effects. In the following sections, let us take a closer look at these by-products and at some provocative examples of the neutrality and opposition that they serve to create.

Neutrality

Neutrality may be defined as the relationship between genes and culture that involves no appreciable difference between the inclusive fitness consequences of allomemes in a population. In this situation, differences between cultural variants do not significantly add to or detract from an individual's state of adaptedness; they are "neutral" with respect to F_g. Notice, however, that neutral allomemes need not have equal *cultural* fitnesses at the same time. Because of the internal, self-selective feature of culture, the comparative evaluation of neutral allomemes may yield substantial F_c differentials, propelling cultural evolution in one or another of several different adaptively neutral directions. In this mode of relationship, cultural change will neither enhance nor oppose adaptation.

A Theoretical Framework for Neutrality

In Fig. 7.1, I propose a theoretical framework for neutrality using the same units and scales as in earlier chapters. Panel A shows hypothetical inclusive fitness functions for two sets of allomemes, I and II. Within either set, there is little difference between the survival and reproduction consequences of the variants 1, 2, and 3, which are defined as neutral with respect to human adaptation. At the same time, their cultural fitnesses may vary widely, as in panel B. There, two hypothetical cultural fitness functions are shown, one with a maximum at variant 1 and the other with a maximum at variant 3.

Differences in social transmission between neutral allomemes, like those shown in panel B, can result from many causes: from the selective influence of secondary values; from chance effects (so-called cultural drift); from the historical sequence in which the alternative forms were introduced; from the imitation of influential persons in whom this idea or belief is apparent—indeed from nearly all of the mechanisms of cultural evolution described in Chapter 4. The one exception, of course, is natural selection: by definition, neutral allomemes are *equally* preserved by the reproduction of their carriers. Note also that if force or coercion is involved in setting cultural fitness, then the variants may not in fact be "neutral," and the situation may be more accurately described as socially imposed opposition.[1]

Looking now at the differences between the sets of allomemes I and II, we can see in panel A that the *absence* of the allomemes in question, here designated as allomeme 0, has very different consequences in the two sets. In set I, the inclusive fitness difference between the presence of any one of the variants 1, 2, or 3, and their absence, 0, is essentially zero. This can be called Type I neutrality—the neutrality of variants with little F_g consequence. In set II, the difference is much greater; indeed the absence

---

[1] Neutral allomemes may or may not remain neutral once F_c differentials develop. Thus a given neutral variant may become a symbol or marker of group identity or affiliation, at which point any attempt to adopt an alternative variant may incur substantial F_g costs. In some indigenous populations, for example, a person who chooses Western clothing over functionally equivalent traditional forms may end up being socially ostracized, disinherited, or both.

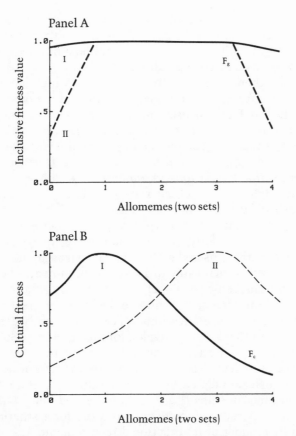

Fig. 7.1. A theoretical framework for neutrality. Panel A shows hypothetical inclusive fitness functions, I and II, for two distinct sets of allomemes arbitrarily numbered o to 4 (o indicates the complete absence of any form of the given meme). Curve I illustrates Type I neutrality: each of the variants 1 to 3 is of little or no consequence on the average to the inclusive fitnesses of its carriers. Curve II represents Type II neutrality: each of the variants 1 to 3 has equal consequence for the inclusive fitnesses of its carriers, and thus they are neutral with respect to one another. However, each also makes a substantial contribution to survival and reproduction when compared to allomemes o or 4. Panel B shows hypothetical cultural fitness functions, I and II, for the same sets of allomemes as in panel A. The curves illustrate the theoretical possibility of significant cultural fitness differentials within groups of neutral allomemes, whether of Type I or Type II. Adapted from Durham 1982: 308.

of the meme in any of its variants is disastrous. In this case, Type II neutrality, the neutral variants have substantial but equal consequences for survival and reproduction. What makes them neutral is the absence of such differences within the set.

To take a hypothetical example, knowing how to make animal-skin parkas in the Arctic may well show a Type II inclusive fitness function. But whether it is knowing how to make parkas of caribou skins (variant 1, say) or to make parkas of musk oxen skins (variant 2) may well be inconsequential, provided supply and assembly costs are roughly equivalent.

An equivalent difference in allomemes at sea level, 30 degrees north or south latitude, would probably have an inclusive fitness function of Type I. In both cases, however, there would be a near-zero F_g difference among the variants undergoing cultural selection.

In neutrality, then, we have a circumstance in which memes may vary without significant impact on human survival and reproduction. The archaeologist Robert Dunnell uses this same criterion when he says that "style denotes those *forms that do not have detectable selective values* [i.e., that do not cause detectable reproduction differentials]. *Function* is manifest as those *forms that directly affect the Darwinian fitness of* [individuals in] *the populations in which they occur.*"[2] (1978: 199, emphasis in the original.) Dunnell also suggests that stylistic elements may be distinguished by their "random behavior" in an evolutionary time frame. Although "capricious behavior" might be a better description, the point is well taken. Similarly, Philip Steadman (1979) argues that the cultural fitnesses of art forms and architectural designs are not a simple by-product of their functional value in a given environment. The persistence of stylistic form, he argues, is largely a matter of cultural preference and what he calls "interference" by human aesthetic or creative impulses. Even where functional specifications appear to be tightly constraining— as, for example, in the design of rigging for sailing ships—Steadman contends that cultural preference is always manifest in at least two ways. First, the design problem itself is "not 'objectively' determined in the first place, but [is instead] created by cultural values and human purposes" (p. 195); other kinds of ships *could* be built. Second, there will inevitably be parts of such a structure where opportunities for aesthetic expression emerge as a by-product of its functional requirements: the ship's design allows, but does not require, a figurehead (on this point, see also Gould and Lewontin 1979).

Neutrality and Cultural Reason

Although a number of authors have made arguments similar to Steadman's for other specific realms of human behavior (see, for instance, Cherfas and Lewin 1980), it is the social anthropologist Marshall Sahlins who states perhaps the most general case for neutrality in the study of culture. Sahlins (1976b: 168) criticizes functional arguments and what he calls "practical reason" as amounting to an "indeterminate explanation of cultural form." In Sahlins's view, inclusive fitness consequences are only pertinent to cultural form at the margins of viability. Within the range of what is possible, an arbitrary "cultural reason" prevails.

Sahlins overstates the case, but on the main point he is surely right:

[2] Dunnell's argument applies to both Type I and Type II neutrality since, as he put it (1978: 199), "specific, adaptively neutral forms may be functionally equivalent manifestations of larger entities." The passage in the text speaks of Darwinian fitness but can easily be generalized to inclusive fitness.

many cultural forms *are* functionally equivalent and are therefore favored, or not favored, in cultural evolution by mechanisms other than natural selection.[3] Consider, for example, his discussion of "the fundamental arbitrariness of the word" in human languages (1976b: 62). Following the arguments of the Swiss linguist Ferdinand de Saussure (1966 [1916]), Sahlins emphasizes that there is "no inherent relation" between a given sound image and the concept it represents. As he notes, "it is not simply that the sound combination 'sheep' has no necessary connection to the animal so designated, any more than does the word '*mouton,*' but that the concept of sheep also varies in different societies." (p. 62.) On the other hand, once a particular association becomes culturally established within a population, the alternatives to it may no longer be functionally equivalent. The point, however, is that there are generally no intrinsic F_g advantages to particular associations.

I can also go along with Sahlins's proposal in some other areas of cultural analysis. On the subject of the American diet, for instance, he argues that by virtue of cultural reason, the memes of food preference are not related to practical benefit. Thus the edibility of certain meats or meat cuts—whether they are "more or less fit for human consumption"—is created by a symbolic association "inversely related to humanity," so that the internal and less desirable parts are more frankly described and compared to parts of the human body, while those on the outside, especially muscle and fat, are considered choice meats (p. 175). But notice, again, that the alternatives are essentially neutral with respect to F_g; in Sahlins's own words, "from the nutritional point of view, such a notion of 'better' and 'inferior' cuts would be difficult to defend." (p. 176.)

In short, I agree with Sahlins that symbolic logic *is* a fundamental organizing principle of cultural systems, and that cultural values *do* reflect the greater systems of meaning within populations. Further, I agree that meaningful differences remain evolutionarily powerful in neutrality, where practical differences and F_g differentials are themselves insignificant. My disagreement is simply over the extent to which this argument generalizes. In particular, I would expect cultural reason to be truly arbitrary and nonpractical only to the degree that the variation on which it acts is, or is perceived to be, adaptively neutral. Among neutral variants in language, meat-cut preferences, art, or fashion, arbitrariness may well be the general rule as Sahlins suggests. But there is certainly nowhere

[3] In the cited passage, Sahlins overstates his case in two ways. First, he misrepresents the concept of "selective advantage," a term that has consistently meant more than "minimum positive functioning" all the way from its very earliest definitions (as in Darwin 1964 [1859]) to its most recent and complex ones (as in Vrba and Eldredge 1984). In fact, judging from the evidence of organic evolution alone, one would have to conclude that "nature" has "ruled" time and time again on specific form. Second, Sahlins is arguing with a straw man's view of adaptation, one in which it is simply "the laws of nature" that shape adaptive forms. Only if we equate adaptation with strictly natural processes and thereby ignore human agency does it follow that "anything within the natural limits . . . is advantageous from the point of view of adaptation."

near this same degree of arbitrariness in the marriage principles of Tibet, the milk-use customs of Europeans, and the incest taboos of the world probability sample.

We will return to this topic later in the chapter. Here it may be noted that my argument with Sahlins can be taken one step further and subjected to direct empirical testing. If, as Sahlins proposes, cultural reason does have free and arbitrary play within the "limit of viability," then we should expect it to cause abundant, sustained examples of yet another mode of gene-culture relations, namely, opposition. In particular, we should expect to find numerous stable examples of opposition by choice, in which people are guided by cultural reason toward viable but relatively maladaptive choices. In contrast, as explained below, my prediction would be that opposition through choice is generally both infrequent and short-lived. I would expect most instances of sustained opposition to result, not from arbitrary cultural reason, but from simple, self-interested imposition.

Opposition

Opposition is the fifth mode of gene-culture relationships in our inventory, and the third of the comparative modes introduced in Chapter 4. I call it "opposition" in order to emphasize the antagonism it represents between the directions of genetic and cultural evolution. In this case, cultural change acts against the ability of human beings to survive and reproduce.

Opposition occurs whenever cultural selection takes place according to an F_c function whose relative maximum (or maxima) favors one or more allomemes that are not the most advantageous in terms of individual inclusive fitness. In other words, for opposition to exist, the ideas and beliefs of highest cultural fitness must actually confer a lower average inclusive fitness upon their carriers than is conferred by some other available option. When this occurs, cultural selection will favor the evolution of phenotypic properties different from those that evolve through the influence of natural selection.

A Theoretical Framework for Opposition

In Fig. 7.2, I propose the comparable framework for opposition. As in earlier models, panel A represents the inclusive fitness consequences of an array of allomemes, 0 to 4; again for purposes of illustration, two different F_g functions are shown, I and II, both with maximum F_g at allomeme 1 while differing in the degree of fitness reduction among suboptimal variants. As shown in panel B, a single cultural fitness function is assumed to apply to both of the F_g curves of panel A, a function whose relative maximum occurs at allomeme 3. Under these conditions, cultural selection

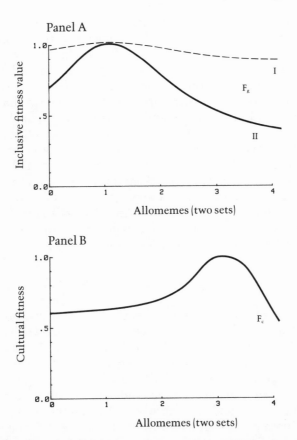

Fig. 7.2. A theoretical framework for opposition. Panel A shows hypothetical inclusive fitness functions, I and II, for two different sets of allomemes numbered 0 to 4 (0 again designates a "null allomeme"). In both cases, the allomeme arbitrarily numbered 1 confers the highest average inclusive fitness upon its carriers. However, the survival and reproduction differentials among allomemes shown by curve II are much more substantial than those shown by curve I. Panel B gives the hypothetical cultural fitness function of both sets of memes (presumed equal for sake of illustration); here, the two allomemes that share the number 3 have the highest expected rates of social transmission. Comparison of panels A and B reveals that in both sets of variants, I and II, cultural selection favors allomemes of suboptimal inclusive fitness for their carriers. Thus set II of panel A shows "major opposition"—that is, the culturally favored variants represent a major reduction of inclusive fitness—while set I shows opposition that is "minor" by comparison but opposition nonetheless. Adapted from Durham 1982: 311.

would favor the evolution of a reproductively suboptimal variant, number 3, despite the coexistence of allomemes with higher F_g. An individual culture carrier would be better off, in reproductive terms, with adherence to one of the available alternative memes or, for that matter, even through a change to allomeme 0 (that is, with dropping the idea or belief altogether) in both cases shown, I and II.[4]

[4] Technically, both may be called opposition. Curve II represents "serious" or "major" opposition because suboptimal allomemes cause a substantial loss of inclusive fitness. Contrast the "minor" opposition indicated by curve I, opposition that grades continuously into

As Fig. 7.2 indicates, for a relationship to qualify as opposition, cultural selection must actually favor an allomeme with less inclusive fitness benefit over an existing option with more. In other words, this relationship (like the others) assumes variation among allomemes and variation among their F_g consequences in the reference group actually under consideration. Given such variation, it can happen that certain allomemes exist within the group and yet remain unavailable to cultural selection because of technological limitations or ideological blinders to novelty; in that case, internal cultural constraints would be the cause of opposition. Similarly, options may exist and yet be unavailable because of power relations between the reference group and some external agency; in that case, external constraints and imposition would be the cause of opposition, as in the example of Central American peasants described earlier. In both of these cases, opposition could be said to stem from "structural" causes as distinct from such "functional" ones as the various forms of choice.

Causes of Opposition

A number of authors have discussed the idea of opposition in human populations, often—like Sahlins—suggesting some kind of harmful internal "reason" to culture. Thus F. T. Cloak (1975: 172) has argued for the "active parasitism" of human beings by their cultural instructions. Cloak suggests that culture evolves with the autonomy of a separate organism, faithful to its own goals and reason, and subject only to the restriction that it cannot destroy its hosts more quickly than they can propagate.

A similar opinion has been offered by the biologist Richard Dawkins, who, as noted in Chapter 4, popularized the term "meme" for the unit of cultural selection. Dawkins uses the term "opposition" in the same sense as I.

Memes and genes may often reinforce each other, but they sometimes come into opposition. . . . I conjecture that co-adapted meme-complexes evolve in the same kind of way as co-adapted gene-complexes. Selection [i.e., differential replication] favors memes which exploit their cultural environment to their own advantage . . . [but] when we look at the evolution of cultural traits and at their survival value, we must be clear whose survival we are talking about . . . [;] a cultural trait may have evolved in the way that it has, simply because it is advantageous to itself. [Dawkins 1976: 213–14]

These "selfish memes" are analogous to Dawkins's well-known "selfish genes" (Dawkins 1976). He joins Sahlins and Cloak in predicting frequent and stable episodes of opposition. According to these authors, people are, as a matter of course, the helpless victims of their own culture.

As I have argued previously (Durham 1976b, 1979b), these views of cul-

neutrality, as we can see by comparing curve I from panel A here with its counterpart in Fig. 7.1. For convenience, however, and because of its greater theoretical significance, I will use the word "opposition" below to mean "major opposition" unless specified otherwise.

tural evolution must be challenged if we are also to accept the argument that our "capacity for culture" evolved under the influence of genetic selection. I agree with Donald Symons, who points out (1979: 308) that Dawkins's analogy of "bits of culture" as "like viruses, self-replicating parasites on human beings" is a good one, but only because it works both ways: "in environments containing pathogenic viruses, [genetic] selection favors the most resistant individuals [and genotypes]" (a similar argument is given by Ball 1984: 148–49). The implication of the genetic evolutionary history of our species is that we should sooner expect active resistance to those "parasites," and I suggest that our principal means of resistance is cultural self-selection.

In my view, opposition is most likely to occur in human populations when cultural selection occurs but circumstances prevent its being reproductively advantageous or neutral. More specifically, my hypotheses are two: first, that most cases of opposition, especially enduring opposition, are socially imposed; and second, that opposition can also occur through selection by choice but only because of the imperfect nature of the human decision system, *not* because we are helplessly parasitized by selfish memes. Of these two pathways to opposition, I give causal priority to imposition because the persistence of suboptimal variants is specifically motivated by the interests of an outside individual or group for whom there generally *are* benefits. At least in principle, imposed opposition is indefinitely sustainable. In contrast, I suggest that opposition by choice is generally a transient side effect of various imperfections in our decision system, four of which are particularly important.[5] They are:

1. *Value blockage.* Though normally strong and effective (in my view), secondary values can be weakened or blocked altogether through such means as brainwashing (that is, the elimination and/or replacement of a given set of cultural values) or addiction to chemical substances.

2. *Value displacement.* Even when effective, secondary values can actively favor maladaptive variants when they are used in novel social-ecological contexts (value disequilibrium); when they are transferred from an appropriate domain of choice to an inappropriate one (value generalization); or when, for whatever reason, one or more are temporarily singled out and given undue weighting (value reification).

3. *Consequence imperception.* Even where secondary values are not blocked or displaced, they can still be ineffective if people do not perceive at least some of the deleterious consequences of a given choice that causes opposition.[6]

---

[5] It should be noted that opposition, like the other interactive and comparative relationships of genes and culture, is defined here as a group-level phenomenon. Specific persons within a given reference group may always deviate from the overall group pattern by virtue of their own idiosyncratic choices.

[6] People, of course, can never perceive *all* of the consequences of their choices, and therefore must necessarily work from incomplete information. My point is simply that selection by choice requires *some* feedback about consequences. (For two provocative examples of op-

4. *Cause imperception.* Finally, even where people do perceive some of the deleterious consequences of their actions, they may fail to link those consequences to one or more allomemes that they have the power to change by their own choice.

Note that each of these imperfections interferes with what I have proposed as the evolved function of our capacity for self-selective cultural evolution.

In the recent literature, the theoretical possibility of opposition has been argued most forcefully by Robert Boyd and Peter J. Richerson (1981, 1985; Richerson and Boyd 1984), who see opposition as a regular, logical consequence of culture's dual inheritance role. They distinguish three mechanisms of cultural evolution that may create opposition. The first one, which they call "frequency-dependent transmission bias," refers to the cultural selection of variants according to their commonness among one's associates: the commoner (or rarer) the variant, the more likely it is to be selected (Boyd and Richerson 1985: 206). The second, "indirect transmission bias," refers to the cultural selection of variants on the basis of an evaluation transferred or generalized from other attributes of their carriers, as when people adopt the style of dress or patterns of speech of persons they admire for their wealth or social position (p. 243). The third, which can (as explained in Chapter 4) be called "role selection," refers to the cultural change that can occur as a consequence of interindividual competition for influential roles in society (p. 178). As one hypothetical example of role selection, Boyd and Richerson suggest the so-called demographic transition of industrialized nations during the last century: norms for small families might have spread, they say, as people imitated professionals and managers whose success in the competition for high status roles had depended upon having few children (see Richerson and Boyd 1984: 433).

Although I agree with Boyd and Richerson that these mechanisms can and do cause opposition, I would characterize them differently. In my view, the first two are simply good examples of the imperfections of choice. In both cases, selection by choice is the mechanism of change; in both cases, choice is guided by specified values (that which is "common" on the one hand and "attractive" on the other); and in both cases, opposition is a by-product of processes that *generally* enhance human adaptation. Consequently, I view Boyd and Richerson's arguments here as reinforcing the larger point that choice, by virtue of its imperfections, is one important source of opposition in human populations. Mechanism three on their list employs a "culling process analogous to natural selection" (1985: 187) that first selects *people* on the basis of certain attributes and then allows them great influence over the course of social transmission. *If*

---

position resulting from consequence imperception, see Whitlaw and Chaniotis 1978; Maramorosch 1987.)

adherence to a particular allomeme of suboptimal F_g makes individuals more likely to achieve certain social roles, and *if* those roles make individuals better-than-average "transmitters" of cultural variants, including the suboptimal one, then the suboptimal allomeme will gain a cultural transmission advantage, creating opposition. I agree with Richerson and Boyd that this is a "logically consistent" hypothesis, and I agree that it could "*sometimes* reduce [carriers'] genetic fitness." (1984: 433, emphasis added.) But notice that it also depends, once again, upon choice: to work, the influential roles must be socially desired in the first place.[7]

Hypotheses for Testing

By these arguments, then, I would expect most instances of opposition to be either the product of imposition, and thus sustainable indefinitely through the exercise of power, or the product of imperfections of choice, and thus relatively unstable and short-lived. In both cases, I would expect some measure of resistance within the affected reference group, although the relations of power, in the case of imposition, might also suppress or obviate any overt reaction. Moreover, I would expect to find few cases, if any, of opposition freely and indefinitely sustained by the symbols, meanings, and "cultural reason" of an autonomous reference group. This would be tantamount, in my view, to imposition without imposers.

The history of our own society would seem to illustrate the sustainability of imposed opposition in the form of slavery and treatment of native peoples. Documented examples from other regions include the Central American case described above (see also Turnbull 1972 on the Ik of east Africa; Jackson 1971, 1979 on the Na-khi of China). The most pressing analytical challenges, then, would seem to lie in the realm of opposition by choice. In particular, there is a need to test two hypotheses: (1) that the imperfections of choice cause opposing relationships that are both unstable and relatively short-lived; and (2) that the indigenous cultural reason of an autonomous reference group, influential though it may be, does not by itself cause stable and long-lasting opposition. Although full, systematic tests of these hypotheses are obviously beyond the scope of this inquiry, let me propose some examples of opposition through choice, and then turn to consider two particular cases in greater detail.

Some Candidate Cases of Opposition Through Choice

Over the years, two levels of opposition through choice have been suggested in the literature. The first level, composed of candidates for general or categorical opposition, includes the following.

---

[7] In this regard, I note that Richerson and Boyd (1984: 434), like Richard Dawkins (1976: 213) before them, suggest that a meme for religious celibacy could be maintained in a population through role selection, since "by avoiding the costs of bearing or supporting children, celibates could devote more resources to spreading their beliefs by nonparental transmis-

1. The introduction and spread of industrial technologies to non-Western peoples, resulting often in "revolutionary confusion" and in disrupted social structure, trading patterns, and even family relations (see Sharp 1952; Farver and Milton 1972).

2. The introduction and spread of cash economies to populations previously characterized by self-provisioning production and a more nearly closed ecosystem, leading to the collapse of the indigenous food production system and drastic nutritional decline (see Bennett 1976; Gudeman 1978; B. Weiss 1980).

The second level, consisting of more specific cases focused on a particular geographical region or on a specific set of allomemes, includes the following.

1. The traditional cultivation of fava beans in Mediterranean populations with relatively high frequencies of persons who, because of their genetically inherited deficiency of the enzyme glucose-6-phosphate dehydrogenase (G-6-PD), tend to suffer from an often fatal type of hemolytic anemia called "favism" after eating those beans (for reviews, see Katz 1987; Katz and Schall 1986; Luzzatto and Battistuzzi 1985).[8]

2. The high cultural fitness of footbinding in certain regions of China for nearly a thousand years, a practice associated with the incapacitation of females and possibly their mortality, morbidity, and suicide (see, for instance, Levy 1966; Dickemann 1981: 428–29).

3. The persistence of beliefs supporting infibulation (a particularly severe form of female "circumcision") among populations in the Sudan region of Africa despite recognized side effects and health hazards (Kennedy 1970; Hosken 1982).

4. Cultural traditions of damaging or addicting drug use, including alcohol and tobacco (see, for example, M. Marshall 1979; McGinnis, Shopland, and Brown 1987).

5. The presumably maladaptive or "wasteful" traditions of abortion, infanticide, adoption, fosterage, and even spouse exchange (see, for ex-

sion." The idea certainly has merit and warrants thorough testing. I note, however, that the cultural evolution of two of the world's largest celibate traditions has already been explained in other terms—terms that qualify, in fact, as imposition; see Goody (1983: 77–81) on Christian religious celibacy, and Goldstein (for example, 1971a: 69–70; see also Chapter 2 of this book) on religious celibacy in Tibet.

[8] Katz and Schall (1979; see also S. Martin 1980) suggest that fava bean consumption by G-6-PD sufficient individuals and heterozygotes (all of whom are non-fava-sensitive) may actually confer a measure of resistance to malaria. If so, then there are two simultaneous but antagonistic adaptations to malaria in these populations, one genetic (genes for G-6-PD deficiency) and one cultural (beliefs promoting fava bean consumption). There are even indications of cultural adaptation to the threat of favism by G-6-PD deficient individuals, including taboos on the consumption of fava beans by pregnant women and children, and the suggestion that the ancient Greek community of Pythagoreans, which as a religious tenet forbade the eating of beans, was a "sheltered environment" for fava-sensitive individuals (see A. Andrews 1949; Lieber 1973; Brumbaugh and Schwartz 1980).

ample, Schneider 1955 on abortion; Sahlins 1976c: ch. 2 on infanticide and adoption; Boyd and Richerson 1981: 108 on spouse exchange).

6. The persistence, in some areas, of folk beliefs incurring substantial health risks, such as the tradition of denying colostrum to newborn children (see, for instance, Fildes 1986: ch. 2) although it is a major source of antibodies and blood clotting factors; or the cutting and treatment of the umbilical cord in such a way as to risk tetanus infection (F. Marshall 1968).

Although reasonable arguments have been made, solid evidence that these are cases of opposition is often difficult to obtain. For many of the suspected cases of opposition by choice, for example, we simply lack adequate demonstration that the three required conditions are met: (1) that the pertinent allomemes do indeed lead to lower F_g values than do other available options; (2) that they have nevertheless been maintained at high F_c values by cultural evolutionary forces; and (3) that the most important of those forces has actually been selection by choice. Let me therefore focus on two candidate examples that seem both to meet these requirements and to have good ethnographic data: the cultural traditions of headhunting among the Mundurucú of the Amazon basin, and of cannibalism among the Fore of highland New Guinea.[9]

Candidate Case 1: Mundurucú Headhunting

In his influential ethnography, *Headhunter's Heritage*, the anthropologist Robert F. Murphy introduced the Mundurucú as follows:

In the Amazon valley, a region where ferociousness was the mode, the Mundurucú Indians enjoyed a reputation for unalloyed, untempered savagery until the turn of the century. Their war parties ranged outward almost every year, striking indiscriminately at tribes anywhere within a radius of five hundred miles, burning the villages, kidnapping children, and taking heads of adults as trophies of their exploits. They did not indulge in cannibalism, as so many of their neighbors, but the terror they inspired was so great that they themselves were seldom preyed upon and eaten. Their homeland on the upper Tapajós River, south of the Amazon, was rarely attacked, and though they no longer go to war their reputation still protects them from the hostile tribes of the region. [1960: 1]

Although warfare had ended by 1912 (Murphy's fieldwork was four decades later), the Mundurucú still talked about it "as if it were yesterday," recounting in "vivid detail [its] techniques and patterned activities."

[9] Choice of the Mundurucú case was prompted by the arguments of a colleague at the University of Michigan who suggested years ago that this was a prime example of (what I would now call) opposition through choice, one that would surely persuade me of the power of cultural reason to routinely depress reproductive fitness in autonomous reference groups. I remain grateful for the suggestion but also, as explained below, unconvinced by that conclusion.

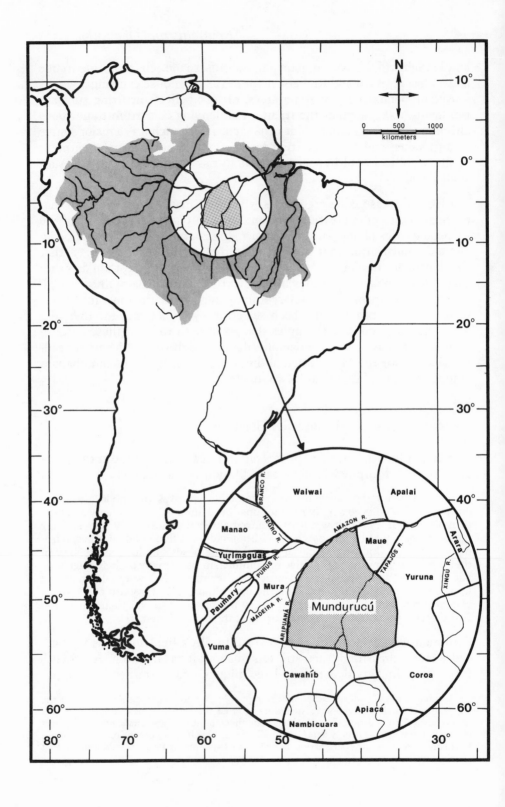

(Murphy and Murphy 1985: 105.) Numbering about 1,250 people at the time of Murphy's work, only one-fourth their estimated population a century earlier, most Mundurucú had abandoned the traditional savannah villages of their homeland (see Fig. 7.3) in favor of scattered single homesteads on the banks of the Tapajós and other nearby rivers. They continued to speak their native language, a member of the South American Tupí language stock, but many other local traditions had lapsed some years earlier.

The Conduct of Mundurucú Warfare

The reports of Murphy's informants confirmed that the Mundurucú reputation for belligerence had been well deserved in its day. According to Murphy, "foreign tribes were attacked because they were enemies by definition. . . . Unless direct, specific questions were asked, the Mundurucú never assigned specific causes to particular wars. The necessity of ever having to defend their home territory was denied and provocation by other groups was not remembered as a cause of war in Mundurucú tradition. It might be said that enemy tribes caused the Mundurucú to go to war simply by existing, and the word for enemy [*pariwat*] meant merely any group that was not Mundurucú." (1957: 1025–26.) On the basis of these reports, Murphy concluded that "the most important single motivation to hostility was a generalized aggressiveness that recognized no specific aims." (p. 1028.)

In contrast, Mundurucú war parties themselves had a very specific focus: the taking of enemy "trophy heads." Organized at village level, the raids commonly began at the instigation of young men who, seeking self-validation and the prestige accorded to trophy takers, appealed to the village chief to take them "to hunt the *pariwat.*" (p. 1022.) If, in consultation with the older men, the chief concluded that the occasion was indeed "auspicious," he would organize a war party, inviting men from his own and other villages, together with their wives and several unmarried women to cook and carry equipment. When preparations were complete, the

Fig. 7.3 (opposite). The location of the Mundurucú and their neighbors at the time of European contact. The large map locates the Mundurucú within the greater Amazon basin of South America (shaded), an area delimited by the line of 600 m altitude. The inset map gives the approximate locations of the Mundurucú and major neighboring populations. The inset is bounded at a radius of 500 miles (806.5 km) from the tribal center, a distance that approximates the maximum reported distance of headhunting raids. According to oral tradition, the Mundurucú waged headhunting raids against all of their contiguous neighbors plus the Nambicuara. The Cawahíb were also once "passionate head hunters" (Nimuendajú 1948a: 291), as were the Yuruna, Arara, and Apiacá, all of the Tupí language stock like the Mundurucú. The population boundaries shown here are first-order approximations: the Mundurucú and their neighbors made little effort to defend exclusive territories, and some of the named groups, such as the Cawahíb, Apiacá, and Yuruna actually consisted of a number of distinct tribes. Adapted from Murdock 1951: 84–85, map P, and 98–99, map Q, using the same orthography.

war party would then set off on the long, surreptitious trek through the forest to the vicinity of a *pariwat* village.[10] There, accompanying women would be left "a safe distance" behind while the men encircled the village under the cover of darkness and waited for the shaman to blow a special sleep trance on the enemy.

When the occupants of the village were benumbed, the warriors waited for the cry of a species of bird that breaks into song at dawn. When this signal was heard, the [raid chiefs] sounded blasts on their horns and cried the order to attack. Incendiary arrows . . . were ignited and loosed at the thatch roofs of the houses. The Mundurucú then broke from cover and dashed into the clearing of the enemy village, emitting wild shouts calculated to terrify the people. Adult males and females were killed and decapitated, and prepubescent children of both sexes were captured by the attackers. The Mundurucú then beat a hasty retreat [followed by] a day and night forced march until they had reached a safe distance from the enemy. At this point, the expedition turned toward home or, frequently, to new fields of conquest. [p. 1023]

Along the way, the trophy heads—said to be "the aboriginal rationale for Mundurucú warfare" (1956: 416)—were treated and preserved according to a strict protocol. Upon return to the village, the trophies were put on display in the men's house and used periodically in ritual observances.

These raids, conducted at the rate of almost one a year according to Murphy, represented a long-standing local tradition. When first encountered by Europeans in the 1760's, "the Mundurucú were [already] a warlike people" (Horton 1948: 271), widely feared by their neighbors. For some time, they had been aggressively expanding to the north, along the Tapajós River, until they were checked by a contingent of the Portuguese colonial army in 1795. But far from being "pacified" by this encounter, the Mundurucú continued raiding for more than a century, for they were actually hired as mercenaries by local traders and government officials. Ironically, then, this period of "peaceful symbiosis" with the whites was marked by renewed intertribal hostility as war parties struck with the added goals of capturing slaves and laborers, and of subduing other hostile Indian groups in the region (Murphy 1956: 415). In this way, the Mundurucú maintained their belligerent tradition through to 1912. All the while, only their employers and the neighboring Apiacá, another group of Tupí-speakers who were reportedly subservient to the Mundurucú and even joined them on raids, were not hunted as enemy.

[10]Although these forays surely did cover considerable distances, Murphy's statement that war parties struck at tribes "anywhere within a radius of five hundred miles" (1960: 1) clearly exaggerates Mundurucú tradition. First, Murphy emphasized in an earlier publication (1957: 1021–22) that the Mundurucú expeditions to locations 500 miles from home were "exceptional journeys." At the same time, he argued that "even short expeditions could well take a party over 100 miles from home," which is still "no mean trip." Second, Mundurucú expeditions since contact with Westerners have surely increased in distance as a function of their employment as mercenaries by the Portuguese (see Murphy 1960: ch. 2). The locations of their traditional enemies (see Fig. 7.3) suggest that average pre-contact raids probably extended even less than 100 miles (160.93 km).

Given this brief portrait of Mundurucú belligerence, one might reasonably ask, What, then, explains the cultural evolution of this tradition? Even if its origins are irrevocably lost in Mundurucú history, what forces acted to perpetuate the headhunting belief complex?[11] Is it truly a case of opposition and, if so, what reasons can be given for the persistence of this particular meme or set of memes? Alternative variants were surely known and available, both other ways of conducting warfare, and, for that matter, other, less violent patterns of collective action; for example, Murphy (1957: 1028) mentions log racing and drinking bouts among certain of their neighbors. Why then headhunting?

In answer to these questions, two points can be made at the outset. First, although imposition became increasingly important in the post-contact period, the tradition certainly persisted for many years as a function of Mundurucú choice. This inference is suggested by the customary village-level organization of the raids, by the relatively simple political system within villages, and by the more-or-less democratic way in which warfare normally originated. Second, although "slave trading for the Portuguese enormously increased the importance of warfare for its economic and social rewards," as Julian Steward and Louis Faron (1959: 339) note, these rewards clearly had not been needed to perpetuate it in the earlier period; the circumstances surrounding pre-contact headhunting somehow provided adequate incentive. The question, then, is simply *how*.

As argued in earlier chapters, a good way to begin looking for answers is with an emic analysis—that is, an analysis of the natives' own views on the matter. Remembering that cultural values describe "the differential standing of a given object in a system of meaningful relationships" (Sahlins 1976b: 36), let us begin with a look at what the Mundurucú themselves regarded as the goals of war.

The Meaning of Mundurucú Warfare

Despite the seeming "undirected aggressiveness" of the Mundurucú, Murphy's informants were able to identify five specific goals of war (1957: 1026). First, during their years of mercenary employment, "the Mundurucú were partially motivated to war by the quest for manufactured goods." (p. 1026.) Second, headhunting was regarded as "a source of sport and excitement" and "a relief from boredom" and the routines of daily life (p. 1028). Third, the captive children seized during a raid were considered "a means of strengthening the group through the addition of new mem-

[11] Headhunting of a similar kind has been described among many, if not most, of the related Tupí-speaking peoples of Amazonia (for example, the Maue, Yuruna, Arara, Apiacá, and Cawahíb peoples of Fig. 7.3). This suggests an early evolutionary origin, before these distinct populations were differentiated. As I have argued elsewhere (Durham 1987), Tupian headhunting is surely another example of cultural homology—that is, of similarity by descent, or what Darwin called "Unity of Type" (1964 [1859]: 206)—as opposed to analogy, or similarity by convergence.

bers." (p. 1027.) Fourth, individual males were motivated by the desire for the prestige and enhanced social status that were accorded to valiant warriors, particularly successful trophy takers. Finally, trophy heads were prized both as a symbol of Mundurucú military prowess and as a key component of several religious rites and observances.

Although it is certainly true that these goals "provide us with an understanding of the incentives that motivated the Mundurucú warrior" (p. 1028), it is also clear that some are more important and revealing than others. The first goal, for example, sheds little light on the formative precontact motives; the second, as Murphy pointed out (p. 1028), is not particularly revealing in a warrior society; and the third conferred "no special honor" on the warrior (p. 1025). In contrast, the taker of trophy heads was accorded "the most important status" in the village (p. 1024), and his accomplishment was thought to be "the ultimate goal of all warfare." (Murphy and Murphy 1985: 106.) Clearly, then, we must give special attention to goals four and five. Although Murphy's account of the Mundurucú was written considerably before the emergence of a school of symbolic or interpretive analysis within anthropology (see Chapter 1), he did provide informative discussion concerning some key symbolic elements. For our purposes, the most important of these symbolic elements relates to both goals four and five. It concerns the taker of a trophy head, who was referred to as *Dajeboiši*.

Literally, the title means "mother of the peccary," an allusion to the Mundurucú view of other tribes as being equivalent to game animals. The "mother" part of the term is derived from the trophy head's power to attract game and to cause their numerical increase, and the headhunter was so titled because of his obvious fertility promoting function; paradoxically for such a seemingly masculine status, he symbolically filled a female role.

The trophy head was believed to exert a powerful charm over the spirit protectors of the animal world and thus improved the supply and availability of game. Each time that the men of the village went hunting, the Dajeboiši took his trophy a short distance into the forest where its magical effect was exercised. [Murphy 1957: 1024–25]

Paradox indeed! In a society that prided itself on military prowess, that distinguished itself for "unalloyed, untempered savagery," and that insisted on a deep and pervasive cleavage between male and female roles, the most vaunted and prized warrior's status was to be the peccary's "mother." The symbolism is fraught with surprising reversals: the *pariwat* are equivalent to game; the hunter is also their mother; the lifeless head causes new life; the deadly warrior promotes fertility; masculine status inheres in a female role; and the quintessentially "human" object influences what is most "wild," but only when the symbol (culture) is brought into the forest (nature). A full-blown symbolic analysis would surely find many more "trophies" of its own in this material.

For present purposes, however, it suffices to say that we have before us a prime example of a symbolic system organized by cultural reason: what is signified in each case (the "concept" or "meaning") is simply not apparent from the physical properties of the signifier. Moreover, each concept certainly "refers in the first place to a code of distinctions proper to the culture in question." (Sahlins 1976b: 123.) All that would seem to be needed to close the case is some solid indication that this is, in fact, an instance of opposition. Murphy continues:

But the supernatural power of the [trophy] head could only be maintained when certain precautions were observed. Both the taker of the head and his wife were prohibited from sexual intercourse and were [even] supposed to avoid looking upon any person who had recently indulged in the act. Accordingly, they lived very restrained and sequestered lives; the Dajeboiši spent most of his time lying in his hammock, and his wife was assigned special assistants to perform her household and garden chores. [1957: 1025]

In fact, "sexuality was considered especially dangerous both to the Dajeboiši and to his wife." Not only was he expected "to have minimal contact with or sight of women other than his wife," but "even she posed a threat to his special status, and they [therefore] ate sitting back to back." (1958: 55.)

I should think one would be hard pressed to find a better candidate for opposition through cultural reason. Of course, one could always ask for better or more complete data so as to ascertain, for example, whether or not the Dajeboiši's sex taboo really did translate into reduced F_g. But given the information we have, virtually all signs point to opposition. Adult males expended considerable time and effort traipsing miles through the rain forest, risking injury, counterattack, and their lives—and so did their accompanying wives, though to a lesser extent—and the reward for all this was status with celibacy for the few who were successful. In addition, noted Murphy, "the taker of the trophy head was further motivated, for the power possessed by him and the head increased the yield of the hunt. . . . [This] magical influence also provided an additional group motivation for warfare and served to root it more firmly in Mundurucú beliefs." (1958: 58.) But, true to form, this power too had its cost: the Dajeboiši was also enjoined from hunting during the three years of his tenure, this time by a belief that, if he journeyed very far into the forest, "he might step in the blood of a game animal and thereby lose the charm of the head." The net result, noted Murphy, was an enhanced status "that endowed his person with an almost sacred aura," but that also "isolated him from normal relations with his fellow Mundurucú."[12] (p. 55.) In this way, cultural reason, empowered by the local system of meanings and values, appears to have maintained the high cultural fitness of headhunting

[12] These observations also eliminate, for this case, the Boyd and Richerson hypothesis of opposition through role selection. Although one might have expected the prohibition against sex and hunting to mean more time and energy for promoting the social transmission of oppositional memes, the Dajeboiši and his wife actually led "very restrained and sequestered lives," as noted above. It is doubtful that the Dajeboiši generated much in the way of transmission force lying on his back in a hammock.

memes while at the same time explicitly discouraging the reproductive fitness of successful warriors.

Explaining the Headhunting Tradition

Murphy, it should be noted, was not persuaded by this line of (cultural) reasoning, "for alternative ways of pleasing the spirits were known and practiced." (1957: 1028.) Chief among them were ceremonial techniques for propitiating the spirit protectors (see 1958: 58–61), techniques that Murphy described as "complex both in practice and in ideational content." (1957: 1028.) In contrast, he argued, "the linkage of the trophy head and the spirits was vague and ephemeral," suggestive of a much more recent emergence in cultural evolution.

Murphy's social cohesion theory. Murphy therefore proposed an alternative explanation focused on the idea of "generalized aggressiveness that recognized no specific aims." (p. 1028.) First, he argued that headhunting was related to the nineteenth-century shift from virilocality to uxorilocality—that is, from residence in the husband's natal household (as discussed in Chapter 2) to residence in the woman's. He traced the cause of this shift to growing trade with Brazilians and the attendant "economic pressures which increased the importance of maintaining the integrity of the female, household work-group." (1956: 430.) But he linked the significance of the shift to two other aspects of Mundurucú kinship and marriage, namely, village exogamy—the requirement, as discussed in Chapter 6, of marrying outside one's natal village—and patrilineality, that is, membership in the descent group of one's father. The unusual juxtaposition of these features, he said, "made male solidarity on the village and tribal level not only possible but a functional necessity." (1957: 1029.) Intervillage conflict had to be rigorously suppressed, lest it pit patrilineal kin against each other and destroy the kinship system. Second, Murphy argued that "latent aggression," under these conditions, must be released "in a socially valued manner upon surrogate objects"—objects such as the *pariwat* and their heads (p. 1032). He therefore interpreted Mundurucú warfare as a "safety valve institution."

Both parts of this thesis have been criticized. On the one hand, the claim of a post-contact switch to uxorilocality has been challenged by persuasive arguments that this was probably a much older tradition among the Mundurucú (Ramos 1978). On the other hand, the social cohesion function has also been questioned (see H. Wilson 1958; Vayda 1961). While it does make a good deal of sense to suggest that internal conflict has real disadvantages in a society with uxorilocal residence and patrilineal descent, one wonders why the general benefits of preserving the kinship system would have prompted the rather specific cultural focus on headhunting. For that matter, why would they have prompted warfare at all? Would not less costly "outlets" be chosen over war if the major benefit were simply the release of internal animosities? Moreover, Murphy's argument neglected to explain "the fact that the Mundurucú were vigorous warriors before their [purported] shift to matrilocality." (1957: 1031.) These concerns led me to propose an alternative explanation for the cultural evolution of Mundurucú warfare.[13]

A resource competition theory. The natives themselves said that they went to the trouble of procuring trophy heads in order to please the spirit protectors and make game more abundant. What if they were right? That is to say, what if trophy heads did, one way or another, have the effect of making game more abundant? Murphy attributed little significance to this belief, calling the linkage between the trophy head and the spirits "vague," "ephemeral," and "magical." But what if those, too, were properties of the linkage in the natives' view? Similarly, the Mundurucú attributed powers over the game supply to the Dajeboiši and his trophy that they did not ascribe to shamans without trophies. Was there some factual basis to this claim? Or was Murphy correct in insisting that shamanistic appeals were "alternate" ways of pleasing the spirits? And if truly alternate, why would the Mundurucú feel compelled to go headhunting, with all the dangers and risks it entailed, rather than simply stay at home and pressure the shamans to tend to the game supply?

Taking the natives at their word, it seemed to me possible that the Mundurucú had long been faced with significant resource competition for their preferred game animals, and that this competition had provided conditions in which the beliefs associated with headhunting had been selected according to their special consequences—consequences that other ceremonial procedures did not have. Indeed, the Mundurucú case seemed to provide a close "fit" to a more general, theoretical model that I had developed earlier, a model for the evolution of aggressive efforts to reduce resource losses to outsiders (Durham 1976a).

Working from the assumptions contained in the model (see App. A.7.1), I was able to show that it is at least theoretically possible for collective

---

[13] The arguments below have been modified from their original publication in Durham 1976a to reflect a number of lessons learned in the course of the Amazonian "protein debate" of the last decade (that debate is reviewed, for example, in Chagnon and Hames 1980; Harris 1984; Good 1987). Specifically, I have been persuaded that the scarce resource of relevance to Mundurucú cultural tradition is *game*, not protein per se (my earlier publication used such phrases as "animal protein" and "high quality protein"). The difference may seem subtle, but I am convinced by the arguments of Beckerman (1979) and A. Johnson (1982) that total available protein may well have been "abundant" (if we sum from all sources) and yet game scarce. For the Mundurucú, I believe the evidence suggests that preferred animals were both scarce in actuality, to the point of constraining average reproductive fitness, and in perception, to the point of motivating efforts to increase local yields. Obviously, I am not suggesting that this conclusion applies to human populations throughout Amazonia. The variability of ecological conditions in the Amazon basin precludes, by itself, any such sweeping generalization; for one example, other regions of Amazonia feature none of the savannah habitat that is the dominant portion of the Mundurucú homeland. By the same token, my conclusions about Mundurucú headhunting are not offered as generalizations about the nature of headhunting in other locations.

aggression in the form of war to have widespread reproductive benefits at the individual level.[14] Of course, it is also theoretically possible for a cultural tradition of warfare to exist as a case of opposition, either as a result of imposition or as a product of selection by choice with the imperfections discussed above. But one implication of the model is that traditions of warfare do not *necessarily* constitute opposition; warfare is surely not a "theoretical embarrassment to a discipline [i.e., anthropology] which has tended to believe that human societies are functionally integrated systems, well-adapted to their environments." (Hallpike 1973: 451.)

Two further implications of the model follow from the average individual "costs" of time, energy, and risk of collective aggression. First, these costs impose a threshold on the amount of resource deprivation that is worth fighting for; the higher the costs of belligerence, the greater the loss to competitors before aggression can, on balance, be beneficial. Thus, from the model, one expects some assessment within local groups as to whether or not conditions are "auspicious" for action, an assessment not unlike that described in the Mundurucú case. Second, under conditions of resource competition, the costs of aggression effectively reduce the magnitude of the potential benefit to be gained from the conflict. In other words, the resource loss to outsiders constitutes a "benefit ceiling" for aggression. Under these conditions, then, one expects warriors to make every effort to reduce the average costs of their campaigns. This, too, is reminiscent of Mundurucú practice, where even ostensibly superstitious measures are taken to ensure that the attacks are a true surprise. So can this model for adaptive intergroup aggression help to explain the Mundurucú case? Ironically, in light of the cultural reason argument, it seems to me that it can.

Intergroup Competition and the Mundurucú

Several aspects of Mundurucú social life closely paralleled the assumptions of the model.

1. The entire tribe, whose pre-1850 population numbered over 5,000, was subdivided into small village social groups of approximately 200 members. These villages were "the basic unit in economy and defense" and also in organizing for war. (Murphy 1960: 148.)

2. One natural resource seems to have been scarcer than any other:

---

[14] To prevent misunderstandings, I should point out that these assumptions, particularly the one about the narrow internal distribution of the limiting resource, are fairly restrictive. In developing the model I wrote: "While not valid in many instances, [this] distribution . . . is a reasonable assumption for *some* [so-called] primitive social groups." (1976a: 393, emphasis added; see also p. 394.) This caution was, however, misinterpreted by a critic, Deborah Gewertz (1978: 578), who wrote: "[Durham] believes that most stateless societies fulfill these requirements," and proceeded to criticize the model for then failing to apply to her chosen New Guinea example. In the same critique, Gewertz seems also to have missed my point about the causal mechanism of *cultural* selection, claiming that I "explained" primitive war by calling it "genotypically selfish" and likewise that I offered "biological imperatives as explanatory panaceas." (1978: 587.) Let me emphasize that this is not my message.

game animals. Aboriginal savannah settlements depended upon game from the surrounding rain forest, and hunting was an almost relentless task.[15] In contrast, the Mundurucú often felt that they had "adequate crops" from their gardens (1960: 62); fishing, too, was "secondary in importance" because of the distance, required for protection, between savannah villages and sizable streams (p. 55). There is also good indirect evidence that game supply was related to reproductive success: in Mundurucú society, as in a number of other Amazonian hunting groups, social relations between the sexes were structured by what Janet Siskind (1973: 226) has called an "economy of sex," including a fairly explicit exchange between hunting and marriage, meat and sex (Murphy 1960: 85).

3. Life in the villages was characterized by "cooperation in production and collectivism in consumption." (p. 148.) Cooperative hunting was particularly beneficial because the principal game animal, peccary, travels in herds. Also the food distribution system closely matched the terms of the model, generating some, but not too much, variance in per capita consumption. According to Murphy (p. 69), "any food that comes into the household is shared by the extended family and if there is a surplus it is distributed to all the households in the village. No one person or family can go hungry if others have food." He adds: "The only exception to this rule is when game is scarce and the day's kill consists only of small animals and birds. On such occasions, the nuclear family of the hunter may consume the food" (p. 112.) This arrangement may slightly have favored the family of a skilled hunter, but the "mutual economic security aspect" of village life meant that individuals would have been affected similarly, if not equally, by increases and decreases in the harvest of game.

4. For a variety of reasons, there was great potential for intergroup competition over game, particularly in the case of villages near the margins of Mundurucú territory. To begin with, virtually every neighboring population harvested most or all of the same animal species as the Mundurucú, and did so using very similar technology.[16] To make matters worse, a number of these animals are known to forage over long distances, particularly white-lipped peccaries, the Mundurucú's "principal game food" (p. 54), who easily travel 10 to 20 km a day in the dry season, often in herds of a hundred or more (Kiltie 1980: 35; Terborgh and Kiltie 1984: 877; see also Sowls 1984: 149). This means, of course, that even distant consumers can compete for these resources and do so unwittingly. Fi-

[15] If anything, hunting has only become more arduous and time-consuming in recent decades. In the 1950's, for example, Murphy noted that the men were "rarely able to relax from hunting for more than two consecutive days." (1960: 54.) Even so, days sometimes passed without meat, making adults depressed and short-tempered, and prompting children to cry a great deal (Murphy and Murphy 1985: 89–90). Moreover, game was prized by the Mundurucú more than any other food (p. 88).

[16] For one example, among the Cawahíb, mortal enemies of the Mundurucú to the southwest (see Fig. 7.3), "Paca, tapir, peccary (collared and white lipped), agouti, and deer are prized, as well as various birds" (Kracke 1978: 10–11; to which Nimuendajú 1948a: 285 adds monkeys). But this list precisely duplicates the inventory of "principal animals" hunted by the Mundurucú (Murphy 1960: 53).

nally, the shortage of game was regarded as particularly serious in the dry season.[17]

Taken together, these four points suggest that competition for game had long been a regular feature of Mundurucú social life, and one particularly important in the years before commercial trading and resettlement near rivers provided alternative ways to obtain meat. Although a substantial proportion of this competition must have come from the overlapping resource demands of adjacent Mundurucú villages, these populations were obviously inappropriate raiding targets because of the kinship links and other interdependencies Murphy describes. My proposal is therefore that competition for game provided the special social and ecological circumstances that favored the cultural selection of memes for intergroup headhunting. I suggest that these memes gained ascendancy in Mundurucú culture through the mechanism of selection by choice because of their beneficial effect in reducing that competition. More specifically, I propose that (1) social groups from other tribes in the area (the "enemies") harvested game from some of the same breeding populations as the Mundurucú, thereby reducing local animal densities; (2) that the resulting loss of game for the Mundurucú meant that headhunting, despite its intrinsic costs, had substantial net inclusive fitness benefits because some competitors were killed and many others fled only to resettle at greater distance from the Mundurucú; and (3) that these benefits came in the form of a perceived and valued, if temporary, improvement in the supply of game for local villages.

In this way, I hypothesize, the memes behind headhunting were actually sustained through the generations by Mundurucú preference. Their high cultural fitness would, much as in cultural reason arguments, have been largely the product of local secondary values, including the value attached to the Dajeboiši's status and "magical influence." But in this case, secondary values seem to have functioned in congruence with the primary values, favoring the retention of a specific set of beliefs that had an average net reproductive benefit under the conditions of resource competition. The implication, to which we return after a brief look at supporting evidence, is that Mundurucú tradition, despite first appearances, is not at all a case of opposition.

Signs and Symbols of Resource Competition

There are clear indications in the ethnographic record that the Mundurucú regarded their game supply as precarious. In particular, we know that "the focus" of Mundurucú religion was the relationship between local villages and the animal world (Murphy 1960: 132), a relationship

---

[17] Such scarcity could drive Mundurucú villagers to establish temporary fishing camps near local rivers, despite the extra danger there of enemy raids (Murphy 1960: 57). For further evidence of seasonal scarcity in the region, see Lévi-Strauss 1944: 21.

mediated by the jealous supernatural "spirit protectors" or "spirit mothers" mentioned earlier. Endowed with the power to create game animals and to regulate their abundance for the hunters, they were also easily offended. Significantly, one of the primary ways to offend them was by "killing an animal for its hide and leaving the carcass to rot" (p. 132); the one exception to this rule encouraged the wanton destruction of a recognized nonhuman competitor, the jaguar (Murphy 1958: 15).[18]

The record also indicates an equivalence in Mundurucú eyes between hunting and headhunting, and between game and enemy. Recall that when the young men pressured the village chief to organize a raid, they would ask him to take them "to hunt" the enemy. Recall also that the successful warrior's title, "mother of the peccary," is said to have stemmed from "the Mundurucú view of other tribes as being equivalent to game animals." (Murphy 1957: 1024.) But even in general conversation, "the enemy was looked upon as game to be hunted, and the Mundurucú still speak of the *pariwat* in the same terms that they reserve for peccary and tapir." (p. 1028.) To this, of course, one might add the "supernatural potency" of the trophy head itself and the whole complex of beliefs and symbolism surrounding the Dajeboiši. But now, when viewed from the perspective of resource competition, we can better understand the special, paradoxical power of these symbols.

Consider the trophy itself, an object that "simply 'pleased' the game spirits and thereby promoted the fertility of the animals and made them more vulnerable to hunting." By the resource competition theory, this "magical influence" would simply reflect an actual reduction, on the average, of game losses to outsiders.[19] To be sure, the *pariwat's* head may well have had additional meanings and emotional effects among the Mundurucú, although these are not spelled out by Murphy. Still, it seems to me that this piece of human anatomy offered one special advantage: quickly removed and easily carried during the forced march away from the enemy village, the head was also incontestable evidence of reduced competition. From this perspective it is no wonder the head "pleased" the game spirits, even if it "did not contain the spirit or soul of the fallen enemy" (Murphy and Murphy 1985: 107): it was the one "signifier" that could, by itself, guarantee the effect "signified."

Turning to the Dajeboiši, we find that this hypothesis also offers an explanation for why "such a seemingly masculine status . . . symbolically

[18] Mythology and ritual confirm that the Mundurucú specifically recognized the predatory competition of the jaguar. Horton (1948: 279), for example, describes an annual Mundurucú dance in which one dancer, imitating a large peccary boar, wrestled with another dancer representing a jaguar, while the remaining "herd" (including young) of other performers escaped. Traditionally, the dance took place each May, celebrating the first hunt following the birth of peccary litters in April.

[19] Technically speaking, this analysis would make the trophy an "index," in the sense of being an object with a factual, nonarbitrary connection to what is signified, rather than a true "symbol" (see, for example, Leach 1976).

filled a female role." (Murphy 1957: 1024.) Here, too, the symbolism would have had a basis in fact: by decapitating an adult consumer from an enemy village, and probably also by scaring the survivors into relocating farther away, each successful trophy taker would have had a positive impact on the population densities of important game species in the area. Singly, and still more in combination, their impact would truly have had the "fertility promoting function" of a "mother" of the peccary and other game. Furthermore, if we assume that game was both a limiting resource and the most highly prized one, we can understand why the Dajeboiši was also "the most important status" in Mundurucú society. True, his power would have been "ephemeral," for surely it did not take more than a year or two for hunting pressure to reabsorb the gains; and surely the connection did seem "vague" and "magical" in the absence of an understanding of resource competition at a distance. But the Dajeboiši's valiant deed would also have been among the most efficacious of all measures at the Mundurucú's disposal for improving their supply of game and therefore their individual reproductive fitnesses (see Irvine 1987 on other "game enhancing" practices in Amazonia). Surely it would have been at least as effective as the shamanistic rites that Murphy described as the "alternate ways of pleasing the spirits."[20] (1957: 1028.) By this account, it is not at all surprising that "the status of the warrior, the power of Mundurucú arms, and the supernatural significance of the trophy head . . . are still considered by the Mundurucú themselves to be the hallmark of traditional Mundurucú culture." (1958: 51.)

Opposition or Enhancement?

To summarize to this point, I propose that the Mundurucú tradition of headhunting evolved under conditions of recurrent competition over the supply of preferred game animals. I must emphasize that this is not an argument concerning competition for land, territory, or *lebensraum* as has been offered for warfare among nonstate societies elsewhere (see, for example, Vayda 1974, 1976). The density of game animals is not reliably proportional to surface area in the interfluvial habitats of the Amazon Basin (Siskind 1973: 229), and indeed the Mundurucú recognized no specific territorial boundaries.[21] It is likely that the maintenance of exclusive control over any territory large enough to ensure a dependable harvest of

[20] In some of these rites, according to Murphy (1960: 133), powerful shamans "used to travel magically to the 'Land of the Game' to 'feed' the animal spirits." A similar kind of "feeding" has been described by Reichel-Dolmatoff (1971) among distant linguistic relatives, the Desana Indians of southern Colombia.

[21] Despite my earlier discussion of this point (Durham 1976a: 407), Chagnon and Hames misrepresent my argument as claiming that the Mundurucú maintained themselves "in a chronic state of war with neighboring tribes in order to extend the size of their own hunting territories." (1980: 350, my translation.) I see absolutely no reason to dispute Murphy's finding that "the necessity of ever having to defend their home territory was denied" (1957: 1026), let alone extend it.

migratory game such as the white-lipped peccary would entail still higher costs than those of the Mundurucú headhunting raids. In such circumstances, selection by choice would predictably favor, as I believe it has, memes encouraging the direct elimination of competitors rather than their exclusion from a protected territory, a harder goal to achieve.

Unfortunately, we know virtually nothing of the specific evolutionary history of Mundurucú aggression, and thus it is impossible to document the actual operation of cultural selection, a problem we have encountered in earlier chapters.[22] Lacking such data, I have tried to compare what we do know about Mundurucú behavior, and the ideology behind it, with a theoretical model for what such behavior would look like if it were, in fact, the product of cultural selection by choice. Such a comparison does not, of course, "prove" that the headhunting tradition evolved in the way the model assumes. But it does have two significant implications. First, it suggests that the resource competition theory is a viable alternative to previous explanations for Mundurucú behavior and one that deserves to be assessed in the same empirical terms. In previous sections, I have attempted to conduct this assessment. Second, and more provocatively, the comparison suggests that headhunting may actually have been an adaptive cultural tradition, one in which the inclusive fitness benefits of reduced competition usually, and for most of the participants, outweighed the costs of belligerence, which were themselves painstakingly minimized. This suggestion rests on the assumption, often made for hunting populations of the Amazon basin (see, for example, Siskind 1973) and certainly reasonable here, that game was an F_g limiting resource; survival, mating, or fertility—all three, even—tended to covary with the harvested supply of forest animals, if only because of local food preferences and the exchange of meat for sex. In effect, this assumption makes it possible for the fitness value of the game diverted by headhunting from *pariwat* populations to the Mundurucú to have paid them back, with profit, for the reproductive costs of waging war.

The Dajeboiši's sex taboo, however, offers one last challenge to the proposal that headhunting was a culturally evolved adaptation. Having literally risked life and limb to "appease the spirits" and increase the supply of game, the trophy taker's reproductive success was, on return to the village, promptly thwarted by a stringent prohibition on all sexual activity. How, one might ask, could that ever be adaptive?

Social distribution of costs and benefits. Paradoxically, the fact that

---

[22] In a review of warfare among Tupí-speaking peoples related to the Mundurucú, particularly those of coastal South America, William Balée (1984) provides evidence that fighting for trophies and to improve access to faunal resources is an ancient tradition in this whole language group of forest dwelling peoples. This fact, with the specific equivalence of enemy and game in the Mundurucú case, makes it tempting to speculate that headhunting evolved culturally as an outgrowth of regular hunting. In a variety of ways, Mundurucú raiding resembled the stalking of just another large predator—one that happened to be social, very dangerous, and human.

the Dajeboiši's sex life mattered at all can, I believe, be taken as further indication both that game supply and reproduction were closely linked and, more importantly, that headhunting actually was carried out with an average net benefit for the participants. My argument hinges on the mechanism of selection by choice and on its implications for the social distribution of the costs and benefits of war. Within an autonomous reference group like a Mundurucú village, headhunting could have evolved through selection by choice (rather than through imposition, for example) provided that the benefits from raiding were fairly evenly distributed among those who paid the costs. Given that the costs of headhunting were widely distributed (in the sense that all warriors took about the same risks, whether successful head takers or not; see additional discussion in Durham 1976a: 406), choice would then have required that the benefits were too. Otherwise, people would have begun opting for less sacrificial courses of action, and the social transmission of the headhunting beliefs would have been disrupted.

Consider the Dajeboiši in this light, then: lounging around the village, without even having to hunt, for more than two years after the successful raid, his sexual activity would surely have threatened to absorb a disproportionate share of the group's potential gains. Assuming that other warriors would have noticed and reacted accordingly, I would suggest that the sex taboo, too, evolved through selection by choice, as a way of trying to distribute the benefits of raiding as equitably as its costs. In the long run, the Dajeboiši's enhanced status in the village may well have had other F_g benefits. But any more immediate self-indulgence after the headhunt would have converted the participation of other, less fortunate members of the raiding party into costly acts of self-sacrifice. In effect, they would have waged war *for* the Dajeboiši much as they had then to hunt for him during the period of his "magical" power.

Support for this hypothesis is provided by an important additional limitation on the Dajeboiši's power. If it is true that game supply and reproduction were closely linked in Mundurucú villages, and if the sexuality of the Dajeboiši did pose a significant threat to the collective gain in game supply, then one might expect violation of the sex taboo to cause a loss in the power of the trophy head. The reason would be simply that the Dajeboiši's dalliance would threaten to replace some or all of the game originally lost to outsiders with an equivalent loss, in effect, from internal competition. Consider, then, the events of the ceremony called *Yašegon*, or "Stripping the Skin from the Head," held the second rainy season after the taking of the trophy head, just over a year later. In the course of this ceremony, "a number of old men, all of whom had at one time taken an enemy head, took the trophy head and tapped its top. If powder or any other matter fell from it, they announced that the *Dajeboiši* had broken an obligation. This was generally interpreted by all to mean that he had

had sexual relations. In such a case his status terminated and no further observances were held since the head had lost its power." (1958: 56.) If, instead, the test "proved" that the owner of the head had abstained as required, the ceremony could continue. At that point, as further illustration of the symbolic equivalence of enemy and game, the head was thrown to the ground and "a group of men called 'Vultures' batted it back and forth with sticks in imitation of the vulture's practice of tossing strips of carrion with its beak." (p. 56.) Finally, provided all had gone smoothly, the head would be boiled and skinned, the skull would be hung in a corner of the men's house, and the Dajeboiši and his trophy would retain their power for another year.

This ceremonial test dramatically emphasized the danger of sexuality to the Dajeboiši's status and reminded him that the mere suspicion of indulgence was considered sufficient to eliminate the "magical" power of the head. Of course, one could always discount as superstition this particular detail of Mundurucú tradition, even while accepting some validity to the other beliefs relating trophies and game. But such an explicit, public test of the Dajeboiši's continence at the hands of elder trophy takers suggests otherwise. There is a persuasive consistency running throughout these various aspects of Mundurucú tradition. Like the pieces of a puzzle, they all fit together in only one way, forming a coherent picture of headhunting as an evolved response to competition for a culturally valued resource, game.[23]

The Fitness Advantages of Headhunting

I conclude that traditional Mundurucú headhunting qualifies as an example not, as it first appeared, of opposition, but of enhancement. In

---

[23] Appearances to the contrary, it seems likely that Mundurucú captive taking was another piece that fit into place. However, I am doubtful of the advantages previously proposed in the literature (see, for example, Murphy 1957: 1027; Oberg 1955: 473). Instead, I believe that captive taking was motivated, before the slave trade, by the same desire to increase the game supply: it is likely that Mundurucú captives were formerly cannibalized. For many years, the Mundurucú have actively denied this suggestion (see Kruse 1934: 53; Murphy 1960: 1), but so have a number of their Tupí-speaking neighbors for whom credible contrary evidence exists (see especially Kracke 1978: 185 and Nimuendajú 1948a: 291 on the Cawahíb; see also Métraux 1949: 399, 402 on the Omagua and Cocama). More important, I feel, are several lines of evidence, both indirect and direct, which I discuss in greater detail elsewhere (see Durham 1987). First, virtually all of the related, coastal Tupí-speakers "executed and ate their prisoners of war" even though, since they lived in villages with several thousand inhabitants, the practice added little to their food supply (Balée 1984: 247; see also Forsyth 1983, 1985). This observation, coupled with reports of captive-cannibalism among forest dwelling Tupí-speakers all across the continent (see Métraux 1949: 402), implies that the practice is an instance of cultural homology; thus it must already have been sanctioned in the ancestral culture of all Tupí-speakers. The only question, then, is how late the descendant Mundurucú gave it up. Second, there is good evidence for the practice among the Apiacá, close neighbors, linguistic relatives, and sometimes co-raiders with the Mundurucú (Nimuendajú 1948c: 318–19). Third, there are tales in Mundurucú folklore of routine, nonchalant cannibalism by legendary ancestors (see, for example, Murphy 1958: 109). Fourth, this hypothesis would provide a direct explanation for why "the enemy was looked upon as

particular, three features of the case imply that this was actually enhancement produced through cultural selection by choice. First, until pacification in 1912, the memes behind headhunting exhibited high fitness in the local cultural system despite the existence of alternative beliefs that were less costly in terms of time, energy, and risk to their bearers. Second, in aboriginal times, this cultural fitness seems to have been the product of autonomous decision making within Mundurucú villages, and not a product of imposition or of natural selection acting on cultural variation. Third, of available options, the allomemes of highest cultural fitness (F_c) appear also to have promoted the highest inclusive fitness (F_g) for their bearers.

My argument, however, is not that each and every warrior recognized these connections and set out on headhunts with the prospects of increased inclusive fitness well in mind. Instead, I believe that the men viewed their participation in terms of culturally defined goals and values, especially the personal goal of lifetime status as a trophy taker and the community goal of appeasing the spirit "mother" of the game. As in the preceding case studies, this analysis shows that it was again the cultural system that provided "the fabric of meaning" and the scale of values in terms of which the natives interpreted their experience and guided their actions (Geertz 1973: 145). But the analysis also suggests that this particular example of cultural reason had adaptive consequences.

Viewed in a cultural evolutionary perspective, this is not entirely surprising. Symbols and meanings always have social histories; these histories necessarily consist of human experience; and human experience always involves evaluation, whether or not—as in this particular example—it also involves choice. Inevitably that evaluation, conscious or unconscious, includes inputs from primary values as well as from the evolving secondary values. Particularly in matters of life and death, such as Mundurucú headhunting, the message of the primary values is unlikely to be forever ignored, repressed, overridden, or blocked. As symbols and meanings evolve subject to the editing hand of primary and secondary values, one would generally expect selection by choice to preserve the positively evaluated—and therefore adaptive—variants. Of course, the system is not flawless and the imperfections of choice, discussed earlier, will cause exceptions to the rule. But if we set aside the exceptions, it remains a plausible hypothesis that the elaboration of symbols and meanings is unlikely to create a logical system that runs persistently contrary to the vital interests of those who edit and sustain it.

---

game to be hunted." (Murphy 1957: 1028.) Fifth and finally, there is the firsthand report of P. J. C. Strömer (1932: 117–18) that, indeed, "the Mundurucú had been headhunters and cannibals. The young people were often told about this by the elders." (Translated from the German by K.A.) Strömer includes an elder's recipe for cooking the heads of slain victims and eating from the pot—a description that parallels independent reports of the same custom among the Cayabí and Tupinambá (see, for example, Nimuendajú 1948c).

In these respects, cultural evolution in the Mundurucú case bears some similarity to other examples we have explored, particularly the Tibetan one. Indeed, I believe that Fig. 2.4 applies equally well to the Mundurucú context. In both cases, I suggest (1) that an enduring set of cultural beliefs gave shape and form to the observable patterns of behavior; (2) that particular consequences of those behaviors (the maintenance of land in one case and of game supply in the other) were both perceived and valued in their respective communities; (3) that this evaluation was the principal reason for the high cultural fitness of the underlying beliefs; and (4) that the valued consequences resulted in net reproductive benefit to those whose evaluations sustained the beliefs. The social and natural contexts are amazingly different, as are the respective beliefs, values, and behaviors. And yet, if my analysis is correct, there is a fundamental underlying similarity of process and product.

In summary, I submit that Mundurucú headhunting had overcompensating inclusive fitness advantages to individual warriors and their mates through the increased abundance of scarce game. This interpretation is consistent with Mundurucú food preferences, the central importance of game in their religion, the "mystical" power of the trophy head, and their common reference to enemy groups in the same terms as game, all of which are unaccounted for in the alternative explanations we have considered. Further, this analysis provides an explanation for the Dajeboiši's sex taboo. Although some questions must, for lack of data, remain unanswered, Mundurucú headhunting is probably *not* a case of opposition.

Candidate Case 2: Fore Cannibalism

A much more likely example of opposition has been documented in the course of a multidisciplinary study of the Fore, a population of some fourteen thousand slash-and-burn horticulturalists living in the Eastern Highlands province of Papua New Guinea (see Fig. 7.4). The case concerns traditional beliefs among the Fore and their neighbors about honoring the dead in mortuary feasts; the cultural evolutionary addition of endocannibalism (the consumption of flesh from deceased kin or co-residents) to those feasts; and a deadly nerve degeneration disease called *kuru*. A connection between these phenomena, strongly indicative of opposition, has been demonstrated by the combined researches of the medical investigators D. Carleton Gajdusek, Clarence Gibbs, Michael Alpers, and their collaborators, and the anthropologists Ronald Berndt, Shirley Lindenbaum, Robert Glasse, and Gillian Gillison. Although our understanding remains tentative, a point emphasized by the arguments of Lyle Steadman and Charles Merbs (1982), the evidence suggests that the beliefs behind cannibalism were maintained at high cultural fitness for at least two

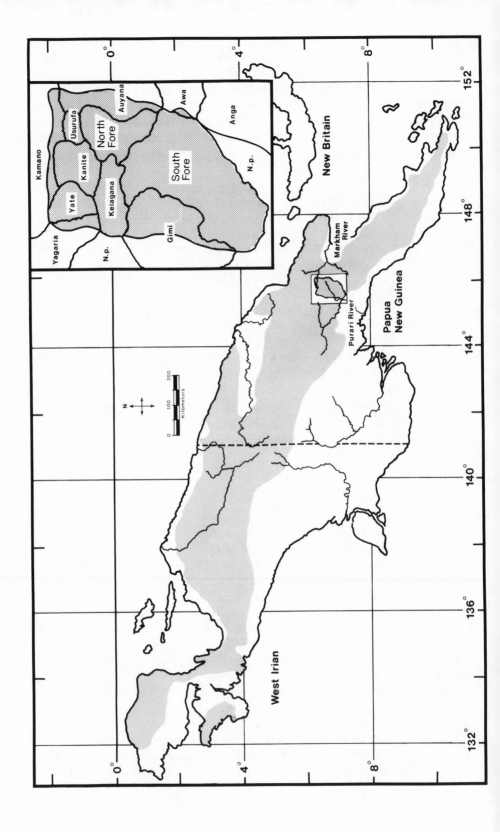

generations of social transmission despite their role in the spread of kuru and the high death rate it created.

Traditional Mortuary Feasts of the Fore

The Fore population represents the southernmost branch of the East New Guinea Highlands language family, which includes all the Fore's immediate neighbors except the Anga to the southeast. Within this family, the Fore and all their neighbors except the Awa and Auyana to the east speak languages of the East Central subfamily, and appear to be closely related by descent from common ancestors. Not surprisingly, these populations traditionally shared a number of distinctive social and cultural features, such as dispersed settlement into many small hamlets of 70 to 120 people, all residing virilocally. When the first missionaries and government officials came into the region in the 1940's, they found clusters of these hamlets, each with its own bamboo stockade, organized into rivalrous war-making units of one to several hamlets called "districts," "parishes," or "sovereignties" (R. Glasse 1967; Robbins 1982). Although the internecine belligerence in this area was obviously very different from Mundurucú warfare, its prominence in social life was certainly parallel (see, for example, Berndt 1954–55: 30).[24]

Given the hostile social environment, it is not particularly surprising that funerary customs were another tradition that the Fore shared with neighboring populations. Death, perceived as a threat to military strength and to the inter-parish alliances fostered by marriage, was commemorated in a mortuary feast that brought together kin, coresidents, and allies, and precipitated certain kinds of economic transactions among

---

[24] In their study of the Fore parish called Wanitabe, Glasse and Lindenbaum (1976) found war injuries to have been the leading cause of death, aside from kuru, in the period before pacification. In particular, they found that interparish fighting accounted for 55 of 326 non-kuru deaths in the years 1900 to 1962. Kuru, by comparison, caused 147 deaths in the same time period (p. 46).

Fig. 7.4 (opposite). The kuru region of New Guinea. In the late 1950's, epidemic frequencies of this fatal nerve degeneration disease were found in the Eastern Highlands of Papua New Guinea (shading indicates areas over 200 m in altitude). The inset map shows the social and geographic distribution of the disease (also shaded), illustrating its confinement to the North and South Fore and neighboring populations with whom the Fore intermarry ("N.p." means no population in the area). All of the affected populations belong to the East New Guinea Highlands language family, and share a number of cultural traditions, including mortuary feasts for honoring the dead. As part of those feasts, the affected populations—except for the Awa and Auyana to the east—also practiced endocannibalism before the establishment of state control in the region between 1950 and 1960. The Awa and Auyana have suffered only a few cases of kuru and only in villages with established marriage ties with the Fore (marriage is virilocal in the region). No cases of kuru have been reported among the Anga (or Kukukuku), who are members of the distinct Angan language family and who, as mortal enemies of the Fore, did not intermarry with them. Adapted from Gajdusek and Gibbs 1977: 19, fig. 2.1; additional data from Lindenbaum 1979: 5, map 2; Hornabrook and Moir 1970: 1177, fig. 5.

them. The events surrounding this kind of feast among the South Fore, a linguistic subgroup of some eight thousand Fore, have been described by Glasse and Lindenbaum.

> When a person dies, news of the event spreads rapidly. . . . Death mobilizes all the people who have been important to the deceased. They come to "see the face" of the dead person for the last time, and to partake in the funerary meal. . . .
> . . . The social status of the deceased substantially determines the magnitude of the death feast. A Big Man's funeral attracts more than 100 mourners representing the numerous parishes with which the deceased man has had social ties. Dozens of pigs are killed to feed the mourners, and food is distributed to parish or [lineage] units rather than to individual persons. The feast may be smaller when a woman or youth dies, because of their inferior status.[25] [1976: 47]

In addition to pig meat during the feast, pigs, goods, and money were distributed in specific mortuary payments, including compensatory ones, after each funeral. Such compensation might go, for example, to the natal parish of a man who had died fighting for an allied settlement. In this way, every death attracted "a large number of people from distant places" and provided "an important occasion for the circulation of pork and vegetables, goods and money." (1976: 48.)

The Cultural Evolution of Fore Cannibalism

That similar mortuary feasts are held throughout the populations of the East Central language subfamily suggests the evolutionary descent with modification of this tradition. Let us now turn to consider one of the more socially significant of these modifications, the rapid cultural evolution of beliefs encouraging routine endocannibalism as an adjunct to the funerary proceedings.[26] On the basis of fieldwork conducted between 1961

[25] Additional details of South Fore feasts are given by R. Glasse (1963: 4). See Berndt (1954–55: 168–69) for a description of parallel mortuary feasts among the neighboring Kamano, Yate, Usurufa, and North Fore; see Gillison (1983: 35–38) on the feasts of the Gimi, and Robbins (1982: 96–97) on those of the Auyana. The starkly contrasting funeral ceremonies of the Anga, who belong to a different language family (that of Central and South New Guinea) and thus a divergent cultural ancestry, are described by Mbaginta'o (1976) and Blackwood (1978: 134–42).

[26] After the publication of Arens's *The Man-Eating Myth* (1979), the evidence for socially sanctioned cannibalism, including the Fore case, was much debated (for reviews, see Kolata 1986, 1987; Harris 1985: ch. 10). The debate served as a reminder that many, many reports of cannibalism have not been confirmed or adequately verified. Indeed, it prompted Lyle Steadman (who had himself conducted fieldwork in the Western Highlands of Papua New Guinea) and Charles Merbs to state that "there is no direct evidence of cannibalism among the Fore." (1982: 616.) It also fueled my own skepticism on the subject in earlier drafts of this manuscript. In this case, however, the latest evidence confirms the earlier claims of cannibalism beyond reasonable doubt (on the veracity of reports from other places, see Forsyth 1985; Sanday 1986). First, there is Gajdusek's brief report of seeing Fore cannibalism for himself (see Klitzman, Alpers, and Gajdusek 1984: 4; Gajdusek 1986). Second, there is the meticulous reconstruction, based on fieldwork, of five endocannibalistic feasts in North and South Fore villages (in 1949, 1950, 1953 or 1954, 1954, and 1955), including cross-checked attendance rosters and some convincingly detailed description of the proceedings (Klitzman, Alpers, and Gajdusek 1984). Third, there is a graphic eyewitness account of ongoing "playlets" among the neighboring Gimi peoples in which women ritually reenact their cannibal feasts

and 1963 among the South Fore, Glasse and Lindenbaum identified five general features of this evolutionary change. First, the change, in relative terms, had been both recent and fast, spreading from the north by cultural diffusion during the last one hundred years or so. All indications were that other East Central groups, namely, the Kamano, Keiagana, and Kanite, had all adopted the custom several generations back; that the North Fore had picked it up from them at about the turn of the century; and that the South Fore had followed suit sometime between about 1910 and 1920 (R. Glasse 1967: 753; Lindenbaum 1979: 22).[27] In the South Fore parish of Wanitabe, for example, base site for Glasse and Lindenbaum's fieldwork, cannibalism reportedly had begun about 1915: "Visitors from Wanitabe to northern hamlets observed the practice there, were invited to participate, and returned home with enthusiasm for the new custom." (R. Glasse and Lindenbaum 1976: 49.) Although there was evidence that exocannibalism (the eating of dead enemies) was also practiced north of the Fore (see Berndt 1954–55: 170–73), in the south "it was usual to eat kin or people of one's own residential group after they had died." (Lindenbaum 1979: 22.)

Second, once the idea was introduced, it seems to have evolved to cultural prominence within each population largely through selection by choice. In one district of North Fore territory, for instance, people reportedly "expressed their approval" the very first time they tasted the cooked flesh of a dead kinsman. "'This is sweet,' they said. 'What is the matter with us, are we mad? Here is good food and we have neglected to eat it. In [the] future we shall always eat the dead, men, women, and children. Why should we throw away good meat? It is not right!'" Following this one initial event, clearly a matter of choice, the dead were virtually "always eaten" until the 1950's, when central government imposition ended the practice (Berndt 1962: 271). This report and others indicate that feedback from primary values, especially taste, was one important reason why the idea was quickly accepted. People were impressed that human flesh compared favorably with pork, their preferred meat, noting in particular that "the layer of fat on those who died rapidly [without wasting away] heighten[ed] the resemblance." (Lindenbaum 1979: 20.)

But even though primary values played an indisputable role, there is

---

of the pre-1960 period (Gillison 1983: 41–43). The details of the playlets, together with other features of these peoples' cannibal tradition and Gillison's symbolic interpretation of the whole package, corroborate the related tradition of the Fore. Finally, the study by Meigs (1984) of the Hua, another linguistically related group, reveals that they, too, believed in the "growth and vitality" effects of cannibalism (p. 110). The study corroborates reports of this kind from both of their neighbors, the Fore and Gimi.

[27] Glasse (1963: 14) notes that the "Keiagana-Kanite and Kamano believe their ancestors have been cannibals for generations. They apparently have no legends of the origin of cannibalism and no myths of an era before the dead were consumed. Cannibalism was a deeply ingrained institution. [In contrast,] North Fore consider [that] cannibalism began when their fathers were young men. . . . South Fore adopted the custom later still and living people recall how the practice began there."

also good evidence that secondary values were the overriding influence. For one thing, the Fore and their neighbors were arguably predisposed toward accepting cannibalism, even before its gastronomic virtues were known, by older cultural values that advocated the use of body substances such as hair and nail clippings for their nourishing and curative effects upon one's relatives (see Meigs 1984: ch. 6). Once introduced, cannibalism was then promptly valued as a means to accelerate the passage of a dead man's spirit to the greater pool of "life-force" for his lineage; ironically, because it defleshed the corpse more quickly than would natural processes, cannibalism was viewed as having a regenerating or revitalizing influence (Gillison 1980: 154, 1983; see also Meigs 1984: 110; Lindenbaum 1979: 22). For this reason, the memes behind the custom were actively promoted and spread even by those who, because of still other secondary values (discussed below), refrained from its practice. Finally, secondary values were also responsible for the one regular exception to the rule that the dead were "always eaten" (Berndt 1962: 271): cannibalism was restricted by cause of death. The Fore simply "did not eat people who died of dysentery or leprosy, or who had had yaws" for the compelling reason that they recognized these conditions as infectious and feared their spread (Lindenbaum 1979: 20). At the same time, few other causes of death deterred the practice (R. Glasse 1963: 4–5). Subject, in this way, to the guiding hand of primary and secondary values, cannibalism spread rapidly in the region through selection by choice.[28]

Third, the consumption of the deceased was simply and smoothly incorporated into the existing routines of the mortuary feast; indeed, "pig and human were dismembered and allocated in similar fashion." (Lindenbaum 1979: 21.) The usual procedure has been summarized from informant accounts by Glasse.

After the funeral, maternal relatives of the dead carried the body to a sugar cane garden. There they dismembered it with a bamboo knife and stone tomahawk, first cutting off the hands and feet. Next they split the arms and legs and stripped them of meat. [Eventually] they severed the head and cracked open the skull to remove the brain. Little was wasted—bone, marrow, viscera, genitalia, brain, even the [chyme] in the gut [was eaten].

[28] Another example of the overriding influence of secondary values comes from the neighboring Gimi. Informants there who remember that human flesh had "a uniquely delectable sweetness" also assert that their "main desire was to prevent the ravages of decomposition." "'We would not have left a man to rot,' they said. 'We took pity on him and pushed him into our bamboo (cooking vessels) and ate him!'" (Gillison 1983: 43.) Gillison's account also confirms that the Gimi viewed cannibalism as a straightforward matter of choice. One female informant, for example, explained as follows their renunciation of cannibalism in the 1950's: "You see, when a man dies that is not the end (of him). He exists. If we do not eat him, he will return (to us as a White man). In the past, we did not understand (this) and so we ate the dead. The White man came and explained these things to us . . . (that) our dead go to stay in Australia and come back (here) later as White men. (Knowing this), we do not cut up the dead anymore." (p. 42, note 10.) At roughly the same time as they were making this "decision," however, native constables of the Australian Administration were going from village to village announcing, "If you eat people we will *kalabus* you (jail you)." (Goodfield 1985: 36.)

Sometimes the body was cooked whole after removing the entrails. This occurred more frequently in the north than in the south where people preferred to cook small pieces of flesh in bamboo tubes together with salt, ginger and leaf vegetables. [1963: 4; for similar descriptions by other investigators, see Berndt 1954–55: 171; 1962: 272–77; Gillison 1983: 35–38]

Fourth, as the idea of funerary cannibalism spread, it was subject to the full set of pre-existing rules and beliefs concerning both the distribution and consumption of meat and the relations between Fore age groups and sexes. In particular, young to middle-aged Fore men—the warriors—generally (but not always) shunned human flesh, claiming a prior right to the pork that was distributed at the funerary feasts. They gave the argument that, as vital community defenders, they were susceptible to the debilitating effects of "pollution" from lesser sources of meat, such as the frogs, small game, insects, and wild pigs that were "appropriate for women, children, and old men."[29] (Lindenbaum 1979: 134.) Consequently, "South Fore men rarely ate human flesh, and those who did (usually old men) said they avoided eating the bodies of women. Young children residing apart from the men in small houses with their mothers, ate what their mothers gave them [whereas] boys moved at about the age of ten to the communal house shared by the adult men of the hamlet. . . . [In this way, cannibalism was] largely limited to adult women, to children of both sexes, and to a few old men."[30] (p. 20.)

In addition, body parts of the deceased were not randomly distributed during the feast but allocated, like pigs and other valuables, according to specific rights of kinship. For example, Table 7.1 lists the body parts that, according to Glasse and Lindenbaum, were reserved for specified kin, all female, during mortuary feasts in the South Fore parish called Wanitabe.[31] As these authors point out, participation in cannibal meals was not confined to the relatives named here but also included so-called fictive or classificatory kin and even some women with little or no relation to the

[29] As Lindenbaum (1979: 130) points out, the ideology of pollution was widely invoked by Fore men to control both subordinates—women, children, and "rubbish men" (sorcerers of ill repute)—and outsiders. However, the Fore men's "fear of contamination by women is not as profound as in some [other] New Guinea societies," where extremely strict rules of avoidance and seclusion are observed (p. 129).

[30] According to the reports of Berndt (1954–55: 172–73; 1962: ch. 13) and Glasse (1963: 5), cannibalism by adult males occurred more frequently among the North Fore and their neighbors to the north and west, as well as among the Gimi. Nevertheless South Fore men did sometimes take part, as the vivid report of Berndt (1958: 12, case B) makes clear.

[31] Robert Glasse (1967: 752) cautions that kinship did *not* provide "a precise model for the allocation of consumption rights [because the rules] seem often to have been violated in practice. [As a further complication], those who did possess rights had to attend the funeral to secure them. Failure to take part in the mortuary rites left the family of the deceased free to dispose of the body" as they saw fit. There was also considerable geographic variation. To take an example of particular relevance to kuru (see below), "the brain of a man in the South Fore [was supposed to be] eaten by his sister; in the North Fore, by his son's wife, sister, and maternal aunts and uncles; in Keiagana-Kanite, by the wife and his male kin; and in the Kamano, by his sister. A woman's brain was often eaten by her son's wife or brother's wife, but there was no strict rule." (p. 752.) Notice, though, that despite the variation, priority commonly went to close female relatives.

TABLE 7.1

Rights of Kin to Human Flesh During Mortuary Feasts
in Wanitabe Parish of the South Fore Population

Kinship relation to deceased[a]	Body parts of deceased	
	Deceased male	Deceased female
Sister	Especially the brain	No specific part
Mother's brother's wife	Especially the legs and buttocks	No specific part
Female matrilateral cousin	Arms and legs	No specific part
Wife	Flesh around pelvic bone and spine	(Not applicable)
Son's wife	Lungs, belly, liver	Arms and legs
Brother's wife	Legs, hands	Buttocks, intestines, vulva
Sister's son's wife	Legs, hands	No specific part

SOURCE: Adapted from R. Glasse and Lindenbaum 1976: 50, table 5. By permission of the Papua New Guinea Institute of Medical Research.

[a]Note that all listed kin are female. The source table by R. Glasse and Lindenbaum also lists "mother's brother," but with the designation "usually did not participate" and no body part mentioned. In addition, their table includes "father's sister," noting for a deceased male that she was "not generally a participant, but sometimes ate the arms and legs" and for a deceased female, "participation optional, no specific part."

dead person. Indeed, "several women at Wanitabe had a reputation for attending funerals of virtual strangers to help dismember and consume the body." Likewise, certain relatives of the dead did not take part in the proceedings: parents, for example, never ate their own children, nor grandparents their own grandchildren (R. Glasse and Lindenbaum 1967: 49).

Fifth and finally, Glasse and Lindenbaum found that the evolutionary spread of cannibalism, though recent, had created a striking correlation in the region.

A variable enthusiasm for human flesh runs from [the northwest] through the Fore area, coming to an abrupt halt in the southeast. . . . This is a gradient that matches an environmental shift from grassland groups for whom hunting plays but a small part in the diet to the Fore . . . for whom until recently wild game was readily available. . . .
Population increases in the region and the conversion to sweet potato as a dietary staple thus appear to have [led] to the progressive removal of forest and animal life. . . . As the forest protein sources became depleted, Fore men met their needs by claiming prior right in pork, while women adopted human flesh as their supplemental *habus*, a [Neo-]Melanesian pidgin term meaning "meat" or "small game." [Lindenbaum 1979: 22–24]

The implication, yet another point of comparison with the Mundurucú, is that the evolutionary addition of cannibalism to pre-existing mortuary traditions was actually a cultural adaptation to the growing scarcity of game in the region. Clearly imposition *had* been involved, at least in the south, in the men's "prior right" to pork. Natural selection, too, in the form of the differential reproduction of practitioners and nonpractitioners, may have played some role during the decades of change, as perhaps did primary value selection. Nevertheless, the suggestion is that this was primarily an evolutionary shift by secondary value selection, wherein people had selected the memes of cannibalism by choice, within constraints, on the basis of the cultural evaluation of consequences. Where meat and game had long been scarce for everybody (to the north), "enthusiasm" ran high and the custom had rapidly become "a deeply ingrained institution" with both males and females taking part (R. Glasse 1963: 14); where meat and game had grown scarce more recently, becoming, because of male domination, a particular problem for women (in the south), adoption was more recent and a matter of mixed emotions; where meat and game were available in stable supply from other sources (as among the Awa), the choice was evidently rejected.[32]

In short, the various requirements seem fulfilled not for opposition, but for enhancement: an introduced custom achieved high cultural fitness in populations where its perceived consequences were highly valued by those making the choice. The pertinent reference groups maintained at least some autonomy on the matter (they certainly could have rejected the introduction). And surely, given the growing scarcity of game, those who adopted and spread the beliefs were in a position to come out ahead in terms of survival and reproduction. Indeed, among the Fore, Gimi, and nearby Hua, cannibalism was viewed as having a "fertilizing effect" on those who took part (Lindenbaum 1979: 22; Gillison 1983: 34; Meigs 1984: 110, 115). All of this would seem, therefore, to qualify as "effective design for reproductive survival," the very definition of reproductive fitness introduced in Chapter 1. How, then, could it be opposition?

The Spread of Kuru Among the Fore

The answer is *kuru*, the deadly nerve degeneration disease first described to the outside world by Berndt (1954: 206; see also 1958) after his fieldwork in Usurufa and Fore communities. He noted that the condition, viewed by the locals as a product of sorcery, "is comparatively common and involves partial paralysis and lack of muscular control; the attacks become more frequent and more intense and finally lead to death." These symptoms were certainly well known to the Fore: "kuru," their word for the condition, means trembling, shivering, fear, and cold.

Writing a few years later, Gajdusek and his colleague Vincent Zigas (1957) described the disease in the medical literature on the basis of their clinical observations and a preliminary survey of the affected region. According to their description, the disease is characterized by fever, tremors,

---

[32] The Awa say they have never practiced cannibalism (Lindenbaum 1979: 25). Instead, they have relied upon free-foraging semidomesticated pigs since the time of "ancient ancestors" (D. Boyd 1985: 122) and upon the *habus* (pig or small game) obtained from hunting and trade. The Auyana, too, seem to have rejected the idea of human flesh consumption; it has not been part of their traditional mortuary customs (described in, for instance, Robbins 1982: 96–97). It may not be coincidental that these two populations also belong to a linguistic subfamily ("Eastern") different from that of the Fore and other groups that adopted cannibalism.

and progressive ataxia, or loss of muscular coordination, which "continue to increase in severity for one to three months from their onset. . . . A month or two later the patient is no longer able to walk or stand at all without considerable support, and equilibrium in the sitting posture is soon thereafter impaired." The helpless patient soon becomes unable to speak or eat, and succumbs shortly thereafter. The disease "rarely lasts much over a year, and is often fatal within three to six months of the onset in the village setting. Remission or recovery is very rare." Sixty percent of the victims are adults and of these over 93 percent are women (1957: 974–75). In addition, autopsies of kuru victims reveal advanced neuronal degeneration of the brain, which had reduced it to a spongy mass riddled with microscopic holes. Moreover, Gajdusek and Zigas noted that at least 1 percent of the entire Fore population were dying each year of the affliction and that, in the populations of certain villages, the prevalence of active cases had reached 5 to 10 percent.

Years of painstaking research subsequent to these first reports have filled in many details about kuru and its impact on the Fore and their neighbors (for illuminating histories of the kuru research effort, see Gajdusek 1975, 1979; Farquhar and Gajdusek 1981; Goodfield 1985; Zigas 1990). To begin with, a considerable amount is now known about the local history of the disease. Working from informant reports, Glasse, Lindenbaum, and their collaborator John D. Mathews have suggested that kuru began as a single case in the North Fore parish of Awande around the turn of the century (see, for example, R. Glasse 1962b, 1963; Lindenbaum 1979: ch. 2; Mathews, Glasse, and Lindenbaum 1968). From there, through some kind of infectious transmission, it seems to have spread simultaneously in three directions: to the northwest into Keiagana and Kanite parishes; to the north into Usurufa and Kamano parishes; and, with greatest frequency, to the south, reaching its first South Fore parish about 1922 (see map 4 in Lindenbaum in 1979: 18). Where it came from before Awande remains a mystery.[33]

In addition, longitudinal data have been collected in the hospital that Gajdusek and his colleagues established in the region. These data provide the following epidemiological sketch of the disease in its first 21 years under medical surveillance, 1957 through 1977 (drawn chiefly from Alpers 1979). First, in this time interval, there were no fewer than 2,464 deaths, of which 61.5 percent were South Fore and another 19.8 percent North Fore. The other 18.7 percent of the cases were all reported among

[33] Circumstantial evidence and comparative pathology suggest that kuru may ultimately have been introduced to humans from sheep, originating as the ruminant disease called scrapie. As Hadlow (1959) first pointed out, scrapie, too, kills its victims through nerve degeneration after a long and variable incubation period. On the basis of this and other evidence, Gajdusek suggests that "butchery accidents" may have caused the first transmission(s) to people (Gajdusek 1977: 958; see also Gajdusek and Gibbs 1977). Detailed electron microscopy confirms the similarity of the two diseases (see, for example, Merz et al. 1984), but further analysis, particularly at the molecular level, is needed for a convincing test of Gajdusek's proposal.

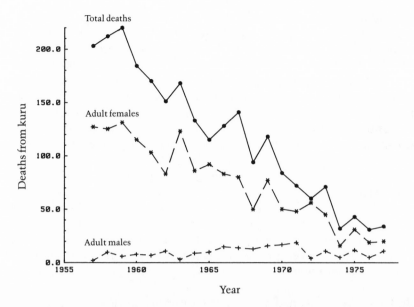

Fig. 7.5. The annual incidence of kuru deaths in all populations of the kuru region during a 21-year period of surveillance, 1957 through 1977. From the top: total deaths per year for all persons regardless of age and sex; total deaths among adult females aged 20 years or more; and total deaths among adult males aged 20 years or more. The graph shows that kuru was primarily a disease of adult women and that, by the early 1970's, virtually all of the females to die of kuru were adults. A total of 2,464 kuru deaths was recorded for this 21-year period. Data from Alpers 1979: 70–71, table 1; Lindenbaum 1979: 90, fig. 2.

their close neighbors in the "kuru region" shown in Fig. 7.4, a pattern indicative of "the most important epidemiological fact" of the case, namely, "the absolute ethnic limitation of the disease to the Fore and the people with whom they have intermarried." (Alpers 1965: 77.) Particularly noteworthy is the absence of kuru from all communities of the Anga population to the southeast. As mortal enemies of the Fore, speakers of an unintelligible language of a different stock (the Angan language family), and parties to a distinctive cultural heritage, though similarly virilocal in marriage, the Anga neither gave nor received marriage partners across that divide.[34]

The annual incidence of kuru deaths, shown in Fig. 7.5 for all populations, adult females, and adult males, has declined dramatically since the 1950's. The peak mortality occurred in 1959, when a total of 220 deaths

[34] Gajdusek and Alpers (1972: S30) note that "the border between Anga [language-speakers] and the Eastern New Guinea Highlands [language-speakers] is one of the sharpest lines of cultural and linguistic discontinuity in the New Guinea highlands." Among the many influences contributing to this discontinuity, two are especially worthy of note. First, the intervening Lamari River (which feeds into the Purari, shown in Fig. 7.4) and its steep valley provide a formidable natural barrier, particularly to populations, like the Fore, who believe that people are incapable of swimming. Second, Anga culture is "closely related to [that of] the lowland inland New Guinea tribes" of the southern coastal plain (p. S30). Evidently, Anga-speakers are relatively recent immigrants into the Highlands area.

were reported, 144 among the South Fore. The local impact of the disease was sometimes even more striking: the South Fore parish of Kamira, with a total population of less than 330, lost 29 inhabitants to kuru in the years 1958–60, and reported 8 additional onsets, for a total mortality rate of over 11 percent. In the region as a whole, during the first seven years of reporting, a full 81.5 percent of all victims were female and the bias was especially pronounced among adults. Over the years, the proportional representation of males has increased slightly, as can be seen in the figure, but this does not detract from the fact, noted early on by Gajdusek and Zigas, that kuru is predominantly a disease affecting Fore females. The longitudinal data also make clear the singular trend in age at death. Adult deaths have consistently made up between 70 and 100 percent of all female mortality, and the general trend has been toward an increasing proportion. When these data are reworked as age-category histograms (Fig. 7.6), it is immediately apparent that the decline in kuru mortality has been especially marked in the younger age groups. Not one case of the disease has been reported since 1974 among persons under twenty years of age.

In short, kuru has had a devastating impact on the Fore, both collectively and individually. Part of that impact, and the most important part for our purposes, has been the unambiguous, widespread reduction of individual inclusive fitness. This reduction has, of course, been most im-

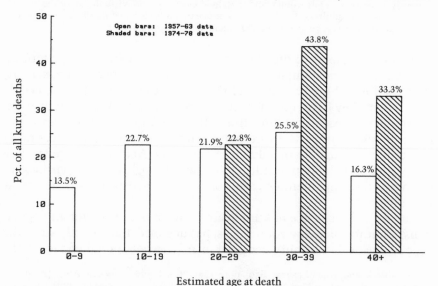

Fig. 7.6. The estimated age at death of kuru victims. Two sets of histograms are shown for the age groups along the *X* axis: the open bars represent the distribution of age at death for the years 1957–63, and the shaded bars show the same distribution for the years 1974–78. Especially noteworthy is the absence of deaths in the 0–9 and 10–19 age classes in the 1974–78 data, suggesting that the transmission of kuru was interrupted late in the 1950's. Data from Alpers 1979: 76, table 3.

mediate and self-evident in the case of adult women, of whom 1,395 died between 1957 and 1978 (Alpers 1979: 76, table 3, from data for females aged 20 and above). But kuru has also caused a significant loss for the men as well: as early as 1962, it was "difficult to find an adult man who [had] not been affected by the loss of immediate kin as a result of kuru." (S. Glasse 1964: 36.) In all, nearly half the adult Fore men lost their wives, not to mention their mothers, sisters, and daughters. The disease provides unequivocal evidence for reduced reproductive fitness, a fundamental requirement for the relationship of opposition. The question remains, Was there a link between kuru and cannibalism?

Theories of the Etiology of Kuru

From the earliest days of their medical investigation, Gajdusek and his colleagues considered the possibility that kuru was somehow related to the practice of cannibalism in the region. One idea, that kuru was simply an acute viral infection transmitted through cannibalism, was quickly dismissed. Kuru produced none of the classic symptoms of infection such as fever, and, in numerous trials in different research institutes, tissue samples from kuru victims failed to produce infection in laboratory animals or in tissue culture. Another idea was the "outlandish hypothesis" that kuru was an allergic encephalitis caused, without infection, by an immunological sensitivity to one's own brain tissue. According to Gajdusek (1963: 162), such an autosensitization could conceivably develop from an initial exposure to foreign brain tissue through cannibalism in early childhood. This hypothesis, too, was rejected when laboratory tests failed to demonstrate antibodies to brain tissue in the blood serum of kuru victims.

Understandably, the investigators turned to follow other leads (reviewed in Gajdusek 1963), including the possibility that kuru was caused by some environmental toxin or dietary deficiency. Again the results were negative: trace metal analyses of everything from the stones used in pit cooking to tissue samples from kuru patients provided no leads, and a detailed study of the Fore diet found all items "to be similarly used by at least one surrounding kuru-free populace" (p. 162.) Consequently, after months of entertaining many working hypotheses at once, Gajdusek and others began to favor a genetic etiology (see Gajdusek and Zigas 1957; Bennett, Rhodes, and Robson 1959; Gajdusek 1963). But that, too, as Ann and Jack Fischer (1961) have argued, involved problems. First, if kuru were genetically transmitted, how did the genes ever evolve to such high frequencies? Heterozygote advantage could always favor a hypothetical kuru gene to some extent, as in the sickle-cell case of Chapter 3, but still not anywhere close to the frequency implied by the kuru deaths in the 1950's. Second, if kuru were genetically transmitted, how could one explain the rapid decline in the onset of new cases during the late 1950's and early

1960's (Fig. 7.5)? Third, how would the genetic hypothesis account for kuru's recent origins, as described in such convincing detail by the Fore (see R. Glasse 1962b)? A genetic disease is simply not expected to come and go in the course of just a few generations.

Growing increasingly skeptical of a genetic explanation, Gajdusek was struck by William J. Hadlow's suggestion in 1959 that kuru was quite similar to scrapie, a disease causing neuronal degeneration in sheep. Scrapie also killed its victims, Hadlow noted, but after a long and variable incubation period ranging from eighteen months to three years or more. There was mounting evidence that scrapie was transmitted by a virus-like agent. Could the same be true for kuru? After visiting Hadlow in 1960, Gajdusek concluded that "we no longer can ignore the possibility that kuru [might be an analogous] slow infection; this even in spite of the convincing genetic model which can be constructed. With this in mind, we have launched an intensive program aimed at exploring this possibility." (Gajdusek 1979: 33.) The program involved attempts to transmit kuru by inoculation to apes, Old and New World monkeys, and eventually also to minks and ferrets.

A first breakthrough came in 1966 when, after eighteen months of incubation, kuru was transmitted experimentally to a chimpanzee. Shortly thereafter two other chimpanzees fell ill and died, as did other hosts on the list (Gajdusek, Gibbs, and Alpers 1966, 1967). In time, repeated inoculation experiments suggested that the pathogen was present at terrifically high densities, on the order of 10^8 infectious doses per gram, in the brain tissue of deceased kuru victims. In contrast, the agent has been found in only a few peripheral tissues, and in much lower concentrations (see Gajdusek 1977: 949). But despite this high concentration in affected tissues, the biochemical nature of the pathogen has proven remarkably resistant to identification. There is still uncertainty on the subject, although most evidence points toward either a "new class of filamentous animal virus" that eventually replicates itself in a host, causing the characteristic nerve degeneration (see, for example, Merz et al. 1984: 439; Gajdusek 1986), or a newly discovered proteinaceous particle called a "prion" that may simply stimulate its own synthesis from one or more of the host's genes (see, for example, Prusiner 1984, 1987; Ciba Foundation 1988.)

Nevertheless, evidence for the actual infectious transmission of kuru by 1966 shifted the focus of the problem back to the question of epidemiology. In particular, the evidence that kuru is caused by a transmissible pathogen reopened the question of cannibalism's role in the spread of the disease.

The cannibalism hypothesis. In 1965, months before the disease was first transmitted to chimpanzees, Gajdusek advanced what I will call the "cannibalism hypothesis": kuru might have spread by a "scrapie-like replicating agent which was transmitted by the oral route from [infected human] meat, cooked or uncooked." But he remained skeptical, emphasizing that the hypothesis was "more in the nature of an embellishment to other etiological hypotheses." (See remarks in Alpers 1965: 82.)

Meanwhile other researchers, especially the Fischers, Glasse, and Lindenbaum, were more convinced (see Fischer and Fischer 1961; R. Glasse 1963, 1967; Mathews, Glasse, and Lindenbaum 1968).[35] To begin with, they argued that cannibalism could explain kuru's recent and rapid spread. Initially, fearing kuru to be yet another infectious disease, the Fore and many of their neighbors had had reservations about eating kuru victims. But when it was observed that "those who ate kuru victims rarely developed kuru immediately . . . the practice [rapidly] became more popular." (R. Glasse 1963: 13.) Further, because of customary virilocality and the tradition of widely attended mortuary feasts, large numbers of persons from many localities, many of them kin, would have been exposed to the pathogen at the same time, giving the epidemic its "explosive" quality (Mathews, Glasse, and Lindenbaum 1968: 450).

In addition, the anthropologists argued that the local form of cannibalism could explain kuru's peculiar distribution by sex and age in the host populations. Consider the case of adult Fore males, for example: to protect their military prowess, as noted earlier, these men rarely participated in any form of cannibalism, let alone kuru cannibalism. This was especially true in the south, where cannibalism was believed to make men vulnerable to enemy attack (R. Glasse 1963: 5). Instead, men laid first claim to the pig meat distributed at the mortuary feasts and avoided all contact with the infected flesh. In contrast, adult females and the children of both sexes in their care must increasingly have had no alternative source of animal protein, or at least no source equally abundant and flavorful. With tragic consequences, South Fore women actually came to view kuru victims as "especially palatable—the wasted corpse was tender, often having a layer of fatty tissue" that increased its resemblance to the men's pork (R. Glasse 1963: 13).

In similar fashion, the anthropologists argued, three aspects of cannibalism could account for the observation that kuru "runs in families." First, as emphasized by Mathews, Glasse, and Lindenbaum (1968: 449), cannibalism was all along a matter of kinship: people "ate their own dead kinfolk for gastronomic reasons, and also to show respect for the dead." In this way, the very fact of attendance at cannibalistic feasts was influenced by family membership. Second, above and beyond attendance, familial patterns of transmission were more or less guaranteed by the culturally prescribed rights of kin to specific portions of the body, particularly to the brain and other tissues in or near the central nervous system (Table 7.1). Third, because women were in charge of the preparation and cooking of the flesh, and because "infants and toddlers were kept in al-

[35] Gajdusek (1979: 30) later commented that the "major contribution" of Glasse and Lindenbaum, in particular, "was to re-emphasize the concern about cannibalism, which we had largely abandoned, at a time when we were beginning to rethink the infectious hypothesis."

most continuous body contact with their mothers or her close associates" (Sorenson 1976: 151), vertical (mother-child) transmission could almost be taken for granted once a given mother was infected.

The cannibalism hypothesis also explained the concentration of kuru among the Fore, particularly the South Fore. Because the disease spread rapidly through the southern parishes in the early years and because, years later, government intervention penetrated from the north, the South Fore had the longest opportunity to practice kuru cannibalism and thus to spread the disease (R. Glasse 1963: 13). Moreover, the hypothesis also explained kuru's correlation with intermarriage. For example, Fore women did not marry and move into the hostile Anga villages to the southeast; this explained why kuru was unknown there, despite the fact that the Anga people apparently did practice their own form of cannibalism (see, for example, Blackwood 1978: 3–4, 122).

Finally, cannibalism could also explain kuru's dramatic decline in recent years, both the downward trend of overall incidence (Fig. 7.5) and the shift in age of kuru victims (Fig. 7.6). As pointed out by Mathews, Glasse, and Lindenbaum (1968: 450), this follows from the fact that cannibalism, and presumably kuru transmission, was "largely suppressed" by administrators and missionaries in the 1950's. In addition, the hypothesis explained why the incidence and age distribution of kuru were slowest to change in isolated South Fore hamlets as well as in those of the neighboring Gimi: cannibalism continued for a longer period in these places (p. 450).

Given the substantial explanatory power of the cannibalism hypothesis on the one hand, and then, in 1966, the successful chimpanzee transmission experiments on the other, medical investigators began to be persuaded that "ingestion of the human brain may have a place in the etiology of the disease." (Alpers 1968: 247.) Indeed, it was not long before Gajdusek and his co-workers began to differentiate two related pathways by which cannibalism could transmit the pathogen: the obvious "oral route," with direct ingestion of infected tissue whether cooked or uncooked (Gibbs, Gajdusek, and Alpers 1969: 536)[36]; and the contamination route, where "extensive contamination of hands during the handling of the deceased kuru relatives' tissues, even by children, could easily result in accidental subcutaneous, conjunctival, respiratory route or oral route infection." (p. 537, emphasis added.) Subsequent experimental work tended to favor the contamination route; direct oral transmission of kuru proved to be remarkably inefficient, having failed to produce even one case of disease in numerous chimpanzee trials (although succeeding in

[36] In regard to cooking, laboratory work has shown the kuru pathogen to be unusually resistant to heat compared with "conventional" viruses (see, for example, Gajdusek 1977). In addition, Gibbs, Gajdusek, and Alpers (1969: 536) note that, among the Fore, "brain and other viscera were eaten with the muscle and skin after very little cooking." They also note, implying an actual field measurement, that "temperatures of only 92° to 95° C were attained in the brief steam cooking of the viscera and brain in bamboo cylinders at elevations of 1,500 to 2,500 meters. It is unlikely that this would totally inactivate the virus."

one squirrel monkey transmission; see Gibbs et al. 1980: 207).[37] Before long, Gajdusek was convinced of both the cannibalism hypothesis and the contamination route. In his Nobel Prize address of 1976 he said simply, "we believe that contamination during the cannibalistic [feast] was the sole source of transmission of kuru from man to man."[38] (Gajdusek 1977: 959; Gajdusek 1979: 28; see also Farquhar and Gajdusek 1981: xxiv.)

In summary, then, there is good evidence that kuru *was* directly related to the evolutionary addition of cannibalism to mortuary practices in the region. All indications are that kuru was indeed transmitted in epidemic proportions among the Fore as the unintended consequence of this recently established cultural "tradition." The memes behind the treatment of the dead appear to have been responsible for nothing short of catastrophic maladaptation, with the result that the case constitutes an exceptionally good candidate for opposition. In the words of Lindenbaum, "when the incidence of kuru reached a peak, in the [late 1950's and] 1960's, the South Fore believed their society was coming to an end." (1979: 6.)

The Fore Reaction to Kuru

The case of kuru clearly demonstrates that opposition by choice can and does occur in the course of human affairs. The case is particularly striking because of the seriousness and magnitude of the disease, and because although it continued to spread, the Fore and many of their neighbors went right on consuming its victims. Equally striking to my mind, however, was the reaction of the Fore in response to kuru. Although a set of cultural beliefs is clearly implicated in the disease, the Fore did not sit passively by as the consequences of those beliefs wrought havoc on their

---

[37] In recent years, careful restudy of the details of the cannibalistic mortuary feasts has added to the likelihood that kuru was most often transmitted by the contamination route: informants say that "desisting from removing debris from their hands and bodies [was part of accepted] mourning practice." (Klitzman, Alpers, and Gajdusek 1984: 19.) However, there is also evidence of the transmission of Creutzfeldt-Jakob disease, a related neural disorder, to human beings through actual consumption of wild animal brains (see Kamin and Patten 1984).

[38] The cannibalism hypothesis has been criticized by Steadman and Merbs (1982; see also Kolata 1986, 1987). Their strongest point is that contamination, the most likely pathway of kuru transmission as all agree, does not require the actual ingestion of flesh. It could be that kuru was transmitted simply by the handling of corpses, particularly skulls, in the course of noncannibalistic mortuary practice. In a brief review of the literature, Steadman and Merbs (1982: 619–20) show that such activity does in fact characterize funeral proceedings among many other ethnolinguistic groups in New Guinea. The problem is, as I explain further in App. A.7.2, that their review ignores descent relationships and thereby lumps together the body-handling practices of widely disparate language groups, many of which shed no light whatsoever on Fore tradition. In contrast, when one compares Fore mortuary practices with others that are truly homologous (and are thus closely related by descent from a common heritage), the conclusion reached is just the opposite: homologous mortuary practices would not have provided direct and intimate contact with infected nervous tissue (see examples in App. A.7.2). Thus, while I agree that flesh consumption itself was probably not the main pathway of disease transmission, I conclude that the preparation of corpses for cannibalism was both necessary and sufficient for that role.

society. Although the example *is* one of opposition, it is not, I contend, a case of a people being commandeered by some "self-interested meme" or "active cultural parasite." Instead, the evidence indicates that the Fore struggled mightily to rid themselves of kuru in a variety of ways, each related to their own theory that the disease was caused by sorcery, that is, by some "magical procedure by which a person can cause harmful effect." (S. Glasse 1964: 40.)

First, the Fore took various steps to avoid ever falling prey to kuru sorcerers, and above all to prevent their getting hold of the personal items—especially clothing, hair, fingernails, and excrement—required to practice the evil magic.[39] Second, "as a measure of their anxiety and frustration," families affected by kuru repeatedly, and often at great expense, sought help from native curers, even while admitting that "no medicine (their own *or* that of Europeans) is strong enough to counteract the work of the sorcerer." (p. 43, emphasis added.) Third, because the Fore consider sorcerers to be "amenable to public persuasion," they used public gatherings, including funerals, as occasions for speeches to denounce the continuing acts of malevolence. Indeed, during the crisis years of 1962 and 1963, the South Fore convened special congresses called *kibungs* to formulate and express their local responses. "Reputed sorcerers made public confessions of their past activities, and Big Men appealed to sorcerers still in hiding to come forth and relinquish their evil practices. All other social events came to a halt." (Lindenbaum 1979: 100.) If, by these efforts, the Fore failed to reduce this opposition between genes and culture, it is at least clear that they tried.

By the mid-to-late 1960's, however, when all else seemed to have failed, many Fore hamlets instituted a stringent, self-imposed "social quarantine" as yet another attempt to curb the plague. Based on the belief that many of the sorcerers were jealous outsiders, these quarantines were designed specifically to reduce contact with neighbors, even those of the same parish (see R. Glasse 1970: 212.) When, largely by coincidence, kuru rapidly declined at the same time, the Fore took this as a sign that their antisorcery efforts had finally succeeded. This, of course, reinforced their belief in the sorcery theory.[40]

[39] These personal materials, although beneficial when used by relatives, are essential for making a kuru sorcery "bundle" as described by Lindenbaum: "A kuru sorcerer is said to steal some physical particle intimately associated with the victim, such as food scraps, fragments of clothing, hair clippings, or excrement. To this he adds pieces of bark, certain leaves, and a power-imbued karena (sorcery) stone, and binds them in a package with vines and canes. Beating the bundle with a stick, he calls the victim's name and recites a spell: 'I break the bones of your arms, I break the bones of your hands, I break the bones of your legs, and finally I make you die.' He then places the bundle in muddy ground, and as the bundle rots, the victim's health deteriorates. [When decay is complete, the victim dies.]" (1979: 65; see also Julius 1981 [1957].) For discussion of the symbolism of the sorcerer's procedures, see Lindenbaum 1979: 65–67.

[40] It is possible that the quarantines did actually play some role, albeit minor, in reducing the spread of infection. Although it is difficult to know just how early they began, during the last years they may well have reduced attendance at the cannibalistic mortuary feasts, particularly the ones that continued on a clandestine basis in remote hamlets after prohibition.

These and other reactions to kuru make it clear that the Fore and their neighbors did not passively accept the circumstances of major opposition. Instead they reacted, understandably in my opinion, with a special intensity and urgency, a reaction that brings us back to the topic of the causes of opposition. Earlier in this chapter, I proposed what might be summarized as a four-way classification of the types of opposition, distinguishing imposed from chosen opposition and, within each of those, an enduring or stable form from one short-lived or unstable. Because of kuru, I suggest, the persistence of Fore cannibalism qualifies as an example of short-lived opposition by choice. As noted earlier, an important degree of imposition was clearly involved: acting as an autonomous reference group, the men claimed priority access to pork, leaving only limited choices—small game and human flesh—for the subordinate reference group of women and children. To be sure, the men argued at the time that their action was also in the women's and children's best interests, the better to fight and defend them from enemy warriors. And certainly the men would have acted differently had they foreseen the dire consequences of their choice. Nevertheless, the men's dietary imposition stands out as the main reason why, once kuru appeared, its victims were primarily adult women. At the same time, an important element of choice was present throughout the history of cannibalism. Certainly no external group forced the Fore—men, women, *or* children—to incorporate flesh into their diet; and even when women's and children's options were foreshortened by the men, the women, at least, still had the option to reject the memes of cannibalism. Tragically, they did not, even after more than twenty years of escalating disease. The crucial question is then, Why not?

In answer to this question, let me return to my earlier discussion of decision system imperfections and eliminate a couple of possibilities that can be ruled out from the start. First, of the four imperfections that I listed as particularly important, "value blockage" seems not to have been involved. The memes of cannibalism, as we have seen, were actively retained because the more obvious of their consequences—such as additional food supply and the speedy defleshing of the corpse to retrieve its "life-force"—were, in fact, positively valued. This was especially true of kuru victims, whose flesh was all the more valued for its palatability. Second, "consequence imperception" is also inappropriate in this case, for the Fore were painfully aware of the devastating effects of kuru within their parishes. This leaves two candidate imperfections, both of which, arguably, were at work. Consider "value displacement." On the argument that cannibalism was adopted in response to the growing scarcity of game (and prior to the first appearance of kuru), it would appear that some time-tested values—for instance, that palatable meat and speedy defleshing are both "good"—came to have maladaptive effects. But they did so only after the social and ecological context changed with the advent of kuru. In other words, opposition resulted, in part, from the (understandable) application of old values in what was a fundamentally new context and a hazardous one.[41]

But far more important, in my assessment, was the remaining imperfection of the system, "cause imperception." Consider, here, the odds against a cause-and-effect understanding by the Fore of how kuru was transmitted. First, we know that kuru was only a recent introduction, having reached South Fore parishes only in 1927 (Lindenbaum 1979: map 4, p. 18). This means that the South Fore had, at most, a single generation's experience with the disease. Because it was both a recent phenomenon and always fatal, they promptly classified it with other "calamities ascribed to sorcery," rather than with "minor afflictions and temporary illness"—a category that included most of the maladies they regarded as having a contagious course (Lindenbaum 1979: 56).

Second, we now realize that the kuru pathogen has a long and highly variable latency period, one of anywhere from 2 to 23 years. Not only did this impede the association of cause and effect by the Fore, it also meant that they had had still less time in which to examine the data. Significantly, when other new epidemics with short latency periods (mumps, measles, whooping cough, and dysentery) swept over the Fore in the 1930's and 1940's, the South Fore noted "with clinical perception" not only that these were contagious conditions (some parishes even imposed quarantines on themselves), but also that "the second wave of some diseases, such as mumps, was less serious than the first." (Lindenbaum 1979: 31.) As Gajdusek pointed out, "were [kuru's] incubation period short, a few days or weeks as with most viruses, the people themselves undoubtedly would have been soon aware of the relationship and fled from both the practice [cannibalism] and the disease successfully. The long, silent, incubation period made the correlation of exposure to human tissue with the occurrence of the disease a problem for them and for us." (1979: 29.) Indeed, it took Western scientists, with all their analytical tools, nearly ten years to document kuru's infectious nature and several years after that to appreciate its connection with cannibalism. Third, the symptoms and epidemiology of kuru fell cleanly outside the patterns of all other diseases known to the Fore. Significantly, the Fore did debate the notion that kuru was a contagious condition, only to convince themselves to the contrary. Lindenbaum described one such discussion, from the time of her fieldwork, thus: "One man noted that whites say kuru is a kind of 'sickness,' a category of ailment Fore attribute to *masalai* spirits of the forest. But women, he pointed out, the main victims of the disease, do not spend their time in the forest. Only men do. Therefore kuru could

---

[41] Gajdusek (1979: 29) has also emphasized that Fore values were not so much to blame as the changed context: "The phenomenon of cannibalism without the presence of a kuru-type virus certainly seems to have been innocuous in many regions of New Guinea, including those adjacent to the kuru region in which it was practiced. The dreadful accident was to have the rare intrusion of Creutzfeldt-Jakob-type virus into a community practicing this sort of cannibalism."

not be a sickness." (1979: 106.) Instead, the patterns of kuru seemed to match in frequency and in detail the suspected activities of sorcerers, also called "hidden men" or "rubbish men." For example, another speaker at the same meeting pointed out that if kuru were a sickness, then infants and toddlers, too, would be affected (of course, in the scientists' view, they were younger than the latency period). That kuru was primarily a disease of adult women clearly showed it to be "the selective aggression of certain sorcerers."[42] (p. 106.)

The Fore explanation of kuru as sorcery was also reinforced by the timing of local events. Initially, the increasing frequency of kuru coincided with rising social inequality and jealousy in Fore society, caused in part by the spread of cash crops. The correlation fit the Fore's theory of etiology. Later on, when many hamlets imposed their own social quarantines and the incidence of kuru simultaneously declined, this too seemed to fit. In time the Fore became so firmly convinced of their explanation that some of them openly feared the consequences should local government officials, who had announced that kuru was a disease, discover that Fore sorcerers really were to blame and punish all of them. (pp. 105–6.) Not even continued exposure to medical researchers could shake this conviction. Instead, by 1970 the very ophthalmoscope became a symbol of hope in the campaign against sorcery: if properly used, some Fore suggested, it would surely reveal "the sorcerer's rotting interior." (p. 124.)

Cultural Selection in the Face of Disaster

The conclusion seems inescapable. On the one hand, the Fore case does constitute opposition. A belief in the cannibalistic consumption of the dead persisted with high cultural fitness despite inclusive fitness reductions of epidemic proportion. Moreover, the case "fits" as an example of impeded cultural selection because of Imperfection 4, according to which people perceive deleterious consequences but do not make the connection to a meme they have the option of changing. Indeed, I have argued that the case also illustrates Imperfection 2, according to which values are influential but actively favor maladaptive memes—in this case, actually promoting the consumption of kuru victims because of their fatty tissue and their life-force for the lineage.

On the other hand, the case makes clear that people also reacted. The Fore did not sit passively by as the threat of kuru advanced, but instead went to considerable lengths in attempting to rid themselves of the pes-

---

[42] Such logic was even more compelling in the case of local "Big Men," whose social position, wealth, and plural wives made them a common target, so it was thought, of envious and covetous sorcerers. The special vulnerability to kuru of their wives (who probably did participate in a greater than average number of mortuary feasts), recognized and widely discussed by the Fore, was clearly not from the random spread of some sickness, but a sure sign of the selective malice of the "rubbish" men (Lindenbaum 1979: 120–22).

tilence. While it is true that their efforts were thwarted by the unusual features of the malady and by a number of pre-existing cultural beliefs about disease, cultural selection was also very much in operation. Among other results, a belief in a self-imposed quarantine was culturally selected because of its (apparent) consequences, and the memes related to sorcery, the "political epidemiology" of the Fore, were strongly reinforced. Had cannibalism not been abolished for other reasons and had the epidemic not subsided, I believe that the Fore would soon have found other ways to honor the dead and dispose of the corpse.[43] As Lindenbaum says, this and the many other responses of the Fore certainly illustrate "the resilience of a community facing apparent disaster. At the peak of the epidemic that was endangering their survival, the Fore spent many days debating how they might survive the holocaust." (p. 144.)

Symbol, Power, and Function in Cultural Evolution

Of all the challenges that present themselves when one is trying to develop a new approach to some subject, two stand out as especially demanding: first, how to establish the intellectual value of the new approach; and second, how to establish its ties to other, more established forms of inquiry. In concluding this chapter on neutrality and opposition, I would like to offer a few points in response to these two challenges, particularly as they relate to my efforts here toward an evolutionary anthropology. (For related attempts to apply evolutionary thinking in other domains see, for example, Oldroyd and Langham 1983; Ruse 1986; Alexander 1987; Hammel and Howell 1987; Radnitzky and Bartley 1987.)

The Value of Evolutionary Cultural Analysis

With respect to the first challenge, I personally feel that the greatest single value of coevolution is the analytic utility of its evolutionary perspective on culture. Consider, for example, how much the preceding analysis contributed to understanding Mundurucú headhunting. As in a number of the earlier chapters, the focus of our attention was on the "persistence question," namely, what forces acted to perpetuate the beliefs behind Mundurucú headhunting and thereby kept the Mundurucú in a perpetual state of war, so it was said, against all of their non-Mundurucú

---

[43] Even as it was, they came close (if only by accident): in the early 1960's, amid the many continuing efforts to curb the epidemic, some women reported that their husbands, many of whom had spurned cannibalism all along, would "not allow them to eat food they [had] received at the death ceremony for a kuru victim." (S. Glasse 1964: 40.) Although this presumably refers to the garden produce distributed at the feast, it would still have been but one small and logical step from there to the abolition of cannibalism itself. True, one cannot be certain of such an outcome. The point remains, however, that a closely associated food restriction was tried.

neighbors? The possible answers we considered were three: (1) that the Mundurucú were motivated to fight by a system of arbitrary "cultural reason" whose symbols and values rewarded valiant warriors with status, prestige, and, curiously, reproductive abstinence; (2) that the Mundurucú fought outsiders in order to release internal hostilities that otherwise would have destroyed the kinship fabric of their society; and (3) that the Mundurucú fought to appease the spirit mother and, in so doing, effectively reduced the competition for preferred game species in their interfluvial habitat. On the argument that some key assumptions behind the second answer are suspect today, we were left with two rival hypotheses, one "cultural" and one functional or "ecological."

As pointed out by the anthropologist Allen Johnson (1982), such an analytical polarization between cultural and ecological positions has been all too common in the anthropological literature, particularly the literature on Amazonia. Calling the former a "structural" position, Johnson notes (p. 417) that "both ecological and structural perspectives sometimes tend to imply that their subjects are mechanical followers of preordained strategies who either blindly pursue adaptive routes or blindly enact cultural rules [and adhere to cultural values]." He not only criticizes structuralists for their "reluctance to ask where values come from" (p. 413), but also chides ecologists for being sometimes too reductionistic (p. 416). He then suggests that improved understanding can come from "working back and forth between levels or orientations" in a way that integrates both kinds of variables (p. 417).

In my opinion, this integration is precisely what a coevolutionary approach can supply. As we have seen in this and earlier chapters, coevolution requires that we do ask where values come from, that we do avoid a presumption that people automatically know and follow "adaptive routes," and that we do integrate both kinds of variables into a more complete and more satisfying kind of explanation. In the case of the Mundurucú, my analysis suggested that both positions, the structural and the functional, are valid as far as they go: on the one hand, cultural values (and the symbols to which they were linked) did motivate the trophy takers; on the other hand, these values also prompted a course of action that had, on the average, adaptive consequences for the participants. But it also suggested that the two were interconnected in the evolutionary history of Mundurucú culture. In particular, the prized status of the Dajeboiši, with all its complex, even contradictory symbolism, involved a paradox, yes, but not an opposition. By my arguments, successful headhunters would certainly have reduced the competition and increased the game supply, particularly of wide-ranging migratory species such as the white-lipped peccary. But these benefits could have been generally enjoyed within the village only under cultural guarantees that the Dajeboiši did not selfishly absorb them. In this way, I argued, it becomes understandable why the Dajeboiši was, at once, a male hero yet a symbol of fertility, a deadly warrior and yet "mother of the peccary," holder of the most valued status in the society and yet subject to a stringent protocol of abstinence.

Thus, a coevolutionary analysis of Mundurucú culture has actually strengthened our interpretation of its symbolism. Behind the cultural evolution of this complex set of symbols, beliefs, and values, it appears, lay years of human experience, trial and error and, evidently, selection by choice. A case that looked at first sight like a striking example of opposition is finally seen, through this analytic lens, to be a rather intricate case of enhancement.

The Relationship of Coevolution to Other Approaches

The second case study of this chapter offers a useful context in which to consider the relationship between coevolution and other theoretical approaches to the analysis of cultural systems. In particular, I would like to use the Fore example to suggest some potential linkages between the evolutionary analysis of cultural systems, as advocated here, and the anthropological traditions of explanatory and interpretive analysis. Figure 7.7 illustrates schematically the relationships described in greater detail below.

In earlier sections, I suggested that the Fore case exemplifies the relationship called opposition through choice. This conclusion was based on a study of the connections between three classes of phenomena: the traditional beliefs among the Fore and their neighbors about honoring the dead in mortuary feasts; the cultural evolutionary addition of endocannibalism to those feasts; and the epidemic of the degenerative disease called kuru. In essence, it was possible to show that the recent "tradition" of Fore cannibalism, itself a product of selection by choice within more-or-less autonomous reference groups, provided a pathway for the selective transmission of the fatal kuru pathogen. Although the kuru epidemic reached catastrophic proportions by the 1950's, the memes behind cannibalism remained a locally valued addition to Fore culture largely because kuru was not consciously linked to cannibalism, but was linked to other culturally valued consequences of a gastronomic and symbolic nature. In this case, we traced opposition to two imperfections of the choice process: value displacement and cause imperception. As was particularly evident in the ethnographers' acounts, the Fore reacted resourcefully and resiliently to the crisis, but were saved, in the end, not by their own considerable ingenuity but by the serendipitous suppression of cannibalism by outside imposition.

Because the Fore case offers convincing evidence for opposition, it is also a useful context in which to consider the relationship between evolutionary analysis and the other, more established dimensions of cultural analysis in anthropology. Indeed there are two reasons why I consider the very existence of opposition to be the strongest of all evidence in these

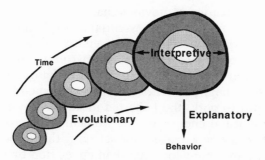

Fig. 7.7.   The three dimensions of cultural analysis. In this schematic rendering, the culture of a human population is represented as a hierarchically arranged conceptual space (with lighter shading at higher levels). The analysis of the symbols and meanings within that culture is called the "interpretive" (or "horizontal") dimension of cultural analysis; the analysis of the behavior patterns guided and shaped by that culture is called the "explanatory" (or "vertical") dimension of cultural analysis; and the analysis of transformational changes through time within that culture is called the "evolutionary" (or "temporal") dimension of cultural analysis. Coevolutionary theory suggests the potential for a mutually beneficial, complementary relationship between these conceptually and historically distinct forms of cultural analysis.

pages for the complementary value of alternative approaches. First, this case of opposition underscores the importance of understanding the system of meaning and values through which people interpret the world and guide their actions. Fore culture found value and meaning in cannibalism; some 2,500 Fore, mostly women and children, died as a result. Surely that gruesome statistic is adequate to persuade even the most skeptical sociobiologist of the causal strength of secondary values in cultural change.

In this particular case, neglect of the symbolic or interpretive dimension of cultural analysis would also make it difficult to understand why cannibalism was accepted, and quickly so, by Fore women while simultaneously rejected, by and large, by the men. But this one differential, subtle enough that its significance was not appreciated by Western investigators for years, proved absolutely crucial in the end to explaining the unique epidemiological pattern of the disease. Similarly, understanding the Fore interpretation of kuru as malicious sorcery, and therefore understanding its connection to local political and economic processes, is crucial to making sense of the Fore reaction to the disease, including their reluctance to accept the Westerners' etiology of it.

Second, the opposition displayed by this case offers particularly clear evidence of the power of cultural beliefs to guide human behavior, and therefore convincing testimonial, if one were needed, of the importance of the explanatory dimension of cultural analysis. Not only have we traced the entire kuru epidemic (and thus the full range of Fore responses) to a small but powerful set of values in Fore culture, but we have also implicated the belief system in the differential adoption of cannibalism by women and men in the first place. The lessons of this case strongly reinforce a major implication of previous chapters: attention to the cultural track of information inheritance is essential for explaining the patterns of human diversity, especially behavioral diversity.

Finally, this example also serves as an instructive microcosm of the power of imposition over the course of cultural change. In the Fore case, adult males largely (and unintentionally) escaped the plague of kuru by laying prior claim to pork, the preferred meat, thereby imposing a narrowed array of cultural choices on the women. As mentioned earlier in this chapter, there are good reasons for believing that imposed opposition is more frequent and more enduring than opposition by choice. Among those reasons is the basic fact that, with imposition, the persistence of suboptimal allomemes can be specifically motivated by the interests of those who benefit. It is this basic fact more than any other that, in my view, guarantees an enduring place for symbol, power, *and* function in the study of cultural evolution.

8 /   CONCLUSION: Evolution in a

Dual Inheritance System

C harles Darwin once wrote that his book, *On the Origin of Species*, had two principal goals, "firstly, to shew that species had not been separately created, and secondly, that natural selection had been the chief agent of change." (1981 [1871] 1: 152). In the preceding chapters, I have attempted to propose a theory of cultural evolution—that is, of descent with modification in the shared conceptual systems we call "cultures"—that is parallel in many ways to Darwin's theory of organic evolution. My goals have been, first, to propose that a process of cultural selection has been the main but not exclusive force of cultural evolution; second, to show that cultural selection gives rise to no fewer than five distinct modes of relationship between organic and cultural change; and third, to suggest that, despite the complexity of their relationship, natural selection (or, more precisely, genetic selection) and cultural selection do tend to cooperate in the evolution of attributes that are adaptively advantageous for some, if not all, of their bearers. I call this theory "coevolution" to emphasize that, for this group of beneficiaries (a group which may or may not be coextensive with the full population), genetic selection and cultural selection have generally harmonious, parallel influences in guiding the evolution of human diversity.

Because of the length and complexity of the arguments already presented, I would like, in this concluding chapter, to summarize the theory and its implications. The following sections therefore review the major assumptions, hypotheses, and implications of coevolution.

Assumptions

Paragenetic Transmission

A basic premise of the theory outlined in these pages is that genes and culture constitute two distinct but interacting systems of information inheritance within human populations. That they are two distinct systems and not somehow one and the same is amply demonstrated by the following observations: first, genes and culture each contain information within codes that have very different biophysical properties (DNA versus memes); second, the information is stored and processed in different, highly specialized structures (cell nuclei versus the brain); third, it is transmitted through space and time by very different mechanisms (sexual versus *social* intercourse); and fourth, the information in either system may undergo lasting, transmissible change without there being a corresponding change in the other.

In addition, I have assumed that genes and culture are both characterized by what Richard Dawkins has called "phenotypic power" (as in 1982a: 91). That is to say, I have assumed that information of both kinds has influence, actual or potential, over the observable phenotypic properties of human beings, particularly their behaviors. In earlier chapters I have argued that this influence creates a real and unambiguous symmetry between genes and phenotypes on the one hand, and culture and phenotypes on the other. To be sure, the two inheritance systems produce their effects in very different ways (compare the influence of the monomarital principle of Chapter 2 with that of the sickling allele, S, in Chapter 3). Nevertheless, the crucial similarities are (1) that both systems, separately or in combination, are capable of causing heritable change in the nature of phenotypes; and (2) that neither system exerts its influence in a way that could accurately be described as "deterministic." In both cases, environment and chance effects (or "developmental noise") are also intimately involved (see Lewontin 1982: ch. 2).

On the basis of these assumptions, I have proposed that genes and culture are best represented as two parallel lines or "tracks" of hereditary influence on phenotypes, a relationship summarized earlier in Fig. 4.3. In this proposal, culture's relationship to phenotypes is structurally symmetrical to that of the genes; it is truly a "paragenetic" transmission system (after Waddington 1961: 72). The proposal builds upon ideational theories of culture and their suggestion that culture provides socially transmitted guides for behavior. In my opinion, these arguments are crucial if social science is to make significant headway past the barriers of the nature/nurture debate.

System Requirements for Evolution

My arguments concerning the dynamics of change within the cultural system and their relationships to genetic change rest upon a number of additional assumptions that serve to ensure that both systems meet the full set of "system requirements" for evolutionary change (as discussed in Chapter 1). I have therefore assumed (1) that both systems can be divided into recognizable subunits of transmission and inheritance; (2) that within all populations there are sources of variation in these units, sources that create alternative forms at least occasionally; and (3) that there exist one or more mechanisms of transmission through which these units are conveyed among the individuals of a population. As concerns the processes of transformation—that is, of evolutionary change *within* genetic and cultural systems—I have assumed (4) that Darwin was right in suggesting natural selection as the main but not exclusive means of modification in organic evolution, and that the principal challenge before me was to elucidate its counterpart or counterparts in cultural evolution. Finally, I have assumed (5) that there exist the necessary sources of isolation such that diversification—the divergence of incipient "daughter systems" from a common ancestor—can occur. As befits my emphasis on the causes of evolutionary change within cultural systems, most of my arguments have concerned Assumptions 1–4; with respect to isolation, I have simply alluded to some of the more obvious candidates—particularly spatial, temporal, and ethnolinguistic separation (see also Hill 1971)—leaving fuller examination of their role for future work.

Units of transmission. Assumption 1 is probably the most important and most controversial of the set. It should be clear by now that the units I have in mind for both systems are the informational entities, whatever their size and complexity, that are differentially transmitted as coherent, functional units. In both cases, it seems wise to avoid an arbitrarily imposed "fundamental bit" or even a fixed, hierarchical inventory of different subunits. Instead, I favor a more elastic conceptualization, one that can vary in size just as much as what is actually transmitted. It also seems wise to avoid traits themselves or other trait-inclusive units even though, historically, these have been among the first and most persistently proposed of all units. As argued in earlier chapters, trait-inclusive units tend to impede the advance of theory: they risk confounding attributes with instructions, genetic effects with cultural effects, and nature with nurture. In the cultural realm, such units ignore the conceptual advances of ideational theory, and they unnecessarily complicate the empirical analysis of transmission for any instructions of variable expression (as in the case of the monomarital rule of Chapter 2).

In contrast, I assume that the units of transmission vary widely with respect to scale and complexity, from the level of introns of DNA to whole genes, chromosomes, genomes, and even gene pools in the genetic system, and from single units of meaning in culture (like the morphemes of language), to more complex ideas, beliefs, and values, and on to entire languages, ideologies, symbol systems, and culture pools. Let me therefore emphasize that in the theory advanced here there is no assumption of a constant, universal "particle" in either system. In a given context, the answer to "What is the relevant unit of transmission?" is essentially an empirical one: "Whatever is both variable and differentially transmitted, regardless of its size and complexity."

In light of this assumption, I have used Richard Dawkins's term "meme" (1976: 206; 1982: 109) to represent the variable unit of transmission in cultural evolution. I have suggested that meme should refer to any kind, amount, and configuration of information in culture that shows both variation and coherent transmission. As explained in Chapter 4, I accept Dawkins's term for this unit both because it has appropriate, if limited, historical precedents and because it lacks everyday connotations with respect to size, organization, and content. My use of this term differs from that of some other authors; for example, John A. Ball (1984: 145) calls memes, quite incorrectly in my view, the "smallest recognizable pieces of cultural information." For these smaller and more uniform subunits a different term is required, perhaps the "menteme" suggested by Martin Stuart-Fox (1986).

It bears emphasis that this definition of "meme" creates an imperfect analogy with the "gene" of genetic theory. On the one hand, there clearly *are* similarities. Both genes and memes are units of information (though of different kinds). Moreover, both are "holons" in the sense of T. F. H. Allen and Thomas B. Starr (1982), that is, both are (1) *parts of* a greater system, and therefore subject to its constraints, and (2) *parts from* that system, and thus capable of semi-independent change. Moreover, by virtue of their (assumed) influence on phenotypes, both genes and memes have what I call the "property of consequences," that is to say, both have the potential for some measure of impact upon the lives of their carriers. As we have seen, this impact may take many specific forms, such as increasing (or reducing) the supply of resources, nutrients, or even mates. But the point is that both genes and culture are capable of some kind of effect, however large or small, on the relationship between individuals (and/or groups of individuals) and their social and natural environments broadly defined. This effect I have called the "ecological consequences" of genes and culture.

On the other hand, there are also major disanalogies, the most important of which concerns the variability of the meme in scale and organization. For largely historical reasons, as we saw in Chapter 3, "gene" has referred to the smallest heritable unit of phenotypic consequence—the length of DNA coding for a polypeptide.[1] The problem is that the smallest units of phenotypic consequence need not be equal to the functional units of transmission (this, of course, is also true of culture). For example, many units of consequence (structural genes) can be linked on a chromosome into one unit of transmission.[2] For this reason, a number of

[1] The problem apparently traces to the early days of the modern synthesis, when Mendel's units (genes, originally *Elemente*) were eagerly plugged in to Darwin's logic. As a result, organic evolution has commonly (but erroneously) been *defined* as gene-frequency change or "allelic substitution." In recent years, a number of theorists have offered worthy arguments for a "pluralistic" theory of evolution by natural selection with a full hierarchy of focal units (see discussion in the conclusion to Chapter 3; see also Gould 1980a, 1982a, 1982b; Arnold and Fristrup 1984; Vrba and Eldredge 1984; Eldredge 1985).

[2] In 1976 Richard Dawkins, like George Williams (1966: 25) before him, bravely attempted to redefine "gene" as a unit with evolutionary significance only to find his efforts

evolutionary theorists speak today not of genes as the transmission unit, but of "selectons," "optimons," or "active germ-line replicators" (see Dawkins 1982a: ch. 5). Ironically, because of its variable size and complexity, "meme" is a better unit for cultural theory than is "gene" for genetic theory.

Sources of variation. In order for a system to evolve through replication, there must obviously exist some degree of variation within these transmission units. By analogy with genes, whose variant forms are called "alleles," I have called the behaviorally expressed variants of any given meme its "allomemes." In both systems, my intention has been to assume only that some amount of variation is available. This assumption is deliberately vague, for I agree with Stephen Jay Gould (1980a: 129) that one cannot assume, either in genetic evolution or in cultural, that "variation is copious, small in increments, and available in all directions." A more realistic assessment is rather that variation is tightly constrained by the effects of circumstances, history, and prevailing structures. Given these constraints, I have assumed only that some sources of variation exist within each system: the primary sources of mutation (genes) and innovation (culture); and the secondary sources of recombination (genes), synthesis (culture), migration (genes and culture), and diffusion (culture). The point is that although variation must not be taken for granted, it still remains essential for any evolutionary process. Since one can speak of evolution if and only if there are unfavored variants left behind, my assumption has been only that variation does sometimes exist within each inheritance system.

The assumption of variation within constraints, however, points out a second disanalogy between genetic and cultural change. In genetic theory (as discussed in Chapter 3), the organic constraints are largely endogenous to the organism; they are "the constraints of inherited form and developmental pathways [that] may so channel any change . . . [as to become] the primary determinant of evolutionary direction." (Gould 1982a: 383; see also Maynard Smith et al. 1985.) In cultural theory, constraints may surely originate from within individuals as well: for example, an individual might have a personal bias toward compliance and conformity with prevailing norms. However, there are two additional sources of constraint. The first of these I have called "cultural constraints," in reference to the limitations imposed upon variation by shared habits of thought, preconceptions and prejudice, existing technology, and the like. The second is a potentially still more powerful set of social constraints arising from the social nature of the transmission process itself. Control by others over any or all aspects of cultural transmission—for example, con-

---

violently criticized by molecular geneticists (see discussion in Dawkins 1982a: ch. 5). In contrast to their unit-of-consequence definition, Dawkins defined a gene as "any portion of chromosomal material which potentially lasts for enough generations to serve as a unit of natural selection." (1976: 30.)

trol over what variants are available to whom, and over which set of values will govern—can, as discussed in Chapter 4, greatly alter the rates and directions of cultural change. Genetic change, then, also differs from cultural change because the actions of other (nonparental) organisms do not ordinarily affect an individual's or group's access to genetic variation. Given that this does occur in culture, our evolutionary models of culture must then embrace the concept of *power* in all of its various dimensions (on which see, for example, Lukes 1974). Because power and attendant social constraints can be highly selective in their influence on culture, I have included them as a force of cultural selection and will review them later in this chapter.

Mechanisms of transmission. Finally, the third assumption simply grants that there are mechanisms for the conveyance through space and time of genetic and cultural variants. Of the two, the genetic mechanisms are perhaps the more thoroughly understood (see, for example, Watson et al. 1987), although there have been significant gains on the cultural side as well (as in T. Williams 1972; Tindall 1976; Cavalli-Sforza and Feldman 1981; Spindler 1987). But surely it is here that disanalogies between genes and culture are most self-evident: we have reproduction versus communication, gametogenesis and syngamy (fertilization) versus teaching and learning, and fixed, vertical (parent-offspring) transmission versus the variable pathways of culture (vertical, horizontal, and oblique). However, the point remains that, in both systems, transmission entails replication, and this means that their respective subunits—germ-line replicators and memes—will all exhibit some degree of fitness, or "appropriateness of design," for the pertinent replication processes. My assumption is simply that, as a general rule in either system, not all variants of a given unit have equal fitness.

The implication is that our evolutionary models of change in human phenotypes must include at least two measures of fitness, one for each kind of transmission unit and hereditary track. On the genetic side, at the level of microevolutionary change, we have spoken of the Darwinian fitness of genotypes—that is, their expected contribution of offspring to the next generation—and we have used W as a measure of that fitness.[3] This measure assesses the relative change in frequency of each genotype during one generation of genetic selection, and standardizes the different values on a scale of 0.0 to 1.0. Similarly, on the cultural side, we have discussed cultural fitness, F_c—that is, the suitability of allomemes for replication and use within a given cultural system—and have defined a mea-

[3] In the emerging hierarchical theories of organic evolution (see note 1), fitness is a property of any and all units that exhibit differential reproduction. Thus one might measure species fitness as "the differential birth and death of species considered as entities." (Gould 1982b: 92.) Because the theory of coevolution concerns changes within human populations, my discussion here focuses on microlevel genetic change and thus on the Darwinian fitnesses of genotypes.

sure of that fitness, namely R—the relative rate of a given allomeme's social transmission per unit of time. Like the W of an optimal genotype, the R of an allomeme is 1.0 if it achieves the highest relative rate of social transmission and use over a particular time interval.[4]

In order to explore relationships between evolutionary changes in the separate tracks, I have also drawn upon a third measure of fitness, namely, W. D. Hamilton's (1964: 8) "inclusive fitness of individuals." As a measure of the relative transmission rates of individuals' genes to the next generation, it is a useful standard for judging adaptation, particularly in social settings where behavioral interactions may frequently contribute to survival and reproduction differentials. Here I have used Hamilton's measure to define the "inclusive fitness value," or F_g, of a given allomeme as the average of the inclusive fitnesses of its bearers in a population or subgroup, standardized on a 0.0 to 1.0 scale relative to the averages for other, coexisting allomemes. F_g is thus a measure of a cultural variant's relative contribution to the "effectiveness of design for reproductive survival" under prevailing conditions (G. Williams 1966: 158).[5]

In summary, this list of assumptions endows both genes and culture with the basic systems requirements for evolutionary change. Table 8.1 summarizes the assumptions pertaining to the transformational components of change and indicates some of the more obvious similarities and differences between the two systems. For example, by summarizing as "communication" the various processes of teaching and learning in the cultural system, the table makes clear that genetic and cultural mechanisms of transmission differ along several important dimensions. These differences are largely responsible for the oft-cited potential of the cultural system to be either faster or slower to change than the genetic system (see also Cavalli-Sforza et al. 1982).

Table 8.1 raises two further points. First, it reminds us that Campbell's rule about false analogies (see p. 187, above) should always be applied to the comparison of genes and culture. The point of the endeavor is not to analogize from genetic theory to cultural change as has so often been

---

[4] Because cultural transmission can be a continuous process, there is no fixed time interval for measuring cultural fitness that could be called equivalent to "generation" in genetic theory. Instead, a cultural "generation" is a highly variable interval; I take it to be the average, over all members of a subpopulation or sample, of the interval between the time of each individual's adoption of any one allomeme and the average time of adoption of that variant among all persons he or she subsequently influences.

[5] In principle, F_g should prove quite useful in comparing the directions and rates of change of cultural evolution with those of organic evolution. It allows one to assess whether or not the variants favored by cultural selection have reproductive effects similar to those of variants favored by genetic selection. Put differently, F_g allows one to ask the hypothetical question, If a particular array of allomemes *were instead* an array of alleles, would genetic selection favor the same variant or variants as are favored by cultural selection? In practice, however, F_g may prove difficult to estimate, particularly if the context requires an accurate assessment of "offspring equivalents" (see Chapter 4, note 31).

TABLE 8.1

System Requirements for Transformational Change
in Genetic and Cultural Systems

Requirement[a]	Genetic system	Cultural system
1. Units of transmission	Genes	Memes
Variant forms	Alleles	Allomemes
Population	Gene pool	Culture pool
2. Sources of variation	Assumed random	Deliberate or random
Primary	Mutation	Innovation
Secondary	Recombination	Synthesis
	Migration	Migration and diffusion
3. Mechanisms of transmission	Reproduction	Communication
Processes	Gametogenesis	Teaching
	Syngamy	Learning
Mode	Vertical	Vertical, horizontal, and oblique
Ratio (receivers: transmitters)	Fixed (1:2)	Variable
4. Processes of transformation	Gene-frequency change	Meme-frequency change
Nonconveyance forces	Mutation	Innovation and synthesis
	Migration	Migration and diffusion
	Genetic drift	Cultural drift
Conveyance forces	Genic selection[b]	Cultural selection
	Genetic selection	Natural selection
	N.e.[c]	Transmission forces
Constraints	Organic constraints	Cultural constraints
	N.e.[c]	Social constraints

[a] The fifth system requirement discussed in Chapter 1—"sources of isolation"—pertains to the diversification component of evolutionary change and is thus not included in this table.

[b] Genic selection refers to natural selection at the level of alternative alleles (after Williams 1966), as contrasted with "genetic selection," the differential reproduction of genotypes.

[c] "N.e." means that no equivalent has been identified.

done; rather, it is to analogize from a general model of evolutionary processes to those features of both systems, genetic and cultural, by which they qualify as evolutionary. Too often we forget that genetic microevolution is, after all, only one specific example of evolutionary process. Upon careful inspection, we can see that cultural evolution is disanalogous in many ways to that example. Yet culture is still an evolutionary system in its own right, and a powerful one at that.

Second, Table 8.1 emphasizes that human evolution is inherently a two-track process. The implication is that we cannot achieve a full understanding of human diversity by using the conceptual tools and principles of either track alone. Theoretical formulations with the equivalent of a single fitness measure—including sociobiology on the one hand, and much of cultural anthropology on the other—are simply incomplete and logically insufficient for the task. Even as first approximations they may be misleading and ultimately counterproductive. Our understanding of human diversity necessarily requires attention to two classes of units, two kinds of variation, two mechanisms of transmission, and two sets of laws of transformation.

Sociological Assumptions

Finally, the theoretical framework presented here assumes a number of attributes in common among individuals in the social aggregates where cultural evolution takes place. First, I have assumed all individuals to have a common "capacity for culture" that is itself the product of organic evolution by genetic selection. This is simply the assumption of "natural origins," namely, that "some of the most distinctive characters of man [specifically those directly involved in cultural transmission] have in all probability been acquired, either directly, or more commonly indirectly, through natural selection" at the individual level (Darwin 1981 [1871] 1: 151). This assumption allows one to begin with the premise that the human decision system—an integral part of our capacity for culture—has been designed to promote decisions that are generally consistent with the selection criterion of genetic microevolution, namely, reproductive fitness. It also allows one to draw inferences about the prehistoric relations of genes and culture from the fossil record for the expansion of the hominid brain. The implications of these suppositions will be discussed in more detail below.

The second assumption is that, for the purposes of analyzing cultural evolution, one can subdivide any population at a given time into one or more reference groups (if necessary, on a meme-by-meme basis). As I use the term, a reference group is a collection of individual culture carriers each of whom has at that time (1) approximately the same range of available allomemes (hence equal constraints and opportunities); (2) about the same "ecological consequences" from those allomemes (hence a uniform inclusive fitness function); and (3) more or less the same value system for comparing the variants (hence a uniform cultural fitness function).[6] This group, which will sometimes be equivalent to a full population, defined by geographic or ethnolinguistic criteria, and at other times equivalent to a specific subset (such as a social class, a caste, a descent group, etc.) is, I believe, the most appropriate unit for the analysis of cultural evolution. The reason is simple: cultural change will run in different directions and at different rates whenever social aggregates differ along any of the three dimensions defining a reference group. I have also found it important to distinguish autonomous reference groups—those in which individuals (called "selectors") are free to adopt or not adopt the given allomemes by their own volition—from the nonautonomous ones in which members (called "compliers") are subject to some degree of imposition for the variants in question. Some of the reasons for these distinctions have been discussed in Chapter 4; others are discussed below.

[6] The term "reference group" has been used with related meaning in sociology and social psychology. In the literature on relative deprivation, for example, the term refers to an individual's "frame of comparative reference" for self-evaluation (see, for example, Merton 1957; Hyman 1960). In my usage, it is a frame of comparative reference for evaluating the direction and rate of cultural change.

The Principal Hypotheses of Coevolution

The remaining systems requirement for evolution is processes of trans-formation—processes that enable one to predict or explain the changes through time in a given system (item 4 in Table 8.1). On this subject, my argument has been that both tracks of information transmission tend to show regular and comprehensible patterns of descent with modification. I have suggested that these regularities result from governing laws of trans-formation that have two key features in common but are different in most other respects. The common features are "multiplicity," or the existence of plural transforming principles within each system, and "selectivity," or a tendency toward the nonrandom, differential transmission of variants. The differences pertain to the directions and rates of change as well as to the whole matter of how selectivity is, in fact, achieved.

With respect to the genetic system, my object has been not to elaborate or extend our understanding of the governing laws, but simply to review what is generally known and hypothesized. Here I have drawn heavily upon Darwin and more recent evolutionary theorists to examine briefly both the range of identified transforming principles and their suspected relative importance. In Chapter 3, for example, we saw that there were four potentially important processes of genetic transformation: mutation, drift, migration, and genetic selection (that is, the differential reproduc-tion of genotypes). The case study of that chapter, on the evolution of ge-netic diversity in specific human hemoglobins, led to the same conclu-sion that Darwin offered over a hundred years ago: that natural selection, or preservation by reproductive advantage, has been "the main but not ex-clusive means of modification." (Darwin 1964 [1859]: 6.) In principle, of course, the potential exists for natural selection to operate at *any* level in the organizational hierarchy of life where there are variable, reproducing entities (see, for example, Brandon and Burian 1984; Vrba and Eldredge 1984; Eldredge 1985).[7] However, we still do not have a clear vision of the relative importance of that process on each of these levels for the shaping of organic diversity, and there remains today considerable debate on this point.

[7] Consider, for example, the three levels "intra-organismic" (or "intra-individual"), "in-terindividual," and "interaggregate." Following the arguments of Dawkins (1976, 1982a) and others, one can imagine gene- or "replicator"-level natural selection that involves the differ-ential reproduction of alleles, linkage groups of genes, or whole chromosomes. Several ex-amples of selection at this level are known or suspected: the case of the "t allele" in the house mouse (reviewed in Sober 1984b: ch. 7); the "segregation distorter" chromosome in the fruit fly (Crow 1979); transposable genetic elements in bacteria and higher organisms (see, for example, Doolittle and Sapienza 1980); and repeated sequences of DNA in higher organisms (Orgel and Crick 1980, among others). Similarly, following the arguments of Gould (1980a, 1982b), Stanley (1979, 1981), and others, one can imagine group- or aggregate-level natural selection, including the differential reproduction of social groups or indeed of whole species in a given phyletic line.

With respect to the cultural system, my objectives have been more comprehensive. Chapter 4 began with a critical review of recently proposed laws of cultural transformation, including some of my own earlier efforts. I then attempted to amend and prioritize the list so as to give the processes of cultural selection the attention and weight I believe they deserve. In Hypothesis 1, reviewed below, I proposed what I regard as the single most important transforming principle in the dynamics of cultural evolution. That hypothesis and its corollaries, together with the assumptions already described, provide the outline for a general theory parallel to its genetic counterpart—a theory of evolution by *cultural* selection. In Hypothesis 2, also reviewed below, I explored the implications of cultural selection for understanding the relationships between genes and culture in human populations. And finally, in Hypothesis 3, I suggested that there is a specific, nonaccidental parallel between the most important of the laws of genetic transformation and the most important of the laws of cultural transformation. Let us now turn to review each of these key hypotheses in turn.

Hypothesis 1: The Main But Not Exclusive Means of Modification

What force or forces cause the preservation of certain variants and the loss of others? This simple but important question was clearly at the forefront of Charles Darwin's thinking when he defined natural selection as the "preservation of [reproductively] favourable variations and the rejection of [reproductively] injurious variations." (1964 [1859]: 81.) Today, this same question should play a leading role in our approach to cultural evolution: we must ask, What force or forces contribute to the differential preservation of allomemes? In other words, what causes some allomemes to attain high frequency in a population while others, at the same time, decrease in prevalence or are eliminated? Why, in short, do some variants show greater staying power than others? The process of answering this question inevitably leads to the search for evolutionary laws of transformation.

My own attempts in this direction have caused me to distinguish two general categories of forces (see Table 8.2). Category A, or "nonconveyance forces," includes the sources of variation in cultural systems, such as innovation, migration, diffusion, and cultural drift, whose role is more to introduce alternatives than to cull them. As in the genetic system, however, such forces can—and no doubt do—contribute to cultural transformation; variants can readily be preserved through their repeated introduction or eliminated by their repeated loss. Category B consists of three kinds of "conveyance forces," all of which can cause meme selection, the differential social transmission of allomemes within a reference group. The first kind, transmission forces or what I think of as "preservation by process" (B.1. in the table), refers to the effects of transmission

TABLE 8.2

Principal Forces of Cultural Evolution

Category and force
A. Nonconveyance forces:
1. Innovation and synthesis
2. Migration and diffusion
3. Cultural drift
B. Conveyance forces:
1. Transmission forces
a. Differential modeling
b. Role selection
2. Natural selection
a. Differential reproduction
b. Societal selection
3. Cultural selection: choice and imposition
a. Primary value selection
b. Secondary value selection

mode (whether vertical, horizontal, or oblique) and ratio (one-to-one, for example, or many-to-one) on the social conveyance of allomemes in a population. In essence, these are forces that arise because cultural transmission does not obey the equivalent of the Hardy-Weinberg law governing genetic transmission.

Instead, cultural transmission is "context-dependent": the rates and directions of change can vary simply as a function of the social situation of allomeme transmission. Thus, for example, differential modeling—the unequal effectiveness of teachers and models—can contribute to the preservation of an allomeme by giving it a transmission ratio advantage. This is particularly true when that advantage is institutionalized through enduring influential roles in society, or what I have called "role selection" (after Boyd and Richerson 1985: ch. 6). The "power of transmission" generated by these forces was first identified by Luigi Cavalli-Sforza and Marcus Feldman (1981: 359); in their opinion, "the mode of transmission is of great importance in determining the rate of change of trait frequencies in populations." (p. 356.) In my view, transmission forces do contribute to F_c differentials, but I see them as having "great importance" only in special circumstances where their influence overrides other, generally more powerful forces.

The second category of conveyance forces (B.2. in Table 8.2) is the familiar one of natural selection or simply preservation by reproductive advantage—here, the natural selection of cultural variation. In this category I include two forces, one intrasocietal and one intersocietal. The intrasocietal force stems from the differential reproduction of individuals, where that reproduction is assumed to be coupled with cultural transmission from parent to offspring. This is the force that F. T. Cloak (1977: 50) was speaking of when he noted that "a cultural instruction whose behavior helps its human carrier-enactor (or his/her relatives) to acquire more children thereby has more little heads to get copied into" and thus has high cultural fitness. The intersocietal force, in contrast, stems from the differential expansion and extinction of whole societies. This force includes various forms of direct conflict, including warfare to annihilation, or what Alfred Keller called "the primordial agency of selection . . . and probably the most efficient that has ever existed" (1915: 62–63; see also Schmookler 1984), and also conquest and subjugation.[8] This force occupies a place in the cultural scheme equivalent to the one that species selection occupies in genetic theory, and thus Keller's term "societal selection" seems appropriate.

In my own estimation, the third category of conveyance forces (B.3 in Table 8.2) is also the most important. It contains the various forces of *cultural* selection or "preservation by preference," including both choice and imposition. My argument here is that allomemes themselves are subject to a weeding-out process in human populations, a process not unlike the natural selection of particular genotypes. However, my proposal is that *people*, not some abstract force called "nature," do most of the selecting; that they achieve this primarily through a range of value-based decision processes; and that their decisions—conscious or unconscious—are heavily influenced by the perceived and valued consequences of the variants. My argument, moreover, locates this selectivity primarily at the "instruction" level—it is usually allomemes rather than individuals or groups that are selected—and ascribes its action potentially to both the "senders" and "receivers" of cultural transmission.[9] Cultural selection thus has much in common with the proposed but controversial idea of "genic selection" in genetic theory (after G. Williams 1966: ch. 4; Dawkins 1976). It is as if individuals could *choose* genes (not to mention chromosomes) for themselves or, for that matter, for the group, population, or even species of which they are a member.

As discussed in earlier chapters, cultural selection includes a range of different decision processes. At one end of this range are the relatively "pure" forms of selection by choice, that is, situations where individuals exert "free choice" and preferentially adopt one or more allomemes of their own accord. Of course, the array of options is limited even in the freest of choices by the cultural constraints of habit, preconception, and technology—constraints analogous to the "organic constraints" of ge-

[8] The relative importance of warfare versus peaceful diffusion has been studied empirically by Naroll and Divale (1976) and Naroll and Wirsing (1976). Contrary to earlier social Darwinist arguments that warfare is "the selective mechanism of cultural evolution" (Naroll and Divale 1976: 100), these studies provide evidence that peaceful diffusion is generally the more important mechanism.

[9] Allomeme frequencies can surely be influenced by "discrimination"—that is, by the actual sorting of individuals or groups according to their attitudes, values, or beliefs. But because this process depends upon coexisting conveyance forces (for the social distribution of variants), and is no match for their potential speed and efficiency, I have not included it in Table 8.2 as one of the principal forces.

netic microtheory (see Fig. 3.3). Nevertheless, at this end of the range, the guiding evolutionary mechanism is differential preservation through choice. I regard this form of cultural selection as the principal cause of cultural evolution in autonomous reference groups.

In contrast, cultural selection at the other end of the range proceeds through relatively pure forms of "selection by imposition," in which constraints of social origin determine the outcome. The various guises of this process (for example, coercion, force, manipulation, and authority) also involve value-based decisions, but they are the decisions of *external* agents imposed upon the members of a nonautonomous reference group. In these cases, individuals face either a narrowly constrained, "unfree" choice or no choice at all. This can happen when options are limited by others, when value systems are manipulated by others, or when the cultural context has been shaped by the actions and interests of others. In this form of cultural selection the guiding evolutionary mechanism is differential preservation through compliance with the choices of others.

Between the two extremes of choice and imposition lie decision processes of various intermediate types, all referred to here as cultural selection. A central argument of this book has been that cultural selection, the preservation of variants through this range of decision processes, is the single most important force of cultural evolution. At an abstract level, of course, genetic selection itself can also be viewed as a decision process: nature effectively chooses on the basis of reproductive value in a given environment. Cultural selection in my view not only continues this basic pattern, it also *internalizes* the process, allowing people to implement decisions long before any choices would be decided "by nature." In contrast, then, to the "selection *by* consequences" of Darwinian theory (after Skinner 1984), cultural selection represents what I have called selection *according to* consequences. At the same time, cultural selection can also *localize* the process of evolutionary change, by enabling (though not necessarily requiring) the choice of one or a few individuals to come to characterize an entire group or population. Again, this forms a striking contrast to evolution by genetic selection, where simultaneous parallel "choices" must be made throughout a population in order for some one genotype, for example, to increase in frequency.

But there is another important difference: in cultural selection, human choices are guided by sets of values whose scales are not generally measured in terms of reproduction (we will return later to the question of why this is so). Specifically, our choices are guided both by what Pugh (1977) has called "primary values," that is, by valuative feedback produced by the nervous system, with or without conscious intervention, and by "secondary values," that is, by the socially transmitted, *cultural* standards derived from primary values through experience, history, and rational thought. This feature gives rise to two intergraded forms of cultural selection as shown in Table 8.2: "primary value selection," in which transmission differentials are most heavily influenced by primary values; and "secondary value selection," in which cultural values play the greater role. Both forms apply to the full range of decision processes, from pure choice to pure imposition, and may be thought of as a perpendicular second axis of cultural selection (see Fig. 4.6).

Following Darwin's lead, then, I have proposed that secondary value selection is the main but not exclusive means of cultural evolutionary change (Hypothesis 1). By this hypothesis, the single most important force in the differential transmission of allomemes is conscious, value-based decision making by culture carriers. Accordingly, the fate of allomemes is predicted to ride on secondary decision criteria whether selection proceeds by choice, imposition, or some mixture of the two. To the extent that choice is involved in a given case, the F_c's of the cultural fitness function should covary with "internal values," that is, with the secondary value preferences of the reference group itself. Thus, in a relatively pure case of selection by choice, Hypothesis 1 predicts that knowledge of internal values will be both necessary for explaining the direction and rates of cultural change, and sufficient to explain most of the variance in F_c values. In contrast, to the extent that imposition is involved, the pertinent F_c's are expected to reflect "external values," that is, the secondary value preferences of the imposers. Imposition succeeds either because manipulation has spread the imposers' values through the reference group, or because the imposers have narrowed the range of choices to those favored by their own values, or both. But whatever the reason, if Hypothesis 1 is valid in cases of imposition, then knowledge of external values should be both necessary for explaining the dynamics of cultural change, and sufficient to explain most of the variance in the F_c curve.

In summary, Fig. 8.1 offers a schematic overview of my proposals concerning the inventory of transformational forces of cultural evolution. For a hypothetical reference group and cultural system (represented for simplicity as a "culture pool" of the pertinent variants), the figure shows changes through time in the prevalence of alternative allomemes specifically showing an increase in allomeme B. The schema includes forces from both categories of Table 8.2: nonconveyance forces (represented by arrows at the edges of the pool) and conveyance forces (represented by the filtering device in the center). The latter include the natural selection of cultural variation (shown as a thin contribution to the filter channels for each allomeme), as well as both forms of cultural selection.[10] Thus selection by imposition blocks off some of the filter channels that would otherwise be available; it may also contribute to the secondary values within

---

[10] In the interest of simplicity, some important forces of cultural evolution—for instance, transmission forces and societal selection—are not shown in Fig. 8.1. Regrettably, clarity has also required allomemes to be portrayed as independent, free-floating circles of uniform size, with distinct boundaries and no discernible internal organization—this despite my own arguments for their interconnected, variably sized, holon-like nature. Suggestions for a more faithful representation would be appreciated.

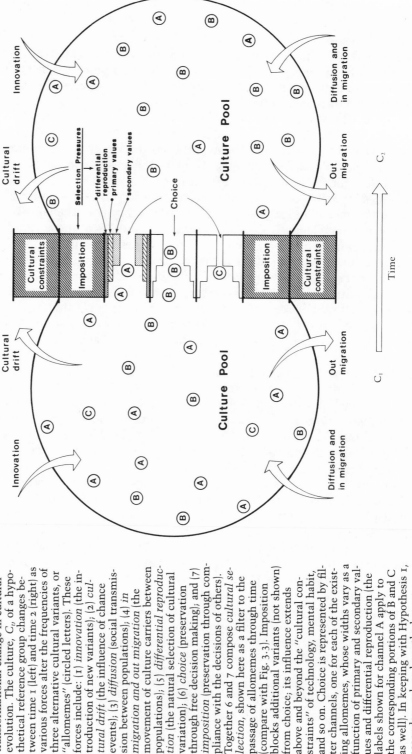

Fig. 8.1. Schematic representation of transformational change in cultural evolution. The culture, C_u of a hypothetical reference group changes between time 1 (left) and time 2 (right) as various forces alter the frequencies of three alternative cultural variants, or "allomemes" (circled letters). These forces include: (1) *innovation* (the introduction of new variants); (2) *cultural drift* (the influence of chance events); (3) *diffusion* (social transmission between populations); (4) *in migration and out migration* (the movement of culture carriers between populations); (5) *differential reproduction* (the natural selection of cultural variation); (6) *choice* (preservation through free decision making); and (7) *imposition* (preservation through compliance with the decisions of others). Together 6 and 7 compose *cultural selection*, shown here as a filter to the passage of allomemes through time (compare with Fig. 3.3). Imposition blocks additional variants (not shown) from choice; its influence extends above and beyond the "cultural constraints" of technology, mental habit, and so on. Choice is represented by filter channels, whose widths vary as a function of primary and secondary values and differential reproduction (the labels shown for channel A apply to the corresponding portions of B and C as well). In keeping with Hypothesis 1, secondary values have the largest effect on the width of the channels.

the channels. Selection by choice operates among the remaining channels, effectively regulating their relative widths through both primary and secondary values (shown as distinct bands in the channel for allomeme A) and thus regulating the rates at which the different allomemes are transmitted through time. The schema also incorporates the effects of "social system" and "environment" within these various conveyance forces. The nature of the existing social system is manifest in the degree and direction of imposition experienced within the reference group (as a general rule, one would expect imposition to have particular force in nonautonomous groups within highly centralized, hierarchical social systems). The influences of environmental conditions are included within two different forces of the figure. First, they are manifest within the force of differential reproduction (which here includes parent-to-offspring social transmission), wherein their role is analogous to that of "selection pressures" in genetic microevolutionary theory (see Fig. 3.3). Second, and more important, they also affect the intended and unintended consequences of allomemes undergoing selection by choice. Environmental conditions thus influence the perceived advantages and disadvantages of alternative choices for the selectors. Here, environment shapes the feedback; it is *people* who do the selecting.

Although each and every one of these processes may contribute to changes in the culture pool, Hypothesis 1 predicts causal priority for cultural selection guided by secondary values. This, too, is shown in Figure 8.1, where secondary value selection, through both choice and imposition, has the most important influence on allomeme frequencies. First, external secondary values are responsible for limiting the number of open channels, thus assuring zero F_c values for the blocked allomemes; second, internal secondary values have the largest effect on the widths of the remaining pores, thereby explaining most of the variance in the nonzero F_c's.[11] By this model, observable changes in human phenotypes will result from the increased frequency of allomeme B in the population. Depending upon such variables as the content and scale of allomeme B, the persistence and stability of secondary values (themselves subject, of course, to cultural evolution), and the history of introduced variation, the change in B could range from slow and gradual to rapid and episodic. In any case, there would be evolution—evolution by cultural selection.

Finally, although my arguments about cultural selection do give weight to the value-based preferences of individuals living within populations, I hope it is also clear that they do not espouse the radical individualism and naive free choice modeling that have plagued so many recent attempts at cultural evolutionary theory. Instead, I conceive of cultural selection as a highly variable process, ranging from pure free choice in

[11] As shown by the "filter channels" of Fig. 8.1, the contributions of differential reproduction, primary values, and secondary values to the net transmission differentials of allomemes may be regarded, for most intents and purposes, as additive. (In earlier chapters I referred to these additive contributions as "partial cultural selection coefficients.")

some circumstances to pure imposition in others, and within choice, from purely individual judgments to collective decision making (as Boehm 1982, for example, has emphasized). Similarly, although my arguments put deliberate weight on conscious thought and rational decision making, I hope it is also clear that this is a matter of emphasis and causal priority rather than exclusivity. I do not doubt, for example, that irrationality is part of social life and a factor in cultural change (on which see Elster 1979). I simply view its role as less important than the more consistent and sustained selective forces of cultural change. Likewise, I do not regard all cultural change as the product of conscious processes and deliberate decisions; I simply regard these as the most important of the forces. Hypothesis 1 implies only that primary value selection, often unconscious, is generally less influential than secondary. But it will surely prove important in special cases, as we saw in the color terms example of Chapter 4.

Hypothesis 2: The Multiple Modes of Gene-Culture Relationship

If Hypothesis 1 is correct and secondary value selection truly is the principal means of modification, then an important property of the cultural system should be the capacity for self-directed change, or what I call "self-selection." In it, previously evolved cultural values themselves play the deciding role in the differential transmission of other memes. There is thus feedback from the cultural pool to the "filter channels" of cultural selection in Fig. 8.1, feedback that provides "a strain toward consistency" within the system (see, for instance, Murdock 1971: 331, citing Sumner) and that gives cultural evolution "a momentum all its own." (Pulliam and Dunford 1980: 8.) In this way, existing memes can become the most important determinants of rates and directions of cultural change.

This capacity for self-directed change leads to Hypothesis 2: The prediction that there should exist no fewer than five distinct modes of relationship between genetic and cultural change in human populations (see Table 8.3). The first two modes represent "interactive" relationships; a change in one system (genetic or cultural) within a population, or a difference between the systems (genetic or cultural) of two populations, causes a change in the fitness values (W or F_c) governing evolution in the other system. Such relationships constitute evolutionary interdependence or what I have called "coevolution in the narrow sense." In contrast, the other three modes of relationship are called "comparative" because of similarities and differences between what is, in principle, favored by "nature's value" (reproductive fitness, measurable at the microlevel by inclusive fitness value, F_g) and what is, in fact, favored by secondary values during cultural selection. In comparative modes there is no interdependent change; instead, culture evolves through self-selection in directions that may or may not be consistent with maximum F_g. Because we do not have, in these last three modes, "two systems mutually altering each

TABLE 8.3

Hypothesized Modes of Relationship Between Genes and Culture

Category and mode of relationship	Description[a]	Example[b]
Category A. Interactive modes		
1. Genetic mediation	Differences in F_c among a set of allomemes vary as a function of primary values and thus as a function of genotype frequencies, G_t.	Cross-cultural similarity in the meaning of basic color terms derives from primary values in the human nervous system.
2. Cultural mediation	Differences in W among a set of genotypes vary as a function of allomeme frequencies, C_t, in a population.	In Old World populations, the reproductive fitness of LA covaries with cultural beliefs about dairying and fresh milk.[c]
Category B. Comparative modes		
3. Enhancement	Differences in F_c among a set of allomemes are greater than, but correlated with, their differences in F_g.	Folk interpretations of inbreeding costs and benefits confer high F_c upon incest taboos that promote optimal outbreeding.
4. Neutrality	Differences in F_c among a set of allomemes exist in the absence (or near absence) of differences in F_g.	The established sound images of a language show high F_c's despite their relatively arbitrary association with concepts.
5. Opposition	Differences in F_c among a set of allomemes vary inversely with their differences in F_g (i.e., high F_c is associated with low F_g).	Beliefs behind endocannibalism had high F_c among the Fore despite their role in the transmission of lethal disease (kuru).

[a] F_c refers to cultural fitness—that is, an allomeme's suitability for replication and use within a given reference group. W refers to a genotype's relative rate of replication in a given generation within a gene pool. F_g refers to inclusive fitness value, the average inclusive fitness of all culture carriers who act on the basis of a given allomeme.

[b] For discussion of these examples and others, see Chapter 4 (genetic mediation); Chapter 5 (cultural mediation); Chapter 6 (enhancement); Chapter 7 (neutrality); and Chapter 7 (opposition).

[c] LA refers to adult lactose absorption.

other" (as in Lumsden and Wilson 1981: 257), I have called this more inclusive view of gene-culture relations "coevolution in the broad sense" or simply "coevolution," in keeping with my own earlier use of the term (Durham 1976a, 1976b).

Hypothesis 2 has served here as, among other things, a useful test of the evolutionary significance of secondary values in the cultural system. Evidence in the preceding chapters documents all five modes of gene-culture relationships and suggests that self-selection *is* a potent force of cultural change. Let us now briefly review each of these relationships together with the supporting evidence from the case studies.

Genetic mediation. This first interactive mode of relationship refers to situations in which a genetic change within one population, or a genetic difference between two populations, is causally related to a difference in primary values and therefore to a difference in the rates and/or directions of cultural evolution. In essence, the idea is that differences in genotype frequencies within or between populations give rise to differences in phenotype frequencies which, in turn, cause differences in primary evaluations and thus in the F_c values of contending allomemes. Obversely, genetic mediation also refers to the situation where the genetic similarity of populations is responsible for their cultural similarity. This mode of relationship is featured prominently in the gene-culture transmission theory of Lumsden and Wilson (1981, 1983) discussed in Chapter 4.

Also in Chapter 4, we examined the basic color terms of human languages as a candidate example of genetic mediation. There I argued that an underlying genetic similarity among human populations is responsible for universal neural structures and functions involved in color vision (for instance, the trichromacy of retinal pigments and the opponent response property of interneurons in the brain). These structures and functions, in turn, appear to have had a common selective effect upon color terms in many different languages, preserving variants whose meaning closely corresponds to the features of neural encoding. In so doing, they have apparently acted as a species-wide primary value "filter" to the evolving pool of lexical variation. The implication is that genes are therefore responsible, through their effects upon primary values, for cross-cultural similarity in the semantics of basic color terms.

Cultural mediation. This second interactive mode refers to the logically symmetrical influence that memes can have on the Darwinian fitnesses of genotypes undergoing differential reproduction. In this case, a cultural difference within or between populations alters one or more of the acting genetic selection pressures, causing a shift in the direction or intensity of genetic selection. Culture, of course, can have this effect in any number of ways (see, for example, Montagu 1962; Dobzhansky 1963b): by changing global environmental properties (as in Livingstone 1958); by relaxing natural hazards or reducing disease (as in R. Post 1971); by redefining diet or subsistence strategy (as in Walcher and Kretchmer 1981); or by setting the standards of mate choice (as in Darwin 1981 [1871]). But in all cases, culture forms part of the selecting environment of the genes, effectively altering the width of the selection filters (as in Fig. 3.3).

In preceding chapters, we have discussed two examples of cultural mediation. The first concerned the case of sickle-cell anemia (Chapter 3) and specifically the role of cultural mediation in resolving the paradox of the S allele, namely, how can so harmful a gene persist? Our answer came from a test of the malaria hypothesis using data from a culturally diverse sample of West African populations. We found that the "balancing" selection pressure of malarial mortality could partially offset the selective force of anemia, favoring the malaria-resistant heterozygote (AS) geno-types and thus the continued persistence of the S allele. In particular, we compared S frequencies among Kwa-speakers and their linguistic brethren, the Kru-speakers, and found that the Kwa had uniformly higher levels, apparently because their yam-based agriculture had increased the mosquito vectoring of the parasite and thus its balancing selection pressure. The implication is that the memes behind yam cultivation have had the effect of redefining the selection pressures operating on the geno-types.

In Chapter 5, we considered a second example of cultural mediation, the evolution of adult lactose absorption. There we examined evidence that cultural differences in dairying and milk use, together with a pronounced gradient in the selection pressures of the natural environment, favored the evolution of diverse frequencies of lactose-absorbing geno-types. In particular we found adult lactose absorption to be most prevalent in populations with both a long cultural history of milk drinking and a chronic vitamin D–calcium deficiency related to low levels of incident ultraviolet light. In this case, cultural mediation seems to have favored the genetic evolution of a special physiological capability that in almost all other mammals is restricted to infancy alone. Just as genes, through their influence on primary values, may affect the directions and rates of cultural evolution, so too may culture, through its impact on behavior, affect the course of gene-frequency change in human populations.

But we have also found that the relationships between genetic and cultural evolution are more complicated than mediation or even reciprocal mediation. Evidence in Chapters 6 and 7 points unequivocally to the capability of the cultural system for self-selection. We have seen that existing memes can have a powerful selective effect in their own right, either by adding to or by subtracting from any differentials caused by genetic mediation and primary values, and so creating cultural fitness values that would otherwise not obtain. Self-selection thereby creates three comparative modes of relationship (see Fig. 8.2).

Enhancement. This first comparative mode may be said to occur whenever secondary values influence social transmission in such a way that differences in the F_c's of a set of allomemes exaggerate the differences in their F_g's. Such a relationship is shown by the comparison of allomemes A and E (or A and D) in the hypothetical example of Fig. 8.2. Because of its consequences, allomeme A produces the highest average inclusive fitness among its carriers; because at least some of those consequences are also highly valued in the population, A is also the variant of highest cultural fitness. At the same time, E has a lower F_g value than A. But its rate of social transmission is reduced still further—that is to say, E lies below the $F_c = F_g$ diagonal—because of the influence of secondary values.

As this example illustrates, secondary values can have two kinds of en-

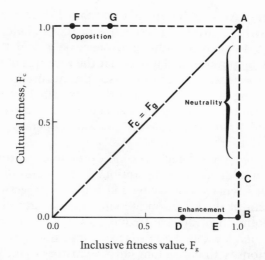

Fig. 8.2. The three comparative modes of gene-culture relations. Shown here are a hypothetical set of allomemes, A through G, each plotted according to both its cultural fitness, F_c (its suitability for replication and use in a given reference group), and its inclusive fitness value, F_g (the average individual inclusive fitness of its carriers). The comparative mode called "enhancement" can be illustrated by the comparison of allomemes A and E (also A and D). While fairly similar to E in its inclusive fitness value, variant A is favored culturally by a wide margin. Two kinds of enhancing effects can be seen: first, cultural evolution actively favors the allomeme A with the higher inclusive fitness benefit to its carriers; and second, cultural evolution creates an F_c differential between A and E larger than their F_g differential. The comparative mode called "neutrality" is illustrated by the allomemes A and C. Although the difference between A and C is adaptively neutral (they have equal F_g values), there is a substantial difference in cultural fitness because of the influence of secondary values. The third mode, "opposition," is shown by the comparison of allomemes F and B (or G and B). F, despite devastating consequences for inclusive fitness ($F_g = 0.1$), is so much favored over B by secondary values that it has the higher cultural fitness ($F_c = 1.0$). The persistence of F over B in the cultural system opposes the successful survival and reproduction of culture carriers. Comparison of G and B also indicates opposition, although to a lesser degree.

hancing effects: first, they can favor the social transmission of allomemes with the highest individual inclusive fitness value; second, they may also enhance the cultural fitness advantages of favored variants by a measure greater than the existing F_g differential (which, after all, equals the difference in F_c that would occur through differential reproduction and vertical social transmission alone). In this mode of relationship, cultural selection actively promotes human survival and reproduction. Accordingly, influential secondary values must be correlated with survival value and/or reproduction value in such a way that culture rewards and encourages the spread of memes that promote high F_g, even if that correlation is not consciously appreciated within the population.

In earlier chapters, we examined two cases highly suggestive of enhancement. The first concerned the monomarital principle among the thongpa serfs of rural Tibet, a meme specifying one and only one marriage with land inheritance per generation (see Chapter 2). In the first part of the analysis ("Explaining Diversity"), we explored the causal influence of the monomarital principle and related memes on the marital diversity of the thongpa. The case offered an example in microcosm of the profound effect that memes can have on the range and frequencies of human behaviors. In all, thirteen different forms of matrimony—including various forms of monogamy, polygyny, polyandry, and polygynandry—were causally related to ideational elements of thongpa culture. In the second part ("Explaining Beliefs"), we turned to consider the social history of the monomarital principle, arguing that the marked persistence of this principle through space and time was itself deserving of explanation. This led to our first consideration of cultural evolution and to a simulation-based test of the hypothesis that, in essence, secondary value selection was responsible for the cultural fitness of the monomarital principle. Finally, in the third part ("Explaining a Special Case") we turned to the case of conjoint marriage among the Nyinba, a population of Tibetan-speaking thongpa in Nepal. There we found evidence suggesting that culturally recognized individual interests in resources and reproduction added still further variation to the thongpa patterns of marriage. The implication was that cultural values guide the Nyinba toward decisions about marriage that have fairly subtle inclusive fitness advantages. In the Tibetan case, in short, we found convincing evidence for enhancement shaped by cultural self-selection.

In Chapter 6, we examined incest taboos for additional evidence of enhancement. After a brief review of incest theory, I proposed the hypothesis that secondary value selection has been the primary cause of the sustained cultural fitnesses of incest taboos in human populations. My argument was that cultural selection has often been conscious and deliberate, guided by socially transmitted concern over the deleterious effects of close inbreeding as balanced against the costs of outbreeding, and by appropriate local interpretations of these consequences (such as the belief that deformity represents the work of angry supernaturals). This secondary value selection may very well have been assisted by primary value selection, particularly by the neurophysiological aversion to sex with intimate childhood associates (the Westermarck effect), and by the greater reproductive success of people who avoided close inbreeding. Nevertheless, we have reviewed two kinds of evidence suggesting that secondary value selection has played the greatest role and contributed most to F_c differentials. First, data from a world probability sample indicate that a majority of human populations do recognize the deleterious phenotypic effects of close inbreeding. Second, other data from the same sample reveal an inverse correlation between the extent of incest taboos and the local costs of outbreeding; as expected, taboos generally extend to distant relatives in populations where the outbreeding costs are low. As in the Tibetan example, these findings confirm not only the strength of secondary value selection, but also its ability to mimic genetic selection. Whenever guided in this way, cultural evolution will favor allomemes whose net effect is genuinely adaptive for their selectors.

Neutrality. This fourth mode of gene-culture relationship refers to the case where cultural variants have closely matched consequences for the inclusive fitnesses of their carriers and yet show substantial differences in cultural fitness. In this instance, cultural selection favors one or more members of a set of adaptively neutral allomemes. This may happen for two reasons: either because of imposition, which is the reduction of choice in a reference group to variants favored by external values; or because internal values guide free choice in some particular direction. Either way, the outcome of the selection process cannot be described as cultural adaptation. This situation is illustrated by allomemes A and C in the hypothetical example of Fig. 8.2. There it can be seen that cultural selection favors allomeme A by a great margin despite the fact that C has equivalent impact upon individual inclusive fitness. Similarly, the comparison of allomemes A and B illustrates neutrality, but this is neutrality in its most extreme form. The two variants have equal inclusive fitness value ($F_g = 1.0$) and yet B exhibits near-zero cultural fitness as a result of prevailing secondary values.

In Chapter 7, we considered a number of candidate cases of neutrality. Concerning the evolution of designs, for example, Philip Steadman (1979) and others have argued that functionally equivalent forms of tools, utensils, machines, and architectural structures often do show great differences in cultural fitness because of aesthetic and stylistic preferences. Of course there are circumstances where functionally equivalent design does not mean equal F_g consequences (as, for example, when designs are markers of strategic alliance or affiliation), but neutrality is surely a possibility as well. Another example concerns the association between linguistic symbols, written or spoken, and their referents. On this subject, Marshall Sahlins (1976b: 62) and others have stressed that the "arbitrariness of the symbol [is] the indicative condition of culture." Although there is considerable evidence that the full symbolic *system* of language is, in fact, nonarbitrary (see Friedrich 1979), many specific, isolated symbols surely do qualify as neutral on the F_g scale.

Opposition. This fifth and final mode of gene-culture relationship is said to occur if and when the differential transmission of allomemes thwarts individual inclusive fitness and reduces the adaptedness of members of a population. The defining condition—that cultural selection should favor instructions that are less adaptive for their bearers than existing alternative variants—is illustrated, for example, by comparing allomemes F and B (or G and B) in Fig. 8.2. F is favored in social transmission ($F_c = 1.0$) despite its serious consequences, on the average, for inclusive fitness; meanwhile variant B of great relative F_g advantage is not very successful in social transmission (its F_c is near zero). In real populations, this condition can be achieved in two ways. First, opposition can be imposed. Through various forms of power, such as coercion or manipulation, compliance with external values can be achieved even when this counters the "latent values" (and reproductive interests) of members of the reference group. Thus, for example, opposition can result when the range of variation freely available to culture carriers is limited to suboptimal forms. In terms of Figure 8.2, opposition would be created if allomemes A through E existed in a population and yet were unavailable to a given reference group because of the actions of others. In Chapter 7, this route to opposition was illustrated with an example from peasant culture in rural El Salvador. Land tenure constraints, socially imposed and legally sanctioned since the 1880's, have resulted in the evolution of a peasant agricultural technology that is decidedly maladaptive at present, although remarkably efficient within the imposed constraints.

The second pathway to opposition is through selection by choice. In Chapter 7, I suggested four conditions under which this might happen: (1) when secondary values are weak or otherwise prevented from guiding choices, as through drug addiction (which suppresses primary values) or brainwashing (which suppresses enculturated secondary values); (2) when secondary values are influential in guiding choices, but actively favor maladaptive memes anyway; (3) when secondary values are influential but people do not perceive the consequences of their choices; and (4) when people perceive deleterious consequences but do not link them to behaviors and memes they could change.

With these conditions in mind, I went on to explore two proposed cases of opposition by choice, namely Mundurucú warfare and the culturally influenced transmission among the Fore of a disease called *kuru*. In the Mundurucú case, I found the evidence for opposition unconvincing and, upon reanalysis, suggested instead that traditional headhunting may well have constituted an enhancing mode of relationship. Linguistic and ethnographic evidence indicated that the memes behind headhunting might well have evolved by secondary value selection for pleasing supernatural spirits and thereby improving the local game supply under conditions of resource competition. In the Fore case, the evidence for opposition was far more convincing, suggesting both that imposition was involved (in the men's pre-emption of pork) and that Condition 4 applied. The Fore readily perceived the threat of kuru, even to the point of feeling that their society was coming to an end; they reacted strongly with Quaker-style mass meetings and a self-imposed quarantine; yet they were blocked in various ways from understanding kuru transmission and their potential ability to control it. The case suggested that Fore secondary values were poised to select against memes of opposition, but that circumstances prevented them from acting effectively.

With respect to Hypothesis 2, then, the preceding chapters suggest that all five modes of relationship do exist in human populations. I believe I have therefore illustrated the need for a broader conceptualization of gene-culture relations than that provided by coevolution in the narrow sense. As a result, we have gained some insight into the validity of Hypothesis 1. At the same time, we have seen that the general theoretical framework behind these modes of gene-culture relationship can be quite useful for unraveling the causes of human diversity.

Hypothesis 3: The Cooperative Evolution of Genes and Culture

The theory proposed here predicts more than simply the existence of these five modes of relationship; it also predicts their relative importance in the ongoing dynamics of cultural evolution. My argument comes in three pieces. First, in Chapter 4, I argued that secondary values are "derived," in the sense of themselves being evolved through the processes of cultural evolution. According to the theory proposed here, that derivation would be an iterative process guided, as in any other instance of cultural change, by the range of selection pressures shown in Fig. 8.1. This means that input from primary values would have been a continuous, integral part of secondary value derivation. Just as "there is no phenotypic characteristic that is unaffected by the genes" (G. Bateson 1979: 179), there would also be no secondary value unaffected by the primaries.

Second, drawing on the work of George Pugh (1977), I have argued that primary values were built into the human decision system through the cumulative action of genetic selection. The implication is that these values and their supporting biological structures have been, in effect, "custom tailored" to motivate and reinforce decisions that are likely to enhance individual inclusive fitness.[12] In the course of cultural selection, therefore, primary values can be expected to act as a bias for variants with high F_g's and this, of course, would include the evolutionary derivation of secondary values. The influence of primary values during that process would also combine with any contribution from the differential reproduction of culture carriers (as shown in the filter pores of Fig. 8.1). Both processes would tend to favor secondary values that have adaptive advantage.

It follows from these considerations that *some degree* of F_g-enhancing bias is built into the human decision system. The question that remains is simply "How much?" Has this bias truly been effective in the evolution of cultural values? Is there evidence for its effectiveness in the past, and is there reason to suspect its continuing effectiveness today? This brings us to the third piece of the argument.

[12] This implication and others to follow are based on the assumption that Darwin was correct in hypothesizing individual-level natural selection to be the major means of modification in human organic evolution. Elsewhere I have suggested that group-level selection, as through warfare, might well have reinforced and accelerated the trends of the individual-level process, given that individual commitment and motivation can be crucial to group success (see Durham 1976a: 387; see also Pitt 1978). This suggestion adds a group selection mechanism but retains reproductive fitness as the effective criterion of genetic selection.

Adaptive selectivity in cultural evolution. For this piece I return to the subject of the genetic evolution of the capacity for culture, and particularly to the rapid expansion of the human brain. In Fig. 8.3, panel A, I have replotted the endocranial volume (ECV) data of Fig. 1.2 for the gracile hominids prior to *Homo sapiens sapiens* (all crania of robust hominids have been excluded). I have also included the best fitting least-squares regression lines for each of the major taxonomic groups represented (the gracile species of *Australopithecus, Homo habilis, Homo erectus,* and Neanderthals; for details see App. A.8.1). Although the data remain insufficient for final resolution of the debate over whether brain expansion was gradual, punctuated, or some combination of the two, the direction and magnitude of the trend are clear (see also Godfrey and Jacobs, 1981; Blumenberg 1984; Falk 1987). The figure amply documents what Phillip Tobias (1971: 114–15), among others, has called "the most strikingly sustained trend" and "the most continuous, long-lasting, and marked hallmark" in all of human evolution.[13]

Still more importantly for our purposes, the figure also allows an inference about the influence of primary values over the course of this three-million-year period. Here let us make the reasonable assumptions that (1) the size and structure of the human brain have evolved primarily through genetic selection; and that (2) the expanding "extrasomatic information system" of culture was one of the brain's most important products during this time period. Let us remember, too, that the brain is, ounce for ounce, the most costly organ in the human body in terms of energy, oxygen, protective bone minerals, and risk. Given all this, Fig. 8.3, panel A, implies that, at each point of change, the reproductive advantages of culture to its beneficiaries must have outweighed the associated costs of a larger brain.[14] In effect, cultural transmission has more than paid for its brain-related costs to these individuals; it has systematically produced net reproductive gains. But who would have been the carriers most likely to benefit from culture in this way? Logic suggests the "selectors"—that is to say, those individuals and groups whose value-guided choices played an active role in shaping the emerging cultural systems. And since primary values would have been instrumental in that process, especially early on, one is brought to an important conclusion: primary values have

[13] It bears emphasizing that little of the increase in ECV in the *Homo* lineage can be explained by allometry, that is, by the correlated enlargement of brain size with body size (see Pilbeam and Gould 1974; Passingham 1975; McHenry 1982). Although there was an increase in average body weight, it was only about 1.5-fold from the *Australopithecines* to the present. Nevertheless, Fig. 8.3A does not control for this trend; existing data do not permit independent estimates of body weight for each of the specimens represented.

[14] As Hockett and Ascher (1964: 145) have well said, "it is utterly out of the question that the growth [of the brain] was fortuitous. A large brain is biologically too expensive. It demands a high percentage of the blood supply . . . and all that blood, in an upright biped, must be pumped uphill. It requires an enlarged skull, which makes for difficulty during parturition. . . . This cost cannot be borne unless there are compensations." (See also Spuhler 1977: 517; Martin 1983.)

Panel A

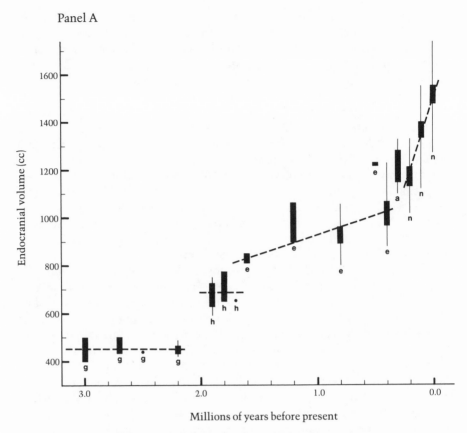

Millions of years before present

Fig. 8.3. Trends in the early evolution of culture and the brain. Panel A shows the expansion of endocranial volume (an indicator of total brain size) during the last 3 million years of evolution in the gracile hominid lineage. For each sample of fossil hominids, the thick bar represents the standard error of mean endocranial volume and the thin bar the range of values. Separate trend lines (dashed) are shown for each of the major taxonomic groups (g = the gracile species of *Australopithecus*, h = *Homo habilis*, e = *Homo erectus*, a = "archaic" *Homo sapiens*, and n = Neanderthals). Trend lines represent least-squares regressions; both the *Homo erectus* and the Neanderthal slopes are significantly different from zero (see App. A.8.1). Panel B is a plot of the increasing complexity of hominid stone tools over the same time interval. Complexity is here measured by the numbers of tool categories used by various investigators to characterize the major so-called tool industries of the interval (Ol-

long been able to bias cultural selection in favor of allomemes that promote the inclusive fitnesses of their selectors. Had this not been the case, and had selectors not derived net reproductive advantage from the cultural systems they were shaping, the organic evolution of ECV would surely have leveled off at some early time.

But more can be said. In Fig. 8.3, panel B, I summarize data presented by the late Glynn Isaac (1972) concerning a trend in the evolution of hominid cultures during the same period. The figure uses stone tool technology, represented by a composite sequence of tool industries, as a conservative indicator of emerging cultural complexity (for similar indicators

Panel B

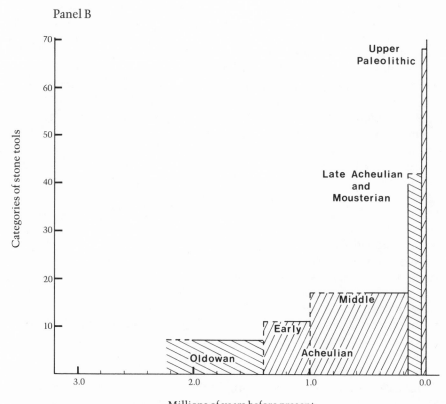

Millions of years before present

dowan, Acheulian, and so on). Although specialists still disagree on the precise number of significant tool categories in each industry, they agree on the trend toward greater complexity in both the tools and the cultural systems that instructed their manufacture. Because there has long been more to culture than stone tool technology, the loose parallelism of panels A and B should not be taken to imply direct causal relations in either direction. Also, because both data bases are small, the trend lines in the two panels should not be taken to represent definitive modes of evolution, either punctuated or gradual. Data for panel A from Fig. 1.2 (excluding the robust species of *Australopithecus*; see App. A.8.1). Data for panel B from Isaac 1972: 394, fig. 5, combining tool categories from Atlantic Europe with those from sub-Saharan Africa.

and arguments, see Blum 1967: 492–96; Holloway 1981: 295–96).[15] Like Ralph Holloway (1969, 1975b), Isaac and I consider these data and the tool record more generally to suggest three important qualities: the capability for symbolization, at least by the time of the Acheulian industry; a degree

[15] Despite the valiant efforts of two student assistants (G.J. and M.C.), I was unsuccessful in an attempt to expand Isaac's data base for finer resolution of the graph in Fig. 8.3, panel B. Problems included gaps in the stone tool record, and what Isaac (1972: 394) refers to as "little agreement" among specialists in the field "about what constitutes a 'significant type category' as opposed to an arbitrary division of a single modality." One consequence is that panel B ignores regional variation and gives the impression—certainly false for at least the more recent periods—of a uniform, stage-like sequence of tool technology.

of selectivity and implied choice, not only in raw materials but also in procedures and operations; and a measure of standardization in the shape and form of the final product.

On the basis of these arguments, panel B suggests that secondary values have long been influential in cultural evolution and that their influence has grown, perhaps with an acceleration parallel to the general trend of the figure. Of course the data do not permit one to estimate with any certainty when secondary values began, or even when they started to gain functional ascendancy over primary ones, although I would think their dominance incontestable by the time of the Upper Paleolithic (see Conkey 1978, 1983, 1985). Nevertheless, their antiquity is implied. As Holloway (1969: 401) has noted, "imitation and observational learning" by themselves do not seem to explain the distribution of certain tool types over time and space; "rules, consensus, [and] syntax" probably existed too.[16] And these, of course, imply the existence of significant socially transmitted values.

From the parallel trends shown in panels A and B of Fig. 8.3 (see also Bordes 1971), it follows that the adaptive selectivity of the cultural system, influenced at first by primary values and then increasingly by secondary values, could not have declined over the last three million years. If anything, that selectivity must have improved, and it must have improved at roughly the same time as secondary values grew in influence (see also Durham 1982: 316). I conclude that the evolutionary emergence of secondary values has generally—though not always—improved the adaptive selectivity of cultural change. From the perspective of Chapter 4, this is not particularly surprising: the human capability to utilize surrogate criteria surely evolved for just this reason, namely, their "help in selecting decision alternatives . . . evaluated as 'good' when measured in terms of the *primary* value structure." (Pugh 1977: 33.) We may therefore expect a general, if imperfect, congruence between evaluations by primary and secondary values—a generalization that I have called, in Chapter 4, the "principle of congruence." The implication is important. For most of the last two million years, the average net effect of secondary values has been to promote decisions that enhanced the reproductive fitnesses of those who guided the evolutionary descent of cultural systems.[17]

[16] Holloway (1969) continues his argument to suggest (1) that the cognitive processes involved in tool making and language are the same; (2) that genetic selection favored their concordant evolution (that is, the three-way coevolution of brain, language, and tool making; and (3) "that a communication system using symbolic language existed at least by the time of handaxes, if not before." (p. 401; see also Spuhler 1977 for a review of arguments on tools and language.) Although currently untestable, these are provocative suggestions, since a symbolic communication system greatly facilitates the social transmission of secondary values.

[17] For ethnographic and recent historical evidence in support of this point see Betzig 1986. This argument, of course, does not mean that secondary values will promote adaptive decisions at all times in all contexts. For example, the arguments of Boyd and Richerson 1985) on "frequency-dependent bias," where the governing secondary value is simple frequency of occurrence, and on "indirect bias," where the governing secondary value is the

Main modes of relationship.   One final conclusion can be drawn from the increasing upward trend of endocranial volume in Fig. 8.3, panel A. It remains unclear at present to what extent the trend was characterized by "phyletic gradualism," that is, by the natural selection of "slight, successive variations"; by "punctuated equilibria," that is, by speciation and the differential success of its products; or by some combination of the two. There is indication, however, that ECV increased in response to positive feedback or "deviation amplification."[18] (Holloway 1981: 293.) The idea is an old one: something about the evolving cultural system, it is suggested, must have set and maintained genetic selection pressures for a larger and larger brain (see Caspari 1963; Gould 1983a traces such feedback arguments to Darwin, Haeckel, and even Engels). Most of the arguments credit the accelerating advantage to some adaptive consequence of behavioral plasticity or what Tobias (1971: x) has called the "ever more diversified and complicated behavior responses" related to tools, weapons, language, food sharing, and so on.[19] But this is, at best, only part of the full story. By themselves, plasticity and complexity can also mean greater error, even—as noted of language by Roy Rappaport (1979: 231)— an overwhelming choice of alternatives. If cultural selection among increasingly complex alternatives had remained governed by the relatively simple sensations of primary values, such an outcome would have been almost inevitable. I therefore take panel A to imply that the evolution of our capacity for culture included the simultaneous evolution of an improved and expanded control system (or a system of "complexity management" as Holloway 1981 put it; see also de Winter 1984). I argue that the accelerating advantage to culture was thus caused by its capacity for internally directed, self-controlled plasticity.

In other words, I suggest that the cultures of our forebears tended to

---

generalized attractiveness of cultural models, suggest that any secondary value can be taken, as it were, too far. Even a generally adaptive secondary value can become maladaptive when reified or pursued too single-mindedly (what we might call the "Scrooge effect"; see "Causes of Opposition" in Chapter 7).

[18] Statistical support for the inference of positive feedback during ECV expansion is somewhat ambiguous. Godfrey and Jacobs (1981), for example, divided an ECV data set like mine into six overlapping time intervals and found statistically significant regression slopes for only two of them. (However, some of their intervals seem peculiarly arbitrary, as when they divide the data for *Homo erectus* among multiple segments.) To take another example, Blumenberg's regressions (1984; see also 1978), using a smaller, more selective data set for the full ECV sequence, support both linear (nonfeedback) and exponential (feedback) models and allow no choice between them (that is, $r^2 = 0.78$ for both). As explained in App. A.8.1, my analysis produced different results: the regressions of Fig. 8.3, panel A, are positive and significant for only *Homo erectus* and Neanderthals.

[19] One good example is the tool-use hypothesis. In the words of Michael Rose (1980: 286), "the most generally credited explanation of human evolution is the hypothesis that tool use engenders a positive feedback selection mechanism, higher levels of tool use increasing the ecological selection pressures for those traits that enable hominids to use tools (Washburn 1957, 1960 . . .). Such traits are of different kinds, from manual anatomy to brain size, but only the latter provides the basis of human mental ability." Lumsden and Wilson (1983: 152 ff.) provide a recent version of the plasticity argument. In their view, "working as a rapid mutator, [culture] throws new variations into the teeth of natural selection and changes the epigenetic rules across generations." (p. 154.)

accumulate ever more refined standards that consciously or unconsciously affected the rates of social transmission of other memes. The governing standards, while almost exclusively dependent upon primary values early on, eventually came to reside within culture itself. Derived through cultural selection with continuous input from primary values, these secondary criteria let culture acquire an increasingly adaptive self-selectivity, at least for the selectors who shaped it. The more standards that accumulated in this fashion, and the more their influence on cultural fitnesses, the more beneficial the "pool" of cultural information, and the more genetically advantageous the capacity for culture—a positive feedback effect of the kind implied by Fig. 8.3. The emerging set of secondary values, though not necessarily using measures of survival and reproduction explicitly, would have constituted an ever more adaptive control system governing cultural transmission. All the while, genetic selection would have favored the genotypes of highest reproductive fitness regardless of how, through secondary values and cultural selection, they achieved that fitness.[20]

By this hypothesis, secondary values would have played an ever-increasing role in cultural evolution. We would expect to find, then, that genes and culture are today most commonly related in the comparative modes, and that the usual state of affairs in autonomous reference groups is enhancement grading into neutrality. This is not to say that gene-culture interaction does not occur in contemporary populations, or that opposition does not exist. First, on the subject of interactive modes, we have already seen striking confirmation in a number of cases: sickle-cell anemia, color terms, and adult lactose absorption. Gene-culture interaction *does* occur at the present time; there *is* a case for coevolution in the narrow sense. However, there is also an answer here to a question that has embarrassed strictly interactional approaches for some time, namely, "Why is there relatively little evidence in contemporary populations for coevolution in the narrow sense?"[21] The reason, I suggest, is that we need a broader analytic framework—one that includes *comparative* modes of relationship in addition to interactions, and that recognizes that comparative modes are actually the more common ones today. In short, the need is for models of coevolutionary relationships in the broad sense.

Second, I have also presented evidence that opposition does exist in

[20]These arguments suggest substantial revision of the "leash metaphor" as a model of relationships between genes and culture (E. O. Wilson 1978: 167; Lumsden and Wilson 1981: 13; see also Chapter 1 of this book). If correct, they suggest that the dog *did* require a leash—a short and taut one, as it were—when first acquired and still a pup. Indeed, the periods of early technological stasis in Fig. 8.3, panel B, suggest that, like many pups, this one was barely able to walk at all at the start. Today, however, after some years of rigorous on-site training, the dog has learned the normal route of the walk and also quite a bit about its underlying rules and contingencies; it is therefore permitted to walk freely and even to run ahead on its own. The dog's understanding remains imperfect, though, and it sometimes strays from the normal course and gets into serious trouble.

[21]I thank Bruce Winterhalder (pers. comm.) for drawing this question to my attention.

contemporary human populations: for example, it can be found in the "backward" agricultural technology of marginalized peasants in El Salvador, and in the ideology of cannibalism that persisted, despite the deadly epidemic of kuru, into the 1950's among the Fore and their close neighbors. Indeed, my view is that opposition and maladaptation are actually quite common in the world today, but mostly because of imposition.[22] More specifically, I believe that the vast majority of cases of enduring opposition result *not* from the imperfections of choice within autonomous reference groups, but from the forced compliance of local groups with the values and desires of one or more external agents. Within autonomous groups, in contrast, I believe that sustained, major opposition is rare although important in special cases. My argument is based on the premise that the selection by choice of a reproductively suboptimal variant entails an intrinsic clash of values, secondary versus primary, and that sooner or later this clash is itself a stimulus to cultural change. The result, I suggest, is that cultural systems tend to evolve toward relationships of enhancement for those who have the power to shape them.[23]

Third and finally, I am convinced that neutrality, too, exists as a mode of gene-culture relations within contemporary human populations. In Chapter 7, we briefly reviewed several candidate examples—involving the cultural evolution of designs, language, and food preferences—from what I think must be a sizable number of such cases in the world today. It is in these cases of neutrality, I further suggested, that we should expect to find the greatest evidence for a truly arbitrary "cultural reason" behind the selective retention of variants. At the same time, I recognize that there is often only a fine line between neutrality, on the one hand, and enhancement of a very minor degree, on the other (i.e., enhancement with only slight F_g advantages to the favored variants). Moreover, I suspect that neutrality—like opposition—is often an unstable, transient condition: people can always add new socially defined consequences to neutral memes, for example (as when a simple pattern on canvas becomes "the flag," a symbol of patriotism); or they can link such memes into a larger,

[22] This statement deliberately contradicts my comment in an earlier publication that "opposition do[es] exist, but rarely." (1982: 313.) The earlier comment was based on an overly narrow definition of cultural selection as a choice process alone; thus "opposition" referred to what I now term "opposition by choice." For reasons explained in Chapter 7, I continue to regard enduring opposition by choice as an unusual occurrence; on the other hand, I am convinced that imposed opposition is commonplace, particularly in societies with state-level organization.

[23] Looking back at the Fore case (Chapter 7) from this vantage point, we can see that we should not have been surprised by the reaction of the Fore to the spread of kuru. Indeed, we should sooner expect all human communities, especially the autonomous ones, to respond with deliberate measures of "resilience" to the threat of equivalent F_g reduction. Along the way, we should also expect people to evaluate all available options using the full array of time-honored standards at their disposal. My proposal is simply that cultural standards have long been instrumental in such circumstances, and that, together with primary values, they have tended to favor variants that enhance the individual inclusive fitnesses of their selectors.

nonneutral ideational package. As a result, there is a certain ambiguous or "slippery" quality to neutrality, in the sense that it is hard for an observer to certify anything as completely neutral, and that neutrality is easily invaded by nonneutral symbolism (see also Durham 1982). My hypothesis therefore predicts that the general distribution of allomemes will show a pattern of "enhancement grading into neutrality."

The steep covariation of F_c and F_g. Thus, in my view, the principal evolutionary advantage of culture has been its ability to favor, in an increasingly selective manner, the accumulation of memes with F_g benefits for their selectors. Accordingly, I take panel A of Fig. 8.3 to mean that the genetic and cultural fitnesses of memes must generally have covaried early in the evolution of culture, only to take on a steeper covariation as self-selection and enhancement became more and more important. I therefore hypothesize that under the influence of secondary value selection, the allomemes of highest cultural fitness ($F_c = 1.0$) tend to be those of highest inclusive fitness value ($F_g = 1.0$) for their selectors. In addition, I hypothesize that secondary value selection causes most allomemes with an F_g below 1.0 for their selectors (i.e., suboptimal variants) to exhibit still lower cultural fitnesses ($F_c < F_g < 1.0$). Because this hypothesis predicts that F_c differentials generally accentuate F_g differentials, I call it the "hypothesis of steep covariation," that is, of steep covariation between the F_c's and F_g's of existing variants.

In Fig. 8.4, panel A, I recast this hypothesis to illustrate its potential testability. The figure assumes, first, a culture that has evolved primarily by secondary value selection operating within a hypothetical autonomous reference group; and second, that one can quantify both kinds of fitness values, F_g and F_c, for each and every meme and allomeme in any given subset of that culture. On the basis of these assumptions, panel A shows the distribution of memes and allomemes that the hypothesis of steep covariation would lead us to expect. Noteworthy features of this distribution include (1) the concentration of memes at the upper right, near $F_g = F_c = 1.0$; (2) the fan-like tail of memes in the "enhancement region" below the diagonal line of $F_c = F_g$; and (3) the general scarcity of memes in the region of opposition at the upper left, near $F_g = 0.0$, $F_c = 1.0$.[24] In this hypothetical case, these features point to the successful operation of secondary value selection. They indicate relatively few examples of opposition, as emphasized by the low "opposition value," O, measured from right to left from $F_g = 1.0$ on the X axis. They also indicate a considerable amount of enhancement, as suggested by the fairly large "enhancement value,"

---

[24] Specifically, in an autonomous reference group I would expect to find few, if any, memes of low F_g at high F_c. In other words, I predict a relative void in the upper left-hand corner of Fig. 8.4, panel A (a region that might be called the "black hole" of culture, although in this case the hypothesized "gravitational gradient"—from secondary value selection—slopes *away* from the hole). The specific size of that void (that is, how low F_g can go before memes become culturally unstable) will vary with such things as the strength and effectiveness of secondary values, and the availability of alternatives.

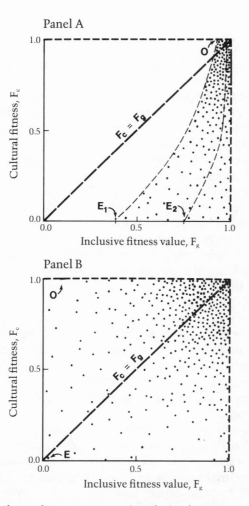

Fig. 8.4. The hypothesis of steep covariation (panel A) and its corresponding null hypothesis (panel B). In both panels, dots represent the memes and allomemes in the culture pool of a hypothetical autonomous reference group; they are plotted according to measures of both their cultural fitnesses (Y axis) and their inclusive fitness values (X axis), as in Fig. 8.2. The line of equal fitnesses ($F_c = F_g$) divides each panel into two regions, a region of enhancement (below the line) and a region of opposition above. In panel A, the influence of cultural selection causes the F_c's of the allomemes to be generally less than their F_g's. Relatively few memes occur in the region of opposition; those that do occur show a low "opposition value," O, measured from the top right corner to the (suboptimal) F_g value of the left-most meme for which $F_c = 1.0$. The great majority of memes indicate enhancement grading into neutrality; their distribution is summarized by the "enhancement value," E_1, measured from the origin to the left-most meme for which $F_c = 0.0$ (for comparison, a higher enhancement value is shown at E_2). In the hypothetical case shown, culture has considerable adaptive selectivity; guided principally by secondary values, cultural dynamics complement the F_g-enhancing action of genetic selection. In panel B, in contrast, there are just as many memes above the diagonal as below it, and these include a considerable number of memes at great opposition to the inclusive fitnesses of individuals. Accordingly, the opposition value, O, is high (near 1.0) and the enhancement value, E, is low (near 0.0). My proposal is that the distribution of memes within autonomous reference groups resembles that of panel A, not B; within nonautonomous groups, I would expect many more memes than shown in A to lie within the region of opposition above the $F_c = F_g$ line.

E_1, measured from left to right from the origin along the X axis. The vast majority of the memes shown illustrate enhancement grading into neutrality.

In contrast, the null hypothesis, namely, that cultural fitnesses vary independently of F_g, is shown in panel B. This distribution of memes is predicted, for example, by the "selfish meme" arguments we encountered earlier, such as Richard Dawkins's claim that "there is no reason why success in a meme should have any connection whatever with [the] genetic success [of its bearers]." (1982a: 110.) Likewise, it is predicted by some "cultural reason" arguments, such as Marshall Sahlins's claim that culture is "an order that enjoys, by its own properties as a symbolic system, a fundamental autonomy" unrelated to matters of survival and reproduction (1976b: 57; for a contrasting view of cultural reason, see Ridington 1982; Biesele 1986). The distribution shown in panel B of Fig. 8.4 shows no evidence for enhancement (the enhancement value, E, is very low) and, at the same time, considerable evidence for opposition (the opposition value, O, is almost 1.0). Nevertheless, the plots of panels A and B do show some degree of similarity in their upper right corners, near $F_c = F_g = 1.0$. Here the arguments almost converge: if each allomeme in a given array has an F_g of over 0.99, for example, and thus selection by choice entails low cost no matter which variant is chosen, then secondary values—and primary ones, for that matter—may very well lack the fine tuning required to detect and favor optimal variants and thus to promote cultural adaptation.

Selfish memes and arbitrary cultural reason *can* prevail in such cases; note, however, that their existence does not destroy a general, overall pattern of steep covariation. In contrast, where reproductive stakes are higher and suboptimal choices include allomemes in the range, say, of $F_g = 0.00$ to 0.90, I would expect less "play" in the system, and greater congruence between the evaluations by primary and secondary values and the F_g's of the alternatives. Were this not the case, the accumulation of high-cost allomemes would almost certainly have interrupted the organic evolution of our expanding cultural capacity, causing a plateau in ECV at some early point in human prehistory (see also Durham 1976b, 1982).

In conclusion, the hypothesis of steep covariation suggests that traditional cultural values are not at all as arbitrary and capricious as they may at first seem. Instead, it proposes that they generally have the effect of promoting the design for reproductive survival of those individuals and groups who are ultimately responsible for the course of cultural evolution within a given population. Three implications follow. First, the hypothesis implies that secondary values generally promote the reproductive fitness "interests" of the pertinent selectors whether or not this effect is ever consciously recognized and appreciated in these terms. Second and more importantly, it also implies that, over time, secondary value selection will tend to pull more and more of a given cultural system into line with the specific reproductive interests of the selectors. A corollary here—that systems of meaning tend to be built around patterns of thought and action that have F_g-promoting benefits to those who make the choices—is, it seems to me, important to *all* dimensions of cultural analysis, interpretive and explanatory as well as evolutionary. Its converse is also important: within autonomous groups, whenever altered conditions cause some part of a valued tradition to become F_g-reducing and thus maladaptive, one expects eventual change in both the tradition and its supporting system of values and meanings ("eventual" because imperfections in the decision system can, as we have seen, delay a response). Once under way, however, such change is predicted to continue until the evolving values and meanings come again to favor variants that are F_g-enhancing to the selectors. Moreover, these changes are expected to take place whether or not the benefits are perceived and consciously evaluated in terms of survival or reproduction.[25]

Third, in many social settings the hypothesis of steep covariation implies cultural conflict. This is particularly true in complex societies in which one or more autonomous groups attempt to impose choices, or values for making choices, upon subordinate groups. On the one hand, such efforts are consistent with the idea of steep covariation: they tend to elevate the F_c's of those variants associated with high F_g for the selectors. On the other hand, however, it is also in the interest of the subordinate groups to detect and, when possible, to resist any and all impositions that come along at their expense. The strength and effectiveness of such resistance will surely vary as a function of many variables, including historical relations and present circumstances. Nevertheless, to the degree that subordinates are successful in resisting, the cultural system of such a population will be or become a contested domain, a virtual ideational battleground between dominant and subordinate interests. "Shared" only by virtue of imposition, the conceptual system of such a population may show, upon close inspection, many deep cleavages.

The "fundamental theorem" of coevolution. If I am correct in the preceding arguments, then an additional theorem follows—a theorem that may be considered analogous to Ronald A. Fisher's "fundamental theorem of Natural Selection." (1958 [1930]; ch. 2; see also Sober 1984b: ch. 6.) Following the arguments of W. D. Hamilton (1964: 8) and George

---

[25] This implication generalizes the earlier arguments of Roy Rappaport (1971a, 1971b, 1979) linking sanctity and adaptation, and those of William Irons (1979a) linking "cultural and biological success." Rappaport speaks, for example, of the "corrective operation through which structures that have become oppressive or maladaptive are divested of their sanctity" by local congregations (1979: 233; see also Durham 1983b). Likewise, Irons hypothesizes that when environmental change erodes the benefits of traditional cultural success, the members of society "gradually redefine their goals to make them correspond with those things which will increase the probability of a high inclusive fitness." (1979a: 258.) Although I do not believe that the process is necessarily gradual, conscious, democratic, or best described in terms of either sanctity or "cultural success," the suggestions of these authors may be viewed as special cases of the more general proposition offered here.

Price (1972: 131), and stated in nontechnical terms, Fisher's theorem proposes that the natural selection of genetic variation always increases the average inclusive fitness of the members of a population to the conditions that existed just prior to selection.[26] In other words, it says that genetic selection continually favors variants that offer an improved design for reproductive survival in the selecting environment. The coevolutionary analog generalizes this prediction to include the influence of culture: it holds that cultural selection, too, generally favors allomemes that improve, or at least do not diminish, the reproductive fitness of their selectors to current conditions. More specifically, it holds that both genetic and cultural selection tend to favor those existing variants whose net effect is to increase the average inclusive fitness of the pertinent selectors to prevailing conditions. Note that this formulation modifies Fisher's proposition from one that is always true—as befits preservation by reproduction—to one that is generally true, but not always, as befits preservation by our imperfect decision making.

More specific versions of this theorem apply to autonomous and nonautonomous reference groups. Within an autonomous group, the prediction is that genetic and cultural change will both tend to increase the average inclusive fitness of individual members. In this instance, genetic selection and cultural selection are expected to cooperate in the evolution of phenotypic properties of adaptive individual advantage (Durham 1982: 320). Within a nonautonomous group, on the other hand, the prediction is that cultural change will tend to improve the inclusive fitnesses of those outside the group who are imposing their preferences on it, at least for the duration of the imposition. Such impositions will generally reduce inclusive fitnesses within the subordinate group because of the goods, services, or other benefits that are extracted by the imposers (should there happen to be some net *increase* in F_g within the nonautonomous group, this would surely be secondary to the imposers' benefit, or even incidental). In short, there is again cooperative evolution in this context, but only from the point of view of the imposers' reference group.

In many ways a capsule summary of the preceding hypotheses, the fun-

---

[26] Fisher's original formulation emphasized the rate of evolutionary change: "The rate of increase in [the reproductive] fitness of any organism at any time is equal to its genetic variance in [reproductive] fitness at that time." (1958 [1930]: 37.) But since the genetic variance in reproductive fitness of a species is unlikely to be zero, as Fisher noted, the theorem predicts "the progressive increase of fitness of each species of organism." (p. 41.) According to Price (1972: 131), Fisher meant to say that natural selection at all times "acts to increase the fitness of a species to live under the conditions that existed an instant earlier. But since the [environment and thus the] standard of 'fitness' changes from instant to instant, this constant improving tendency of natural selection does not necessarily get anywhere in terms of increasing 'fitness' as measured by any fixed standard." Thus, says Price, what the fundamental theorem means is that "in any species at any time, the rate of change of fitness *ascribable to natural selection* is equal to the (additive) genetic variance in fitness at that time." (1972: 132, emphasis added.) This rate, he notes, is generally opposed by the rate of change of fitness ascribable to environmental change, a phenomenon sometimes called the "Red Queen hypothesis" (see, for example, Daly and Wilson 1983: 68).

damental theorem points to a number of the special features of coevolutionary theory. First, the theorem emphasizes the fact that, despite the complexity of possible modes of gene-culture relationship, genetic selection and cultural selection are generally expected to cooperate in the evolution of attributes that, from the point of view of their selectors, are adaptively advantageous. This prediction is important, for it places the two tracks of human inheritance in a relationship that is both complementary and supplementary. It means that cultural dynamics, while governed in day-to-day operation to a very high degree by self-selection and internal cultural values, generally come out doing the genes one better. The potential for opposition by choice is there, and we have seen that it can and does happen. The point, however, is that the human decision system has been, in effect, designed by genetic selection to resist it. Although the system remains imperfect and can thus be fooled or blindfolded in a number of ways, I contend that secondary value selection is actually geared to work against F_g-reducing allomemes. The demonstration that either the decision system has not been designed during evolution to resist opposition, or that opposition by choice is not, in all cases, a product of the remaining imperfections in that system, would be sufficient to refute my arguments.[27]

Second, the theorem emphasizes the importance of the locus of choice for the outcome of cultural change. It says, effectively, that cultural selection proceeds according to the consequences of variants for those with the power to choose, whether that is the given reference group itself or an outside, imposing group. Importantly, when imposition is involved, the predicted F_g-enhancing benefits of change are expected to accrue *outside* the reference group in which the cultural dynamics, and costs, are most pronounced. One implication is simply that the question, "Who benefits and who pays the costs?" should always accompany the analysis of cultural change. A second implication is a corollary to the theorem: imposition is expected to account for the vast majority of all cases of opposition in human populations.

Third, the theorem emphasizes the case made here that genetic and cultural change are both "evolutionary" in the same sense ("descent with modification" or "sequential transformation in a system of replicating entities," as in Chapter 1); that they stand in symmetrical, "instructive" relationship to human phenotypes; and yet that they are not complete or

[27] It should be noted that this conclusion, dubbed the "Jonestown hypothesis" by students in my undergraduate anthropology class, is not negated by the mere existence within a cultural system of one or more allomemes of suboptimal F_g; negation requires that those allomemes also exhibit high F_c as the result of voluntary choice by carriers. Thus, the refutation of my arguments is not implied by cases where reproductively suboptimal variants are characterized by little or no social transmission. Such cases include the Shakers and the religious sect in nineteenth-century Russia "whose cultural pool contained a total ban on sexual intercourse. Lacking an alternate method of recruitment, the sect disappeared and the idea [naturally] selected itself out." (Ruyle 1973: 206.)

perfect analogs. Indeed, the theorem underscores this last point through the implication that cultural change tends to be F_g-enhancing—but only for those in the position to choose among variants. In my view it is people, not "nature," who do most of the selecting in cultural evolution, and it is communication, not reproduction, that is the principal mechanism of transmission.

Finally, the theorem also draws attention to both the structural and functional components of evolutionary change in the two inheritance systems. First, with respect to function, the theorem predicts that evolution in both systems tends to preserve variants that promote effective design for reproductive survival. In other words, it suggests that our genetic and cultural inheritances are shaped by the reproductive results they bring—genetic inheritance because reproduction is the main pathway to preservation, and cultural inheritance because success in social transmission requires positive evaluation by secondary values, and that is likely to be correlated with reproductive fitness. In this respect, my arguments can be termed "functionalist" or—better, using Jon Elster's (1979) terminology—"intentional." Although this is not the kind of "system-serving" functionalism found elsewhere in the social sciences (see, for example, Turner and Maryanski 1979), I do consider the perceived consequences of cultural variants to be among the main determinants of their persistence or elimination.

Second, there is also a significant structural component to the theorem: genetic and cultural selection can sort only among the limited array of actually "existing variants" in their respective systems. Within the genetic track, for example, existing variation is always subject to what I have called the "organic constraints" of inherited form. In the earlier case study of genetically evolved resistance to malaria, for example, we did not find genetic selection to act as an engineer might in a similar situation— that is, by redesigning the whole organism to create some radically new solution. Instead, we found genetic selection to act as the "tinkerer" in François Jacob's (1977) fitting metaphor, leaving the organism basically intact and reworking only one small aspect, namely, the amino acid composition of the protein hemoglobin. As concerns evolution in the cultural track, we have seen that *two* sets of structural constraints may apply: the "cultural constraints" of existing conceptual frameworks and technology, and the "social constraints" of power relations among groups within a population. The two sets often work in tandem, narrowing the field of options available for selection by choice within any given reference group; in this way, the structural component of change can have a strong channeling effect upon its functional counterpart. My arguments therefore have a "structuralist" side to them as well; in my view, evolutionary change is always the product of an interaction between structural and functional components.[28] Understanding evolution, whether genetic, cul-

---

[28] Note that two kinds of *revolutionary* change are readily accommodated within this evolutionary framework: revolutionary change in the social constraints that may limit a

tural, or some combination, inevitably requires attention to both the principles of descent and the principles of selection.

Implications

In Chapter 1, I reviewed five of the most important issues that an evolutionary perspective on human diversity raises for anthropology and related behavioral sciences. In these concluding pages, let us return to those issues and to a comparison of the pertinent insights offered by coevolution and by the other theories reviewed in Chapter 4 (in the interest of brevity, my comparisons here must also be selective).

Distinction

The first issue is that of distinction: does culture provide human populations with a second system of information inheritance that is truly distinct from the genes? Is it really necessary to treat culture as a separate system? In this book, I have answered both questions in the affirmative. Among the many reasons for making this distinction (including several discussed in the opening paragraphs of this chapter), I find two related ones to be particularly compelling. The first is simply that culture consists of information that is *socially* conveyed: allomemes are either transmitted through space and time by teaching and learning or else they are lost. Generally speaking, they cannot be maintained through gene transmission—as if generated in one grand last step of the Central Dogma (as implied by Wind 1984: 10, for example)—nor do they persist by virtue of individual trial-and-error learning. Human languages offer prime examples: it is only through persistent social transmission that these important cultural subsystems survive. In short, cultural systems warrant distinction by virtue of their own special kind of transmission.

Second, as a result of social conveyance, cultural systems are also subject to processes of transformation that are separate and distinct from those operating on the genes. In particular, I have argued that the persistence or elimination of cultural entities is not, in the main, governed by natural selection, or "preservation by reproductive advantage." Instead, I have proposed that the single most important process is cultural selection, or "preservation by preference"—the preservation of variants through the value-driven decisions of human beings. This process can certainly promote variants with reproductive advantage to their selectors; indeed, I have offered that proposition as one of my three principal hypotheses. However, I believe that the "main means of modification" is

---

group's freedom of choice, and in the pre-existing ideological or technological limitations that may constrain their recognition or conceptualization of options (for discussion and examples of the latter see, for example, Cohen 1985). As defined and used in this book, there is nothing intrinsically gradual about evolutionary change.

here decision making and human preference, not reproduction and "selection by nature." It is, again, selection *according* to consequences, not selection *by* consequences. If correct, this argument implies not only that culture warrants distinction as a separate track of inheritance with its own special processes of transformation; it also implies a supplementary form of adaptation—and exaptation—in human populations. Thus, to offer a parallel to the arguments of Stephen Jay Gould and Elizabeth Vrba (1982: 6), we may define a "cultural adaptation" as any feature of a human phenotype that promotes reproductive fitness *and* was built by cultural selection for its current consequences, at least some of which are locally valued. No longer can we say that "adaptations are features of living organisms [that are] spread by natural selection" (as in Hawkes 1987: 343); nor can we continue to insist that "natural selection is the only acceptable explanation for the genesis and maintenance of adaptation" (as in Williams 1966: vii). If I am right, cultural selection is also a perfectly acceptable explanation.

Independence

The second issue raised in Chapter 1 is that of independence: Given the organic evolution of our capacity for culture, to what degree is cultural change a truly distinct and autonomous force in the shaping of human diversity? That is, in what ways is culture "tied" to the genes, and in what ways is it independent? In this book, I have tried to suggest that the answer to these questions is both complex and dualistic. On the one hand, cultural systems are clearly dependent upon genes in a variety of ways, both physiologically and anatomically. Thus, for example, culture remains tied to the genes through the structures and functions of the human decision system, including the important primary values that were built into that system by genetic selection. On the other hand, I have argued that cultural systems also exhibit a high degree of independence owing to the process of self-selection in which change is guided by socially transmitted secondary values. Such independence is aptly illustrated by, for example, the role of "critical values" for hypothesis testing, like $p < 0.05$, in the cultural evolution of Western science. Moreover, I have argued that this dualistic relationship—that is, culture's being independent in some respects and dependent in others—was essential to the phylogenetic expansion of the capacity for culture in the first place. In other words, a rather ambiguous answer to the independence issue was itself built right into the dual inheritance system.

The duality described here is also a feature of the "programmed learning" model of H. Ronald Pulliam and Christopher Dunford. Building on a comparable start in decision theory, complete with primary and secondary "reinforcers," Pulliam and Dunford (1980: 8) argue that cultural evolution "owes its origin and its rules to genetic evolution, but it has a momentum all its own." But the implications are not, in my view, adequately developed. In part, this is because the authors (by their own admission) shy away from a theory of cultural selection. Perhaps more importantly, it is also because they assume that cognitive consistency is a primary value with a very strong influence. As a result, secondary values all but disappear from their formulation, and culture is left to evolve as selfish, parasitic memes: "Ideas can motivate people to behave in certain ways that, in turn, perpetuate those ideas from generation to generation." (p. 101.)

The issue of independence is also raised by Charles Lumsden and Edward O. Wilson (1981, 1983) in their gene-culture transmission model, particularly in their use of Wilson's earlier metaphor (discussed in Chapter 1) of genes holding culture "on a leash." In their analysis, pulls come from both ends of the "leash": from genes through epigenetic rules to culture, and from culture through behavioral plasticity back to the genes (see, for example, Lumsden and Wilson 1983: 153–54). But culture's tug of independence is manifest only in variation, not in selection: culture is described as "working as a rapid mutator" (p. 154) rather than as a source of values and guidance. Consequently, their arguments neglect all but the interactive modes, which are only two of the five presented here. Moreover, they define coevolution as the "reciprocal effects of genetic and cultural change within the human species" (Lumsden and Wilson 1983: 206), and that is coevolution in a narrow and restrictive sense. Although there are parallels here with some of my examples and logic (for instance, with basic color terms as genetic mediation), I part company with them at the point where I propose cultural self-selection.

Transformation

Turning now to the third special issue, let us consider again the matter of transformation: What is the range of evolutionary forces that cause sequential modification in cultural systems, and which of these have been most important in the evolutionary descent of cultures as we know them today? In this book, I have tried both to inventory the principal forces of cultural transformation and to identify the ones I believe to have the greatest significance. As noted earlier, Table 8.2 summarizes what I view as the two most important categories of transforming processes, the conveyance and nonconveyance forces. Of these, I have further suggested that cultural selection, or value-guided decision making by human beings, has been the most important general process of cultural transformation. In addition, I have subdivided cultural selection into two subprocesses, primary and secondary value selection, according to the nature of the dominant decision criteria. This has allowed me to suggest, in Hypothesis 1, that secondary value selection has long been the single most important process of cultural transformation in human populations.

In a related argument, I have suggested that cultural divergence—that is, the historical branching and differentiation of cultures—has chiefly been the product of two processes, namely, cultural isolation and the independent transformation of the isolates. Here again I have proposed that cultural selection has been the main means of transformation, guiding the evolutionary divergence of cultures from a hypothetical universal ancestor to the wide diversity of forms observable in the world today. Although it has not been possible for me to offer some kind of representative world sample of cultural diversity, and to show how the tools of analysis offered here could be systematically applied to that sample, I do hope the range of examples I have tried to examine—from incest and marriage to headhunting and color terms—will not be seen as narrow, but will encourage yet other case studies more refined and more complex. I hope part of that effort will include attention to the analysis of culture within modern nation-states, which for want of expertise, first, and time, second, I have largely avoided. Until then, it bears re-emphasis that my hypotheses assign causal priority to the processes of decision making, including both choice and imposition, by human actors, and that I view secondary value selection as the chief agent of cultural change.

The specific inventory of forces I propose above shows considerable similarity to at least two previously described inventories, both noteworthy for their multiplicity of change mechanisms. First, there is overlap between Table 8.2 and the range of forces outlined by L. L. Cavalli-Sforza and M. W. Feldman in their "cultural transmission" model. As discussed in Chapter 4, these authors regard "the cultural differences between human populations . . . as the outcome of the balance of several evolutionary forces." Among them they list mutation, including innovation and copy error; transmission; cultural drift; cultural selection (defined as "decisions by individuals"); and natural selection (1981: 351). On the items given here, the main differences between us concern their "cultural selection," which ignores group decision making and does not distinguish the primary and secondary values. In addition, it does not include imposition and thus the forced compliance of some individuals with the decisions of others. Not surprisingly, the authors' quantitative models also ignore this difference, lumping together the effects of imposition and choice, as well as other forces, into unitary transmission coefficients. This, in turn, prevents their approach from supplying a satisfactory solution to the very "cultural transmission paradox" it raises, namely, how can the capacity for culture have had both "natural origins" in genetic selection and yet such great potential for maladaptive consequences? I believe the paradox is resolved by carefully distinguishing imposition from choice. If I am right, most cases of cultural maladaptation, particularly the enduring ones, will prove to be impositions that actually do have inclusive fitness benefits to those who have made—and imposed—a given choice.

Turning to the second similar inventory, there is again overlap between my Table 8.2 and the five forces described in the "Darwinian culture theory" of Boyd and Richerson (1985: 9–11). First, we agree about a subcategory of mutation-like forces ("innovation" and "synthesis" in my rendering, "random variation" in theirs), and about cultural drift. Second, we also agree about the "natural selection of cultural variation" (conveyance force B.2. in Table 8.2), particularly with respect to differential reproduction at the individual level (see their examples, pp. 175– 78). I would, however, separate out two nonreproductive components included in "natural selection" by Boyd and Richerson, namely, differential modeling and what I have called role selection, and include them under "transmission forces" (B.1.).[29] Finally, we also agree about a category of decision-making forces—although, again, I subdivide it differently. Whereas I draw a distinction between the sources of values used in decision making, calling them "primary" and "secondary," Boyd and Richerson distinguish the sources of variation, differentiating "guided variation" (in which variants come from individual learning) from "biased transmission" (in which variants come from social conveyance). While basically a matter of emphasis, the "fundamental similarity" that they see between guided variation and biased transmission (p. 136) leads me to suspect that the distinction between types of values may be more fruitful.

Where we differ is in what has been omitted from their list and in the related matter of causal priority among the various forces. Put differently, we agree that cultural processes can and do create maladaptive traits in human populations; but we disagree about both the range of processes that have that effect and about the specific nature of the ones that are most important. Thus, despite Boyd and Richerson's claim that they enumerate "all of the conceivable processes that can change culture through time" (1985: 9), imposition, once again, is lacking from the list. One result of this oversight is that their models always have maladaptation evolving out of some form of individual choice. Not only does this give the work the taint of radical individualism, but it also contributes to the misleading impression that a group of people have only their own biases to blame if their culture has wasteful, irrational, or oppressive features. In

[29] To Boyd and Richerson (1985: 175) the "natural selection of cultural variation" refers to the situation where "individuals characterized by different variants of the culturally transmitted trait have different probabilities of becoming cultural parents," that is, of becoming teachers or models for "naive" individuals. To prevent confusion I prefer to subdivide this force between actual differential reproduction (coupled with parent-offspring social transmission) and the differential effectiveness of nonparental models and teachers, whom Boyd and Richerson call "cultural parents." (p. 175.) Thus, when the preservation of one or more allomemes arises from differential biological parenting—that is, from "rates of fertility and mortality . . . the basic stuff of ordinary Darwinian (genetic) fitness" (p. 175)—combined with assumed vertical transmission, I would go ahead and call this cultural evolution through natural selection, specifically through individual-level differential reproduction (B.2.a. in Table 8.2). On the other hand, when the preservation of one or more allomemes occurs because of differential "cultural parenting"—that is, because of differentials in the ratio and mode of transmission—I would call that a transmission force, for reasons discussed in Chapter 4. As in the arguments of Cavalli-Sforza and Feldman, for this force to be important, value-driven decision making must be weak.

some few selected cases of maladaptation, the Boyd and Richerson models may well apply. But again, as noted above, I personally look to imposition as a more important general cause of enduring maladaptation.

There is another area in which I disagree with Boyd and Richerson, one that brings us to Issue 4.

Difference

The fourth issue concerns the question of difference: Can culture be incorporated into evolutionary models without invoking forces or principles that are either unprecedented in the evolution of living forms, or at least qualitatively different in their logic or function? As mentioned in Chapter 4, Boyd and Richerson had, as one of their principal goals, to show "that the existence of culture causes human evolution to be fundamentally different from that of noncultural organisms" in the sense that "cultural evolution leads to the evolution of genetically maladaptive traits" (1985: 99.) This is a central argument in their theory and models; it is also one that, for several reasons, I think is wrong.

First, I disagree that culturally produced maladaptive traits constitute evidence that human evolution is "fundamentally different." As we have seen in the case of sickle-cell anemia (Chapter 3), organic evolution, too, can promote genetically maladaptive traits in a population, both slightly maladaptive (nonsicklers compared with carriers) and seriously maladaptive but nonetheless recurrent (the anemics themselves). Moreover, all evidence suggests that the maladaptations of this example are sustained within populations by ordinary genetic selection, which is only one force of many in organic evolution and arguably one of the least likely to produce maladaptations. Surely, then, the cultural evolution of maladaptive traits does not in any way suggest that human evolution is qualitatively different. Cultural mechanisms may well produce maladaptations more frequently than genetic mechanisms, and they may well spread them more widely within and between populations. But it is simply an error to suggest that culturally induced maladaptations provide "the strongest indication that the forces of genetic and cultural evolution do not always coincide." (p. 99.)

Second, I contend that the forces in culture that lead to maladaptive traits are, in fact, *fundamentally similar* to the forces at work in the evolution of noncultural organisms. Consider, for example, the two forces that I have proposed as the most important of all in this regard, both of which were involved in the epidemic of kuru among the Fore of highland New Guinea. One is maladaptation by choice (or, more precisely, by the confounding of choice): during the first several decades of the kuru epidemic, it was clearly the Fore's own choice whether or not to perpetuate cannibalism within their cultural system. The second is imposition: the pre-emption of pork by Fore men had the effect of making cannibalism a relatively attractive choice for women, which in turn provided a deadly transmission route for kuru among them. But the crucial point here is that both forces, choice and imposition, entail a process of selection among alternatives. In this fundamental respect, both are similar to genetic selection. In the latter, as we have seen, "nature" selects and does so according to the criterion of reproductive advantage; in the former, people select, whether consciously or unconsciously, and are guided in their choices by the various primary and secondary values at their disposal. The agents are different, to be sure, but the processes are strictly parallel (see also Rescher 1977: 133). They are similar in what Andrew Schmookler (1984: 6) calls "that most essential Darwinian sense of postulating a process of selection among alternatives to account for the overall trends" of evolutionary change. The point, then, is that neither of these mechanisms involves an unprecedented or "fundamentally different" process.[30]

It should also be noted that some of the most important cultural and noncultural forces are so similar that, in fact, the latter have actually been named after the former. Thus, Darwin (1964 [1859]: 61) deliberately called his most important principle natural selection "in order to mark its relation to man's power of selection," a power readily apparent in the value-driven choices of animal breeders. To show today that "man's power of selection" can propel the evolution of maladaptive traits in a population, as Boyd and Richerson have done, is hardly grounds, then, for asserting a "fundamental difference" from its namesake. This is especially true in light of such cases as sickle-cell anemia, which show that genetic selection can do the very same thing.

In short, I think Boyd and Richerson are mistaken on the issue of difference.[31] I do give them credit for establishing, quantitatively, that a capacity for culture featuring secondary value selection and its inevitable mal-

[30] Boyd and Richerson's mechanisms of frequency-dependent bias and indirect bias are excellent cases in point. Both are simply decision-making processes governed, they assume, by what I have called secondary values—namely, by the socially acquired values that to be "common" or "attractive," respectively, is to be "good." In other words, they are simply special cases of secondary value selection. Important special cases they may be; but they are certainly not exceptional with respect to mechanism. Given the imperfect nature of our human decision system, *of course* they can generate maladaptation. Virtually any secondary value can have this effect. What Boyd and Richerson neglect to explain is that, as secondary values, both criteria must themselves have evolved to cultural prominence in local populations in the face of both primary values and their effective, already established cultural surrogates. In my view, this means that such criteria will generally conform to the principle of congruence; if so, then it would surely be a distortion to label the resulting mechanisms as "maladaptive processes" (Boyd and Richerson 1985: 166). To identify the maladaptive by-products of these forces as their most important aspect would be tantamount, as Richard Alexander (1979a: 76) points out, "to supposing that the function of appetite is obesity."

[31] Another problem, in my estimation, is that Boyd and Richerson identify their forces of direct bias and guided variation too closely with primary values and therefore with sociobiology (see 1985: 133). This makes it easy for them to call into question the relative strength of these mechanisms, and thus to exaggerate the importance of other, supposedly renegade forces. But surely both direct bias and guided variation can also be guided by secondary values—not to mention by the conjunction of both primary and secondary values—in which case their influence is certainly much stronger than Boyd and Richerson allow.

adaptive side effects could, in fact, have evolved by Darwinian natural selection. Moreover, I also give them credit for emphasizing that the strength of decision-making values is an important variable governing the outcome of cultural selection. But it should be clear from arguments and examples in this book why I disagree with their assertion that decision-making forces are "weak compared to [natural] selection [acting on cultural variation] because the traits seem to be transmitted without much choice or because it is difficult to believe that people are aware of the consequences of their behavior." (Boyd and Richerson 1985: 175.)

Coexistence

We come to the fifth and last issue, coexistence: What is the range of possible relationships between the genetic and cultural "channels" of evolution, and which of these relationships are most important to our understanding of human diversity? On this subject, I have offered two hypotheses and several supporting arguments and examples. First, I have argued that cultural selection, as the principal mechanism of cultural change, gives rise to no fewer than five distinct modes of relationship, two interactive and three comparative, between genetic and cultural change (see Table 8.3). In earlier chapters, I have tried to illustrate each of these modes with an eye to demonstrating their utility in the challenge of explaining human diversity. Second, I have argued that genetic selection and cultural selection do tend to cooperate within autonomous reference groups. The results, I maintain, are that comparative modes of gene-culture relationship are the most common, and that the vast majority of all memes within autonomous groups will reflect enhancement grading into neutrality. This conclusion does not rule out opposition for, as we have seen, imperfections in the human decision system can all too readily impede its evolved functionality. The argument does suggest, however, that most instances of lasting opposition in human populations are the product of cultural imposition upon nonautonomous groups. With respect to coexistence, then, I would locate coevolution in "explanation space" somewhere between the Lumsden-Wilson model, where genes and culture are tightly linked in interactive modes, and the Boyd-Richerson model, where culture runs readily away into opposition. Of the existing arguments, I believe coevolution alone is able to predict the pattern of Fig. 8.4, panel A.

To conclude, I hope these arguments will eventually be seen as strengthening the concept of culture and clarifying its legitimate place in the explanation of human diversity. On the one hand, I have tried to argue that anthropology and cognate social sciences need urgently to add a genuine evolutionary dimension to cultural analysis, a dimension characterized by descent with modification and "branching trees" rather than by universal stages. I see this dimension as complementing, yes, and as supplementing with a stronger temporal emphasis the more conventional vertical-explanatory and horizontal-symbolic dimensions of cultural study. Contrary to a widely held view in social science, I also think this dimension will actually help to further define and refine our conceptualization of culture, even to the benefit of the other dimensions (in some ways, the conceptualization of culture is really *the* issue in all three dimensions). On the other hand, I have tried to illustrate what I regard as culture's key role in the shaping of human diversity. On this topic, I hope I have argued convincingly that culture constitutes an "intermediate" force behind diversity, neither as ultimate as the genes from which its capacity is derived, nor as proximate as the individual learning and experience from which its variation is supplied. And I hope that, by argument and example, I have given appropriate weighting—prominent but not excessive—to the influence culture exerts in the shaping of human diversity. In the last analysis, any model of gene-culture relations is only as good as its case for culture.

Finally, I hope to have shed new light on human differences and their history. The reader will please forgive me if I find the evolution of human diversity, not merely the production of higher animals, the most exalted object that we are capable of conceiving, and if I find the control and direction of that process not simply in the war of nature, from famine and death, but also in ourselves, from choice and imposition. Nevertheless, Darwin did have it right: there *is* grandeur in this view of life.

APPENDIXES

A /   Methods and Supporting Analysis

This appendix summarizes some of the more detailed and technical information pertinent to the case studies of Chapters 2 through 7. The material is organized by chapter.

A.2.1. Candidate Explanations of Marriage in Tibet: A Critique

Apart from the general problem that they focus too narrowly on polyandry, many previous explanations of *thongpa* marital customs are subject to additional, more specific criticisms. Here follows a brief summary of these criticisms, organized by the categories of explanation used in Chapter 2.

The suggestion in the first category, that Tibetans practice polyandry because they "borrowed it from their cousins of Kham" to the east (as discussed by Prince Peter 1963: 553), is of course no explanation at all. The argument begs two questions: Why did the inhabitants of Kham marry polyandrously in the first place? and, Why did other Tibetans choose to adopt this practice from them? Similarly, the notion that Tibetan society represents some kind of "cultural fossil" or throwback to an earlier stage of social evolution is completely unacceptable in contemporary social science (although such a view was espoused by the nineteenth-century anthropologist John F. McLennan and by Darwin himself). Not only is there virtually no evidence *for* this kind of explanation, there is also considerable evidence *against* it, including the simultaneous existence in Tibet of the other, supposedly more advanced forms of matrimony.

The sex ratio theory (Category 2) also runs into problems of evidence in the Tibetan context. Competition for spouses may very well be a factor behind polyandry among the Marquesan Islanders of Polynesia, for instance (see Linton 1939: 155; contrast Otterbein 1968), but it is apparently not a major force in Tibet. Sex ratios in the Tibetan communities studied to date range from an amazingly balanced 1.008 in Ladak (Prince Peter 1963: 556; see also Nag 1960 on neighboring Lahul) to figures well below 1.000 in the pertinent adult age classes (see Goldstein 1976). Far from documenting a chronic scarcity of women, these studies point instead to an unfavorable marriage market for females and to numbers of unwed adults, such as the *luba*, or "left-over" women, among the Nyinba (see Levine 1977: 310).

Similarly, two key aspects of Prince Peter's own psychological explanation (Category 6) are contradicted by the data from Tibet. First, the only unambiguous reports of male homosexuality in Tibet, including those mentioned by Prince Peter himself (1963: 385), concern monks in monasteries—that is, persons largely buffered from the "difficult and insecure natural environment" that supposedly promotes this tendency in the lay population. Second, the suggestion of pervasive incestuous desires among Tibetans is contradicted by Prince Peter's own findings (1963: 468–69) that (1) the shared wife in father-son marriage "must never be" the actual mother of the son or sons, a point also repeated forcefully by Aziz's informants (1978: 153); that (2) local inhabitants of Western Tibet viewed the few occurrences of bigenerational polygyny as "rather strange and even repulsive"; and that (3) a common insult directed at central Tibetans was the term "stepmother-sharing people" (Prince Peter 1963: 468). These are hardly the signs of an irrepressible incestuous desire in the population.

Still other problems have surfaced for the sociological (Category 3) and sociobiological (Category 8) explanations, including some compelling counterevidence in Goldstein's refugee study. To begin with, informants told Goldstein that polyandry was anything but prestigious; in fact, they regarded it as "a difficult form of marriage which produced stresses and anxieties and which required considerable adjustment by the participants. It was perceived by the thoughtful more as the lesser of two evils than as the prized form of marriage." (1971a: 73.) Second, Goldstein found that thongpa refugees from the Gyantse District voluntarily gave up polyandrous marriage within a single generation of their settlement in India. On the one hand, this indicates that neither the alleged prestige value nor the sibling solidarity involved in polyandry were strong enough to perpetuate the institution. On the other hand, it also casts doubt on the existence of what Hiatt (1980: 598) called "some specific genetic basis for fraternal sexual sharing" among the thongpa. In India, thongpa refugees were given permanent but nonhereditary rights to the land, an arrangement that "fits precisely into the tied dü-jung land-tenure pattern in Tibet." (Goldstein 1971a: 73.) That refugee marriages quickly conformed to the traditional dü-jung pattern undermines the argument that thongpa polyandry reflected some special genes for sexual tolerance.

A similar problem confronts the political-economic type of explanation (Category 7), that is, the argument that polyandry is forced upon the thongpa by the tax and inheritance requirements of Tibetan overlords seeking to maintain a fixed tax roll. Although patterns of marriage among the recent, post-1959 immigrants in India would seem to be consistent with this argument (namely, that away from Tibetan landlords, marriage is monogamous), patterns among long-established Tibetans in Nepal, Ladak, and elsewhere are not. Indeed, some of the best descriptions we have of the Tibetan marriage system come from communities that have lived for hundreds of years outside the reach of Tibetan overlords, including some, like the Nyinba, who were ruled by Hindu overlords with very different ideas about taxation and land inheritance (see, for example, Levine 1988: 90–93).

On the other hand, one could always attempt to rationalize these exceptions as cases of cultural inertia, maintained either (1) by highly conservative mechanisms of cultural transmission (à la Cavalli-Sforza and Feldman 1981) or (2) by virtue of their "embeddedness" within the greater logical structure of Tibetan culture. But these arguments, too, involve problems. The first rationalization is contradicted by the degree of nonconservative cultural transmission in Nepal: in every generation remembered by the Nyinba, for example, there have been experiments with divisive, monogamous marriages (see the discussion under "A Simulation Study" in the section "Explaining Beliefs"). If the general tendency remains conservative, it is because of the devastating consequences of such experiments to thongpa households themselves, not because of the mechanism of cultural transmission per se. The second rationalization is contradicted by the experience of Tibetan refugees in India. Today, monogamy prevails even where much of the fabric of Tibetan culture remains intact (see Nowak 1984).

In short, Category 7 explanations do not fit the facts. The landed elite may sometimes have recognized that thongpa polygamy was consonant with their economic interests, and they may well have taken advantage of the system; the laws of Bhutan (Carrasco 1959: 61, 88) and the decrees of King Trhisong Detsen (Toussaint 1933: 269; Stein 1972: 98) are cases in point. But this was not universal. Despite any vested interest of the landlords, *legal* fraternal polyandry, according to Dargyay, "was not practiced by subjects of the monastic and noble landlords," only informal "quasi-fraternal" polyandry. (1982: 34.) Moreover, even where $M = 1$ was a legal requirement, there is reason to believe that the landlords did little but formalize an existing tradition (Levine, pers. comm. 1983). In Nepal, thongpa marital diversity persists today completely outside the sphere of the landlords' influence, and sometimes even in violation of Nepali law.

The personal explanations (Category 5) and at least some of the economic ones (Category 4) are also hard to reconcile with the facts. Personal reasons, while certainly valid in individual cases, would tend, if truly personal, to create variation that was random, not patterned, in any sizable sample of marriages. Because, as we have seen, the variation in Tibetan tradition is far from random, we must conclude either that some other set of forces or "needs" is involved, or else that the "personal needs" of the Tibetans are too widely shared to be called idiosyncratic.

The Tibetan data are also problematic for the hypothesis that polyandry forms a *pis aller*, or last resort, as when destitute males recognize that "half a loaf is better than none" (Symons 1979: 225). In the first place, polyandry simply does not covary with economic circumstances in the predicted direction; the thongpa, after all, are the wealthier stratum in rural Tibet (see also Briffault 1927: 662–63; Beall and Goldstein 1981: 19). Second, the marriage form of thongpa families can and does vary independently of resources, as when polyandry in one generation is replaced by monogamy or polygyny in the next (subject only to variation in the sibship), or when polyandry is converted to polygynandry in the same generation with the same resources (see Levine 1977: 217–21). In short, there is clearly something more to the Tibetan case than the last resort of "shared loaves."

The second economic argument is a hypothesis by the anthropologist Edmund Leach that fraternal polyandry "is consistently associated with systems in which women as well as men are the bearers of property rights." (1955: 185.) In such systems, says Leach, polyandry avoids a potential conflict of interests among the children of brothers: it prevents heirs with common patrimony from having separate inheritances from their mothers. While plausible in other contexts (among the Kandyan Sinhalese of Sri Lanka, for example), the hypothesis runs into problems in Tibet. Among the thongpa, fraternal polyandry is found only in families specifically *lacking* matrilineal land inheritance; in cases where residual land rights do pass to daughters (as in *magpa* marriages), the only recorded polyandry is nonfraternal.

A.2.2. *Further Evidence for the Antiquity of the Marital System*

In addition to the early reports of Chinese annalists, several other lines of evidence suggest an ancient origin for the thongpa marital system. Perhaps the most convincing of these is the evidence for common origins: so similar are the marital customs of the thongpa from across the length and breadth of ethnic Tibet that we may regard them all as the modified descendants of a common ancestral tradition. From Kinnaur to Kham, in other words, thongpa marriage customs are evidently homologous (i.e., derived from the same origin) and therefore quite old. If, for example, we use J. Fisher's (1986: 209) timeline for evolutionary divergence in the Tibetan language family, then the existence of homologous marital customs in different language subgroups implies an origin well before 1500 B.C.

The following more specific lines of evidence also point to an early origin:

1. *Religious inference.* Numerous arguments in the literature assert that Tibetan polyandry is both older than Buddhism, which was introduced about 640 A.D. (see Koeppen 1857: 476; A. Wilson 1886: 185; Kawaguchi 1909: 373; Nag 1960: 195), and actually antithetical to Buddhist doctrine (Prince Peter 1948: 217). The beliefs behind polyandry, and perhaps other forms of marriage as well, may thus trace to the earlier Bon religion, an indigenous cult of demons and ancestral deities.

2. *Legal inference.* An early Tibetan king, Trhisong Detsen (740 to about 798 A.D.), decreed as part of his legal code that "if there be several sons, let the oldest sons establish themselves permanently [i.e., in the estate household]; let the younger enter religion!" (Toussaint 1933: 269, translated from French by D. P.; see also Stein 1972: 98.) Implicitly, since other marital arrangements would almost invariably have created conflicting inheritance claims among the heirs and threatened the permanence of the arrangement, it seems also to condone fraternal polyandry. The proclamation, therefore, like most others in Trhison Detsen's code, seems to have been an attempt to formalize pre-existing Tibetan custom.

3. *Linguistic inference.* On the basis of a comparative study of Tibetan and Chinese kinship terms, Paul Benedict presented evidence for "an ancient cultural stratum" (but he does not say how ancient), common to both the Chinese and Tibeto-Burman cultures, in which matrilateral cross-cousin marriage (that is, marriage of a man to his mother's brother's daughter) was "a conspicuous feature." (1942: 337.) One piece of the evidence concerned a shift in the meaning of the Tibeto-Burman root word *k'u* from "mother's brother," its original and still more widespread meaning, to "father's brother." Benedict concluded that "this development, peculiar to Tibetan, is to be interpreted as the product of that distinctively Tibetan feature, fraternal polyandry." (pp. 317–18.) This shift and others imply considerable antiquity for polyandry, particularly if there is truth to the report of Das (1902: 251–52) that polyandry "is said to have had its origin in Khams [easternmost Tibet, in archaic spelling]." Benedict found that *k'u* was semantically expanded "especially in western Tibetan dialects" like those in Ladak and Lahul, maximally distant from Kham.

A.2.3. *Additional Evidence for the Domestic Economy Theory*

Although Goldstein (1971a) found an explicit "folk articulation" of the domestic economy theory among the refugees from Chimdro, this may have been a special case. We need to know whether or not the conservation of family property has the same conscious and deliberate motivation in D'ing-ri, Barkhang, and the various regions of Tibet discussed by Prince Peter. Do the same beliefs exist in other communities, and do they explain the inter-regional similarity we have seen in marital diversity? The answer, as discussed below, is basically yes, but there are some noteworthy modifications.

Aziz's study of migrants from D'ing-ri provides perhaps the best confirming case to date. According to her informants, the observed patterns of marriage among the thongpa are directly fostered by two related sets of "underlying ideals." The first of these is "the indivisibility of the plot of land attached to the household. Brothers must not separate nor the land be divided." (1978: 105.) Related to this is a second ideal that advocates the concentration of labor available to the family to work their common holdings. "Polygamous ideals are fostered by underlying ideals concerning residence: brothers should remain together; a father and son should not separate and co-residents should work for and share the common prosperity of the unit." (p. 139.) It is clear from the ethnographer's reports that both of these overlapping ideals are fully conscious and expressly articulated, since "D'ing-ri agriculturalists keep the economic benefits of polygamy in the forefront of their thought." (p. 140.)

Guiding thongpa marriages in D'ing-ri in general accord with these ideals are, once again, three explicit principles that closely parallel Goldstein's finding in Chimdro. Aziz summarizes the principles as follows, continuing the first passage quoted above.

> Brothers must not separate nor their land be divided. Therefore when sons mature they remain in the natal houses to which the land is attached, if they wish to retain their rightful share and status. All sons have an equal interest [in the estate] if they do so. When this rule is combined with the one that allows only one daughter-in-law (*na-ma*) per generation into the household, the result is fraternal polyandry, and as Tibetans see it, an increase in the household's labor force. [p. 105]

The passage clearly points to beliefs like those in Chimdro, but here they are broken down slightly differently. First, the patrilineal inheritance rule is clearly present, guaranteeing each brother a "rightful share and status" in the household and "an equal interest." The monomarital principle is also expressed, although subdivided into ideals that (1) brothers must not separate and that (2) normally there must be only one daughter-in-law (wife) per generation. The latter is related to the third ideal, namely, that domestic units should exhibit "household solidarity." There is an explicit concern for a single, relatively noncontentious set of heirs per thongpa household. At the same time, there is a stated desire to increase, within evident limits, the household labor supply. A young man is therefore discreetly "coerced and caressed" into a harmonious partnership with his older brother(s) and wife. But should the opportunity arise for him to marry in the magpa fashion (and thereby reduce tensions in the patrilocal "fold"), a marriage outside is "happily arranged." (p. 144.) As in the previous example, both property conservation and labor optimization contribute to the structure and frequency of thongpa marriages.

When all of these beliefs work as they are supposed to, the thongpa household in D'ing-ri will remain a dynamically stable single entity in space and time. Exceptions, of course, do occur, especially in recent years when "independent-minded individuals do not acquiesce to the polyandric ideology." (p. 109). However, considerable effort is exerted to prevent this by the combined actions of parents, other siblings, and existing spouses. Aziz notes that "succeeding generations ideally carry on in the same apartment, around the same hearth and without any structural alterations in the house or in land-holdings. Every attempt is made to coerce brothers to adhere to this ideal. Where a family fails—and that happens not infrequently—they release a member with a feeling of regret and a certain amount of shame." (p. 106.)

Prince Peter documented many of the same phenomena in the course of his travels in and around Tibet, confirming the validity of the property conservation hypothesis despite his own predilection for the psychological explanation described in Chapter 2. Writing of Central Tibetans, for example, he stated that

> all laymen, from the nobility down to the most humble serfs, herdsmen or members of the outcaste classes (butchers, hunters, metalworkers, beggars and disposers of the dead), are organized according to the principle which we already encountered earlier in Lahul and Ladak, of the conservation of property which must remain undivided. . . . Property, mainly immovable, but also movable in the case of nomads (except for some individual items) is shared undivided and is handed down to the next generation preferably through male heirs, if they exist; if they do not, then the device of making the eldest daughter the sole heiress is resorted to and she becomes a sort of stand-in for a male heir until one becomes available again among her descendants. [1963: 414]

This statement, ironically, can be seen as a better explanation for the full Tibetan marriage system than can his own views on the reasons for polyandry. His informants, moreover, were insistent on this matter. One local chieftain in Lahul, for example, summarized his own understanding of polyandry, commenting that "the system worked pretty smoothly on the whole. There was little quarreling and not much jealousy. The reason for which this matrimonial custom was practised was an economic one: the soil was poor, the holdings small, and there was little possibility of acquiring other arable land. Each family had to hang on to what it owned; partition was strenuously avoided." (1963: 326.) When Prince Peter pressed this informant and others on the subject of jealousy among co-husbands, he was repeatedly told that few males could actually afford the "luxury" of that emotion under the circumstances. The overriding concern was clearly to avoid dividing up family property and the subsequent impoverishment that this would entail.

According to the anthropologist Robert Ekvall, marriage patterns among Tibetan nomads appear to reflect a similar set of basic "guiding principles" in the minds of the actors. However, the principles do seem to differ from Goldstein's in a number of ways related to nomadism, although Ekvall's discussion of the issues is much less explicit. First, there is a form of partible inheritance among the nomads, but here it is defined to include all siblings, daughters as well as sons. Among the siblings of a herding family,

> each one has right to an equal share of the common wealth, and the father and mother each have a right to two such units. In a family of six—parents, two sons, and two daughters—when the eldest son marries, he receives one-eighth of the [so-called] livestock fields of his family. . . . Each of the other

siblings at marriage also gets one-eighth. When all marry or leave, the father and mother still have four-eighths of the original production wealth of the family [plus any natural increase].

Ideally, at the death of the parents, this wealth should be devoted to religious observances. . . . In actual practice . . . much of it is divided among the siblings. [Ekvall 1968: 25]

One reason why this expanded inheritance rule is workable for the nomads is that what Ekvall calls "fields on the hoof," unlike normal agricultural plots, are movable property. Thus, when the eldest son of Ekvall's hypothetical family marries, his bride brings with her a dowry consisting of one share of her family's wealth, and this provides the new family with a resource base potentially much greater than the son's one-eighth share alone.

This modified inheritance rule, together with the movable, renewable nature of the nomads' resources, renders the partitioning of family wealth and the formation of nuclear tentholds a more viable option for herders than it is for agriculturalists. True, there is a local belief that "the family should not break up while the parents are alive" (p. 25), which sounds like the nomads' version of the monomarital principle. Nevertheless, the economic inducements for plural marriages are surely reduced in this context and, not surprisingly, the "great majority" of herders' marriages are monogamous.

At the same time, however, there is evidence that conservation of property remains an issue for nomadic families. First, herders say that property conservation is the main reason behind such polyandrous unions as are formed. "Quite frequently, two brothers decide not to divide the family herds and, since both sense and experience are against there being two tent mistresses [see below], they agree to share one wife." (p. 27; see also Prince Peter 1963: 559–60.) Thus, despite other differences from agriculturalists, the stated motive for polyandry among nomads is the same as Goldstein described in Chimdro.

Second, concern for property conservation is also expressed in the context of magpa marriages among the nomads. According to Ekvall, "the 'called-in-son-in-law' monogamous marriage is of particular interest for it is also devised to preserve family wealth intact and results in an extended family." (1968: 27.) Moreover, a nomad's son-in-law does not have the right to his own tenthold and share of the herd. Ekvall's information thus suggests that here, too, magpa marriage is a mechanism for conserving family property through vulnerable, sonless generations of uxorilocality. This inference is strengthened by his observation that nomadic magpa arrangements occur "mostly in affluent tentholds" that have especially attractive estates for would-be sons-in-law. (p. 27.)

Finally, Ekvall's discussion also reveals that the desire for family harmony has its own influence on the structure of nomadic families, particularly in wealthy polygynous tentholds. In only two cases, the sororal and the mother-stepdaughter forms of polygyny, is an attempt made to preserve a one-tent ownership of livestock. "Two sisters can possibly function as comistresses of the tent—though even then, control of the churn may pose greater problems than sexual jealousy— but no man in his senses should expect to keep two nonsibling women in the same tent." (p. 26.) It is for this reason that polygynous nomadic families generally consist of two tents, the "big" tent of the first wife and the "little" tent of the newcomer.

A.2.4. Assumptions and Checks in the Simulation Study

In an attempt to test Hypothesis 5 of the Tibetan study—namely, that the culturally valued consequences of the monomarital principle actually confer net reproductive benefits upon its carriers—my student assistants (B.C. and H.H.) and I developed a computer simulation of thongpa family demography and land inheritance. This section summarizes both the assumptions behind the simulation and the tests we performed to assess the robustness of our results.

Assumptions. At the outset, the simulation approach required a number of assumptions, including two about thongpa history (Assumptions 1 and 2) that could not be made lightly or without justification.

1. I had to assume that the contemporary consequences of the monomarital principle (for family structure, domestic economy, household demography, etc.) offer a reasonable approximation of its consequences in previous generations.

2. I had to assume that the traditional value system for evaluating such consequences, including the economic payoff discussed in Chapter 2, had also not drastically changed from earlier times. In other words, I was required to assume that the past and present consequences of $M = 1$ were both (a) more or less equal and (b) more or less equally valued.[1]

3. To keep the model tractable and yet as realistic as possible, I designed the simulation to represent the conditions facing thongpa households in the upper valleys of Nepal, most notably conditions like those in Limi Valley (especially Tsang), Barkhang in Humla District, and the Khumbu area of Sherpa inhabitants (see Fig. 2.1). This decision was prompted by the considerations (a) that better and more complete empirical data were available for these areas, allowing the use of actual data-based parameters in the simulation; (b) that the predictions of the model had the best chance for empirical rejection or verification in areas where field research can still be conducted; and (c) that the monomarital principle had not been externally imposed upon the agriculturalists of these regions for at least several hundred years.[2] As Goldstein (1976) has emphasized, in these areas marriage forms are "consciously selected" by the thongpa; the questions are only Why? and With what consequence?

4. I assumed that the thongpa situation could be fairly represented by a deterministic model, that is, one in which key variables were fully specified by simple difference equations with average parameter values and no stochastic terms. My sense was that a deterministic model of the "average case," while adopted pri-

---

[1] The vulnerability of research based upon "extrapolation of the present" has been persuasively argued by Diener and collaborators (1978, 1980, for example), and I am mindful of their critique. In this case, however, many of their concerns have already been addressed by previous researchers, and notably by Beall and Goldstein, who argue (1981: 11) that "traditional circumstances" live on in Limi Valley, Nepal, allowing one to read with accuracy what Kottack (1980) calls "the past in the present." Accordingly, I believe that Assumptions 1 and 2 are reasonably justified in this case. Certainly there is nothing in the folk history of contemporary Tibetans to challenge them; today's thongpa believe that the arguments they give on the subject of marriage do in fact represent the long-standing "traditional wisdom" of their forebears.

[2] In some parts of Tibet and Tibetan-speaking Bhutan, the monomarital principle was formalized some years ago into an official legal code (see App. A.2.2, above). Although the sanctions behind the code are not described, the possibility remains that these added significant force to the persistence of the principle in these regions. By modeling the simulation after Tibetan communities in Nepal, I am able to set aside any additional motivation from this source and to focus on the locally reinforced motivations of the thongpa.

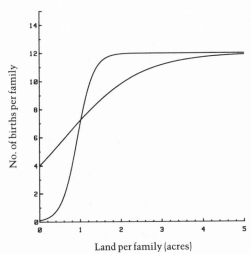

No. of births per family

Land per family (acres)

Fig. A.2.1. Sample fertility functions used in the simulation of thongpa family demography. Both curves represent the average number of children ever born to married, reproducing females as a function of the family's land resources. A wide range of different "logistic," or S-shaped, fertility functions were used in the simulations, all subject to a maximum potential fertility of 12.0 births and to a total realized fertility of 7.4 births at a family land base of 1.0 acre (the actual fertility and land averages for Tsang, Humla District, Nepal; see Goldstein 1981a). The average total fertility at land base 0.0 acres was varied from an average of 0.01 to 5.0 births with little effect on the results of the simulation.

marily for simplicity and ease of programming, would also give appropriately conservative predictions—conservative because a number of key environmental parameters (like rainfall, for example) are subject to highly skewed distributions in this high desert habitat. As part of this decision, I assumed also a small and homogeneous population of thongpa households, each with a single reproducing female. This assumption allowed the simulation to preserve the full range of reported marriage forms and at the same time to simplify the specification of household fertility. Furthermore, each household was assigned a land base by the model (ranging from 0 to 20 acres depending on the run) whose productivity was assumed to be the average of today's yields—about 70 *khal* (or 2,800 pints) of barley per acre per year.[3]

5. I assumed that the demographic properties of these households were subject to the simple arithmetic functions shown in Figs. A.2.1 and A.2.2. More specifically, I assumed a standard logistic-type fertility function centered on an average total fertility of 7.4 children at a land base of 1.0 acre (based on data for Tsang; see Beall and Goldstein 1981: 8). I also assumed a negative exponential child mortality function based upon (1) the average childhood mortality of 40 percent among the thongpa families of Tsang (see, for example, Beall and Goldstein 1981: 8); and (2) the calculated average land base (0.40 acres) required just to sustain the simplest hypothetical family of two parents. Average rates of fertility and mortality similar to those used here have been documented among other Tibetan-speaking populations of Nepal (see, for example, the compilation in Goldstein 1981a: 728). Thus in the simulations total fertility, *f*, varied as the following function of household land resources, *l*:

$$f = \frac{K}{1 + \dfrac{(K - f_0)}{f_0} \times \exp(-r \times l)} \tag{A.1}$$

[3] The range of initial estate sizes used in the simulation was deliberately generous. Actual thongpa estates average on the order of 1 to 3 acres in the Nepalese valley areas (Goldstein 1974: 262; Ross 1981: 152; Levine 1977: 51). For comparison, the average land area of thongpa serfs in Kham (eastern Tibet) was calculated at 3.33 acres in 1940 (Carrasco 1959:

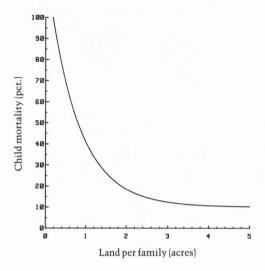

Child mortality (pct.)

Land per family (acres)

Fig. A.2.2. A sample mortality function used in the simulation of thongpa family demography. The curve represents the proportion of all children to die before reproductive age in a given generation as a function of the family's land resources. Mortality functions used in the simulations were based on the assumption that (1) below some minimal threshold of land area, l_0, child mortality is 100 percent; (2) above a land base of l_0 acres, child mortality decreases in a negative exponential fashion, as shown; and (3) the mortality figure does not drop below 10 percent even at very large estate sizes. In the simulations, l_0 was varied from 0.01 to 0.95 acres, but all mortality functions were required to meet the condition of 40 percent mortality at a land base of 1.0 acre, a figure based on the average of the mortality rates reported by all married women aged 45 or more in Tsang (see Beall and Goldstein 1981; Goldstein 1981a). Results of the simulations were qualitatively similar for the full range of these mortality functions.

where K represented the maximum total fertility, f_0 represented total fertility at 0.0 acres of land, and r was a constant adjusted to fit the curve to the empirical value of 7.4 births at 1.0 acre. Child mortality also varied as a function of the land base:

$$m = \{m_0 + \exp[-(l - l_0) \times \rho]\} \times 100 \qquad (A.2)$$

where m_0 was the asymptotic mortality rate experienced on very large estates, l_0 was the land base at which mortality reached 100 percent, and ρ was a constant adjusted to fit the curve to the empirical value of 40 percent at 1.0 acre. The use of a negative exponential mortality function was suggested by the demographic studies of Stys (1957, 1959) and Durham (1979a) in other agricultural populations.

6. I assumed that the rule of partible, patrilineal inheritance was observed each generation in simulations where the marriage principle, M, had a value greater than 1.0. In other words, corporate estates were partitioned evenly among all surviving male heirs allowed by the marriage rule of the simulation. Thus in simulations with $M = 2.0$, each of two surviving heirs in a given generation received exactly one-half of the land base of the preceding generation. Because departing heirs often received less than an equal share (see Chapter 2, note 15), this, too, is a conservative assumption.

7. I assumed that the total land base of the fictitious valley portrayed in the simulations was rigidly inelastic. Building on the observation that "all arable land has long since passed into family holdings" (see Hypothesis 2 in Chapter 2), I allowed a given estate to increase in total size only when it inherited the land of

67). Agricultural yields and household consumption rates were based on figures given in Levine 1977: 51; Cassinelli and Ekvall 1969: 279; and Ross 1981: 154–55.

another estate that had already become extinct. Here I was following actual case descriptions by Goldstein (1971b: 524) and Levine (1977: 270ff.).

Checks. To assess the robustness of the results of the Type 1 simulations described in Chapter 2 (the ones that projected numbers of surviving descendants per household as a function of the assumed marriage principle), my student assistants (B.C. and H.H.) and I performed a series of additional simulations in which we systematically varied each of the parameters in the fertility and mortality equations and studied the impact upon the number of generations to household extinction. Values tested and found to produce results equivalent to those discussed in Chapter 2, plus or minus one generation of simulation time, were: l_0 from 0.01 to 0.95; m_0 from 0.01 to 0.399; and f_0 from 0.01 to 5.00 (with corresponding adjustments in ρ and r as required to fit the curves to the empirical data described under Assumption 5 above). This procedure confirmed that the simulation results apply to a fairly wide and, in my judgment, realistic range of parameter values.

CHAPTER 3

A.3.1. A Brief Research History of Sickle-Cell Anemia Since 1910

The research history of sickle-cell anemia makes a fascinating story almost equal to that of the double helix (for detailed reviews, see Raw 1975; Dickerson and Geis 1983; Honig and Adams 1986; for a nontechnical account see Edelstein 1986). The highlights subsequent to Herrick's report in 1910 can be condensed and summarized as follows.

1. By 1923, genealogical evidence suggested that sickle-cell anemia was an inherited disorder caused by a single dominant allele (see Taliaferro and Huck 1923). It was also known that the sickling property occurred in two forms. In contrast to anemic persons with 30 to 60 percent sickled erythrocytes in venous blood, their "asymptomatic" close kin often showed less than 1 percent sickling in vivo. However, when a sample of the latter's blood was subjected in the laboratory to low oxygen pressures, similarly high rates of sickling could be induced. This condition came to be called "sickle-cell trait" or "sicklemia," to distinguish it from the more serious anemic disease. Before long, evidence suggested that the trait form was present among U.S. blacks at a frequency of about 75 per thousand compared to the anemic form at 2 per thousand.

2. In 1947, the human geneticist James V. Neel proposed that both conditions were caused not by a dominant allele but by a recessive one, "a certain factor which when heterozygous may have no discernible effects but usually results in sickling [under laboratory conditions], and when homozygous tends to result in sickle-cell anemia." (1947: 129.) The inference was based on an analogy to another congenital anemia, common in Mediterranean populations, called thalassemia major, or Cooley's anemia, which was linked to recessive inheritance in an earlier study by Neel and his colleagues. In subsequent papers, Neel (1949, 1951) presented genealogical evidence supporting the recessive gene hypothesis.

3. In 1949, Linus Pauling and his colleagues reported "a significant difference between the electrophoretic mobilities [rates of movement in a charged field] of hemoglobin derived from the erythrocytes of normal individuals and from those of sickle-cell anemic individuals." (p. 544.) These results indicated a chemical difference between "normal" hemoglobin (Hb A) and sickling hemoglobin (Hb S),

confirming Herrick's suggestion from 1910 of a "change in the composition of the corpuscle itself." Moreover, from their analysis of blood from persons with sickle-cell trait, Pauling and his colleagues (p. 547) concluded "it appears quite certain that normal hemoglobin and sickle-cell anemia hemoglobin coexist within each sicklemia cell" in roughly equal proportions. This finding essentially offered molecular proof of Neel's recessive gene theory and enabled the complete specification of the relevant genotypes and phenotypes. By a rather unorthodox convention, "A" has since been used to represent the allele coding for Hb A and "S" the allele for Hb S even though the latter is recessive (the use of S dates to the period when the allele was thought to be dominant; see, for instance, Beet 1949). Thus the genotypes and corresponding phenotypes given in Chapter 3 were known by 1949.

4. Another breakthrough came in 1957. Using a technique called "fingerprinting," Vernon M. Ingram subjected short fragments, or peptides, of hemoglobins Hb A and Hb S to treatment by both electrophoresis (separation by charge) and chromatography (separation by diffusion) at the same time. The technique "showed all peptides to have identical electrophoretic and chromatographic properties, except for one." (1957: 326.) Further fragmentation and fingerprinting of the exceptional peptide, moreover, led to the conclusion "that out of nearly 300 amino acids in the two proteins, only one is different; one of the glutamic acid residues [amino acids] of normal haemoglobin is replaced by a valine residue in sickle-cell anaemia haemoglobin." (p. 326.) That is to say, the substitution of a single amino acid in the large and complex molecule of hemoglobin was sufficient

Fig. A.3.1 (opposite). Simplified molecular genetics of the human hemoglobins A and S. At left: a segment of the DNA molecule from the A allele, its messenger RNA (mRNA), and its product, a portion of the β polypeptide of hemoglobin A (Hb A). The DNA consists of a double helical "backbone" of sugars and phosphate groups between which lie the organic bases of the code itself—adenine (A), thymine (T), cytosine (C), and guanine (G)—in a paired stair-step arrangement. Details (not shown) in the bonding of sugars and phosphates give the two strands "antiparallel" directionality as indicated by the end markers, 3' and 5' (read "three prime" and "five prime"). During gene expression, the 3'-to-5' "coding strand" (shaded) of DNA serves as a chemical template for the synthesis of a complementary strand of mRNA—complementary in that all A's, T's, C's, and G's in the DNA are represented in the mRNA by U's, A's, G's, and C's respectively ("U" stands for uracil, another organic base). After a step called "RNA processing" (not shown) to remove extraneous bases, the mRNA molecule serves, in turn, as a template for the synthesis of the β polypeptide. In this operation, triplet sequences, or "codons," of mRNA bases (indicated by numbered brackets) specify the order of amino acids to be bonded together. Thus mRNA codon 1—GUG—calls for a molecule of valine to start the chain; codon 2—CAC—then adds a molecule of histidine; codon 3—CUG—adds leucine, and so on. For simplicity, only the first 7 of 146 amino acids in the β polypeptide of Hb A are shown. At right: the matching segment of the DNA molecule from the S allele, its mRNA, and its product, a portion of the β polypeptide of sickling hemoglobin (Hb S). As in the case of Hb A, a single strand of DNA (shaded) serves as a template for the synthesis of an mRNA whose codons (numbered) then specify the order of amino acids in the β polypeptide of Hb S. However, there is a small but significant difference in the DNA's of the A and S alleles: at codon 6 in the S allele, the sequence of bases is CAC rather than CTC. This difference causes a corresponding change in the mRNA codon (to GUG instead of GAG), which then specifies the amino acid valine rather than glutamic acid (both shaded) at position 6 in the polypeptide. The presence of valine at this location, in turn, promotes the crystallization of Hb S into long strands—strands that distort red blood cells to the characteristic sickle shape. Adapted from Chambon (1981: 62) with additional data from Honig and Adams (1986).

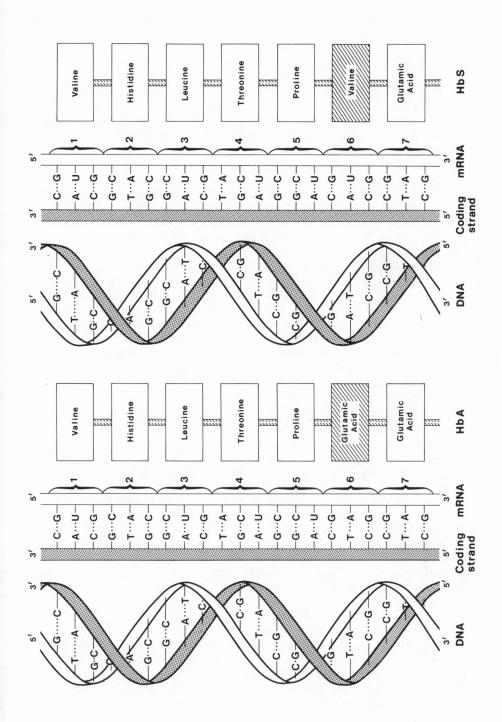

to cause drastic differences among the phenotypes, including all the symptoms of sickle-cell anemia.

5. In the years since Ingram's discovery, the complete molecular structures of Hb A and Hb S have been elucidated. Both are known to consist of four chains, or polypeptides, of amino acids—two α chains of 141 amino acids each and two β chains of 146—and four iron-containing "heme" groups, each a site of oxygen attachment (for details see Dickerson and Geis 1983; Stryer 1988: ch. 7). Moreover, the amino acid sequences of both the α and β chains have been determined, revealing that the substitution of valine for glutamic acid takes place at the sixth amino acid position of the β chains of hemoglobin. It has also been shown that the amino acid difference of Hb S is caused, in turn, by only a single nucleotide substitution in the corresponding gene of DNA (see Fig. A.3.1). The two alleles, A and S, therefore differ only in their sixth codon from the start of the sequence: the CTC of the A form has been replaced by CAC in the S. In accordance with the "central dogma" (see App. B.1), this variant codon is transcribed to GUG (instead of GAG) in the mRNA, which then "attracts" a valine-bearing tRNA in the course of protein synthesis.

6. Thus, by the early 1970's, sickling hemoglobin was regarded as a textbook case of "molecular disease," a phenotypic impairment whose etiology could be traced all the way down to the sequential nucleotides of the double helix. Scores of other hemoglobin variants had also been identified over the years and linked to a growing array of alternative alleles such as C, D, E, F. In each case, differences in the amino acid composition of the protein could be traced to molecular alterations in the nucleotide sequence of DNA (for sample listings of these variants, see McKusick 1986 and Bowman 1983; for a detailed study of one variant, Hb E, see Flatz 1967). In 1977, however, a surprise finding was announced: using recombinant DNA techniques, Alec Jeffreys and R. A. Flavell found that the gene for the β polypeptide in rabbits contained "a large insert" of nucleotides that were not translated into the protein structure. The finding was quickly verified in other mammalian species, including humans (see Efstratiadis et al. 1980), and indeed *two* "intervening sequences" of nucleotides were identified in both the α- and the β-globin genes. These intervening sequences are now called "introns" (after Gilbert 1978), as distinguished from the translated code or "exons."

7. Further use of recombinant DNA techniques has clarified the nature and structure of human globin genes, although many of the fine details remain to be investigated. It is now known that we have nine functional globin genes subdivided into two closely related gene "families" or clusters, one α and one β, as shown in Fig. A.3.2. In both clusters, member genes are arranged in order of their activation during development. Moreover, surprisingly little of the total DNA of the clusters is used for protein synthesis: only 8 percent of the nucleotides are part of the globin exons, while another 8 percent lie within the introns, and the remaining 84 percent are "a complex mixture of unique sequence and repetitive DNAs" whose functions, if any, are unknown (Jeffreys et al. 1983: 180).

8. The structure and organization of the two gene clusters contain valuable information concerning their evolutionary history. For example, nucleotide sequence similarities among the various genes in a given family indicate that "both clusters have clearly evolved by a series of tandem globin gene duplications." (Jeffreys 1982: 81.) Moreover, nucleotide similarities among *all* of the globin

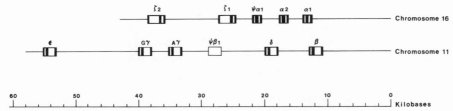

Fig. A.3.2. The organization of the human globin genes on chromosomes 16 and 11. Each chromosome contains a distinct cluster of genes (shown here as rectangular boxes) that are both arranged in developmental sequence, with embryonic genes preceding adult genes, and internally related by descent. By convention, distances are measured in kilobases of DNA from the right or 3' end. Chromosome 16 includes the α-globin gene cluster: two genes, ζ1 and ζ2, whose products are part of embryonic hemoglobin; a nonfunctional "pseudogene," ψ α1; and two genes, α1 and α2, whose products, the α polypeptides, are part of adult hemoglobin (Hb A). Likewise, chromosome 11 includes the β-globin gene cluster: one gene, ε, that contributes polypeptides to embryonic hemoglobin; two genes, Gγ and Aγ, that contribute to foetal hemoglobin; a pseudogene ψ β1; and two genes, δ and β, that contribute to adult hemoglobins, the latter being the source of the β polypeptide of Hb A. Note that each functional globin gene is composed of three "exons," or coding regions (shown as shaded areas within the boxes), interrupted by two "introns," or intervening sequences (open areas), that are not used in polypeptide synthesis. Redrawn from Dickerson and Geis 1983: 83.

genes suggest their evolutionary divergence from a common ancestral DNA sequence (see Jeffreys et al. 1983 for a globin phylogeny). An initial α-β duplication some 500 million years ago allowed the subsequent expansion and differentiation of both α- and β-globin families. Interestingly, the basic intron-exon structure of each gene has not changed in the interim. According to Jeffreys and his colleagues, "every vertebrate alpha- and beta-globin gene so far examined in species ranging from amphibians to mammals contains [the same] two introns at precisely homologous intragenic locations. This suggests that the number and positions of introns within globin genes are stable in evolution and were established before the alpha-beta duplication. . . . Despite this stability, no functions of these globin introns have yet been discovered." (1983: 178.) Similarly, DNA sequences between the genes of a cluster also show long periods of stable organization (for instance, the β-globin cluster is organizationally the same for gorillas, chimpanzees, baboons, and humans), and their rates of molecular divergence are much slower than "silent" base substitutions within functional genes. Jeffreys and his colleagues suggest that these intergene sequences are probably not a simple matter of "junk" in the genome—that is, they are probably not functionless copies of purely "selfish DNA" in the sense of Orgel and Crick (1980). Instead, "it seems more likely that the cluster in its entirety, including the intergenic DNA, has some functional significance and might represent a single coadapted supergene." (Jeffreys et al. 1983: 183; for a similar view, see Bodmer 1983.)

A.3.2. Procedures Used in Testing the Malaria Hypothesis

Data of three kinds were assembled in preparation for the test of the malaria hypothesis described in Chapter 3: gene frequencies for the A, S, and C alleles in a diverse sample of West African populations; meteorological data for the same populations, as a source of potential surrogates for the intensity of malarial selec-

TABLE A.3.1

Subsamples of 157 West African Populations
Used in Testing the Malaria Hypothesis,
by Language Group and Agricultural Emphasis

(number of populations)

I. CONGO-KORDOFANIAN ($N = 145$)
   I.A. Niger-Congo ($N = 145$)
      I.A.1. *West Atlantic* ($N = 44$)
        a. Rice cultivators ($N = 31$)
        b. Sorghum and millet cultivators ($N = 6$)
        c. Nomadic herders ($N = 7$)
      I.A.2. *Mande* ($N = 40$)
        a. Rice cultivators ($N = 24$)
        b. Sorghum and millet cultivators ($N = 16$)
      I.A.3. *Voltaic* ($N = 19$)
        a. Sorghum and millet cultivators ($N = 14$)
        b. Sorghum, millet, and yam cultivators ($N = 5$)
      I.A.4. *Kwa* ($N = 42$)
        a. Yam cultivators ($N = 29$)
        b. Rice cultivators ($N = 13$)
II. NILO-SAHARAN ($N = 4$)
   II.A. Songhai ($N = 2$)
   II.B. Saharan ($N = 2$)
III. AFROASIATIC ($N = 8$)
   III.E. Chad ($N = 8$)

SOURCE: Data from Livingstone 1967, 1973.

tion; and descriptive statistics on population size, settlement pattern, and subsistence practices for use in subdividing the data set and in retesting the arguments of Wiesenfeld (1967). Whereas the descriptive statistics could simply be culled from Murdock's compilations (1967 and 1981), additional methods were required for the other two kinds of data.

Gene-frequency data. Following the format used by Rucknagel and Neel (1961), and with the help of student assistants (E.L., J.G., P.I., and R.W.), I compiled hemoglobinopathy tallies for all West African populations listed in the tables published by Livingstone (1967, 1973). Data from multiple entries for the same population, compiled by Livingstone from independent studies, were pooled except in the case of the Malinke (Mandingo) and Fulani peoples, each of whom spans a great geographical range. From preliminary tallies, only those populations with a pooled sample of 30 or more subjects were retained for statistical analysis (a precaution also used by Rucknagel and Neel 1961 in order to reduce sampling error); moreover, samples of persons of European descent living in the region were omitted. This resulted in a final data base of 157 different population samples. Using the language classification of Fivaz and Scott (1977), and maps of language affiliation and agricultural zones (Figs. 3.5 and 3.6), I then subdivided the data into subsamples as shown in Table A.3.1.

The frequencies of S and C alleles were then calculated for each of the populations in the data base following a conservative estimation procedure. The frequency of S was calculated as one-half the frequency of all S-carriers in the pooled samples—that is, as one-half the total frequency of Livingstone's "S," AS, and SC hemoglobin types plus one-half the frequency of his generic "sickle-cell" category of unspecified hemoglobin types. In counting all S-carriers as if they possessed but a single S allele, this procedure slightly underestimates q. To check its validity, I calculated a second estimate of q by ignoring the generic "sickle-cell" data and treating all "S" hemoglobin types as homozygous SS's. The correlation of these two estimates across the sample, as measured by a Pearson's correlation coefficient of 0.99, confirms the validity of the first and more conservative measure. I then used parallel procedures to provide a conservative estimate of r, the frequency of C, for each of the pooled samples. The frequency, p, of the A allele could then be estimated for each population as $1.0 - (q + r)$. Copies of the resulting data table are available from the author upon request.

Meteorological data. In order to estimate the severity of malarial selection for each of the 157 populations in the data base, I had little choice but to search for a surrogate measure in the weather data available for West Africa. Fortunately, the region is well represented in the World Meteorological Organization's (WMO's) network of weather stations, so I had a reliable set of standard measures from which to work. I therefore added weather data to the gene-frequency data base in the following way. First I estimated coordinates for the geographic center of each population in the sample, using the maps in Westermann and Bryan (1952), Murdock (1959), and Dalby (1977) plus, in the case of populations in Ghana, those in Dickson (1969). These coordinates were then compared by computer to the coordinates for all WMO weather stations in the region, and the nearest station was determined by planar triangulation. Populations whose nearest weather station proved to be more than one hundred miles away were dropped from the analysis. Second, weather data from the nearest station were then added to the data base for each population; taken from U.S. Department of Commerce Environmental Data Service (1967), each variable was represented by its average value for the ten years from 1951 to 1960. Third, to provide a semi-independent check on any results I might get with WMO data, I repeated this procedure using an additional set of weather data from the "crop ecological survey" of Papadakis (1966). Not only did Papadakis provide data from additional, presumably smaller weather stations in the region, but he also added a number of useful variables including "water surplus" described in Chapter 3. A table summarizing the selection of both sets of weather stations is available from the author upon request.

As mentioned in Chapter 3, I expected the variable "maximum monthly rainfall"—that is, the average total rainfall in the wettest month—to be the best surrogate in the WMO data for the severity of malaria in an area. My reasoning was that West Africa is characterized by a pronounced seasonality in rainfall such that there is a sharp increase each summer in conditions (such as relative humidity and area in standing water) favorable to the proliferation of *Anopheles* vectors. Other things being equal, one therefore expects that (1) the higher the rainfall in summer months, the more the vectors, and (2) the more the vectors, the higher the incidence of malaria in local populations. Field data from West Africa support both parts of this assertion. Fig. 3.8, discussed in Chapter 3, supports the first part; Fig. A.3.3 supports the second using data pertaining to the Yoruba of southern Nigeria (see also Durham 1983a). The figure shows a single annual peak in the parasite rate of both mothers and their infants—a peak that follows, at an appropriate three-to-four week lag, the rainfall and mosquito peaks at the same location. Under these conditions, rates of malarial mortality are likely to be closely

Panel A

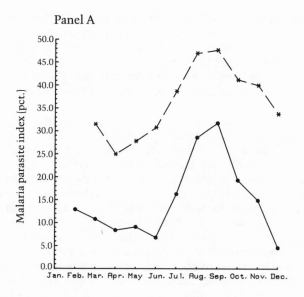

Panel B

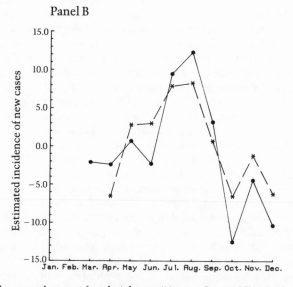

Fig. A.3.3. The annual wave of malarial parasitism at Lagos, Nigeria, in 1929. Panel A shows the variation in the malaria parasite index—that is, in the percentage of persons with malaria parasites in peripheral blood—among Yoruba mothers (broken line, N = 865) and their three-to-four-month-old infants (solid line, N = 1, 108). Both curves have a single peak, from August to September. Panel B shows the estimated incidence of new cases of malaria in the same sample, as measured by the monthly change in the parasite indexes for the mothers (broken line) and their infants (solid line). Again, both curves have a single peak, here from July to August. The curve for infant malaria has slightly steeper ascending and descending slopes, indicating severer impact. Panel A redrawn by permission of the publisher from Durham 1983a: 57. Copyright 1983 by Elsevier Science Publishing Co., Inc. Panel B data from Barber and Olinger 1931.

correlated with maximum monthly rainfall. By the same token, other weather variables cannot be expected to work as well. Total annual rainfall, for instance, is a statistic heavily influenced by the September and October rains that come after the mosquito bottleneck and have little impact on their population, and temperature measurements are much more uniform across the whole region. This expectation was confirmed in the course of the study.

Statistical analysis. The pattern of covariation between the gene-frequency data and the malarial surrogates was explored on a Hewlett-Packard 9845B computer using regression analysis software developed by the manufacturer and plotting programs written specifically for this task by the author. The data set was partitioned into subfiles, according to the categories of Table A.3.1, to allow separate analysis by linguistic affiliation and agricultural emphasis.

CHAPTER 4

A.4.1. Earlier Models of Selective Cultural Change

In addition to Albert Keller's (1915) theory of "social selection," briefly discussed in Chapter 4, three earlier models of culture change stand as important "conceptual ancestors" to the idea of evolution by cultural selection. In all three, I believe it is fair to say, selective transformational mechanisms are proposed as important though not exclusive sources of evolutionary change.

Model 1: Hoebel's theory of "imperative selection." In 1954, E. Adamson Hoebel published an influential treatise on what he called "comparative legal dynamics." In an opening chapter on the cultural background of law, Hoebel outlines a "theory of imperative selection" to account for the evolutionary coherence and selectivity of social norms, particularly legal ones. The theory stemmed from two premises: that "man is truly capable of many things—perhaps not in infinite variety, for his finite body and the physical universe do impose real limitations—but the range is impressively wide"; and that "the capacity of each individual culture is inherently finite and can never be an omnibus for all possibilities." (1954: 10.) The consequence of these premises is what he terms "the imperative of selection," which is "the proposition that every society must of necessity choose a limited number of behavior possibilities for incorporation in its culture." (p. 12.)

To this chain of reasoning, Hoebel adds a third important premise, "that selection is by no means ever wholly fortuitous." (p. 13.) Instead, it is guided and given specific direction by a very basic set of values he calls "postulates."

> Once a culture gets under way (and all the cultures with which social science has to deal are under way) there are always some criteria of choice that govern or influence selection. These criteria are broadly generalized propositions held by the members of a society as to the nature of things and as to what is qualitatively desirable and undesirable. We prefer to call these basic propositions "postulates". . . . The particular formulations of specific customs and patterns for behavior that go into a given culture are more or less explicitly shaped by the precepts given in the basic postulates of that specific culture. New patterns are accepted, rejected, or modified with reference to the basic postulates. [pp. 12–13]

In this way, Hoebel proposes that cultures are transformed through time by a selective process of evaluation. Consciously or unconsciously, new or variant behavior possibilities are compared against socially accepted standards—the postulates—and thereby "selected for" or "selected against" within the population. The process gives a directional bias to cultural change so long as the postulates themselves remain invariant.

Hoebel's theory is certainly a model for the selective transformation of cultural systems; indeed it inspired my concept of the mechanism I call "secondary value selection." However, the theory does not address two key questions about selective evolutionary change. First, it does not answer Philip Burnham's (1973: 95) question about cultural adaptation. Arguing that culture is "man's primary means of adapting to changing environmental and social circumstances," Burnham points out that "if men make decisions on the basis of culturally defined scales of values which have no necessary relation to the adaptive significance of the trait from a biological point of view, one is thrown back on the dilemma of explaining how 'an adaptative solution to an ecological problem' (Carneiro 1968: 553) is regularly reached." In other words, Hoebel's theory offers nothing to keep a culture from "getting under way" with maladaptive postulates for its carriers, postulates that would cause people far greater harm than good. Second, the whole subject of how such postulates arise and how they may change in time (or not change, as the case may be) is not sufficiently explored. The result is a selective model with seemingly arbitrary direction. This shortcoming is partly alleviated in Model 2.

Model 2: Murdock's theory of "selective elimination." Two years after Hoebel's theory was proposed, George P. Murdock published a more comprehensive account of "how culture changes" (the title of his article). Murdock's model features four processes: (1) innovation, "the formation of a new habit by a single individual which is subsequently accepted or learned by other members of society" (1971 [1956]: 322); (2) social acceptance, "the adoption of a new habit" by other individuals (p. 329); (3) selective elimination, the "competition for survival" in society among innovations (p. 330); and (4) integration, the process by which "shared habits . . . become progressively adapted to one another so that they tend to form an integrated whole." (p. 331.) Murdock makes very clear his view that the transformation of the cultural system through time is achieved by two processes, selective elimination and integration. But just as the "shared habits . . . become progressively adapted to one another" via integration, so those habits on the whole tend to adapt via selective elimination to the environment of the population.

Murdock is quite explicit on this point:

Every innovation that has been socially accepted enters, as it were, into a competition for survival. So long as it proves more rewarding than its alternatives a cultural habit will endure, but when it ceases to bring comparable satisfactions it dwindles and eventually disappears. The process superficially resembles that of natural selection in organic evolution. It should be noted, however, that cultural traits do not compete directly with one another but are competitively tested in the experience of those who practice them. . . . By and large, the cultural elements that are eliminated through trial and error or social competition are the less adaptive ones, so that the process is as definitely one of the survival of the fittest as is that of natural selection. [pp. 330–31]

According to Murdock, then, this aspect of culture's evolutionary transformation is both selective, owing to the competition of habitual forms, and directional, in tending to promote adaptation.

The directionality of the scheme arises from the consequences of the habits or traits, and from two kinds of consequences at that. Within populations, by Murdock's theory, selective elimination proceeds on the basis of the comparative satisfaction that variants bring to individuals. Between populations, selective elimination depends upon social competition where "the issue is decided indirectly by the victory of one group over the other." (p. 330.) As a result of selection at both levels, Murdock proposes, the tendency will be for the most adaptive forms to prevail.

Unfortunately, Murdock was not very explicit about the nature of the "satisfaction" that played so central a role in his theory. He neglected to identify the satisfying features of successful innovations and failed to specify the kinds of satisfactions they entailed. Later, when other authors attempted to carry forward this line of reasoning, they ran into some serious difficulties on this very point (see for example, Ruyle 1973; Ruyle et al. 1977). Depending on how satisfaction is defined and measured, it may or may not provide adaptive directionality to cultural change.

Nevertheless, Murdock's theory helped to draw attention to the mechanisms of adaptive selectivity in cultural evolution. It also pointed out that selective elimination "superficially resembles" the transforming principle of natural selection in genetic evolution (see Chapter 3 of this book). That similarity, noted independently by another author, led the way to a third model of cultural evolution.

Model 3: Campbell's theory of "selective retention." In an influential paper of 1965, the psychologist Donald Campbell pointed out that a very general evolutionary logic is contained within the theory of organic evolution developed in biology. His argument, which follows the lead of Alfred Keller (1915), is that Darwin's mechanism of natural selection is but a single, special case of a more general evolutionary transformation, a principle he calls "variation and selective retention." According to Campbell, selective evolutionary change should characterize any system of phenomena that has four elements: (1) a population of some kind of replicable units; (2) one or more sources of variation in those units; (3) consistent selection of certain types of variants; and (4) a mechanism for the transmission of positively selected forms.[1]

Campbell's proposition is clearly inspired by genetic evolutionary theory, but his point is that culture, too, is capable of this same general kind of transformation. In a preliminary manner, he identifies "representatives" in the cultural inheritance system for each of the four logical elements of the model. He speaks of (1) social forms and customs as the replicable units; (2) "variations among social units, variations among occasions within a social unit, and variations among the members of a social unit" (1965: 29); (3) several kinds of "potential selective systems";[2] and of (4) a retention system that includes indoctrination and education.

---

[1] Although Campbell actually speaks of "three basic requirements," not four, I have expanded his list on the grounds that his Requirement 1, "the occurrence of variations," implies both a unit *and* some degree of variability in that unit.

[2] Campbell (1965: 29) notes that "the potential selective systems are so numerous and so intertwined, and the selective criteria so difficult to specify, that quite responsible intellectual grounds are provided for a denial of the existence of a socio-cultural evolutionary pro-

He notes a number of the ways in which these representatives are different in form and function from their counterparts in genetic evolution. Nevertheless, he insists on logical grounds that these differences do not prevent culture from having its own kind of evolutionary process based on variation and selective retention. Because both sets of processes, the genetic and the cultural, are manifestations of the same general evolutionary model, one would expect to find "specific embodiments of the process in organic evolution [that] have no counterpart in sociocultural evolution, and vice versa." (p. 42.) Campbell elaborates and extends his model in more recent papers (see especially 1975b, 1979), backing off, in response to criticisms by Corning (1974) and Boehm (1978), from his earlier emphasis on "blind" and "random" variation in cultural innovations. But the central idea of selective retention remains: "The slogan perhaps should not be *blind* or *random* variation and selective retention, but it certainly should be *even-if-blind-or-random-variation* and selective retention." (1979: 41.)

A.4.2. Parallels in the Neural and Semantic Coding of Color

In the case study at the end of Chapter 4, I suggest that the basic color terms of different languages have evolved their similar spectral meanings under the guidance of primary value selection. Here I explain in greater detail the three data sets that are crucial to the argument. For more information on color, see Rossotti 1985; on color vision, see Boynton 1979 and 1988; Jacobs 1981; Hurvich 1981; Mollon and Sharpe 1983.

Consider, first, the color-naming experiment of Boynton and Gordon (1965). As shown in Fig. A.4.1, this experiment establishes that each of the four basic hues— blue, green, yellow, and red—is perceived as a "fuzzy," or graded, set within which membership is a matter of degree. Thus the sensation "yellow" varies, for example, from "slightly yellowish" (as at 520 nm, for example), to "very yellowish" (as at 560 nm), to "pure yellow" (580 nm), and back down again to "slightly yellowish" (as at 640 nm). The data plotted here were obtained by asking experimental subjects to name the one or two component hues visible in a light of given wavelength. Each hue was then awarded 1 to 3 points depending upon its intensity in the stimulus, and the tallies for each were then totaled at each wavelength of light. Other authors have criticized Boynton and Gordon's procedure, noting that subjects can perform finer discriminations than the 1-to-3 point scale allows (see, for example, Wooten 1970: 93–94). Nevertheless, the curves generated by alternative scaling procedures (Wooten 1970: 116) preserve much the same location and shape as those shown here.

The second crucial data set came from the work of De Valois et al. (1966) on the coding of color in nerve cells of the lateral geniculate nucleus (LGN) of the macaque monkey (*Macaca irus*). In the course of recording from 147 different cells, the authors found 103 of the cells to have the property of so-called spectral oppo-

---

cess." His own list includes no fewer than six selective systems: (1) "the selective survival of complete social organizations"; (2) "selective diffusion or borrowing between social groups"; (3) "selective propagation of temporal variations"; (4) "selective imitation of interindividual variations"; (5) "selective promotion to leadership and educational roles"; and (6) the older idea of "rational selection" (from Keller 1915). Campbell's (1965: 30–31) predictions about selective systems 4 and 5 have been studied in detail by Boyd and Richerson (1985) in their models of "indirect bias" and "natural selection of cultural variation." The latter are discussed under "Darwinian Culture Theory" in Chapter 4 of this book.

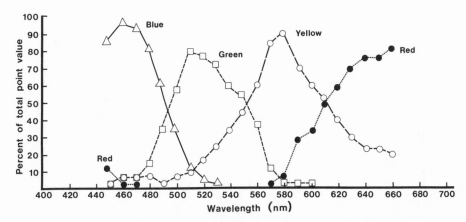

Fig. A.4.1. The semantic coding of color by native English-speakers. The graph plots the results of a color-naming experiment in which participants were asked to describe mono-chromatic lights of various wavelengths, using only the four basic color terms shown. The participants were instructed to use single color terms whenever they saw only one hue (in which case three points were tallied for the chosen term) and otherwise to use them in pairs, naming the "primary component of the sensation" first (two points) and the less intense component second (one point). Point tallies were then averaged across participants and the score for each term converted to a percentage of the total at each wavelength of light. Similar results were obtained at two retinal illuminances (100 and 1000 trolands); the data shown here are from the higher illuminance trials. Redrawn from De Valois et al. (1966: 975); original data from Boynton and Gordon (1965).

nency—that is, they responded with excitation (i.e., an increased rate of nerve impulse propagation) when one set of wavelengths was shown to the macaque and with inhibition when another set of wavelengths was viewed. Moreover, four distinct types of opponent cells were found: (1) "+R−G" cells, with an excitatory response to "red" wavelengths (from 600 to 700 nm), coupled with an inhibitory response to "green" wavelengths (from 400 to 600 nm); (2) "+G−R" cells, characterized by the reverse activity pattern; (3) "+Y−B" cells, with excitatory response to "yellow" wavelengths (500 to 700 nm) and inhibitory response to "blue" wavelengths (400 to 500 nm); and (4) "+B−Y" cells, characterized by the reverse activity pattern. When the neural responses of these cells (measured by the *total* change, excitatory or inhibitory, from spontaneous spike rate) were first averaged and then added together by wavelength, an overall spectral activity pattern was obtained (Fig. A.4.2; see also De Valois et al. 1966: 976). The figure shows that the continuous spectrum of visible light is actually subdivided into four discrete categories by the LGN—"blueness," "greenness," "yellowness," and "redness"—each of which is neurally encoded as a fuzzy set. The correlations between this figure and Fig. A.4.1 suggest a neurophysiological basis to the semantic coding of color.

That suggestion is confirmed by the third data set (Fig. A.4.3). The figure plots the spectral location of the color-term foci of the twenty distinct human languages studied by Berlin and Kay (1969; as explained in Chapter 4, "foci" are colors identified by native speakers as "the best, most typical examples" of a given color term). As shown by breaks in heavy black shading along the horizontal axis, the Berlin and Kay color palette contained a number of wavelength gaps, which

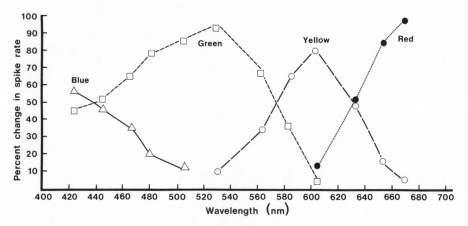

Fig. A.4.2. The neural coding of color by the lateral geniculate nucleus (LGN) of the macaque. This graph shows the average activity pattern of the opponent cell system of the LGN in response to monochromatic lights of varying wavelengths, all at relatively low intensity. Here neural activity is measured as the percentage of total change, whether excitatory or inhibitory, in the "spike rate"—the rate of nerve impulse propagation—of the spectrally opponent cells (i.e., nerve cells that respond with excitation to some wavelengths and with inhibition to others). In effect, the plot shows the focal wavelengths and ranges of light that the macaque's opponent cells code as "blue," "green," "yellow," and "red." Because the visual systems of macaques and humans are similar, this activity pattern is believed to be a reasonable model for the output of the human LGN; note that the curves closely parallel those of Fig. A.4.1. Redrawn from De Valois et al. (1966: 976).

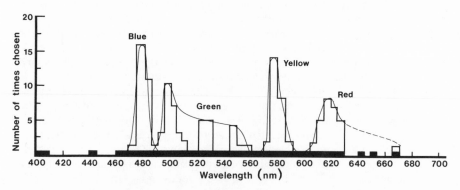

Fig. A.4.3. The color-term foci of 20 human languages. Using a wavelength scale, this graph locates, for each of the languages, the focal hues of basic color terms that most closely correspond to the English words shown. The heavy line along the horizontal axis indicates the "dominant," or characteristic, wavelengths included in the full set of stimulus colors used to solicit these foci. Despite a number of gaps in the stimulus wavelengths, the shapes of these curves show close correspondence with the neural response curves of Fig. A.4.2. The correlation indicates that cultural evolution has systematically favored color terms whose spectral meanings are a close match to the neural coding patterns of the LGN. Data on color-term foci from appendix I of Berlin and Kay (1969); data on the dominant wavelengths of the stimulus colors from Munsell Color Co. (1976b).

precluded some hues from consideration as possible foci. Nevertheless, the correspondence with Fig. A.4.2 is reasonably close, and all the more striking since that figure is based on data for the macaque. Similarly, there is a close match between the wavelength *boundaries* of the basic color terms, presented in Chapter 4 (Fig. 4.8), and the wavelength boundaries of the LGN response categories in Fig. A.4.2. We may reasonably conclude, therefore, that these cross-cultural similarities in the semantic coding of color reflect universal processes within the neural coding of color.

CHAPTER 5

A.5.1. Procedures for Quantifying the Genetic and Cultural Diversity of the Adult Lactose Absorption Case

Genetic diversity. The analysis in Chapter 5 makes an assumption of genetic covariation (for which see Chapter 2) between the phenotypic difference, LM and LA, and one or more corresponding genotypic differences. I therefore use the frequency of LA phenotypes in human populations as a measure of the frequency of the presumed LA genotypes. The LA phenotype data were compiled as follows.

First, from Simoons's compilation (1978a), I extracted a list of all sample populations whose native homeland lay between 60 degrees east and west longitude, or roughly from Greenland to Saudi Arabia (see Fig. 5.3). In this selection, I was guided by the argument of Flatz and Rotthauwe (1977: 237–38) that "distribution studies of the lactase phenotypes in the Old World are of particular interest, because the populations of this region have been exposed to the environmental conditions of their present habitats for a long time." I was also guided by the desire to preserve (1) the diversity of subsistence modes represented in Simoons's compilation (including hunter-gatherers and pastoralists, for example); and (2) the range of habitats and latitudes included in the sample populations (from the Kalahari Desert of southern Africa to the arctic tundra of northern Greenland). The choice of 60-degree meridians was largely arbitrary, except that I wanted to exclude from the subsample the Indian subcontinent, China, and Southeast Asia because of the uncertain agricultural history of some areas and the lack of reliable data from others, especially China. (Since I assembled this subsample, however, information has become available for some of these areas; see Simoons 1981a.) From the list of populations within this area I dropped any with unspecified ancestry (e.g., "Europeans") whose homeland latitudes could not be determined with accuracy. I then pooled the data concerning lactose absorption and malabsorption from all samples drawn from the same population. Finally, as a step to reduce sampling error, I discarded all populations whose total sample size then included fewer than 10 persons.

This procedure generated a cross-sectional subsample of 60 populations, 59 from the Old World plus the Eskimos (Inuit) of Greenland, representing the full range of adult lactose absorbing capability, from 0 to 100 percent (see Table A.5.1). Following Simoons's (1978a) example, I further subdivided these populations into seven categories according to subsistence technology and geographic location. The thirteen groups of "mixed" ancestry (that is, groups in which a dairying and a nondairying population have interbred) were omitted from the final analysis, leaving a final sample size of 47 populations.

Cultural diversity. The analysis of Chapter 5 also required comparative in-

TABLE A.5.1

Sixty Human Populations, by Means of Subsistence:
Their Lactose Absorbing Capacity, Geographic Latitude, and Annual Exposure to Ultraviolet Radiation

Category and population[a]	Sample(s) in Simoons 1978a[b]	Number of persons in study	Age range	Lactose absorbers		Approximate latitude (degrees)[c]	Approximate annual UV-B (wattsec/cm²)[d]
				Number	Percent		
Category A. Hunter-gatherers (traditionally lacking dairy animals): N = 4							
1. Eskimos of Greenland	1,2,3	119	1	18	15.1%	69.2 N	50
2. Twa Pygmies of Rwanda	7	22	15–58	5	22.7	1.6 S	400
3. !Kung Bushmen of S.W. Africa	8	40	Adults	1	2.5	19.6 S	350
4. ‡huá Bushmen of Botswana	9	25	10	2	8.0	23.0 S	350
TOTAL		206		26	12.6%		
Category B. Nondairying agriculturalists: N = 5							
5. Yoruba	18,23,24	100	3	9	9.0%	6.3 N	350
6. Ibo	19,22	15	13	3	20.0	4.4 N	350
7. Children in Ghana	20	100	2–6	27	27.0	5.3 N	350
8. Bantu of various tribes, Zaire	21	52	Adults	1	1.9	4.2 S	350
9. Hausa[e]	194	17	4	4	23.5	12.0 N	375
TOTAL		284		44	15.5%		
Category C. Recently dairying agriculturalists: N = 5[f]							
10. Kenyans (mainly Kikuyu, Kamba, & other Bantu)	51	71	5–15	19	26.8%	1.2 S	400
11. Bantu of Zambia	52	26	17–59	0	0.0	15.3 S	400
12. Bantu of South Africa	53	31	Adults?[g]	3	9.7	26.1 S	300
13. Shi, Bantu of Lake Kivu area	54	28	Adults	1	3.6	1.6 S	400
14. Ganda, other Bantu of Uganda	55,56,57	70	5–70	4	5.7	0.2 N	400
TOTAL		226		27	11.9%		
Category D. Milk-dependent pastoralists: N = 5							
15. Arabs of Saudi Arabia	59,60	22	17	19	86.4%	24.4 N	375
16. Hima pastoralists	61	11	6–53	10	90.9	1.0 S	400
17. Tussi pastoralists in Uganda	62,65	17	10–50	15	88.2	0.2 N	400

TABLE A.5.1 (continued)

Category and population[a]	Sample(s) in Simoons 1978a[b]	Number of persons in study	Age range	Lactose absorbers		Approximate latitude (degrees)[c]	Approximate annual UV-B (wattsec/cm²)[d]
				Number	Percent		
18. Tussi, in Congo	63	15	Adults	15	100.0	4.1 S	350
19. Tussi, in Rwanda	64	27	Adults	25	92.6	1.6 S	400
TOTAL		92		84	91.3%		
Category E. Dairying peoples of North Africa and the Mediterranean (from 0° to 40° N): N = 16[h]							
20. Jews in Israel	150,151,152	201	8	82	40.8%	32.1 N	250
21. Ashkenazic Jews	153	53	20–70	11	20.8	32.1 N	250
22. N. African Sephardim (from Morocco, Tripoli, & Tunis)	154	32	19–65	12	37.5	33.4 N	250
23. Other Sephardim (from Turkey, Bulgaria, & Greece)	155	36	17–69	10	27.8	37.0 N	250
24. Iraqi Jews	157	38	17–65	6	15.8	33.2 N	350
25. Other Oriental Jews (mainly Persian)	158	20	Adults	3	15.0	35.4 N	300
26. Arab villagers in Israel	159	67	Adults	13	19.4	32.1 N	250
27. Syrian Arabs	160	40	Adults	2	5.0	33.3 N	300
28. Jordanian Arabs	161	56	17–48	13	23.2	31.6 N	300
29. Arabs from Jordan, Syria, & Morocco	162	19	Adults	0	0.0	31.6 N	300
30. Arabs from Jordan, Syria, Saudi Arabia, Egypt, Iraq, Tunisia, & Libya	163	26	Adults	5	19.2	33.3 N	300
31. Egyptian fellahin	164	14	13–65	1	7.1	30.0 N	300
32. Greeks (mostly mainland)	167–71	730	1	380	52.1	37.6 N	200
33. Greek Cretans	172	50	Adults	22	44.0	35.2 N	250
34. Greek Cypriots	173,174	67	Unspecified	19	28.4	35.1 N	250
35. Ethiopians/Eritreans (mainly Amhara & Tigre)	192	58	7–13	6	10.3	13.0 N	400
TOTAL		1,507		585	38.8%		

TABLE A.5.1 (continued)

Category and population[a]	Sample(s) in Simoons 1978a[b]	Number of persons in study	Age range	Lactose absorbers Number	Lactose absorbers Percent	Approximate latitude (degrees)[c]	Approximate annual UV-B (wattsec/cm²)[d]
Category F. Dairying peoples of northern Europe (over 40° N): N = 12							
36. Danes	66,67	761	Adults	742	97.5%	55.4 N	100
37. Swedes	68,69	491	Adults	480?[g]	97.8	59.2 N	50
38. Finns	70,71,72,73	578	7	492	85.1[i]	60.1 N	50
39. Northwest Europeans	74,75,88	158	3	138	87.3	51.3 N	100
40. French	96	14	Adults	13	92.9	48.5 N	150
41. Germans from Central Europe	97	55	Adults	47	85.5	52.3 N	150
42. Dutch (living in Surinam)	98	14	Adults	12?[g]	85.7	52.2 N	150
43. Poles (living in Canada)	99	21	17–65	15	71.4	52.2 N	150
44. Czechs (living in Canada)	100	17	17–65	14	82.4	50.1 N	150
45. Czechs from Bohemia & Moravia	101	20	Adults	20	100.0	49.1 N	150
46. Spaniards	102	265	Adults	226	85.3	40.2 N	200
47. North Italians (Ligurians)	165	40	Adults	28	70.0	44.2 N	200
TOTAL		2,434		2,227	91.5%		
Category G. Populations of "mixed" ancestry (dairying and nondairying): N = 13							
48. Iru	109	13	7–60	8	61.5%	0.2 N	400
49. Hutu	110,111	51	8	25	49.0	1.6 S	400
50. Hutu/Tussi mixed persons	112	11	Adults	5	45.5	1.6 S	400
51. Fulani/Hausa	113,114	39	4	13	33.3	12.0 N	375
52. Yoruba/European mixed persons	115	43	3	24	55.8	6.3 N	350
53. Nama Hottentots	116	18	Adults	9	50.0	26.0 S	300
54. Greenland Eskimo / Northwest European mixed persons	134,135,136	108	1	67	62.0	69.2 N	50
55. Yemen Jews (mixed with Arabs)[e]	156	36	20–70	20	55.6	32.1 N	400
56. Skolt Lapps in Finland[e]	188	176	15	[70][j]	39.8	69.5 N	25
57. Mountain Lapps in Finland[e]	189	75	15	[47][j]	62.7	69.0 N	25

TABLE A.5.1 (continued)

Category and population[a]	Sample(s) in Simoons 1978a[b]	Number of persons in study	Age range	Lactose absorbers		Approximate latitude (degrees)[c]	Approximate annual UV-B (wattsec/cm²)[d]
				Number	Percent		
58. Fisher Lapps in Finland[e]	190	110	15	[82][f]	74.5	68.0 N	25
59. Mountain Lapps, some with Fisher Lapp ancestry[e]	191	160	15	[106][f]	66.3	69.5 N	25
60. Rehoboth Basters[e] (50% Caucasoid, 50% Hottentot?)	197	20	Adults?[g]	7	35.0	26.1 N	300
TOTAL		860		483	56.2%		
GRAND TOTAL (All categories, 60 populations)[k] 5,609				3,476	62.0%		

SOURCE: Lactose absorption data from Simoons 1978a; latitudes from *Rand McNally New International Atlas* 1980; data on UV-B from Schulze and Gräfe 1969.

[a] Categories have been renamed and reorganized from those in Simoons (1978a), but the original population names have been preserved to facilitate identification and cross-referencing.

[b] To reduce sampling error and to prevent the overrepresentation of some populations in the final tally, this table pools data from different samples of the same population.

[c] Based on actual sampling locations in the case of small, nonstate populations, and on the location of the largest city in the case of large, state populations.

[d] Approximate annual sum of incident solar radiation, direct beam plus diffuse, for a 10 nm bandwidth centered at 307.5 nm. The data shown here represent the conservative, lower bounding isogram for each population as estimated from the map in Schulze and Gräfe (1969: 367).

[e] Listed in Simoons (1978a) under a different category but included here on the basis of more recent information.

[f] According to Simoons (1978a: 974) and others, these populations adopted dairying and milk use within the last two thousand years.

[g] Question mark in the original (Simoons 1978a).

[h] Entries here have been taken from the Categories F ("Peoples who have used milk since antiquity but who do not meet conditions of strong selective pressures against LM") and G ("Problems") in Simoons (1978a).

[i] This sample may well include persons of mixed Finn and "Lapp" ancestry.

[j] Brackets in the original (Simoons 1978a).

[k] Because of relatively large sample sizes in Category F, northern European populations are overrepresented in these totals.

dicators of the cultural differences between populations in the subsample in regard to beliefs about milk production, processing, and consumption. For measures of contemporary cultural differences, and with the help of student assistant E.L., I compiled national-level statistics for the baseline year 1978 (the same year as Simoons's compilation of LA data) from the publications of the United Nations Food and Agriculture Organization (United Nations FAO 1979a, 1979b). For each population in the subsample (Table 5.1), I used the data of the most closely corresponding "homeland country," which is admittedly only a first approximation. In cases where the subjects of the lactose absorption studies came from more than one country (for example, North African Sephardi, population 22), the country whose citizens comprised the largest proportion of the sample was used. Where per capita measures were needed, I used the 1978 population estimates for each country provided by UNESCO (1982).

Indicators of cultural diversity were tabulated for each population in the subsample aside from those in Categories A (hunters and gatherers, traditionally lacking in dairy animals) and D (milk-dependent pastoralists, for whom national-level statistics on milk production and consumption do not apply). The specific indicator variables were as follows: (1) number of dairy cows per thousand people; (2) total fresh milk production in millions of liters per year, including the milk of cows, goats, sheep, and buffalo, and the milk used to make butter, but not including the milk used for cheese production; (3) implied total milk consumption in liters per person per year, calculated as the total domestic production of all milk from cows, sheep, goats, and buffalo plus imports, minus exports, and then divided by 1978 population size; (4) implied cheese consumption in kilograms per capita per year, calculated again as the total domestic production of cheeses of all kinds plus imports, minus exports, and then divided by the 1978 population size; (5) cheese production as a percentage of milk production, calculated on the basis of domestic cheese production in kilograms and assuming that 9.5 kg of fresh whole milk yields an average of 1.0 kg of cheese (following the procedure of McCracken 1971); and (6) average fresh milk yield in kilograms per cow per year. Copies of the resulting data table are available upon request.

A.5.2. *The Genetic Evolution of Human Epidermal Pigmentation*

In the course of analyzing the phenotypic diversity of adult lactose absorption in Chapter 5, the question arose, Is there other evidence that vitamin D deficiency has acted as a genetic selection pressure in human evolution? The answer is important not only for assessing the overall potential for natural selection caused by calcium deficiency diseases, but also to ascertain the geographic pattern of its magnitude. Specifically, we need to know if the selective effects of vitamin D deficiency covary with latitude in a pattern inverse to that of the UV-B gradient. As shown in Chapter 5, that gradient features high values across an equatorial "plateau" of latitudes out to 30 degrees north or south. From there, incident UV-B radiation drops sharply toward the poles, reaching by 67 degrees north or south only about one-fourth of the equatorial intensity. Given that UV-B (as explained in the chapter) is critical for the photosynthesis of vitamin D, is there an inverse pattern in the severity of calcium deficiency diseases?

Probably the best evidence in this regard comes from the study of geographic patterns in human skin pigmentation and specifically from the growing body of data in support of Frederick G. Murray's "vitamin D hypothesis." Writing in 1934, shortly after the first experimental verification of the antirachitic effect of vitamin D, Murray predicted that a general latitudinal gradient should exist in human skin color when the effect of "recent" (that is, post-1492) migrations was taken into account. His reasoning was that relatively low levels of ultraviolet radiation at high latitudes could induce vitamin D deficiency diseases, primarily rickets and osteomalacia, among peoples with heavily pigmented skin. These diseases would act as forces of genetic selection causing the progressive evolution of lighter pigmentation and enhanced UV absorption in northern and southern regions. The effect of the UV gradient by latitude, moreover, would be multiplied by a similar temperature gradient because "thermal protection" (clothing) would further reduce UV exposure. At the same time, Murray argued that genetic selection would favor dark pigmentation because of its protective value in regions of intense equatorial sun. He cautiously proposed sunlight-induced neurasthenia (nervous exhaustion) as one selection pressure, but concluded that "fuller explanation of negroid pigmentation may come with more extended knowledge of the metabolic effects of prolonged exposure to excessive sunlight." (p. 445.)

Today, there are four main sources of evidence in support of Murray's vitamin D hypothesis, and all four lend additional credibility to the calcium absorption proposal of Chapter 5 (for discussion of the evolution of skin color, see Fleure 1945; Blum 1969; Daniels, Post, and Johnson 1972; W. T. Hamilton 1973; Loomis 1967; P. Post 1975; Quevedo et al. 1975; Neer 1975; Roberts 1977; Quevedo, Fitzpatrick, and Jimbow 1985). The first source of evidence is indirect, consisting of experimental verification of Murray's assumptions concerning the optical and physiological properties of human skin. The principal pigment of the human skin, melanin, has been found to be particularly effective at absorbing UV-B wavelengths (see summaries in Urbach 1969a; Parrish et al. 1978). In a complex biochemical process, that compound is enzymatically synthesized from the amino acid tyrosine within special cells, called melanocytes, at the base of the epidermis. The melanocytes are themselves dispersed at varying densities in the skin, but they also contain fingerlike projections that distribute particles of melanin, called melanosomes, widely throughout the overlying skin cells. Consequently, the epidermis of individuals with relatively unmelanized or "white" skin transmits as much as double the amount of UV-B as does an equal thickness of epidermis from individuals of more heavily melanized or "black" pigmentation. This suggests that whites may require shorter exposure to UV-B than blacks, for example, in order to convert equal proportions of pro-D_3 to pre-D_3 in the first steps of vitamin D_3 synthesis. This prediction, consistent with Murray's hypothesis, has been confirmed experimentally by Holick, MacLaughlin, and Doppelt (1981), providing at least partial explanation for the high incidence of rickets among black infants compared to white infants in New York and other northern cities (for discussion, see Levinsohn 1927). It has also been shown that facultative melanin production in white skin (that is, suntanning or "seasonal melanization") is activated by the very same range of wavelengths that promote vitamin D synthesis. However, this happens only when light of those wavelengths is especially direct and intense, as during the summer months in temperate zones. These observations and others support Murray's assumption that "the pigmented skin offers added resistance to ultra violet rays, so that it takes a much greater intensity [or duration] of light on the pigmented, than on the unpigmented skin to produce the same antirachitic effect; that is to cure or prevent rickets." (p. 439.)

Second, there is also more direct evidence for Murray's proposition. In 1959, a global skin color map was published by Biasutti. It was based upon his compilation of subjective data for many populations of the world. Although occasionally criticized for the assumptions and generalizations it entails (see, for instance, Coon 1965: 211 ff.), the map has been widely accepted as a first approximation of the pre-1492 world distribution of skin pigmentation. As can be seen in Fig. 5.9, an enlargement of the portion of Biasutti's map that corresponds to Fig. 5.3, there is a striking correlation of latitude with subjective skin shade as measured by the von Luschan scale. The pattern in the Old World has been interpreted, reasonably I feel, as evidence for a progressive evolutionary depigmentation as our hominid ancestors, beginning with *Homo erectus*, migrated north and northeast out of Africa (see Loomis 1967). This interpretation fits with evidence that European Neanderthals at a later stage (from 100,000 to 35,000 B.P.) were afflicted with rickets in rough proportion to the latitude of their habitat. In fact, Ivanhoe (1970: 578) claims that every Neanderthal child's skull he has examined shows characteristics of vitamin D deficiency.

A similar but less pronounced gradient of skin color in the New World has been received as evidence of a later repigmentation after traversal of the Bering land bridge by waves of relatively light-skinned ancestors. The resultant global pattern, almost a "natural experiment" if the assumptions are warranted, provides notable confirmation of Murray's proposal. Indeed, the subjective evidence holds up well even in finer-scale analysis, such as that of Fig. 5.10. Based on Biasutti's 8-point condensation of the von Luschan scale (8 being darkest, 1 lightest), the plot shows a pronounced latitudinal gradient strikingly parallel to the independently derived UV-B curve presented in Fig. 5.8. Both plots are characterized by a low-latitude plateau of high values followed by a steep decline of decreasing slope as latitudes approach the polar circles. This correlation indicates that Murray's hypothesis accounts statistically for the greater share of variance in subjectively appraised skin pigment.

The third line of evidence for the vitamin D hypothesis confirms this trend by using more objective measures of skin pigmentation. The human geneticists D. F. Roberts and D. P. S. Kahlon (1976) have reviewed the data available from field studies in which pigmentation of the upper inner arm, an area affected little by facultative pigmentation, was measured through the use of a portable reflectance spectrophotometer. Earlier studies had established that the amount of melanin present in the basal layer of the epidermis is linearly related to the reciprocal of the reflectance value of red light of 685 nm in wavelength. Roberts and Kahlon therefore used 685 nm reflectance data from 77 samples (females and males) around the globe to calculate a correlation coefficient of 0.835 with latitude, a correlation that accounts statistically for about 70 percent of the variance in skin pigmentation (see also Tasa et al. 1985).[1] But this conclusion, too, holds on a smaller scale. Following the lead of Roberts and Kahlon, I compiled published reflectance data of the same wavelength from 26 populations within the subsample region of the lactose study (copies of the data tables and plots are available on re-

[1] When Roberts and Kahlon repeated the analysis for other wavelengths (425 to 655 nm) of test light, incorporating reflectance from other skin pigments such as hemoglobin and beta-carotene, the resulting correlations were even stronger. Stepwise regression calculations confirmed that these correlations were not explained by temperature or humidity, among other variables.

quest). Statistical analysis and scatterplots showed precisely the expected pattern: a plateau of low reflectances (meaning heavy pigmentation) extending from the equator to 20 degrees north or south latitude, followed by an almost linear increase in reflectance to peak values (light pigmentation) at 50 to 60 degrees north latitude. When the reflectance data were replotted as a function of incident ultraviolet light (UV-B), I found a strong and very linear association (with a Pearson's r of -0.92). Thus, in the words of Roberts and Kahlon (1976: 16), "there is no doubt about the dominating influence of the latitudinal associations."

The final source of evidence in favor of Murray's argument comes from the study of the harmful biological effects of excessive UV exposure. As noted above, Murray hypothesized that dark pigmentation conferred a selective advantage in equatorial areas through protection against strong UV radiation. But he was unable to specify the nature of those harmful effects. Considerably more is known today, substantiating Murray's proposition, but the matter is complex and not yet fully resolved. Recent reviews suggest three principal classes of harmful effects of UV light with actual or potential consequence to human survival and reproduction (for more information see Giese 1976; Harm 1980; Parrish et al. 1978; Urbach 1969a). The first concerns UV-induced genetic damage. Studies of irradiated mouse, hamster, and bacterial cells, for example, or of cell-free DNA extracts indicate that UV radiation can damage both DNA and its various enzymatic repair systems. The damage may take several forms—breaks in the phosphate-sugar chains of DNA, chemical bonding or "dimerization" of adjacent nucleic acids, or disruption of the AT/CG hydrogen bonds (see App. B.1)—but the effect is often DNA inactivation, cell death, and mutagenesis (see Deering 1962). According to Webb and Brown (1982: 992), "there is little doubt that similar DNA lesions are produced in human cells," where they may cause germ cell mutations (largely deleterious), aging, and/or cancers.

This leads us to the second class of documented harmful effects, namely, UV-induced carcinogenesis in human populations. There is now abundant evidence relating sunlight exposure to human skin cancers—basal cell epitheliomas, squamous cell carcinomas, and melanomas of several kinds (see summary in Harm 1980: 192 ff.). First, people with light skin are much more susceptible to skin cancer than people with dark; the incidence of malignant melanomas in the United States in recent years has averaged 4.1 to 4.4 per 100,000 whites compared to 0.6 to 0.7 per 100,000 blacks. Second, there is a higher incidence of skin cancer among people who spend a good portion of their daytime outdoors compared to those living mostly indoors. Third, skin cancers are more common in the sun-exposed parts of the body, particularly in the less pigmented areas normally exposed, or overexposed, while sunbathing (see Harm 1980: 194). Finally, and perhaps most significantly, both the frequency of skin cancer and its associated mortality among light-skinned persons increase exponentially with decreasing latitude (see also Crombie 1979b; McGovern 1977). In the United States, for example, annual melanoma rates vary sharply from lows in the northern states (Montana, Washington, and Wisconsin, for instance, have fewer than 1.2 cases among white males per 100,000 population per year) to highs in the southern states (Texas and Florida, by the same measure, have over 2.0 cases per year). The implication is that ultraviolet light, especially UV-B, is responsible. Blum (1961), among others, has suggested that UV-induced cancer and other skin changes usually occur too late in life to act as agents of genetic selection, but studies of light-skinned persons and pigmentless albinos in the tropics indicate otherwise (see, for example, McFadden 1961; Keeler 1970).

The third and final harmful effect now documented for UV exposure has been called "nutrient photolysis." Branda and Eaton (1978) have presented experimental evidence for the photodecomposition of a vitamin, folate, upon exposure to light of 360 nm in wavelength. (Folate and folic acid, which is related to it, are essential to cell growth and replication; their deficiency has been linked to maternal and newborn mortality, birth complications, and growth retardation.) In addition, they have pointed out that, because the earth's ozone layer acts as a short-wavelength radiation shield, there is much more incident radiation at the earth's surface at 360 nm than there is in the carcinogenic range (290–320 nm), and that melanized skin has an even greater relative absorbency advantage over "white" skin at that wavelength. They conclude (p. 625) that "prevention of ultraviolet photolysis of folate and other light-sensitive nutrients by dark skin may be sufficient explanation (by itself) for the maintenance of this characteristic in human groups indigenous to regions of intense solar radiation."

Other harmful effects of overexposure to ultraviolet light have been proposed—hypervitaminosis D, for instance (Loomis 1967)—but none have been so clearly established as these three. There may well remain some disagreement among investigators about which, if any, has been the predominant force behind equatorial melanization. But there is no reason to assume that they have acted separately in the course of human history, or that, given the drastic changes in clothing, housing, and diet in particular, their relative strengths have always been what they might be now. Instead, it appears likely that some combination of effects, probably shifting from place to place and from time to time, caused the genetic evolution of the skin color gradient proposed by Murray in 1934 and substantiated today.

In summary, we may safely conclude that ultraviolet radiation creates not one but two special biological problems for human skin. If too much UV is transmitted through the epidermis, then damage to DNA, to cell repair and regulation mechanisms, and to crucial metabolites can result. If too little UV is allowed through, insufficient vitamin D may be synthesized, a result that leads to rickets, osteomalacia, neuromuscular trauma, and psychological distress. If we assume both that constitutive skin color is genetically variable, and that ample genetic variability has been available during the evolutionary history of pigmentation, then by Murray's hypothesis genetic selection would favor a different compromise solution to these problems at every intensity of UV. Depigmentation would evolve as a function of latitude to the point where the reproductive fitness benefits of additional vitamin D synthesis would be balanced by the costs of additional UV-induced gene damage, skin cancer, and nutrient photolysis.

The expected result of these arguments, a geographic cline in the degree of skin pigmentation, is very much the general pattern we observe today among native populations. Murray's hypothesis may thus be said to account for a major portion of the variance in human skin pigmentation, somewhere in the range of 70 to 90 percent depending on the sampling techniques and measurements used. There are, of course, such exceptions as the relatively light pigmentation of equatorial peoples of insular Southeast Asia or the unexpectedly heavy pigmentation of populations of northern China. However, most of these exceptions can be explained by the history of population movements and by the duration of settled occupation (see the discussion of Brace and Montagu 1977). There may also have operated additional selection pressures, such as those proposed from frostbite and cold injury, infectious diseases, sexual selection, and possibly even from the visual properties of eye coloration (Daniels et al. 1972). These other forces would effectively contribute to the "residual variance" not explained by Murray's hypothesis. Nevertheless, the available evidence does suggest that vitamin D deficiency has acted as the most important selection pressure in the evolution of patterns in human pigmentation. There would seem to be ample potential there to propel the evolution of adult lactose absorption as well.

A.5.3. Evolutionary Transformations in the Indo-European Myth of Creation

In the course of the analysis of Chapter 5, it became important to investigate the cultural diversity in attitudes and beliefs toward dairying and milk drinking in the subsample populations. A historical assessment of that diversity was made possible by the comparative analysis of Indo-European creation myths. This appendix summarizes the specific myths and correspondences established by Bruce Lincoln (1981), together with my extensions and elaborations on the mythic role of bovines and dairying.

As noted in Chapter 6, the reconstructed "Proto-Indo-European" creation myth of Lincoln's analysis features a primordial sacrifice in which the figure *Manu ("man") kills his twin brother *Yemo ("twin"), and fashions the earth, the heavens, and human society from the dismembered body. According to Lincoln, as well as other analysts of the so-called genetic school of Indo-European myth, this basic mythical story was transformed over space and time through the dispersion of Indo-European peoples and their eventual differentiation into more recent and distinct descendant populations. The resulting correspondences both with the original proto-myth and with each other may be summarized as follows.

In old Indic texts to begin with, particularly the *Rig-Veda* (composed sometime between the sixteenth and twelfth centuries B.C.), six ancient gods play the part of *Manu. According to Lincoln and other scholars, this group of deities takes the place in Indian mythology of an older, otiose sky god named Dyaus who, in turn, is related to the ancestral Indo-European sovereign *Dieu-s. The six are led by three brothers, Varuna (god of truth and order), Mitra (guardian of bonds and social contracts), and Indra (god of war), to carry out the first sacrifice upon a giant primordial being named Puruṣa (derived from words for men, *pu-*, and bull, *vṛṣa-*).

> From that sacrifice, offered completely, the curdled butter was collected.
> It made the animals of the air, those of the forest, and those of the village.
>
> . . .
>
> The priest was his mouth, the warrior was made from his arms;
> His thighs were the commoner, and the untouchable was born from his feet.
> The moon was born of his mind: of his eye, the sun was born. . . .
>
> [from Lincoln 1981: 70–71]

The personages of first king, *Yemo, and first bovine, the ox, of the prototype myth were apparently fused over time in India into one sacrificial being. The dismemberment of this first being, literally an act of destruction, is allegorically the act of the world's creation.

In the myth, Puruṣa is the initial being and substance out of which the creation is fashioned—the sun, the moon, the earth, the earth's inhabitants, and even their preformed social organization. The first bovine–first man is literally raw material in the hands of the gods, a source of body parts that serve to form landscape, cosmos, and society. Curiously, the myth mentions a single dairy product among those parts, the "curdled butter" that is the source of all animals. The substance is poorly defined in the tale. It may, despite Puruṣa's otherwise masculine constitution, mean curdled milk, in reference to the role of bovines and other "animals of the village" in Indo-Iranian subsistence. (The word translated "butter" in the Old Testament similarly referred to curdled milk, as Michell 1957 [1940]: 62 has pointed out.) Alternatively, "curdled butter" may refer to blood or even semen to judge from the related Iranian text described below. Either way, the life-giving substance of the first bovine is symbolically represented in the myth as a dairy product. The creation is formed, in part, from processed milk.

In Iranian texts the basic plot reflects another set of modifications, some of which were introduced when the prophet Zarathustra (Zoroaster) officially condemned religious cattle sacrifice about 1000–900 B.C. Instead of a primordial sacrifice at the hands of gods as in India, a demonic figure named Ahriman appears in the *Greater Bundahhishn*, written about the ninth century A.D. Ahriman dismembers both the first mortal, Gayōmart, and what is called the "sole-created ox," at the beginning of the world.

> When the sole-created ox passed away, there where it sent forth its marrow, the fifty-five species of grain grew up, and the twelve species of healing plants. . . .
> The semen of the ox was borne up to the moon station. There they purified it, and he [Ohrmazd] created domestic animals of all species [from it]. First [he created] two bovines, one male and one female; then a pair of every species in the earth appeared in the Aryan home. . . . Because of the value of cattle, they were created twice—once in the [sole-created] ox, and once with the domestic animals of all species. [from Lincoln 1981: 72–73, brackets in the original]

From Gayōmart, in turn, were formed metals, minerals, the sun, and diverse populations of humanity.

Unlike the Indic tale, Iranian tradition does not fuse the first bovine with the *Yemo figure. Instead, it makes the two play complementary roles, and sacrifices both to make source material for the creation. Once again, the original ox is sacrificed, dismembered, and destroyed, but this time from the slaughter only two body parts are used. From the marrow of the ox are formed grains and medicinal plants; from the semen emerge other animal species and re-created bovines. It is important to note in both of these mythical traditions, the Indic and Iranian, that the sex of the first bovine is male (so that this detail of the prototype myth is preserved), and that its mythical role is that of source, or "seed," of all living things, particularly those valued in the local human economy.

These myths form a striking contrast when compared on these points to their more northerly Indo-European relatives. In the case of Italy, next, Lincoln builds a persuasive case that the founding myth of Rome is actually a "historicized reflex" of the original Proto-Indo-European tale. In that well-known story, the twins Romulus (supposedly a "back-formation" from "Roma") and Remus (derived from *Yemo, says Lincoln, with the *y* changed to *r* under the influence of "Roma" and "Romulus") are nurtured as infants by a she-wolf who appears to take the place of the Indo-Iranian male bovine. The body of the she-wolf does provide resources for the "creation," here transformed somewhat immodestly to the founding of Rome. But the resources are not plants, animals, minerals and the like; instead, the animal provides fresh milk to infants.

Later, when matured, Romulus and Remus become rivals for kingly power and for dominion over the growing new city.

> Then they turned from wrangling and angry words to bloodshed, and in the uproar, Remus was struck down. The more common [version] is that Remus leapt mockingly over the new walls of his brother, and therefore was slain by the enraged Romulus, who added, calling loudly with these words: "Thus hereafter to whoever leaps over my protective walls."
> Thus the sole power over the realm was Romulus, and the city thus founded was called by the name of its founder. [from Lincoln 1981: 85]

The similarity to the Indo-Iranian versions is thereby completed. The death of Remus, the twin, may be seen as the sacrifice that established the creation of Rome. Lincoln notes that even the motif of dismemberment is present in some versions of the tale.

For our purposes, the significant transformation manifest in the Roman myth concerns the nutritive symbolism of she-wolf and fresh milk. The myth makes clear not only that nonhuman milk sustained the very founders of Rome, but that Romulus and Remus grew thereby into tall, strong, and valiant warriors. Why is the mythical animal transformed to a she-wolf? Lincoln suggests that Roman national pride substituted the fierce and fearsome she-wolf for more docile bovines, particularly cows (see below), as a means of explaining Roman military prowess.

The same theme, nurturance of infant heroes, is also found in different guise in the creation mythology of ancient Greece—another variation, I submit, on the Proto-Indo-European myth of first sacrifice. In this version, the infant Zeus, later king of the gods, derived nurturance and strength from the milk of a female bovine named Amalthea during his early years in Crete. As befits a country where the milk of sheep and goats has long had special importance, Amalthea, the "first bovine," was a she-goat, esteemed by Zeus and later cast among the stars by him as Capricorn. Zeus, in turn, shared the position of *Manu with his two brothers, Hades (god of the underworld) and Poseidon (god of seas and waters), in a brotherhood that "recalls that of the Vedic male trinity—Mitra, Varuna, and Indra," as noted by Robert Graves (1960, 1: 43). At maturity, the brothers led their three sisters, other gods, and assorted demigods in a ten-year-long battle to overthrow their own tyrannical father, Cronos, king of the Titans. In the end, the gods emerged victorious over the Titans; Cronos, the *Yemo figure of the tale, was destroyed—flung, according to some accounts, into the abyss of Tartarus. Hamilton (1940: 67) notes that "the world, now cleared of the monsters, was ready for mankind." The gods then turned to creating humanity, delegating, by some accounts, the specifics to their allies the renegade Titans Prometheus and Epimetheus or, in other accounts, making mortals themselves from a sequence of metals (gold, silver, brass, and iron).

The mythical correspondences are several. Zeus, to begin with, can be related via the reconstructed Indo-European sky god, *Dieu-s, to the otiose Indic god, *Dyaus, and hence to the gods who slew Puruṣa. Zeus's role as "first priest" is shared with five siblings, just as in the Vedic version, and the sacrificial "first king" is again a giant. As in the Iranian tale, moreover, the creation of humanity follows from the destruction of the giant, and is related to precious metals. For our purposes, however, the apparent transformations of the ancestral myth are equally noteworthy. The "first bovine" is female, she is a goat, and she is not sacrificed as part of the creation. On the contrary, she is immortalized in the stars in appreciation for her role as nurturer and provider. The sacrifice itself is cast in the image of a great battle, one that, we are told, almost destroyed the universe, and the key antagonists are related as part of a mythical "first family." Some of these transformations are no doubt "historicized" in Greece, because of the mixing of Indo-European tradition with that of the original Old European culture in the area. But some of them, as described below, recur in other variants to the north.

In summary, then, the two southern European variants, the Greek and the Roman, suggest that we are dealing with a true case of cultural "descent with modification" from a common ancestor. However, the modifications of the prototype myth in this region emphasize the female form of the "original animal" and the value of her milk for infant gods and culture heroes. The role of the first animal (or first bovine) is one of direct nurturance through lactation, but no mention is made of adult consumption of that milk. In both cases it goes to infants. This point is underscored by the observation of Michell (1957 [1940]: 63) that "it is curious to note that there are few references in Greek, or indeed in any ancient literature, to the drinking of milk, except by infants. Plutarch [for example] . . . regards it as an unhealthy article of food [presumably for adults, the vast majority of whom would have been, and are, lactose malabsorbers]." One of the few exceptions, Michell notes, is the mythical giant Cyclops of the *Odyssey*, who milked sheep and goats and used half of the product for drinking and half for making cheese. Interestingly, some scholars suggest that the Grecian Cyclops actually symbolized to the Greeks a prototypical barbarian from the north.

Turning, next, to the northern branch of Indo-European mythology, we find still further transformations of importance. Possibly the most impressive of these is the origin myth from the body of northern mythology that is variously called Germanic, Icelandic, Old Norse, Scandinavian, and the like (see, for example, Davidson 1964; Crossley-Holland 1977). A lucid version of that myth was recorded by the Icelandic scholar, Snorri Sturluson, in his text known as the *Prose Edda* (about 1220 A.D.). The first section of Sturluson's text describes the legendary visit of one Gangleri, a prehistoric Swedish king in disguise, to Iceland to learn the secrets of the Aesir (the Norse gods). He is received by three knowledgeable beings called the High Ones, who recount for him a creation story of the world. They explain that the first of all beings, formed from the melting ice, was a giant by the name of Ýmir (derived from *Yemo). From the ooze of Ýmir's sweat, Gangleri is told, grew the first man and woman; from his two legs appeared a large and unruly family of frost giants.

> Then Gangleri said, "Where did Ýmir dwell, and what did he live on?" [High One said:] "Thereafter, when the frost fell, there was a cow, who was called Auðhumla, and four streams of milk ran from her [teats], and she fed Ýmir."
>
> Then Gangleri said, "On what did the cow feed?" High One said, "She licked frost stones which were salty and the first day on which she licked the stone a man's hair, the next day a man's head, and on the third day all of the man was there: he was named Buri. He was fair in appearance [light pigmentation], tall and mighty. He begat a son, then, who was called Bǫr. That

one took himself a wife who was called Besla, the daughter of the giant Bǫlthorn, and they had three sons. One was called Óðinn [Odin], the next Vili, and the third Ve. [from Lincoln 1981: 73–74]

Just as in the Grecian myth, these three sons were the first gods; indeed, Odin was later father to Thor. They grew to hate and despise the menacing frost giants, and in the end they attacked and killed the original giant, Ýmir. As in the other myths, the three took his corpse, according to High One, "'and made the earth of him: of his blood, the sea and waters; of his flesh, the earth was made; and mountains of bones. They made rocks and stones of teeth and jawbones and of the bones which were broken. . . . And they took up his skull, and made heaven [the sky] of it, and set it up over the earth with its four corners, and under each corner they set a dwarf. These were called East, West, North, and South.'" (from Lincoln 1981: 74.) The central theme is immediately recognizable: Ýmir in the role of *Yemo is sacrificed by Bǫr's sons, the *Manu, and from the dismembered body is created the world. The first bovine, once again, is not sacrificed; she lives on as "the cow of abundance . . . nurse and mother of heroes." (Gubernatis 1872: 221.) There is certainly a correspondence to be made here between Auðhumla and Amalthea, and probably between both of those and a celestial cow in Vedic, Slavic, and Iranian myth whose name, in translation, is Aurora. However, the noteworthy features here are (1) that Auðhumla, like Amalthea but unlike Aurora, is elevated to the role of first animal—first bovine in the world; (2) that she provided great quantities of milk (four streams) to the very first being, a giant no less; and (3) that she is the mythical mother, in a sense, to both the gods and giants. For his part, Ýmir is from the first an adult milk drinker, a tremendous giant, and without doubt a lactose absorber! In these transformed myths of the north, the theme of adult milk consumption is given central importance, providing both legitimacy and precedent for the practice among mortals.

Fresh cow milk is also valued for adult consumption in the Celtic myths handed down from prehistoric Gauls, Britons, and Gaels. Here Lincoln pursues the Proto-Indo-European correspondences to an Irish tale, "The Cattle Raid of Cooley," in which the Irish landscape is created from the slaying and dismemberment of one bull, the fabled Findbennach Aí, by another, Donn Cúailnge, in a heroic battle. In this version, the first bovines are both male and there is little discussion of fresh milk, but, as Lincoln notes (p. 92), the myth has been "relegated to a position as prologue and postscript to [a greater] epic tale of battle and adventure."

Both the correspondences and the role of female bovines in ancient Ireland are, I feel, more clearly illustrated by versions of the myth that Squire (1905: 233) has called "the central incident of Gaelic mythology, the mysterious birth of the sungod from demoniac parentage, and his eventual slaying of his grandfather when he came to full age." According to both early texts and more recent peasant folklore, Lugh, the sun-god, slays Balor, his grandfather and king of the menacing Fomors, in a fight over a legendary gray cow that could fill twenty barrels at a single milking.[2] In this tale, Balor, a giant, plays the Indo-European mythological role of "first king." He is said to be the son of one Buarainech, the "cow-faced" (p. 48)—a name possibly derived from *Yemo—much as the Norse giant Bolthorn was descended

[2] I thank Moses Moon (pers. comm.) for drawing my attention to the Irish saga of Balor and his legendary cow. I thank also student assistant M.H. for tracking down several extant variants of the tale, the longest of which is given in Squire (1905: 78–118).

from Ýmir. Balor, moreover, was essentially a cyclops figure, for "though he had two eyes, one was always kept shut, for it was so venomous that it slew anyone on whom its look fell." (pp. 48–49.) Balor's daughter, in turn, married the son of the ancient god of health and medicine and begat Lugh (compare the Norse version, in which Bolthorn's daughter married the son of the first man, Bor, and begat Odin and his two brothers). The correspondence of Lugh and Odin is further suggested (p. 85) by Lugh's alternative name Ioldanach, or "Master of all Arts."

Lugh, then, in the Gaelic tale goes on to play the part of the "first priest," *Manu; indeed, in some versions of the myth, Lugh is raised by a foster father named Manannan. Zeus, it will be remembered, destroyed Cronos, his father, and Odin killed Ýmir, effectively his great-grandfather. Lugh slays his grandfather, the giant Balor, with a hot firebrand or fiery magic stone delivered directly into the "evil eye." In one version, the slaying takes place at the end of an epic battle between the gods and the Fomor giants (which also recalls the Greek tale), and in the preparations for that battle the sorcerers and cupbearers promise to work magic upon the landscape of Ireland, altering its major mountains, streams, and lakes.

I submit that this myth, too, represents an evolutionary transformation of the original Proto-Indo-European creation myth. There are, on the one hand, too many correspondences with other geographic variants from as far away as India and Iran to claim separate and independent origins for the tradition. On the other hand, the variation presented here includes important transformations, particularly concerning bovines. It should be noted that the "first bovine," here Balor's gray cow, is valued—indeed fought over—for her productive potential and nurturance. A symbol as well as a productive resource, her loss or theft actually motivates the sacrificial killing in some of the tales. What is so valued, the myths make clear, is fresh or "new" milk, the base ingredient of porridge throughout the land and what is called "the main source of food." (Squire 1905: 79.) Moreover, the myths leave little doubt that this product is fit for adult consumption. At one point Dagda, the second greatest of the Gaelic gods, who is at once "gray-headed," "a sturdy porridge eater," and a "formidable fighter," gains time in the battle with the Fomors by consuming singlehandedly a porridge of "fourscore gallons of new milk with meal and bacon in proportion," to which were also added whole carcasses of goats, sheep, and pigs (pp. 54, 107).

CHAPTER 6

A.6.1. Incest Myths in the Sixty Cultures Sample

At an early stage of research on incest taboos, I was impressed by Segner's (1968: 37) claim that "almost one-third of the [31] cultures examined possessed myths in which incest results in the birth of inferior offspring." Upon examination of Segner's methods, however, I found suspiciously little description of procedures used to generate the study's "cross-cultural sample" (see 1968: 30); in addition, I found that coding procedures allowed one to treat as myth *any* folk belief "in which it was clearly stated that incest leads to degeneration of the stock." (p. 31.) Thus, before citing this work as solid support for an inbreeding theory of incest taboos, I felt it important to check its findings against a genuine world probability sample. After considering various options, I chose the "Sixty Cultures" collection (Lagacé 1977) in order to take full advantage of the Human Relations Area Files (HRAF).

In this effort, I was fortunate to have the dedicated assistance of five Stanford undergraduate students (F.H., D.G., J.B., P.S., and C.S.), all either anthropology or human biology majors, who together spent over 2,500 hours in the course of two years studying both the myths and incest taboos of the Sixty Cultures populations (listed, for example, in Table A.6.1). This study of incest myths was conducted in two phases. In the first phase, the students read all material under category 773, "Mythology," in the HRAF files for all of the Sixty Cultures populations in a given world area. They then transcribed and coded any material pertaining to incest in the myths of each population. At the end of this first full reading, the students exchanged notebooks and double-checked each other's codes and conclusions, returning to HRAF to resolve discrepancies.

Second, one student (D.G.) undertook the heroic task of rereading all the HRAF files and all the coding notebooks. Her purpose was both to correct any inconsistencies in the coding procedures of the other students and to carry out a more detailed coding of the incest taboos for all 60 populations (see section A.6.2). Once this review was completed, the same student conducted an additional search for each population still lacking one or more incest myths. Intentionally limited to three hours of effort per case, this search was carried out with the ethnographic literature in the Stanford library system. Student efforts in this second phase spanned the course of a full academic year.

Finally, my own efforts went into rechecking all the notes and decisions made by all the coders. Given this system of checks and cross-checks, I believe our results, summarized in the penultimate section of Chapter 6 under the heading "The 'incest myth' hypothesis," are about as reliable as can be obtained for this kind of effort. A table summarizing all the incest myths we found is available upon request.

A.6.2. *Incest Taboos in the Sixty Cultures Sample*

One of the challenges facing cross-cultural research on incest taboos is how to measure existing variation in the "extent," or range, of different prohibitions. For the test of optimal outbreeding theory described in Chapter 6, I devised a set of related measures of extent, each based on the "coefficient of relationship," r, which represents the average proportion of all genes that are identical by descent in two relatives (see Fig. 6.4 for sample values of r). These measures are summarized in Table A.6.1 for all populations in the Sixty Cultures sample. The two most important measures of extent, r_s and r_m, refer to the r value of the most distant consanguineous relative, not including lineage mates, with whom sex or marriage, respectively, is forbidden. The definition includes two deliberate simplifications: first, it includes only consanguineal relatives and not in-laws, fictive kin, foster children, and the like, simply because the ethnographic record is too fragmentary in its coverage of incest rules for these kinds of relatives; second, I have deliberately excluded lineage mates on the grounds that rules of lineage exogamy—that is, rules prohibiting marriage to members of one's entire descent group—are distinct in both theory and practice from incest taboos (see discussion in Fox 1983). In the vast majority of populations there are categories of kin outside one's descent group to whom the local incest prohibition applies; the goal of the analysis here is to explain interpopulational variation in the range of consanguines included in those categories.

In many instances, I found it possible to estimate r_s directly from ethnographic descriptions of prohibited sexual partners. In other cases, the literature spoke of incest prohibitions only in terms of prohibited marriages, requiring me to use r_m

TABLE A.6.1

Key Features of the Incest Taboos in the "Sixty Cultures" Sample

Population	Descent system	Exogamous lineages	Sex regulation[a] $s = m$	Sex regulation[a] r_s	Marriage regulation[b] r_m	r_{dg}	r_{mat}	r_{pat}	Emotional intensity[c]	Consequence of incest — Social sanction	Consequence of incest — Supernatural sanction	Consequence of incest — Inbreeding depression[d]
Asia												
1. Korea	Patri.	Fa.	Yes	.062	.062	.001	.062	.062		Death		MD + I
2. Taiwan Hokkien	Patri.	Fa.		[.250]	.250	.001	.250	(.250)		Ostra.		MD
3. Central Thai	Bilat.	—	No	[.250]	.250	.250	(.250)	(.250)				
4. Garo	Matri.	Mo.		.500	.500	.001	(.250)	.500	"Social sin"	Death	Various	
5. Khasi	Matri.	Mo.		[.250]	.250	.001	(.250)	.250	"Worst sin"	Ostra.		I
6. Santal	Patri.	Fa.	Yes	.125	.125	.001	.125	.125	"Detested"	Ostra.		
7. Sinhalese	Bilat.	—	Yes	.250	.250	.250	(.250)	.125	"Scandalous"	Ostra.	Disease	
8. Andamanese	Bilat.	—	Yes	.001	.001	.001	.001	.001	"Objection-able"	Ostra.		
Europe												
9. Serbs	Patri.	Fa.	Yes	.125	.125	.001	.125	.125	"Sinful"			
10. Lapps	Bilat.	—	No	.250	.125	.125	.125	.125				MD
11. Highland Scots	Patri.	None		[.250]	.250	.250	.250	.250				PD
Africa												
12. Dogon	Patri.	Fa.	Yes	.125	.125	.001	.125	.125	"Scandalous"	Ostra.		I (PD)
13. Ashanti	Double	Mo. + Fa.	Yes	.250	.250	.001	(.250)	(.250)	"Evokes horror"	Death	Chaos	I
14. Tiv	Patri.	Fa.	No	.062	.062	.001	.062	.062				PD
15. Ganda	Patri.	Mo. + Fa.	Yes	[.125]	(.125)	.001	(.125)	(.125)	"Real horror"	Death	Anger	
16. Masai	Patri.	Mo. + Fa.	Yes	.031	.031	.001	.031	.008		Beating		
17. Mbuti	Bilat.	—	Yes	.125	.125	.125	.125	.125		Ostra.		
18. Azande	Patri.	Mo. + Fa.	Yes	.125	.125	.001	.125	.125			Various	
19. Bemba	Matri.	Mo. + Fa.		[.250]	.250	.001	(.250)	.125		Death	Disease	(PD)
20. Lozi	Ambil.	Mo. + Fa.		[.031]	.031	.031	.031	.031				
Middle East												
21. Kurd	Bilat.	—		[.250]	.250	.250	.250	.250				
22. Somali	Patri.	Fa.	No	.250	.031	.001	.031	.031	"Fear"			(PD)
23. Amhara	Bilat.	—		[.004]	.004	.004	.004	.004				
24. Hausa	Patri.	(Fa.)[e]	Yes	.250	.250	(.001)	.250	(.250)				

Population	Descent system	Exogamous lineages	Sex regulation[a]: s = m	Sex regulation[a]: r_s	Marriage regulation[b]: r_m	Marriage regulation[b]: r_{dg}	Marriage regulation[b]: r_{mat}	Marriage regulation[b]: r_{pat}	Emotional intensity[c]	Consequence of incest: Social sanction	Consequence of incest: Supernatural sanction	Consequence of incest: Inbreeding depression[d]
25. Kanuri	Bilat.	—		[.250]	.250	.125	.125	.250				
26. Wolof	Double	—		[.125]	.125	.125	.125	.125				
27. Libyan Bedouin	Patri.	(Fa.)[e]										
28. Shluh	Patri.	Fa.		[.250]	.250	(.001)	.250	(.250)	"Dangerous"	Death		(PD)
North America												
29. Tlingit	Matri.	Mo.		[.500]	.500	.001	(.250)	.500		Death		PD
30. Copper Eskimo	Bilat.	—										
31. Blackfoot	Bilat.	—		[.125]	.125	.125	.125	.125				
32. Ojibwa	Patri.	Fa.	Yes	[.031]	.031	.031	.031	.031	"Shocking"	Death		P + MD
33. Iroquois	Matri.	Mo.		.125	.125	.001	.125	.125	"Ridiculed"			P + MD
34. Pawnee	Matri.	Mo.	Yes	.125	.125	.001	.125	.125				
35. Klamath	Bilat.	—		[.001]	.001	.001	.001	.001				
36. Hopi	Matri.	Mo. + Fa.	No	.500	.125	.001	.001	.125	"Special anger"			
37. Tarahumara	Bilat.	—	Yes	.125	.125	.125	.125	.125		Ostra.		PD + I
38. Tzeltal	Patri.	Fa.		[.250]	.250	.001	.125	.250			Vague	
Oceania												
39. Ifugao	Bilat.	—		[.008]	.008	.008	.008	.008	"Horror"			
40. Iban	Bilat.	—	Yes	.250	.250	.250	.250	.250	"Moral shock"	Death	Various	
41. Toradja	Bilat.	—	Yes	.062	.062	.062	.062	.062	"Grave"	Death	Various	P + MD + I
42. Aranda	Double	Mo. + Fa.	(Yes)	.031	.031	.031	.031	.031	"Heinous"	Death		I
43. Kapauku	Patri.	Fa.	Yes	[.062]	.062	.001	.062	.062	"Horror"	Death	Death	
44. Trobrianders	Matri.	Mo.	Yes	.500	.500	.001	.125	.500	"Horror"	Death		
45. Lau Fijians	Patri.	Fa.	Yes	.250	.250	.001	.125	(.250)		Ostra.	Disease	
46. Trukese	Matri.	Mo. + Fa.	Yes	.125	.125	.001	.125	.125	"Reprehensible"	Death		
47. Tikopia	Patri.	None	Yes	.125	.125	.125	.125	.125	"Disgust"	Ostra.		P + MD + I
Russia												
48. Yakut	Patri.	Fa.		[.500]	.500	.001	.500	(.250)				PD
49. Chukchee	Bilat.	—		[.250]	.250	.250	.250	.250				
South America												
50. Kuna	Bilat.	—		[.125]	.125	.125	.125	.125			Purgatory	
51. Cagaba	Bilat.	—	Yes	.125	.125	.125	.125	.125	"Sinful"	Expia.	Various	I (MD)

TABLE A.6.1 (*continued*)

Population	Descent system	Exogamous lineages	Sex regulation[a] s = m	Sex regulation[a] r_s	Marriage regulation[b] r_m	Marriage regulation[b] r_{dg}	Marriage regulation[b] r_{mat}	Marriage regulation[b] r_{pat}	Emotional intensity[c]	Consequence of incest Social sanction	Consequence of incest Supernatural sanction	Consequence of incest Inbreeding depression[d]
52. Aymara	Patri.	Fa.		[.031]	.031	.001	.031	.031	"Sorrowful"			M + PD
53. Ona	Bilat.	—		[.008]	.008	.008	.008	.008	"Abhorrence"			
54. Mataco	Bilat.	—	Yes	.125	.125	.001	.125	.125	"Foolish"			
55. Guarani	Bilat.	—		[.125]	.125	.125	.125	.125			Death	
56. Bahia Brazilians	(Bilat.)	—		[.500]	.500	.500	.500	.500				
57. Bororo	Matri.	Mo.	No	.500	.500	.001	(.250)	.500	"Great crime"	Gang rape		
58. Yanomamo	Patri.	Fa.	Yes	.250	.250	.001	.125	(.250)	"Shameful"	Ostra.	Loss of soul	I + PD
59. Tucano	Patri.	Fa.	Yes	.250	.250	.001	.250	(.250)	"Horror"	Death	Disease or death	I + PD
60. Bush Negroes	Matri.	Mo. + Fa.		[.250]	.250	.001	(.250)	.125	"Greatest sin"	Labor		
TOTALS	23 Patri. 11 Matri. 22 Bilat. 3 Double 1 Ambil.		26 Yes 6 No							15 Death 10 Ostra. 4 Other	16	20

SOURCE: Data from Human Relations Area Files.

NOTE: Parentheses indicate uncertainty resulting from ambiguous or unclear reporting in the literature. Entries in parentheses are not included in column totals.

[a] These columns refer to rules regulating sexual activity. The column labeled $s = m$ indicates whether or not, according to HRAF sources, the rules regulating sex are congruent with the rules regulating marriage. The values in the column labeled r_s represent the coefficient of relationship, r, corresponding to the most distant consanguineous relative included in the taboo on sex (aside from lineage mates treated separately). Square brackets indicate that r_m values from column 6 have also been used for r_s because separate information on sexual taboos is not contained in the available literature.

[b] These columns refer to rules regulating marriage. The first, r_m, designates the higher r value of the columns r_{mat} and r_{pat}; it indicates that at least one relative of the next lower r value is permitted as a marriage partner. The second, r_{dg}, designates the r value of the most distant member of an ego's descent group to be included in rules governing descent group exogamy (0.001 is used for prohibitions that apply to all descent group members). Finally, r_{mat} and r_{pat} respectively designate the r values of the most distant matrilateral and patrilateral relatives that are prohibited from marriage, setting aside descent group members.

[c] Entries on emotional intensity are taken directly from ethnographers' descriptions of the strongest affective response of population members to the idea of incest. As Murdock (1949) pointed out, this response is generally most intense in the case of nuclear-family incest and tends to diminish rapidly as a function of the genealogical distance between participants.

[d] Entries in this column indicate that, according to HRAF sources, members of the given population recognize physical defects, PD; mental defects, MD; or infertility or fertility impairment, I, as consequences of inbreeding.

[e] Because references are vague on this subject, I have assumed that the exogamous lineage is that of the father.

in the place of r_s (as indicated by brackets around r_s entries in Table A.6.1). In still other cases, sex and marriage prohibitions were said to be congruent (as indicated by a "Yes" in column 4 of the table), allowing me to use the same value for both measures. Values of r_m were estimated in a similar manner. First, r_{pat} and r_{mat} were defined as the r values of the most distant patrilateral and matrilateral relatives prohibited as marriage partners within a given society, setting aside ego's own descent group members. These values were estimated directly from the literature in HRAF. Second, I set r_m equal to the higher of the two (i.e., to the r value of the closer relative); r_m therefore indicates that at least one relative of the next lower r value is a permitted marriage partner. To facilitate the distinction of incest prohibitions from lineage exogamy, I also coded the measure r_{dg} as the r value of the most distant relative of ego's descent group to be excluded from marriage by the rules of exogamy. In most cases, ethnographers reported that marriage was prohibited among *all* members of a given patrilineage or matrilineage, in which case I entered the value $r_{dg} = 0.001$ and identified (in column 3) the exogamous lineage ("Mother's," "Father's," or "Both").

In addition to measures of extent, Table A.6.1 also compiles information about the local emotional reaction to incest as described in the literature, and about the reported consequences of taboo violations, including social sanctions, supernatural sanctions, and recognized inbreeding depression. These entries were also gleaned from the information in HRAF following the same general procedure outlined in App. A.6.1, except that HRAF was here the exclusive source of information (i.e., we conducted no supplemental library search), and all of the following HRAF code categories were scrutinized by student researchers:

143 Genetics	732 Defectives
582 Regulation of Marriage	826 Ethnoanatomy
588 Irregular Unions	834 General Sex Restrictions
593 Family Relationships	835 Kinship Regulation of Sex
684 Sex and Marital Offenses	837 Ethnophysiology

The same team of student assistants helped with this task, one of whom (D.G.) also helped with the coding of r_s and r_m. As before, my own role was to supervise the work of the team and then to recheck all coded information. Although every effort has been made to ensure the accuracy of Table A.6.1, any additions and corrections would be greatly appreciated.

As part of the same effort, I also asked the students to transcribe from HRAF all information on community endogamy, agamy, or exogamy for each population and then to assign a single code number to each (where 1 = local endogamy, 2 = local agamy, and 3 = local exogamy). Where possible, these codes were checked against Murdock's (1967) data for "community organization" by means of Ember's (1975: 259) procedure, which recodes column 19 of the *Ethnographic Atlas*. (The procedure takes Murdock's "C," "E," and "T" to mean local exogamy; "A" and "S" to mean local agamy; and "D" to mean local endogamy.) As before, my role was to recheck the codes and comparisons, and then to resolve any remaining discrepancies. These data, too, are available on request.

A.6.3. Additional Evidence for Recognition and Interpretation

In Chapter 6, under "An Optimal Outbreeding Theory of Incest Taboos," I describe two hypotheses about the role of human cognition in the cultural evolution of incest taboos. First, in the "recognition hypothesis," I propose that cultural beliefs about incest generally reflect a recognition of the major reproductive costs of inbreeding and outbreeding in local populations. Second, in the "interpretation hypothesis," I suggest that people also elaborate an appropriate cultural interpretation of the inbreeding costs they experience, where "appropriate" denotes both "locally meaningful" and "negatively valued." Also in Chapter 6, I summarize HRAF data for populations in the Sixty Cultures sample that support these hypotheses. Here let me summarize additional evidence from other populations, most of which I came across while researching the case studies for the other chapters.

Consider, first, the evidence for recognition within the folk beliefs of the Tibetan-speaking Nyinba of Chapter 2, who

> see themselves as linked to their fathers through a heredity of bone. . . . It is the belief in the common physical makeup of agnates [patrilineal relatives] that explains proscriptions on clan endogamy. Although the community has not had to deal with any proven case of incest within living memory, it is said that violations of this rule would be cause for serious punishment. Incest is thought to evoke mystical sanctions as well: the transgressors are left marked by a condition of cleft bones observable in their skeleton after death, and *their children born malformed, stillborn or so sickly as to be unable to survive past infancy.* [Levine 1981b: 56–57, emphasis added]

Similarly, among the Tibetan-speaking Lepchas of Sikkim incest is called "horrifying." The term applies to "any sexual connection with blood relations for nine generations on the father's side and four on the mother's side," except among children under the age of puberty. Should offspring result from such a union, it is said, "they would be allowed to live, but they would either be of an evil mind or idiots, and would be short-lived." (Gorer 1967 [1938]: 151.) In addition, Lepcha mythology features a creation story in which numerous fearsome monsters are born to an original brother-sister union.

Another example comes from a population included in the analysis of Chapter 3, the Kwa-speaking Yoruba of southern Nigeria. Every summer, the Yoruba honor the god Obatala as part of their annual New Yam Festival.

> Obatala, known also as Orisa-nla, Orisala, Ogiyan, and, in some places, Olufon, is called by Idowu [1963] "the arch-divinity" of Yorubaland. *If displeased by the breaking of some taboo, he has the power to mold the human foetus in ways that cause a defective child to be born.* Hunchbacks, cripples, albinos, and deaf-mutes are thought to have been shaped by Obatala. Not infrequently Obatala is appealed to when a woman has been unable to give birth to a child. [Simpson 1964: 323, emphasis added; see also Awolalu 1979: 21ff.]

Simpson's informants (pers. comm., 1983) did not specifically mention incest or exogamy as the taboos whose breaking displeases Obatala. That remains a reasonable inference, however, particularly given the special abhorrence of incest among the Yoruba, and also the fact that "Orisa-nla represents . . . the idea of ritual and ethical purity, and therefore the demands and sanctions of high morality." (Idowu 1963: 73.) Ellis (1894: 39) points out that "albinoism and congenital deformities are regarded as his handiwork." These powers must be especially impressive in a population where deliberate steps are taken each generation to ensure the "soundness of stock" of potential marriage partners (see Fadipe 1970: 70–71).

A third example came to light in the course of my research on Amazonian headhunting for Chapter 7. Among the fabled headhunters of the region are the Shuar or Jivaro (Jibaro) of eastern Ecuador, a non-Tupí-speaking population. The Shuar

> are firmly convinced that children who are born deformed or defective in any way have been begotten by demoniacal operation [i.e., by spirits]. Such a child is called *nētsi*, *pasúna*, "deformed," "monstrous," or *iguánchi uchi*[,] "the son of a demon." . . . Most generally the birth of a *nētsi*, *pasúna*, or *iguánchi uchi* follows as the consequence of unlawful marriage, especially a marriage within the forbidden degrees of relationship, when brother and sister, or cousins on the male side marry, or when a man marries his niece or a woman her nephew. *Such marriages are therefore looked upon with horror and strictly prohibited by Jibaro custom.* [Karsten 1935: 222, emphasis added]

Unlike the Tikopia described in Chapter 6, however, the Shuar do not leave punishment to the spirits alone: "Incest and any illicit sexual intercourse is regarded with the greatest horror and severely punished by cruel ill-treatment, sometimes even by both parties being put to death." (p. 184.)

A fourth example turned up during the literature search for incest myths described in section A.6.1. It concerns the people of Ulithi, an atoll in the Caroline Islands of Micronesia, who believe that "the child of an incestuous marriage will be stupid, and its toes may be joined together, its fingers twisted or bent, and its buttocks almost missing." As in Tikopia, locals regard this as "the work of indignant family ghosts, who in this manner show their disapproval of the forbidden union." (Lessa 1961: 50; see also Monberg 1976: 250–51 for a report of similar beliefs among the Bellona Islanders of Melanesia.) Because Ulithians and their neighbors on Truk (population number 46 in Table A.6.1) are closely related by descent, it seems likely that a similar interpretation exists among the Trukese; however, I was unable to confirm this using HRAF and have thus not included Trukese in the tallies of Tables 6.5 and A.6.1.

Fifth and finally, there is the case of the Yapese, neighbors to the Ulithians but from a different language family, who regard incestuous behavior as tantamount to sexual cannibalism, "a kind of survival through self-consumption." (Labby 1976: 179.) On the one hand, sexual relations within the basic residential unit, or "land-estate," were punished by "ancestral ghosts who lived on the land and watched over it," punishing transgressors with sickness, injury, or calamity (pp. 172–73). On the other hand, sexual relations within the matrilineal clan were said to "result in the extinction of that clan. People were not exactly sure how or when it would 'die out' . . . but it was felt generally that the women of the clan would cease to become pregnant or would bear only sickly or weak children." (p. 172.) These consequences were further related to the view that since a child was, in effect, "planted by [its father] on the woman's reproductive 'land,'" the child belonged to the mother's clan as "an extension of [the clan's] natural fertility." (p. 174.) Sex within the clan was thus viewed as

> an attempt to produce from the "land," from "nature," alone, without its being culturally labored upon [by another clan]. It followed that anything that grew from this attempt would have grown "wildly," would lack the transforming input of labor and thus might be sickly and weak. . . . [Thus,

just as] cannibals appear to survive by eating off themselves, by self-consumption, rather than by working the land and receiving food from it in exchange, so incest attempts to perpetuate the clan [or the land-estate] by sexual self-consumption rather than through the cultural exchange with other groups. [Labby 1976: 174]

This is a striking example of appropriate interpretation. The case emphasizes that the "attribution hypothesis" of Roger Burton (1973; discussed in Chapter 6) simply does not allow a wide enough range of local meanings to be attached to the costs of inbreeding.

For additional examples of recognition and interpretation, see Devereux (1939: 527) on the Mojave Indians; Kaberry (1969: 179) on the Nso of Western Cameroon; Krige (1936: 224) on the Zulu of South Africa; Hutton (1921; 134) on the Sema Nagas of northeast India; and Jochelson (1926: 80) on the Yukaghir of Siberia, not to mention Westermarck (1922 [1891], 2: ch. 20) for a compilation of examples (quoted, in part, in Chapter 6 of this book).

CHAPTER 7

A.7.1. A Model for the Evolution of Adaptive Intergroup Aggression

Some years back, while working on the "early coevolution model" described in Chapter 4, I was attracted to the study of human intergroup aggression because of its inherent challenge to my arguments. I felt that "group-level aggression, in the form of warfare, is particularly appropriate for [evolutionary] analysis because it is often considered dysfunctional from a participant's point of view. If it can be shown that warfare generally has net fitness benefits for the individuals involved, despite its high phenotypic costs, then other less costly forms of human social behavior may also prove to be adaptive in this way." (Durham 1976a: 388.) Although my efforts fell well short of this goal (for the very good reason, I now realize, that belligerence is often imposed), I was able to formulate a model for the evolution of adaptive intergroup aggression under conditions of resource competition. The model is helpful for understanding why the headhunting of the Mundurucú, described in Chapter 7, fails to qualify as a case of opposition, and so I include a brief description of it here. For further discussion and elaboration, see Durham (1976a, 1976b) and Ruse (1979: ch. 8).

Assumptions. The model begins with four assumptions. First, let us assume a hypothetical breeding population or deme, A, that is subdivided into smaller social units, A_1, A_2, A_3, etc., like villages or camps, within which individuals participate in some form of collective resource procurement and distribution. Second, let us also assume that a given "limiting," or scarce, resource constrains the average reproductive success of the members of each of the social groups within the deme. In other words, we will assume that individuals could, on average, leave behind greater numbers of surviving descendants if they could also sustain a greater per capita yield of the limiting resource. It is important to note that this assumption does *not* require abject poverty in the population nor yet a stark physiological limitation of human fertility. Surely it is more common in human populations for reproductive success to be constrained by culturally defined standards of resource availability, standards with thresholds that stand well above those defined by viability alone (in an agricultural population, for example, the marriageability of young men might depend on their acquiring a land base large enough to support a family). For simplicity, let us assume that the average number of surviving decendants, S, of individuals in A varies in a sigmoidal, or S-shaped, manner with the average per capita yield, Y_c, of the limiting resource. In other words, we will assume that S grows relatively rapidly between two thresholds of Y_c: a lower threshold, L, required for nonzero reproductive success, and an upper threshold, U, where some other resource or constraint becomes limiting.

Third, for simplicity, let us also assume a narrow social distribution of the limiting resource within each social group, narrow enough for all members to be similarly affected by gains and losses in the collective resource supply. While surely not valid in complex, stratified societies, a narrow distribution of resources characterizes some (though not all) of the "relatively small, stateless societies traditionally studied by anthropologists." (Vayda 1968: 86.) Fourth and finally, let us assume that a number of social groups, B_1, B_2, B_3, etc., of at least one other deme, B, consume the same limiting resource in an amount that would substantially reduce A's supply were B to harvest from the same source. In other words, we assume there is "niche overlap," or potential for resource competition, between the social groups of A and B (on niche overlap, see Arthur 1987).

Conditions favoring aggression. Consider, now, the hypothetical situation where the resources available to a given group, A_1, are reduced by the activities of a neighboring group from the other deme, B_1. This could happen if B_1 were to intrude upon A_1's "home range" (that is, its normal resource acquisition space) and harvest resources there; or it could happen through harvest without intrusion if the resource were highly mobile and therefore part of the supply available to A_1. Either way, the effect of B_1's activity will be to reduce the average per capita yield rate within A_1 from its precompetition level, $Y_c = a$, to a new and lower value, $Y_c = b$ (where $L < b < a < U$). But this lower resource yield threatens to reduce, or actually reduces, the average reproductive success in A_1 from an earlier level S_a to a corresponding level S_b (according to the sigmoidal curve relating S to Y_c). Moreover, because we have assumed a narrow distribution of yield within A_1, the competition from B_1 translates into a roughly equivalent loss of S for each and every member of A_1.

Provided that no alternative supply of the resource is available, this threat of reduced S places the members of A_1 in a position to derive individual-level benefits from aggressive behavior that reduces their loss of resource to B_1. In effect, the loss in Y_c suffered by members of A_1 constitutes a potential benefit (equal to $S_a - S_b$) that can be gained back by reducing or eliminating the competition. But from this benefit must be subtracted, of course, the various direct and indirect reproductive *costs* pertaining to aggression, such as risk of injury or death, or the time and energy consumed by belligerence that could be put to other uses. Still, there may well be the prospect of net gain: resource competition may threaten losses so great that they more than compensate for the inherent costs of war. In short, competition from B_1 can create in A_1 a "fitness budget for fighting" (Parker 1974: 236), particularly when strategy and armaments are sufficient to keep average costs low.

To this basic argument let us now add a few degrees of complexity. First, remembering that A_1 is not the sole social group in A, let us allow for simultaneous competition from other codemic social units (A_2, A_3, etc.) such that the per capita yield values in A_1 are well below U even before B_1 has its effect. In fact, because these other units belong to the same deme and have, presumably, the same resource preferences, technology, language, etc. as A_1, one might reasonably expect A_1 to lose more yield to each of them than it loses to B_1. Although this line of reasoning seems to suggest that intrademic competition would also generate large budgets for intrademic fighting, it is also likely that the reproductive *costs* of intrademic aggression are much higher, because of the interdependencies among such groups arising from trade relations, mate acquisition, kin dispersal, etc. Consequently, the effect of added intrademic competition may be not so much to fuel the evolution of war among intrademic groups—although that surely can and does happen—as to make A_1 extra-sensitive to any real or suspected loss of resources to outsiders.

As a second degree of complexity, let us also allow for simultaneous competition from other groups in B, as would be the case if B_2, B_3, etc., harvested resources from the same mobile population as did A_1 and B_1. In this instance, A_1's fitness budget for fighting could be large enough to fuel customary aggression toward a number of outside groups, and also large enough to promote A_1's collaboration with A_2, say, in campaigns of the latter's own initiative. As a result, A_1 might begin to appear perpetually hostile to all outsiders.

To this set of conditions one need add only time plus a cultural system meeting the basic requirements for evolutionary change (see Chapter 1)—including a mechanism for value-guided selection by choice—to make possible the cultural evolution of traditional warfare with individual-level reproductive benefits.

Implications. This model for the cultural evolution of adaptive intergroup aggression has important implications for understanding human belligerence. First, it suggests that cultural traditions of warfare are not necessarily dysfunctional as is so often assumed. The model describes conditions under which intergroup aggression can contribute positively to the survival and reproduction of the warriors and their families. Second, it challenges the presumption that traditional warfare in nonstate societies has generally evolved for some transcendent group-level function requiring individual sacrifice (as suggested, for example, by Divale 1973). At least in circumstances of resource competition, it is possible for aggressive intergroup behavior to have real benefits in reproductive success for participating individuals. My argument, of course, does not discuss the mechanics of collective aggression; owing to the influence of environment, cultural descent, and the local history of interaction tactics, they will be specific to each case. The point is simply that many traditions of collective aggression in nonstate societies may actually represent cultural adaptations to intergroup competition (for further discussion of the implications, see Durham 1976a).

A.7.2. Fore Mortuary Customs Before Cannibalism

In their critique of the cannibalism hypothesis for the transmission of kuru, Steadman and Merbs (1982: 623–24) argue that "the mortuary practices of the Fore, which included the handling of bodies and skulls of dead kin and affines, provided an unusually direct mode of transmission for the [kuru] disease agent. Under these conditions only one [initial] case . . . would be sufficient to lead to the epidemic of kuru." Given the lack of information about actual Fore practices before cannibalism, Steadman and Merbs base their argument on selected ethnographic descriptions of other societies, which indicate that "the handling of dead kin and affines in mortuary activities, especially by women, occurs throughout New Guinea, without cannibalism." (p. 619.) Among the more convincing of such descriptions are those of the Anga and Hewa peoples, both of whom escaped the ravages of kuru. Among the former, they note, a corpse is traditionally suspended for a week or more over a hearth in the women's house, during which time "the widow remains under her dead husband's body, while the fluids from the putrefying corpse drip down the *nambai* [bark cape] over her back. Her *nambai*, so spattered with fluids and grease from the decaying corpse, symbolizes her status as a widow in mourning." (Mbaginta'o 1976: 302, cited in Steadman and Merbs 1982: 620.) In the Hewa case, Steadman and Merbs report, it is a sign of respect that "the rotting skull of a dead kinsman is regularly retrieved from the grave one or two months after burial, placed in a small shrine near the house, and later hung on a wall inside the house. This task is normally performed only by women. . . . [If the kuru agent had been present in the population] this activity could easily have resulted in transmission of the disease." (p. 620.)

Although initially impressed by Steadman and Merbs's arguments, I had second thoughts upon considering the linguistic diversity in their ethnographic sample. Whereas the Fore and other populations affected with kuru are all speakers of East New Guinea Highlands languages, the majority of the Steadman and Merbs examples, and certainly most of the convincing ones, are all from other language families; the Anga, for instance, belong to the Angan language family and the Hewa belong to a family called Sepik Hill (see, for example, Ruhlen 1987: 354–61 on language classification in New Guinea). This means that these authors' inferences depend upon cases that are not closely related by descent and are therefore not homologous. While I empathize with the problem they encountered, namely, that they "could find nowhere a detailed description of the traditional [precannibalism] mortuary activities of the Fore themselves" (Steadman and Merbs 1982: 620), I also find their solution to that problem to be misleading.

With the assistance of two student researchers, M.T. and Q.T., I therefore searched the ethnographic record anew to see what was known about traditional mortuary activities *within* the East New Guinea Highlands language family. I found two particularly revealing accounts, the first of which was published only after the Steadman and Merbs analysis. It is Gillian Gillison's 1983 account of funeral activities among the Gimi, close linguistic relatives and neighbors of the Fore (see Fig. 7.4) who also suffered from kuru in earlier decades.

> When a man dies, men carry his body inside his mother's or wife's house and lay him on a mat of dried pandanus leaves. In the small dark hut, his female relatives crowd around him, swatting away flies, lifting and caressing his limbs, pressing their mouths onto his face and chest, beating their breasts, throwing themselves onto the hard-packed mud floor, and wailing for long periods of the day and night. After about four or five days, his male matrikin move him on a litter to his garden and [nowadays] bury him in a wooden chamber built inside a hillside vault. In the past, they installed him on a wooden platform built two or three meters off the ground amid a stand of sugarcane or bamboo (once a standard method of disposing of the dead in many parts of the Eastern Highlands). . . . [The] men left the body there slowly to decompose among the man's own produce. [Gillison 1983: 35]

The account speaks only of male corpses but, to judge from other related cases (e.g., the Auyana as described by Robbins 1982: 96–97), the same general procedure was probably followed for deceased women and children as well. According to Gillison's male informants, moreover, cannibalism actually began as an adjunct to this tradition: on one occasion, years ago, "the women, unable to contain their sorrow, secretly dragged [a man] off the funeral bed and ate him." (p. 35.)

The second account comes from a population called the Maring, who live outside the kuru region, northwest of the Fore, and are more distantly related members of the Eastern Highlands language family. According to Georgeda Buchbinder and Roy Rappaport (1976: 22), "the burden of funerary responsibilities falls upon women," just as Steadman and Merbs suggest. However, Buchbinder and Rappaport indicate that, once decomposition is under way (to the extent that body handling might entail exposure to decayed nervous tissue), corpses are regarded as dangerous and polluting, and are therefore handled as little as possible. By their account, when a man dies,

> women bring the corpse of the deceased man into his wife's house, or if the deceased was not a married man, into the house of a close kinswoman. There the body is laid out for two or three days or more. . . . The corpse is washed, its knees are flexed, and the legs tied together, its wrists are crossed and bound. It is adorned with paint and valuables, and a constant stream of female mourners passes in and out of the house to fondle the corpse and to cry. Men also come to pay their respects, but they remain outside the house. . . .
>
> Two or three days after death, soon after dawn, the corpse is carried to the place where its clan traditionally exposes their dead. There it is laid out on a platform, newly erected for the purpose. Ten to 15 feet above the ground, these platforms have low side walls and the area below them is fenced in to prevent both *Koimps* (witches) and wild pigs and other animals that might be eaten by men from consuming the decayed matter that leaks to the ground.
>
> While the men build the platforms and enclose the area below them, women place the body upon it, cover it with fern leaves and watch to see that *Koimps*, who can assume the shape of animals, do not disturb it. They may also rearrange it from time to time to speed its dissolution. As the body decays, it becomes more and more dangerous, for the odor of decomposition attracts *Koimps*. The process of decay seems to take four to six weeks to complete, for that is how long the corpse remains exposed. [Buchbinder and Rappaport 1976: 22–23]

The account is more detailed than that of the Gimi and it, too, is focused on male deaths alone. But the general procedure is very much the same: following a few days of mourning and direct contact with the corpse, the body is removed to a distant platform where it decomposes and is viewed, not unrealistically, as becoming more and more dangerous. Among the Maring, women sometimes "rearrange" the body, but their contact with it is both limited and fraught with perceived danger. In fact, the Maring say that

> while the corpse remains on the platform the women attending it are in an extreme state of pollution. They may not enter gardens, lest the crops rot in the ground, and they handle and cook food only for themselves. They should not touch men [for] not only may contact with a widow attract the jealous wrath of the deceased, but anyone in contact with a corpse carries the contagion of its corruption. Hence, women tending corpses remain confined, by

and large, to the enclosure of the women's house in which the corpse was laid out, except for their short trips to the funerary platform.

When the corpse has dissolved, the bones are removed from the platform and cleaned [presumably by women], and a night-long ritual called *Ngimbai* is held in the men's house of those closest to the deceased. Only men attend the *Ngimbai*, during which shamans summon the ancestral spirits to take the deceased into their company and depart with him or her. At dawn, after their night of chanting, the men burst out of the house to purify the women who had tended the corpse, and to cleanse the women's house enclosure in which they remained, of the supernatural corruption called *tukump* [the term is also used for the mold that develops on some rotting articles]. [p. 23]

Then, after a feast, the women [except for the widow, if there is one] return to their normal lives. Today, at least, "the bones of the young, the unmarried, and of women, are usually buried [thereafter] with little delay." (p. 23.) In contrast, the bones of married men remain in their widow's custody until buried in a special ceremony two years or so later.

In short, the Buchbinder-Rappaport description certainly confirms that Maring women do have a special association with the dead. But it also emphasizes that the decaying corpses under their care are regarded as dangerous and worthy of special, infrequent handling. Importantly, routine contact with brain cases is delayed until the internal tissues are decomposed and drained, whereupon the skulls *are* handled, even cleaned. But this cleaning brings with it the resumption of "normal association and duties" following the *Ngimbai*, including close contact again with the men. If one were to argue from this that Maring women would have been regularly exposed to the kuru agent during the cleaning of the bones [had kuru existed in this population], then one would also have to expect its regular transmission at the same time to adult men. With tragic irony, efforts to "cleanse" the women would only have contaminated the men.

To return now to the Fore context, we may ask, What are the implications of these accounts for our understanding of kuru transmission? First, if I am correct that Fore mortuary tradition was closer to Gimi and Maring customs than to those of the Anga, Hewa, and other non-Eastern-Highlands speakers, then the accounts here cast doubt on the idea that traditional mortuary customs [i.e., pre-cannibalism] were the central pathway for the spread of kuru. Paradoxically, the very fact that adult men only rarely contracted the disease [see Fig. 7.5] suggests that traditional mortuary practice was not, contra Steadman and Merbs [1982: 619], "the most likely source" of kuru transmission. I conclude that kuru was most often transmitted through the added direct handling of brain tissue in preparation for cannibalism. Second, the Gimi account also supports the cannibalism hypothesis by providing an institutional context that can explain the persistently low rates of kuru transmission to adult males. According to Gillison's informants [1983: 36], from the very first act of cannibalism, mortuary practice changed in another significant way: women secluded themselves within the men's house "for as long as it took to eat and digest" the deceased. Interpreting the occupation as a deliberate [and polluting] provocation, the men as a group remained outside the structure for the duration, but "kept track of the women's meal by sending into the men's house as observers several men of low status and several boys who also ate the human meat." In this way, not only did high-status men shun human flesh itself (for reasons discussed in Chapter 7), but they also remained physically separated from the proceedings. If there are similar seclusion practices among the Fore, they would help to explain the characteristic age and sex asymmetries of kuru epidemiology.

CHAPTER 8

A.8.1. The Evolution of Human Endocranial Volume

On several occasions in Chapters 1 and 8, I discuss the evolution of human cranial capacity or endocranial volume (ECV), a measure of brain size. My arguments and illustrations (Figs. 1.2 and 8.3, panel A) are based on published data for the estimated date (in millions of years before present) and ECV (in cubic centimeters) of hominid crania in the fossil record. With the help of student assistants (B.B., J.K., and M.Q.), I compiled these data from Parenti (1973), Holloway (1975a, 1978, 1983), Olivier and Tissier (1975), Lestrel (1975), Zindler (1978), Wolpoff (1980), Beals et al. (1984), Blumenberg (1978, 1983, 1984), Bräuer (1984), Stringer (1984), Day (1986), and Falk (1987), using information from primary sources as needed to resolve discrepancies (a complete list of data and sources is available upon request). The full sample included 88 specimens subdivided as follows: gracile species of *Australopithecus* ($N = 9$), robust species of *Australopithecus* ($N = 11$), *Homo habilis* ($N = 7$), *Homo erectus* ($N = 21$), "archaic" *Homo sapiens* ($N = 3$), and Neanderthals ($N = 37$; note that the taxonomic status of Neanderthals is uncertain at present, with some scholars favoring *Homo sapiens neanderthalensis* and others *Homo neanderthalensis*). One specimen known as ER = 1813 was dropped from analysis because of ambiguity surrounding its genus and species designation.

Because the sample was already small and also plagued by conflicting age and sex determinations, I opted to include *all* remaining specimens in the quantitative analysis. However, for those few specimens widely accepted as juvenile (e.g., Taung), I used published estimates of their adult EVC's. These data were then analyzed on an IBM personal computer using the multiple regression procedure contained within SPSS/PC+, a statistical software package. The following regression equations, corresponding to the dashed lines of Fig. 8.3, were obtained:

1. Gracile Australopithecines: ECV =   413 + 14.8 × (Date)   (n.s.)
2. Robust Australopithecines: ECV =   781 − 146 × (Date)   (n.s.)
3. *Homo habilis*:   ECV =   393 + 161 × (Date)   (n.s.)
4. *Homo erectus*:   ECV = 1093 − 172 × (Date)   (p < 0.05)
5. *Homo neanderthalensis*:   ECV = 1547 − 1604 × (Date)   (p < 0.05)

It should be noted that only equations 4 and 5 feature regression coefficients for "Date" that are significantly different from zero. Those coefficients are negative numbers because the dates of the fossil specimens are estimated in millions of years B.P. ("before present").

B /   First Principles of Genetics

This appendix is intended as an introductory guide to some first principles of modern genetics. Section B.1 reviews the basic molecular biology of the gene, including the chemical code of DNA, the genetic control of protein synthesis, and some special properties of the DNA molecule. Section B.2 reviews introductory population genetics, including the Hardy-Weinberg law and the first principles of selection kinetics. (For more advanced treatment of molecular genetics see B. Lewin 1983; Hawkins 1985; Watson et al. 1987. On population genetics see Roughgarden 1979; Falconer 1981; Christiansen and Feldman 1986. On the link between these fields today see Hunkapiller et al. 1982; Nei and Koehn 1983; Rose and Doolittle 1983.)

B.1. FIRST PRINCIPLES OF MOLECULAR GENETICS

As befits their evolutionary descent from one universal ancestor, all living things contain genes composed of either DNA (deoxyribonucleic acid) or its relative RNA (ribonucleic acid). Of the two, DNA is far more common among existing species and is considered to be the prime genetic material.[1] Its general structure was first outlined by James Watson and Francis Crick (1953; for the history of this discovery see Sayre 1975; Watson 1980). Their model has since been refined but not replaced (see, for example, Watson et al. 1987: ch. 9). Formed of double helical strands, the DNA molecule is present within each and every living cell of multicellular organisms, wrapped with proteins into discrete bundles, or chromosomes, within the nucleus. An organism is said to be diploid if it has two copies of each chromosome and haploid if it has a single copy; humans are diploid with 46 such DNA-containing chromosomes, two each of 23 types.

B.1.1. The Genetic Code of DNA

Four properties of the DNA molecule are especially important for understanding its role in genetic evolution. The first of these is the property of *information*:

[1] To date, all organisms with genes composed of RNA, including the deadly AIDS retrovirus (see Gallo 1987), have turned out to be dependent parasites on organisms with genes of DNA. Thus, in the words of Holland et al. (1982: 1577), "the entire present-day biosphere is based on DNA."

DNA contains a very specific, detailed set of chemical instructions for the activation and control of the biochemical processes of life. This "genetic code," as it is generally known, resides within specific chemical subunits of the DNA molecule called nucleotides, each of which contains one of four organic "bases": adenine (abbreviated A), thymine (T), cytosine (C), and guanine (G)—see, for example, Fig. A.3.1. Specific arrangements of A, T, C, and G take on a meaning that is analogous in biochemical terms to the words, sentences, and even whole texts of written language.[2]

A second key property of the DNA molecule, *linearity*, is the one from which the genetic code derives its organization. In each strand of the double helix, nucleotides are arranged in an orderly linear sequence such as CACGTG-GACTGAGGACTCCTCTTC . . . (part of an actual sequence from the DNA that codes for the beta chains of human hemoglobins). The linear organization of this code greatly increases its specificity, further strengthening the analogy between the genetic code and written language.

These first two properties have major biological significance (we return below, in Section B.1.3, to properties three and four). They render DNA molecules capable of serving as "blueprints," or instructions, for the synthesis of another class of compounds called polypeptides, the molecular building blocks of life. It is by virtue of these properties, in other words, that DNA has been able to influence the morphology, physiology, and behavior of living organisms, including ourselves. The chemical sequence of nucleotides in DNA constitutes an individual's genotype, serving as chemical instructions for the assembly of his or her phenotype.

Originally it was assumed that the information in DNA was nearly all functional, either coding for polypeptides or regulating that process, and nearly all continuous, as appears to be the case in simple bacteria. Beginning in 1977, however, studies of complex multicellular organisms have found the coding sequences to be markedly discontinuous. Functional nucleotide sequences called "exons" are commonly interrupted by one or more stretches of noncoding nucleotides called "introns" or intervening sequences (the hemoglobin genes are a good example—see App. A.3.1). This pattern, of course, adds another layer of complexity to the genetic code, one whose evolutionary significance remains to be discovered.

B.1.2. The Genetic Control of Protein Synthesis

In both simple and complex organisms, polypeptides are themselves constructed from smaller compounds, the amino acids, according to the instructional code of the DNA. Amino acids are capable of forming great chainlike strands whose links are formed by peptide bonds between adjacent acids (hence the name polypeptides). Some sense of how very specifically these polypeptides are organized can, in turn, be gained by noting (1) that more than 20 distinct amino acids are known; (2) that many polypeptides contain sequences of 100 to 300 of these subunits; and (3) that a difference of as little as 1 amino acid in a long chain of 100 or more can drastically alter the structural and/or functional nature of the polypeptide. For instance, one of the molecular subunits of human hemoglobin A, the

---

[2] The analogy between the genetic code and human language is an old and useful one (see, for example, Gerard, Kluckhohn, and Rapoport 1956; Masters 1970; Bender 1976; Hoenigswald and Wiener 1987). As emphasized by Colin Pittendrigh, a former colleague in Human Biology at Stanford, in a 1980 lecture, "the two most important events in the history of life on earth were the origin of DNA and the origin of human language."

so-called β polypeptide, consists of 146 amino acids linked together in a particular order; the substitution of one single amino acid (valine) for another (glutamic acid) at position 6 in that chain is sufficient to cause the lethal disease known as sickle-cell anemia (see Chapter 3 and App. A.3.1). But, as the example of hemoglobin A also shows, the specificity of molecular organization is often compounded one further step, by the chemical bonding of two or more polypeptides into a single protein molecule. In the case of hemoglobin A, there are actually four interbonded polypeptides—two called α and two β—for a total of 574 amino acids. Moreover, only two of these amino acids are different in the hemoglobin that sickles, one in each of the two β polypeptides. It follows that Hb A, like all other proteins, is a highly organized biochemical compound.

The genetic control of protein synthesis is therefore a matter of fundamental importance to the structures and functions of living organisms. A general outline of the process first occurred to Watson in the early 1950's (see Watson 1980), but was more fully described in a later paper by Crick (1958; see also Hunt, Prentis, and Tooze 1983). In essence, Watson's proposal contained two related hypotheses. The first, called the Sequence Hypothesis (Crick 1958: 152), proposed that the order of amino acids in a given polypeptide is specified by the order of nucleotides in DNA taken three at a time, a unit called a "codon." The second hypothesis, known widely as the Central Dogma, stated that "once 'information' has passed into protein *it cannot get out again.*" (p. 153, emphasis in the original.) The point was that information transfer was unidirectional: the code was expressed only from the nucleic acids to the proteins and not back again.[3] Otherwise, as Watson and Crick realized, the system would provide a biochemical pathway for the Lamarckian inheritance of acquired characteristics.

Fig. B.1 summarizes the basic features of Watson's proposals as they are understood today, illustrated again by hemoglobin A. The figure outlines the flow of information from the codons of DNA in the nucleus of a cell (top), to the codons of chemical intermediaries of RNA, including messenger RNA (mRNA), ribosomal RNA (rRNA), and transfer RNA (tRNA)—and from there to the sequence of amino acids in a polypeptide (center). Hemoglobin A is then assembled (bottom) from four polypeptides, two alpha chains and two beta, all of which are synthesized in accordance with Watson's model. With the sole exception of timing, the basic steps of the process shown in the figure are believed to be the same for other proteins. Hemoglobin A biosynthesis takes place only within immature blood cells because, for reasons not yet fully understood, the nucleii and the DNA are extruded from mature cells before they enter into circulation (see, for example, Harris and Kellermeyer 1970: ch. 6).

The first step of protein synthesis, shown within the cell nucleus of Fig. B.1, is called "transcription." In this step, the information of the DNA code is transcribed with high fidelity from one strand of the double helix to a corresponding RNA molecule called a "primary RNA transcript." The information of the nucleotide sequence is conserved, subject only to the modification that the original nucleotides A, T, C, and G of the DNA are represented in the RNA by their "binding partners," or chemical complements, U (uracil), A, G, and C respectively.

---

[3] Note that the Central Dogma did not propose that "DNA makes RNA makes protein" in all cases, as is so often claimed. Hence the discovery in 1970 of an enzyme, reverse transcriptase, that synthesizes DNA from RNA did not falsify the dogma as some suggested (see discussion in Hunt 1983).

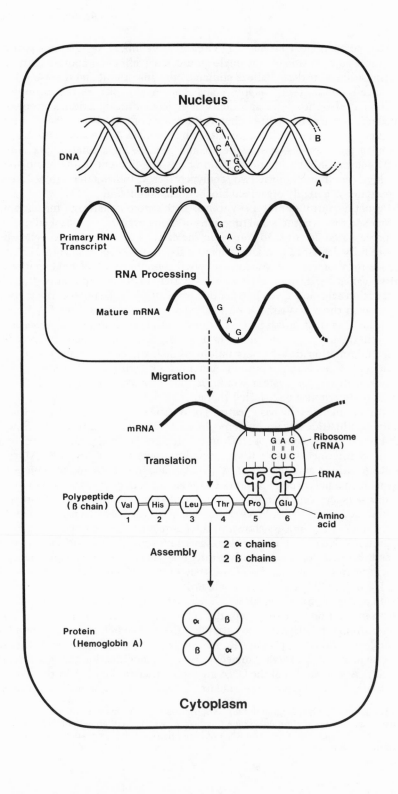

After transcription, a step called "RNA processing," or splicing, eliminates the noncoding introns from the RNA to produce a "mature" mRNA molecule (see Darnell 1983, 1985). As a result of transcription and RNA processing, then, the DNA remains intact, protected within the nucleus; only its chemical message is ferried out into the cytoplasm where protein synthesis takes place.

The second step of information transfer, called "translation," takes place in the cytoplasm at the site of subcellular granules, made of rRNA, that are called "ribosomes" (one of which is shown, greatly enlarged, in the center of the figure). Here the information of the mRNA transcript is "translated" from the chemical language of the nucleic acids DNA and RNA into the chemical language of the polypeptides. The translation proceeds in an orderly fashion by taking one codon of mRNA at a time. Once a given codon of mRNA has moved into place on the ribosome, its triplet sequence is matched by an "anticodon" of tRNA. Again the matching proceeds on the basis of complementary binding partners. The anticodon of the tRNA now matches the corresponding sequence of the original DNA code, except that, as shown, the role of thymine in DNA is played by uracil in the RNA's. The specificity is again important since the triplet anticodons of tRNA are each associated with particular amino acids.[4] The outcome, then, is that the mRNA codon specifies that a particular amino acid be added to the growing polypeptide chain. The process continues until the full sequence of nucleotides in the

---

[4] The genetic code is said to be "degenerate": although there are $4 \times 4 \times 4 = 64$ possible codons, there are only some twenty distinct amino acids. As a result, more than one codon may specify a given amino acid, and this means that some mutational changes in DNA may be functionally "silent," that is, they may cause no change in the polypeptide sequence.

Fig. B.1 (opposite). Basic steps of protein synthesis within the cells of a complex organism (as illustrated for the human protein, hemoglobin A). Through the sequence of information transfers summarized here, the genetic code of DNA instructs the synthesis of "polypeptides," or amino acid chains, from which proteins are made. In the first step, called "transcription," the sequence of nucleotides (A's, T's, C's, and G's) in one strand (A) of DNA is copied into a complementary sequence of nucleotides in a molecule called a primary RNA transcript; in this way, the sequence labeled CTC in the DNA molecule is represented by GAG in the RNA. Following transcription, the newly formed mRNA is spliced and shortened during RNA processing to remove "introns," which are extraneous sequences of nucleotides that may lie between the ones coding for the given polypeptide. The "mature" transcript of messenger RNA (mRNA), then migrates out of the nucleus and into the "cytoplasm" (surrounding cell matrix), where it becomes attached to one or more granules called ribosomes (shown larger than scale for clarity), composed of specialized proteins and ribosomal RNA (rRNA). Here the second step of information transfer, "translation," takes place: the messenger RNA serves as a template for the synthesis of a polypeptide (here the β chain of hemoglobin A). During translation, ribosomes move along the mRNA molecule one "codon," or nucleotide triplet, at a time (from left to right as shown here). As they go, complementary base pairing takes place once again, this time between a given codon (such as GAG in the diagram) and a corresponding triplet sequence, or "anticodon" (such as CUC) of a transfer RNA (tRNA) molecule. Because there is a specific amino acid (or, in a few cases, a stop signal) associated with each type of anticodon, the information of the mRNA template is translated into a specific sequence of amino acids which are linked by peptide bonds (shown here as double horizontal lines) to form a polypeptide. In the figure, glutamic acid has just been brought into position to become the sixth amino acid in the growing β chain polypeptide. Shortly afterwards, glutamic acid will be joined to the β chain by another peptide bond and the ribosome will shift right to the next codon of mRNA. When all of the necessary polypeptides have been synthesized in this manner, the final product—a protein—will be assembled in the cytoplasm. Adapted from Darnell 1983: 92.

RNA messenger has been matched three to one by a corresponding chain of amino acids.

In the final stage of the process, which I have labeled "assembly," the freshly synthesized polypeptides twist and fold into three-dimensional configurations and go on to bond, where appropriate, into proteins. As shown schematically in Fig. B.1, for example, hemoglobin A forms from two alpha chains and two beta chains. The final result of this synthesis, a veritable molecular assembly line, is a fully assembled protein whose amino acid composition has been specified point by point by the chemical code of the DNA. Because of this great specificity, a gene has been defined as "any sequence of DNA bases that codes for a complete polypeptide."

In summary, Watson's proposal provides for the orderly transcription and translation of the genetic code into macromolecular proteins. Genes therefore play a key "instructional role" in the development of phenotypic properties. They instruct the orderly synthesis of proteins much in the way that blueprints instruct the building of an edifice. The analogy is particularly apt in this case because it emphasizes the indirect, guiding role played by the genes. Just as a blueprint, because of the materials available, the effects of weathering, wear and tear, and so on, does not completely determine the appearance and functionality of an edifice, so too the genes cannot fully determine the nature and form of a phenotype, which will always be subject to extragenetic, environmental influences. As Fig. B.1 implies, some environmental conditions (including, for example, the availability of A, U, G, and C precursors and a reaction catalyst) begin to influence the building of phenotypes as early as transcription. So pervasive are such influences on gene expression that geneticists speak of "the norm of reaction" of a given genotype, that is to say, the *range* of phenotypes produced by a given genotype under different environmental conditions (for further discussion, see Lewontin 1982: ch. 2). It is therefore most accurate to describe the role of genes not as "determining" the phenotype but as "instructing" it. In this respect, the influence of genes closely parallels the instructional role of cultural beliefs discussed in Chapter 2.

B.1.3. *Other Special Properties of DNA*

Two other properties of the DNA molecule are important for understanding its role in genetics and organic evolution. The first of these—let us call it key property number three—is *mutability*: small but lasting chemical changes are possible within the sequences of nucleotide subunits of DNA. Some mutations result from the simple replacement of a single nucleotide by another of a different kind, others from inversions, deletions, and translocations in the chemical code (for more information see, for example, Bodmer and Cavalli-Sforza 1976: ch. 4; Hartl 1983: chs. 7 and 11). Furthermore, these changes may be random and accidental, or they may be induced by the environment, either chemically or by radiation from various sources. But the point is that once the nucleotide sequence is changed, then the polypeptides synthesized from the mutated DNA may also change, with lasting, heritable effects on the phenotype. In this way, the mutability of DNA is responsible for genetic variation among organisms, variation that is the raw material of organic evolutionary change.

The fourth and final key property of DNA from the point of view of genetic evolution is its *capacity for faithful, semiconservative replication*. In addition to serving as templates for mRNA's and thus for protein synthesis, DNA molecules also serve as templates for their own replication. In higher organisms the process takes place before cell division (as in the formation of egg and sperm cells); the "parental" strands of the double helix are chemically separated, whereupon each serves as a template for the synthesis of a complementary "daughter" strand. Along the way, except in the rare event of copy error, A's are faithfully matched to T's and C's to G's, in much the same way as in transcription. In replication, however, the byproducts are always DNA, not RNA, and both strands are copied at the same time. Replication is thus semiconservative: one parental strand is conserved in each new molecule. The evolutionary consequences are also distinct. It is this process that provides for the highly regular transmission of genetic instructions from parents to offspring down through the generations. And it is this property of DNA that provides the continuity of genetic evolution, bestowing upon genes what Richard Dawkins (1976) has called their own special kind of immortality.

B.1.4. Some Helpful Definitions

In order to keep track of the variation in DNA molecules, geneticists have adopted a number of terminological conventions that are also helpful in evolutionary theory. To begin with, the word "allele" is used to refer to the alternative forms of a gene that may exist within a given population, each form differing by at least one nucleotide in the sequence. In diploid organisms like ourselves, most genes are present in the individual's "genome" (the full set of genetic instructions) in two copies, normally one inherited from each parent. Diploidy allows for the possibility that the two copies may be different, each coding for a distinct amino acid sequence. In addition, the location of a gene on a chromosome is called its "locus"; geneticists often speak of "the alleles at a given locus" to refer to the full range of variation that exists for a given gene in a specified population at a particular time. The chromosomes themselves are differentiated into either "sex chromosomes" (those chromosomes, like the human X and Y, that carry the genes that influence the sex of the organism) or "autosomes" (all others).

To keep track of plural alleles, it is customary to represent each variant by a letter of the alphabet, either alone or with a numeric subscript (A_1, A_2, etc.), usually chosen to be mnemonic for the phenotype under study. Thus, to take a simple example, "B" and "b" are sometimes used to represent the alleles that code for brown and blue eye color respectively. When the two alleles of a diploid individual are alike, such as BB or bb, he or she is said to be a "homozygote" ("bearer of same alleles"). When the two alleles are different, such as Bb, the individual is called a "heterozygote." Another convention is that capital letters are usually used for "dominant" alleles—that is, alleles whose phenotypic effects are the same in homozygotes and heterozygotes—and lower-case letters are used for "recessives"—alleles whose effects are masked in the heterozygote.

B.2. FIRST PRINCIPLES OF POPULATION GENETICS

This section reviews some basic logic and mathematics of selection theory in population genetics. In particular, it provides a derivation for the Hardy-Weinberg law and for the Δq (read "delta q") equations of gene-frequency change used in Chapter 3.

B.2.1. Calculating Genotype and Gene Frequencies

For purposes of illustration, consider a hypothetical sample of individuals from a given gene pool, each with one of the three genotypes, **AA**, **Aa**, and **aa**, where the **A** allele is dominant over **a**.

Genotype frequencies. The genotype frequency is simply the proportion of each genotype found in a given sample. Letting N refer to the total number of persons in a sample and Σ (read "the sum of all") refer to the number of individuals of the specified genotype, we can calculate genotype frequencies as follows.

Genotypes	Proportions	Frequencies
AA	$\dfrac{\Sigma \mathbf{AA}}{N}$	u
Aa	$\dfrac{\Sigma \mathbf{Aa}}{N}$	v
aa	$\dfrac{\Sigma \mathbf{aa}}{N}$	w

Note that genotype frequencies are usually expressed as percentages or their decimal equivalents. As a check against miscalculations, one can always confirm that the sum of the calculated frequencies, $u + v + w$, equals 1.0.

Gene frequencies. The gene frequencies for the same sample of N individuals can readily be found from the genotype frequencies. Letting $2N$ represent the total number of alleles in the sample and p the frequency of the allele **A**, then

$$p = \frac{2(\Sigma\mathbf{AA}) + 1(\Sigma\mathbf{Aa})}{2N} = \frac{\Sigma\mathbf{AA}}{N} + \frac{\Sigma\mathbf{Aa}}{2N}$$

$$= u + \frac{v}{2} \tag{B.1}$$

Likewise, if we let q be the frequency of **a**, then

$$q = \frac{2(\Sigma\mathbf{aa}) + 1(\Sigma\mathbf{Aa})}{2N} = \frac{\Sigma\mathbf{aa}}{N} + \frac{\Sigma\mathbf{Aa}}{2N}$$

$$= w + \frac{v}{2} \tag{B.2}$$

As a check, one can always confirm that the calculated values of p and q sum to 1.0.

B.2.2. Derivation of the Hardy-Weinberg Law

Following the rediscovery of Gregor Mendel's "laws" of inheritance early this century, it became important to know whether heredity itself causes intergenerational change in gene frequencies and thus qualifies as an evolutionary process. For example, does Mendelian "segregation" during germ cell formation—that is, the separation of the alleles at a given locus into equal numbers of distinct gametes—cause p and q to change between generations?

As several investigators discovered by 1908, the answer is no: Mendel's laws do not, by themselves, cause evolutionary change. Called the Hardy-Weinberg law after two of its codiscoverers, this deduction can be derived as follows. First, let us assume that two alleles, **A** and **a**, are present with frequencies p and q, respectively, in both sexes of a hypothetical population. Second, let us assume that no other candidate forces of evolutionary change are operating, so that mating is random and there is no discernible migration, mutation, drift, or genetic selection. Third, let us assume that these two alleles do obey Mendel's law of segregation, so that in germ cell formation, or "gametogenesis," they form **A**-bearing eggs of frequency p, **a**-bearing eggs of frequency q, **A**-bearing sperm of frequency p, and **a**-bearing sperm of frequency q. Now under the assumption of random mating, and in the absence of other evolutionary forces, these gametes will combine to produce the genotypes of the next generation in the proportions: p^2 of **AA** individuals (calculated as the frequency of **A**-bearing eggs, p, times the frequency of **A**-bearing sperm, p); q^2 of **aa** individuals; and $2pq$ of **Aa** individuals ($2pq$ because two different combinations of eggs and sperm will produce **Aa** genotypes). We may then ask, What is the gene frequency of **a**—call it "q final" or q_f—in this new generation? Using Eq. B.2 above and setting w equal to q^2 and v equal to $2pq$, we can write

$$q_f = w + \frac{v}{2}$$
$$= q^2 + pq$$
$$= q(q + p)$$
$$= q$$

In other words, there has been no gene-frequency change between generations: Mendelian segregation does not cause evolution.

B.2.3. Uses of the Hardy-Weinberg Law

The Hardy-Weinberg law may now be formally stated in order to emphasize its utility as a test for organic evolution within a given gene pool.

For a diallelic system. In a population with two co-alleles, **A** and **a**, present at frequencies p and q, if the genotypes occur within reasonable sampling error of the frequencies p^2 of **AA**, $2pq$ of **Aa**, and q^2 of **aa**, then no organic evolution is taking place at that locus, and the population is said to be "in Hardy-Weinberg equilibrium." Note that the equilibrium is specific to the locus in question; alleles at other loci in the population may or may not be in equilibrium at the same time.

For a multi-allelic system. If the genotype frequencies in a population with multiple alleles (of frequencies p,q,r,s . . .) occur within reasonable sampling error of the values given by the expanded polynomial expression $(p + q + r + s + . . .)^2$, then we may conclude that evolutionary forces are not operating on these alleles in the population.

Departures from Hardy-Weinberg equilibrium. If the genotype frequencies observed within a population are significantly different from those predicted from the gene frequencies according to the Hardy-Weinberg law, then we may conclude that *one or more* evolutionary forces are at work in the population. Possible forces at work would include mutation, migration, drift, and genetic selection of various forms. The data may or may not contain clues as to which of these forces are involved.

Procedure to test for Hardy-Weinberg equilibrium. The following steps are recommended in testing for Hardy-Weinberg equilibrium in a gene pool.

1. Use information about genotypes to calculate the gene frequencies of relevant alleles in a population.

2. Calculate the genotype frequencies to be expected from the gene frequencies were the population in HW equilibrium (that is, from p and q calculate p^2, $2pq$, and q^2).

3. Finally, go back and compare these expected values with the original observed values. If the differences are large and not ascribable to chance effects (as determined, for example, by a chi-square statistic), the population is not in equilibrium and evolution is under way. If the observed values are a close match to the expected values, then one may conclude that organic evolution is not taking place.

4. A useful shortcut: A population is in HW equilibrium if v (the frequency of **Aa**) is within reasonable sampling error of the calculated value

$$v = 2\sqrt{uw} \tag{B.3}$$

B.2.4. *Genetic Selection Against Recessive Homozygotes*

Let p represent the initial frequency of an allele **A** and let q represent the initial frequency of allele **a** in a population. Let us also assume that an environmental change causes the differential reproduction of genotypes within a gene pool that has been in Hardy-Weinberg equilibrium previously. Let us further assume that genetic selection disadvantages the recessive homozygote **aa**, and only **aa**, by an amount t, called a "selection coefficient" (as shown, for example, in Fig. 3.4, panel A). Our goal is to derive an algebraic expression representing the fate of the **a** allele in the gene pool in future generations. Commonly, such expressions relate the change of **a**'s frequency per generation, Δq, to the variables p, q, and the selection pressures in effect.

This information can be incorporated into the following table. Again, t represents the selection coefficient reducing the relative fitness of the genotype **aa**.

	Genotypes			
	AA	**Aa**	**aa**	Total
Frequency before selection	p^2	$2pq$	q^2	1
Darwinian fitness (W)	1	1	$1 - t$	
Representation after selection	p^2	$2pq$	$q^2(1 - t)$	$1 - tq^2$
Frequency after selection	$\dfrac{p^2}{1 - tq^2}$	$\dfrac{2pq}{1 - tq^2}$	$\dfrac{q^2(1 - t)}{1 - tq^2}$	$\dfrac{1 - tq^2}{1 - tq^2}$

Now we may ask, What is the frequency of the allele **a** after one generation of selection given by the coefficient t? Let us designate the new frequency of **a** by the expression q_f (q "final") in order to distinguish it from q, the initial frequency of **a**. The frequency q_f can be calculated from the table by using Eq. B.2, above, as follows. Let q_f be the frequency of **a** alleles in the gene pool after one generation of selection of magnitude t. Then

$$q_f = \frac{pq + q^2(1 - t)}{1 - tq^2} = \frac{pq + q^2 - tq^2}{1 - tq^2} = \frac{q(p + q - tq)}{1 - tq^2}$$

$$= \frac{q(1 - tq)}{1 - tq^2} \quad \text{(Remember, } p + q \text{ always equals 1.)}$$

The *change* in the frequency of **a** after one generation of selection is $q_f - q$. Let Δq be this change in q. Then

$$\Delta q = \frac{q(1 - tq)}{1 - tq^2} - q = \frac{q - tq^2 - q(1 - tq^2)}{t - tq^2}$$

$$= \frac{q - tq^2 - q + tq^3}{1 - tq^2}$$

$$= \frac{-tq^2(1 - q)}{1 - tq^2} \qquad \text{(B.4a)}$$

This algebraic expression has two noteworthy features. First, it expresses the change in the a allele frequency in one generation as a function of only two quantities: t, the selection coefficient acting against aa; and q, the starting frequency of a. Second, the numerator shows that Δq will be negative for all values of t greater than 0.0 (q, of course, is always a number between 0.0 and 1.0). In other words, this equation states that under the action of t alone, the a allele will always *decrease* in frequency, no matter what its initial value. It also states that the loss of a in each generation, the Δq, will be proportional to q^2 as seen in the numerator. This means that the higher the starting value of q, the steeper its rate of reduction.

Fortunately, this equation simplifies still further for the special case in which recessive homozygotes are lethal and therefore have zero fitness ($t = 1.0$). Substituting $t = 1$ into Eq. B.4a gives us

$$\Delta q = \frac{-q^2(1 - q)}{1 - q^2} = \frac{-q^2(1 - q)}{(1 + q)(1 - q)}$$

$$= \frac{-q^2}{1 + q} \qquad \text{(B.4b)}$$

The predictions of this equation are shown in Fig. B.2, which uses (for the sake of illustration) two different initial values of q, 0.100 and 0.999. The figure makes clear that the behavior of this simplified Δq equation retains the main features of the preceding gene-frequency response. The rate of change of q (indicated by the slope of the curve) is everywhere decreasing—and decreasing in a decelerating fashion.[5]

As a consequence of this asymptotic behavior, the number of generations of selection, n, required to produce a given change in gene frequency varies inversely with q. More specifically, it can be shown that when $t = 1.0$,

$$n = \frac{1}{q_n} - \frac{1}{q_o} \qquad \text{(B.4c)}$$

where q_o and q_n are the original and final frequencies respectively of the allele **a**. Thus to reduce q from 0.5 to 0.25 it would take n generations = $1/0.25 - 1/0.5 = 4 - 2 = 2$. But to then reduce q in half again, from 0.25 to 0.125, it would take

[5] Among its other implications, this equation points to the logical futility of attempts at "eugenics" (artificial gene pool manipulation) through the sterilization of recessive homozygotes. As the frequency of the allele gets lower and lower, essentially a greater proportion of the total number of the alleles is contained within heterozygotes and therefore unavailable to selection or eugenic efforts. Quite apart from the ethical issues of the idea, Fig. B.2 shows that recessive eradication is not a realistic course of action.

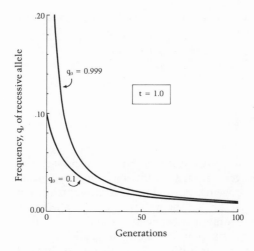

Fig. B.2. Genetic selection against recessive homozygotes in a hypothetical population. The plot shows a computer simulation of changes in the frequency, q, of a recessive allele resulting from a single selection coefficient t of value 1.0 operating against the recessive homozygote genotype. Two different starting values are shown, $q_0 = 0.1$ and $q_0 = 0.999$. Both curves show a steep initial decline followed by an asymptotic approach to $q = 0.0$. Data from Eq. B.4b.

$1/0.125 - 1/0.25 = 8 - 4 = 4$ generations. Thus the number of generations of selection to effect a given proportional change in q, given that $t = 1.0$, increases rapidly as q diminishes. In short, natural selection against a homozygous recessive genotype causes a progressively decelerating elimination of the recessive allele from the population.

B.2.5. *Genetic Selection Against Both Homozygotes*

Again let us take p to represent the initial frequency of an allele **A** and q to represent the initial frequency of allele **a** in a hypothetical gene pool. Assume that the gene pool is in Hardy-Weinberg equilibrium before the onset of genetic selection. But this time let us assume that there are *two* selection pressures operating: one against the **AA** genotype, measured by the selection coefficient s, and one against the **aa** genotype as before, measured by the selection coefficient t (see Fig. 3.4, panel B). The challenge here is to derive an expression for Δq when these two selection pressures are operating.

This information may be summarized as follows for any given generation of genetic selection.

	Genotypes			
	AA	**Aa**	**aa**	Total
Frequency before selection	p^2	$2pq$	q^2	1
Darwinian fitness (W)	$1 - s$	1	$1 - t$	
Representation after selection	$p^2(1 - s)$	$2pq$	$q^2(1 - t)$	$1 - sp^2 - tq^2$
Frequency after selection	$\dfrac{p^2(1 - s)}{1 - sp^2 - tq^2}$	$\dfrac{2pq}{1 - sp^2 - tq^2}$	$\dfrac{q^2(1 - t)}{1 - sp^2 - tq^2}$	$\dfrac{1 - sp^2 - tq^2}{1 - sp^2 - tq^2}$

As in section B.2.4 above, we can now use this information to calculate the change in a frequency, Δq, after one generation of genetic selection according to the coefficients s and t. As before, we will make use of Eq. B.2 for this purpose. Let

q_f be the frequency of **a** alleles in the gene pool after one generation of selection of magnitude s (against **AA**) and t (against **aa**). Then

$$q_f = \frac{pq + q^2(1 - t)}{1 - sp^2 - tq^2}$$

Again we can calculate Δq as the difference $q_f - q$:

$$\Delta q = \frac{pq + q^2(1 - t)}{1 - sp^2 - tq^2} - q$$

This expression can be rewritten as

$$\Delta q = \frac{pq(sp - tq)}{1 - sp^2 - tq^2} \tag{B.5a}$$

The change in gene frequency is thus a function of four variables: p (the initial frequency of **A**), q (the initial frequency of **a**), s, and t. Fig. B.3 illustrates the fate of the **a** allele according to this equation using, as sample values, $s = 0.20$ and $t = 1.00$. Two trajectories are shown, one for a starting q, or q_0, of 0.500 and the other for a q_0 of 0.001. An interesting feature is immediately clear: both trajectories converge on the same intermediate frequency (0.167) of the **a** allele. In other words, even when the homozygous recessive genotype (**aa**) is assumed lethal, the **a** allele can still persist at substantial frequency in a population because of the balancing effect of selection against the other homozygote (**AA**). Moreover, the frequency of **a** eventually reaches the same value regardless of whether the starting q was as low as 0.001 or as high as 0.500. The plateau frequency is reached more quickly from $q_0 = 0.500$, owing to the assumption that t is greater than s, but both curves do flatten out at the same constant value.

Fig. B.3 therefore indicates that a new genetic equilibrium may be reached within in a population subject to balancing selection pressures. Because this new equilibrium depends on the existence of selection coefficients (s and t) not equal

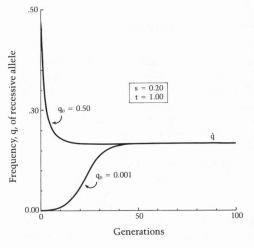

Fig. B.3. Genetic selection against both types of homozygotes in a hypothetical population. The plot shows a computer simulation of changes in the frequency, q, of a recessive allele resulting from the action of the two selection coefficients, s and t. The coefficient s is assumed to lower the Darwinian fitness of the homozygous dominant genotype to 0.80; similarly, t is assumed to reduce the recessive homozygote's fitness to 0.20. Two different starting values are shown, $q_0 = 0.50$ and $q_0 = 0.001$. Both curves show a period of initial gene-frequency change followed by an approach toward a common equilibrium value of q labeled $\hat{q}$. In this way, two balancing selection pressures are able to maintain the frequencies of two alleles in a population at levels well above those expected by mutation. Data from Eq. B.5a.

to zero, it may be called a "selectional equilibrium," not to be confused with the Hardy-Weinberg equilibrium. At this equilibrium, genetic selection prevents the genotypes from existing at the frequencies p^2 of **AA**, $2pq$ of **Aa**, and q^2 of **aa**.

Some important features of this second, selectional type of equilibrium can be inferred from the numerator of the Δq formula above (Eq. B.5a). Remembering that a gene-frequency equilibrium will exist in a given gene pool whenever $\Delta q = 0$, the preceding formula suggests two conditions for equilibrium: the relatively obvious case where p or q equals o (that is to say where there is no genetic variation in the population and hence nothing for genetic selection to operate on); and where the expression $(sp - tq)$ of the numerator equals o. This second possibility implies a genetic equilibrium whenever $sp - tq$. If we now call the special values of p and q where this occurs by the names $\hat{p}$ (read "p-hat") and $\hat{q}$ (read "q-hat"), then

$$s\hat{p} - t\hat{q} = 0$$

from the numerator of Eq. B.5a, so

$$s(1 - \hat{q}) - t\hat{q} = 0$$
$$s - s\hat{q} - t\hat{q} = 0$$
$$s = s\hat{q} + t\hat{q}$$

which can be rearranged and written

$$\hat{q} = \frac{s}{s + t} \qquad\qquad (B.5b)$$

That is to say, the equilibrium value of q, reached after many generations of selection, is fully determined by the two selection coefficients s and t (ignoring stochastic effects). In the sample plots of Fig. B.3, this is why the frequency of **a** leveled out at 0.167 for all initial q's. According to the equation, $\hat{q} = 0.20/(1.20) = 0.167$. More generally, the relationship between $\hat{q}$, s, and t is that shown in Fig. 3.7. In that figure, $\hat{q}$ values (represented by the curved lines) vary as a function of s for selected values of t, $t = 0.7$ and $t = 1.0$.

B.2.6. Comparing the Change Between Generations in Gene and Genotype Frequencies

As shown in section B.2.5, a rare recessive allele can sometimes increase in frequency under conditions of heterozygote advantage. When that happens, it stands to reason that the frequency before selection of the homozygous recessive genotype will also increase. As it turns out, however, the proportional increase in the preselectional genotype frequency is even greater than that for the gene. In the case of sickle-cell anemia, for example, the frequency of **SS** births in a population will rise faster than the frequency of the **S** allele itself.

To see why this is so, consider a hypothetical population in which the allele **a** increases between generations 1 and 2 by an amount Δq. The frequency of **a** in generation 2 will be $q + \Delta q$, which represents a proportional increase of $(q + \Delta q)/q$. At the same time, the frequency of **aa** zygotes formed by the chance encounters of gametes before selection will be equal to the new **a** frequency squared, or $(q + \Delta q)^2$. The proportional increase in the frequency of **aa** before selection will thus be $(q + \Delta q)^2/q^2$.

Let x equal the ratio between the proportional increases in frequency of the genotype and gene. Then

$$x = \frac{(q + \Delta q)^2}{q^2} \Bigg/ \frac{(q + \Delta q)}{q}$$

$$= \frac{(q + \Delta q)}{q}$$

But this last line implies that x will be greater than 1.0 for all values of Δq above 0.0, and hence that the proportional genotype frequency change is always the greater of the two.

REFERENCE MATTER

BIBLIOGRAPHY

Aberle, D., et al. 1963. The incest taboo and the mating patterns of animals. *Am. Anthropologist* 65: 253–65.

Abernethy, V. 1981. Comments on Tibetan fraternal polyandry. *Am. Anthropologist* 83: 895.

Abramov, I., and J. Gordon. 1973a. Seeing. In E. C. Carterette and M. P. Friedman, eds., *Handbook of Perception*, vol. 3. New York.

——. 1973b. Vision. In E. C. Carterette and M. P. Friedman, eds., *Handbook of Perception*, vol. 3. New York.

Abramson, H., I. F. Bertles, and D. L. Wethers, eds. 1973. *Sickle-Cell Disease*. St. Louis, Mo.

Ackerknecht, E. H. 1965. *History and Geography of the Most Important Diseases*. New York.

Adam, A. 1969. A further query on color blindness and natural selection. *Social Biology* 16: 197–202.

——. 1973. Color blindness and gene flow in Alaskans. *Am. J. Hum. Genetics* 25: 564–66.

Adams, F. M., and C. E. Osgood. 1973. A cross-cultural study of the affective meanings of color. *J. Cross-Cultural Psychology* 4: 135–56.

Adams, M. S., and J. V. Neel. 1967. Children of incest. *Pediatrics* 40: 55–62.

Adams, R. N. 1981. Natural selection, energetics and "cultural materialism." *Current Anthropology* 22 (no. 6): 603–24.

Adriani, N., and A. C. Kruyt. 1950–51. *De Bare'e sprekende Toradjas van Midden-Celebes (de Oost-toradjas)* [The Bare'e-speaking Toradja of Central Celebes (the East Toradja)]. 3 vols., with vol. 1 published in 1950. Amsterdam. 2d ed.

Ajayi, J. F. A., and M. Crowder, eds. 1976. *History of West Africa*. 2 vols. London.

Ajose, O. A. 1957. Preventive medicine and superstition in Nigeria. *Africa* 27: 268–74.

Aldridge, A. O. 1951. The meaning of incest from Hutcheson to Gibbon. *Ethics* 61: 309–13.

Alexander, J., and D. G. Coursey. 1969. The origins of yam cultivation. In P. J. Ucko and G. W. Dimbleby, eds., *The Domestication and Exploitation of Plants and Animals*. London.

Alexander, R. D. 1971. The search for an evolutionary philosophy of man. *Proc. Royal Soc. Victoria, Melbourne* 84: 99–120.

————. 1974. The evolution of social behavior. *Ann. Rev. Ecology and Systematics* 5: 325–83.

————. 1977. Natural selection and the analysis of human sociality. In C. E. Goulden, ed., *Changing Scenes in the Natural Sciences: 1776–1976*. Philadelphia, Pa.

————. 1979a. *Darwinism and Human Affairs*. Seattle, Wash.

————. 1979b. Evolution and culture. In N. A. Chagnon and W. Irons, eds., *Evolutionary Biology and Human Social Behavior: An Anthropological Perspective*. North Scituate, Mass.

————. 1981. Evolution, culture, and human behavior: Some general considerations. In R. D. Alexander and D. W. Tinkle, eds., *Natural Selection and Social Behavior*. New York.

————. 1987. *The Biology of Moral Systems*. New York.

Alexander, R. D., and D. W. Tinkle, eds. 1981. *Natural Selection and Social Behavior*. New York.

Alland, A. 1966. Medical anthropology and the study of biological and cultural adaptation. *Am. Anthropologist* 68: 40–51.

————. 1970. *Adaptation in Cultural Evolution: An Approach to Medical Anthropology*. New York.

————. 1972a. Cultural evolution: The Darwinian model. *Social Biology* 19: 227–39.

————. 1972b. *The Human Imperative*. New York.

————. 1972c. "C'est ainsi que faisaient nos grandpères," enquête en ethnoignorance. *L'Homme* 12: 111–18.

————. 1973. *Evolution and Human Behavior*. Garden City, N.Y.

————. 1976. Adaptation. *Ann. Rev. Anthropology* 4: 59–73.

Alland, A., and B. McCay. 1973. The concept of adaptation in biological and cultural evolution. In J. J. Honigmann, ed., *Handbook of Social and Cultural Anthropology*. Chicago, Ill.

Allen, C. J. 1981. To be Quechua: The symbolism of coca chewing in highland Peru. *Am. Ethnologist* 8: 157–71.

Allen, L. H. 1982. Calcium bioavailability and absorption: A review. *Am. J. Clin. Nutrition* 35: 783–808.

Allen, T. F. H., and T. B. Starr. 1982. *Hierarchy: Perspectives for Ecological Complexity*. Chicago, Ill.

Allison, A. C. 1954a. Protection afforded by sickle-cell trait against subtertian malarial infection. *Brit. Medical J.* 1 (no. 4857): 290–94.

————. 1954b. The distribution of the sickle-cell trait in East Africa and elsewhere, and its apparent relationship to the incidence of subtertian malaria. *Tr. Royal Soc. Trop. Medicine and Hygiene* 48: 312–18.

————. 1955. Aspects of polymorphism in man. *Cold Spring Harbor Symposia on Quantitative Biology* 20: 239–55.

————. 1956a. Sickle cells and evolution. *Scientific American* 195 (no. 2): 87–94.

————. 1956b. Population genetics of abnormal human haemoglobins. *Acta Genetica et Statistica Medica* 6: 430–34.

————. 1961a. Abnormal haemoglobin and erythrocyte enzyme-deficiency traits. In G. A. Harrison, ed., *Genetical Variation in Human Populations*. Oxford, Eng.

————. 1961b. Genetic factors in resistance to malaria. *Ann. N.Y. Acad. Sciences* 91: 710–29.

———. 1964. Polymorphism and natural selection in human populations. *Cold Spring Harbor Symp. on Quantitative Biology* 29: 137–49.

———. 1965. Population genetics of abnormal haemoglobins and glucose-6-phosphate dehydrogenase deficiency. In J. H. P. Jonxis, ed., *Abnormal Haemoglobins in Africa*. Oxford, Eng.

Alpers, M. P. 1965. Epidemiological changes in kuru, 1957 to 1963. In D. C. Gajdusek, C. J. Gibbs, and M. Alpers, eds., *Slow, Latent, and Temperate Virus Infections*. Washington, D.C.

———. 1968. Kuru: Implications of its transmissibility for the interpretation of its changing epidemiological pattern. In O. T. Bailey and D. E. Smith, eds., *The Central Nervous System: Some Experimental Models of Neurological Diseases*. Baltimore, Md.

———. 1970. Kuru in New Guinea: Its changing pattern and etiologic elucidation. *Am. J. Trop. Medicine and Hygiene* 19: 133:37.

———. 1979. Epidemiology and ecology of kuru. In S. B. Prusiner and W. J. Hadlow, eds., *Slow Transmissible Diseases of the Nervous System*. New York.

———. 1981. Carbohydrate digestion: Effects of monosaccharide inhibition and enzyme degradation on lactase activity. In D. M. Paige and T. M. Bayless, eds., *Lactose Digestion*. Baltimore, Md.

Ammerman, A., and L. Cavalli-Sforza. 1971. Measuring the rate of spread of early farming in Europe. *Man* (n.s.) 6: 674–88.

———. 1973. A population model for the diffusion of early farming in Europe. In C. Renfrew, ed., *The Explanation of Culture Change: Models in Prehistory*. London.

———. 1979. The wave of advance model for the spread of agriculture in Europe. In C. Renfrew and K. L. Cooke, eds., *Transformations: Mathematical Approaches to Culture Change*. New York.

———. 1984. *The Neolithic Transition and the Genetics of Populations in Europe*. Princeton, N.J.

Anderson, A. R., and O. K. Moore. 1962. Toward a formal analysis of cultural objects. *Synthèse* 14: 144–70.

Anderson, E. N., Jr., and M. L. Anderson. 1977. Modern China: South. In K. C. Chang, ed., *Food in Chinese Culture*. New Haven, Conn.

Anderson, P. 1983. The reproductive role of the human breast. *Current Anthropology* 24: 25–45.

Andrews, A. C. 1949. The bean and Indo-European totemism. *Am. Anthropologist* 51: 274–92.

Angel, J. L. 1966. Porotic hyperostosis, anemias, malarias and marshes in the prehistoric eastern Mediterranean. *Science* 153: 760–73.

Aoki, K. 1986. A stochastic model of gene-culture coevolution suggested by the "culture historical hypothesis" for the evolution of adult lactose absorption in humans. *Proc. Nat. Acad. Sciences* 83: 2929–2933.

Arens, W. 1979. *The Man-Eating Myth*. New York.

———. 1986. *The Original Sin: Incest and Its Meaning*. New York.

Armbrecht, H. J., and R. H. Wasserman. 1976. Enhancement of Ca^{++} uptake by lactose in the rat small intestine. *J. Nutrition* 106: 1265–71.

Armelagos, G. J., and J. R. Dewey. 1970. Evolutionary response to human infectious diseases. *Bioscience* 20: 271–75.

Armelagos, G. J., and A. McArdle. 1975. Population, disease and evolution. *Am. Antiquity* 40: 1–10.

Armstrong, E., and D. Falk. 1982. *Primate Brain Evolution.* New York.

Arnold, A. J., and K. Fristrup. 1984. The theory of evolution by natural selection: A hierarchical expansion. In R. N. Brandon and R. M. Burian, eds., *Genes, Organisms, Populations: Controversies over the Units of Selection.* Cambridge, Mass.

Arthur, W. 1984. *Mechanisms of Morphological Evolution.* New York.

———. 1987. *The Niche in Competition and Evolution.* New York.

Ashbel, D., et al. 1965. *Solar Radiation in Different Latitudes.* Jerusalem.

Attah, E. B., and M. C. Ekere. 1975. Death patterns in sickle-cell anemia. *J. Am. Medical Assn.* 233: 889–96.

Awolalu, J. O. 1979. *Yoruba Beliefs and Sacrificial Rites.* London.

Ayala, F. J. 1982. *Population and Evolutionary Genetics: A Primer.* Menlo Park, Calif.

———. 1983. Microevolution and macroevolution. In D. S. Bendall, ed., *Evolution from Molecules to Men.* New York.

Aziz, B. N. 1978. *Tibetan Frontier Families: Reflections of Three Generations from Ding-ri.* Durham, N.C.

Baber, E. C. 1886. Travels and researches in western China. *Royal Geographical Soc.* (Supp. Papers) 1: 1–201.

Baer, D. 1970. Lactase deficiency and yogurt. *Social Biology* 17: 143.

Bagley, C. 1969. Incest behavior and incest taboo. *Social Problems* 16: 505–19.

Bailit, H. L. 1968. A possible benefit from tooth-blackening. *Am. Anthropologist* 70: 348–53.

Baines, J. 1985. Color terminology and color classification: ancient Egyptian color terminology and polysony. *Am. Anthropologist* 87: 282–97.

Baird, P. A., and B. McGillivray. 1982. Children of incest. *J. Pediatrics* 101: 854–57.

Bajema, C. J., ed. 1971a. *Natural Selection in Human Populations.* New York.

———. 1971b. Natural selection in relation to human behavior. In C. J. Bajema, ed., *Natural Selection in Human Populations.* New York.

———. 1978. Differential transmission of genetic and cultural information about the environment: A cybernetic view of genetic and cultural evolution in animal species. In R. Meier, C. Otten, and F. Abdel-Hameed, eds., *Evolutionary Models and Studies in Human Diversity.* The Hague.

Bajpai, S. C. 1981. *Kinnaur in the Himalayas.* New Delhi.

Baker, P. T. 1960. Climate, culture and evolution. *Hum. Biology* 32: 3–16.

———. 1966a. Ecological and physiological adaptation in indigenous South Americans. In P. T. Baker and J. S. Weiner, eds., *The Biology of Human Adaptability.* Oxford, Eng.

———. 1966b. Human biological variation as an adaptive response to the environment. *Eugenics Q.* 13: 461–508.

———. 1969. Human adaptation to high altitude. *Science* 163: 1149–56.

———, ed., 1978. *The Biology of High-Altitude Peoples.* Cambridge, Eng.

Baker, P. T., and M. A. Little, eds. 1976. *Man in the Andes: A Multidisciplinary Study of High Altitude Quechua.* Stroudsberg, Pa.

Baker, P. T., and J. S. Weiner, eds. 1966. *The Biology of Human Adaptability.* Oxford, Eng.

Baldwin, D. E., and C. M. Baldwin. 1976. *The Yoruba of Southwestern Nigeria: An Indexed Bibliography.* Boston, Mass.

Baldwin, J. D., and J. I. Baldwin. 1981. *Beyond Sociobiology*. New York.

Balée, W. 1984. The ecology of ancient Tupi warfare. In R. B. Ferguson, ed., *Warfare, Culture, and Environment*. New York.

Ball, J. A. 1984. Memes as replicators. *Ethology and Sociobiology* 5: 145–61.

Bandura, A. 1977. *Social Learning Theory*. Englewood Cliffs, N.J.

Bang, H. O., et al. 1976. The composition of food consumed by Greenland Eskimos. *Acta Medica Scandinavica* 200: 69–73.

Bank, A., J. G. Mears, and F. Ramirez. 1980. Disorders of human hemoglobin. *Science* 207: 486–93.

Banton, M., ed. 1961. *Darwinism and the Study of Society*. London.

Barash, D. P. 1977. *Sociobiology and Behavior*. New York.

———. 1979. *The Whisperings Within: Evolution and the Origins of Human Nature*. New York.

———. 1980. Human behavior: Do the genes have it? *Nature* 287: 173–74.

———. 1982. *Sociobiology and Behavior*. New York. 2d rev. ed. of work first published in 1977.

———. 1986. *The Hare and the Tortoise: Culture, Biology, and Human Nature*. New York.

Barber, M. A., and M. T. Olinger. 1931. Studies on malaria in southern Nigeria. *Anns. Trop. Medicine and Parasitology* 25: 461–508.

Barber, M. A., J. B. Rice, and J. Y. Brown. 1932. Malaria studies on the Firestone rubber plantations in Liberia, West Africa. *Am. J. Hygiene* 15: 601–33.

Bargatzky, T. 1984. Culture, environment, and the ills of adaptationism. *Current Anthropology* 25: 399–415.

Barker, L. M., ed. 1982. *The Psychobiology of Human Food Selection*. Westport, Conn.

Barkow, J. H. 1984. The distance between genes and culture. *J. Anthropological Research* 40: 367–79.

Barlow, G. W., and J. Silverberg. 1980. *Sociobiology: Beyond Nature/Nurture*. Boulder, Colo.

Barnard, A., and A. Good. 1984. *Research Practices in the Study of Kinship*. New York.

Barnett, H. G. 1953. *Innovation: The Basis of Cultural Change*. New York.

Barnicot, N. A. 1957. Human pigmentation. *Man* 57: 114–20.

———. 1958. Reflectometry of the skin in southern Nigerians and in some mulattoes. *Hum. Biology* 30: 150–60.

———. 1959. Climatic factors in the evolution of human populations. *Cold Spring Harbor Symposia on Quantitative Biology* 24: 115–29.

Barth, F. 1966. *Models of Social Organization*. Glasgow, Scot.

Barton, N. H., and B. Charlesworth. 1984. Genetic revolutions, founder effects, and speciation. *Ann. Rev. Ecology and Systematics* 15: 133–64.

Bascom, W. 1969. *The Yoruba of Southwestern Nigeria*. New York.

Basden, G. T. 1966. *Niger Ibos*. London. Reprint with new biblio. note of work first published in 1938.

Bassett, E. J., et al. 1980. Tetrocycline-labeled human bone from ancient Sudanese Nubia (A.D. 350). *Science* 209: 1532–34.

Bateson, G. 1972a. The role of somatic change in evolution. In G. Bateson, ed., *Steps to an Ecology of Mind*. New York.

———. 1972b. *Steps to an Ecology of Mind*. New York.

———. 1979. *Mind and Nature: A Necessary Unity*. New York.

Bateson, P. 1983a. Optimal outbreeding. In P. Bateson, ed., *Mate Choice.* Cambridge, Eng.

———. 1983b. Rules for changing the rules. In D. S. Bendall, ed., *Evolution from Molecules to Men.* Cambridge, Eng.

Bayless, T. M. 1981. Lactose malabsorption, milk intolerance, and symptom awareness in adults. In D. M. Paige and T. M. Bayless, eds., *Lactose Digestion.* Baltimore, Md.

Bayoumi, R. A. L., et al. 1981. Distribution of the lactase phenotypes in the population of the Democratic Republic of the Sudan. *Hum. Genetics* 57: 279–84.

Beall, C. M., and M. C. Goldstein. 1981. Tibetan fraternal polyandry: A test of sociobiological theory. *Am. Anthropologist* 83: 5–12.

Beals, K. L., and A. J. Kelso. 1975. Genetic variation and cultural evolution. *Am. Anthropologist* 77: 566–79.

Beals, K. L., C. L. Smith, and S. M. Dodd. 1984. Brain size, cranial morphology, climate and time machines. *Current Anthropology* 25: 301–30.

Beckerman, S. 1979. The abundance of protein in Amazonia: A reply to Gross. *Am. Anthropologist* 81: 533–60.

Beet, E. A. 1946. Sickle-cell disease in the Balovale District of northern Rhodesia. *East African Medical J.* 23: 75–86.

———. 1947. Sickle-cell disease in northern Rhodesia. *East African Medical J.* 24: 212–22.

———. 1949. The genetics of the sickle-cell trait in a Bantu tribe. *Anns. Eugenics* 14: 279–84.

Beier, H. U. 1960. Obatala: Five myths about the Yoruba creator god. *Black Orpheus* 7: 34–35.

Bell, C. 1928. *The People of Tibet.* Oxford, Eng.

Bell, G. 1982. *The Masterpiece of Nature: The Evolution and Genetics of Sexuality.* Berkeley, Calif.

Bellig, R., and G. Stevens, eds. 1988. *The Evolution of Sex.* San Francisco, Calif.

Belsey, M. A. 1973. The epidemiology of favism. *Bull. World Health Organization* 48: 1–13.

Bemiss, S. M. 1858. Report on influence of marriages of consanguinity upon offspring. *Tr. Am. Medical Assn.* 11: 319–425.

Bendall, D. S., ed. 1983. *Evolution from Molecules to Men.* Cambridge, Eng.

Bender, M. L. 1976. Genetic classification of languages: Genotype vs. phenotype. *Language Sciences* 43: 4–6.

Benedict, P. K. 1942. Tibetan and Chinese kinship terms. *Harvard J. Asiatic Stud.* 6: 313–37.

Benedict, R. F. 1934. *Patterns of Culture.* New York.

Bener, P. 1972. *Approximate Values of Intensity of Natural Ultraviolet Radiation for Different Amounts of Atmospheric Ozone.* London.

Bengtsson, B. O. 1978. Avoiding inbreeding: At what cost? *J. Theoretical Biology* 73: 439–44.

Bennett, J. H., F. A. Rhodes, and H. N. Robson. 1959. A possible genetic basis for kuru. *Am. J. Hum. Genetics* 11: 169–87.

Bennett, J. W. 1970. The significance of the concept of adaptation for contemporary socio-cultural anthropology. In *Proc. Eighth Congress of Anthropological and Ethnological Sciences* (Tokyo), symposium 7.

———. 1976a. *The Ecological Transition: Cultural Anthropology and Human Adaptation.* New York.

————. 1976b. Anticipation, adaptation, and the concept of culture in anthropology. *Science* 192: 847–53.

Bennett, K. A., R. H. Osborne, and R. J. Miller. 1975. Biocultural ecology. *Ann. Rev. Anthropology* 4: 163–81.

Berlin, B., and P. Kay. 1969. *Basic Color Terms: Their Universality and Evolution.* Berkeley, Calif.

Bernardi, B., ed. 1977. *The Concept and Dynamics of Culture.* The Hague.

Berndt, R. M. 1952. A Cargo Movement in the Eastern Central Highlands of New Guinea. *Oceania* 23: 40–65.

————. 1954. Reaction to contact in the Eastern Highlands of New Guinea. *Oceania* 24 (nos. 3–4): 190–228, 255–74.

————. 1954–55. Kamano, Jate, Usurufa and Fore Kinship of the Eastern Highlands of New Guinea: A preliminary account. *Oceania* 25 (nos. 1–3): 23–53, 156–87.

————. 1958. A devastating disease syndrome: Kuru sorcery in the Eastern Central Highlands of New Guinea. *Sociologus* 8: 4–28.

————. 1962. *Excess and Restraint.* Chicago, Ill.

Berreman, G. D. 1962. Pahari polyandry: A comparison. *Am. Anthropologist* 64: 60–75.

————. 1975. Himalayan polyandry and the domestic cycle. *Am. Ethnologist* 2: 127–38.

————. 1978. Ecology, demography and domestic strategies in the western Himalayas. *J. Anthropological Res.* 34: 326–68.

Bertles, J. F. 1973. Multiple hemoglobins in cells: Significance and genetic control. In H. Abramson et al., eds., *Sickle Cell Disease.* St. Louis, Mo.

Betzig, L. 1986. *Despotism and Differential Reproduction: A Darwinian View of History.* Hawthorne, N.Y.

Betzig, L., M. Borgerhoff Mulder, and P. Turke, eds. 1988. *Human Reproductive Behavior: A Darwinian Perspective.* Cambridge, Eng.

Biasutti, R. 1959. *Le razze i popoli della terra,* Turin, Italy. 3d rev. ed. of work first published in 1940.

Bienen, L. B. 1981. The incest statutes. Appendix in J. L. Herman and L. Hirschmann, *Father-Daughter Incest.* Cambridge, Mass.

Bienzle, U., V. C. N. Okoye, and H. Gogler. 1972. Haemoglobin and glucose-6-phosphate dehydrogenase variants: Distribution in relation to malaria endemicity in a Togolese population. *Zeitschrift für Tropenmedizin und Parasitologie* 23: 56–62.

Biesele, M. 1986. How Hunter-gatherers' stories "make sense": Semantics and adaptation. *Cultural Anthropology* 1: 157–70.

Billings, W. D. 1979. High mountain ecosystems: Evolution, structure, operation and maintenance. In P. J. Webber, ed., *High Altitude Geoecology.* Washington, D.C.

Bilsborough, A. 1976. Patterns of evolution in Middle Pleistocene hominids. *J. Hum. Evolution* 5: 423–39.

Binford, L. R. 1969. Conceptual problems in dealing with units and rates of cultural evolution. *Anthropology UCLA* 1: 27–35.

Biondi, G., et al. 1980. Distribution of the S and C hemoglobins in Atkora District (Benin). *Hum. Biology* 52: 205–13.

Birge, S. J., et al. 1967. Osteoporosis, intestinal lactase deficiency and low dietary calcium intake. *New England J. Medicine* 276: 445–48.

Bischof, N. 1972. The biological foundations of the incest taboo. *Social Science Information* 11 (no. 6): 7–36.

———. 1975. Comparative ethology of incest avoidance. In R. Fox, ed., *Biosocial Anthropology*. New York.

Bittles, A. H., and E. Makov. 1988. Inbreeding in human populations: An assessment of the costs. In C. G. N. Mascie-Taylor and A. J. Boyce, eds., *Human Mating Patterns*. Cambridge, Eng.

Bixler, R. H. 1981a. Incest avoidance as a function of environment and heredity. *Current Anthropology* 22: 639–54.

———. 1981b. The incest controversy. *Psychological Reports* 49: 267–83.

Blackwood, B. 1978. *The Kukukuku of the Upper Watut*. Oxford, Eng.

Blakely, R. L., ed. 1977. *Biocultural Adaptation in Prehistoric America*. Athens, Ga.

Bleibtreu, H. K. 1969. *Evolutionary Anthropology*. Boston.

Bloch, M. 1971. *Placing the Dead: Tombs, Ancestral Villages and Kinship Organization in Madagascar*. New York.

Blois, M. S., H. F. Blum, and W. F. Loomis. 1968. Vitamin D, sunlight and natural selection. *Science* 159: 652–53.

Blum, H. F. 1961. Does the melanin pigment of human skin have adaptive value? An essay in human ecology and the evolution of race. *Q. Rev. Biology* 36: 50–63.

———. 1963. On the origin and evolution of human culture. *Am. Scientist* 51: 32–47.

———. 1967. Humanity in the perspective of time. *Anns. N.Y. Acad. Sciences* 138: 489–503.

———. 1968. *Time's Arrow and Evolution*. Princeton, N.J.

———. 1969. Is sunlight a factor in the geographical distribution of human skin color? *Geographical Rev.* 59: 557–81.

———. 1978. Uncertainty in interplay of biological and cultural evolution: Man's view of himself. *Q. Rev. Biology* 53: 29–40.

Blumenberg, B. 1978. Hominid ECV versus time: Available data does not permit a choice of model. *J. Hum. Evolution* 7: 425–36.

———. 1983. The evolution of the advanced hominid brain. *Current Anthropology* 24: 589–623.

———. 1984. Allometry and evolution of Tertiary hominoids. *J. Hum. Evolution* 13: 613–76.

Blurton Jones, N. G. 1976. Growing points in human ethology: Another link between ethology and the social sciences? In P. Bateson and R. A. Hinde, eds., *Growing Points in Ethology*. Cambridge, Eng.

Blust, R. 1981. Linguistic evidence for some early Austronesian taboos. *Am. Anthropologist* 83: 285–319.

Blute, M. 1979. Sociocultural evolutionism: An untried theory. *Behavioral Science* 24: 46–59.

———. 1984. The sociobiology of sex and sexes today. *Current Anthropology* 25: 193–212.

Bocock, R. 1986. *Hegemony*. New York.

Bodley, J. H. 1982. *Victims of Progress*. Menlo Park, Calif.

Bodmer, W. F. 1965. Differential fertility in population genetics models. *Genetics* 51: 411–24.

————. 1983. Gene clusters and genome evolution. In D. S. Bendall, ed., *Evolution from Molecules to Men*. Cambridge, Eng.

Bodmer, W. F., and L. Cavalli-Sforza. 1976. *Genetics, Evolution, and Man*. San Francisco, Calif.

Boehm, C. 1978. Rational preselection from Hamadryas to Homo sapiens: The place of decisions in adaptive processes. *Am. Anthropologist* 80: 265–96.

————. 1982. A fresh outlook on cultural selection. *Am. Anthropologist* 84: 105–25.

Bogucki, P., and Grygiel, R. 1983. Early farmers of the north European plain. *Scientific American* 248 (no. 4): 104–12.

Bohannan, P. 1965. The Tiv of Nigeria. In J. L. Gibbs, Jr., ed., *Peoples of Africa*. New York.

————. 1973. Rethinking culture: A project for current anthropologists. *Current Anthropology* 14: 357–72.

Bolin, T. D., and A. E. Davis. 1970. Primary lactase deficiency: Genetic or acquired? *Digestive Diseases* 15: 679–92.

Bolton, R. 1976. Andean coca chewing: A metabolic perspective. *Am. Anthropologist* 78: 630–34.

————. 1978. Black, white and red all over: The riddle of color term salience. *Ethnology* 17: 287–311.

————. 1979. On coca chewing and high-altitude stress. *Current Anthropology* 20: 418–20.

Bolton, R., and D. Crisp. 1979. Color terms in folk tales: A cross-cultural study. *Behavior Science Res.* 14: 231–53.

Bonner, J. T. 1980. *The Evolution of Culture in Animals*. Princeton, N.J.

Bookstein, F. L., P. D. Gingerich, and A. G. Kluge. 1978. Hierarchical linear modeling of the tempo and mode of evolution. *Paleobiology* 4: 120–34.

Bordes, F. 1971. Physical evolution and technological evolution in man: A parallelism. *World Archaeology* 3: 1–5.

Borgerhoff Mulder, M. 1987a. Adaptation and evolutionary approaches to anthropology. *Man* (n.s.) 22: 25–41.

————. 1987b. Progress in human sociobiology. *Anthropology Today* no. 3: 5–8.

Bornstein, M. H. 1973a. Color vision and color naming: A psychophysiological hypothesis of cultural difference. *Psychological Bull.* 80: 257–85.

————. 1973b. The psychophysiological component of cultural differences in color naming and illusion susceptibility. *Behavior Science Notes* 8: 41–101.

————. 1975. The influence of visual perception on culture. *Am. Anthropologist* 77: 774–98.

————. 1979. Perceptual development: Stability and change in infant perception. In M. H. Bornstein and W. Kessen, eds. *Psychological Development from Infancy: Image to Intention*. Hillsdale, N.J.

Bornstein, M. H., W. Kessen, and S. Weiskopf. 1976. The categories of hue in infancy. *Science* 191: 201–2.

Bourguignon, E., et al. 1983. Women, possession trance cults, and the extended nutrient-deficiency hypothesis. *Am. Anthropologist* 85: 413–16.

Bowler, P. J. 1989. *Evolution: The History of an Idea*. Berkeley, Calif. 2d rev. ed. of work first published in 1983.

Bowman, J. E. 1964. Comments on abnormal erythrocytes and malaria. *Am. J. Trop. Medicine and Hygiene* 13: 159–61.

————, ed. 1983. *Distribution and Evolution of Hemoglobin and Globin Loci.* New York.

Boyd, D. J. 1985. "We must follow the Fore": Pig husbandry intensification and ritual diffusion among the Irakia Awa, Papua New Guinea. *Am. Ethnologist* 12: 119–36.

Boyd, M. F. 1949a. Epidemiology: Factors related to the definitive host. In M. F. Boyd, ed., *Malariology.* Philadelphia, Pa.

————. 1949b. Epidemiology of malaria: Factors related to the intermediate host. In M. F. Boyd, ed., *Malariology.* Philadelphia, Pa.

————, ed. 1949c. *Malariology: A Comprehensive Survey of All Aspects of This Group of Diseases from a Global Standpoint.* 2 vols. Philadelphia, Pa.

Boyd, R., and P. J. Richerson. 1976. A simple dual inheritance model of the conflict between social and biological evolution. *Zygon* 11: 254–62.

————. 1980. Sociobiology, culture and economic theory. *J. Econ. Behavior and Organization* 1: 97–121.

————. 1981. Culture, biology and the evolution of variation between human groups. In M. S. Collins, I. W. Wainer, and T. A. Bremner, eds., *Science and the Question of Human Equality.* Boulder, Colo.

————. 1982. Cultural transmission and the evolution of cooperative behavior. *Hum. Ecology* 10: 325–51.

————. 1983. Why is culture adaptive? *Q. Rev. Biology* 58: 209–14.

————. 1985. *Culture and the Evolutionary Process.* Chicago.

Boynton, R. M. 1975. Color, hue, and wavelength. In E. C. Carterette and M. P. Friedman, eds., *Handbook of Perception,* vol. 5. New York.

————. 1979. *Human Color Vision.* New York.

————. 1988. Color vision. *Ann. Rev. Psychology* 39: 69–100.

Boynton, R. M., and J. Gordon. 1965. Bezold-Brücke hue shift measured by color-naming technique. *J. Optical Soc. America* 55: 78–86.

Boyo, A. E. 1972. Malariometric indices and hemoglobin type. *Am. J. Trop. Medicine and Hygiene* 21: 863–67.

Brace, C. L., and M. F. A. Montagu. 1977. *Human Evolution: An Introduction to Biological Anthropology.* New York.

Branda, R. F., and J. W. Eaton. 1978. Skin color and nutrient photolysis: An evolutionary hypothesis. *Science* 201: 625–26.

Brandon, R. N. 1978. Adaptation and evolutionary theory. *Stud. History and Philosophy of Science* 9: 181–206.

————. 1985. Adaptation explanations: Are adaptations for the good of replicators or interactors? In D. J. Depew and B. H. Weber, eds., *Evolution at a Crossroads.* Cambridge, Mass.

Brandon, R. N., and R. M. Burian, eds. 1984. *Genes, Organisms, Populations: Controversies over the Units of Selection.* Cambridge, Mass.

Bräuer, G. 1984. A craniological approach to the origin of anatomically modern *Homo sapiens* in Africa and implications for the appearance of modern Europeans. In F. H. Smith and F. Spencer, eds., *The Origins of Modern Humans.* New York.

Bray, W. 1973. The biological basis of culture. In C. Renfrew, ed., *Explanations of Culture Change: Models in Prehistory.* Pittsburgh, Pa.

Bray, W., and C. Dollery. 1983. Coca chewing and high-altitude stress: A spurious correlation. *Current Anthropology* 24: 269–82.

Bressani, R., and N. S. Scrimshaw. 1958. Effect of lime treatment on in vitro availability of essential amino acids and solubility of protein fractions in corn. *J. Agr. and Food Chemistry* 6: 774–78.

Bressani, R., R. Paz y Paz, and N. S. Scrimshaw. 1958. Chemical changes in corn during preparation of tortillas. *J. Agr. and Food Chemistry* 6: 770–74.

Briffault, R. 1927. *The Mothers*. New York.

Bright, M. 1984. *Animal Communication*. Ithaca, N.Y.

Brown, K. H., et al. 1980. Nutritional consequences of low dose milk supplements consumed by lactose-malabsorbing children. *Am. J. Clin. Nutrition* 33: 1054–63.

Brown, P., and D. Tuzin, eds. 1983. *The Ethnography of Cannibalism*. Washington, D.C.

Brown, P. J. 1979. Cultural adaptations to endemic malaria and the socioeconomic effects of malaria eradication in Sardinia. Ph.D. diss., State University of New York, Stony Brook.

———. 1981a. Cultural adaptation to endemic malaria in Sardinia. *Medical Anthropology* 5: 313–39.

———. 1981b. New considerations on the distribution of malaria, thalassemia, and glucose-6-phosphate dehydrogenase deficiency in Sardinia. *Hum. Biology* 53: 367–82.

———. 1986. Cultural and genetic adaptations to malaria: Problems of comparison. *Hum. Ecology* 14: 311–32.

Browning, D. 1971. *El Salvador: Landscape and Society*. Oxford, Eng.

Bruce-Chwatt, L. J. 1951. Malaria in Nigeria. *Bull. World Health Organization* 4: 301–27.

———. 1952. Malaria in African infants and children in southern Nigeria. *Anns. Trop. Medicine and Parasitology* 46: 173–200.

———. 1980. *Essential Malariology*. London.

———. 1987. Malaria and its control: Present situation and future prospects. *Ann. Rev. Public Health* 8: 75–110.

Brumbaugh, R. S., and J. Schwartz. 1980. Pythagoras and beans: A medical explanation. *The Classic World* 73: 421–22.

Buchbinder, G., and R. A. Rappaport. 1976. Fertility and death among the Maring. In P. Brown and G. Buchbinder, eds., *Man and Woman in the New Guinea Highlands*. Washington, D.C.

Bunn, H. F., B. G. Forget, and H. M. Ranney. 1977. *Human Hemoglobins*. Philadelphia, Pa.

Burchard, R. E. 1975. Coca chewing: A new perspective. In V. Rubin, ed., *Cannabis and Culture*. The Hague.

———. 1976. Myths of the sacred leaf: Ecological perspectives on coca and peasant biocultural adaptation in Peru. Ph.D. diss., Indiana University.

———. 1980. On coca chewing and the polycythemia hypothesis. *Current Anthropology* 2: 108–9.

Burger, J. 1987. *Report from the Frontier: The State of the World's Indigenous Peoples*. Cambridge, Mass.

Burgess, D., et al. 1983. Tarahumara color modifiers: category structure presaging evolutionary change. *Am. Ethnologist* 10: 133–49.

Burkill, I. H. 1960. The organography and the evolution of the Dioscoreaceae, the family of the yams. *J. Linnean Society* 56: 319–412.

Burnet, G. M. 1971. Reflections on kuru. *Human Biology in Oceania* 1: 3–9.

Burnham, J. T. 1975. Incest avoidance and social evolution. *Mankind* 10: 93–98.

Burnham, P. 1973. The explanatory value of the concept of adaptation in studies of culture change. In C. Renfrew, ed., *Explanations of Culture Change: Models in Prehistory*. Pittsburgh, Pa.

Burrow, J. W. 1966. *Evolution and Society: A Study in Victorian Social Theory.* Cambridge, Eng.

Burton, R. V. 1973. Folk theory and the incest taboo. *Ethos* 1: 504–16.

Bush, G. 1975. Modes of animal speciation. *Ann. Rev. Ecology and Systematics* 6: 339–64.

Bushnell, P. J., and H. F. DeLuca. 1981. Lactose facilitates the intestinal absorption of lead in weanling rats. *Science* 211: 61–63.

Bushnell, S. W. 1880. The early history of Tibet from Chinese sources. *J. Royal Asiatic Soc.* 12: 435–541.

Butzer, K. 1977. Environment, culture and human evolution. *Am. Scientist* 65: 572–84.

Caldwell, M. M., R. Robberecht, and W. D. Billings. 1980. A steep latitudinal gradient of solar ultraviolet-B radiation in the arctic-alpine life zone. *Ecology* 61: 600–611.

Campbell, D. T. 1960. Blind variation and selective retention in creative thought as in other knowledge processes. *Psychological Rev.* 67: 380–400.

———. 1965. Variation and selective retention in sociocultural evolution. In H. R. Barringer, G. I. Blanksten, and R. W. Mack, eds., *Social Change in Developing Areas: A Reinterpretation of Evolutionary Theory*. Cambridge, Mass.

———. 1970. Natural selection as an epistemological model. In R. Naroll and R. Cohen, eds., *A Handbook of Method in Cultural Anthropology*. Garden City, N.Y.

———. 1972. On the genetics of altruism and the counter-hedonic components in human culture. *J. Social Issues* 28: 21–37.

———. 1974. Evolutionary epistemology. In P. A. Schilpp, ed., *The Philosophy of Karl Popper*. La Salle, Ill.

———. 1975a. The conflict between social and biological evolution and the concept of original sin. *Zygon* 10: 234–49.

———. 1975b. On the conflicts between biological and social evolution and between psychology and moral tradition. *Am. Psychologist* 30: 1103–26.

———. 1979. Comments on the sociobiology of ethics and moralizing. *Behavioral Science* 24: 37–45.

Cancian, F. 1979. *The Innovator's Situation*. Stanford, Calif.

Cannon, W. B. 1963. *The Wisdom of the Body*. New York. Reprint of 1939 ed., rev. and enlarged from work first published in 1932.

Caplan, A. L., ed. 1978. *The Sociobiology Debate*. New York.

Caplan, A. T. 1983. Out with the old and in with the new: The evolution and refinement of sociobiological theory. In D. W. Pfaff, ed., *Ethical Questions in Brain and Behavior*. New York.

Carneiro, R. L. 1968. Culture: Cultural adaptation. In D. L. Sills, ed., *International Encyclopedia of the Social Sciences*, vol. 3.

———. 1970. Foreword to Keith F. Otterbein, *The Evolution of War: A Cross-Cultural Study*. New Haven, Conn.

———. 1972. The devolution of evolution. *Social Biology* 19: 248–58.

———. 1973a. Classical evolution. In R. Naroll and F. Naroll, eds., *Main Currents in Cultural Anthropology.* New York.

———. 1973b. The four faces of evolution. In J. Honigman, ed., *Handbook of Social and Cultural Anthropology.* Chicago, Ill.

Caro, T. M., and M. Borgerhoff Mulder. 1987. The problem of adaptation in the study of human behavior. *Ethology and Sociobiology* 8: 61–72.

Carrasco, Pedro. 1959. *Land and Polity in Tibet.* Seattle, Wash.

Carroll, V., ed. 1972. *Adoption in Eastern Oceania.* Honolulu, Hawaii.

Carterette, E. C., and M. P. Friedman, eds. 1975. *Handbook of Perception,* vol. 5. New York.

Caspari, E. 1963. Selective forces in the evolution of man. *Am. Naturalist* 97: 5–14.

Cassinelli, C. W., and R. B. Ekvall. 1969. *A Tibetan Principality: The Political System of Sa sKya.* Ithaca, N.Y.

Caton, H., and F. K. Salter. 1988. *A Bibliography of Biosocial Science.* Brisbane, Aus.

Cavalli-Sforza, L. L. 1971. Similarities and dissimilarities of sociocultural and biological evolution. In F. R. Hodson, et al., eds., *Mathematics in the Archaeological and Social Sciences.* Edinburgh, Scot.

———. 1973. Analytic review: Some current problems of human population genetics. *Am. J. Hum. Genetics* 25: 82–104.

———. 1974. The genetics of human populations. *Scientific American* 231 (no. 3): 80–89.

———. 1986. Cultural evolution. *Am. Zoologist* 26: 845–55.

Cavalli-Sforza, L. L., and W. F. Bodmer. 1971. *The Genetics of Human Populations.* San Francisco, Calif.

Cavalli-Sforza, L. L., and M. W. Feldman. 1973a. Cultural versus biological inheritance: Phenotypic transmission from parents to children. *Am. J. Hum. Genetics* 25: 618–37.

———. 1973b. Models for cultural inheritance, I: Group mean and within group variation. *Theoretical Population Biology* 4: 42–55.

———. 1976. Cultural and biological evolutionary processes, selection for a trait under complex transmission. *Theoretical Population Biology* 9: 238–59.

———. 1978. Towards a theory of cultural evolution. *Interdisciplinary Science Reviews* 3: 99–107.

———. 1981. *Cultural Transmission and Evolution.* Princeton, N.J.

Cavalli-Sforza, L. L., et al. 1982. Theory and observation in cultural transmission. *Science* 218: 19–27.

———. 1988. Reconstruction of human evolution: Bringing together genetic, archeological, and linguistic data. *Proc. Nat. Acad. Sciences* 85: 6002–6.

Cerny, J. 1954. Consanguineous marriages in pharaonic Egypt. *J. Egyptian Archaeology* 40: 23–9.

Chagnon, N. A., and R. B. Hames. 1979. Protein deficiency and tribal warfare in Amazonia: New data. *Science* 203: 910–13.

———. 1980. La "hipótesis proteica" y la adaptación indigena a la cuenca del Amazonas: Una revisión crítica de los datos y la teoría. *Interciencia* (Caracas) 5: 346–58.

Chagnon, N. A., and W. Irons, eds. 1979. *Evolutionary Biology and Human Social Behavior: An Anthropological Perspective.* North Scituate, Mass.

Chambon, P. 1981. Split genes. *Scientific American* 244 (no. 5): 60–71.

Chandra, R. 1973. Types and forms of marriage in a Kinnaur village. *Man in India* 53: 176–87.

———. 1981. Sex role arrangement to achieve economic security in the North Himalayas. In C. von Fürer-Haimendorf, ed., *Asian Highland Societies.* New Delhi.

———, ed. 1984. *Food Intolerance.* New York.

Chapple, E. D. 1970. *Culture and Biological Man: Explanations in Behavioral Anthropology.* New York.

Charlesworth, D., and B. Charlesworth. 1987. Inbreeding depression and its evolutionary consequences. *Ann. Rev. Ecology and Systematics* 18: 237–68.

Charney, M., and R. D. McCracken. 1971. Intestinal lactase deficiency in adult nonhuman primates: Implications for selection pressures in man. *Social Biology* 18: 416–21.

Chasan, D. J. 1983. Milk. *Science 83* 4: 67–74.

Cherfas, J., and R. Lewin, eds. 1980. *Not Work Alone: A Cross-Cultural View of Activities Superfluous to Survival.* Beverly Hills, Calif.

Chibnik, M. 1981. The evolution of cultural rules. *J. Anthropological Res.* 37: 256–68.

Chick, H. 1932. The relation of ultraviolet light to nutrition: Lecture II, Influence of vitamin D on mineral metabolism. *Lancet* 2 (no. 5685): 377–84.

Childe, V. G. 1951. *Social Evolution.* New York.

Ch'ing-yuan Yu. 1936. "Wei Hsi Chien Wen Chi" [A Descriptive account of Weihsi, Yunnan]. In *Travel to Dali and Five Other Descriptive Accounts.* Shanghai. Reprint of work first published in 1770.

Christiansen, F. B., and M. W. Feldman. 1986. *Population Genetics.* Palo Alto, Calif.

Church, R. J. H. 1974. *West Africa.* London.

Ciba Foundation. 1988. *Novel Infectious Agents and the Central Nervous System.* Ciba Foundation Symposium 135. Chichester, Eng., and New York.

Cloak, F. T., Jr. 1975. Is a cultural ethology possible? *Hum. Ecology* 3: 161–82.

———. 1977. Comment. In E. E. Ruyle et al., The adaptive significance of cultural behavior: Comments and a reply. *Hum. Ecology* 5: 49–68.

———. 1986. The causal logic of natural selection: A general theory. *Oxford Surveys in Evolutionary Biology* 3: 132–86.

Cloninger, C. R., and S. Yokoyama. 1981. The channeling of social behavior. *Science* 213: 749–51.

Clutton-Brock, T. H., and P. H. Harvey, eds. 1978. *Readings in Sociobiology.* San Francisco, Calif.

Coatney, G. R., et al., eds. 1971. *The Primate Malarias.* Bethesda, Md.

Cochet, B., et al. 1983. Effects of lactose on intestinal calcium absorption in normal and lactase-deficient subjects. *Gastroenterology* 84: 935–40.

Cohen, A. 1974. *Two-Dimensional Man: An Essay on the Anthropology of Power and Symbolism in Complex Society.* Berkeley, Calif.

Cohen, I. B. 1985. *Revolution in Science.* Cambridge, Mass.

Cohen, R. 1962. The strategy of social evolution. *Anthropologica* 4: 321–48.

———. 1981. Evolutionary epistemology and human values. *Current Anthropology* 22: 201–18.

Cohen, Y. A. 1969. Ends and means in political control: State organization and the punishment of adultery, incest, and violation of celibacy. *Am. Anthropologist* 71: 658–87.

———. 1974a. Culture as adaptation. In Y. A. Cohen, ed., *Man in Adaptation: The Cultural Present.* Chicago, Ill.

———, ed. 1974b. *Man in Adaptation: The Cultural Present.* Chicago, Ill.

———. 1978. The disappearance of the incest taboo. *Hum. Nature* 1 (no. 7): 72–78.

Colbourne, M. J. 1966. *Malaria in Africa.* London.

Colbourne, M. J., and G. M. Edington. 1954. Mortality from malaria in Accra. *J. Trop. Medicine and Hygiene* 57: 203–10.

———. 1955a. Malaria in the Gold Coast, Part 1. *West African Medical J.* 4: 3–17.

———. 1955b. Malaria in the Gold Coast, Part 2. *West African Medical J.* 4: 161–74.

———. 1956. Sickling and malaria in the Gold Coast. *Brit. Medical J.* 1 (no. 4970): 784–86.

Collier, G. A. 1975. A reinterpretation of color nomenclature systems. *Am. Ethnologist* 2: 111–25.

Collier, G. A., et al. 1976. Further evidence for universal color categories. *Language* 52: 884–90.

Condon, J. R., et al. 1970. Calcium and phosphorus metabolism in relation to lactose tolerance. *Lancet* 1 (no. 7655): 1027–29.

Cone, T. E., Jr. 1970. The treatment of rickets as suggested by Boerhaave and Glisson and interpreted by Dr. John Theobald of London in 1764. *Pediatrics* 46: 619.

———. 1980. A rachitic infant painted by Burgkmair 136 years before Dr. Whistler described rickets. *Clinical Pediatrics* 19: 194.

Conkey, M. W. 1978. Style and information in cultural evolution: Toward a predictive model for the Paleolithic. In C. L. Redman et al., eds., *Social Archaeology.* New York.

———. 1983. On the origins of Paleolithic art: A review and some critical thoughts. In E. Trinkhaus, ed., *The Mousterian Legacy.* Oxford, Eng.

———. 1985. Ritual communication, social elaboration and the variable trajectories of Paleolithic material culture. In T. D. Price and J. A. Brown, eds., *Prehistoric Hunter-Gatherers: The Emergence of Social and Cultural Complexity.* New York.

Conklin, H. C. 1955. Hanunoo color categories. *Southwestern J. Anthropology* 11: 339–44.

———. 1973. Color categorization. *Am. Anthropologist* 75: 931–42.

Cook, G. C. 1969. Lactase deficiency: A probable ethnological marker in East Africa. *Man* (n.s.) 4: 265–67.

———. 1978. Did persistence of intestinal lactase into adult life originate on the Arabian peninsula? *Man* (n.s.) 13: 418–27.

Cook, G. C., and M. T. Al-Torki. 1975. High intestinal lactase concentrations in adult Arabs in Saudi Arabia. *Brit. Medical J.* 3 (no. 5976): 135–36.

Cook, G. C., and S. K. Kajubi. 1966. Tribal incidence of lactase deficiency in Uganda. *Lancet* 1 (no. 7440): 725–30.

Coon, C. S. 1956. *The Races of Europe.* New York. 2d rev. ed. of work first published in 1939.

———. 1965. *The Living Races of Man.* New York.

Cooper, J. M. 1932. Incest prohibitions in primitive culture. *Primitive Man* 5: 1–20.

Cornille-Brøgger, R., et al. 1979. Abnormal hemoglobins in the Sudan savannah of Nigeria, 2: Immunological response to malaria in normals and subjects with sickle-cell trait. *Anns. Trop. Medicine and Parasitology* 73: 173–83.

Corning, P. A. 1974. Politics and the evolutionary process. In T. Dobzhansky et al., eds., *Evolutionary Biology*, vol. 7. New York.

Cosmides, L., and J. Tooby. 1987. From evolution to behavior: Evolutionary psychology as the missing link. In J. Dupré, ed., *The Latest on the Best: Essays on Evolution and Optimality*. Cambridge, Mass.

Coursey, D. G. 1967. *Yams: An Account of the Nature, Origins, Cultivation and Utilization of the Useful Members of the Dioscoreaceae*. London.

———. 1972. The civilizations of the yam: Interrelationships of man and yams in Africa and the Indo-Pacific region. *Archaeology and Physical Anthropology in Oceania* 7: 215–33.

———. 1976a. The origins and domestication of yams in Africa. In J. R. Harlan et al., eds., *Origins of African Plant Domestication*. The Hague.

———. 1976b. Yams. In N. W. Simmonds, ed., *Evolution of Crop Plants*. New York.

———. 1980. The origins and domestication of yams in Africa. In B. K. Swartz, Jr., and R. E. Dumett, eds., *West African Culture Dynamics*. The Hague.

Coursey, D. G., and C. K. Coursey. 1971. The new yam festivals of West Africa. *Anthropos* 66: 444–84.

Cowles, R. B. 1959. Some ecological factors bearing on the origin and evolution of pigment in the human skin. *Am. Naturalist* 93: 283–93.

Crawford, M., and P. Workman, eds. 1973. *Methods and Theories in Anthropological Genetics*. Albuquerque, N.Mex.

Crick, F. 1958. On protein synthesis. *Symp. Soc. for Experimental Biology* 12: 138–63.

Crombie, I. K. 1979a. Racial differences in melanoma incidence. *Brit. J. of Cancer* 40: 185–93.

———. 1979b. Variation of melanoma incidence with latitude in North America and Europe. *Brit. J. Cancer* 40: 774–81.

Cronin, J. E., et al. 1981. Tempo and mode in hominid evolution. *Nature* 292: 113–22.

Crook, J. H. 1980a. *The Evolution of Human Consciousness*. Oxford, Eng.

———. 1980b. Social change in Indian Tibet. *Social Science Information* 19: 139–66.

Crook, J. H., and S. J. Crook. 1987. Explaining Tibetan polyandry: Sociocultural, demographic, and biological perspectives. Unpublished manuscript.

———. 1988. Tibetan polyandry: Problems of adaptation and fitness. In L. Betzig, M. Borgerhoff Mulder, and P. Turke, eds., *Human Reproductive Behavior: A Darwinian Perspective*. Cambridge, Eng.

Crosignani, P. G., and C. Robyn, eds. 1977. *Prolactin and Human Reproduction*. New York.

Crossley-Holland, K., ed. 1977. *The Faber Book of Northern Legends*. London.

Crow, J. F. 1979. Genes that violate Mendel's rules. *Scientific American* 240 (no. 2): 134–46.

Crow, J. F., and M. Kimura. 1970. *An Introduction to Population Genetics Theory.* New York.

Cuatrecasas, P., D. H. Lockwood, and J. R. Caldwell. 1965. Lactase deficiency in the adult. *Lancet* 1 (no. 7375): 14–18.

Cumming, C. F. G. 1884. *In the Himalayas and on the Indian Plains.* London.

Czelusniak, J., et al. 1982. Phylogenetic origins and adaptive evolution of avian and mammalian hemoglobin genes. *Nature* 289: 297–300.

Dacke, C. G. 1979. *Calcium Regulation in Sub-Mammalian Vertebrates.* New York.

Daiger, S. P., M. S. Schanfield, and L. L. Cavalli-Sforza. 1975. Group specific component (Gc) proteins bind vitamin D and 25-hydroxyvitamin D. *Proc. Nat. Acad. Sciences* 72: 2076–80.

Dalby, D. 1977. *Language Map of Africa and the Adjacent Islands.* London.

Daly, M. 1982. Some caveats about cultural transmission models. *Hum. Ecology* 10: 401–8.

Daly, M., and M. Wilson. 1983. *Sex, Evolution, and Behavior.* Boston. 2d rev. ed. of work first published in 1978.

———. 1984. A sociobiological analysis of human infanticide. In G. Hausfater and S. B. Hrdy, eds., *Infanticide: Comparative and Evolutionary Perspectives.* New York.

Damon, A., ed. 1975. *Physiological Anthropology.* New York.

D'Andrade, R. G. 1981. The cultural part of cognition. *Cognitive Science* 5: 179–95.

———. 1984. Cultural meaning systems. In R. A. Shweder and R. A. LeVine, eds., *Culture Theory.* Cambridge, Eng.

Danielli, J. S. 1980. Altruism and the internal reward system, or the opium of the people. *J. Social and Biological Structures* 3: 87–94.

Daniels, F., P. W. Post, and B. E. Johnson. 1972. Theories of the role of pigment in the evolution of human races. In V. Riley, ed., *Pigmentation: Its Genesis and Biologic Control.* New York.

D'Aquili, E. G. 1972. *The Biopsychological Determinants of Culture.* Reading, Mass.

D'Aquili, E. G., C. D. Laughlin, and J. McManus. 1979. *The Spectrum of Ritual: A Biogenetic Structural Analysis.* New York.

Dargyay, E. K. 1982. *Tibetan Village Communities: Structure and Change.* Warminster, Eng.

Darlington, C. D. 1955. The genetic component of language. *Nature* 175: 178.

———. 1960. Cousin marriage and the evolution of the breeding system in man. *Heredity* 14: 297–332.

Darnell, J. E. 1983. The processing of RNA. *Scientific American* 249 (no. 4): 90–100.

———. 1985. RNA. *Scientific American* 253 (no. 4): 68–78.

Darwin, C. 1859. *On the Origin of Species.* London.

———. 1889. *The Effects of Cross and Self-Fertilization in the Vegetable Kingdom.* New York. First published in 1876.

———. 1890. *The Variation of Animals and Plants Under Domestication.* 2 vols. New York. 2d ed., rev., of work first published in 1868.

———. 1922. *The Descent of Man, and Selection in Relation to Sex.* New York. Reprint of 2d ed., rev. 1874, of work first published in 1871.

———. 1964. *On the Origin of Species.* Cambridge, Mass. Photoreproduction of work first published in 1859.

———. 1981. *The Descent of Man, and Selection in Relation to Sex.* Princeton, N.J. Photoreproduction of work first published in 1871.

Darwin, G. 1875. Marriages between first cousins in England and their effects. *J. Statistical Soc.* 38: 153–84.

Das, S. C. 1893. The marriage customs of Tibet. *J. Asiatic Soc. of Bengal* (Calcutta) 62: 8–19.

———. 1902. *Journey to Lhasa and Central Tibet.* London.

Davidson, H. R. E. 1964. *Gods and Myths of Northern Europe.* Baltimore, Md.

Dawkins, R. 1976. *The Selfish Gene.* New York.

———. 1979. Defining sociobiology. *Nature* 280: 427–28.

———. 1982a. *The Extended Phenotype: The Gene as the Unit of Selection.* San Francisco.

———. 1982b. Replicators and vehicles. In King's College Sociobiology Group, eds., *Current Problems in Sociobiology.* Cambridge, Eng.

———. 1986. *The Blind Watchmaker: Why the Evidence of Evolution Reveals a Universe Without Design.* New York.

Dawson, J. B., et al. 1980. A theoretical and experimental study of light absorption and scattering by in vivo skin. *Physics in Medicine and Biology* 25: 695–709.

Day, M. H. 1986. *Guide to Fossil Man.* Chicago. 4th ed. of work first published in 1965.

Deering, R. A. 1962. Ultraviolet radiation and nucleic acid. *Scientific American* 207 (no. 6): 135–44.

De Filippi, F., ed. 1971. *An Account of Tibet: The Travels of Ippolito Desideri of Pistoia, S. J., 1712–1727.* Taipei. Photoreproduction of work first published in 1932.

Delmont, J., ed. 1983. *Milk Intolerances and Rejection.* New York.

DeLuca, H. F. 1979. The vitamin D system in the regulation of calcium and phosphorus metabolism. *Nutrition Revs.* 37: 161–93.

———. 1986. The metabolism and functions of vitamin D. *Advances in Experimental Medicine and Biology* 196: 361–75.

DeLuca, H. F., et al. 1982. Molecular events involved in 1, 25-dihydroxyvitamin D_3 stimulation of intestinal calcium transport. *Fed. of Am. Soc. for Experimental Biology Proc.* 41: 66–71.

Demarest, W. J. 1977. Incest avoidance among human and nonhuman primates. In S. Chevalier-Skolnicoff and F. E. Poirier, eds., *Primate Biosocial Development: Biological, Social and Ecological Determinants.* New York.

———. 1982. Left-handedness and right-handedness in Guatemalan populations: A cross-cultural examination of Marian Annett's single gene / right shift theory. Ph.D. diss. Stanford University.

De Meillon, B. 1951. Species and varieties of malaria vectors in Africa and their bionomics. *Bull. World Health Organization* 4: 419–41.

De Mott, B. 1980. The pro-incest lobby. *Psychology Today* 13 (no. 10): 11–16.

Dent, C. E. 1970. Rickets (and osteomalacia), nutritional and metabolic (1919–1969). *Proc. Royal Soc. Medicine* 63: 401–8.

Deol, M. S. 1975. Racial differences in pigmentation and natural selection. *Anns. Hum. Genetics* 38: 501–3. London.

De Saussure, F. 1966. *Course in General Linguistics.* Tr. Wade Baskin. New York. Posthumous work edited from students' notes and first published in 1916.

Desowitz, R. S. 1981. *New Guinea Tapeworms and Jewish Grandmothers: Tales of Parasites and People.* New York.

De Valois, R. L., and K. K. De Valois. 1975. Neural coding of color. From E. C. Carterette and M. P. Friedman, eds., *Seeing: Handbook of Perception,* vol. 5. New York.

De Valois, R. L., and G. H. Jacobs. 1968. Primate color vision. *Science* 162: 533–40.

De Valois, R. L., I. Abramov, and G. H. Jacobs. 1966. Analysis of response patterns of LGN cells. *J. Optical Soc. America* 56: 966–77.

Devereux, G. 1939. The social and cultural implications of incest among the Mohave Indians. *Psychoanalytic Q.* 8: 510–33.

De Winter, K. 1984. Biological and cultural evolution: Different manifestations of the same principle. *J. Hum. Evolution* 13: 61–70.

Dewsbury, D. A. 1982. Avoidance of incestuous breeding between siblings in two species of *Peromyscus* mice. *Biology of Behavior* 7: 157–69.

Dickemann, M. 1979. Female infanticide, reproductive strategies, and social stratification: A preliminary model. In N. A. Chagnon and W. Irons, eds., *Evolutionary Biology and Human Social Behavior.* North Scituate, Mass.

———. 1981. Paternal confidence and dowry competition: A biocultural analysis of purdah. In R. D. Alexander and D. W. Tinkle, eds., *Natural Selection and Social Behavior.* New York.

———. 1985. Human sociobiology: The first decade. *New Scientist* 108 (no. 1477): 38–42.

Dickerson, R. E., and I. Geis. 1983. *Hemoglobin: Structure, Function, Evolution, and Pathology.* Menlo Park, Calif.

Dickson, K. B. 1969. *A Historical Geography of Ghana.* Cambridge, Eng.

Diener, P. 1974. Ecology or evolution? The Hutterite case. *Am. Ethnologist* 1: 601–18.

———. 1980. Quantum adjustment, macroevolution and the social field: Some comments on evolution and culture. *Current Anthropology* 21: 423–43.

Diener, P., D. Nonini, and E. E. Robkin. 1978. The dialectics of the sacred cow: Ecological adaptation versus political appropriation in the origins of India's cattle complex. *Dialectical Anthropology* 3: 221–41.

———. 1980. Ecology and evolution in cultural anthropology. *Man* 15 (n.s.): 1–31.

Diener, T. O. 1980. Viroids. *Scientific American* 244 (no. 1): 67–73.

Diggs, L. W. 1973. Anatomic lesions in sickle-cell diseases. In H. Abramson et al., eds., *Sickle-Cell Disease.* St. Louis, Mo.

Divale, W. T. 1973. *Warfare in Primitive Societies: A Bibliography.* Santa Barbara, Calif.

Dobzhansky, T. 1951. Human diversity and adaptation. *Cold Spring Harbor Symposia on Quantitative Biology* 15: 385–400.

———. 1961. Man and natural selection. *Am. Scientist* 49: 285–99.

———. 1962. *Mankind Evolving: The Evolution of the Human Species.* New Haven, Conn.

———. 1963a. Anthropology and the natural sciences—the problem of human evolution. *Current Anthropology* 4: 138–48.

———. 1963b. Cultural direction of human evolution: A summation. *Hum. Biology* 35: 311–16.

———. 1964. *Heredity and the Nature of Man.* New York.

———. 1972a. On the evolutionary uniqueness of man. In T. Dobzhansky, M. K. Hecht, and W. C. Steere, eds., *Evolutionary Biology,* vol. 6. New York.

———. 1972b. Unique aspects of man's evolution. In J. W. S. Pringle, ed., *Biology and the Human Sciences.* Oxford, Eng.

Dobzhansky, T., and E. Boesiger. 1983. *Human Culture: A Moment in Evolution.* New York.

Dobzhansky, T., and M. F. A. Montagu. 1947. Natural selection and the mental capacities of mankind. *Science* 105: 587–90.

Dobzhansky, T., et al. 1977. *Evolution.* San Francisco.

Dole, G. E. 1973. Foundations of contemporary evolutionism. In R. Naroll and F. Naroll, eds., *Main Currents in Cultural Anthropology.* Englewood Cliffs, N.J.

Doolittle, W. F., and C. Sapienza. 1980. Selfish genes, the phenotype paradigm and genome evolution. *Nature* 284: 601–3.

Dornstreich, M. D., and G. E. B. Morren. 1974. Does New Guinea cannibalism have nutritional value? *Hum. Ecology* 2: 1–12.

Douglas, M. 1970. *Purity and Danger: An Analysis of Concepts of Pollution and Taboo.* Harmondsworth, Eng.

———. 1971. Deciphering a meal. In C. Geertz, ed., *Myth, Symbol, and Culture.* New York.

Dover, G. J., S. H. Boyer, and M. E. Pembrey. 1981. F-cell production in sickle-cell anemia: Regulation by genes linked to B-Hemoglobin locus. *Science* 211: 1441–44.

Dow, J. 1983. Woman capture as a motivation for warfare: A comparative analysis of intra-cultural variation and a critique of the "male supremacist complex." In R. Dyson-Hudson and M. A. Little, eds., *Rethinking Human Adaptation.* Boulder, Colo.

Downs, J. F. 1964. Livestock, production, and social mobility in high altitude Tibet. *Am. Anthropologist* 66: 1115–59.

Draper, H. H. 1977. Aboriginal Eskimo diet in modern perspective. *Am. Anthropologist* 79: 309–16.

———. 1980. Nutrition. In F. A. Milan, ed., *The Human Biology of Circumpolar Populations.* Cambridge, Eng.

Drummond, J. C., and A. Wilbraham. 1958. *The Englishman's Food: A History of Five Centuries of English Diet.* London. 2d ed., rev., of work first published in 1939.

Dunn, F. L. 1965. On the antiquity of malaria in the western hemisphere. *Hum. Biology* 37: 385–92.

Dunnell, R. C. 1978. Style and function: A fundamental dichotomy. *Am. Antiquity* 43: 192–202.

———. 1980. Evolutionary theory and archaeology. *Advances in Achaeological Method and Theory* 3: 35–99.

Durham, W. H. 1976a. Resource competition and human aggression, Part I: A review of primitive war. *Q. Rev. Biology* 51: 385–415.

———. 1976b. The adaptive significance of cultural behavior. *Hum. Ecology* 4: 89–121.

———. 1977. Reply. In E. E. Ruyle et al., The adaptive significance of cultural behavior: Comments and reply. *Hum. Ecology* 5: 49–68.

———. 1978. The coevolution of human biology and culture. In V. Reynolds and N. B. Jones, eds., *Hum. Behavior and Adaptation.* London.

———. 1979a. *Scarcity and Survival in Central America: The Ecological Origins of the Soccer War*. Stanford, Calif.

———. 1979b. Toward a coevolutionary theory of human biology and culture. In N. A. Chagnon and W. Irons, eds., *Evolutionary Biology and Human Social Behavior: An Anthropological Perspective*. North Scituate, Mass.

———. 1980. The coevolution of dairying and adult lactose absorption. Paper presented at the 79th Annual Meeting of the American Anthropological Association, Washington, D.C.

———. 1981. Coevolution and law: The new yam festivals of West Africa. Paper presented at the Hutchins Center and Goethe Institute Conference on Law and Behavioral Research, Monterey Dunes, Calif.

———. 1982. Interactions of genetic and cultural evolution: Models and examples. *Hum. Ecology* 10: 289–323.

———. 1983a. Testing the malaria hypothesis in West Africa. In J. E. Bowman, ed., *Distribution and Evolution of Hemoglobin and Globin Loci*. New York.

———. 1983b. Review of *Ecology, Meaning, and Religion* by Roy A. Rappaport. *Hum. Ecology* 11: 105–10.

———. 1987. Imposition versus choice in the cultural evolution of Mundurucú warfare. Paper presented at the 86th Annual Meeting of the American Anthropological Association, Chicago.

———. 1990. Advances in evolutionary culture theory. *Ann. Rev. Anthropology* 19: 187–210.

Dyson-Hudson, R. 1983. An interactive model of human biological and behavioral adaptation. In R. Dyson-Hudson and M. A. Little, eds. 1983. *Rethinking Human Adaptation: Biological and Cultural Models*. Boulder, Colo.

Dyson-Hudson, R., and E. A. Smith. 1978. Human territoriality: An ecological reassessment. *Am. Anthropologist* 80: 21–41.

Eastman, N. J. 1956. *Williams Obstetrics*. New York. 11th ed., rev., of work first published in 1906.

Eberhard, W. 1937. Early Chinese cultures and their development: A new working-hypothesis. In publication 3451, *Ann. Rep. Board of Regents of the Smithsonian Institution*. Washington, D.C.

———. 1942. Kultur und Siedlung der Randvölker Chinas. T'oung Pao (Leiden, Neth.) 35, supplement.

———. 1982. *China's Minorities: Yesterday and Today*. Belmont, Calif.

Eccles, J. C. 1973. Cultural evolution versus biological evolution. *Zygon* 8: 282–93.

Eckholm, E. 1982. *Down to Earth: Environment and Human Needs*. New York.

Eckland, B. K. 1972. Trends in the intensity and direction of natural selection. *Social Biology* 19: 215–23.

Edelstein, S. J. 1986. *The Sickled Cell: From Myths to Molecules*. Cambridge, Mass.

Eder, J. F. 1987. *On the Road to Tribal Extinction*. Berkeley, Calif.

Edgerton, R. B. 1971. *The Individual in Cultural Adaptation: A Study of Four East African Tribes*. Berkeley, Calif.

Edington, G. M., and N. Lehmann. 1955. Expression of sickle-cell gene in Africa. *Brit. Medical J.* 1 (no. 4925): 1308–11.

Edington, G. M., and E. J. Watson-Williams. 1965. Sickling, haemoglobin C, glucose-6-phosphate dehydrogenase deficiency and malaria in western Nigeria. In J. H. P. Jonxis, ed., *Abnormal Haemoglobins in Africa*. Oxford, Eng.

Efstratiadis, A., et al. 1980. The structure and evolution of the human (beta)-globin gene family. *Cell* 21: 653–68.

Ehrlich, P. R., and S. S. Feldman. 1977. *The Race Bomb: Skin Color, Prejudice, and Intelligence*. New York.

Ehrlich, P. R., and P. H. Raven. 1964. Butterflies and plants: A study in coevolution. *Evolution* 18: 586–608.

Ekvall, R. B. 1954. Some differences in Tibetan land tenure and utilization. *Sinologica* 4: 39–48.

———. 1968. *Fields on the Hoof: The Nexus of Tibetan Nomadic Pastoralism.* New York.

Eldredge, N. 1985. *Unfinished Synthesis: Biological Hierarchies and Modern Evolutionary Thought.* New York.

Eldredge, N., and J. Cracraft. 1980. *Phylogenetic Patterns and the Evolutionary Process.* New York.

Eldredge, N., and S. J. Gould. 1972. Punctuated equilibria: An alternative to phyletic gradualism. In T. J. M. Schopf, ed., *Models in Paleobiology.* San Francisco, Calif.

Eldredge, N., and I. Tattersall. 1982. *The Myths of Human Evolution.* New York.

Ellis, A. B. 1894. *The Yoruba-Speaking Peoples of the Slave Coast of Africa.* London.

Elster, J. 1979. *Ulysses and the Sirens: Studies in Rationality and Irrationality.* Cambridge, Eng.

———. 1985. *Making Sense of Marx.* Cambridge, Eng.

Ember, M. 1974. Warfare, sex ratio, and polygyny. *Ethnology* 13: 197–206.

———. 1975. On the origin and extension of the incest taboo. *Behavior Science Res.* 10: 249–81.

———. 1978. Size of color lexicon: Interaction of cultural and biological factors. *Am. Anthropologist* 80: 364–67.

Embury, S. H., et al. 1982. Concurrent sickle-cell anemia and alpha thalassemia. *New England J. Medicine* 306: 270–74.

Emerson, A. 1956. Homeostasis and comparison of systems. In R. R. Grinker, ed., *Toward a Unified Theory of Behavior.* New York.

———. 1965. Human cultural evolution and its relation to organic evolution of insect societies. In H. Barringer et al., *Social Change in Developing Areas: A Reinterpretation of Evolutionary Theory.* Cambridge, Mass.

Emmett, E. D. 1973. Ultraviolet radiation as a cause of skin tumors. *CRC Revs. Toxicology* 2: 211–55.

Emlen, S. T., and L. W. Oring. 1977. Ecology, sexual selection, and the evolution of mating systems. *Science* 197: 215–23.

Endler, J. A. 1986. *Natural Selection in the Wild.* Princeton, N.J.

Epling, P. J., et al. 1973. Genetic relations of Polynesian sibling terminologies. *Am. Anthropologist* 75: 1596–1625.

Erikson, A. W., W. Lehmann, and N. E. Simpson. 1980. Genetic studies on circumpolar populations. In F. A. Milan, ed., *The Human Biology of Circumpolar Populations.* Cambridge, Eng.

Escudie, A., and J. Hamon. 1961. Le paludisme en Afrique Occidentale d'expression française. *Médecine Tropicale* 21: 661–87.

Etkin, N. L. 1979. Indigenous medicine among the Hausa of northern Nigeria: Laboratory evolution for potential therapeutic efficacy of antimalarial plant medicinals. *Medical Anthropology* 3: 401–29.

———. 1981. A Hausa herbal pharmacopoeia: Biomedical evaluation of commonly used plant medicines. *J. Ethnopharmacology* 4: 75–98.

Etkin, N. L., and P. J. Ross. 1983. Malaria, medicine, and meals: Plant use among the Hausa and its impact on disease. In L. Romanucci-Ross, ed., *The Anthropology of Medicine: From Culture to Method*. New York.

Etkin, W. 1954. Social behavior and the evolution of man's mental facilities. *Am. Naturalist* 88: 129–42.

Evans-Pritchard, E. E. 1940. *The Nuer*. Oxford, Eng.

———. 1951. *Kinship and Marriage Among the Nuer*. Oxford, Eng.

———. 1956. *Nuer Religion*. Oxford, Eng.

———. 1963. Nuer rules of exogamy and incest. In M. Fortes, ed., *Social Structure*. New York.

Fabrega, H. 1977. Culture, behavior, and the nervous system. *Ann. Rev. Anthropology* 6: 419–55.

Fadipe, N. A. 1970. *The Sociology of the Yoruba*. Ibadan, Nigeria.

Falconer, D. S. 1981. *Introduction to Quantitative Genetics*. New York.

Falk, D. 1987. Hominid paleoneurology. *Ann. Rev. Anthropology* 16: 13–30.

Farb, P., and G. Armelagos. 1980. *Consuming Passions: The Anthropology of Eating*. Boston.

Farnsworth, D. 1943. The Farnsworth-Munsell 100 hue and dichotomous tests for color vision. *J. Optical Soc. America* 33: 568–78.

Farquhar, J., and D. C. Gajdusek, eds. 1981. *Kuru: Early Letters and Field Notes from the Collection of D. Carleton Gajdusek*. New York.

Farver, M. T., and J. P. Milton, eds. 1972. *The Careless Technology*. Garden City, N.Y.

Fein, A., E. Z. Szuts. 1982. *Photoreceptors: Their Role in Vision*. Cambridge, Eng.

Feldman, M. W., and L. L. Cavalli-Sforza. 1975. Models for cultural inheritance: A general linear model. *Anns. Hum. Biology* 2: 215–26.

Felsenstein, J. 1985. Recombination and sex: Is Maynard Smith necessary? In P. J. Greenwood et al., eds., *Evolution: Essays in Honor of John Maynard Smith*. Cambridge, Eng.

Ferguson, A., and J. D. Maxwell. 1967. Genetic aetiology of lactose intolerance. *Lancet* 2 (no. 7508): 188–91.

Fernandez, R. L. 1981. Comments on Tibetan polyandry: A test of sociobiological theory. *Am. Anthropologist* 83: 896–97.

Ferré, C. D. 1982. Lactose absorption: Population variations, calcium physiology and biocultural evolution. Paper presented at the 51st Annual Meeting of the American Association of Physical Anthropologists, Eugene, Oreg.

Fetzer, J. H., ed. 1985. *Sociobiology and Epistemology*. Dordrecht, Neth.

Fildes, V. A. 1986. *Breasts, Bottles, and Babies: A History of Infant Feeding*. Edinburgh, Scot.

Firth, R. 1930. Marriage and the classificatory system of relationship. *J. Royal Anthropological Institute* 60: 235–68.

———. 1957. *We, the Tikopia*. London. 2d ed., abridged by the author, of work first published in 1936.

Fischer, A., and J. L. Fischer. 1960. Aetiology of kuru. *Lancet* 1 (no. 7139): 1417–18.

———. 1961. Culture and epidemiology: A theoretical investigation of kuru. *J. Health and Human Behavior* 2: 16–25.

Fisher, J. F. 1986. *Trans-Himalayan Traders: Economy, Society, and Culture in Northwest Nepal.* Berkeley, Calif.

Fisher, R. A. 1958. *The Genetical Theory of Natural Selection.* New York. 2d (revised) ed. of work first published 1930.

Fitzpatrick, T. B. 1971. The biology of pigmentation. In D. Bergsma et al., eds., *The Clinical Delineation of Birth Defects.* Baltimore, Md.

Fitzpatrick, T. B., et al., eds. 1974. *Sunlight and Man.* Tokyo.

Fivaz, D., and P. E. Scott. 1977. *African Languages: A Genetic and Decimalized Classification for Bibliographic and General Reference.* Boston, Mass.

Flannery, K. V. 1972. The cultural evolution of civilizations. *Ann. Rev. Ecology and Systematics* 3: 399–426.

———. 1973. The origins of agriculture. *Ann. Rev. Anthropology* 2: 271–310.

Flatz, G. 1967. Hemoglobin E: Distribution and population dynamics. *Humangenetik* 3: 189–234.

———. 1983. Genetics of the human adult lactase polymorphism. In J. Delmont, ed., *Milk Intolerances and Rejection.* New York.

———. 1987. Genetics of lactose digestion in humans. *Advances in Hum. Genetics* 16: 1–77.

Flatz, G., and H. W. Rotthauwe. 1971. Evidence against nutritional adaptation of tolerance to lactose. *Humangenetik* 13: 118–25.

———. 1973. Lactose nutrition and natural selection. *Lancet* 2 (no. 7820): 76–77.

———. 1977. The human lactase polymorphism: Physiology and genetics of lactose absorption and malabsorption. In A. G. Steinberg et al., eds., *Progress in Medical Genetics.* Philadelphia.

———. 1979. Geography and lactose malabsorption. *Digestive Diseases and Sciences* 24: 492.

Fleising, U. 1982. The dialectics of reproductive effort. *Am. Anthropologist* 84: 408–10.

Fleming, A. F., et al. 1979. Abnormal hemoglobins in the Sudan savannah of Nigeria, Part 1: Prevalence of hemoglobins and relationships between sickle-cell trait, malaria and survival. *Anns. Trop. Medicine and Parasitology* 73: 161–72.

Fleure, H. J. 1945. The distribution of types of skin color. *Geographical Rev.* 35: 580–95.

Flinn, M. V., and R. D. Alexander. 1982. Culture theory: The developing synthesis from biology. *Hum. Ecology* 10: 383–400.

Foley, R. 1987. *Another Unique Species: Patterns in Human Evolutionary Ecology.* Harlow, Essex, Eng.

Foote, J. A. 1927. Evidence of rickets prior to 1650. *Am. J. Diseases of Children* 34: 443–52.

Ford, C. S. 1960. Sex offenses: An anthropological perspective. *Law and Contemporary Problems* 25: 225–43.

Ford, E. B. 1940. Polymorphism and taxonomy. In J. S. Huxley, ed., *The New Systematics.* Oxford, Eng.

Forde, C. D. 1953. The cultural map of West Africa: Successive adaptations to tropical forests and grasslands. *Tr. N.Y. Acad. Sciences* 15: 206–19.

Forsyth, D. 1983. The beginnings of Brazilian anthropology: Jesuits and Tupinambá cannibalism. *J. Anthropological Research* 39: 147–78.

———. 1985. Three cheers for Hans Staden: The case for Brazilian cannibalism. *Ethnohistory* 32: 17–36.

Fortes, M. 1935. Kinship, incest and exogamy among the Tallensi of the northern territories of the Gold Coast. In L. H. Dudley Buxton, ed., *Where Custom Is King*. London.

———. 1937. Ritual festivals and social cohesion in the hinterland of the Gold Coast. *Am. Anthropologist* 38: 590–604.

Fortes, M., and S. L. Fortes. 1936. Food in the domestic economy of the Tallensi. *Africa* 9: 237–76.

Foulks, E. F. 1972. *The Arctic Hysterias of the North Alaskan Eskimo*. Washington, D.C.

Foulks, E. F., and S. H. Katz. 1975. Biobehavioral adaptation in the Arctic. In E. S. Watts, F. E. Johnston, and G. W. Losher, eds., *Biosocial Interrelations in Population Adaptation*. The Hague.

———. 1977. Nutrition, behavior, and culture. In L. S. Greene, ed., *Malnutrition, Behavior, and Social Organization*. New York.

Fournier, P., Y. Dupuis, and A. Fournier. 1975. L'absorption, par le rat, du calcium de divers laits examinée en fonction de leur teneur en phosphore total et en lactose. *Annales de la Nutrition et de l'Alimentation* 29: 421–38.

Fournier, P., et al. 1971. Effect of lactose on the absorption of alkaline earth metals and intestinal lactase activity. *Israel J. Medical Science* 7: 389.

Fox, J. R. 1962. Sibling incest. *Brit. J. Sociology* 13: 128–50.

Fox, R. 1971. The cultural animal. In J. F. Eisenberg and W. S. Dillon, eds., *Man and Beast: Comparative Social Behavior*. Washington, D.C.

———. 1980. *The Red Lamp of Incest*. New York.

———. 1983. *Kinship and Marriage*. Cambridge, Eng. Reprint with new preface of work first published in 1967.

Franklin, I., and R. C. Lewontin. 1970. Is the gene the unit of selection? *Genetics* 65: 707–34.

Fraser, F. C., and C. J. Biddle. 1976. Estimating the risks for offspring of first-cousin matings. *Am. J. Hum. Genetics* 28: 522–26.

Frazer, J. G. 1910. *Totemism and Exogamy*. London.

Freeman, J. D. 1958. The family system of the Iban of Borneo. In J. Goody, ed., *The Developmental Cycle in Domestic Groups*. Cambridge, Eng.

Freilich, M. 1977. The meaning of "sociocultural." In B. Bernardi, ed., *The Concept and Dynamics of Culture*. The Hague.

Freud, S. 1950. *Totem and Taboo*. London. Translation of work first published in 1938.

Fricke, T. E. 1986. *Himalayan Households: Tamang Demography and Domestic Processes*. Ann Arbor, Mich.

Fried, K., and A. M. Davies. 1974. Some effects on the offspring of uncle-niece marriage in the Moroccan Jewish community in Jerusalem. *Am. J. Hum. Genetics* 26: 65–72.

Fried, M. 1968. *The Evolution of Political Society*. New York.

Friedman, J., and M. J. Rowlands, eds. 1977. *The Evolution of Social Systems*. London.

Friedman, M. J. 1978. Erythrocyte mechanism of sickle-cell resistance to malaria. *Proc. Nat. Acad. Sciences* 75: 1994–97.

———. 1981. Inherited resistance to malaria. In M. Levandowsky and S. H. Hunter, eds., *Biochemistry and Physiology of Protozoa*, vol. 4. New York.

Friedman, M. J., and W. Trager. 1981. The biochemistry of resistance to malaria. *Scientific American* 244 (no. 3): 154–64.

Friedman, M. J., et al. 1979. *Plasmodium falciparum*: Physiological interactions with the human sickle cell. *Experimental Parasitology* 47: 73–80.

Friedrich, P. 1979. *Language, Context, and the Imagination*. Stanford, Calif.

Frisancho, A. R. 1975. Functional adaptation to high altitude hypoxia. *Science* 187: 313–19.

———. 1979. *Human Adaptation: A Functional Perspective*. St. Louis, Mo.

Frisancho, A. R., and P. T. Baker. 1970. Altitude and growth: A study of the pattern of physical growth of a high altitude Peruvian Quechua population. *Am. J. Physical Anthropology* 32: 279–92.

Fuchs, A. 1978. Coca chewing and high-altitude stress: Possible effects of coca alkaloids on erythropoiesis. *Current Anthropology* 19: 277–91.

Fürer-Haimendorf, C. von. 1955–56. Ethnographic notes on the Tamangs of Nepal. *Eastern Anthropologist* 9: 166–77.

———. 1964. *The Sherpas of Nepal*. Berkeley, Calif.

Futuyma, D. J. 1986. *Evolutionary Biology*. Sunderland, Mass. 2d (rev.) ed. of work first published in 1979.

Futuyma, D. J., and M. Slatkin, eds. 1983. *Coevolution*. Sunderland, Mass.

Gagliano, J. A. 1976. Coca and popular medicine in Peru: An historical analysis of attitudes. In F. X. Grollig and H. B. Harley, eds., *Medical Anthropology*. New York.

Gajdusek, D. C. 1963. Kuru. *Tr. Royal Soc. Trop. Medicine and Hygiene* 57: 151–69.

———. 1973. Kuru in the New Guinea Highlands. In J. D. Spillane, ed., *Tropical Neurology*. Oxford, Eng.

———, ed. 1975. *Correspondence on the Discovery and Original Investigations on Kuru*. Bethesda, Md.

———. 1977. Unconventional viruses and the origin and disappearance of kuru. *Science* 197: 943–60.

———. 1979. Observations on the early history of kuru investigation. In S. B. Prusiner and W. J. Hadlow, eds., *Slow Transmissible Diseases of the Nervous System*, vol. 1. New York.

———. 1986. Kuru: Lessons from a plague in a primitive New Guinea people. Lecture 2 of the 1986 Prather Lectures in Biology, Harvard University. March 1986. Video. Harvard Archives.

Gajdusek, D. C., and M. Alpers. 1965. Changing patterns of kuru. *Am. J. Trop. Medicine and Hygiene* 14: 852–79.

———. 1972. Genetic studies in relation to kuru. I. Cultural, historical, and demographic background. *Am. J. Hum. Genetics* 24 (supp.): S1–S38.

Gajdusek, D. C., and C. J. Gibbs [Jr.]. 1964. Attempts to demonstrate a transmissible agent in kuru, amyotrophic lateral sclerosis, and other subacute and chronic nervous system degenerations of man. *Nature* 204: 257–59.

———. 1973. Kuru and virus dementias. In *Biohazards in Biological Research: Proceedings of a Conference in Pacific Grove, California, January 22–24, 1973*. Typescript. Cold Spring Harbor, N.Y.

———. 1977. Kuru, Creutzfeldt-Jakob disease, and transmissible presenile dementias. In V. ter Meulen and M. Katz, eds., *Slow Virus Infections of the Central Nervous System*. New York.

Gajdusek, D. C., and V. Zigas. 1957. Degenerative disease of the central nervous system in New Guinea. The endemic occurrence of "kuru" in the native population. *New England J. Medicine* 257: 974–78.

Gajdusek, D. C., C. J. Gibbs, Jr., and M. Alpers. 1966. Experimental transmission of a kuru-line syndrome to chimpanzees. *Nature* 209: 794–96.

———. 1967. Transmission and passage of experimental "kuru" to chimpanzees. *Science* 155: 212–14.

Gajdusek, D. C., E. R. Sorenson, and J. Meyer. 1970. A comprehensive cinema record of disappearing kuru. *Brain* 93: 65–76.

Galef, B. G. 1976. Social transmission of acquired behavior: A discussion of tradition and social learning in vertebrates. *Advances in the Study of Behavior* 6: 77–100.

Gallagher, C., A. L. Molleson, and J. H. Caldwell. 1974. Lactose intolerance and fermented dairy products. *American Dietetic Assn. J.* 65: 418–19.

Gallo, R. C. 1987. The AIDS virus. *Scientific American* 256 (no. 1): 47–56.

Ganshof, F. L. 1971. *The Carolingians and the Frankish Monarchy.* Ithaca, N.Y.

Garn, S. M., ed. 1964. *Culture and the Direction of Human Evolution.* Detroit, Mich.

Geertz, C. 1962. The growth of culture and the evolution of mind. In J. M. Scher, ed., *Theories of Mind.* New York.

———. 1964. The transition to humanity. In S. Tax, ed., *Horizons of Anthropology.* Chicago, Ill.

———. 1965. The impact of the concept of culture on the concept of man. In Y. Cohen, ed., *Man in Adaptation: The Cultural Present.* Chicago.

———. 1966. *Person, Time, and Conduct in Bali: An Essay in Cultural Analysis.* New Haven, Conn.

———. 1973. *The Interpretation of Culture.* New York.

———. 1983. *Local Knowledge: Further Essays in Interpretive Anthropology.* New York.

Gerard, R. W., C. Kluckhohn, and A. Rapoport. 1956. Biological and cultural evolution: Some analogies and explorations. *Behavioral Science* 1: 6–34.

Gewertz, D. 1978. The myth of the blood-men: An explanation of Chambri warfare. *J. Anthropological Res.* 34: 577–88.

Ghosh, A. K., and P. P. Majumder. 1979. Genetic load in an isolated population of South India. *Hum. Genetics* 51: 203–8.

Gibbs, C. J., and D. C. Gajdusek. 1970. Kuru: pathogenesis and characterization of virus. *Am. J. Trop. Medicine and Hygiene* 19: 138–45.

Gibbs, C. J., D. C. Gajdusek, and M. P. Alpers. 1969. Attempts to transmit subacute and chronic neurological diseases to animals. *Int. Arch. Allergy* 36 (supp.): 519–22.

Gibbs, C. J., et al. 1980. Oral transmission of kuru, Creutzfeldt-Jakob disease, and scrapie to nonhuman primates. *J. Infectious Diseases* 142: 205–8.

Gibbs, J. L. 1965. *Peoples of Africa.* New York.

Giddens, A. 1984. *The Constitution of Society: Outline of the Theory of Structuration.* Berkeley, Calif.

Giese, A. 1976. *Living with Our Sun's Ultraviolet Rays.* New York.

Gilat, T., et al. 1970. Lactase deficiency in Jewish communities in Israel. *Am. J. Digestive Diseases* 15: 895–904.

———. 1971. Lactose tolerance in an Arab population. *Am. J. Digestive Diseases* 16: 203–6.

Gilbert, W. 1978. Why genes in pieces? *Nature* 271: 501.

Giles, E. 1970. Culture and genetics. In A. Fischer, ed., *Current Directions in Anthropology*, vol. 3. Washington, D.C.

Gill, C. A. 1938. *The Seasonal Periodicity of Malaria and the Mechanism of the Epidemic Wave*. London.

Gillette, P. N., et al. 1974. Sodium cyanate as a potential treatment for sickle-cell disease. *New England J. Medicine* 290: 654–59.

Gillison, G. 1980. Images of nature in Gimi thought. In C. MacCormack and M. Strathern, eds., *Nature, Culture, and Gender*. Cambridge, Eng.

———. 1983. Cannibalism among women in the Eastern Highlands of Papua New Guinea. In P. Brown and D. Tuzin, eds., *The Ethnography of Cannibalism*. Washington, D.C.

Gimbutas, M. 1963. The Indo-Europeans: Archaeological problems. *Am. Anthropologist* 65: 815–36.

———. 1970. Proto-Indo-European Culture: The Kurgan culture during the fifth, fourth, and third millennia B.C. In H. Hoenigswald, ed., *Indo-European and Indo-Europeans*. Philadelphia, Pa.

———. 1973. The beginning of the Bronze Age in Europe and the Indo-Europeans: 3500–2500. *J. Indo-European Studies* 1: 163–214.

———. 1974. *The Gods and Goddesses of Old Europe*. Berkeley, Calif.

———. 1977. The first wave of Eurasian steppe pastoralists into Copper Age Europe. *J. Indo-European Studies* 5: 277–338.

Glasse, R. M. 1962a. South Fore society: A preliminary report. Mimeo. report, Territory of Papua and New Guinea. Reissued by National Institutes of Health, Bethesda, Md.

———. 1962b. The spread of kuru among the Fore. Mimeo. report, Territory of Papua and New Guinea. Reissued by National Institutes of Health, Bethesda, Md.

———. 1963. Cannibalism in the kuru region. Mimeo. report, Territory of Papua and New Guinea. Reissued by National Institutes of Health, Bethesda, Md.

———. 1967. Cannibalism in the kuru region of New Guinea. *Tr. N.Y. Acad. Sciences* 29: 748–54.

———. 1970. Some recent observations on kuru. *Oceania* 40 (no. 3): 210–13.

Glasse, R. M., and S. Lindenbaum. 1976. Kuru at Wanitabe. In R. W. Hornabrook, ed., *Essays on Kuru*. Faringdon, Eng.

Glasse, S. 1962. The social effects of kuru. Mimeo. report, Territory of Papua and New Guinea. Reissued by National Institutes of Health, Bethesda, Md.

———. 1963a. A note on Fore medicine and sorcery, with an ethnobotanical list. Mimeo. report, Territory of Papua and New Guinea. Reissued by National Institutes of Health, Bethesda, Md.

———. 1963b. The social life of women in the South Fore. Mimeo. report, Territory of Papua and New Guinea. Reissued by National Institutes of Health, Bethesda, Md.

———. 1964. The social effects of Kuru. *Papua and New Guinea Medical J.* 7: 36–47.

Godelier, M. 1974. Anthropology and biology: Towards a new form of cooperation. *International Social Science J.* 26: 611–35.

Godfrey, L., and K. H. Jacobs. 1981. Gradual, autocatalytic and punctuational models of hominid brain evolution: A cautionary tale. *J. Hum. Evolution* 10: 255–72.

Goffman, I. 1963. *The Cubeo: Indians of the Northwest Amazon.* Urbana, Ill.

Goggin, J. M., and W. C. Sturtevant. 1964. The Calusa. In W. H. Goodenough, ed., *Explorations in Cultural Anthropology.* New York.

Goh, S. T. 1970. The logic of explanation in anthropology. *Inquiry* 13: 339–59.

Goldschmidt, W. 1964. Theory and strategy in the study of cultural adaptability. *Am. Anthropologist* 67: 402–8.

———. 1974. Ethology, ecology and ethnological realities. In D. A. Hamburg et al., eds., *Coping and Adaptation.* New York.

———. 1986. *The Sebei: A Study in Adaptation.* New York.

Goldstein, M. C. 1971a. Stratification, polyandry and family structure in central Tibet. *Southwestern J. Anthropology* 27: 64–74.

———. 1971b. Serfdom and mobility: An examination of the institution of "human lease" in traditional Tibetan society. *J. Asian Stud.* 30: 521–34.

———. 1971c. Taxation and the structure of a Tibetan village. *Central Asiatic J.* 15: 1–27.

———. 1971d. The balance between centralization and decentralization in the traditional Tibetan political system. *Central Asiatic J.* 15: 170–82.

———. 1973. The circulation of estates in Tibet: Reincarnation, land, and politics. *J. Asian Stud.* 32 (no. 3): 445–55.

———. 1974. Tibetan-speaking agro-pastoralists of Limi: A cultural ecological overview of high altitude adaptation in the northwest Himalayas. *Objets et Mondes* 14: 259–68.

———. 1975. A report on Limi Panchayat, Humla District, Karnali Zone. *Contrib. Nepalese Stud.* 2: 89–101.

———. 1976. Fraternal polyandry and fertility in a high Himalayan valley in northwest Nepal. *Hum. Ecology* 4: 223–33.

———. 1977. Population, social structure and strategic behavior: An essay on polyandry, fertility and change in Limi Panchayat. *Contrib. Nepalese Stud.* 4: 47–62.

———. 1978a. Adjudication and partition in the Tibetan stem family. In D. C. Buxbaum, ed., *Chinese Family Law and Social Change.* Seattle.

———. 1978b. Pahari and Tibetan polyandry revisited. *Ethnology* 17: 325–37.

———. 1981a. New perspectives on Tibetan fertility and population decline. *Am. Ethnologist* 8: 721–38.

———. 1981b. High altitude Tibetan populations in the remote Himalaya: Social transformation and its demographic, economic and ecological consequences. *Mountain Research and Development* 1: 5–18.

———. 1987. When brothers share a wife. *Natural History* 96 (no. 3): 39–48.

Goldstein, M. C., and C. M. Beall. 1982. Tibetan fraternal polyandry and sociology: A rejoinder to Abernethy and Fernandez. *Am. Anthropologist* 84: 898–901.

Goldstein, M. C., and D. A. Messerschmidt. 1980. The significance of latitudinality in Himalayan mountain ecosystems. *Hum. Ecology* 8: 117–34.

Good, K. R. 1987. Limiting factors in Amazonian ecology. In M. Harris and E. B. Ross, eds., *Food and Evolution.* Philadelphia.

Goodenough, W. H. 1981. *Culture, Language, and Society.* Menlo Park, Calif.

Goodfield, J. 1985. *Quest for the Killers.* Boston.

Goodhart, C. B. 1960. The evolutionary significance of human hair patterns and skin coloring. *The Advancement of Science* 17: 53–59.

Goody, J. 1956. A comparative approach to incest and adultery. *Brit. J. Sociology* 7: 286–305.

———. 1969. Inheritance, property and marriage in Africa and Eurasia. *Sociology* 3: 55–76.

———. 1976. *Production and Reproduction*. Cambridge, Eng.

———. 1983. *The Development of the Family and Marriage in Europe*. Cambridge, Eng.

Gordon, R. M., E. P. Hicks, T. H. Davey, and M. Watson. 1932. A study of the house-haunting culicidae occurring in Freetown, Sierra Leone. *Anns. Trop. Medicine and Parasitology* 25: 273–345.

Gordon, S. 1988. Why does *Homo sapiens* differ? *J. Social and Biological Structures* 11: 427–41.

Gorer, G. 1967. *Himalayan Village: An Account of the Lepchas of Sikkim*. New York. Reprint, with new foreword, of work first published in 1938.

Gottesman, I. I., and L. L. Heston, eds. 1973. *Summary of the Conference on Lactose and Milk Intolerance*. Washington, D.C. A publication of the Office of Child Development, U.S. Dept. of Health, Education, and Welfare.

Gough, E. K. 1959. The Nayars and the definition of marriage. *J. Royal Anthropological Inst.* 89: 23–34.

Gould, S. J. 1977. *Ever Since Darwin*. New York.

———. 1978. Sociobiology: The art of storytelling. *New Scientist* 80: 530–33.

———. 1980a. Is a new and general theory of evolution emerging? *Paleobiology* 6: 119–30.

———. 1980b. Sociobiology and human nature: A postpanglossian vision. In A. Montagu, ed., *Sociobiology Examined*. Oxford, Eng.

———. 1982a. Darwinism and the expansion of evolutionary theory. *Science* 216: 380–87.

———. 1982b. The meaning of punctuated equilibrium and its role in validating a hierarchical approach to macroevolution. In R. Milkman, ed., *Perspectives on Evolution*. Sunderland, Mass.

———. 1982c. Introduction to T. Dobzhansky, *Genetics and the Origin of Species*. New York.

———. 1983a. Genes on the brain. *New York Rev. Books* 30 (no. 11): 5–10.

———. 1983b. Irrelevance, submission, and partnership: The changing place of palaeontology in Darwin's three centennials, and a modest proposal for macroevolution. In D. S. Bendall, ed., *Evolution from Molecules to Men*. Cambridge, Eng.

———. 1985. Wallace's fatal flaw. In L. R. Godfrey, ed., *What Darwin Began*. Boston.

———. 1987. The panda's thumb of technology. *Natural History* 96: 14–23.

Gould, S. J., and N. Eldredge. 1977. Punctuated equilibria: The tempo and mode of evolution reconsidered. *Paleobiology* 3: 115–51.

Gould, S. J., and R. C. Lewontin. 1979. The spandrels of San Marco and the Panglossian paradigm: A critique of the adaptionist programme. *Proc. Royal Soc. of London*, series B, 205: 581–98.

Gould, S. J., and E. S. Vrba. 1982. Exaptation—a missing term in the science of form. *Paleobiology* 8: 4–15.

Grafen, A. 1982. How not to measure inclusive fitness. *Nature* 298: 425–26.

Graubard, M. 1985. The biological foundation of culture. *J. Social and Biological Structures* 8: 109–28.

Graves, R. 1960. *The Greek Myths.* 2 vols. New York. Rev. ed. of work first published in 1955.

Gray, J. P., ed. 1984. *A Guide to Primate Sociobiological Theory and Research.* New Haven, Conn.

———. 1985. *Primate Sociobiology.* New Haven, Conn.

Green, R. L., R. G. Huntsman, and G. R. Serjeant. 1971. The sickle cell and altitude. *Brit. Medical J.* 4 (no. 5787): 593–95.

Greenberg, J. H. 1957. Language and evolutionary theory. In J. H. Greenberg, *Essays in Linguistics.* Chicago.

———. 1959. Language and evolution. In Meggers, B. J., ed., *Evolution and Anthropology: A Centennial Appraisal.* Washington, D.C.

———. 1966a. *The Languages of Africa.* Bloomington, Ind.

———. 1966b. *Language Universals.* The Hague.

———. 1975. Research on language universals. *Ann. Rev. Anthropology* 4: 75–94.

———. 1987. *Language in the Americas.* Stanford, Calif.

Greenfield, H. J. 1988. The origins of milk and wool production in the Old World. *Current Anthropology* 29: 573–93.

Greenwood, D. J. 1984. *The Taming of Evolution: The Persistence of Nonevolutionary Views in the Study of Humans.* Ithaca, N.Y.

Greenwood, D. J., and W. A. Stini. 1977. *Nature, Culture, and Human History: A Bio-Cultural Introduction to Anthropology.* New York.

Gregory, R. L. 1978. *Eye and Brain.* New York. 3d ed., rev., of work first published in 1966.

Grenard, F. 1904. *Tibet: The Country and Its Inhabitants.* London.

Grimshaw, A. 1983. Celibacy, religion, and economic activity in a monastic community of Ladakh. In D. Kantowsky and R. Sander, eds., *Recent Research on Ladakh: History, Culture, Sociology, Ecology.* Munich, W. Ger.

Gross, D. R. 1975. Protein capture and cultural development in the Amazon Basin. *Am. Anthropologist* 77: 526–49.

Grover, R. F. 1979. High altitude physiology. In P. J. Webber, ed., *High Altitude Geoecology.* Washington, D.C.

Gruter, M., and P. Bohannan, eds. 1983. *Law, Biology and Culture: The Evolution of Culture.* Santa Barbara, Calif.

Gubernatis, A. 1872. *Zoological Mythology.* London.

Gudeman, S. 1978. *The Demise of a Rural Economy: From Subsistence to Capitalism in a Latin American Village.* Boston.

Guillet, D. 1983. Toward a cultural ecology of mountains: The central Andes and the Himalayas compared. *Current Anthropology* 24: 561–74.

Gupta, R. 1980a. Altitude and demography among the Sherpas. *J. Biosocial Science* 12: 103–14.

———. 1980b. Selection intensity in the Sherpas. *Current Anthropology* 21: 136–37.

Haas, J. D., and G. G. Harrison. 1977. Nutritional anthropology and biological adaptation. *Ann. Rev. Anthropology* 6: 69–101.

Hackett, L. W. 1937. *Malaria in Europe: An Ecological Study.* London.

———. 1949. Distribution of malaria. In M. F. Boyd, ed., *Malariology.* Philadelphia.

Hadlow, W. J. 1959. Scrapie and kuru. *Lancet* 2 (no. 7097): 289–90.

Hainline, J. 1965. Culture and biological adaptation. *Am. Anthropologist* 67: 1174–97.

Haldane, J. B. S. 1932. *The Causes of Evolution*. London.

———. 1948. The rate of mutation of human genes. *Proc. Eighth Int. Congress of Genetics*, pp. 267–73.

———. 1985. A defense of beanbag genetics. In E. D. Garber, ed., *Genetic Perspectives in Biology and Medicine*. Chicago. Reprint of a paper first published in 1964.

Halliday, W. R. 1933. *Indo-European Folk-Tales and Greek Legend*. London.

Hallowell, A. I. 1962. The protocultural foundations of human adaptation. In S. L. Washburn, ed., *Social Life of Early Man*. London.

Hallpike, C. R. 1973. Functionalist interpretations of primitive war. *Man* 8 (n.s.): 451–70.

———. 1984. The relevance of the theory of inclusive fitness to human society. *J. Social and Biological Structures* 7: 131–44.

———. 1986. *The Principles of Social Evolution*. Oxford, Eng.

Hambraeus, L. 1984. Human milk composition. *Nutrition Abstracts and Revs.* 54: 219–35.

Hamburg, D. A., G. V. Coelho, and T. E. Adams, eds. 1974. *Coping and Adaptation*. New York.

Hamilton, E. 1940. *Mythology*. Boston.

Hamilton, W. D. 1964. The genetical evolution of social behavior. I and II. *J. Theoretical Biology* 7: 1–52.

———. 1982. Pathogens as causes of genetic diversity in their host populations. In R. M. Anderson and R. M. May, eds., *Population Biology of Infectious Diseases*. New York.

Hamilton, W. T. 1973. *Life's Color Code*. New York.

Hammel, E. A. 1968. Anthropological explanation: Style in discourse. *Southwestern J. Anthropology* 24: 155–69.

Hammel, E. A., and N. Howell. 1987. Research in population and culture: An evolutionary framework. *Current Anthropology* 28: 141–60.

Hammel, E. A., et al. 1979. Demographic consequences of incest tabus: A microsimulation analysis. *Science* 205: 972–77.

Hanna, J. M. 1974. Coca leaf use in southern Peru: Some biosocial aspects. *Am. Anthropologist* 76: 281–95.

Hanson, E. D. 1981. *Understanding Evolution*. New York.

Hardesty, D. L. 1977. *Ecological Anthropology*. New York.

Harding, T. G. 1960. Adaptation and stability. In M. D. Sahlins and E. R. Service, eds., *Evolution and Culture*. Ann Arbor, Mich.

Hardy, A. C. 1936. *Handbook of Colorimetry*. Cambridge, Mass.

Harkness, S. 1973. Universal aspects of learning color codes: A study in two cultures. *Ethos* 1: 175–200.

Harlan, J. R., J. M. J. de Wet, and A. B. L. Stemler, eds. 1976. *Origins of African Plant Domestication*. The Hague.

Harm, W. 1980. *Biological Effects of Ultraviolet Radiation*. Cambridge, Eng.

Harmse, N. S. 1964. Reflectometry of the bloodless living human skin. *Proc. Koninklijke Nederlandse Akademie van Wetenschappen*, series C, 67: 138–43.

Harnad, S. R., H. D. Steklis, and J. Lancaster, eds. 1976. Origins and evolution of language and speech. *Anns. N.Y. Acad. Sciences* 280: 1–915.

Harpending, H. 1980. Perspectives on the theory of social evolution. In J. H. Mielke and M. H. Crawford, eds., *Current Developments in Anthropological Genetics, Vol. I: Theory and Methods*. New York.

Harrell, B. 1981. Lactation and menstruation in cultural perspective. *Am. Anthropologist* 83: 796–823.

Harrer, H. 1982. *Seven Years in Tibet*. Los Angeles. Reprint of 1953 work.

Harris, D. R. 1976. Traditional systems of plant food production and origins of agriculture in west Africa. In J. R. Harlan, J. M. J. de Wet, and A. B. L. Stemler, eds., *Origins of African Plant Domestication*. The Hague.

Harris, J. W., and R. W. Kellermeyer. 1970. *The Red Cell*. Cambridge, Mass.

Harris, M. 1960. Adaptation in biological and cultural science. *Tr. N.Y. Acad. Sciences* 23: 59–65.

———. 1964. *The Nature of Cultural Things*. New York.

———. 1968. *The Rise of Anthropological Theory*. New York.

———. 1979. *Cultural Materialism*. New York.

———. 1984. Animal capture and Yanomamö warfare: Retrospect and new evidence. *J. Anthropological Research* 40: 183–201.

———. 1985. *Good to Eat: Riddles of Food and Culture*. New York.

Harrison, G. 1978. *Mosquitoes, Malaria, and Man: A History of the Hostilities Since 1880*. New York.

Harrison, G. A. 1961a. Pigmentation. In D. F. Roberts, ed., *Human Variation and Natural Selection*. London.

———, ed. 1961b. *Genetical Variation in Human Populations*. Oxford, Eng.

———. 1973. Differences in human pigmentation: Measurement, geographic variation, and causes. *J. Investigative Dermatology* 60: 418–26.

Harrison, G. A., and Owen, J. J. T. 1956–57. The application of spectrophotometry to the study of skin color inheritance. *Acta Genetica et Statistica Medica* 6: 481–84.

———. 1964. Studies on the inheritance of human skin color. *Anns. Hum. Genetics* 28: 27–37.

Harrison, G. G. 1975. Primary adult lactase deficiency: A problem in anthropological genetics. *Am. Anthropologist* 77: 812–35.

Hartl, D. L. 1980. *Principles of Population Genetics*. Sunderland, Mass.

———. 1983. *Human Genetics*. New York.

Haussler, M. R., et al. 1988. Molecular biology of the vitamin D hormone. *Recent Progress in Hormone Research* 44: 263–305.

Hawkes, K. 1983. Kin selection and culture. *Am. Ethnologist* 10: 345–63.

———. 1987. How much food do foragers need? In M. Harris and E. B. Ross, eds., *Food and Evolution: Toward a Theory of Human Food Habits*. Philadelphia, Pa.

Hawkins, J. D. 1985. *Gene Structure and Expression*. Cambridge, Eng.

Hays, D. G., et al. 1972. Color term salience. *Am. Anthropologist* 74: 1107–21.

Heath, A. 1976. *Rational Choice and Social Exchange: A Critique of Exchange Theory*. Cambridge, Eng.

Heller, P. 1974. Does the sickle-cell trait have pathogenic significance? In J. I. Hercules et al., eds., *Proc. First Nat. Symp. on Sickle-Cell Disease*. Bethesda, Md.

Sponsored by the Sickle-Cell Disease Branch of the National Heart and Lung Institute, National Institutes of Health.

Hempel, C. G. 1965. *Aspects of Scientific Explanation.* New York.

Henderson, N. D. 1982. Human behavior genetics. *Ann. Rev. Psychology* 33: 403–40.

Henderson, R. N. 1972. *The King in Every Man: Evolutionary Trends in Onitsha Ibo Society and Culture.* New Haven, Conn.

Hendrickse, R. G., et al. 1971. Malaria in early childhood. *Anns. Trop. Medicine and Parasitology* 65: 1–20.

Hercules, J. I., et al., eds. 1974. *Proc. First Nat. Symp. on Sickle-Cell Disease.* Bethesda, Md. See Heller 1974.

Herman, J. L. 1981. *Father-Daughter Incest.* Cambridge, Mass.

Herman, R. H. 1981. Epilogue. In D. M. Paige and T. M. Bayless, eds., *Lactose Digestion.* Baltimore, Md.

Herrick, J. B. 1910. Peculiar elongated and sickle-shaped red corpuscles in a case of severe anemia. *Arch. Internal Medicine* 6: 517–21.

Herskovits, M. J. 1945. The processes of cultural change. In R. Linton, ed., *The Science of Man in the World Crisis.* New York.

Heston, L. L., and I. I. Gottesman. 1973. The evolution of lactose tolerance. In I. I. Gottesman and L. L. Heston, eds., *Summary of the Conference on Lactose and Milk Intolerance.* Washington, D.C. See Gottesman and Heston 1973.

Hiatt, L. R. 1980. Polyandry in Sri Lanka: A test case for parental investment theory. *Man* 15 (n.s.): 583–602.

Hiernaux, J. 1976. Skin color and climate in central Africa: A comparison of three populations. *Hum. Ecology* 4: 69–73.

Hiernaux, J., and A. Froment. 1976. The correlations between anthropobiological and climatic variables in sub-Saharan Africa: Revised estimates. *Hum. Biology* 48: 757–67.

Higham, C., and M. Message. 1969. An assessment of a prehistoric technique of bovine husbandry. In D. Bromwell and E. Higgs, eds., *Science in Archaeology.* London.

Hilgard, E. R., and G. H. Bower, eds. 1975. *Theories of Learning.* Englewood Cliffs, N.J.

Hill, J. 1971. A model for social evolution. *Sociological Analysis* 1: 61–76.

———. 1978. The origin of sociocultural evolution. *J. Social and Biological Structures* 1: 377–86.

———. 1984. Human altruism and sociocultural fitness. *J. Social and Biological Structures* 7: 17–35.

Hill, M. J. 1983. Bacterial adaptation to lactase deficiency. In J. Delmont, ed., *Milk Intolerances and Rejection.* New York.

Hinde, R. A. 1982. *Ethology: Its Nature and Relations with Other Sciences.* New York.

Hinde, R. A., and J. Stevenson-Hinde. 1973. *Constraints on Learning: Limitations and Predispositions.* New York.

Ho, M. W., S. Povey, and D. Swallow. 1982. Lactase polymorphism in adult British natives: Estimating allele frequencies in enzyme assays in autopsy samples. *Am. J. Hum. Genetics* 34: 650–57.

Hock, R. J. 1970. The physiology of high altitude. In A. J. Vander, ed., *Human Physiology and the Environment.* San Francisco, Calif.

Hockett, C. F., and R. Ascher. 1964. The human revolution. *Current Anthropology* 5: 135–68.

Hoebel, E. A. 1954. *The Law of Primitive Man: A Study in Comparative Legal Dynamics*. Cambridge, Mass.

———. 1971. The nature of culture. In H. L. Shapiro, ed., *Man, Culture and Society*. New York. Rev. ed. of symposium first published in 1956.

Hoenigswald, H. M., and L. F. Wiener, eds. 1987. *Biological Metaphor and Cladistic Classification*. Philadelphia, Pa.

Holick, M. F. 1985. The photobiology of vitamin D and its consequences for humans. *Anns. N. Y. Acad. Sciences* 453: 1–13.

Holick, M. F., J. A. MacLaughlin, and S. H. Doppelt. 1981. Regulation of cutaneous previtamin D_3 photosynthesis in man: Skin pigment is not an essential regulator. *Science* 211: 590–93.

Holland, J. H. 1975. *Adaptation in Natural and Artificial Systems*. Ann Arbor, Mich.

Holland, J. H., et al. 1982. Rapid evolution of RNA genomes. *Science* 215: 1577–85.

Holloway, R. L. 1966. Cranial capacity, neural reorganization, and hominid evolution: A search for more suitable parameters. *Am. Anthropologist* 68: 103–21.

———. 1969. Culture: A human domain. *Current Anthropology* 10: 395–412.

———. 1972. Australopithecine endocasts, brain evolution in the Hominoidea, and a model of hominid evolution. In R. Tuttle, ed., *The Functional and Evolutionary Biology of Primates*. Chicago.

———. 1973. Endocranial volumes of early African hominids, and the role of the brain in human mosaic evolution. *J. Hum. Evolution* 2: 449–59.

———. 1975a. Early hominid endocasts: Volumes, morphology, and significance for hominid evolution. In R. H. Tuttle, ed., *Primate Functional Morphology and Evolution*. The Hague.

———. 1975b. *The Role of Human Social Behavior in the Evolution of the Brain*. New York. 43d James Arthur Lecture at Am. Museum of Natural History.

———. 1976. Paleoneurological evidence for language origins. *Ann. N.Y. Acad. Sciences* 280: 330–48.

———. 1978. Problems of brain endocast interpretation and African hominid evolution. In C. J. Jolly, ed., *Early Hominids of Africa*. New York.

———. 1981. Cultural symbols and brain evolution: A synthesis. *Dialectical Anthropology* 5: 287–303.

———. 1983. Human brain evolution: A search for units, models and synthesis. *Canadian J. Anthropology* 3: 215–30.

Holm, G. 1914. Ethnological sketch of the Angmagsalik Eskimo. *Meddelelser om Grönland* 39: 65–70.

Holmes, I. H., et al. 1976. Is lactase the receptor and uncoating enzyme for infantile enteritis (rota) viruses? *Lancet* 1 (no. 7974): 1387–89.

Holmes, W. G., and P. W. Sherman. 1983. Kin recognition in animals. *Am. Scientist* 71: 46–55.

Holstein, M. H. 1954. *Biology of Anopheles Gambiae*. Geneva, Switz.

Honig, G. R., and J. G. Adams. 1986. *Human Hemoglobin Genetics*. New York.

Hoogland, J. L. 1982. Prairie dogs avoid extreme inbreeding. *Science* 215: 1639–41.

Hooker, J. D. 1855. *Himalayan Journals*. London.

Hooper, A. 1976. "Eating blood": Tahitian concepts of incest. *J. Polynesian Soc.* 85: 227–41.

Hopkins, A. G. 1973. *An Economic History of West Africa.* New York.

Hopkins, K. 1980. Brother-sister marriage in Roman Egypt. *Comp. Stud. Society and History* 22: 303–54.

Hore, P., and M. Messer. 1968. Studies on disaccharidase activities of the small intestine of the domestic cat and other carnivorous mammals. *Comp. Biochemistry and Physiology* 24: 717–25.

Hornabrook, R. W. 1976. *Essays on Kuru.* Faringdon, Eng.

Hornabrook, R. W., and D. J. Moir. 1970. Kuru: Epidemiological trends. *Lancet* 2 (no. 7684): 1175–79.

Horton, D. 1948. The Mundurucú. In J. H. Steward, ed., *Handbook of South American Indians: Vol. 3, The Tropical Forest Tribes.* Washington, D.C.

Hosken, F. P. 1982. *The Hosken Report: Genital and Sexual Mutilation of Females.* Lexington, Mass.

Høygaard, A. 1941. Studies on the nutrition and physio-pathology of Eskimos. *Norske Videnskaps-akademi i Oslo: I. Matematisk-Naturvidenskapelig Klasse.* No. 9.

Hrdy, S. B., and G. C. Williams. 1983. Behavioral biology and the double standard. In S. K. Wasser, ed., *Social Behavior of Female Vertebrates.* New York.

Hubel, D. H. 1988. *Eye, Brain, and Vision.* New York.

Hubel, D. H., and T. N. Wiesel. 1979. Brain mechanisms of vision. *Scientific American* 241 (no. 3): 150–62.

Hughes, A. L. 1980. Preferential first-cousin marriage and inclusive fitness. *Ethology and Sociobiology* 1: 311–17.

———. 1981. Female infanticide: Sex ratio manipulation in humans. *Ethology and Sociobiology* 2: 109–12.

Huizinga, J. 1975. Cultural and biological adaptation in man. In F. M. Salzano, ed., *The Role of Natural Selection in Human Evolution.* New York.

Hull, D. L. 1982. The naked meme. In H. C. Plotkin, ed., *Learning, Development, and Culture.* New York.

Hulse, F. S. 1960. Adaptation, selection and plasticity in ongoing human evolution. *Hum. Biology* 32: 63–79.

Hunkapiller, T., et al. 1982. The impact of modern genetics on evolutionary theory. In R. Milkman, ed., *Perspectives on Evolution.* Sunderland, Mass.

Hunt, T. 1983. The general idea. In T. Hunt, S. Prentis, and J. Tooze, eds., *DNA Makes RNA Makes Protein.* New York.

Hunt, T., S. Prentis, and J. Tooze, eds. 1983. *DNA Makes RNA Makes Protein.* New York.

Hurvich, L. M. 1981. *Color Vision.* Sunderland, Mass.

Hurvich, L. M., and D. Jameson. 1955. Some quantitative aspects of an opponent-colors theory: 2. Brightness, saturation and hue in normal and dichromatic vision. *J. Optical Soc. America* 45: 602–16.

Huss-Ashmore, R., et al. 1982. Nutritional inference from paleopathology. In M. B. Schiffer, ed., *Advances in Archaeological Method and Theory*, vol. 5. New York.

Hussein, L., et al. 1982. Distribution of human adult lactose phenotypes in Egypt. *Hum. Heredity* 32: 94–99.

Hutchinson, S. 1985. Changing concepts of incest among the Nuer. *Am. Ethnologist* 12: 625–41.

Huth, A. H. 1875. *The Marriage of Near Kin.* London.

Hutton, J. H. 1921. *The Sema Nagas.* London.

Huxley, J. S. 1955. Evolution, cultural and biological. *Ybk. Anthropology* 1: 3–25.

———. 1958. Cultural processes and evolution. In A. Roe and G. G. Simpson, eds., *Behavior and Evolution.* New Haven, Conn.

———. 1962. Evolution: Biological and human. *Nature* 196: 203–4.

Hyman, H. 1960. Reflections on reference groups. *Public Opinion Q.* 24: 383–96.

Idowu, E. B. 1963. *Olodumare: God in Yoruba Belief.* New York.

Ihde, A. J. 1974. Studies on the history of rickets, I. Recognition of rickets as a deficiency disease. *Pharmacy in History* 16: 83–88.

———. 1975. Studies on the history of rickets, II. The roles of cod liver oil and light. *Pharmacy in History* 17: 13–20.

Ingold, T. 1986. *Evolution and Social Life.* Cambridge, Eng.

Ingram, V. M. 1957. Gene mutation in human hemoglobin—chemical difference between normal and sickle-cell hemoglobin. *Nature* 180: 326–28.

———. 1981. Molecular disease. In P. B. Sigler, ed., *The Molecular Basis of Mutant Hemoglobin Dysfunction.* New York.

Ireland, D. H. 1962. The little dry season of southern Nigeria. *Nigerian Geographical J.* 5: 7–21.

Irons, W. 1979a. Cultural and biological success. In N. A. Chagnon and W. Irons, eds., *Evolutionary Biology and Human Social Behavior: An Anthropological Perspective.* North Scituate, Mass.

———. 1979b. Natural selection, adaptation, and human social behavior. In N. A. Chagnon and W. Irons, eds., *Evolutionary Biology and Human Social Behavior: An Anthropological Perspective.* North Scituate, Mass.

———. 1981. Why lineage exogamy? In R. D. Alexander and D. W. Tinkle, eds., *Natural Selection and Social Behavior.* New York.

———. 1983. Human female reproductive strategies. In S. K. Wasser, ed., *Social Behavior of Female Vertebrates.* New York.

Irvine, M. 1987. Resource management by the Runa Indians of the Ecuadorian Amazon. Ph.D. diss., Stanford University.

Isaac, E. 1970. *Geography of Domestication.* Englewood Cliffs, N.J.

Isaac, G. L. 1972. Chronology and the tempo of cultural change during the Pleistocene. In W. W. Bishop and J. A. Miller, eds., *Calibration of Hominoid Evolution.* Toronto, Can.

———. 1976. Early stone tools—an adaptive threshold? In G. de G. Sieveking, I. H. Longworth and K. E. Wilson, eds., *Problems in Economic and Social Archaeology.* London.

———. 1983. Aspects of human evolution. In D. S. Bendall, ed., *Evolution from Molecules to Men.* Cambridge, Eng.

Itani, J. 1972. A preliminary essay on the relationship between social organization and incest avoidance in nonhuman primates. In F. E. Poirier, ed., *Primate Socialization.* New York.

Ivanhoe, F. 1970. Was Virchow right about Neanderthal? *Nature* 227: 577–79.

Jackson, A. 1971. Kinship, suicide and pictographs among the Na-khi (S. W. China). *Ethnos* 36: 52–93.

———. 1979. *Na-khi Religion.* The Hague.

Jackson, L. C. 1981. The relationship of certain genetic traits to the incidence and intensity of malaria in Liberia, West Africa. Ph.D. diss., Cornell University.

————. 1986. Sociocultural and ethnohistorical influence on genetic diversity in Liberia. *Am. Anthropologist* 88: 825–42.

Jackson, R. T., and M. C. Latham. 1979. Lactose malabsorption among Masai children of east Africa. *Am. J. Clin. Nutrition* 23: 779–82.

Jacob, F. 1977. Evolution and tinkering. *Science* 196: 1161–66.

Jacob, G. F. 1957. A study of the survival rate of cases of sickle-cell anaemia. *Brit. Medical J.* 1 (no. 5021): 738–39.

Jacobs, G. H. 1981. *Comparative Color Vision.* New York.

Jaffe, R. B., ed. 1981. *Prolactin.* New York.

Jameson, D., and L. M. Hurvich. 1955. Some quantitative aspects of an opponent-colors theory: 1. Chromatic responses and spectral saturation. *J. Optical Soc. of America* 45: 546–52.

————. 1968. Opponent-response functions related to measured cone photopigments. *J. Optical Soc. America* 58: 429–30.

Janzen, D. H. 1973. Social systems, sex, and survival. *Natural History* 82 (no. 2): 86–90.

Jeffreys, A. J. 1982. Evolution of globin genes. In J. Maynard Smith, ed., *Evolution Now.* San Francisco.

Jeffreys, A. J., and R. A. Flavell. 1977. The rabbit β-globin gene contains a large insert in the coding sequence. *Cell* 12: 1097–1108.

Jeffreys, A. J., et al. 1983. Evolution of gene families: The globin genes. In D. S. Bendall, ed., *Evolution from Molecules to Men.* Cambridge, Eng.

Jeri, F. R., ed. 1980. *Cocaine 1980: Proceedings of the Interamerican Seminar on Coca and Cocaine.* Lima, Peru.

Jerison, H. J. 1973. *Evolution of the Brain and Intelligence.* New York.

————. 1975a. Evolution of the brain and intelligence. *Current Anthropology* 16: 403–26.

————. 1975b. Fossil evidence of the evolution of the human brain. *Ann. Rev. Anthropology* 4: 27–58.

Jochelson, W. 1906. Kumiss festivals of the Yakut and the decoration of kumiss vessels. *Boas Anniversary Volume.* New York.

————. 1926. The Yukaghir and Yukaghirized Tungus. *Memoirs of the American Museum of Natural History* 13: 1–469.

Johanson, D. C., and T. D. White. 1979. A systematic assessment of early African hominids. *Science* 203: 321–30.

Johnson, A. W. 1972. Individuality and experimentation in traditional agriculture. *Hum. Ecology* 1: 149–59.

————. 1982. Reductionism in cultural ecology: The Amazon case. *Current Anthropology* 23: 413–28.

Johnson, A. W., and T. Earl. 1987. *The Evolution of Human Societies: From Foraging Group to Agrarian State.* Stanford, Calif.

Johnson, E. G. 1977. The development of color knowledge in preschool children. *Child Development* 48: 308–11.

Johnson, J. D. 1981. The regional and ethnic distribution of lactose malabsorption: Adaptive and genetic hypotheses. In D. M. Paige and T. M. Bayless, eds., *Lactose Digestion: Clinical and Nutritional Implications.* Baltimore, Md.

Johnson, J. D., N. Kretchmer, and F. J. Simoons. 1974. Lactose malabsorption: Its biology and history. *Advances in Pediatrics* 21: 197–237.

Johnson, J. D., et al. 1977. Lactose malabsorption among the Pima Indians of Arizona. *Gastroenterology* 73: 1299–1304.

Johnson, R. C., R. E. Cole, and F. M. Ahern. 1981. Genetic interpretation of racial/ethnic differences in lactose absorption and tolerance: A review. *Hum. Biology* 53: 1–13.

Johnson, R. C., et al. 1987. Environmental influences on lactose tolerance. *Behavior Genetics* 17: 313–330.

Johnston, B. F. 1958. *The Staple Food Economies of Western Tropical Africa*. Stanford, Calif.

Johnston, F. E., and S. M. Low. 1984. Biomedical anthropology: An emerging synthesis in anthropology. *Ybk. Physical Anthropology* 27: 215–27.

Jones, S. R., et al. 1970. Sudden death in sickle-cell trait. *New England J. Medicine* 282: 323–25.

Jones, T. A. 1971. Operant psychology and the study of culture. *Current Anthropology* 12: 171–89.

Jonxis, J. H. P. 1961. Some investigations on rickets. *J. Pediatrics* 59: 607–15.

———, ed. 1965. *Abnormal Haemoglobins in Africa*. Oxford, Eng.

Jorgensen, J. G. 1972. *Biology and Culture in Modern Perspective*. San Francisco, Calif.

Julius, C. 1981. Sorcery among the South Fore, with special reference to kuru. In J. Farquhar and D. C. Gajdusek, eds., *Kuru: Early Letters and Field Notes from the Collection of D. Carleton Gajdusek*. New York. Reprint of work first published in 1957.

Jürgens, H. W. 1970. Anthropologische Indikatoren für die Wanderungsbewegungen in Westafrika. *Homo* 2: 33–40.

Justice, B., and R. Justice. 1979. *The Broken Taboo: Sex in the Family*. New York.

Kaberry, P. M. 1969. Witchcraft of the sun: Incest in Nso. In M. Douglas and P. M. Kaberry, eds., *Man in Africa*. London.

Kaffman, M. 1977. Sexual standards and behavior of the Kibbutz adolescent. *Am. J. Orthopsychiatry* 47: 207–17.

Kalmus, H. 1965. *Diagnosis and Genetics of Defective Colour Vision*. Oxford, Eng.

Kamin, M., and B. M. Patten. 1984. Creutzfeldt-Jakob disease: Possible transmission to humans by consumption of wild animal brains. *Am. J. Medicine* 76: 142–45.

Kan, Y. W., and A. M. Dozy. 1980. Evolution of the hemoglobin S and L genes in world populations. *Science* 209: 388–91.

Kanaghinis, T., et al. 1974. Primary lactase deficiency in Greek adults. *Am. J. Digestive Diseases and Nutrition* 19: 1021–27.

Kantowsky, D., and R. Sander, eds. 1983. *Recent Research on Ladakh: History, Culture, Sociology, Ecology*. Munich, W. Ger.

Kaplan, D., and R. A. Manners. 1972. *Culture Theory*. Englewood Cliffs, N.J.

Karan, P. P. 1960. *Nepal: A Cultural and Physical Geography*. Lexington, Ky.

Karsten, R. 1935. The head-hunters of western Amazonas: The life and culture of the Jibaro Indians of eastern Ecuador and Peru. *Societas Scientiarum Fennica, Commentationes Humanarum Litterarum* 7 (no. 1): 1–598.

Katz, R. S. 1981. Dairy council perspective on lactose intolerance. In D. M. Paige and T. M. Bayless, eds., *Lactose Digestion*. Baltimore, Md.

Katz, S. H. 1973a. Evolutionary perspectives on purpose and man. *Zygon* 8: 325–40.

————. 1973b. Genetic adaptation in twentieth-century man. In M. H. Crawford and P. L. Workman, eds., *Methods and Theories of Anthropological Genetics*. Albuquerque, N.Mex.

————, ed. 1975. *Biological Anthropology*. San Francisco, Calif.

————. 1982. Food, behavior, and biocultural evolution. In L. M. Barker, ed., *The Psychobiology of Human Food Selection*. Westport, Conn.

————. 1987. Fava bean consumption: A case for the coevolution of genes and culture. In M. Harris and E. B. Ross, eds., *Food and Evolution*. Philadelphia, Pa.

Katz, S. H., and E. F. Foulks. 1970. Mineral metabolism and behavior: Abnormalities of calcium homeostasis. *Am. J. Physical Anthropology* 32: 299–304.

Katz, S. H., and J. Schall. 1979. Fava bean consumption and biocultural evolution. *Medical Anthropology* 3: 459–76.

————. 1986. Favism and malaria: A model of nutritional and biocultural evolution. In N. Etkin, ed., *Plants in Indigenous Medicine and Diet*. Bedford Hills, N.Y.

Katz, S. H., M. L. Hediger, and L. A. Valleroy. 1974. Traditional maize processing techniques in the new world. *Science* 184: 765–73.

Kaufman, S. 1983. Phenylketonuria and its variants. *Advances in Human Genetics* 13: 217–97.

Kawaguchi, E. 1909. *Three Years in Tibet*. Adyar, Madras, India.

Kay, P. 1975. Synchronic variability and diachronic change in basic color terms. *Language in Society* 4: 257–70.

Kay, P., and C. K. McDaniel. 1978. The linguistic significance of the meanings of basic color terms. *Language* 54: 610–46.

Keeler, C. E. 1950. The Caribe-Cuna moon-child: A demonstration of pigment-gene pleiotropy in Man. *Bull. Georgia Acad. Science* 8: 3–6.

————. 1953. The Caribe Cuna moon-child and its heredity. *J. Heredity* 44: 163–71.

————. 1956. *Land of the Moon-Children*. Athens, Ga.

————. 1964. The incidence of Cuna moon-child albinos. *J. Heredity* 55: 115–20.

————. 1970. Cuna moon-child albinism 1950–70. *J. Heredity* 61: 272–78.

————. 1973. The incidence of Cuna moon-child albinos. In J. B. Bresler, ed., *Genetics and Society*. Reading, Mass.

Keesing, R. 1974. Theories of culture. *Ann. Rev. Anthropology* 3: 73–97.

————. 1980. Review of *Culture and Practical Reason* by Marshall Sahlins. *Am. Anthropologist* 82: 130–31.

Kehoe, A. B., and D. H. Giletti. 1981. Women's preponderance in possession cults: The calcium-deficiency hypothesis explained. *Am. Anthropologist* 83: 549–61.

Keller, A. G. 1915. *Societal Evolution: A Study of the Evolutionary Basis of the Science of Society*. New York.

Kennedy, J. G. 1970. Circumcision and excision in Egyptian Nubia. *Man* 5 (n.s.): 175–91.

Kiltie, R. A. 1980. Seed predation and group size in rain forest peccaries. Ph.D. diss., Princeton University.

Kimball, H. H. 1935. Intensity of solar radiation at the surface of the earth and its variation with latitude, altitude, season and time of day. *Monthly Weather Rev.* 63: 1–4.

Kingsley, M. H. 1899. *West African Studies*. London.

Kirch, P. V. 1980. The archaeological study of adaptation: Theoretical and methodological issues. *Advances in Archaeological Method and Theory* 3: 101–56.

———. 1984. *The Evolution of the Polynesian Chiefdoms*. Cambridge, Eng.

Kirch, P. V., and R. C. Green. 1987. History, phylogeny, and evolution in Polynesia. *Current Anthropology* 28: 431–56.

Kirchhoff, P. 1931. Die Verwandschaftsorganisation der Unwaldstämme Südamerikas. *Zeitschrift für Ethnologie* 63: 85–193.

Kiste, R. C., and M. A. Rynkiewich. 1976. Incest and exogamy: A comparative study of two Marshall Island populations. *J. Polynesian Society* 85: 209–26.

Kitcher, P. 1985. *Vaulting Ambition: Sociobiology and the Quest for Human Nature*. Cambridge, Mass.

Klitzman, R. L., M. P. Alpers, and D. C. Gajdusek. 1984. The natural incubation period of kuru and the episodes of transmission in three clusters of patients. *Neuroepidemiology* 3: 3–20.

Kloster, J. 1931. The distribution and frequency of rickets in one of the fishery districts of Finmark and relation of diet to the disorder. *Acta Paediatrica* 12 (supp. 3): 1–82.

Kluckhohn, C. 1951. The study of culture. In D. Lerner and H. Lasswell, eds., *The Policy Sciences*. Stanford, Calif.

———. 1960. Recurrent themes in myths and myth making. In H. A. Murray, ed., *Myth and Myth Making*. New York.

Knight, E. F. 1897. *Where Three Empires Meet*. London.

Kobayashi, A., et al. 1975. Effects of dietary lactose and lactase preparation on the intestinal absorption of calcium and magnesium in normal infants. *Am. J. Clin. Nutrition* 28 (no. 7): 681–93.

Koch, K. F. 1974. Incest and its punishment in Jale society. *J. Polynesian Society* 83: 84–91.

Koeppen, C. F. 1857. *Die Religion des Buddha und ihre Entstehung*. 2 vols. Berlin.

Kohn, D., ed. 1985. *The Darwinian Heritage*. Princeton, N.J.

Kolars, J. C., et al. 1984. Yogurt—an autodigesting source of lactose. *New England J. Medicine* 310: 1–3.

Kolata, G. B. 1983. Dietary dogma disproved. *Science* 220: 487–88.

———. 1986. Anthropologists suggest cannibalism is a myth. *Science* 232: 1497–1500.

———. 1987. Are the horrors of cannibalism fact—or fiction? *Smithsonian* 17: 151–70.

Kon, S. K. 1972. *Milk and Milk Products in Human Nutrition*. Rome.

Kon, S. K., and A. T. Cowie. 1961. *Milk: The Mammary Gland and Its Secretion*. 2 vols. New York.

Konner, M. 1982. *The Tangled Wing: Biological Constraints on the Human Spirit*. New York.

Konotey-Ahulu, F. I. D. 1968. Hereditary qualitative and quantitative erythrocyte defects in Ghana: An historical and geographical survey. *Ghana Medical J.* 7: 118–19.

———. 1970. Maintenance of the high sickling rate in Africa—role of polygamy. *J. Trop. Medicine and Hygiene* 73: 19–21.

———. 1971. Malaria and sickle-cell disease. *Brit. Medical J.* 2 (no. 5763): 710–11.

———. 1972a. Balanced polymorphism and hereditary qualitative and quantitative erythrocyte defects. *Ghana Medical J.* 11: 274–85.

———. 1972b. Management of patients with sickle-cell disease. *Lancet* 2 (no. 7800): 772.

———. 1973. Effect of environment on sickle-cell disease in west Africa: Epidemiologic and clinical considerations. In H. Abramson et al., eds., *Sickle-Cell Disease*. St. Louis, Mo.

———. 1974a. The sickle-cell diseases: Clinical manifestations including the "sickle crisis." *Arch. Internal Medicine* 133: 611–19.

———. 1974b. The sickle-cell patient: A native habitat profile. In J. I. Hercules et al., eds. *Proc. First Nat. Symp. Sickle-Cell Disease*. Bethesda, Md.

Konotey-Ahulu, F. I. D., and B. Ringelhann. 1969. Sickle-cell anemia, sickle-cell thalassaemia, sickle-cell haemoglobin C disease, and asymptomatic haemoglobin C thalassaemia in one Ghanaian family. *Brit. Medical J.* 1 (no. 5644): 607–12.

Kortlandt, A. 1965. Comment on the essential morphological basis for human culture. *Current Anthropology* 6: 320–25.

Kortmulder, K. 1968. An ethological theory of the incest taboo and exogamy. *Current Anthropology* 9: 437–49.

Kosikowski, F. V. 1985. Cheese. *Scientific American* 252 (no. 5): 88–99.

Kottack, C. P. 1971. Cultural adaptation, kinship and descent in Madagascar. *Southwestern J. Anthropology* 27: 129–47.

———. 1980. *The Past in the Present: History, Ecology, and Cultural Variation in Highland Madagascar*. Ann Arbor, Mich.

Kovach, J. K. 1980. Mendelian units of inheritance control color preferences in quail chicks (*Coturnix coturnix japonica*). *Science* 207: 549–51.

Kracke, W. H. 1978. *Force and Persuasion: Leadership in an Amazonian Society*. Chicago.

Kreier, J. P., ed. 1980. *Malaria*. 3 vols. New York.

Kretchmer, N. 1971. Lactose and lactase—a historical perspective. *Gastroenterology* 61: 805–13.

———. 1972. Lactose and lactase. *Scientific American* 227 (no. 4): 70–78.

———. 1977. The geography and biology of lactose digestion and malabsorption. *Postgraduate Medical J.* (supp. 2) 53: 65–72.

———. 1981a. Food: A selective agent in evolution. In D. N. Walsher and N. Kretchmer, eds., *Food, Nutrition and Evolution*. New York.

———. 1981b. The significance of lactose intolerance: An overview. In D. M. Paige and T. M. Bayless, eds., *Lactose Digestion: Clinical and Nutritional Implications*. Baltimore, Md.

Kretchmer, N., and P. Sunshine. 1967. Intestinal disaccharidase deficiency in the sea lion. *Gastroenterology* 53: 123–29.

Krige, E. J. 1936. *The Social System of the Zulus*. New York.

Kroeber, A. L. 1960. Evolution, history, and culture. In S. Tax, ed., *The Evolution of Man: Mind, Culture and Society*. Chicago, Ill.

———. 1962. *A Roster of Civilizations and Culture*. New York.

———. 1963. *Anthropology: Culture Patterns and Processes*. New York. Abridged version of work first published in 1923 and revised in 1948.

Kroeber, A. L., and C. Kluckhohn. 1952. *Culture: A Critical Review of Concepts and Definitions*. Cambridge, Mass.

Kruse. A. 1934. Mundurucú moieties. *Primitive Man* 7: 51–57.

Kuhn, N. J., D. T. Carrick, and C. J. Wilde. 1980. Lactose synthesis: The possibilities of regulation. *J. Dairy Science* 63: 328–36.

Kummer, H. 1971. *Primate Societies: Group Techniques of Ecological Adaptation.* Chicago.

Kuttner, R. 1968. Cultural selection of human psychological types. In M. F. A. Montagu, ed., *Culture: Man's Adaptive Dimension.* New York. Reprint of a paper first published in 1960.

Labby, D. 1976. Incest as cannibalism: The Yapese analysis. *J. Polynesian Society* 85: 171–79.

Lagacé, R. O., ed. 1977. *Sixty Cultures: A Guide to the HRAF Probability Sample Files* (part A). New Haven, Conn.

Laguna, J., and K. J. Carpenter. 1951. Raw versus processed corn in niacin-deficient diets. *J. Nutrition* 45: 21–28.

Land, E. H. 1977. The retinex theory of color vision. *Scientific American* 237 (no. 6): 108–28.

Lang, S. D. R., and A. Lang. 1971. The Kunde hospital and a demographic survey of the upper Khumbu, Nepal. *New Zealand Medical J.* 74: 1–8.

Larson, G. J. 1974a. Introduction: The study of mythology and comparative mythology. In G. J. Larson, ed., *Myth in Indo-European Antiquity.* Berkeley, Calif.

———. 1974b. *Myth in Indo-European Antiquity.* Berkeley, Calif.

Lasker, G. 1969. Human biological adaptability. *Science* 166: 1480–86.

Latham, M. C., and L. S. Stephenson. 1974. Theories of milk use and lactose intolerance. *Ecology of Food and Nutrition* 3: 156–58.

Laughlin, C. D., and E. G. D'Aquili. 1974. *Biogenetic Structuralism.* New York.

Lawrence, T. L. 1977. Physical and social deviance: A study of health related attitudes, perceptions and practices within a San Blas Cuna Village, Panama. Ph.D. diss. University of North Carolina at Chapel Hill.

Leach, E. R. 1955. Polyandry, inheritance and the definition of marriage. *Man* 55: 182–86.

———. 1976. *Culture and Communication: The Logic by Which Symbols Are Connected.* Cambridge, Eng.

———. 1981. Biology and social science: Wedding or rape? *Nature* 291: 267–68.

Leach, M. ed. 1949. Brother-sister incest. In M. Leach, ed., *Funk and Wagnalls Standard Dictionary of Folklore, Mythology, and Legend,* vol. 1. New York.

Lebenthal, E., C. I. Antonowicz, and H. Schwachman. 1975. Correlation of lactase activity, lactose tolerance and milk consumption in different age groups. *Am. J. Clin. Nutrition* 28: 595–600.

Leguebe, A. 1976. Skin pigmentation variability. *Zeitschrift für Morphologie und Anthropologie* 67: 181–92.

———. 1979. Analysis of the worldwide variability of skin pigmentation. *Société d'Anthropologie de Paris: Bulletins et Mémoires,* 6: 161–70.

Lehmann, H., and R. G. Huntsman. 1974. *Man's Haemoglobins.* Amsterdam, Neth.

Lehmann, H., and A. B. Raper. 1956. Maintenance of high sickling rate in an African community. *Brit. Medical J.* 2 (no. 4988): 333–36.

Lehninger, A. L. 1975. *Biochemistry.* New York.

Leichter, J., and A. F. Tolensky, 1975. Effect of dietary lactose on the absorption of protein, fat and calcium in the postweaning rat. *Am. J. Clin. Nutrition* 28: 238–41.

Leloir, L. F., and C. E. Cardini. 1961. The biosynthesis of lactose. In S. K. Kon and A. T. Cowie, eds., *Milk: The Mammary Gland and Its Secretion.* New York.

Lennenberg, E. H. 1957. A probabilistic approach to language learning. *Behavioral Science* 2: 1–12.

———. 1960. Language, evolution, and purposive behavior. In S. Diamond, ed., 1960. *Culture in History.* New York.

———. 1961. Color naming, color recognition, color discrimination: A reappraisal. *Perceptual and Motor Skills* 12: 375–82.

———. 1967. *Biological Foundations of Language.* New York.

Lenski, G. 1970. *Human Societies.* New York.

Lenski, G., and J. Lenski. 1982. *Human Societies: An Introduction to Macrosociology.* New York. 4th ed. of work first published in 1970.

Lerner, I. M., and W. J. Libby. 1976. *Heredity, Evolution, and Society.* San Francisco, Calif. 2d ed. of work first published in 1968.

Lessa, W. A. 1961. *Tales from Ulithi Atoll.* Berkeley, Calif.

Lestrel, P. E. 1975. Hominid brain size versus time: Revised regression estimates. *J. Hum. Evolution* 5: 207–12.

Lestrel, P. E., and D. W. Read. 1973. Hominid cranial capacity versus time: A regression approach. *J. Hum. Evolution* 2: 405–11.

Le Vay, D. 1975. On the derivation of the name "rickets." *Proc. Royal Soc. Medicine* 8: 46–50.

Levine, A. S., and M. Murayama. 1975. Solubility of sickle-cell hemoglobin: Inhibitors of the sickling process. *J. Molecular Medicine* 1: 27–34.

Levine, A. S., F. Hasegawa, and M. Murayama. 1974. Perturbants affecting gelation, rates of aggregation and solubility of sickle-cell hemoglobin. In J. I. Hercules, et al., eds., *Proc. First Nat. Symp. Sickle-Cell Disease.* Bethesda, Md.

Levine, N. E. 1976. The origin of *sTod-pa*: A Nyinba clan legend. *Contrib. Nepalese Stud.* 4: 57–75.

———. 1977. The Nyinba: Population and social structure in a polyandrous society. Ph.D. diss., University of Rochester.

———. 1980. Nyinba polyandry and the allocation of paternity. *J. Comp. Family Structures* 11: 283–98.

———. 1981a. Perspectives on love: Morality and effect in Nyinba interpersonal relationships. In A. C. Mayer, ed., *Culture and Morality.* New York.

———. 1981b. The theory of *rü* kinship, descent and status in a Tibetan society. In C. von Fürer-Haimendorf, ed., *Asian Highland Societies.* New Delhi.

———. 1981–82. Social structure, fertility and the value of children in northwestern Nepal. *Contrib. Nepalese Stud.* 9: 1–19.

———. 1987. Fathers and sons: Kinship value and validation in Tibetan polyandry. *Man* (n.s.) 22: 267–86.

———. 1988. *The Dynamics of Polyandry: Kinship, Domesticity, and Population on the Tibetan Border.* Chicago.

Levine, N. E., and W. H. Sangree, eds. 1980. Women with many husbands: Polyandrous alliance and marital flexibility in Africa and Asia. *J. Comp. Family Stud.* 11: 283–410.

LeVine, R. A. 1984. Properties of culture: An ethnographic view. In R. A. Shweder and R. A. LeVine, eds., *Culture Theory: Essays on Mind, Self, and Emotion.* Cambridge, Mass.

Levins, R. 1966. Strategy of model building in population biology. *Am. Scientist* 54: 421–31.

Levinsohn, S. A. 1927. Rickets in the Negro: Effect of treatment with ultraviolet rays. *Am. J. Diseases of Children* 34: 955–61.

Lévi-Strauss, C. 1944. The social and psychological aspects of chieftainship in a primitive tribe: The Nambikuara of Northwestern Mato Grosso. *Tr. N.Y. Acad. Sciences* 7: 16–32.

———. 1969. *The Elementary Structures of Kinship.* Boston, Mass. Translation of work first published 1949.

———. 1971. The family. In H. L. Shapiro, ed., *Man, Culture and Society.* New York. Rev. ed. of symposium first published in 1956.

Levy, H. S. 1966. *Chinese Footbinding: The History of a Curious Erotic Custom.* New York.

Lewin, B. 1983. *Genes.* New York.

Lewin, R. 1981. Do jumping genes make evolutionary leaps? *Science* 213: 634–36.

Lewis, I. 1983. Spirit possession and biological reductionism: A rejoinder to Kehoe and Giletti. *Am. Anthropologist* 85: 412–13.

Lewontin, R. C. 1968. Evolution: The concept of evolution. In D. L. Sills, ed., *International Encyclopedia of the Social Sciences,* vol 5. New York.

———. 1972. The apportionment of human diversity. *Evolutionary Biology* 6: 381–98.

———. 1974. *The Genetic Basis of Evolutionary Change.* New York.

———. 1979a. Fitness, survival and optimality. In D. J. Horn et al., eds., *Analysis of Ecological Systems.* Columbus, Ohio.

———. 1979b. Sociobiology as an adaptationist program. *Behavioral Science* 24: 5–14.

———. 1982. *Human Diversity.* San Francisco, Calif.

———. 1984. Adaptation. In E. Sober, ed., *Conceptual Issues in Evolutionary Biology.* Cambridge, Mass.

Lewontin, R. C., S. Rose, and L. F. Kamin. 1984. *Not in Our Genes: Biology, Ideology, and Human Nature.* New York.

Li, W.-H. 1983. Evolution of duplicate genes and pseudogenes. In M. Nei and R. K. Koehn, eds., *Evolution of Genes and Proteins.* Sunderland, Mass.

Lieber, E. 1973. The Pythagorean community as a sheltered environment for the handicapped. In H. Karplus, ed., *Int. Symp. Society, Medicine and Law.* Amsterdam, Neth.

Lieberman, M., and D. Lieberman. 1978. Lactose deficiency: A genetic mechanism which regulates the time of weaning. *Am. Naturalist* 112: 625–27.

Lieberman, P. 1975. *On the Origins of Language: An Introduction to the Evolution of Human Speech.* New York.

———. 1984. *The Biology and Evolution of Language.* Cambridge, Mass.

Lifshitz, F. 1984. Disaccharide intolerance. In R. K. Chandra, ed., *Food Intolerance.* New York.

Linares, O. F., and A. J. Ranere, eds. 1980. *Adaptive Radiations in Prehistoric Panama.* Cambridge, Mass.

Lincoln, B. 1975. The Indo-European myth of creation. *History of Religions* 15: 121–45.

———. 1981. *Priests, Warriors and Cattle: A Study in the Ecology of Religion.* Berkeley, Calif.

———. 1986. *Myth, Cosmos, and Society: Indo-European Themes of Creation and Destruction.* Cambridge, Mass.

Lindenbaum, S. 1979. *Kuru Sorcery: Disease and Danger in the New Guinea Highlands.* Palo Alto, Calif.

———. 1980. On Fore kinship and kuru sorcery. *Am. Anthropologist* 82: 858–59.

Lindholm, C., and C. Lindholm. 1985. What price freedom? In D. Hunter and P. Whitten, eds., *Anthropology: Contemporary Perspectives.* Boston, Mass.

Lindzey, G. 1967. Some remarks concerning incest, the incest taboo, and psychoanalytic theory. *Am. Psychologist* 22: 1051–59.

Linton, R. 1936. *The Study of Man.* New York.

———. 1939. Marquesan culture. In A. Kardiner, ed., *The Individual and His Society.* New York.

Little, M. A. 1983. An overview of adaptation. In R. Dyson-Hudson and M. A. Little, eds., *Rethinking Human Adaptation.* Boulder, Colo.

Littleton, C. S. 1973. *The New Comparative Mythology.* Berkeley, Calif.

Livingstone, F. B. 1957. Sickling and malaria. *Brit. Medical J.* 1 (no. 5021): 762–63.

———. 1958. Anthropological implications of sickle-cell distribution in West Africa. *Am. Anthropologist* 60: 533–62.

———. 1960. The wave of advance of an advantageous gene: The sickle-cell gene in Liberia. *Hum. Biology* 2: 197–202.

———. 1961. Balancing the human hemoglobin polymorphism. *Hum. Biology* 33: 205–19.

———. 1967. *Abnormal Haemoglobins in Human Populations.* Chicago, Ill.

———. 1969a. Gene frequency clines of the beta hemoglobin locus in various human populations and their simulation by models involving differential selection. *Human Biology* 41: 223–36.

———. 1969b. Genetics, ecology and the origins of incest and exogamy. *Current Anthropology* 10: 45–61.

———. 1969c. Polygenic models for the evolution of human skin color differences. *Hum. Biology* 41: 480–93.

———. 1971. Malaria and human polymorphisms. *Ann. Rev. Genetics* 5: 33–64.

———. 1973. Data on the abnormal hemoglobins and glucose-6-phosphate dehydrogenase deficiency in human populations. *Technical Report Number 3, Museum of Anthropology, University of Michigan.* Ann Arbor, Mich.

———. 1976. Hemoglobin history in west Africa. *Hum. Biology* 48: 487–500.

———. 1980. Cultural causes of genetic change. In G. W. Barlow and J. Silverberg, eds., *Sociobiology: Beyond Nature/Nurture?* Boulder, Colo.

———. 1981. Comment on "Incest avoidance as a function of heredity and environment" by R. H. Bixler. *Current Anthropology* 22: 645–46.

———. 1983. The malaria hypothesis. In J. Bowman, ed., *Distribution and Evolution of Hemoglobin and Globin Loci.* New York.

———. 1989. Who gave whom hemoglobin S: The use of restriction site haplotype variation for the interpretation of the evolution of the β^s-globin gene. *Am. J. Hum. Biology* 1: 289–302.

Livingstone, F. B., and J. N. Spuhler. 1965. Cultural determinants in natural selection. *International Social Science Journal* 17: 118–20.

Livingstone, M. S., and D. H. Hubel. 1984. Anatomy and physiology of a color system in the primate visual cortex. *J. Neuroscience* 4: 309–56.

Lloyd, B. 1977. Culture and color coding. In G. Vesey, ed., *Communication and Understanding*. Atlantic Highlands, N.J.

Lockard, J. S., ed. 1980. *Evolution of Human Social Behavior*. New York.

Lockard, J. S., et al. 1976. Panhandling: Sharing of resources. *Science* 19: 406–8.

Loomis, W. F. 1967. Skin-pigment regulation of vitamin D biosynthesis in man. *Science* 157: 501–6.

———. 1970. Rickets. *Scientific American* 223 (no. 6): 77–91.

Lopreato, J. 1984. *Human Nature and Biocultural Evolution*. Winchester, Mass.

Lorinet, A. 1975. Etude comparée de l'effet du glucose et du fructose libres et combinés sur l'absorption et la retention du calcium. *Annales de la Nutrition et de l'Alimentation* 29: 313–19.

Losco, J. 1981. Ultimate vs. proximate explanation: Explanatory modes in sociology and the social sciences. *J. Social and Biological Structures* 4: 329–46.

Louw, G. N., and M. K. Seely. 1982. *Ecology of Desert Organisms*. New York.

Lukes, S. 1974. *Power: A Radical View*. London.

Lumsden, C. J. 1985. Color categorization: A possible concordance between genes and culture. *Proc. Nat. Acad. Sciences* 82: 5805–8.

Lumsden, C. J., and A. C. Gushurst. 1985. Gene-culture coevolution: Humankind in the making. In J. H. Fetzer, ed., *Sociobiology and Epistemology*. Boston, Mass.

Lumsden, C. J., and E. O. Wilson. 1980a. Gene-culture translation in the avoidance of sibling incest. *Proc. Nat. Acad. Sciences* 77: 6248–50.

———. 1980b. Translation of epigenetic rules of individual behavior into ethnographic patterns. *Proc. Nat. Acad. Sciences* 77 (no. 7): 4382–86.

———. 1981. *Genes, Mind and Culture*. Cambridge, Mass.

———. 1982. Precis of *Genes, Mind, and Culture*. *Behavioral and Brain Sciences* 5: 1–37.

———. 1983. *Promethean Fire: Reflections on the Origin of Mind*. Cambridge, Mass.

———. 1985. The relation between biological and cultural evolution. *J. Social and Biological Structures* 8: 343–59.

Luzzatto, L. V. 1974. Genetic factors in malaria. *Bull. World Health Organization* 50: 195–202.

———. 1979. Genetics of red cells and susceptibility to malaria. *Blood* 54: 961–76.

Luzzatto, L., and G. Battistuzzi. 1985. Glucose-6-phosphate dehydrogenase. *Advances in Hum. Genetics* 14: 217–329.

Luzzatto, L. V., et al. 1970. Increased sickling rate of parasitized erythrocytes as mechanism of resistance against malaria in the sickling trait. *Lancet* 1 (no. 7642): 319–21.

Lyons, J. 1968. *Introduction to Theoretical Linguistics*. Cambridge, Eng.

Mabayoje, J. O. 1956. Sickle-cell anaemia: A major disease in west Africa. *Brit. Medical J.* 1 (no. 4960): 194–96.

McBride, G. 1971. The nature-nurture problem in social evolution. In J. F. Eisenberg and W. S. Dillon, eds., *Man and Beast: Comparative Social Behavior*. Washington, D.C.

McCabe, J. 1983. FBD Marriage: Further support for the Westermarck hypothesis of the incest taboo? *Am. Anthropologist* 85: 50–69.

McCarron, D. A., C. D. Morris, and C. Cole. 1982. Dietary calcium in human hypertension. *Science* 217: 267–69.

MacCormack, C. P., ed. 1982. *Ethnography of Fertility and Birth*. New York.

McCracken, R. D. 1971. Lactase deficiency: An example of dietary evolution. *Current Anthropology* 12: 479–517.

McCullough, J. M. 1978. Phenylketonuria: A balanced polymorphism in Europe? *J. Hum. Evolution* 7: 231–37.

McDonald, D. R. 1977. Food taboos: A primitive environmental protection agency (South America). *Anthropos* 72: 734–48.

MacDonald, K. 1984. An ethological-social learning theory of the development of altruism: Implications for human sociobiology. *Ethology and Sociobiology* 5: 97–110.

McFadden, A. W. 1961. Skin disease in the Cuna Indians. *Arch. Dermatology* 84: 1013–23.

McGill, D. B. 1983. Diagnostic tests for lactase deficiency. In J. Delmont, ed., *Milk Intolerances and Rejection*. New York.

McGinnis, J. M., D. Shopland, and C. Brown. 1987. Tobacco and health: Trends in smoking and smokeless tobacco consumption in the United States. *Ann. Rev. Public Health* 8: 441–67.

McGovern, V. J. 1977. Epidemiological aspects of melanoma: A review. *Pathology* 9: 233–41.

McGrew, W. C., and C. E. G. Tutin. 1978. Evidence for a social custom in chimpanzees? *Man* (n.s.) 13: 234–51.

McHenry, H. 1982. The pattern of human evolution: Studies on bipedalism, mastication, and encephalization. *Ann. Rev. Anthropology* 11: 151–73.

MacIntyre, I., I. M. A. Evans, and R. G. Larkins. 1977. Vitamin D. *Clinical Endocrinology* 6: 65–79.

MacKay, D. M. 1969. *Information, Mechanism and Meaning*. Cambridge, Mass.

McKinley, R. 1976. Human and proud of it! A structural treatment of headhunting rites and the social definition of enemies. In G. N. Appell, ed., *Studies in Borneo Societies: Social Process and Anthropological Explanation*. Northern Illinois University, Special Report no. 12.

McKusick, V. A. 1986. *Mendelian Inheritance in Man*. Baltimore, Md. 7th ed. of work first published in 1966.

MacLachlan, M. D. 1983. *Why They Did Not Starve: Biocultural Adaptation in a South Indian Village*. Philadelphia, Pa.

MacLaughlin, J. A., R. R. Anderson, M. F. Holick. 1982. Spectral character of sunlight modulates photosynthesis of previtamin D and its photoisomers in human skin. *Science* 216: 1001–3.

MacLaury, R. E. 1987. Color-category evolution and Shuswap yellow-with-green. *Am. Anthropologist* 89: 107–24.

McLennan, J. F. 1865. *Primitive Marriage*. Edinburgh, Scot.

MacNichol, E. F., Jr. 1964. Three-pigment color vision. *Scientific American* 211 (no. 6): 48–56.

Mager, J., M. Chevion, and G. Glaser. 1980. Favism. In I. E. Liener, ed., *Toxic Constituents of Plant Foodstuffs*. New York.

Magnus, K. 1977. Incidence of malignant melanoma of the skin in five Nordic countries: Significance of solar radiation. *International Journal of Cancer* 20: 477.

Mainardi, D. 1980. Tradition and the social transmission of behavior in animals. In G. W. Barlow and J. Silverberg, eds., *Sociobiology: Beyond Nature/Nurture*. Boulder, Colo.

Maisch, H. 1972. *Incest*. New York.

Majumdar, D. N. 1955. Family and marriage in a polyandrous society. *Eastern Anthropologist* 8: 85–110.

———. 1962. *Himalayan Polyandry*. London.

Malinowski, B. 1929. *The Sexual Life of Savages*. New York.

———. 1955. *Sex and Repression in Savage Society*. New York. Reprint of work first published in 1927.

———. 1965. *The Dynamics of Culture Change: An Inquiry into Race Relations in Africa*. New Haven, Conn. First published in 1945; here, edited and with a new introduction by P. M. Kaberry.

Mallory, J. P. 1989. *In Search of the Indo-Europeans: Language, Archaeology, and Myth*. London.

Maniatis, T., et al. 1980. The molecular genetics of human hemoglobins. *Ann. Rev. Genetics* 14: 145–78.

Mankin, H. J. 1974. Rickets, osteomalacia, and renal osteodystrophy: Part 1. *J. Bone and Joint Surgery* 56-A: 101–28.

Mann, A. 1972. Hominid and cultural origins. *Man* (n.s.) 7: 379–86.

Mann, R. S. 1978. Ladakhi polyandry reinterpreted. *Indian Anthropologist* 8: 17–30.

Manoukian, M. 1950. *Akan and Ga-Adangme Peoples of the Gold Coast*. London.

Maramorosch, K. 1987. The curse of *Cadang-cadang*. *Natural History* 96 (no. 7): 20–22.

Marcus, R. 1982. The relationship of dietary calcium to the maintenance of skeletal integrity in man—an interface of endocrinology and nutrition. *Metabolism* 31: 93–102.

Marshall, F. N. 1968. Tetanus of the newborn, with special reference to experiences in Haiti, W.I. *Advances in Pediatrics* 15: 65–110.

Marshall, M., ed. 1979. *Beliefs, Behaviors, and Alcoholic Beverages: A Cross-cultural Survey*. Ann Arbor, Mich.

———. 1984. Structural patterns of sibling classification in island Oceania: Implications for culture history. *Current Anthropology* 25: 597–637.

Martin, R. D. 1983. *Human Brain Evolution in an Ecological Context*. New York.

Martin, S. K. 1980. Modified G-6-PD/malaria hypothesis. *Lancet* 1 (no. 8158): 51.

Masters, R. D. 1970. Genes, language and evolution. *Semiotica* 2: 295–320.

———. 1982. Is sociobiology reactionary? The political implications of inclusive fitness theory. *Q. R. Biology* 57: 275–92.

Masters, R. E. L. 1963. *Patterns of Incest*. New York.

Matessi, C. R. G., C. Viganotti, and L. L. Cavalli-Sforza. 1983. *Spatial Distributions of Cultural Traits in Africa*. Pavia, Italy.

Mather, K. 1964. *Human Diversity*. Edinburgh, Scot.

Mathews, J. D., R. Glasse, and S. Lindenbaum. 1968. Kuru and cannibalism. *Lancet* 2 (no. 7565): 449–52.

Mattingly, P. F. 1974. Origins and evolution of the human malarias. *Parassitologia* 15: 169–72.

Maugh, T. H. 1977. Malaria: Resurgence in research brightens prospects. *Science* 196: 413–16.

———. 1981. A new understanding of sickle cell emerges. *Science* 211: 265–67.

Maxwell, J. P. 1930. Further studies in osteomalacia. *Proc. Royal Soc. Medicine* 23: 639–52.

May, J. M. 1951. Map of the world distribution of malaria vectors. *Geographical Rev.* 41: 638–39.

———. 1954. The cultural aspects of tropical medicine. *Am. J. Trop. Medicine and Hygiene* 3: 422–30.

———. 1958. *Ecology of Human Disease.* New York.

———. 1972. Influence of environmental transformation in changing the map of disease. In M. T. Farvar and J. P. Milton, eds., *The Careless Technology.* Garden City, N.Y.

May, R. M. 1979. When to be incestuous. *Nature* 279: 192–94.

Maynard Smith, J. 1961. Evolution and history. In M. Banton, ed., *Darwinism and the Study of Society.* Chicago.

———. 1966. *The Theory of Evolution.* Baltimore, Md.

———. 1971. What use is sex? *J. Theoretical Biology* 30: 319–35.

———. 1978. *The Evolution of Sex.* Cambridge, Eng.

———. 1982. *Evolution Now.* San Francisco.

———. 1984. The ecology of sex. In J. R. Krebs and N. B. Davies, eds., *Behavioural Ecology: An Evolutionary Approach.* Sunderland, Mass.

Maynard Smith, J., and N. Warren. 1982. Models of cultural and genetic change. *Evolution* 36: 620–27.

Maynard Smith, J., et al. 1985. Developmental constraints and evolution. *Q. Rev. Biology* 60: 265–87.

Mayo, O. 1983. *Natural Selection and Its Constraints.* New York.

Mayr, E. 1961. Cause and effect in biology. *Science* 134: 1501–6.

———. 1972. Lamarck revised. *J. History of Biology* 5: 55–94.

———. 1974. Behavior programs and evolutionary strategies. *Am. Scientist* 62: 650–59.

———. 1976a. Change of genetic environment and evolution. In E. Mayr, *Evolution and the Diversity of Life.* Cambridge, Mass. Reprint of article first published in 1954.

———. 1976b. Where are we? In E. Mayr, *Evolution and the Diversity of Life.* Cambridge, Mass. Reprint of article first published in 1959.

———. 1982. *The Growth of Biological Thought: Diversity, Evolution, and Inheritance.* Cambridge, Mass.

———. 1983. How to carry out the adaptationist program. *Am. Naturalist* 121: 324–34.

Mazess, R. B. 1975. Human adaptation to high altitude. In A. Damon, ed., *Physiological Anthropology.* New York.

Mbaginta'o, I. 1976. Medical practices and funerary ceremony of the Dunkwi Anga. *J. de la Societé des Oceanistes* 53: 299–305.

Mead, M. 1958. Cultural determinants of behavior. In A. Roe and G. Simpson, eds., *Behavior and Evolution.* New Haven, Conn.

———. 1964. *Continuities in Cultural Evolution.* New Haven, Conn.

Mears, J. G., et al. 1983. Alpha-thalassemia is related to prolonged survival in sickle-cell anemia. *Blood* 62: 286–90.

Medawar, P. B. 1960. *The Future of Man*. New York.

———. 1981. Stretch genes. *New York Rev. Books* 28: 45–48.

Meggers, B. J., ed. 1959. *Evolution and Anthropology: A Centennial Appraisal*. Washington, D.C.

Meier, R. J., C. M. Otten, and F. Abdel-Hameed, eds. 1978. *Evolutionary Models and Studies in Human Diversity*. New York.

Meigs, A. S. 1984. *Food, Sex and Pollution: A New Guinea Religion*. New Brunswick, N.J.

Melotti, U. 1981. Towards a new theory of the origin of the family. *Current Anthropology* 22: 625–38.

———. 1984. A sociobiological interpretation of the structures and functions of the human family. *J. Hum. Evolution* 13: 81–90.

Menozzi, P., A. Piazza, and L. Cavalli-Sforza. 1978. Synthetic human gene frequency maps of Europe. *Science* 201: 786–92.

Mentzer, W. C., et al. 1981. Covalent inhibitors of sickling. In P. B. Sigler, ed., *The Molecular Basis of Mutant Hemoglobin Dysfunction*. New York.

Merlini, S. 1978. La storia del rachitismo. *Minerva Dietologica e Gastroenterologica* 24: 175–79.

Merton, R. K. 1957. *Social Theory and Social Structure*. Glencoe, Ill.

Merz, P. A., et al. 1984. Infection-specific particle from the unconventional slow virus diseases. *Science* 225: 437–40.

Métraux, A. 1948. Tribes of the middle and upper Amazon River. In J. H. Steward, ed., *Handbook of South American Indians: Vol. 3, The Tropical Forest Tribes*. Washington, D.C.

———. 1949. Warfare, cannibalism, and human trophies. In J. H. Steward, ed., *Handbook of South American Indians: Vol. 5, The Comparative Ethnology of South American Indians*. Washington, D.C.

Mettler, F. A. 1962. Culture and the structural evolution of the nervous system. In M. F. A. Montagu, ed., *Culture and the Evolution of Man*. New York.

Mettler, L. E., and T. G. Gregg. 1969. *Population Genetics and Evolution*. Englewood Cliffs, N.J.

Michell, H. 1957. *The Economics of Ancient Greece*. New York: Facsimile reprint of work first published in 1940.

Michod, R. E., and B. R. Levin, eds. 1988. *The Evolution of Sex*. Sunderland, Mass.

Middleton, R. 1962. Brother-sister and father-daughter marriage in ancient Egypt. *American Sociological Review* 27: 603–11.

Miège, J. 1952. L'importance économique des ignames en Côte-d'Ivoire. *Revue Internationale de Botanique Appliqué et d'Agriculture Tropicale* 32: 144–55.

———. 1954. Les cultures vivrières en Afrique occidentale. *Les Cahiers d'Outre Mer* 7: 25–50.

Milan, F. A. 1980. *The Human Biology of Circumpolar Populations*. Cambridge, Eng.

Milisankas, S. 1978. *European Prehistory*. New York.

Miller, C. H., and R. Carter. 1976. *Innate resistance in malaria: A review*. Experimental Parasitology 40: 132–46.

Miller, R. 1952. The climate of Nigeria. *Geography* 37: 198–213.

Minsky, M. 1986. *The Society of Mind*. New York.

Mitchell, S. D. 1987. "Why" functions (in evolutionary biology and cultural anthropology). Ph.D. diss. University of Pittsburgh.

Molineaux, L., and G. Gramiccia. 1980. *The Garki Project: Research on the Epidemiology and Control of Malaria in the Sudan Savanna of West Africa.* Geneva, Switz.

Molineaux, L., et al. 1979. Abnormal hemoglobins in the Sudan savannah of Nigeria: III. Malaria, immunoglobins and antimalarial antibodies in sickle-cell disease. *Anns. Trop. Medicine and Parasitology* 73: 301–10.

Mollon, J. D. 1980. Post-receptoral processes in color vision. *Nature* 283: 623–24.

———. 1982a. Color vision. *Ann. Rev. Psychology* 33: 41–85.

———. 1982b. Color vision and color blindness. In H. B. Barlow and J. D. Mollon, eds., *The Senses.* Cambridge, Eng.

Mollon, J. D., and L. T. Sharpe, eds. 1983. *Colour Vision: Physiology and Psychophysics.* London, Eng.

Monberg, T. 1976. Ungrammatical "love" on Bellona (Mungiki). *J. Polynesian Society* 85: 243–55.

Monod, Jacques. 1971. *Chance and Necessity.* New York.

Montagu, M. F. A. 1937. Physiological paternity in Australia. *Am. Anthropologist* 39: 175–83.

———. 1962. *Culture and the Evolution of Man.* New York.

———, ed. 1968a. *Culture: Man's Adaptive Dimension.* New York.

———. 1968b. Brains, genes, culture, immaturity and gestation. In M. F. A. Montagu, ed., *Culture: Man's Adaptive Dimension.* New York.

———, ed. 1980. *Sociobiology Examined.* New York.

Moog, F. 1981. The lining of the small intestine. *Scientific American* 245 (no. 5): 154–76.

Moore, J. H. 1974. The culture concept as ideology. *Am. Ethnologist* 1: 537–49.

Moore, S. F. 1964. Descent and symbolic filiation. *Am. Anthropologist* 66: 1308–20.

Morgan, L. H. 1985. *Ancient Society.* Tucson, Ariz. Photoreproduction of corrected 1878 edition of work first published in 1877.

Morgan, W. B., and J. C. Pugh. 1969. *West Africa.* London.

Morton, N. E. 1961. Morbidity of children from consanguineous marriages. In A. G. Steinberg, ed., *Progress in Medical Genetics*, vol 1. New York.

Motulsky, A. G. 1960. Metabolic polymorphisms and the role of infectious diseases in human evolution. *Hum. Biology* 32: 28–62.

———. 1975. Glucose-6-phosphate dehydrogenase and abnormal hemoglobin polymorphisms—evidence regarding malarial selection. In F. M. Salzano, ed., *The Role of Natural Selection in Human Evolution.* New York.

Mourant, A. E., et al. 1976. Sunshine and the geographical distribution of the Gc system of plasma proteins. *Hum. Genetics* 33: 307–14.

Muller, H. F. 1913. A chronological note on the physiological explanation of the prohibition of incest. *J. Religious Psychology* 6: 294–95.

Mundinger, P. C. 1980. Animal cultures and a general theory of cultural evolution. *Ethology and Sociobiology* 1: 183–223.

Munsell Color Co. 1976a. *Munsell Book of Color.* Baltimore, Md.

———. 1976b. *Dominant Wavelength and Excitation Purity for Munsell Color Standards.* Baltimore, Md.

Murdock, G. P. 1949. *Social Structure.* New York.

———. 1951. *Outline of South American Cultures.* New Haven, Conn.

———. 1959a. *Africa: Its Peoples and Their Culture History.* New York.

———. 1959b. Evolution in social organization. In B. J. Meggers, ed., *Evolution and Anthropology: A Centennial Appraisal*. Washington, D.C.

———. 1967. *Ethnographic Atlas*. Pittsburgh, Pa.

———. 1971. How culture changes. In H. C. Shapiro, ed., *Man, Culture and Society*. New York. Reprint of article first published in 1956.

———. 1981. *Atlas of World Cultures*. Pittsburgh, Pa.

Murphy, R. F. 1956. Matrilocality and patrilineality in Mundurucú society. *Am. Anthropologist* 58: 414–34.

———. 1957. Intergroup hostility and social cohesion. *Am. Anthropologist* 59: 1018–35.

———. 1958. Mundurucú religion. *U. California Pub. Am. Archaeology and Ethnology* 49: 1–154.

———. 1960. *Headhunter's Heritage*. Berkeley, Calif.

Murphy, Y., and R. F. Murphy. 1985. *Women of the Forest*. New York. 2d ed. of work first published in 1974.

Murray, F. G. 1934. Pigmentation, sunlight and nutritional disease. *Am. Anthropologist* 36: 438–45.

Murray, R. D. 1980. The evolution and functional significance of incest avoidance. *J. Hum. Evolution* 9: 173–78.

Murray, R. D., and E. O. Smith. 1983. The role of dominance and intrafamilial bonding in the avoidance of close inbreeding. *J. Hum. Evolution* 12: 481–86.

Nag, N. G. 1960. Family and marriage in Lahul Valley. *Eastern Anthropologist* 13 (no. 4): 185–202.

Nakane, C. 1966. A plural society in Sikkim: A study of the interrelations of Lepchas, Bhotias, and Nepalis. In C. von Fürer-Haimendorf, ed., *Caste and Kin in Nepal, India, and Ceylon*. New York.

Nance, W. E., and J. Grove. 1972. Genetic determination of phenotypic variation in sickle-cell trait. *Science* 177: 716–18.

Nardin, E. H., et al. 1979. Antibodies to sporozoites: Their frequent occurrence in individuals living in an area of hyperendemic malaria. *Science* 206: 597–99.

Naroll, R., and W. T. Divale. 1976. Natural selection in cultural evolution: Warfare versus peaceful diffusion. *Am. Ethnologist* 3: 97–129.

Naroll, R., and R. Wirsing. 1976. Borrowing versus migration as selection factors in cultural evolution. *J. Conflict Resolution* 20: 187–212.

Nathans, J. 1987. Molecular biology of visual pigments. *Ann. Rev. Neuroscience* 10: 163–94.

Nathans, J., et al. 1986a. Molecular genetics of human color vision: The genes encoding blue, green, and red pigments. *Science* 232: 193–202.

———. 1986b. Molecular genetics of inherited variation in human color vision. *Science* 232: 203–10.

Nayal, A. S., et al. 1978a. Correlation between vitamin D intake, sunlight exposure and plasma levels of 25(OH)D$_3$. *Gerontology* 24: 117–22.

———. 1978b. 25-hydroxy-vitamin D, diet and sunlight exposure in patients admitted to a geriatric unit. *Gerontology* 24: 117–22.

Neel, J. V. 1947. The clinical detection of the genetic carriers of inherited disease. *Medicine* 26: 115–53.

———. 1949. The inheritance of sickle-cell anemia. *Science* 110: 64–66.

———. 1951. The inheritance of the sickling phenomenon, with particular reference to sickle-cell disease. *Blood* 6: 389–412.

Neel, J. V., and R. Post. 1963. Transitory "positive" selection for color-blindness? *Eugenics Q.* 10: 33–35.

Neer, R. M. 1975. The evolutionary significance of vitamin D, skin pigment and ultraviolet light. *Am. J. Physical Anthropology* 43: 409–16.

Nei, M., and R. K. Koehn, eds. 1983. *Evolution of Genes and Proteins.* Sunderland, Mass.

Netting, R. McC. 1981. *Balancing on an Alp: Ecological Change and Continuity in a Swiss Mountain Community.* Cambridge, Eng.

Neumann, T. W. 1977. A biocultural approach to salt taboos: The case of the Southeastern United States. *Current Anthropology* 18: 289–308.

Newcomer, A. D., et al. 1978. Lactase deficiency: Prevalence in osteoporosis. *Anns. Internal Medicine* 89: 218–20.

Newman, C., J. E. Cohen, and C. Kipnis. 1985. Neo-darwinian evolution implies punctuated equilibria. *Nature* 315: 400–401.

Nickerson, T. A. 1974. Lactose. In B. H. Webb, A. H. Johnson, and J. A. Alford, eds., *Fundamentals of Dairy Chemistry.* Westport, Conn.

Nigh, R. B. 1975. Evolutionary ecology of Maya agriculture in highland Chiapas, Mexico. Ph.D. diss., Stanford University.

Nimuendajú, C. 1948a. The Cawahíb, Parintintin, and their neighbors. In J. H. Steward, ed., *Handbook of South American Indians: Vol. 3, The Tropical Forest Tribes.* Washington, D.C.

———. 1948b. The Mura and Piraha. In J. H. Steward, ed., *Handbook of South American Indians: Vol. 3, The Tropical Forest Tribes.* Washington, D.C.

———. 1948c. The Cayabí, Tapanyuna, and Apiacá. In J. H. Steward, ed., *Handbook of South American Indians: Vol. 3, The Tropical Forest Tribes.* Washington, D.C.

Nordenskiold, E. 1938. *An Historical and Ethnological Survey of the Cuna Indians.* Göteborg, Swed.

Norman, A. W. 1979. *Vitamin D: The Calcium Homeostatic Steroid Hormone.* New York.

———. 1985. The vitamin D endocrine system. *Physiologist* 28: 219–32.

Norman, A. W., et al. 1980. Vitamin D deficiency inhibits pancreatic secretion of insulin. *Science* 209: 823–25.

Nowak, M. 1984. *Tibetan Refugees.* New Brunswick, N.J.

Nurse, G. T. 1979. Iron, the thalassaemias, and malaria. *Lancet* 2 (no. 8149): 938–40.

Oberg, K. 1955. Types of social structure among the lowland tribes of South and Central America. *Am. Anthropologist* 57: 472–87.

O'Brien, D. F. 1982. The chemistry of vision. *Science* 218: 961–66.

O'Donald, P. 1982. The concept of fitness in population genetics and sociobiology. In King's College Sociobiology Group, eds., *Current Problems in Sociobiology.* Cambridge, Eng.

Ogbu, J. M. 1973. Seasonal hunger in tropical Africa as a cultural phenomenon. *Africa* 13: 317–32.

Ogburn, W. F. 1950. *Social Change with Respect to Culture and Original Nature.* New York. 2d ed. of work first published in 1922.

Ojikutu, R. O. 1965. Die Rolle von Hautpigment und Schweissdrüsen in der Klimaanpassung des Menschen. *Homo* 16: 77–95.

Ojo, O. 1977. *The Climates of West Africa.* London.

O'Keefe, D. 1978. *The Cheese Buyer's Handbook*. New York.

Olby, R. 1985. *Origins of Mendelism*. Chicago.

Oldroyd, D., and I. Langham, eds. 1983. *The Wider Domain of Evolutionary Thought*. Dordrecht, Neth.

Oliver, D. L., and W. W. Howells. 1957. Micro-evolution: Cultural elements in physical variation. *Am. Anthropologist* 59: 965–78.

Olivier, G. 1973. Hominization and cranial capacity. In M. H. Day, ed., *Hum. Evolution*. London.

Olivier, G., and G. Devigne. 1983. Biology and social structure. *J. Biosocial Science* 15: 379–89.

Olivier, G., and H. Tissier. 1975. Determination of cranial capacity in fossil men. *Am. J. Physical Anthropology* 43: 353–62.

Onwubalili, J. K. 1983. Sickle-cell anaemia: An explanation for the ancient myth of reincarnation in Nigeria. *Lancet* 2 (no. 8348): 503–5.

Ophuls, W. 1977. *Ecology and the Politics of Scarcity*. San Francisco, Calif.

Opler, M. E. 1945. Themes as dynamic forces in culture. *Am. J. Sociology* 51: 198–206.

———. 1964. Cause, process, and dynamics in the evolutionism of E. B. Tylor. *Southwestern J. Anthropology* 20: 123–44.

———. 1965. Cultural dynamics and evolutionary theory. In H. R. Barringer et al., eds., *Social Change in Developing Areas: A Reinterpretation of Evolutionary Theory*. Cambridge, Mass.

Orgel, L. E., and F. H. C. Crick. 1980. Selfish DNA: The ultimate parasite. *Nature* 284: 604–7.

Orkin, S. H., and H. H. Kazazian, Jr. 1984. The mutation and polymorphism of the human β-globin gene and its surrounding DNA. *Ann. Rev. Genetics* 18: 131–71.

Orlove, B. S. 1980. Ecological anthropology. *Ann. Rev. Anthropology* 9: 235–73.

Ortner, D. J. 1983. Biocultural interaction in human adaptation. In D. J. Ortner, ed., *How Humans Adapt: A Biocultural Odyssey*. Washington, D.C.

Ortner, S. B. 1975. God's bodies, God's food: A symbolic analysis of a Sherpa ritual. In R. Willis, ed., *The Interpretation of Symbolism*. New York.

———. 1978. *Sherpas Through Their Rituals*. Cambridge, Eng.

———. 1984. Theory in anthropology since the sixties. *Comp. Stud. Society and History* 26: 126–66.

Osgood, C. E., W. H. May, and M. S. Miron. 1975. *Cross-cultural Universals of Affective Meaning*. Urbana, Ill.

Otterbein, K. F. 1968. Marquesan polyandry. In P. Bohannan and J. Middleton, eds., *Marriage, Family, and Residence*. Garden City, N.Y.

Oyama, S. 1985. *The Ontogeny of Information*. Cambridge, Eng.

Packer, C. 1979. Inter-troop transfer and inbreeding avoidance in Papio anubis. *Animal Behavior* 27: 1–36.

Page, H. J., and R. Lesthaeghe, eds. 1981. *Child-spacing in Tropical Africa*. New York.

Pagnier, J., et al. 1983. Human globin gene polymorphisms in West and Equatorial Africa. In J. E. Bowman, ed., *Distribution and Evolution of Hemoglobin and Globin Loci*. New York.

———. 1984. Evidence for the multicentric origin of the sickle-cell hemoglobin gene in Africa. *Proc. Nat. Acad. Sciences* 81: 1771–73.

Paige, D. M., and T. M. Bayless, eds. 1981. *Lactose Digestion: Clinical and Nutritional Implications*. Baltimore, Md.

Palmiter, R. D. 1969. What regulates lactose content in milk? *Nature* 221: 912–14.

Papadakis, J. 1966. *Crop Ecological Survey in West Africa*, vols. 1 and 2. Rome.

Paque, C. 1984. Infant salt taboos in Morocco. *Current Anthropology* 25: 237–38.

Parascandola, J., and A. J. Ihde. 1977. Edward Mellanby and the antirachitic factor. *Bull. History of Medicine* 51: 507–15.

Parenti, R. 1973. Quantitative and qualitative trends in human sapientization. *J. Hum. Evolution* 2: 499–508.

Parker, G. A. 1974. Assessment strategy and the evolution of fighting behavior. *J. Theoretical Biology* 47: 223–43.

Parker, S. 1976. The precultural basis of the incest taboo: Toward a biosocial theory. *Am. Anthropologist* 78: 285–305.

Parmar, Y. S. 1975. *Polyandry in the Himalayas*. New Delhi.

Parrish, J. A., et al. 1978. *UV-A: Biological Effects of Ultraviolet Radiation with Emphasis on Human Responses to Longwave Ultraviolet*. New York.

Parsons, T. 1951. *The Social System*. New York.

———. 1954. The incest taboo in relation to social structure and the socialization of the child. *Brit. J. Sociology* 5: 101–17.

Partridge, L. 1983. Non-random mating and offspring fitness. In P. Bateson, ed., *Mate Choice*. Cambridge, Eng.

Passingham, R. E. 1975. Changes in the size and organization of the brain in man and his ancestors. *Brain, Behavior and Evolution* 11: 73–90.

Pasternak, B. 1976. *Introduction to Kinship and Social Organization*. Englewood Cliffs, N.J.

Pasvol, G., D. J. Weatherall, and R. J. M. Wilson. 1979. Haemoglobin S and *P. falciparum* malaria. *Nature* 280: 613–14.

Patton, Stuart. 1969. Milk. *Scientific American* 221 (no. 2): 59–68.

Paul, R. A. 1982. *The Tibetan Symbolic World: Psychoanalytic Explanations*. Chicago, Ill.

Pauling, L., et al. 1949. Sickle-cell anemia, a molecular disease. *Science* 110: 543–48.

Pawson, I. G. 1974. Skin color in Alaskan eskimos. *Am. J. Physical Anthropology* 40: 147.

Peacock, J. L., and A. T. Kirsch. 1980. *The Human Direction: An Evolutionary Approach to Social and Cultural Anthropology*. Englewood, Cliffs, N.J.

Peel, J. D. Y., and P. Richards. 1981. Introduction to rice and yams in west Africa. *Africa* 51: 553–56.

Peña Yañez, A., J. F. Peña Angulo, and J. Rico Irles. 1971. Malabsorción de lactosa en árabes. *Revista Española de las Enfermedades del Aparato Digestivo y de la Nutrición* 34: 13–24.

Perrill, D. M. 1976. Tropical diets and human ecology: A consideration for the Hb S allele. *Am. J. Physical Anthropology* 44: 198. Abstract of unpublished paper.

Perutz, M. F. 1963. X-ray analysis of hemoglobin. *Science* 146: 863–69.

———. 1964. The hemoglobin molecule. *Scientific American* 211 (no. 5): 64–76.

Peter, K., and N. Petryszak. 1980. Sociobiology versus biosociology. In A. Montagu, ed., *Sociobiology Examined*. New York.

Peters, S. M. 1982. The concept of evolution and its application to cultural phenomena: A critical and historical assessment. Ph.D. diss., State University of New York, Stony Brook.

Pettigrew, J. D. 1972. The neurophysiology of binocular vision. *Scientific American* 227 (no. 2): 84–95.

Phillips, C. S., Jr. 1971. The revival of cultural evolution in social science theory. *J. Developing Areas* 5: 337–69.

Phillips, S. F. 1981. Lactose malabsorption and gastrointestinal function: Effects on gastrointestinal transit and the absorption of other nutrients. In D. M. Paige and T. M. Bayless, eds., *Lactose Digestion: Clinical and Nutritional Implications.* Baltimore, Md.

Phillipson, D. W. 1975. The chronology of the iron age in Bantu Africa. *J. African History* 16: 321–42.

———. 1977. The spread of the Bantu language. *Scientific American* 236 (no. 4): 106–44.

Pilbeam, D., and S. J. Gould. 1974. Size and scaling in human evolution. *Science* 186: 892–901.

Pitt, R. 1978. Warfare and hominid brain evolution. *J. Theoretical Biology* 72: 551–75.

Pittendrigh, C. S. 1958. Adaptation, natural selection, and behavior. In A. Roe and G. G. Simpson, eds., *Behavior and Evolution.* New Haven, Conn.

Plotkin, H. C., ed. 1982. *Learning, Development, and Culture: Essays in Evolutionary Epistemology.* New York.

Plotkin, H. C., and F. J. Odling-Smee. 1981. A multiple-level model of evolution and its implications for sociobiology. *Behavioral and Brain Sciences* 4: 225–68.

Pollitzer, W. S. 1970. Some interactions of culture and genetics. *Current Directions in Anthropology* 3: 69–86.

Popper, K. R. 1959. *The Logic of Scientific Discovery.* New York. Rev. ed. of work first published in German in 1935 and in English in 1959.

———. 1963. *Conjectures and Refutations: The Growth of Scientific Knowledge.* New York.

———. 1972. *Objective Knowledge: An Evolutionary Approach.* Oxford, Eng.

———. 1976. *Unended Quest: An Intellectual Autobiography.* London.

———. 1984. Evolutionary Epistemology. In J. W. Pollard, ed., *Evolutionary Theory: Paths into the Future.* New York.

Portères, R. 1958–59. Les appellations des céréales en Afrique. *Journal d'Agriculture Tropicale et de Botanique Appliquée* 5 and 6: 1–286.

———. 1976. African cereals: Eleusine, fonio, black fonio, teff, Brachiaria, paspalum, Pennisetum and African rice. In J. R. Harlan, J. M. J. de Wet, and A. B. L. Stemler, eds., *Origins of African Plant Domestication.* The Hague.

Posnansky, M. 1969. Yams and the origins of West African agriculture. *Odu* 1: 101–7.

Pospisil, L. 1958. *Kapauku Papuans and Their Law.* New Haven, Conn.

Post, P. W. 1975. Anthropological aspects of pigmentation. *Am. J. Physical Anthropology* 43: 383–86.

Post, P. W., F. Daniels, and R. T. Binford. 1975. Cold injury and the evolution of "white" skin. *Hum. Biology* 47: 65–80.

Post, R. H. 1962a. Population differences in red and green color vision deficiency: A review and a query on selection relaxation. *Eugenics Q.* 9: 131–46.

———. 1962b. Population differences in vision acuity: A review with speculative notes on selection relaxation. *Eugenics Q.* 9: 189–212.

———. 1971. Possible cases of relaxed selection in civilized populations. *Humangenetik* 13: 253–84.

Potter, V. R. 1964. Society and science. *Science* 146: 1018–22.

Price, B. 1982. Cultural materialism: A theoretical review. *Am. Antiquity* 47: 709–41.

Price, G. R. 1972. Fisher's "Fundamental Theorem" made clear. *Ann. Hum. Genetics* 36: 129–40.

Prince Peter of Greece and Denmark. 1948. Tibetan, Toda, and Tiya polyandry: A report on field investigations. *Tr. N.Y. Acad. Sciences* 10: 210–25.

———. 1955. Polyandry and the kinship group. *Man* 55: 179–81.

———. 1963. *A Study of Polyandry.* The Hague.

———. 1965. The Tibetan family system. In M. F. Nimkoff, ed., *Comparative Family Systems.* Boston, Mass.

Pringle, J. W. S. 1972. *Biology and the Human Sciences.* Oxford, Eng.

Pritchard, J. A. 1973. The effects of maternal sickle-cell hemoglobinopathies and sickle-cell trait on reproductive performance. *Am. J. Obstetrics and Gynecology* 117: 662–70.

Protsch, R., and R. Berger. 1973. Earliest radiocarbon dates for domesticated animals. *Science* 179: 235–39.

Provine, W. B. 1971. *The Origins of Theoretical Population Genetics.* Chicago.

Prusiner, S. B. 1982. Novel proteinaceous infectious particles cause scrapie. *Science* 216: 136–44.

———. 1984. Prions. *Scientific American* 251 (no. 4): 50–59.

———. 1987. Prions causing degenerative neurological diseases. *Ann. Rev. Medicine* 38: 381–98.

Prusiner, S. B., and W. J. Hadlow. 1979. *Slow Transmissible Diseases of the Nervous System.* 2 vols. New York.

Prusiner, S. B., et al. 1981. Scrapie agent contains a hydrophobic protein. *Proc. Nat. Acad. Sciences* 78: 6675–79.

Pugh, G. E. 1977. *The Biological Origin of Human Values.* New York.

Puini, C. 1904. Il Tibet (geografia, storia, religione, costumi) secondo la relazione del viaggio del P. Ippolito Desideri (1715–1721). *Memorie della Società Geographica Italiana*, vol. 10.

Pulliam, H. R., and C. Dunford. 1980. *Programmed to Learn: An Essay on the Evolution of Culture.* New York.

Pusey, A. E. 1980. Inbreeding avoidance in chimpanzees. *Animal Behavior* 28: 543–52.

Quadagno, J. S. 1979. Paradigms in evolutionary theory: The sociobiological model of natural selection. *Am. Sociological Rev.* 44: 100–109.

Quevedo, W. C., Jr., T. B. Fitzpatrick, and K. Jimbow. 1985. Human skin color: Origin, variation and significance. *J. Hum. Evolution* 14: 43–56.

Quevedo, W. C., Jr., et al. 1974. Light and skin color. In T. B. Fitzpatrick, ed., *Sunlight and Man.* Tokyo.

———. 1975. Role of light in human skin color variation. *Am. J. Physical Anthropology* 43: 393–408.

Rabin, D. L., et al. 1965. Untreated congenital hip disease: A study of the epidemiology, natural history, and social aspects of the disease in a Navajo population. *Am. J. Public Health* 55 (supp.): 1–44.

Radcliffe-Brown, A. R. 1965. *Structure and Function in Primitive Society*. New York. U.S. ed. of essays and addresses first published 1923–49.

Radnitzky, G., and W. W. Bartley, eds. 1987. *Evolutionary Epistemology, Rationality, and the Sociology of Knowledge*. La Salle, Ill.

Raha, M. K. 1978. Stratification and religion in a Himalayan society. In J. Fischer, ed., *Himalayan Anthropology*. The Hague.

Räihä, N. C. R. 1981. Comparative composition of animal milks in relationship to environment and pattern of infant metabolism and growth. In D. Walcher and N. Kretchmer, eds., *Food, Nutrition, and Evolution*. New York.

Ralls, K., et al. 1979. Inbreeding and juvenile mortality in small populations of ungulates. *Science* 206: 1101–3.

——. 1988. Estimates of lethal equivalents and the cost of inbreeding in mammals. *Conservation Biology* 2: 185–93.

Ramos, A. 1978. Mundurucú: Social change or false problem? *Am. Ethnologist* 5: 675–89.

Ramot, B., ed. 1974. *Genetic Polymorphisms and Disease in Man*. New York.

Rand McNally & Co. 1980. *Rand McNally New International Atlas*. Chicago.

Ransome-Kuti, O. 1977. Lactose intolerance—a review. *Postgraduate Medical J.*, supp. 2, 53: 73–87.

Rao, P. S. 1984. Inbreeding in India: Concepts and consequences. In J. R. Lukacs, ed., *The People of South Asia*. New York

Rao, P. S., and S. G. Inbaraj. 1980. Inbreeding effects on fetal growth and development. *J. Medical Genetics* 17: 27–33.

Raper, A. B. 1960. Sickling and malaria. *Tr. Royal Soc. Trop. Medicine and Hygiene* 54: 503–4.

Rappaport, R. A. 1969. *Sanctity and Adaptation*. New York.

——. 1971a. Ritual, sanctity, and cybernetics. *Am. Anthropologist* 73: 59–76.

——. 1971b. The sacred in human evolution. *Ann. Rev. Ecology and Systematics* 2: 23–44.

——. 1977. Maladaptation in social systems. In J. Friedman and M. J. Rowlands, eds., *The Evolution of Social Systems*. London.

——. 1979. *Ecology, Meaning and Religion*. Richmond, Calif.

Ratliff, F. 1976. On the psychophysiological basis of universal color terms. *Proc. Am. Philosophical Soc.* 120: 311–30.

Raw, I. 1975. *Anemia: From Molecules to Medicine*. Boston, Mass.

Ray, V. F. 1952. Techniques and problems in the study of human color perception. *Southwestern J. Anthropology* 8: 251–59.

——. 1953. Human color perception and behavioral response. *Tr. N.Y. Acad. Sciences* 16: 98–104.

Read, A. F., and P. H. Harvey. 1988. Genetic relatedness and the evolution of animal mating patterns. In C. G. N. Mascie-Taylor and A. J. Boyce, eds., *Human Mating Patterns*. Cambridge, Eng.

Records, R. E., ed. 1979. *Physiology of the Human Eye and Visual System*. Hagerstown, Md.

Reichel-Dolmatoff, G. 1971. *Amazonian Cosmos*. Chicago, Ill.

Reid, R. M. 1973. Inbreeding in human populations. In M. H. Crawford and P. L.

Workman, eds., *Methods and Theories of Anthropological Genetics*. Albuquerque, N.Mex.

———. 1976. Effects of consanguineous marriage and inbreeding on couple fertility and offspring mortality in rural Sri Lanka. In B. A. Kaplan, ed., *Anthropological Studies of Human Fertility*. Detroit, Mich.

Renfrew, C., ed. 1973. *The Explanation of Culture Change: Models in Prehistory*. Pittsburgh, Pa.

———. 1988. *Archaeology and Language: The Puzzle of Indo-European Origins*. Cambridge, Eng.

———. 1989. The origins of Indo-European languages. *Scientific Am.* 261 (no. 4): 106–14.

Renfrew, C., and K. L. Cooke. 1979. *Transformations: Mathematical Approaches to Culture Change*. New York.

Rescher, N. 1977. *Methodological Pragmatism*. New York.

Revusky, S., and E. W. Bedarf. 1967. Association of illness with prior ingestion of novel foods. *Science* 155: 219–20.

Reyna, S. P. 1979. Social evolution: a learning theory approach. *J. Anthropological Research* 35: 336–49.

Reynolds, V. 1976. *The Biology of Human Action*. San Francisco, Calif.

———. 1984. The relationship between biological and cultural evolution. *J. Hum. Evolution* 13: 71–79.

Reynolds, V., and R. E. S. Tanner. 1983. *The Biology of Religion*. New York.

Richards, G. 1987. *Human Evolution: An Introduction for the Behavioural Sciences*. London.

Richards, N. L. 1980. *Erythroxylon coca* in the Peruvian highlands: Practices and beliefs. Ph.D. diss., University of California, Irvine.

Richerson, P. J. 1977. Ecology and human ecology: A comparison of theories in the biological and social sciences. *Am. Ethnologist* 4: 1–26.

Richerson, P. J., and R. Boyd. 1978. A dual inheritance model of the human evolutionary process: I. Basic postulates and a simple model. *J. Social and Biological Structures* 1: 127–54.

———. 1984. Natural selection and culture. *Bioscience* 34: 430–34.

———. 1989. A Darwinian theory for the evolution of symbolic cultural traits. In M. Freilich, ed., *The Relevance of Culture*. New York.

Ridington, R. 1982. Technology, world view, and adaptation strategy in a Northern hunting society. *Canadian Rev. Sociology and Anthropology* 19: 469–81.

Rightmire, G. P. 1981. Patterns in the evolution of *Homo erectus. Paleobiology* 7: 241–46.

Riley, V., ed. 1972. *Pigmentation: Its Genesis and Biologic Control*. New York.

Rindos, D. 1984. *The Origins of Agriculture: An Evolutionary Perspective*. New York.

———. 1985. Darwinian selection, symbolic variation, and the evolution of culture. *Current Anthropology* 26: 65–88.

———. 1986a. The evolution of the capacity for culture: Sociobiology, structuralism, and cultural selectionism. *Current Anthropology* 27: 315–32.

———. 1986b. The genetics of cultural anthropology: Toward a genetic model for the origin of the capacity for culture. *J. Anthropological Archaeology* 5: 1–38.

Ringelhann, B., et al. 1976. A new look at the protection of hemoglobin AS and

AC genotypes against *Plasmodium falciparum* infection: A census tract approach. *Am. J. Hum. Genetics* 28: 270–79.

Ritenbaugh, C. 1978. Human foodways: A window on evolution. In E. E. Bauwens, ed., *The Anthropology of Health*. St. Louis, Mo.

Rivier, L., ed. 1981. Coca and cocaine—1981: A special issue. *J. Ethnopharmacology* 3 (nos. 2–3).

Robbins, S. 1982. *Auyana: Those Who Held onto Home*. Seattle, Wash.

Roberts, D. F., ed. 1975. *Human Variation and Natural Selection*. London.

———. 1977. Human pigmentation: Its geographical and racial distribution and biological significance. *J. Soc. Cosmetic Chemists* 28: 329–42.

———. 1978. *Climate and Human Variability*. Menlo Park, Calif.

———. 1981. Selection and body size. In D. N. Walcher and N. Kretchmer, eds., *Food, Nutrition, and Evolution*. New York.

Roberts, D. F., and A. E. Boyd. 1960. On the stability of haemoglobin gene frequencies in West Africa. *Anns. Hum. Genetics* 24: 375–87.

Roberts, D. F., and D. P. S. Kahlon. 1976. Environmental correlations of skin color. *Anns. Hum. Biology* 3: 11–22.

Rockhill, W. W. 1891. *The Land of the Lamas*. London.

Rodieck, R. W. 1973. *The Vertebrate Retina*. San Francisco, Calif.

———. 1979. Visual pathways. *Ann. Rev. Neuroscience* 2: 193–225.

Roe, A., and G. Simpson, eds. 1958. *Behavior and Evolution*. New Haven, Conn.

Roe, D. A. 1973. *A Plague of Corn: The Social History of Pellagra*. Ithaca, N.Y.

Rogers, E. M. 1983. *Diffusion of Innovations*. New York. 3d ed. of work first published in 1962.

Rogers, E. M., and F. F. Shoemaker. 1971. *Communication of Innovations: A Cross-Cultural Approach*. New York. 2d ed. of Rogers 1962.

Rosaldo, M. Z. 1980. *Knowledge and Passion: Ilongot Notions of Self and Social Life*. Cambridge, Eng.

Rosch, E. 1973. Natural categories. *Cognitive Psychology* 4: 328–50.

Rose, M. R. 1980. The mental arms race amplifier. *Hum. Ecology* 8: 285–93.

Rose, M. R., and W. F. Doolittle. 1983. Molecular biological mechanisms of speciation. *Science* 220: 157–62.

Rosenberg, A. 1980. *Sociobiology and the Preemption of Social Science*. Baltimore, Md.

Ross, E. B. 1978. Food taboos, diet, and hunting strategy: The adaptation to animals in Amazon cultural ecology. *Current Anthropology* 19: 1–36.

———. 1980. Patterns of diet and forces of production: An economic and ecological history of the ascendancy of beef in the United States diet. In E. B. Ross, ed., *Beyond the Myths of Culture*. New York.

Ross, J. L. 1981. Hindu and Tibetan reproduction and fertility in northwestern Nepal: A study of population, ecology, and economics. Ph.D. diss., Case Western Reserve University.

Rossotti, H. 1985. *Colour: Why the World Isn't Grey*. Princeton, N.J. Reprint with corrections of work first published in 1983.

Roth, E. F., et al. 1978. Sickling rates of human AS red cells infected in vitro with *Plasmodium falciparum* malaria. *Science* 202: 650–52.

Rotthauwe, H. W., M. O. El-Schallah, and G. Flatz. 1971. Lactose intolerance in Arabs. *Humangenetik* 13: 344–46.

Roughgarten, J. 1979. *Theory of Population Genetics and Evolutionary Ecology: An Introduction*. New York.

Rozin, P. 1976. The selection of foods by rats, humans, and other animals. *Advances in the Study of Behavior* 6: 21–76.

———. 1982. Human food selection: The interaction of biology, culture, and individual experience. In L. M. Barker, ed., *The Psychobiology of Food Selection*. Westport, Conn.

Rozin, P., and J. W. Kalat. 1971. Specific hungers and poison avoidance as adaptive specializations of learning. *Psychological Rev.* 78: 459–86.

Rubin, R., and G. Byerly. 1983. *Incest: The Last Taboo (An Annotated Bibliography)*. New York.

Rucknagel, D. L., and J. V. Neel. 1961. The hemoglobinopathies. In A. G. Steinberg, ed., *Progress in Medical Genetics*. New York.

Ruffer, M. A. 1921. On the physical effects of consanguineous marriages in the royal families of ancient Egypt. In M. A. Ruffer, ed., *Studies in the Paleopathology of Egypt*. Chicago, Ill.

Ruhlen, M. 1987. *A Guide to the World's Languages: Vol. 1, Classification*. Stanford, Calif.

Ruse, M. 1974. Cultural evolution. *Theory and Decision* 5: 413–40.

———. 1979. *Sociobiology: Sense or Nonsense?* Dordrecht, Neth.

———. 1981. Is human sociobiology a new paradigm? *Philosophical Forum* 13: 119–43.

———. 1986. *Taking Darwin Seriously: A Naturalistic Approach to Philosophy*. New York.

Ruse, M., and E. O. Wilson. 1986. Moral philosophy as applied science. *Philosophy* 61: 173–92.

Rushton, W. A. H. 1962. Visual pigments in man. *Scientific American* 207 (no. 5): 120–32.

Rutz, H. J. 1977. Individual decisions and functional systems: Economic rationality and environmental adaptation. *Am. Ethnologist* 4: 156–74.

Ruyle, E. E. 1973. Genetic and cultural pools: Some suggestions for a unified theory of biocultural evolution. *Hum. Ecology* 1: 201–15.

Ruyle, E. E., et al. 1977. The adaptive significance of cultural behavior: Comments and reply. *Hum. Ecology* 5: 49–68.

Sacherer, J. 1977. The Sherpas of Rolwaling, north Nepal: A study in cultural ecology. Ph.D. diss., Ecole des Hautes Etudes en Sciences Sociales, Paris.

Sahi, T. 1974. The inheritance of selective adult-type lactose malabsorption. *Scandinavian J. Gastroenterology* 9 (supp. 30): 1–73.

———. 1978. Dietary lactose and aetiology of human small intestinal hypolactasia. *Gut* 19: 1074–86.

Sahi, T., et al. 1973. Recessive inheritance of adult type lactose malabsorption. *Lancet* 2 (no. 7833): 823–26.

Sahlins, M. D. 1957. Differentiation by adaptation in Polynesian societies. *J. Polynesian Society* 66: 291–300.

———. 1958. *Social Stratification in Polynesia*. Seattle, Wash.

———. 1976a. Colors and cultures. *Semiotica* 16: 1–22.

———. 1976b. *Culture and Practical Reason*. Chicago, Ill.

———. 1976c. *The Use and Abuse of Biology: An Anthropological Critique of Sociobiology*. Ann Arbor, Mich.

Sahlins, M. D., and E. R. Service, eds. 1960. *Evolution and Culture.* Ann Arbor, Mich.

Saksena, R. N. 1962. *Social Economy of a Polyandrous People.* New York.

Salzano, F. M., ed. 1975. *The Role of Natural Selection in Human Populations.* New York.

Salzano, F. M., et al. 1962. Genetic load in Brazilian Indians. *Acta Genetica et Statistica Medica* 12: 212–18.

Samuels, M. L. 1972. *Linguistic Evolution.* Cambridge, Eng.

Sanday, P. R. 1986. *Divine Hunger: Cannibalism as a Cultural System.* Cambridge, Eng.

Sander, R. 1983. Three generations in the Wanla Valley. In D. Kantowsky and R. Sander, eds., *Recent Research on Ladakh: History, Culture, Sociology, Ecology.* Munich, W. Ger.

Sanderson, L. P. 1986. *Female Genital Mutilation, Excision and Infibulation: A Bibliography.* London, Eng.

Sanghvi, L. D. 1975. The genetic consequences of inbreeding. In F. M. Salzano, ed., *The Role of Natural Selection in Human Evolution.* New York.

Santiago, L. P. R. 1973. *The Children of Oedipus.* Roslyn Heights, N.Y.

Sayre, A. 1975. *Rosalind Franklin and DNA.* New York.

Schaafsma, G., and R. Visser. 1980. Nutritional interrelationships between calcium, phosphorus and lactose in rats. *J. Nutrition* 110: 1101–11.

Schappera, I. 1963. The Tswana conception of incest. In M. Fortes, ed., *Social Structure.* New York.

Schmid, M., and F. M. Wuketits, eds. 1987. *Evolutionary Theory in Social Science.* Dordrecht, Neth.

Schmookler, A. B. 1984. *The Parable of the Tribes.* Boston, Mass.

Schneider, D. M. 1955. Abortion and depopulation on a Pacific island. In B. Paul, ed., *Health, Culture, and Community.* New York.

———. 1976a. The meaning of incest. *J. Polynesian Soc.* 85: 149–69.

———. 1976b. Notes toward a theory of culture. In K. H. Basso and H. A. Selby, eds., *Meaning in Anthropology.* Albuquerque, N.Mex.

Schreider, E. 1950. Geographical distribution of the body-weight / body-surface ratio. *Nature* 165: 286.

———. 1951. Anatomical factors of body-heat regulation. *Nature* 167: 823–24.

Schroeder, T. 1915. Incest in Mormonism. *Am. J. Urology and Sexology* 11: 409–16.

Schuler, S. R. 1987. *The Other Side of Polyandry: Property, Stratification, and Nonmarriage in the Nepal Himalayas.* Boulder, Colo.

Schull, W. J. 1958. Empirical risks in consanguineous marriages: Sex ratio, malformation, and viability. *Am. J. Hum. Genetics* 10: 294–343.

———. 1972. Genetic implications of population breeding structure. In G. A. Harrison and A. J. Boyce, eds., *The Structure of Human Populations.* Oxford, Eng.

Schull, W. J., and J. V. Neel. 1965. *The Effects of Inbreeding on Japanese Children.* New York.

———. 1966. Some further observations on the effect of inbreeding on mortality in Kure, Japan. *Am. J. Hum. Genetics* 18: 144–52.

Schulze, R., and K. Gräfe. 1969. Consideration of sky ultraviolet radiation in the measurement of solar ultraviolet radiation. In F. Urbach, ed., *The Biologic Effects of Ultraviolet Radiation.* Oxford, Eng.

Schwerin, K. H. 1980. Incest and kinship structure. In L. S. Cordell and S. Becker-man, eds., *The Versatility of Kinship*. New York.

Scott-Emuakpor, A. B. 1974. The mutation load in an African population: 1. An analysis of consanguineous marriages in Nigeria. *Am. J. Hum. Genetics* 26: (no. 6): 674–82.

Scrimshaw, N. S., and E. B. Murray. 1988. The acceptability of milk and milk products in populations with a high prevalence of lactose tolerance. *Am. J. Clinical Nutrition* 48: 1083–1159.

Scrimshaw, N. S., and V. R. Young. 1976. The requirements of human nutrition. *Scientific American* 235 (no. 3): 51–64.

Seemanová, E. 1971. A study of children of incestuous matings. *Hum. Heredity* 21: 108–28.

Segner, L. L. 1968. Two studies of the incest taboo: 1. Sexual activity of mice (*Mus musculus*) as a function of familiarity; 2. A cross-cultural investigation of the correlates of incest in myth. Ph.D. diss., University of Texas at Austin.

Seligman, B. 1935. The incest taboo as a social regulation. *Sociological Rev.* 27: 75–93.

———. 1950. Incest and exogamy: A reconsideration. *Am. Anthropologist* 52: 305–16.

Seligman, M. E. P. 1971. Phobias and preparedness. *Behavior Therapy* 2: 307–20.

Seligman, M. E. P., and J. L. Hager, eds., 1972. *Biological Boundaries of Learning*. New York.

Semon, R. 1921. *The Mneme*. New York.

Serjeant, G. R. 1973. Sickle-cell anemia: Clinical features in adulthood and old age. In H. Abramson, J. F. Bertles, and D. L. Wethers, eds., *Sickle-Cell Disease*. St. Louis, Mo.

Serjeant, G. R., et al. 1968. Relatively benign sickle-cell anemia in sixty patients aged over thirty in the West Indies. *Brit. Medical J.* 3: 86–91.

Service, E. R. 1962. *Primitive Social Organization: An Evolutionary Perspective*. New York.

———. 1966. Forms of kinship. In E. R. Service, ed., *The Hunters*. Englewood Cliffs, N.J.

———. 1968. The prime-mover of cultural evolution. *Southwestern J. Anthropology* 24: 396–409.

———. 1971. *Cultural Evolutionism*. New York.

———. 1975. *Origins of the State and Civilization: The Process of Cultural Evolution*. New York.

Sharp, L. 1952. Steel axes for stone age Australians. In E. H. Spicer, ed., *Human Problems in Technological Change*. New York.

Shatin, R. 1966. Lactase deficiency in Uganda. *Lancet* 2 (no. 7461): 498.

———. 1967. The transition from food-gathering to food-production in evolution and disease. *Vitalstoffe-Zivilisationskrankheiten* 12: 104–7.

———. 1968. Evolution and lactase deficiency. *Gastroenterology* 54: 992–93.

Shepher, J. 1971. Mate selection among second-generation Kibbutz adolescents and adults: Incest avoidance and negative imprinting. *Arch. Sexual Behavior* 1: 293–307.

Shepher, J. 1983. *Incest: The Biosocial View*. Cambridge, Mass.

Sherratt, A. 1981. Plough and pastoralism: Aspects of the secondary products revolution. In I. Hodder et al., eds., *Pattern of the Past*. Cambridge, Eng.

Shettleworth, S. J. 1972. Constraints on learning. *Advances in the Study of Behavior* 4: 1–68.

Shields, W. M. 1982. *Philopatry, Inbreeding, and the Evolution of Sex.* Albany, N.Y.

Short, G. B. 1975. Iris pigmentation and photopic visual acuity: A preliminary study. *Am. J. Physical Anthropology* 43: 425–33.

Shorter, E. 1982. *A History of Women's Bodies.* New York.

Shrader, D. 1980. The evolutionary development of science. *Rev. Metaphysics* 34: 273–96.

Shweder, R. A., and R. A. LeVine, eds. 1984. *Culture Theory: Essays on Mind, Self and Emotion.* Cambridge, Eng.

Siegel, B. J. 1969. Defensive cultural adaptation. In H. D. Graham and T. R. Gurr, eds., *Violence in America.* New York.

Silk, J. B. 1980. Adoption and kinship in Oceania. *Am. Anthropologist* 82: 799–820.

———. 1987. Adoption and fosterage in human societies: Adaptations or enigmas? *Cultural Anthropology* 2: 39–49.

Simon, H. A. 1955. A behavioral model of rational choice. *Quarterly J. Economics* 69: 99–118.

Simoons, F. J. 1954. The non-milking area of Africa. *Anthropos* 49: 58–66.

———. 1969. Primary adult lactose intolerance and the milking habit: A problem in biological and cultural interrelations: 1. Review of the medical research. *Am. J. Digestive Diseases* 14: 819–36.

———. 1970a. Primary adult lactose intolerance and the milking habit: A problem in biologic and cultural interrelations: II. A culture historical hypothesis. *Am. J. Digestive Diseases* 15: 695–710.

———. 1970b. The traditional limits of milking and milk use in southern Asia. *Anthropos* 65: 547–93.

———. 1971. The antiquity of dairying in Asia and Africa. *Geographical Review* 61: 431–39.

———. 1973. The determinants of dairying and milk use in the Old World: Ecological, physiological and cultural. *Ecology of Food and Nutrition* 2: 83–90.

———. 1974. Snails, yogurt and lactose intolerance: Reply to Latham and Stephenson. *Ecology of Food and Nutrition* 3: 158–64.

———. 1978a. The geographic hypothesis and lactose malabsorption. *Am. J. Digestive Diseases* 23: 963–80.

———. 1978b. Lactose malabsorption in Africa. *African Econ. History* 5: 16–34.

———. 1978c. Traditional use and avoidance of foods of animal origin: A culture historical view. *Bioscience* 28: 178–84.

———. 1979a. Dairying, milk use, and lactose malabsorption in Eurasia: A problem in culture history. *Anthropos* 74: 61–80.

———. 1979b. Geography and lactose malabsorption: Response to Flatz and Rotthauwe. *Digestive Diseases and Sciences* 24: 493–94.

———. 1980a. Age of onset of lactose malabsorption. *Pediatrics* 66: 646–48.

———. 1980b. Effects of culture: Geographical and historical approaches. *Int. J. Obesity* 4: 387–94.

———. 1981a. Geographic patterns of primary adult lactose malabsorption: A further interpretation of evidence for the Old World. In D. M. Paige and T. M.

Bayless, eds., *Lactose Digestion: Clinical and Nutritional Implications.* Baltimore, Md.

———. 1981b. Celiac disease as a geographic problem. In D. N. Walcher and N. Kretchmer, eds., *Food, Nutrition and Evolution.* New York.

———. 1982a. Geography and genetics as factors in the psychobiology of human food selection. In L. M. Barker, ed., *The Psychobiology of Human Food Selection.* Westport, Conn.

———. 1982b. A geographic approach to senile cataracts: Possible links with milk consumption, lactase activity, and galactose metabolism. *Digestive Diseases and Sciences* 27: 257–64.

Simoons, F. J., J. D. Johnson, and N. Kretchmer. 1977. Perspectives on milk-drinking and malabsorption of lactose. *Pediatrics* 59: 98–109.

Simpson, G. E. 1964. Selected Yoruba rituals. *Nigerian J. Econ. and Social Stud.* 7: 311–24.

———. 1980. *Yoruba Religion and Medicine in Ibadan.* Ibadan, Nigeria.

Simpson, G. G. 1944. *Tempo and Mode in Evolution.* New York.

———. 1949. *The Meaning of Evolution.* New York.

———. 1966. The biological nature of man. *Science* 152: 472–78.

———. 1972. The evolutionary concept of man. In B. Campbell, ed., *Sexual Selection and the Descent of Man.* Chicago, Ill.

Siniscalco, M., et al. 1961. Favism and thalassemia in Sardinia and their relationship to malaria. *Nature* 190: 1179–80.

Siskind, J. 1973. Tropical forest hunters and the economy of sex. In D. R. Gross, ed., *Peoples and Cultures of Native South America.* Garden City, N.Y.

Skinner, B. F. 1984. Selection by consequences. *Behavioral and Brain Sciences* 7: 477–510. Reprint of 1981 article with 20 pages of pertinent reviewer comments.

Slater, M. K. 1959. Ecological factors in the origin of incest. *Am. Anthropologist* 61: 1042–59.

Slatkin, M. 1987. Gene flow and the geographic structure of natural populations. *Science* 236: 787–92.

Slicher Van Bath, B. H. 1963. *The Agrarian History of Western Europe, A.D. 500–1850.* London.

Slobodkin, L. B. 1968. Toward a predictive theory of evolution. In R. Lewontin, ed., *Population Biology and Evolution.* Syracuse, N.Y.

Slobodkin, L. B., and A. Rapoport. 1974. An optimal strategy of evolution. *Q. Rev. Biology* 49: 181–200.

Slotkin, J. S. 1947. On a possible lack of incest regulations in Old Iran. *Am. Anthropologist* 49: 612–17.

Smith, A. G., and J. P. Kennedy. 1960. The extension of incest taboos in the Woleai Micronesia. *Am. Anthropologist* 62: 643–47.

Smith, E. A. 1980. Evolutionary ecology and the analysis of human social behavior. In R. Dyson-Hudson and M. A. Little, eds. *Rethinking Human Adaptation: Biological and Cultural Models.* Boulder, Colo.

Snellgrove, D., and H. Richardson. 1980. *A Cultural History of Tibet.* Boulder, Colo.

So, J. K. 1980. Human biological adaptation to arctic and subarctic zones. *Ann. Rev. Anthropology* 9: 63–82.

Sober, E., ed. 1984a. *Conceptual Issues in Evolutionary Biology.* Cambridge, Mass.

———. 1984b. *The Nature of Selection: Evolutionary Theory in Philosophical Focus.* Cambridge, Mass.

Sofowora, E. A., and W. A. Isaacs. 1971. Reversal of sickling and crenation in erythrocytes by the root extract of *Fagara zanthoxyloides. Lloydia* 34: 383–85.

Solien de Gonzalez, N. L. 1964. Lactation and pregnancy: A hypothesis. *Am. Anthropologist* 66: 873–78.

Song, J. 1971. *Pathology of Sickle-Cell Disease.* Springfield, Ill.

Sorenson, E. R. 1972. Socio-ecological change among the Fore of New Guinea. *Current Anthropology* 13: 349–83.

———. 1976. *The Edge of the Forest.* Washington, D.C.

Sorenson, E. R., and D. C. Gajdusek. 1969. Nutrition in the kuru region: 1. gardening, food handling, and diet of the Fore people. *Acta Tropica* 26: 281–330.

Sotiroff-Junker, J. 1978. *A Bibliography on the Behavioral, Social, and Economic Aspects of Malaria and Its Control.* Geneva, Switz.

Sowls, L. K. 1984. *The Peccaries.* Tucson, Ariz.

Spain, D. H. 1987. The Westermarck-Freud incest-theory debate. *Current Anthropology* 28: 623–45.

Spencer, R. F. 1968. Spouse-exchange among the North Alaskan Eskimo. In P. Bohannan and J. Middleton, eds., *Marriage, Family and Residence.* Garden City, N.Y.

Spindler, G. D., ed. 1987. *Education and Cultural Process: Anthropological Approaches.* Prospect Heights, Ill. 2d ed.

Spiro, M. F. 1958. *Children of the Kibbutz.* Cambridge, Mass.

———. 1982. *Oedipus in the Trobriands.* Chicago, Ill.

Spuhler, J. N., ed. 1959a. *The Evolution of Man's Capacity for Culture.* Detroit, Mich.

———. 1959b. Somatic paths to culture. In J. N. Spuhler, ed., *The Evolution of Man's Capacity for Culture.* Detroit, Mich.

———. 1977. Biology, speech and language. *Ann. Rev. Anthropology* 6: 509–61.

Squire, C. 1905. *Celtic Myth and Legend, Poetry and Romance.* London.

Staddon, J. E. R. 1981. On a possible relation between cultural transmission and genetic evolution. In P. P. G. Bateson and P. H. Klopfer, eds., *Perspectives in Ethology: Vol. 4. Advantages of Diversity.* New York.

———. 1983. *Adaptive Behavior and Learning.* Cambridge, Eng.

Stamatoyannopoulos, G., and P. Fessas. 1964. Thalassaemia, glucose-6-phosphate dehydrogenase deficiency, sickling, and malarial endemicity in Greece: A study of five areas. *Brit. Medical J.* 1 (no. 5387): 875–79.

Stamatoyannopoulos, G., et al. 1966a. On the familial predisposition to favism. *Am. J. Hum. Genetics* 18: 253–63.

———. 1966b. The distribution of glucose-6-phosphate dehydrogenase deficiency in Greece. *Am. J. Hum. Genetics* 18: 296–308.

Stamp, L. D., and W. T. W. Morgan. 1972. *Africa: A Study in Tropical Development.* New York.

Stanley, S. M. 1979. *Macroevolution: Pattern and Process.* San Francisco, Calif.

———. 1981. *The New Evolutionary Timetable.* New York.

Steadman, L. B., and C. F. Merbs. 1982. Kuru and cannibalism? *Am. Anthropologist* 84: 611–27.

Steadman, P. 1979. *The Evolution of Designs.* Cambridge, Eng.

Stebbins, G. L. 1971. *Processes of Organic Evolution.* Englewood Cliffs, N.J.

Stebbins, G. L., and F. J. Ayala. 1981. Is a new evolutionary synthesis necessary? *Science* 213: 967–71.

———. 1985. The evolution of Darwinism. *Scientific American* 253 (no. 1): 72–82.

Steffanson, V. 1960. Food and food habits in Alaska and northern Canada. In I. Galdston, ed., *Human Nutrition: Historic and Scientific*. New York.

Stein, R. A. 1972. *Tibetan Civilization*. Stanford, Calif.

Steinbock, R. T. 1976. *Paleopathological Diagnosis and Interpretation*. Springfield, Ill.

Stent, G. S. 1975. Limits to the scientific understanding of man. *Science* 187: 1052–57.

Stephenson, P. H. 1973. The evolution of color vision in the primates. *J. Hum. Evolution* 2: 379–86.

Stern, C. 1960. *Principles of Human Genetics*. San Francisco, Calif.

Stern, C., and E. R. Sherwood, eds. 1966. *The Origin of Genetics*. San Francisco, Calif.

Stern, J. J. 1970. The meaning of "adaptation" and its relation to the phenomenon of natural selection. In T. H. Dobzhansky, ed., *Evolutionary Biology*, vol. 4. New York.

Steward, J. H., ed. 1948. *Handbook of South American Indians: Vol. 3. The Tropical Forest Tribes*. Washington, D.C.

———. 1955. *Theory of Culture Change: The Methodology of Multilinear Evolution*. Urbana, Ill.

———. 1956. Cultural evolution. *Scientific American* 194 (no. 5): 69–80.

———. 1958. Problems of Cultural Evolution. *Evolution* 12: 206–10.

———. 1960. Evolutionary principles and social types. In S. Tax, ed., *Evolution After Darwin*, vol. 2. Chicago, Ill.

Steward, J. H., and L. C. Faron. 1959. *Native Peoples of South America*. New York.

Steward, J. H., and D. B. Shimkin. 1962. Some mechanisms of sociocultural evolution. In H. Hoagland and R. W. Burhoe, eds., *Evolution and Man's Progress*. New York.

Stini, W. A. 1971. Evolutionary implications of changing nutritional patterns in human populations. *Am. Anthropologist* 73: 1019–30.

———. 1975. *Ecology and Human Adaptation*. Dubuque, Iowa.

———, ed. 1979. *Physiological and Morphological Adaptation and Evolution*. New York.

Stocking, G. W. 1968. *Race, Culture, and Evolution: Essays in the History of Anthropology*. Chicago, Ill.

———. 1986. Review of D. J. Greenwood, *The Taming of Evolution*. *Am. Anthropologist*. 88: 505–6.

———. 1987. *Victorian Anthropology*. New York.

Storey, J., et al. 1979. Abnormal haemoglobins in the Sudan savannah of Nigeria: IV. Malaria, immunoglobins, and anti-malarial antibodies in haemoglobin AC individuals. *Anns. Trop. Medicine and Parasitology* 73: 311–15.

Stout, D. B. 1946. Further notes on albinism among the San Blas Cuna, Panama. *Am. J. Physical Anthropology* 4: 483–90.

———. 1947. *San Blas Cuna Acculturation: An Introduction*. New York.

Strathern, A. 1982. Witchcraft, greed, cannibalism and death. In M. Bloch and J. Parry, eds., *Death and the Regeneration of Life*. Cambridge, Eng.

Stringer, C. 1984. Human evolution and biological adaptation in the Pleistocene. In R. Foley, ed., *Hominid Evolution and Community Ecology*. New York.

Strömer, [P. J.] C. 1932. *Die Sprache der Mundurukú: Wörterbuch, Grammatik und Texte eines Indianeridioms am Oberen Tapajoz, Amazonasgebiet*. Vol. 11, *Anthropos* International Collection of Linguistic Monographs. Mödling, Austria.

Stryer, L. 1988. *Biochemistry*. New York. 3d ed. of work first published in 1975.

Stuart-Fox, M. 1986. The unit of replication in socio-cultural evolution. *J. Social and Biological Structures*. 9: 67–89.

Styś, W. 1957. The influence of economic conditions on the fertility of peasant women. *Population Stud*. 11: 136–48.

———. 1959. Wspólzależność rozwoju rodziny chłopskiej i jej gospodarstwa [Relationship between size of peasant families and size of their farmsteads]. *Prace Wrocławskiego Towarzystwa Naukowego*, series A (no. 62).

Sumner, W. G. 1907. *Folkways: A Study of the Sociological Importance of Usages, Manners, Customs, Mores and Morals*. Boston, Mass.

Sumner, W. G., and A. G. Keller. 1927. *The Science of Society*. New Haven, Conn.

Sunshine, P., and N. Kretchmer. 1964. Intestinal disaccharidases: Absence in two species of sea lions. *Science* 144: 850–51.

Swadesh, M. 1971. *The Origin and Diversification of Language*. Chicago.

Swanson, C. 1983. *Ever-Expanding Horizons: The Dual Informational Sources of Human Evolution*. Amherst, Mass.

Swartz, B. K., and R. A. Dummett, eds. 1980. *West African Culture Dynamics*. New York.

Symons, D. 1979. *The Evolution of Human Sexuality*. New York.

Syvanen, M. 1984. The evolutionary implications of mobile genetic elements. *Ann. Rev. Genetics* 18: 271–93.

Taliaferro, W. H., and J. G. Huck. 1923. The inheritance of sickle-cell anemia in man. *Genetics* 8: 594–98.

Talmon, Y. 1972. *Family and Community in the Kibbutz*. Cambridge, Mass.

Tambiah, S. J. 1966. Polyandry in Ceylon. In C. von Fürer-Haimendorf, *Caste and Kin in Nepal, India, and Ceylon*. London.

Tannahill, R. 1973. *Food in History*. London.

Tasa, G. L., et al. 1985. Reflectometer reports on human pigmentation. *Current Anthropology* 26: 511–12.

Tattah, E. B., and M. C. Ekere. 1975. Death patterns in sickle-cell anemia. *J. Am. Medical Assn*. 233: 889–90.

Taylor, A. N., and R. H. Wasserman. 1969. Correlations between the vitamin D–induced calcium binding protein and intestinal absorption of calcium. *Proc. 34th Ann. Poultry Nutrition Conf.: Nutrition Soc. Symp*. 28: 1834–38.

Taylor, A. W. 1930. Domestic mosquitoes of Gadau, Northern Nigeria and their relation to malaria and filariasis. *Anns. Trop. Medicine and Parasitology* 24: 425–35.

Temin, H. M., and W. Engels. 1984. Movable genetic elements and evolution. In J. W. Pollard, ed., *Evolutionary Theory: Paths into the Future*. New York.

Templeton, A. R. 1982. Adaptation and the integration of evolutionary forces. In R. Milkman, ed., *Perspectives on Evolution*. Sunderland, Mass.

Terborgh, J., and R. A. Kiltie. 1984. Ecology and behavior of rain forest peccaries in Southeastern Peru. *Nat. Geographic Soc. Research Reports* 17: 873–82.

ter Meulen, V., and M. Katz. 1977. *Slow Virus Infections of the Central Nervous System.* New York.

Thomas, A., and L. Krieger. 1976. Jamaican vomiting sickness: A theoretical investigation. *Social Science and Medicine* 10: 177–83.

Thomas, R. B. 1979. Effects of change on high mountain human adaptive patterns. In P. J. Webber, ed., *High Altitude Geoecology.* Washington, D.C.

Thompson, G. R. 1962. Significance of haemoglobins S and C in Ghana. *Brit. Medical J.* 1 (no. 5279): 682–85.

Thompson, S. 1966. *Tales of the North American Indians.* Bloomington, Ind.

Thomson, A. M., F. E. Hytten, and A. E. Black. 1975. Lactation and reproduction. *Bull. World Health Organization* 52: 337–49.

Thornton, J. E., and E. N. Pugh. 1983. Red/green color opponency at detection threshold. *Science* 219: 191–93.

Tindall, B. A. 1976. Theory in the study of cultural transmission. *Ann. Rev. Anthropology* 5: 195–208.

Tobias, P. V. 1961. New evidence and new views on the evolution of man in Africa. *South African J. Science* 52: 25–38.

———. 1971. *The Brain in Hominid Evolution.* New York.

———. 1974. An anthropologist looks at malaria. *South African Medical J.* 48: 1124–27.

———. 1975. Brain evolution in the Hominoidea. In R. H. Tuttle, ed., *Primate Functional Morphology and Evolution.* The Hague.

Tooby, J. 1982. Pathogens, polymorphism, and the evolution of sex. *J. Theoretical Biology* 97: 557–76.

Tooby, J., and L. Cosmides. 1989. Evolutionary psychology and the generation of culture. Part I: Theoretical considerations. *Ethology and Sociobiology* 10: 29–49.

Tootell, R. B. H., et al. 1982. Deoxyglucose analysis of retinotopic organization in primate striate cortex. *Science* 218: 902–4.

Torún, B., N. W. Solomons, and F. E. Viteri. 1979. Lactose malabsorption and lactose intolerance: Implications for general milk consumption. *Archivos Latinoamericanos de Nutrición* 29: 445–94.

Toulmin, S. 1961. *Foresight and Understanding: An Inquiry into the Aims of Science.* Bloomington, Ind.

———. 1967. The evolutionary development of natural science. *Am. Scientist* 55: 456–71.

———. 1972. *Human Understanding.* Princeton, N.J.

Toussaint, G.-C. 1933. *Le Dict de Padma.* Paris.

Trakas, D. J. 1981. Favism and GCPD deficiency in Rhodes, Greece. The interaction of environment, inheritance and culture. Ph.D. diss., Michigan State University.

Trewartha, G. T. 1961. *The Earth's Problem Climates.* Madison, Wis.

Trivers, R. L. 1971. The evolution of reciprocal altruism. *Q. Rev. Biology* 46: 35–57.

———. 1985. *Social Evolution.* Menlo Park, Calif.

Trump, D. H. 1980. *The Prehistory of the Mediterranean.* New Haven, Conn.

Tucci, G. 1980. *The Religions of Tibet.* Berkeley, Calif. English translation of work first published in German in 1970.

Tunnell, G. 1973. *Culture and Biology: Becoming Human.* Minneapolis, Minn.

Turnbull, C. M. 1972. *The Mountain People*. New York.

Turner, J. H., and A. Maryanski. 1979. *Functionalism*. Menlo Park, Calif.

Turner, V. 1977. Process, system and symbol: A new anthropological synthesis. *Daedalus* 1: 61–80.

Tylor, E. B. 1865. *Researches into the Early History of Mankind and the Development of Civilization*. New York.

———. 1871. *Primitive Culture*. 2 vols. London.

———. 1888. On a method of investigating the development of institutions: Applied to laws of marriage and descent. *J. Royal Anthropological Inst.* 18: 245–69.

Underwood, J. H. 1975. *Biocultural Interactions and Human Variation*. Dubuque, Iowa.

———. 1979. *Human Variation and Human Microevolution*. Englewood Cliffs, N.J.

United Nations, Food and Agricultural Organization (FAO). 1979a. *1978 FAO Production Ybk*. Rome.

———. 1979b. *1978 FAO Trade Ybk*. Rome.

United Nations, Protein Advisory Group (PAG). 1972. PAG ad hoc working group on milk intolerance—nutritional implications. *PAG Bulletin* 2 (no. 2): 7–11.

United Nations Educational, Scientific and Cultural Organization (UNESCO). 1980. *Statistical Ybk., 1979*. Paris.

———. 1982. *Statistical Ybk., 1981*. Paris.

United States Department of Commerce, Environmental Data Service. 1967. *World Weather Records, 1951–1960: Vol. 5, Africa*. Washington, D.C.

United States Public Health Service. 1979. *Smoking and Health: A Report of the Surgeon General*. Bethesda, Md.

Urbach, F., ed. 1969a. *The Biologic Effects of Ultraviolet Radiation*. Oxford, Eng.

———. 1969b. Geographic pathology of skin cancer. In F. Urbach, ed., *The Biologic Effects of Ultraviolet Radiation*. Oxford, Eng.

Urbach, F., et al. 1974. Ultraviolet carcinogenesis: Experimental, global and genetic aspects. In T. B. Fitzpatrick, ed., *Sunlight and Man*. Tokyo.

Ursprung, H. W. 1988. Evolution and the economic approach to human behavior. *J. Social and Biological Structures* 11: 257–79.

Vahlquist, B. 1975. A two-century perspective of some major nutritional deficiency diseases in childhood. *Acta Paediatrica Scandinavica* 64: 161–71.

van den Berghe, P. L. 1979. *Human Family Systems: An Evolutionary View*. New York.

———. 1980. Incest and exogamy: A sociobiological reconsideration. *Ethology and Sociobiology* 1: 151–62.

———. 1983. Human inbreeding avoidance: Culture in nature. *Behavioral and Brain Sciences* 6: 91–123.

van den Berghe, P. L., and D. Barash. 1977. Inclusive fitness and human family structure. *Am. Anthropologist* 79: 809–23.

van den Berghe, P. L., and G. M. Mesher. 1980. Royal incest and inclusive fitness. *Am. Ethnologist* 7: 300–317.

Vandermeer, J. H. 1972. The farming practices of local campesinos and their effect on the ecology of dry tropics. In Organization for Tropical Studies [ed.], *Tropical Biology: An Ecological Approach*. San Jose, Costa Rica.

Van Essen, D. C. 1979. Visual areas of the mammalian cerebral cortex. *Ann. Rev. Neuroscience* 2: 227–63.

Van Parijs, P. 1981. *Evolutionary Explanation in the Social Sciences: An Emerging Paradigm.* Totowa, N.J.

Vayda, A. P. 1961. Expansion and warfare among swidden agriculturalists. *Am. Anthropologist* 63: 346–58.

———. 1968. Hypotheses about functions of war. In M. Fried, M. Harris, and R. Murphy, eds., *War: The Anthropology of Armed Conflict and Aggression.* Garden City, N.Y.

———. 1974. Warfare in ecological perspective. *Ann. Rev. Ecology and Systematics* 5: 183–93.

———. 1976. *War in Ecological Perspective.* New York.

Vehrencamp, S. L., and J. W. Bradbury. 1984. Mating systems and ecology. In J. R. Krebs and N. B. Davies, eds., *Behavioral Ecology: An Evolutionary Approach.* Sunderland, Mass.

Vermeersch, E. 1977. An analysis of the concept of culture. In B. Bernardi, ed., *The Concept and Dynamics of Culture.* The Hague.

Vogel, F., and A. G. Motulsky. 1979. *Human Genetics: Problems and Approaches.* New York.

Von Wattenwyl, A., and H. Zollinger. 1979. Color-term salience and neurophysiology of color vision. *Am. Anthropologist* 81: 279–88.

Vrba, E. S., and N. Eldredge. 1984. Individuals, hierarchies, and processes: Towards a more complete evolutionary theory. *Paleobiology* 10: 146–71.

Waddington, C. H. 1961. The human evolutionary system. In M. Banton, ed., *Darwinism and the Study of Society.* Chicago, Ill.

Wagner, R. 1972. Incest and identity: A critique and theory on the subject of exogamy and incest prohibition. *Man* (n.s.) 7: 601–13.

Walcher, D. N., and N. Kretchmer, eds. 1981. *Food, Nutrition and Evolution: Food as an Environmental Factor in the Genesis of Human Variability.* New York.

Wald, G. 1964. The receptors of human color vision. *Science* 145: 1007–16.

Walker, H. O. 1962. Weather and climate. In J. B. Wills, ed., *Agriculture and Land Use in Ghana.* London.

Walker-Smith, J. A. 1984. Cow's milk protein intolerance in infancy. In R. K. Chandra, ed., *Food Intolerance.* New York.

Wallace, A. F. C. 1961. Mental illness, biology and culture. In F. L. K. Hsu, ed., *Psychological Anthropology.* Cambridge, Mass.

Wallace, A. F. C., and R. E. Ackerman. 1960. An interdisciplinary approach to mental disorder among the polar Eskimos of Northwest Greenland. *Anthropologica* (Ottawa) 2: 249–60.

Wallace, A. R. 1891. *Darwinism: An Exposition of the Theory of Natural Selection.* London.

Walter, M. W. 1967. The length of the rainy season in Nigeria. *Nigerian Geographical J.* 10: 123–28.

Walter, V. H. 1958. Der Zusammenhang von Hautfarbenverteilung und Intensität der ultravioletten Strahlung. *Homo* 9: 1–13.

Warner, K. E. 1981. Cigarette smoking in the 1970's: The impact of the antismoking campaign on consumption. *Science* 211: 729–30.

Washburn, S. L. 1957. Speculations on the interrelations of the history of tools and biological evolution. In J. N. Spuhler, ed., *The Evolution of Man's Capacity for Culture*. Detroit, Mich.

———. 1960. Tools and human evolution. *Scientific American* 203 (no. 3): 63–75.

Washburn, S. L., and F. C. Howell. 1960. Human evolution and culture. In S. Tax, ed., *Evolution After Darwin: Vol. 2, The Evolution of Man*. Chicago, Ill.

Wasserman, R. H. 1981. Intestinal absorption of calcium and phosphorus. *Fed. Am. Soc. Experimental Biology Proc.* 40: 68–72.

Wasserman, R. H., and A. N. Taylor. 1969. Some aspects of the intestinal absorption of calcium, with special reference to vitamin D. In C. L. Comar and F. Bronner, eds. *Mineral Metabolism: An Advanced Treatise*. New York.

Watson, J. B. 1952. Cayua culture change: A study in acculturation and methodology. *Am. Anthropological Assn. Memoir* no. 73.

Watson, J. D. 1980. *The Double Helix*. Gunther S. Stent, ed. New York. Critical edition, with reviews and original papers, of work first published in 1968.

Watson, J. D., and F. H. C. Crick. 1953. A structure of deoxyribose nucleic acid. *Nature* 171: 737–38.

Watson, J. D., et al. 1987. *Molecular Biology of the Gene*. 2 vols. Menlo Park, Calif. 4th ed. of work first published in 1965.

Watts, E. S., F. E. Johnston, and G. W. Lasker, eds. 1975. *Biosocial Interrelations in Population Adaptation*. Chicago, Ill.

Weale, R. A. 1955. The absolute threshold of vision. *Physiological Rev.* 35: 233–46.

Weatherall, D. J., and J. B. Clegg. 1981. *The Thalassaemia Syndromes*. Oxford, Eng.

Webb, R. B., and M. S. Brown. 1982. Genetic damage in *Escherichia coli* K12 AB2480 by broad-spectrum near-ultraviolet radiation. *Science* 215: 991–93.

Webber, P. J., ed. 1979. *High Altitude Geoecology*. Washington, D.C.

Weibel, E. R. 1984. *The Pathway for Oxygen: Structure and Function in the Mammalian Respiratory System*. Cambridge, Mass.

Weigel, R. M., and M. M. Taylor. 1982. Testing sociobiological theory with respect to human polyandry: A reply to Beall and Goldstein. *Am. Anthropologist* 84: 406–8.

Weigel, R. M., and M. M. Weigel. 1987. Demographic factors affecting the fitness of polyandry for human males: A mathematical model and computer simulation. *Ethology and Sociobiology* 8: 93–133.

Weinberg, S. K. 1963. *Incest Behavior*. New York.

Weiss, B. 1980. Nutritional adaptation and cultural maladaptation: An evolutionary view. In N. W. Jerome, R. F. Kandel, and G. H. Pelto, eds., *Nutritional Anthropology: Contemporary Approaches to Diet and Culture*. Pleasantville, N.Y.

Weiss, G. 1973. A scientific concept of culture. *Am. Anthropologist* 75: 376–413.

Weiss, K. M. 1976. Demographic theory and anthropological inference. *Ann. Rev. Anthropology* 5: 351–81.

Weiss, M. L., and A. E. Mann. 1975. *Human Biology and Behavior: An Anthropological Perspective*. Boston.

Weitz, C. A., et al. 1978. Cultural factors affecting the demographic structure of a high altitude Nepalese population. *Social Biology* 25: 179–95.

Wei Zheng et al. 1973. *Sui Shu* [History of the Sui dynasty]. Beijing.

Welsh, J. D. 1981. Causes of isolated low lactase levels and lactose intolerance. In

D. M. Paige and T. M. Bayless, eds., *Lactose Digestion: Clinical and Nutritional Perspectives.* Baltimore, Md.

Wenegrat, B. 1984. *Sociobiology and Mental Disorder: A New View.* Menlo Park, Calif.

Wenke, R. J. 1981. Explaining the evolution of cultural complexity: A review. In M. B. Schiffer, *Advances in Archaeological Method and Theory,* vol. 4. New York.

Werner, W. T. C. 1922. *Myths and Legends of China.* London.

Wernsdorfer, W. H. 1980. The importance of malaria in the world. In J. P. Kreier, ed., *Malaria,* vol. 1. New York.

Werren, J. H., and H. R. Pulliam. 1981. An intergenerational model of the cultural evolution of helping behavior. *Hum. Ecology* 9: 465–83.

Wessels, C. 1924. *Early Jesuit Travellers in Central Asia, 1603–1721.* The Hague.

West Eberhard, M. J. 1975. The evolution of social behavior by kin selection. *Q. Rev. Biology* 50: 1–33.

Westermann, D., and M. A. Bryan. 1952. *The Languages of West Africa.* New York.

Westermarck, E. 1891. *The History of Human Marriage.* London.

———. 1906–1908. *The Origin and Development of the Moral Ideas.* 2 vols. London.

———. 1922. *The History of Human Marriage.* 3 vols. New York. 5th ed., rev., of work first published in 1 vol. in 1891.

———. 1929. *Marriage.* New York. An abridgement of *A Short History of Marriage,* first published in 1926, which in turn is based on *The History of Human Marriage.*

———. 1934. *Three Essays on Sex and Marriage.* London.

White, L. A. 1948. The definition and prohibition of incest. *Am. Anthropologist* 50: 416–35.

———. 1949a. Energy and the evolution of culture. In L. A. White, ed., *The Science of Culture.* New York.

———, ed. 1949b. *The Science of Culture.* New York.

———. 1959a. *The Evolution of Culture.* New York.

———. 1959b. The concept of culture. *Am. Anthropologist* 61: 227–51.

———. 1959c. The concept of evolution in cultural anthropology. In B. J. Meggers, ed., *Evolution and Anthropology: A Centennial Appraisal.* Brooklyn, N.Y.

———. 1960. Foreword to M. Sahlins and E. Service, eds., *Evolution and Culture.* Ann Arbor, Mich.

Whiting, J. W. M. 1964. Effects of climate on certain cultural practices. In W. H. Goodenough, ed. *Explorations in Cultural Anthropology.* New York.

Whitlaw, J. T., Jr., and B. N. Chaniotis. 1978. Palm trees and Chagas' disease in Panama. *Am. J. Trop. Medicine and Hygiene* 27: 873–81.

Wiesenfeld, S. L. 1967. Sickle-cell trait in human biological and cultural evolution. *Science* 157: 1134–40.

———. 1968. African agricultural patterns and the sickle cell. *Science* 160: 1474–75.

Wiesenfeld, S. L., and D. C. Gajdusek. 1975. Genetic studies in relation to kuru: VI. Evaluation of increased liability to kuru in Gc Ab-Ab individuals. *Am. J. Hum. Genetics* 27: 498–504.

Williams, B. J. 1979. *Evolution and Human Origins: An Introduction to Physical Anthropology.* New York.

Williams, C. A. 1986. Metabolism of lactose and galactose in man. *Progress in Biochemical Pharmacology* 21: 219–47.

Williams, G. C. 1966. *Adaptation and Natural Selection*. Princeton, N.J.

———. 1975. *Sex and Evolution*. Princeton, N.J.

Williams, T. R. 1972. *Introduction to Socialization: Human Culture Transmitted*. St. Louis, Mo.

Willner, D. 1983. Definition and violation: Incest and the incest taboos. *Man* (n.s.) 18: 134–59.

Wills, J. B., ed. 1962. *Agriculture and Land Use in Ghana*. London.

Wilson, A. 1886. *The Abode of Snow*. New York.

Wilson, A. C. 1985. The molecular basis of evolution. *Scientific American* 253 (no. 4): 164–73.

Wilson, D. B., et al. 1950. A review of hyperendemic malaria. *Trop. Diseases Bull.* 47: 677–98.

Wilson, D. S. 1978. A cultural route to biological fitness. *Evolutionary Theory* 3: 235–36.

———. 1983. The group selection controversy: History and current status. *Ann. Rev. Ecology and Systematics* 14: 159–87.

Wilson, E. O. 1975. *Sociobiology: The New Synthesis*. Cambridge, Mass.

———. 1976. The central problems of sociobiology. In R. M. May, ed., *Theoretical Ecology*. Philadelphia, Pa.

———. 1978. *On Human Nature*. Cambridge, Mass.

———. 1982. Foreword. In D. P. Barash, *Sociobiology and Behavior*. New York.

Wilson, E. O., and W. H. Bossert. 1971. *A Primer of Population Biology*. Stamford, Conn.

Wilson, H. C. 1958. Regarding the causes of Mundurucú warfare. *Am. Anthropologist* 60: 1193–96.

Wilson, P. J. 1961. Incest: A case study. *Social and Econ. Stud.* 12: 200–209.

Wind, J. 1984. Sociobiology and the human sciences: An introduction. *J. Hum. Evolution* 13: 3–24.

Wing, E., and A. Brown. 1979. *Paleonutrition*. New York.

Winterhalder, B., and E. A. Smith, eds. 1981. *Hunter-Gatherer Foraging Strategies: Ethnographic and Archaeological Analyses*. Chicago, Ill.

Witkop, C. J., Jr. 1971. Albinism. In H. Harris and K. Hirschorn, eds., *Advances in Human Genetics*, vol. 2.

Witkop, C. J., Jr., W. C. Quevedo, and T. B. Fitzpatrick. 1983. Albinism and other disorders of pigment metabolism. In J. B. Stanbury et al., eds., *The Metabolic Basis of Inherited Disease*. New York.

Witkowski, S. R., and C. H. Brown. 1977. An explanation of color nomenclature universals. *Am. Anthropologist* 79: 50–57.

———. 1978. Lexical universals. *Ann. Rev. Anthropology* 7: 427–51.

———. 1982. Whorf and universals of color nomenclature. *J. Anthropological Res.* 38: 411–20.

Wittenberger, J. F. 1979. The evolution of mating systems in birds and mammals. In P. Marler and J. G. Vandenbergh, eds., *Handbook of Behavioral Neurobiology: Vol. 3, Social Behavior and Communication*. New York.

———. 1981. *Animal Social Behavior*. Boston.

Wobst, H. M. 1975. The demography of finite populations and the origins of the incest tabu. *Am. Antiquity* 40: 75–81.

Wolf, A. P. 1964. Marriage and adoption in a Hokkien village. Ph.D. diss., Cornell University.

———. 1966. Childhood association, sexual attraction, and the incest taboo: A Chinese case. *Am. Anthropologist* 68: 883–98.

———. 1968. Adopt a daughter-in-law, marry a sister: A Chinese solution to the problem of the incest taboo. *Am. Anthropologist* 70: 864–74.

———. 1970. Childhood association and sexual attraction: A further test of the Westermarck hypothesis. *Am. Anthropologist* 72: 503–15.

———. 1976. Childhood association, sexual attraction, and fertility in Taiwan. In E. F. Zubrow, ed., *Demographic Anthropology: Quantitative Approaches.* Albuquerque, N. Mex.

Wolf, A. P., and C. Huang. 1980. *Marriage and Adoption in China, 1845–1945.* Stanford, Calif.

Wolpoff, M. 1980. *Paleoanthropology.* New York.

———. 1984. Evolution in *Homo erectus*: the question of stasis. *Paleobiology* 10: 389–406.

Wood, C. S. 1979. *Human Sickness and Health: A Biocultural View.* Palo Alto, Calif.

Woodworth, R. S. 1970. The puzzle of color vocabularies. In I. Al-Issa and W. Dennis, eds., *Cross-Cultural Studies of Behavior.* New York.

Woolf, L. I., W. I. Cranston, and B. L. Goodwin. 1967. Genetics of phenylkentonuria. *Nature* 213: 882–85.

Wooten, B. R. 1970. The effects of simultaneous and successive chromatic constraint on spectral hue. Ph.D. diss., Brown University.

World Health Organization. 1966. *Haemoglobinopathies and Allied Disorders.* Technical Report 338. Geneva, Switz.

Wright, S. 1921a. Systems of mating: General considerations. *Genetics* 6: 167–78.

———. 1921b. Systems of mating: II. The effects of inbreeding on the genetic composition of a population. *Genetics* 6: 124–43.

———. 1922. Coefficients of inbreeding and relationship. *Am. Naturalist* 56: 330–38.

———. 1933. Inbreeding and homozygosis. *Proc. Nat. Acad. Sciences* 19: 411–20.

———. 1968. *Evolution and the Genetics of Populations: Vol. 1, Genetic and Biometric Foundations.* Chicago, Ill.

———. 1969. *Evolution and the Genetics of Populations: Vol. 2, Theory of Gene Frequencies.* Chicago, Ill.

———. 1977. *Evolution and the Genetics of Populations: Vol. 3, Experimental Results and Evolutionary Deductions.* Chicago, Ill.

Wyszecki, G., and W. S. Stiles, eds. 1982. *Color Science: Concepts and Methods, Quantitative Data and Formulae.* New York.

Yokoyama, S. 1983. Social selection and evolution of human diseases. *Am. J. Physical Anthropology* 62: 61–66.

Young, J. Z. 1978. *Programs of the Brain.* New York.

Young, R. M. 1985. *Darwin's Metaphor: Nature's Place in Victorian Culture.* Cambridge, Eng.

Yule, H. 1903. *The Book of Ser Marco Polo.* London.

Zeuner, F. 1963. *A History of Domesticated Animals.* New York.

Zigas, V. 1970. Kuru in New Guinea: Discovery and epidemiology. *Am. J. Trop. Medicine and Hygiene* 19: 130–32.

————. 1990. *Laughing Death: The Untold Story of Kuru.* Clifton, N.J.

Zihlman, A. L. 1982. *The Human Evolution Coloring Book.* New York.

Zindler, R. E. 1978. On the increase of cranial capacity in mankind's lineage: Arguments and elaborations. *J. Hum. Evolution* 7: 295–305.

Zinn, K. M., and M. F. Marmar, eds. 1979. *The Retinal Pigment Epithelium.* Cambridge, Mass.

Zollinger, H. 1979. Correlations between the neurobiology of color vision and the psycholinguistics of color naming. *Experientia* 35: 1–8.

Zrenner, E. 1983. *Neurophysiological Aspects of Color Vision in Primates.* New York.

Zuckerkandl, E. 1965. The evolution of hemoglobin. *Scientific American* 212 (no. 5): 110–18.

INDEX

Library of Congress Cataloging-in-Publication Data

Durham, William H.
   Coevolution : genes, culture, and human diversity /
by William H. Durham.
      p.   cm.
   Includes bibliographical references and index.
   ISBN 0-8047-1537-8 (cloth : acid-free paper)
      1. Culture.   2. Social evolution.   3. Human population genetics—
Social aspects.   4. Human behavior.   5. Sociobiology.   I. Title.
GN360.D87   1991
304.5—dc20   90-43867

   ⊗ This book is printed on acid-free paper

DATE DUE

MaK DUE	MAY 0 5 2005	
MaK DUE	MAY 0 1 2006	
ICK PAID	MAR 0 2 2006	